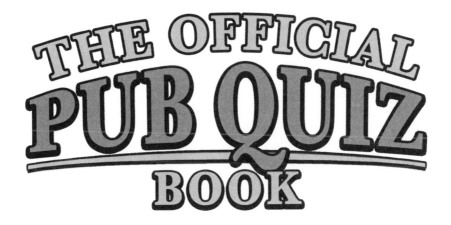

THIS IS A CARLTON BOOK

This edition published in 2012 by Carlton Books Ltd
A Division of the Carlton Publishing Group
20 Mortimer Street
London W1T 3JW

ISBN 978-1-84732-985-1

Printed in Dubai

The puzzles in this book were previously published in *The Biggest Pub Quiz Book Ever*, *The Biggest Pub Quiz
Book Ever 2*, *The Biggest Movie and TV Pub Quiz Book Ever*

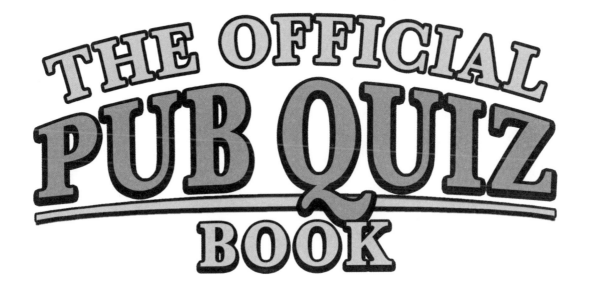

THE OFFICIAL PUB QUIZ BOOK

THE ULTIMATE QUIZ-MASTER'S GUIDE

CARLTON

Contents

Introduction   8

THE QUIZZES

 Sport

Music

Movies

 Geography

 Pot Luck

Animal, Vegetable or Mineral

Introduction

Over the past few years snugs and lounges in pubs, clubs and bars the length and breadth of the country have become akin to seats of learning, or at least seats of intellect. Which makes a change from seats of worn leatherette (although these still prevail in some areas). The popularity of the Pub Quiz has meant that the bar has transformed itself into an arena of knowledge where beery brethren battle to the final bell.

Running a Pub Quiz is simple: you just need some participants, a questioner, some paper, a collection of pens, a barrel of booze and some questions are all that is needed to create the perfect evening's entertainment. Wits are challenged, heads are huddled and patience is tested as teams attempt to outdo each other in their show of trivia retention. At these events you will learn that no fact is too small, no sport star too obscure and no war too insignificant to test the pub crowd's grey matter. In fact, the more obscure and wide-ranging the questions the greater the chance of involving the entire barroom. And that's where this book comes in. Chock full of questions and all the answers too, it will fulfill your every Pub Quiz need, whether you fancy running your own or you just want to brush up on your answering skills.

Remember: the main aim of a Pub Quiz is to entertain, so it is important that you retain a sense of humour and good sportsmanship as you play along, whether you are testing friends at home or setting a quiz for your local. That aside, you also have to ensure that you are fully in control of your questions and players: remain calm, speak in a steady voice and be constantly unflapped when challenged by any of the more heavily imbibed, as indeed you will be eventually.

We have divided this book into three sections: Easy, Medium and Hard questions, which are all subdivided by specialist subject, as well as a Pot Luck section. Specialist subjects can be chosen either to help or hinder players; giving Easy TV questions to the rabid sports fans is bound to reveal some interesting answers but it is possibly more challenging to tailor your questions so that the experts receive the brain-teasing Hard questions and the novice the stupefyingly simple Easy questions. Nothing hurts a fanatic more than being beaten on their specialist subject.

In the interest of further clarification there follows a brief run-down of each section that is contained in this book:

EASY

In this primary round the main objective is to keep scribbling down the answers, as these questions are so easy that even the most docile pub-goer could gurgle their way through them in the time it takes to down a glass of red and still have time left to knock over the stack of pennies on the bar.

MEDIUM

On your toes, things are getting tricky. By now even the ringers on the out-of-towners' team will be sweating. These questions make for a challenge, but you are bound to get the odd smug bar steward who will fancy his chances, for which you should continue on to the next section.

HARD

Let off a full salvo of these questions and only the shrill wail of the pub cat fighting in the yard will be heard, brows will be furrowed, glances exchanged and beer stared into. To set an entire quiz using just these questions is a form of evil so dark-hearted it should be strapped to a rocket and flown to the sun.

All that is left to say is good luck with your quizzing – whichever side of the counter you are on – and if you can't keep your spirits up at least try to keep them down.

www.officialpubquizassociation.co.uk

1
PENALTY KICKS

1. Who missed a penalty kick and put a bag on his head in a pizza place?
2. Beardsley and Shearer have been on the spot for which club?
3. Andy Brehme scored a World Cup final penalty for which country?
4. Where should a goalkeeper stand for a penalty?
5. Who made the first Wembley save from an FA Cup final penalty kick?
6. Ron Flowers has been on the spot for which country?
7. Which England player missed in a shoot-out in Italy in 1990 but scored in Euro 96?
8. Which Julian became a 1990s penalty expert for West Ham?
9. Yorke and Townsend have been on the spot for which club?
10. Robbie Rensenbrink scored four penalties in the 1978 World Cup finals for which team?
11. Which London team won the UEFA Cup final of 1984 after a shoot-out?
12. Who missed from the spot for Scotland against England in Euro 96?
13. Which country did the Republic of Ireland beat in a 1990 World Cup shoot-out?
14. Who scored two penalty kicks in an FA Cup final for Manchester United in the 1990s?
15. Wise and Hughes have been on the spot for which club?
16. Which country was awarded a penalty in the Euro 96 final?
17. In 1994, the final of which major tournament was decided on a penalty shoot-out for the first time ever?
18. Which Tottenham Hotspur player failed to score from the spot in the 1991 FA Cup final?
19. In a league game, can a penalty taker score from a rebound off the keeper?
20. Which Francis was a penalty-kick king for Manchester City in the 1970s?
21. Who scored a Champions League semi-final penalty for Chelsea in April 2008?
22. Which Jerzy saved two penalties in the 2005 Champions League Final shoot-out?
23. Which country has been in two World Cup Final penalty shoot-outs?
24. Who scored a penalty in the 2006 World Cup Final and was later sent off?
25. Which team lost an FA Cup Final on penalties after drawing 3–3 in 120 minutes?
26. Which club lost the 2005 FA Cup Final to Arsenal in a penalty shoot-out?
27. Can you name the team that lost the 2008 Community Shield in a penalty shoot-out?
28. Who missed the penalty that would have won the 2007–08 UEFA Champions League for Chelsea?
29. Who was the first player to miss a penalty kick in an FA Cup Final at Wembley?
30. Which side put Chelsea out of the 2008–09 Carling Cup in a penalty shoot-out?

 Answers on page 189

2
SUMMER SPORTS

1. Which sport are the Lord's Taverners famous for playing?
2. Which Denise won European gold in the heptathlon in 1988?
3. Which Australian bowler was first to pass 700 Test wickets?
4. Sergey Bubka has set a world record in which field event over 30 times?
5. Which British tennis star reached the Wimbledon semi-finals in 1998?
6. Which summer sport did Kerry Packer revolutionise in the 70s?
7. Did Lance Armstrong dominate the Tour de France or Tour of Italy?
8. Chris Boardman suffered an accident riding what in summer 1998?
9. Which country staged the summer Olympics in 1984 and 1996?
10. Between 1990 and 1998 all Ladies Wimbledon Singles champions were born in which continent?
11. The summer Olympics are held every how many years?
12. In cricket, what must a ball not do to score six runs?
13. Jonathan Edwards specialises in what type of jump?
14. For which international side did Shane Warne play cricket?
15. Which golfer is known as the Great White Shark?
16. Which Martina did Martinez beat in the 1994 Wimbledon final?
17. Which Tour is the world's premier cycling event?
18. Which German tennis player's father Peter was jailed for tax fraud?
19. Sonia O'Sullivan races for which country?
20. How many runners are there in the 400m relay team?
21. Which Jana won Wimbledon in 1998 after her third final?
22. You would do a Fosbury flop in which athletics event?
23. Which cricket club is nicknamed the "Cradle of Cricket"?
24. How many balls an over are there in cricket?
25. Who told a Wimbledon umpire "You cannot be serious!"?
26. Which West Indian cricketer was called Vivian?
27. Who was top National Hunt jockey from 1999–2000 through to 2005?
28. Which Jimmy won Wimbledon doubles with Ilie Nastase?
29. What was the nationality of tennis pin-up Gabriela Sabatini?
30. Which team competes against America in the Ryder Cup?

 Answers on page 189

3 QUOTE UNQUOTE

1 Which Manchester City manager said, "We've got 1 point from 27 but it's not as bad as that"?

2 According to Eric Cantona what would be thrown off the trawler?

3 Which Gary said, "This is not a normal injury. Fashanu was playing without due care and attention"?

4 Whose departure from Lazio caused the president to remark, "He will only return to Rome as a tourist"?

5 Which Liverpool player was supposedly, "happier at Southend"?

6 Which company decided that, "1966 was a great year for English football. Eric was born"?

7 Which ex-Arsenal boss said, "I am as weak as the next man when it comes to temptation"?

8 Which manager suffered from the *Sun*'s turnip jibes?

9 Which Brazilian great talked of "the beautiful game"?

10 Which short-stay boss Phil said, "Watching Manchester City is probably the best laxative you can take"?

11 Which England international Peter said, "I often get called Quasimodo"?

12 Which modest '60s player said in the 90s, "I'd be worth around £14 to £15 million by today's prices"?

13 Who claimed in 1996 that he had "given up beer and guzzling"?

14 Which German said in 1994, "Me dive? Never!"?

15 What did Arrigo Sacchi say might be thrown at him after Euro 96?

16 When did Terry Venables say, "It's a football match, not a war"?

17 Which team did Alf Ramsey liken to "Animals"?

18 Who in 1996 took "the only job I would have left Chelsea for"?

19 Who said, "I've only taken one penalty before, for Crystal Palace"?

20 "As daft as a brush". Who was Bobby Robson talking about?

21 Who, in 2007, said, "I believe I am a better manager than I was 18 months ago"?

22 Who said, "I am special for my friends and for my family. As a manager, so-so"?

23 Which boss said, "You cannot say that you are happy when you don't win"?

24 Which Gordon said, "The Celtic job has to be the best job in the world. I love it"?

25 What did Jose Mourinho say Spurs left in front of the goal after a 0–0 draw?

26 Who said "I feel like Superman" after scoring against his former club Arsenal?

27 Which West Ham Utd boss said "I know I am not the most experienced manager"?

28 Who said "I'm now a dad who can't take his kids to a football game"?

29 Name the Spurs boss who said "I haven't seen my missus, Sandra, all week."

30 Which Blackburn boss said, "Football is not a game for women"?

4 THE '80S

1 Which Gary was England's top soccer marksman of the 1980s?

2 Who fought back from cancer to win the Grand National?

3 Which English batsman became the highest run getter in Test history?

4 Which Steve was Sebastian Coe's great rival in mid-distance races?

5 Which club were English soccer champions six times in the 80s?

6 Which Steve became snooker World Champion in 1981?

7 The America's Cup left home for the first time ever to go to where?

8 Which motor-cycle legend Mike was killed in a motor accident in 1981?

9 Which Tom won both the US and British Opens in the same year?

10 Which team were English soccer champions under Howard Kendall?

11 Which Martina dominated Wimbledon in the 1980s?

12 Which piece of music by Ravel did Torvill and Dean use in winning an Olympic gold for ice dancing?

13 Which country beat West Germany to win the 1982 soccer World Cup?

14 The *Daily Mail* ran a campaign to get which South African athlete to receive a British passport?

15 Where in the USA was the centre for the 1984 Olympic Games?

16 In golf, which Sandy won the 1988 US Masters?

17 Which country is motor racing's Nelson Piquet from?

18 Who became a world snooker champion wearing "upside-down" glasses?

19 In which country was the 1985 Heysel Stadium soccer tragedy?

20 In which event did Tessa Sanderson win Olympic gold?

21 What was Barry McGuigan's sport?

22 Which 17-year-old German won the Wimbledon men's singles?

23 Which Diego benefited from "The hand of God"?

24 What was the nickname of sprinter Florence Griffith-Joyner?

25 Who in soccer was known as "Captain Marvel"?

26 Viv Richards and Ian Botham played together for which county?

27 Which team won the Five Nations tournament from 1986 to 1989?

28 Which country does Ivan Lendl originate from?

29 Which Scottish soccer team was managed by Graeme Souness?

30 Which Englishman became soccer boss of the Republic of Ireland?

 **Answers on page 189**

 Answers on page 189

5 HORSE RACING

1 Who returned to racing in 1990 when he was over 50?
2 Which horse was the first to win the Grand National three times?
3 Where is the William Hill Lincoln Handicap held?
4 Trainers Lynda and John Ramsden won a libel case against which paper?
5 In which country was Shergar captured?
6 In which month is the Melbourne Cup held?
7 Who was National Hunt champion jockey from 1986 to 1992?
8 Which horse Benny won the 1997 English Derby?
9 Which English classic is held at Doncaster?
10 Which 100-1 shot won the 2009 Grand National?
11 Which horse race was abandoned in 1997 after a bomb scare?
12 The Prix du Jockey-Club is held at which race course?
13 Which horse had the nickname Corky?
14 Which Gordon, a trainer of over 2000 winners, died in September 1998?
15 Which country hosts the Belmont and Preakness Stakes?
16 Which race meeting is described as Glorious?
17 The 12th Earl of where gave his name to a famous race?
18 The Curragh is in which Irish County?
19 Where did Frankie Dettori have his record-breaking seven wins?
20 In which country is Flemington Park race course?
21 The Velka Pardubice is the top steeplechase race in which European country?
22 Which jockey was retired because of his injuries in the 2008 Grand National?
23 In which Irish county is Aidan O'Brien's yard situated?
24 In which Middle East country is the world's richest race held?
25 On which famous race course do horses cross The Chair and Melling Road?
26 Which horse won the Cheltenham Gold Cup in 2007?
27 Which American thoroughbred was the subject of a major film in 2003?
28 Which Southampton footballer went on to become a successful racehorse trainer?
29 How much would you be betting if you put a "Monkey" on a horse?
30 On which French race course is the Prix de l'Arc de Triomphe run?

6 FOOTBALL

1 Which team is known as the Magpies?
2 Which Patrick was Arsenal skipper when they went a season unbeaten in the Premiership?
3 What two colours are in Blackburn's home strip?
4 Which Gerard was the first Frenchman to manage Liverpool?
5 In which country were the 1994 World Cup finals held?
6 Which city has teams called Rovers and City?
7 What position did Peter Shilton play?
8 At which club did Shearer and Owen line up in the same side?
9 Which surname is shared by England players Ashley and Joe?
10 Which club is linked with the playing career of Jimmy Armfield?
11 Which Peter kept goal for both Man Utd and Man City?
12 Which country do Real Madrid come from?
13 In QPR what does the letter R stand for?
14 Which club did Steve Bruce play for in a Premiership-winning season?
15 Which country did George Best play for?
16 What is the home colour of Nottingham Forest?
17 Which country does David Ginola come from?
18 At which club did Terry Venables and Alan Sugar clash?
19 Which club appointed former player Sam Allardyce as manager in October 1999?
20 Why did France not play in qualifying games for the 98 World Cup?
21 Which David has managed Spurs, Luton and Sheffield Wednesday?
22 What do the letters o.g. stand for?
23 In which year did Roy Keane end his playing days with Man Utd?
24 Which Kevin has managed Newcastle, Fulham, Man City and England?
25 Which Lane do Sheffield United play at?
26 Which club is associated with the song "You'll Never Walk Alone"?
27 What is the traditional kick-off time for Saturday League games?
28 Edwin Van der Sar left Fulham to join which other Premiership club?
29 David Moyes first managed in the Premiership at which club?
30 Which London side did Ruud Gullit join in 1995?

  Answers on page 189

 Answers on page 189

7 FOOTBALL LEGENDS

1 What position did Stanley Matthews play?
2 Which legend married a 23-year-old air hostess on his 49th birthday?
3 Which Dutch international player went on to managerial success at Barcelona in the 1990s?
4 With which London club did Jimmy Greaves begin his career?
5 Who was the first England captain of a World Cup-winning team?
6 Which country did Zbigniew Boniek play for?
7 Which League club did Billy Wright play for?
8 Who was "Wor Jackie"?
9 In which country was Ferenc Puskas born?
10 At which club did Denis Law finish his career?
11 Who was "Kaiser Franz"?
12 How many clubs did Tom Finney play for?
13 Who was known as "The Black Panther"?
14 Who was England's keeper in the 1966 World Cup-winning side?
15 How did Edson Arantes do Nascimento become better known?
16 Which goalkeeper with Christian names Patrick Anthony played over 100 times for his country?
17 Which French midfielder of the 70s and 80s became France's top scorer?
18 In which city did Billy Meredith play his soccer?
19 Which player turned out in a record 21 World Cup finals matches for Argentina?
20 At which club did Stanley Matthews begin and end his career?
21 Which flame-haired England World Cup winner died in 2007?
22 Which Matthew was known to Southampton fans as "Le God"?
23 What was Celtic and Scotland winger Jimmy Johnstone's nickname?
24 At which London club did French legend David Ginola play 100 League games?
25 Which Chelsea legend was a former teammate of Diego Maradona at Napoli?
26 Name the 1995 World Player of the Year who joined Manchester City in 2005.
27 Which England international won the inaugural European Player of the Year award?
28 Who won the European Player of the Year award in 1968?
29 Who won the championship with Leeds United and Manchester United in the 1990s?
30 Which Dutch striker won two European Cups before joining Chelsea in 1995?

8 WHO'S WHO?

1 Whom was tennis star Martina Hingis named after?
2 Which lauded soccer star was born Edson Arantes do Nascimento?
3 Which French footballer David advertised L'Oreal hair products?
4 Golfer Ernie Els is from which African country?
5 Which British tennis player was born on Greg Rusedski's first birthday?
6 Jonah Lomu played for which international side?
7 Athlete Kelly Holmes was formerly a member of which armed service?
8 Which Paula had a hat-trick of London Marathon wins this millennium?
9 Which snooker champ Ray was nicknamed Dracula?
10 What sort of eye accessory does Chris Eubank wear?
11 At which sport was Nokolai Valuev a world champion?
12 Which Monica was stabbed in the back by a fanatical Graf supporter?
13 Was tennis's Michael Chang from Hong Kong or the USA?
14 Which racing driver was first to clock up more than 75 F1 wins?
15 Rahul Dravid captained which international cricket team?
16 Which four-legged, three-times Grand National winner died in 1995?
17 Which Greg rejected a maple leaf for a Union Jack in the 1990s?
18 Who founded the book known as "the cricketer's Bible"?
19 Rachel Hayhoe Flint is a famous name in which sport?
20 Who was Ben Johnson running for when disqualified in Seoul?
21 Which Princess won the 1971 European Three Day Event?
22 Which David has kept goal for Liverpool, West Ham, Manchester City and Portsmouth?
23 Which temperamental tennis player was dubbed Superbrat?
24 Which Jenny was the first woman to train a Grand National winner?
25 Who was Australia's cricket captain in the 2006 ICC Trophy final?
26 Which boxer's catchphrase was "Know what I mean 'Arry"?
27 Which disappearing horse last won the Derby in 1981?
28 Who founded the Stewart motor racing team?
29 What was cricket umpire Harold Bird's nickname?
30 Who became the first black manager of a Premiership club when he took over at Chelsea in 1996?

 Answers on page 189

9 THE '70S

1 Bobby Moore captained which country in the 1970 World Cup?

2 Which British golfer Tony won the US Open Championship?

3 In 1970 Margaret Court won four major tournaments in which sport?

4 Which horse-riding princess was voted Sportswoman of the Year?

5 At which Scottish stadium was there a crowd disaster in 1971?

6 Which Sebastian completed a hat-trick of running records in 1979?

7 John Conteh became a champion in which sport?

8 Which London team won the League and FA Cup double in 1971?

9 What was the sport of Britain's David Wilkie?

10 In 1976 which cricketer Viv hit 291 runs in an innings against England?

11 Which 19-year-old Evonne triumphed at Wimbledon in 1971?

12 Which Ray was the most successful snooker player of the 70s?

13 Which soccer team won the Scottish League every season from 1970 to 1974?

14 Which horse won the Grand National three times?

15 Who was manager of Nottingham Forest when they won the European Cup?

16 Which Brendan won the only British track and field medal of the 1976 Olympic Games?

17 Bjorn Borg comes from which country?

18 Which Barry became world 500cc motor-cycling champion?

19 Which Daley became the youngest ever athlete to represent Britain in the decathlon?

20 Which British player won the 1977 women's singles at Wimbledon?

21 Which English soccer side twice won the European Cup?

22 In which sport was Mike Brearley an England captain?

23 Which country outside the UK won the Grand Slam in 1977?

24 Which Suffolk soccer side won the FA Cup in 1978?

25 Which team won the 1978 soccer World Cup staged in Argentina?

26 In 1978–9 Hull Kingston Rovers were champions in which sport?

27 Which Niki was badly burnt in the 1976 German Grand Prix?

28 Which TV mogul started his own cricket unofficial Test series?

29 Which Jackie was world champion motor racing driver in 1971 and 1973?

30 Ally MacLeod was manager of which national soccer side?

10 MANCHESTER UNITED

1 Which United manager signed Eric Cantona?

2 How old was Ryan Giggs when he made his first-team debut?

3 Who wrote the autobiography *The Good, the Bad and the Bubbly*?

4 Which player went to Newcastle as part of the deal that bought Andy Cole to Old Trafford?

5 In which country was Sir Matt Busby born?

6 Which club was Paul Ince bought from?

7 Mark Hughes has moved from Manchester Utd twice. Which clubs did he join?

8 Which team were the opponents in the Cantona Kung-Fu spectator attack in January 1995?

9 Alex Ferguson sold his son Darren to which club?

10 Who is the elder of the Neville brothers?

11 What was Denis Law's usual shirt number?

12 What infamous first went to Kevin Moran in the 1985 FA Cup Final?

13 What is the surname of 1970s brothers Brian and Jimmy?

14 Which United manager signed Bryan Robson?

15 Who was the scoring skipper in the 1996 FA Cup Final?

16 Paddy Roche was an international keeper for which country?

17 Who was dubbed "El Beatle" after a '60s European triumph?

18 Which forename links Beckham, May and Saddler?

19 Which two United players were members of England's World Cup-winning team?

20 Who was the first Manchester Utd player to hit five goals in a Premier League match?

21 From which club did United sign Michael Carrick in 2006?

22 Which teenage striker was signed from Everton in 2004?

23 What was the score in the 1999 FA Cup Final against Newcastle United?

24 Who passed Sir Bobby Charlton as United's appearances record-holder?

25 Assistant manager Carlos Queiroz became coach of which national team in 2008?

26 What is the club's nickname?

27 How many times had United won the Premier League up to the end of 2007–08?

28 Name any year in which United won the European Cup/ UEFA Champions League.

29 Can you name United's talismanic French striker from 1992–97?

30 Who did Alex Ferguson replace as the manager of Manchester United?

 Answers on page 189

 Answers on page 189

11 CRICKET

1 Which international teams contest the Ashes?
2 In which city is the ground Old Trafford?
3 In LBW what does the B stand for?
4 Which bowler Dominic took a Test hat-trick in 1995?
5 Which cricketer was voted BBC Sports Personality for 2005?
6 Which English wicket keeper shares his name with a breed of dog?
7 The Nursery End, the Pavilion End and St John's Wood Road are all linked with which ground?
8 Which former England batsman Derek was known as "Rags"?
9 Which patriotic song was adopted by England in the 2005 Ashes?
10 Robin Smith is an international for which country?
11 How many bails are there on a set of wickets?
12 Which county does Geoff Boycott come from?
13 What was the specialist position of Australia's Rodney Marsh?
14 Trent Bridge is in which English city?
15 How many runs are scored in a maiden over?
16 Which country was captained by Kapil Dev?
17 What were the initials of legendary Victorian cricketer Dr Grace?
18 Which county did Michael Vaughan play for?
19 In the 1990s, which Alec opened and kept wicket for England?
20 In scoring, what does c & b stand for?
21 Was David Gower a left- or right-handed batsman?
22 Which English county did West Indies skipper Clive Lloyd play for?
23 On which day of the week were John Player League games played?
24 How many valid deliveries are sent down in a Test cricket over?
25 Which cricket commentator on radio was known as "Johnners"?
26 What does the initial T stand for in I. T. Botham's name?
27 In which country do Sheffield Shield games take place?
28 What does the batsman score for a shot that sends the ball over the boundary without touching the ground?
29 England skippers Brearley and Gatting have both captained which county?
30 How many Tests did England win on the tour of Pakistan late in 2005?

12 RECORD BREAKERS

1 Mark Spitz won seven Olympic golds at record speeds doing what?
2 Which South American soccer team has won most World Cups?
3 How many seasons did Alan Shearer play for Newcastle – 3, 6 or 10?
4 Lyn Davies broke the British record in which jump event?
5 David Campese was leading try scorer for which country?
6 Which Sally was a world record hurdler and 1992 Olympic champion?
7 Who was made England's youngest ever football coach in 1996?
8 Did Roger Bannister run the first four-minute mile in Oxford or Cambridge?
9 Was Martina Hingis 13, 15 or 17 when she first won Wimbledon doubles?
10 Who was the first Rugby Union player to win 100 England caps?
11 Which Nigel was the first to win both F1 and Indy Car world championships?
12 Which record breaker Sebastian went on to become a Tory MP?
13 Which Tony made the first televised hole in one in Britain?
14 Who won the 100m in Seoul in record time before being disqualified?
15 Which Steve was six times World Snooker Champion in the 1980s?
16 For which former Iron Curtain country did Marita Koch break records?
17 Jerry Rice set a career touchdown record in which sport?
18 How many events were in Daley Thompson's speciality event?
19 Which Pete equalled Borg's five Wimbledon singles wins in 1998?
20 Which Gareth became Wales's youngest ever Rugby captain in 1968?
21 Alain Prost was the first to win the F1 world title for which country?
22 Bob Beaman held which Olympic jump record for over 20 years?
23 Who was Britain's only Men's 100m world record holder between 1983 and 1993?
24 Which David did Graham Gooch overtake to become England's highestscoring Test player?
25 World record breaker Kip Keino is from which continent?
26 Did Nadia Comaneci first score a perfect Olympic 10 at 14, 18 or 21?
27 Which golfer Jack was first to achieve 15 career professional majors?
28 Colin Jackson was a world record holder in which event?
29 Who was the first player to score 100 goals in the Premiership?
30 Duncan Goodhew held British records in which sport?

 Answers on page 190

 Answers on page 190

13
THE '80S 2

1 Which club did both Malcolm Allison and John Bond manage?

2 What changed from two to three in all games at the start of the 1981–82 campaign?

3 Which London team were hailed as "The Team of the Eighties"?

4 Which tycoon became Oxford chairman?

5 Which team was top of the First Division during 1981 but back in the Fourth Division by 1986?

6 Who won the 1982 World Cup?

7 What was the League Cup known as after a deal with the National Dairy Board?

8 Who retired as Liverpool boss after a season in which both the championship and League Cup were won?

9 Garth Crooks and Steve Archibald played together at which club?

10 Which former England captain ended his playing days at Newcastle Utd?

11 Which Englishman was the top scorer in the 1986 World Cup finals?

12 Who did Wimbledon beat in their first FA Cup Final victory?

13 Which manager collapsed and died seconds before the end of the Wales v Scotland World Cup qualifying game?

14 On leaving Tottenham Hotspur, Chris Waddle moved to which country?

15 UEFA banned the clubs of which country from participation in European competitions?

16 Which host nation won the 1984 European Championship?

17 Which British manager took over at Barcelona?

18 Which team won the 1988–89 championship in the last minute of the season?

19 Kerry Dixon was Division 1 top scorer in 1984–85 with which team?

20 Which extra games were introduced to decide promotion?

21 Which Hertfordshire team lost the 1984 FA Cup Final?

22 Which club were known as the "Crazy Gang"?

23 Which club completed a League and FA Cup double in the 1980s?

24 Which dreadlocked striker scored in the 1988 European Championship Final?

25 Which club won their first League Championship for 18 years in 1989?

26 Who replaced Ron Greenwood as the England manager in 1982?

27 Can you name the British club which won the European Cup in 1982?

28 Name the London club which beat Arsenal in the 1980 FA Cup Final.

29 Which Town lifted the Uefa Cup in 1981?

30 Which club lost the 1983 League Cup Final but won the 1983 FA Cup?

Answers on page 190

14
MOURINHO'S CHELSEA

1 Did Mourinho join Chelsea in 2000, 2002 or 2004?

2 Which club was Damian Duff sold to in 2006?

3 Mourinho was dubbed the "Special" what?

4 Who was skipper of Jose's first Premiership-winning side?

5 Shaun Wright-Phillips was bought from which City club?

6 Which country did Claude Makelele play for?

7 Which midfielder was top scorer in 2005 and 2006?

8 Petr Cech keeps goal for which international Republic?

9 Who went to Arsenal when Ashley Cole came to Chelsea?

10 Mourinho joined Chelsea from which Portuguese club?

11 Who was not signed by Jose – Michael Ballack, Michael Essien or John Terry?

12 Did Crespo play for Argentina or Russia?

13 Joe Cole and Frank Lampard were at which other London club?

14 Carvalho and Ferreira play for which European country?

15 Who bankrolled Chelsea's success?

16 Which Carlo was number-two keeper in 2005 and 2006?

17 Does Andriy Shevchenko play for Bulgaria or the Ukraine?

18 Was Mourinho born in the 1940s, 1960s or 1970s?

19 Which Claudio was boss before Mourinho?

20 Which English team dumped Chelsea out of 2005's Champions League?

21 Who, in November 2006, beat Chelsea at home for the first time in 19 seasons?

22 Scott Parker moved on to which club?

23 Does Michael Essien play for France or Ghana?

24 When did Chelsea last win the league before 2005 – 1930s or 1950s?

25 Which Chelsea player Wayne had a link to the ground name?

26 Which Liverpool boss was part of the "no handshake" row?

27 Adrian Mutu's contract was cancelled after a scandal involving what?

28 Did Mourinho first win the League Cup or the FA Cup?

29 Arjen Robben plays international soccer with which country?

30 Which Norwegian club held Chelsea to a draw in what became Mourinho's final match?

Answers on page 190

15
CRICKET 2

1 When did England last win the Ashes before 2005 – was it 1967, 1977 or 1987?

2 The Oval is the home of which county?

3 What bird is linked to a score of nought?

4 Which 1990s English Test pace bowler has the same first name as an English county?

5 Which county has been captained by Mike Atherton?

6 Which Donald became the first Australian to score 300 test runs in a day?

7 At most, how many wickets can fall in a two-innings game?

8 Which former England all-rounder earned the nickname "Beefy"?

9 Which term describes a ball bowled out of the striker's reach?

10 Which specialist position does Adam Gilchrist take when fielding?

11 How many stumps are there on a set of wickets?

12 Which Aussie player is known – among other things – as Shanie?

13 What term describes fielders positioned closely behind the batsmen?

14 Grace Road is the ground of which county?

15 What must an umpire raise to show that a player is out?

16 Which country did all rounder Richard Hadlee play for?

17 What is the surname of Australian brothers Gregg and Ian?

18 Which county side did Fred Trueman play most of his cricket for?

19 Which West Indian batsman Brian started rewriting the record books in 1994?

20 What is added to the scores of the batsmen to make the total?

21 What does the abbreviation "st" stand for?

22 Which country did Abdul Qadir play for?

23 If the umpire raises both arms above his head what is he signalling?

24 What is a batsman said to collect if he scores 0 twice in a match?

25 Which radio commentator is known as "Aggers"?

26 Which Warwickshire ground hosts Test cricket?

27 Lillee and Thomson formed a deadly pace attack for which country?

28 Can a Test Match end in a tie?

29 Which world-class fast bowler made his last visit to England for the 2005 Ashes?

30 In 2005 which Welsh bowler Simon was injured and missed the final Ashes Test?

16
MIDFIELD MEN

1 Tim Sherwood led which club to the Premiership?

2 David Platt, Ray Parlour and Liam Brady have all played for which club?

3 Which French superstar was European Player of the Year three times in the 80s?

4 According to song, who was dreaming of Wembley with Tottenham Hotspur?

5 Which Billy was at the heart of Leeds's success in the 1960s and 70s?

6 Which English club did Kazimierz Denya join in the 70s?

7 Which former Liverpool skipper moved to Sampdoria?

8 Which midfield dynamo captained the West Germans in Italia 90?

9 Which Gary has played for Luton, Forest, Villa and Leicester?

10 Which London team did Stefan Schwartz play for?

11 What name is shared by Minto and Sellars?

12 Enzo Scifo has played for which country?

13 Which was Johnny Haynes's only English club?

14 Which long-serving Celtic and Scotland skipper first played back in 1982?

15 Michael Thomas has scored an FA Cup Final goal for which team?

16 What is the first name of West German '60s and 70s stalwart Overath?

17 Who was England's "Captain Marvel"?

18 Which club had the dream midfield of Ball, Harvey and Kendall?

19 Paul Ince was at which club when he made his England debut?

20 Has Robert Lee ever played for England?

21 In which year did Owen Hargreaves first play for Manchester United?

22 Which Frank scored in the 2008 Champions League Final?

23 Which club did Gareth Barry play for in 2007?

24 What country did Senegalese ex-Arsenal captain Patrick Vieira play for?

25 Which England midfielder won his 100th international cap in 2008?

26 Which Liverpool player was linked with a move to Chelsea in 2005?

27 At what London club did Joe Cole begin his professional career?

28 Who began his career at Nottingham Forest and ended it with Glasgow Celtic?

29 Name the attacking Australian midfielder who joined Everton in 2004.

30 Which ex-West Ham Utd and Spurs midfielder joined Man Utd in 2006?

 Answers on page 190

 Answers on page 190

17
FOOTBALL UK

1 Messrs Docherty, Atkinson and Ferguson have all managed which team?

2 Who was the first football boss to marry one of her former players?

3 Who stood down at Charlton in 2006 after more than ten years as manager?

4 Which Stanley was first winner of the European Footballer of the Year award?

5 Which was the first Rovers side to win the Premiership?

6 Graham Taylor was likened to a turnip after a defeat in which Scandinavian country?

7 Whom did Ruud Gullit replace as manager of Newcastle Utd?

8 In which Asian country did Gary Lineker play club soccer?

9 What colour are the stripes on Newcastle Utd's first choice shirts?

10 Which side moved from Roker Park to the Stadium of Light?

11 Was Alan Shearer sold to Newcastle for £5 million, £15 million or £25 million?

12 In which country was George Best born?

13 What is the nationality of Dennis Bergkamp?

14 Which Premiership keeper fractured his skull in a game in 2006?

15 Which manager took Wigan into the Premiership for the first time?

16 Which Yorkshire side was involved in a plane crash in March 1988?

17 Which Paul was the first black player to captain England?

18 Who was known as El Tel when he managed Barcelona?

19 Who in 1997 became Arsenal's all-time leading goal scorer?

20 How is the Football Association Challenge Cup better known?

21 Which Welshman Ian said living in Italy was like "living in a foreign country"?

22 Which club Charlton were promoted to the Premier League in 1998?

23 Which colour links shirts at Liverpool, Middlesbrough and Southampton?

24 Which Brian managed Notts Forest for 18 years?

25 Gareth Southgate finished his playing career at which club?

26 Which Charlton brother was the first to be knighted?

27 Which Eric was the first overseas PFA Player of the Year winner?

28 Who was dubbed "Duncan Disorderly"?

29 Paul Le Guen took over as boss of which Scottish giants?

30 Which club did Martin O'Neill manage after Celtic?

18
FOOTBALL 2

1 Who plays home games at Ewood Park?

2 Which team are known as the "Gunners"?

3 What colour are Manchester United's home shirts?

4 Which European country was drawn in the group with England in the 2006 World Cup in Germany?

5 Wayne Rooney joined Man Utd from which club?

6 Which city has teams called Wednesday and United?

7 Jose Mourinho joined Chelsea from which club in Portugal?

8 Who plays against Rangers in an Auld Firm derby match?

9 How many minutes in the second half of a Premier League match?

10 What name is shared by Birmingham, Coventry and Leicester?

11 Which colour card is used to send a player off?

12 Which German city hosted the final of the 2006 World Cup?

13 Which country does Ryan Giggs play for?

14 Which Graeme has managed Blackburn, Liverpool, Newcastle and Rangers?

15 Which East Anglian team is nicknamed the Canaries?

16 How many players should be on the pitch at the start of a game?

17 Who won the World Cup in 1958, 1962, 1970, 1994 and 2002?

18 Which team plays home games at Villa Park?

19 Raphael Benitez managed which British club to win the 2005 Champions League?

20 Hearts and Hibs come from which Scottish city?

21 What number is traditionally worn on the goalie's shirt?

22 Which England keeper Paul moved from Leeds to Spurs?

23 Which country did Freddie Ljungberg play for?

24 If you were at Goodison Park who would be playing at home?

25 Martin O'Neill managed which club to the Scottish title?

26 Which Nottingham club was managed by Brian Clough?

27 What is the colour of the home strip of both Everton and Chelsea?

28 Who managed England during the 2002 World Cup campaign?

29 Can a goalkeeper score a goal for his own team?

30 At which Lane do Spurs play when at home?

   Answers on page 190

 Answers on page 190

19
THE '90S

1 Which team scored 50 points in the 1999 Rugby League Challenge Cup Final?

2 What international Southern Hemisphere rugby union cup began in 1996?

3 What are the initials of champion jump jockey McCoy?

4 Which Australian golfer Ian won the British Open golf championship in 1991?

5 In which New Zealand city were the 1990 Commonwealth Games held?

6 In 1994 which rugby-playing Gavin was made an OBE?

7 Which Scottish soccer side monopolized the championship throughout the first half of the 1990s?

8 Which Phil was world darts champion in 1990 and 1992?

9 Which country returned to playing international sport in the 90s?

10 Which city hosted the 1996 Olympic Games?

11 Which steeplechase did Party Politics win in election year 1992?

12 Which rugby league team won the Challenge Cup every year for the first half of the 1990s?

13 Which Sally won Olympic gold in the 400-metre hurdles?

14 Which manager left Arsenal after taking a "bung"?

15 Why did no horse win the 1993 Grand National?

16 What is the first name of the athlete Akabusi?

17 At which sport did Karen Pickering excel?

18 Which country did Sonia O'Sullivan race for?

19 Which former Villa player David became England's soccer captain?

20 What does Alberto Tomba wear on his feet when he competes?

21 Who does Mary Pierce play tennis for?

22 Which country is snooker star Stephen Hendry from?

23 Which Kenny took Blackburn to the Premiership championship?

24 What is the first name of the athlete Regis?

25 Which Miss Martinez beat Martina in a Wimbledon final?

26 Who won the World Drivers' Championship in 1994–95?

27 Which English team won the European Cup Winners' Cup in 1991?

28 In which event was Jonathan Edwards world champion in 1995?

29 What does Steve Backley throw?

30 Which soccer nation were surprise winners of the 1992 European Championship?

20
DAVID BECKHAM

1 Which shirt number was linked with David Beckham at Man Utd?

2 In which area of London was David born?

3 Who was Man Utd boss when Beckham broke into Man Utd's team?

4 Beckham was first sent off for England in 1998, against which country?

5 What was wife Victoria's nickname in the Spice Girls?

6 Is Beckham's middle name Alex, Edward or Joseph?

7 The Beckham's first son was named after an area of which American city?

8 David's autobiography was called *My...* what?

9 Which Beckham baby shares a name with a Shakespeare character?

10 What was the second country in which Beckham played domestic football?

11 How many players before Beckham had been sent off twice playing for England?

12 What was Mrs Beckham's original surname?

13 Which TV soccer pundit Alan got it hopelessly wrong about Man Utd "kids" not winning anything?

14 What was the usual colour of the shorts during Beckham's Man Utd days?

15 Who are Ted and Sandra in relation to David?

16 Which country beginning with a "C" did Becks score against in France '98?

17 Victoria and David married at a castle in which country?

18 Which England soccer boss gave Beckham the captaincy?

19 Young Beckham was part of a side known as Fergie's what?

20 What was the nickname of the Beckhams' palatial home in Hertfordshire?

21 Beckham was sent off a second time for England against which country?

22 What was David's squad number at Real Madrid – 13, 23 or 43?

23 Against which Premiership side did David score from the half-way line in the 1996/7 season?

24 In which major 2002 sporting opening ceremony was David involved?

25 Was Beckham's transfer fee moving to Real Madrid £10m, £15m or £25m?

26 Which team ended Beckham's and England's World Cup hopes in 2002?

27 Why was the game against Getafe on 3 December 2005 significant for Beckham?

28 Which English international Michael was with Becks at Real Madrid?

29 Which Englishman was England boss when Becks was first capped?

30 Who is the older – David or Victoria Beckham?

Answers on page 190

21
LONDON CLUBS

1 Who became the first goalie to save a penalty in a Wembley FA Cup Final?

2 Which Northern Ireland star is QPR's most capped player?

3 What nationality is West Ham United's Slaven Bilic?

4 If you were walking down South Africa Road, which London club's ground would you be nearest?

5 Have Millwall ever won the FA Cup?

6 Which London side did Johnny Haynes play for?

7 Who holds Chelsea's record for the most League appearances?

8 Goalie Pat Jennings played for which three London area sides?

9 Which London side defeated Wales in a friendly in May 1996?

10 Who play in red and white vertical striped shirts?

11 Chelsea's Dennis Wise was transferred from which other London club?

12 Who was Trevor Brooking's "minder" on the pitch at West Ham?

13 Who scored the final goal to win Arsenal the title in 1989?

14 Who moved from West Ham United to Celtic for £1.5 million in 1992?

15 At which club did John Barnes make his League debut?

16 Who became the chairman of Leyton Orient in 1996?

17 Which Wimbledon player joined them from Brentford in 1992?

18 Name the London team whose address is 748 High Road?

19 Who did Crystal Palace beat in the 1990 FA Cup semi-final?

20 Frank Clark managed which London side?

21 Which London club ground has the largest capacity?

22 Which club successively had Italian, Portuguese, Israeli and Brazilian managers?

23 Brentford and which other London club are nicknamed "The Bees"?

24 Which London club sacked Peter Taylor as manager in 2007?

25 Which London club plays home games close to South Bermondsey rail station?

26 How many professional teams can London boast?

27 By what name was Arsenal originally known when it was first founded?

28 Which London club was the first to win the FA Cup?

29 Name the London club which has had almost 20 home grounds.

30 Which London club calls Griffin Park home?

22
RUGBY

1 Which country won League's World Cup from 1975 to 1995?

2 Which Scot was British Lions captain for the '93 New Zealand tour?

3 How old was Will Carling when he first captained England?

4 Who was top try scorer on the Lions 2005 tour of New Zealand?

5 How many countries had won the expanded Six Nations before Wales?

6 On his return to Union which Jonathan said, "It's a challenge I don't particularly need"?

7 Who did not play in 2005 after being named Great Britain league captain?

8 Where was Jeremy Guscott born?

9 Alphabetically, which team was last in the 2003 rugby union World Cup?

10 Which stadium hosted the League's 1995 World Cup Final?

11 The Ranfurly Shield is contested in which country?

12 Over half of the 1997 Lions squad came from which country?

13 In which decade was the John Player/Pilkington Cup begun?

14 Which English club did Franco Botica join when he left Wigan?

15 Which Michael has scored most points for Australia?

16 Which team ended Wigan's Challenge Cup record run in the 90s?

17 Which club were in the Heineken Cup finals of 2003, 2004 and 2005?

18 Which was the first team in the 90s other than Bath to win the Pilkington Cup?

19 Which two countries contest the Bledisloe Cup?

20 In the 1995 World Cup who were on the wrong end of an 89-0 score to Scotland?

21 What position did Sir Clive Woodward play at rugby?

22 In which decade was Fran Cotton born?

23 Which country did Grant Fox play for?

24 Gareth Thomas and which player captained Wales to 2005 Six Nations glory?

25 What was Martin Offiah's first League side?

26 Which player – a Frenchman – became the first to win 100 caps?

27 Which Belfast-born solicitor went on five British Lions tours?

28 Which Nick captained Australia from 1984 to 1992?

29 How many teams took part in the 2003 Rugby Union World Cup?

30 Where do St Helens play?

  Answers on page 191

 Answers on page 191

23
WHO'S WHO? 2

1 Whom did Muhammad Ali beat when he first became World Champion?

2 Who was runner up to Jana Novotna in the Wimbledon final in 1998?

3 Who was the first heavyweight boxing champion to retire undefeated?

4 Who was the late Flo Jo's husband?

5 Which husband of Marilyn Monroe was elected to the Baseball Hall of Fame?

6 Whose life was recorded on film in *Raging Bull*?

7 What colour individual medal did Sharron Davies win at the Moscow Olympics?

8 Which snooker champion was unkindly nicknamed "Dracula"?

9 Who beat Phil Taylor in the 2007 World Professional Darts Championship Final?

10 Whom did Zola Budd trip up at the Los Angeles Olympics in 1984?

11 British-born long jumper Fiona May represents which country in international athletics?

12 Which South African golfer's real first name is Theodore?

13 Which golfer split with his coach and his girlfriend in September 98?

14 Whom did Stephen Hendry replace as world No. 1 in the 1989–90 season?

15 Away from cricket, what sort of book did Aussie Matthew Hayden write?

16 Who was appointed USA captain for the 2008 Ryder Cup?

17 Who lost most Ladies Singles finals at Wimbledon in the 80s?

18 Which surname has been shared by three world snooker champions?

19 Peter Nicol won Commonwealth gold for Scotland in which sport?

20 Who successfully defended her heptathlon title at the 1998 Commonwealth Games?

21 Which cricketer with a very English surname was made South Africa captain in 2003?

22 Which Gladiator competed in the heptathlon in the 1998 Commonwealth Games?

23 Which Liverpudlian won the WBC Light Heavyweight Title in 1974?

24 Sharron Davies' one time fiancé Neil Adams was an international in which sport?

25 Who replaced Leon Spinks as Heavyweight Champion in 1987?

26 Who defeated Navratilova in the final at her last Wimbledon?

27 Who captained Europe to Ryder Cup success in 1995?

28 Allison Fisher is a former world champion in which sport?

29 With whom did John McEnroe win five Wimbledon Doubles titles?

30 Which boxer is nicknamed "The Dark Destroyer"?

24
SPORTING RECORDS

1 Who was Barcelona's boss for their record fourth European Cup Winner's Cup Final triumph in 1997?

2 In November '95 Jansher Khan won his seventh World Open title in which sport?

3 Which Derbyshire wicket-keeper set a career record number of dismissals from 1960 to 1988?

4 David Watkins scored 221 goals in a season for which rugby league club?

5 Which team were the first this century to win successive Super Bowl finals?

6 Who was the first overseas manager to win the FA Cup?

7 At which venue did Greg Norman set a lowest four-round Bittish Open total in 1993?

8 What record will Alf Common always hold?

9 Who was the first rugby union player to reach 50 international tries?

10 Who overtook Sunil Gavaskar's Test appearance record for India?

11 Sergei Bubka has broken a record over 30 times in which event?

12 Peter Shilton played his 1,000th league game with which club?

13 What was athlete Kathy Cook's maiden name?

14 Fred Perry was world champion in which sport before becoming a major tennis star?

15 Which soccer club is generally accepted to be the oldest in England?

16 Who is the youngest ever winner of the US Masters?

17 In which decade did Clive Lloyd first play Test cricket?

18 Who was the first player to hit 100 Premiership goals?

19 Bob Nudd had been a world champion in which sport?

20 Which British driver was the first to have seven Grand Prix wins in a year?

21 Francis Chichester made his '60s solo round-the-world trip in which boat?

22 Which Billy set an appearance record for West Ham?

23 Who set a new record of 9.77 seconds for the Men's 100m in June 2005?

24 Who in the 80s and early 90s set a record for captaining Pakistan at cricket?

25 Who in 1972 became the youngest F1 Motor Racing world champ?

26 Which record beaker won the first major Marathon she entered?

27 George Lee has been three time world champ in which sport?

28 Which Australian holds the world record for most Test runs in cricket?

29 In Jan 2005 Joachim Johansson set which new world record in tennis?

30 What is Seb Coe's middle name?

  Answers on page 191

25
SPORTING LEGENDS

1 Which Spaniard became the youngest golfer to win the British Open in the 20th century?

2 What was Roger Bannister's "day job"?

3 Which English club did George Best join immediately after leaving school?

4 In which decade did Ian Botham make his Test debut?

5 How many times did Will Carling lead England to the Five Nations title?

6 In which city did Shane Warne play his last Test match?

7 In which decade did Henry Cooper win his first British heavyweight championship?

8 Which side did Alex Ferguson manage before he went to Manchester United?

9 For which club did Jimmy Greaves make his Football League debut?

10 In which decade did Wayne Gretzky make his professional debut?

11 What was Sally Gunnell's Olympic gold medal-winning event?

12 Mike Hailwood won how many Isle of Man TT races in the period 1961–1979?

13 Who was the first snooker player to win all nine world ranking tournaments?

14 Who was the European Ryder Cup team's captain from 1983 to 1989?

15 Which Welsh Rugby player scored a record 90 points for his country between 1966 and 1972?

16 Who was the first man to hold the world record at 200m and 400m simultaneously?

17 Who led India to victory in the Cricket World Cup in 1983?

18 Anatoli Karpov was world champion in what?

19 Which team on the European mainland did Kevin Keegan play for?

20 Which sport did Jahangir Khan play?

21 How many Wimbledon titles did Billie Jean King win?

22 Who broke Fred Perry's record of three consecutive Wimbledon titles?

23 To the nearest 50 how many runs did Don Bradman make on his first innings for New South Wales?

24 In 1990 John McEnroe was expelled from which Grand Slam Open for swearing?

25 Which music did Torvill & Dean use when they scored a full hand of perfect scores at the 1984 Olympics?

26 Which team did Alf Ramsey take to the First Division Championship?

27 Which sport did Hank Aaron play?

28 Why was Muhammad Ali stripped of his World Heavyweight tile in 1967?

29 Which was the only Grand Slam title Pete Sampras did not win?

30 Which former Scottish jockey has the first names William Hunter Fisher?

26
HORSE RACING

1 In 1990 Mr Frisk set a record time in which major race?

2 Which Earl of Derby gave his name to the race?

3 To a year each way, when was Red Rum's third Grand National win?

4 Which jockey rode Best Mate to a hat-trick of Cheltenham Gold Cup wins?

5 Which three races make up the English Triple Crown?

6 How did 19th-century jockey Fred Archer die?

7 Which Irish rider won the Prix de L'Arc de Triomphe four times?

8 To two years each way, when did Lester Piggott first win the Derby?

9 Which classic race was sponsored by Gold Seal from 1984–92?

10 Who rode Devon Loch in the sensational 1956 Grand National?

11 What colour was Arkle?

12 How long is the Derby?

13 Sceptre managed to win how many classics outright in a season?

14 Shergar won the 1981 Derby by a record of how many lengths?

15 Which National Hunt jockey retired in 1993 with most ever wins?

16 What was the nickname of Corbiere?

17 Who rode Nijinsky to victory in the Derby?

18 In which decade was the Prix de L'Arc de Triomphe first run?

19 Who triumphed in the Oaks on Ballanchine and Moonshell?

20 Which horse was National Hunt Champion of the Year four times in a row from 1987 on?

21 Which horse stopped Red Rum getting three in a row Grand National wins?

22 How many times did the great Sir Gordon Richards win the Epsom Derby?

23 The Preakness Stakes, Belmont Stakes plus which other race make up the American Triple Crown?

24 Which Frank established a record nine victories in the Oaks?

25 Which jockey was the first ever winner of the Derby?

26 What actually is Frankie Detorri's first name?

27 Who holds the world record of riding 9,531 winners?

28 Which horse was the first Derby winner ridden by Kieren Fallon?

29 What colour was Red Rum?

30 How old was Lester Piggott when he returned to racing in 1990?

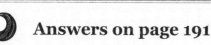 **Answers on page 191**

 Answers on page 191

27 WORLD FOOTBALL

1 In which country is the club Grampus Eight?

2 Which Italian team did Gazza play for?

3 Who was Dutch captain when they won the European Championship in 1988?

4 Who was leading scorer in the 1986 World Cup finals?

5 Which international side did Venables manage after England?

6 Who won the third-place final in the 1998 World Cup?

7 Which side did Cruyff move to from Ajax in 1973?

8 Dukla and Sparta are from which European city?

9 In a 2006 game, which British ref. showed three yellow cards to the same player?

10 Which Brazilian football coach was sacked after France 98?

11 Which Portuguese side did Graeme Souness manage?

12 Which country ran a full-page "thank you" ad in *The Times* after Euro 96?

13 Who won the Golden Boot in the 1998 World Cup?

14 Cesar Menotti managed which victorious World Cup side?

15 Who is the oldest player ever to score in the World Cup finals?

16 Penarol is a club side in which country?

17 Which Frenchman moved to Liverpool when Ronnie Moran retired?

18 What is Pele's full name?

19 Who, with England and Holland, was eliminated from France 98 on penalties?

20 Which country does Arsenal's Philippe Senderos represent?

21 Who scored the last goal in France 98?

22 Whose much-seen girlfriend in France 98 was Suzana Werner?

23 Who received the Golden Ball as outstanding player of the 2006 World Cup?

24 Which overseas star won most Premiership Player of the Month awards in 1997–98?

25 Which German won European Player of the Year in 1996?

26 In which stadium was the opening match of France 98?

27 Who captained Brazil in the 1998 World Cup Finals?

28 Who was the first European Footballer of the Year?

29 Who scored Italy's open play goal in the 2006 World Cup Final?

30 Which US star of the 1994 World Cup became the first American player to take part in Italy's Serie A?

28 GOLDEN OLDIES

1 Who was born on Feb. 1, 1915, in Hanley, Stoke on Trent?

2 Bobby Charlton came out of retirement to play for which League club?

3 Which club had goalkeepers Banks and Shilton on their books in the 1960s?

4 Which was the third London side that Jimmy Greaves played for?

5 Who was travelling on a bus when he learnt that he had been made England skipper?

6 Who fractured his skull in a motorbike accident in the 1920s?

7 With which League club did Denis Law make his debut?

8 Who hit 42 goals in a season for Arsenal in the 1930s?

9 Who was aged 60 when he became England's caretaker manager?

10 Who bagged 255 League goals for Bolton in the 1940s and 1950s?

11 To two each way, how many years did Stanley Matthews play League soccer in England?

12 Who became Britain's most expensive player when he moved from Preston North End to Arsenal in 1929?

13 Which Dave of Tottenham Hotspur broke his left leg twice in a year in the 1960s?

14 Hughie Gallacher hit 36 League goals in a season for which club?

15 Where was Wilf Mannion born?

16 At which club did Brian Kidd begin his career?

17 Liverpool's legendary striker Billy Liddell came from which country?

18 Which country developed the deep-lying centre forward role just after World War II?

19 Which great goalkeeper was born in Newry on June 12, 1945?

20 Did Matt Busby ever play international soccer?

21 By what non-PC nickname was England goalkeeper Willie Foulke known?

22 Who was England's first £10,000 footballer?

23 Who was Manchester United's captain when they won the FA Cup in 1948?

24 Which 1940s and 1950s star was known as "The Clown Prince of Football"?

25 Which future England manager won a League title with Spurs in 1951?

26 Who won the inaugural FWA Player of the Year Award in 1948?

27 Who scored England's only goal when they lost 7–1 away to Hungary in 1954?

28 Name the player who captained Spurs to the League and Cup double in 1960–61.

29 Name the Arsenal star of the 1940s who went on to manage Man. City and England.

30 Which German international broke his neck in the 1956 FA Cup Final?

  Answers on page 191

  Answers on page 191

29
WORLD FOOTBALL 2

1 What colour did the legendary keeper Lev Yashin play in?
2 Which host city was the most northerly in Germany 2006?
3 Bobby Robson left which club to join Barcelona?
4 Oscar Ruggeri became the highest-capped player for which country?
5 Who had the final kick of the 1994 World Cup Final?
6 In which decade did Bayern Munich first win the UEFA Cup?
7 Former Italian prime minister Silvio Berlusconi took over which club?
8 Thomas Ravelli became the most-capped player for which country?
9 The stadium the Monumental is in which country?
10 Which Dutchman came with Arnold Muhren to Ipswich in the 80s?
11 Alfredo di Stefano played for Argentina, Spain and which other country?
12 Which country does Andrei Shevchenko play for?
13 The club Feyenoord is based in which city?
14 Which club play at the Bernabeu Stadium?
15 Who was UK's first European Footballer of the Year this century?
16 What colour are Brazil's shorts?
17 How old was Maradona when he first played for Argentina?
18 Who captained Italy in the 1994 World Cup Final?
19 Gullit, Van Basten and Rijkaard lined up at which non-Dutch club?
20 The Fritz-Walter Stadium is in which German venue?
21 Who was first player from Ghana to play in the English league?
22 Which Arsenal manager signed Dennis Bergkamp?
23 How often is the African Nations Cup staged?
24 Which was the first African country to reach the World Cup quarter finals?
25 Lars Lagerback took which country to Germany 2006?
26 Which club play at the Olympiastadion?
27 Which city hosted the final of Euro 2004?
28 What colour are Portugal's shorts?
29 Which country did Mario Kempes play for?
30 Since the 1950s, in which decade did Brazil not win the World Cup?

30
FOOTBALL: ITALY

1 What was Paolo Maldini's first club?
2 Which club have won the League most times?
3 Who was Italy's top scorer in the 1994 World Cup in the USA?
4 How old was Paolo Rossi when he retired from playing?
5 Which club did Graeme Souness join in Italy?
6 German imports Klinsmann and Matthaus brought which club the League title in 1989?
7 Which team are known as the Zebras?
8 Dino Zoff became coach and later president of which club?
9 Which team knocked Italy out of Italia 90?
10 The import of what was banned in 1964, only to be lifted in the 1980s?
11 Who were the opponents for Cesare Maldini's first match as coach?
12 Who was Italy's top scorer in the 1982 World Cup tournament?
13 Michel Platini inspired Juventus to European Cup Final victory over which English side?
14 Gianfranco Zola took over the number 10 shirt at Napoli from which superstar?
15 In which decade did the Italians first win the World Cup?
16 Who were champions of Serie A in 1995–96?
17 Thomas Brolin joined Leeds United from which Italian club?
18 Who missed the final penalty for Italy in the 1994 World Cup Final?
19 Lazio play in which Italian city?
20 Who was in charge of Italy for Euro 96?
21 In which city is the Stadio Delle Alpi?
22 Who is Italy's all-time leader in international appearances?
23 Who knocked Italy out of the 2002 World Cup?
24 Which Italian international had Allan Border as his favourite sportsman?
25 Which Fabio scored the decisive penalty in the 2006 World Cup Final?
26 Who aged 40 became the oldest winner of the World Cup in 1982?
27 Name the former Middlesbrough player nicknamed "The White Feather".
28 Which player's mother refused a lucrative offer from AC Milan before he joined Roma in 1989?
29 Name the ex-Juventus and FC Barcelona defender who joined AC Milan in 2008.
30 Who played for Modena in 1994 and made Bayern Munich his 10th club in 2007?

  Answers on page 191

 Answers on page 191

31 FOOTBALL: GOLDEN GOALS

1 Which Cliff set a career goals record at Arsenal?
2 Dennis Bergkamp's goals led which team to Euro success in 1992?
3 Who is credited – or blamed – for bringing the shirt-over-the-head-after-scoring routine to English soccer?
4 Which player of the 1950s and '60s set up Chelsea's record for most League goals for the club?
5 Whose amazing Euro 96 lob knocked out Portugal?
6 Neil Shipperley's goals kept which side in the Premiership in 1995–96?
7 Which German striker was known as "Der Bomber"?
8 Steve Bloomer notched 292 League goals for which club?
9 Who dived full-length on the pitch after his first goal for Tottenham Hotspur in the Premiership?
10 To 20 each way, what was Dixie Dean's Everton League goals total?
11 Which two clubs has Ian Wright scored for in FA Cup Finals?
12 A Brett Angell goal took which team to the Coca-Cola Cup semi-final in 1997?
13 A Charlie George goal won the FA Cup for which team?
14 A fine Davor Suker shot bamboozled which Danish keeper in Euro 96?
15 Who scored a last-gasp equalizer for Manchester Utd v Oldham in a 1990s semi-final?
16 Who was the Brazilian top scorer in the 1994 World Cup tournament?
17 Andy Linighan scored a last-minute FA Cup Final winner for which team?
18 Craig Brewster scored the only goal to win the Scottish League Cup for which club in 1993–94?
19 Which Scot was Europe's top league scorer in 1991–92?
20 Who scored England's first in the 1966 World Cup Final?
21 Whose handball gave France a golden goal penalty at the Euro 2000 semi-final?
22 Which country conceded the first World Cup finals golden goal?
23 Who scored the golden goal winner of the Euro 2000 final?
24 What replaced the golden goal at Euro 2004?
25 In which year did the UEFA Cup Final end 5–4 on a golden goal?
26 In what year did FIFA first introduce the golden goal system?
27 What was the first major tournament played using the golden goal rule?
28 Which French defender scored the first ever golden goal in the World Cup?
29 Which sandy 2008 FIFA-recognized tournament still uses the golden goal rule?
30 Who scored the golden goal decider in the final of Euro 1996?

32 WAYNE ROONEY

1 In which city was Wayne born?
2 Rooney scored his first England goal against which country?
3 Which Everton manager gave Rooney his debut?
4 In which year was Rooney born?
5 Where did Everton finish in the Premiership in Rooney's first season?
6 Against which country did Rooney make his England debut?
7 Rooney was first sent off against which Premiership side?
8 Which BBC award did he win in 2002?
9 Which squad number did Rooney take at Man Utd?
10 Which player left Man Utd to make Rooney's number available?
11 Wayne first played in an FA Cup Final against which team?
12 Who was Everton's regular keeper in Rooney's first season?
13 What is Wayne's star sign – Taurus or Scorpio?
14 Who were the opponents in Euro 2004 when Rooney was injured?
15 Which other club bid for Rooney before the Man Utd move?
16 Who were the opposition in Rooney's Man Utd debut?
17 How many goals did he score in his Man Utd debut game?
18 His first Premiership goal was against which club?
19 Rooney was booked against which country in Euro 2004?
20 Which animated character gives Rooney one of his nicknames?
21 Against which European club team was he red carded in Sept. 2005?
22 What was the score in the England v. Croatia Euro 2004 game?
23 What number does Rooney usually wear for England?
24 In his first season did Rooney score 6, 9, or 16 league goals?
25 A goal against which team made Wayne the youngest ever Premiership scorer?
26 He was 17 years and how many days old on his England debut – 111, 222 or 333?
27 Which Tomasz was Everton's top scorer in Wayne's first season?
28 Where did Man Utd finish in the Premiership in Wayne's first season?
29 What is Wayne's middle name?
30 Wayne's first Everton goals were in the League Cup against which club?

 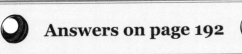 **Answers on page 192**

Answers on page 192

33
FOOTBALL UK 2

1 Who succeeded Ossie Ardiles as Spurs manager?

2 Which football team plays its home matches at Love Street?

3 Which English international played for three Italian clubs before moving to Arsenal?

4 Who was fined £20,000 for making a video on how to foul players?

5 Whose 1996 penalty miss prompted Des Lynam to say "You can come out from behind your sofas now"?

6 Who was PFA Young Player of the Year in 95 and 96?

7 Who left Tottenham immediately before George Graham took over?

8 Which football manager is singer Louise's father-in-law?

9 Which club side was Alan Ball playing for during the 1966 World Cup?

10 What is Glenn Hoddle in the cockney rhyming slang dictionary?

11 Which was the first Lancashire side Kenny Dalglish managed?

12 How is Mrs Paul Peschisolido better known?

13 Wayne Rooney was doubtful for Germany 2006 after an injury sustained in which match?

14 Who was Man Utd manager immediately prior to Alex Ferguson?

15 Which team did Arsenal beat in the 2006 Champions League semi-finals?

16 Who was the first UK manager to walk out on a contract and work abroad?

17 Who has managed Internazionale of Milan and Blackburn Rovers?

18 Which 1980s FA Cup winners came nearest the start of the alphabet?

19 Who was Blackburn's top scorer in 2005–06, his only season at the club?

20 Who stayed longer as Newcastle boss – Sir Bobby Robson or Graeme Souness?

21 Who became Everton's record signing in June 2006?

22 Who was made Northern Ireland manager in February 1998?

23 Which England player was seen on the town wearing a sarong prior to France 98?

24 Who should Scotland have been playing when they arrived for a World Cup qualifier with no opposition?

25 Which ex-international managed Burnley in the 1997–98 season?

26 Whom did Jack Charlton play all his League football with?

27 George Graham was accused of taking a "bung" in the transfer of which player?

28 Whom did David O'Leary take over from as Aston Villa boss?

29 In which season did evergreen Ryan Giggs make his Man Utd league debut?

30 Which team beat Middlesbrough in the 2006 UEFA Cup Final?

 Answers on page 192

34
AMERICAN SPORT

1 How many of their 16 NFL regular season games did New England win in 2007?

2 Which team won their first NBA Championship for more than 20 years in 2008?

3 Who replaced Winston as headline sponsors of NASCAR's main championship?

4 Which Canadian province had runners-up in the Stanley Cup twice in the 2000s?

5 Which Chicago baseball team won the World Series in 2005?

6 In which sport is the Stanley Cup awarded?

7 Where are the Astros baseball team from?

8 Which city do the Redskins American football team come from?

9 What were "Babe" Ruth's real first names?

10 Which two countries other than the US have won Olympic gold medals at basketball?

11 Which US soccer player was with Blackburn and Coventry?

12 The First Budweiser Bowl in the UK in 1986 was won by which team?

13 The Princetown College rules drawn up in 1867 affect which sport?

14 Which US soccer team plays at Anaheim Stadium?

15 In American football in which year did the AFL and the NFL merge?

16 How many people are there in an ice hockey team?

17 What game is played by the Detroit Pistons?

18 What was the nickname of baseball's Lawrence Peter Berra?

19 Giants and Jets have triumphed in the Super Bowl for which city?

20 The invention of which sport is credited to Dr J. A. Naismith?

21 In baseball, which team bats first?

22 Which year were American professionals first allowed to enter the World Basketball Championships?

23 Which sport do the Miami Dolphins play?

24 In which country were the rules for modern ice hockey formulated?

25 Which two American men won ice skating Olympic gold in the 1980s?

26 Which trophy do teams from AFC and NFC players contest?

27 Which two US women skaters had a battle on and off the rink in 1994?

28 Which team won the first Super Bowl?

29 Which sport do the Atlanta Braves play?

30 How many players are there in a baseball team?

 Answers on page 192

35 SPEED STARS

1 Which country did motor racing's Juan Manuel Fangio come from?

2 Who set a world record for the fastest ever maximum snooker break at the Crucible in April 1997?

3 Which England fast bowler received damages from *Wisden Cricket Monthly* over the article "Is It in the Blood?"?

4 What was the nost notable thing about Julio McCaw who raced against Jesse Owens?

5 In which event did Redgrave and Pinsent win Olympic gold?

6 Who was the first driver to register 50 Grand Prix victories?

7 In which British city did Kelly Holmes first race after Athens Gold?

8 In motor cycling, at what cc level was Barry Sheene world champ?

9 What was Mary Slaney's surname before her marriage?

10 Which Australian quick bowler is known as Pigeon?

11 To a year each way, when was James Hunt Formula 1 world champ?

12 Graeme Obree is connected with which sport?

13 Stephane Peterhansel won his second successive what in Jan. 2005?

14 To a year each way, how old was Nigel Mansell when he was F1 world champion?

15 What famous first will Diomed always hold?

16 Finishing third in which race made Fernando Alonso F1 world champ?

17 In April 1997 what did younger brother Florian give to Niki Lauda?

18 Colin Jackson's 60m hurdle record was set in Sindelfingen – in which country?

19 Whom did Frank Williams recruit from IndyCar for the 1996 GP season?

20 Who succeeded Linford Christie as England's athletics team captain?

21 Which country does Donovan Bailey run for?

22 What nationality is Keke Rosberg?

23 Where in 1996 did Oliver Panis have his debut Grand Prix victory?

24 Who was the first man to swim 100m in less than a minute?

25 Who was Man. Utd's left winger in the '60s European Cup triumph?

26 What are Daley Thompson's first two names?

27 Which Grand Prix did Damon Hill win first when he became 1996 world champion?

28 Which England fast bowler was nicknamed George?

29 Which horse was Lester Piggott's first Derby winner?

30 Bode Miller is associated with which sport?

36 CRICKET 3

1 Which county were admitted to the County Championship in 1992?

2 Who was Australia's Man of the Series in the 2005 Ashes?

3 In 2005, who became the fourth quickest England player to 1,000 Test runs?

4 What was Alfred Freeman's nickname?

5 Which county has its HQ at Sophia Gardens?

6 Which county did Dermot Reeve take to the championship?

7 What creature is on the Somerset badge?

8 Which pair of spinners – both with surnames beginning with an E – dominated the 80s at Middlesex?

9 Which country did Martin Crowe play for?

10 What is the colour of the *Wisden Cricketers' Almanac*?

11 Which county has its headquarters in Nottingham Road?

12 Which country won their first ever Test in January 2005?

13 Which country was first to win a Test in the 2005 Ashes series?

14 Which cricket personality is known as "Bumble"?

15 Who was the first Scotsman to captain England?

16 Who became the first Test bowler to take 19 wickets in a game?

17 Which county did Ian Botham join on leaving Somerset?

18 Is Brian Lara a right- or left-handed batsman?

19 What did the St Lawrence Ground in Canterbury lose in Jan. 2005?

20 Which England fast bowler took Dylan as a middle name in honour of Bob Dylan?

21 How old was Mike Atherton when he was made England captain?

22 In 1995, which Englishman took a Test hat-trick against the West Indies?

23 Shane Warne first captained which Australian state side?

24 Which county did Nasser Hussain play for?

25 In what year was the series that became known as "Botham's Ashes"?

26 Which county did Malcolm Marshall and Gordon Greenidge play for?

27 In which decade did the first Australia v. England Test take place?

28 Which English bowler took 12 for 205 against South Africa in 2005?

29 Which country did Ian Redpath play for?

30 Did Geoff Boycott ever captain England?

 Answers on page 192

 Answers on page 192

37
FOOTBALL: INTERNATIONALS

1 Who is the oldest player to turn out for Wales?

2 In which decade did Wales first beat England at Wembley?

3 Who became manager of Northern Ireland in 1994?

4 Which ex-Liverpool player has managed Wales?

5 At which ground do the Republic of Ireland play home matches?

6 Which Peter scored twice for Northern Ireland in their magnificent draw with West Germany in the 1958 World Cup?

7 Who was Tony Cascarino playing for when he won his first cap?

8 When did the Republic of Ireland first qualify for the World Cup finals?

9 Which country has Vinnie Jones played for?

10 Which Welsh player was the most capped before Neville Southall?

11 Which Christian names link Northern Ireland's McIlroy and Quinn?

12 Which Northern Ireland skipper said, "Our tactics are to equalize before the other side scores"?

13 Which Republic of Ireland player was nicknamed "Chippy"?

14 In 1992 Michael Hughes made his debut for which country?

15 Which Republic of Ireland player appeared in five FA Cup Finals between 1963 and 1973?

16 In which year did Jack Charlton become manager of the Republic of Ireland?

17 Which home international countries were present in the 1982 World Cup finals?

18 Which Arsenal and Tottenham Hotspur manager was also team boss of Northern Ireland?

19 Which London-based striker captained Northern Ireland in 1996?

20 When did Wales last qualify for the World Cup?

21 In which city did England inflict a first competitive home loss for Croatia in 2008?

22 Which country moved to the top of the FIFA World Rankings in July 2008?

23 Which club did Craig Burley leave to take over as Scotland's manager?

24 Where was Croatia's Josip Simunic, who received three yellow cards against Australia in 2006, born?

25 Who was the first England manager to make David Beckham captain?

26 Which former West Ham player guided Croatia to two famous wins over England?

27 Who is the only player to score 100 League goals in England and Scotland?

28 Which ex-member of Chelsea's foreign brigade was awarded an OBE in 2004?

29 Name the Italian who broke Irish hearts at the 1990 World Cup finals.

30 Which ex-Premiership star played for Russia, Ukraine and the CIS?

38
RUGBY 2

1 Which Australian was the first to score 60 tries in international rugby?

2 Who was the first Englishman to reach 750 points in major internationals?

3 Who was the first English player to play in 50 internationals?

4 Which country in 1995 asked to increase the number of teams in the Five Nations Cup?

5 Which colours do Bath play in?

6 Which Welsh Union player was a regular captain on *A Question of Sport*?

7 In which part of London did the London Broncos start out?

8 Who won the Man of Steel in 1996 and 2004?

9 For which side did Brian Bevan score 740 tries in 620 matches?

10 What were Bradford before they were Bulls?

11 Who retired as Scottish captain after the 1995 World Cup?

12 Who was Wigan's leading try scorer in the 1994/95 season?

13 Where would you watch Rhinos playing rugby?

14 Paul Sackey was at which club when he first won a cap, aged 27?

15 Which international side has the shortest name?

16 Who are the two sides in the Varsity Match?

17 Which rugby team plays its home games at Welford Road?

18 Who was leading try scorer in the 1995 rugby union World Cup?

19 In 1998 what colour cards were substituted for yellow ones?

20 Who joined Leeds in 1991 after playing on the other side of the Pennines since 1984?

21 What did Bath Football Club change its name to in the mid-90s?

22 Who was the first non-white Springbok, before the end of apartheid?

23 Which rugby side added Warriors to its name?

24 In which decade was Rugby Union last played in the Olympics?

25 How old was Will Carling when he was first made England captain?

26 Who played a record-breaking 69 times at fly half for England between 1985 and 1995?

27 In 1980 who led England to their first Grand Slam in 23 years?

28 Where is the annual Varsity match played?

29 How many years had Wigan's unbeaten run in the FA Challenge Cup lasted when it ended in 1996?

30 Whom did Martin Offiah play for in his first years as a League player?

  Answers on page 192

39
CRICKET 4

1 Where was the first Test played in the 2006–7 Ashes?

2 Who was Geraint Jones's main rival as keeper in the 2006–7 Ashes?

3 Which former test cricketer became President of the MCC in 1998?

4 Which newsreader has written biographies of Viv Richards and Clive Lloyd?

5 What is Ian Botham's middle name?

6 Which Indian was the second bowler to reach 400 Test wickets?

7 Which English county did Viv Richards play for?

8 Which cricketer was the first British sportsman to appear in a major advertising campaign?

9 Which umpire did Gatting publicly argue with in Faisalabad?

10 Which Australian was the first man to take 300 wickets in Test cricket?

11 Who played in the most tests as England captain?

12 Which is the most southerly of the six regular English Test grounds?

13 Which cricketer's initials are GAG?

14 In Aussie opening partnerships, who are Justin and Matthew?

15 At which ground did England beat South Africa to clinch the 1998 series?

16 David Lloyd was reprimanded for criticising which Sri Lankan bowler in 1998?

17 What were WG Grace's first two names?

18 Whose record did Graham Gooch pass when he became England's leading run scorer?

19 Which county does Monty Panesar play for?

20 Who won the 1998 Nat West Trophy?

21 In 1996 Darren Gough became the first England bowler to bowl wearing what?

22 Which Indian cricketer scored 10,122 runs in 125 matches between 1971 and 1987?

23 Who captained the South Africans on their 1998 England tour?

24 Which cricketer's bat was auctioned for £23,000 in 1997?

25 Which Rhodesian became Zimbabwe's youngest professional at the age of 17 in 1985?

26 Who captained Pakistan in the 1992 World Cup victory?

27 On which island did Brian Lara make his record-breaking 375?

28 In which newspaper was it announced that English cricket had died, leading to competition for the Ashes?

29 In which country is Khettarama Stadium?

30 Which hand does David Gower write with?

40
FOOTBALL: HAT TRICKS

1 Who scored five Premiership hat-tricks in 1995–96?

2 Who finished Southampton's joint top scorer in 1995–96 with seven goals, having hit a hat-trick in the first game?

3 Which Leeds Utd midfielder hit a 1995 hat-trick against Coventry City?

4 Which Stan hit an FA Cup Final hat-trick in the 1950s?

5 Geoff Hurst hit his first England hat-trick against which team?

6 Who was Andy Gray playing for when he hit a mid-1980s European Cup Winners' Cup treble?

7 Which Ipswich player hit two hat-tricks in 1980–81 UEFA Cup games?

8 Which England player got four against San Marino in November 1993?

9 Who was Dion Dublin playing for when he hit three against Sheffield Wednesday in 1995, ending up on the losing side?

10 Robert Fleck has hit three in a Euro game for which club?

11 Who hit a 1997 hat-trick for Newcastle Utd, who were losing 3–1, leading to a 4–3 victory over Leicester City?

12 Bryan Robson got his only England hat-trick in an 8–0 rout of which country in 1984?

13 Who hit Blackburn Rovers' hat-trick in the 1995–96 European Cup?

14 Who hit three-plus as Man Utd beat Ipswich Town 9–0 in 1995?

15 Which England player hit hat-tricks against Turkey in 1985 and 1987?

16 Adcock, Stewart and White each hit three for which team in the same game in 1987?

17 Who hit a Scottish FA Cup Final hat-trick in 1996?

18 Which player hit his first Newcastle Utd hat-trick against Wimbledon in October 1995?

19 Which player hit six England hat-tricks from 1960 to 1966?

20 Who hit a Charity Shield hat-trick for Leeds Utd in 1992?

21 Who scored the only hat-trick of the Euro 2008 finals?

22 Which 21st-century player scored a hat-trick for England in his second start?

23 Which post-war player has scored the most hat-tricks for Arsenal with 11?

24 Who scored a hat-trick of penalties for Brazil against Argentina in 2004?

25 In which city did Michael Owen score his first England hat-trick?

26 Which Man Utd player scored a hat-trick on his debut for the club in 2004?

27 Who scored a hat-trick for Real Madrid in a 4–3 defeat to Man. Utd in 2003?

28 In 2008, he scored consecutive home hat-tricks for his Premiership club. Who is he?

29 Who scored a hat-trick for England against Jamaica in 2006?

30 Which Spurs player scored a hat-trick in their 4–0 win over Dinamo Zagreb in 2008?

  Answers on page 192

 Answers on page 192

41
FOOTBALL 3

1 Nanninga was the first sub to score in a World Cup Final ... for whom?

2 Which team are known as the "Cherries"?

3 What was strange about the tackle that ended the career of keeper Chic Brodie of Brentford back in 1970?

4 How many countries played in World Cup 2002 in Japan and South Korea?

5 Which club did Glenn Hoddle leave to become England manager?

6 Which country won the first World Cup held in 1930?

7 Which German club did Kevin Keegan play for?

8 Mike Walker and Martin O'Neill walked out on which chairman?

9 Who was the first uncapped player sold for over £1,000,000 in Britain?

10 What name is shared by Scunthorpe, Southend and Rotherham?

11 Fabien Barthez began his career with which French club?

12 Who was England's final substitute in the 2002 quarter-final defeat by Brazil?

13 Which country did Emlyn Hughes play for?

14 Emmanuel Petit joined Arsenal from which soccer club?

15 Which 4th Division team reached the first League Cup Final in 1962?

16 Who played in the first FA Cup Final ever to end 3–3?

17 Which team paid a record £1,000 for Alf Common in 1905?

18 Newcastle play at St James' Park but who plays at St James Park?

19 Who captained the Man Utd team that won the 1968 European Cup?

20 Who scored Scotland's only goal in the 1986 World Cup Finals in Mexico?

21 Where in England do you go to shout "Come on, you greens"?

22 An Italian boss replacing a Dutchman was a first at which English club?

23 Stokoe (Sunderland) and Revie (Leeds) were rival managers in the 1973 FA Cup Final. For which teams were they rivals as Cup Final players?

24 If you are at Turf Moor who is playing at home?

25 Which keeper played three games for Man Utd in the early 1990s and 23 games in 1999–2000?

26 Which club has been managed by Brian Clough and Jimmy Armfield?

27 Which player went from Juventus to Real Madrid for £46.5m in 2001?

28 Which team is known as "The Bairns"?

29 Which non-League team held Man Utd to a 0–0 draw in the third round of the 2005/6 FA Cup?

30 At which Lane did Wimbledon play when they entered the League?

42
FOOTBALL 4

1 Who preceded Frank O'Farrell as Man Utd manager?

2 How did Joan Bazely make history in 1976?

3 Who were the opponents in Peter Shilton's last game for England?

4 Which Premiership side lost nine of its last ten games in 2006 and stayed up?

5 Who offered the England and Scotland squads a week on his Caribbean island if they won the World Cup in 1998?

6 Roy Keane played his last Premiership game for Man Utd against which team?

7 Which club's motto is *Nil Satis Nisi Optimum*?

8 John Benson, Bruce Rioch and Steve Bruce have all managed which club?

9 To three, for how many games was Sven-Goran Eriksson in charge of England?

10 Ray Wilkins was sent off while playing for England against which country?

11 Who did Denis Law play for immediately before Man Utd?

12 Who was the only side to beat England over 90 minutes when Venables was manager?

13 Who appeared in a TV ad for bacon before the 1998 World Cup?

14 Who is Sweden's most capped player of all time?

15 Who led Naples to their first ever Italian championship?

16 Which of the Italian sides David Platt played for had the shortest name?

17 Bolton's Kevin Davies has played over 100 games for three clubs – which was first?

18 Who was fourth in the 1994 World Cup?

19 Roy Hodgson joined Blackburn Rovers from which club?

20 What was Arsenal tube station called before it was called Arsenal?

21 Who was the first Dutchman to play in an FA Cup Final?

22 Whom were Man Utd playing when George Best made his debut?

23 Which sides competed in the first all-British UEFA Cup Final?

24 Who were the first winners of the Inter Toto Cup?

25 How many times did Bobby Moore captain England in 108 internationals?

26 Who was Reading's only ever-present in their 2005–06 Championship win?

27 Where did Paul Ince captain England for the first time?

28 Which club side were the first to win the South American Cup?

29 Which defender scored his only England goal in Sven-Goran Eriksson's first game?

30 Which two Scottish sides did Antti Niemi play for prior to moving to England?

 Answers on page 193

 Answers on page 192

43
FOOTBALL: WORLD CUP

1 Oman Biyik played in the World Cup for which country?

2 In 1994, Leonardo of Brazil was sent off against which country?

3 Which French player was victim of Schumacher's appalling challenge in 1984?

4 Which country took the first penalty in the 1994 final shoot-out?

5 20 of the Republic of Ireland's 22-man USA 94 squad played in the English league – which two didn't?

6 Which country, other than the Republic of Ireland, included a high proportion of English League players in USA in 1994?

7 Which Czechoslovakian player was second-top scorer in Italia 90?

8 In USA 94 which country scored most goals in the group games yet still went out?

9 How many games did England lose in Spain in 1982?

10 Which was the first host country to win the World Cup?

11 What was the half-time score in the 1994 third-place match?

12 Olguin, Gallego and Ortiz played for which World Cup-winning team?

13 In 1982, what was the nickname of England's mascot?

14 Felix was in goal for which World Cup winners?

15 Who were Scotland's joint top scorers in Italia 90?

16 Whose last international goal was a World Cup Final winner?

17 Which country was top of the Republic of Ireland's Group in USA 1994?

18 Who were the only team to beat West Germany in the 1974 finals?

19 In Italia 90 who scored England's winner against Egypt?

20 Which country failed to score in the USA in 1994?

21 In which country was 2006 World Cup Final referee Horacio Elizondo born?

22 Who scored in the opening 15 seconds of the 2002 third-place play-off?

23 What was the score when Scotland lost to Morocco in France 98?

24 Against which country was Thierry Henry red-carded in 2002?

25 How many players received yellow cards when Portugal played Holland in 2006?

26 Apart from Brazil, which is the only other country to successfully retain the trophy?

27 Name the Russian who holds the record for the most goals in a single game (five).

28 Which South American country holds the record for the most defeats (20)?

29 What is the most number of red cards shown in a World Cup final stages game?

30 Name the European debutants at the 2006 World Cup finals.

Answers on page 193

44
RUGBY 3

1 Which country was the first to play in two union World Cup Finals?

2 As a player Willie John McBride went on how many Lions tours?

3 To five years, when did France first win the Five Nations outright?

4 Who won the league's first Man of Steel award?

5 Lawrence Dallaglio's Lions tour ended in June 2005 in a game against which side?

6 Who is Argentina's leading all-time point-scorer?

7 Who didn't collect his loser's medal after the 1996 Pilkington Cup Final?

8 Keith Elwell played in 239 consecutive games for which league side?

9 Who scored 45 individual points for New Zealand against Japan in 1995?

10 Which university did Will Carling go to?

11 Who is the only person to captain the Lions and the English cricket team?

12 Who said at the wedding of the All-Black Glen Osborne, "I'm not the best man: I'm one of the security guards"?

13 Who scored most tries in the first Super League season?

14 Which country first completed the Grand Slam in 1968?

15 How old was Barry John when he retired from playing rugby?

16 Which coach was sacked by St Helens for gross misconduct in May 2005?

17 Rory Underwood began his senior career with which club?

18 What is Martin Offiah's middle name?

19 Gavin Hastings scored how many points in the 1995 World Cup game against Ivory Coast?

20 Ellery Hanley first won the Man of Steel award while with which club?

21 In which decade were Orrell founded?

22 Which club did Gareth Edwards play for?

23 Who was Warrington's first player to win the Man of Steel award?

24 In the 1995 World Cup which two players scored seven tries?

25 Who set a new Super League record with six tries in a September 2005 game?

26 Which team won the league's Challenge Cup before Wigan's eight-in-a-row run?

27 The full-back J. P. R. Williams played once in a 1978 international in which position?

28 Who was the first man to play for, then coach an England Grand Slam team?

29 Where was Tony Underwood born?

30 Andrew Johns's much-heralded move to Warrington Wolves lasted how many games?

Answers on page 193

45
OLYMPICS

1 In which country did the final vote about hosting the 2012 Olympics take place?

2 At which sport did future tennis star Drobny win a medal in 1948?

3 Windsurfing is included in the Olympics as part of which sport's events?

4 Where were the Winter Olympics held in 1928 and 1948?

5 On which apparatus did Nadia Comaneci score perfect tens in 1976?

6 Who was the first man to win Olympic gold at 200m and 400m?

7 In which event did Carl Lewis win his ninth and final gold medal?

8 Who won the first of four discus golds in Melbourne in 1956?

9 How many silver medals did skier Raisa Smetanina win with her four golds and one bronze?

10 How many gold medals did Mark Spitz win in his first Olympics?

11 Which amazing treble did Emil Zatopek achieve at the 1952 Games?

12 Who carried the torch into the stadium at the Atlanta games?

13 On which lake did Steve Redgrave win his record-breaking fourth gold medal?

14 Who was the only British woman sprinter to compete in all Olympics between 1984 and 1996?

15 Under what name did Mrs Erik de Bruin win gold at Atlanta?

16 What was the name of the Olympic mascot in Atlanta?

17 Where did Linford Christie run his first Olympic race?

18 Who was the oldest Olympic 100m champion when he won in 1980?

19 Who won women's gold in hockey in Barcelona?

20 Which is the only Olympic yachting event for three-person crews?

21 Who won the first medal at the Atlanta games?

22 Who won Britain's first tennis medal since 1924 in Atlanta?

23 Who replaced her partner Michael Hutchinson before winning gold in 1984?

24 Other than 400m hurdles, for which event did Sally Gunnell win a medal in Barcelona?

25 In which year did women first compete in the Olympics?

26 Why were equestrian events held in Sweden in 1956 when the Games were held in Australia?

27 Who was Britain's only female medallist at the Atlanta games?

28 Where did Daley Thompson compete in his first Olympics?

29 Which son of a former Millwall goalie won gold in the USA in 1980?

30 What was the first Asian country to have staged the Winter Olympics?

46
GOLF

1 At which course did the US regain the Ryder Cup in 2008?

2 Who won the European Tour Order of Merit in 2007?

3 Which South African won the British Open in 1949, 1950, 1952 and 1957?

4 Which comedian took his name from the 1912 British Open?

5 Who was the first non-American postwar winner of the US Masters?

6 Which American played in the British Open only once and won it?

7 Faldo won the British Open in 1990 and 1992. Who won in 1991?

8 Who was the first Englishman to win the US Open after World War II?

9 What is Lee Trevino's nickname?

10 For which sport is Graham Marsh's brother famous?

11 Which US golfer had 11 successive tournament wins in 1945?

12 In which town is Royal Birkdale golf course?

13 Over which course is the World Matchplay Championship played?

14 Who won the US Masters in 1986 for a record sixth time?

15 In which country is Penina golf course?

16 Where was the first-ever US Open played in 1895?

17 What name did Jack Nicklaus give to his own golf course in honour of his favourite British course?

18 Who opposed the US in the Ryder Cup between 1973 and 1977?

19 Who won the English Amateur Championship in 1975 aged 18?

20 Which trophy is played for by women golfers from the US in competition with Britain and Ireland?

21 Which is the oldest open championship in the world?

22 Which England cricket captain is an amateur golf champion?

23 Which golfer was responsible for the the US Masters?

24 What is the status of competitors in the Walker Cup?

25 In 1971 who won the US Open, the Canadian Open and the British Open?

26 Which actor shared his name with the winner of the 1939 British Open?

27 Which Irish golfer played in ten successive Ryder Cup teams?

28 Who captained the European team to victory in the 1995 Ryder Cup?

29 Who headed the European Order of Merit between 1971 and 1974?

30 Which US president's home was alongside the course on which the US Masters is played?

 Answers on page 193

 Answers on page 193

47
OLYMPICS 2

1 Which race gave Michelle Smith her third gold medal in Atlanta?

2 Who was the first Olympic athlete to win the 200m/400m double gold?

3 Who were the finalists in basketball in the 1996 Games?

4 On which Olympic lake did Steve Redgrave win a fourth gold?

5 With whom did Britain tie for 35th place in the medals table in Atlanta?

6 Who defeated Amir Khan in the 2004 Olympic final?

7 Where were the 1936 Winter Olympics held?

8 Who were beaten by the Woodies in the 1996 men's doubles final?

9 Who was the first woman to win gold at winter and summer Games?

10 Before Turin where was the last Winter Olympics to be held in Italy?

11 Between 1928 and 1948 where were the Winter Olympics held twice?

12 How many times have the Olympics been held in Britain?

13 What were victors given in the ancient Olympics?

14 How many of Mark Spitz's seven golds in 1972 were for team events?

15 In which event did Hilda Johnstone compete in the 1972 Games aged 70?

16 Which two countries beginning with A won first-time medals in 1996?

17 Who beat Jonathan Edwards in the Triple Jump final in Atlanta?

18 In Atlanta who became South Africa's first gold medallist since 1952?

19 In which year were the Winter Olympics first held in the middle of the four-year cycle of the summer games?

20 Who was the second track and field athlete in Olympic history to win four successive titles in the same event?

21 Who won silver medals for Britain for yachting in Atlanta?

22 Whom did Steve Backley beat into third place in 1996?

23 Whose horse Cartier forced him to withdraw from the Three-Day Event competition in 1988?

24 Who won Britain's first medal of the Atlanta Games?

25 Who carried the Olympic flag for the UK in Barcelona?

26 In which event, new in Atlanta, did Paolo Pezzo win gold?

27 Why did the Modern Pentathletes stage a sit-down protest at Atlanta?

28 How many people died because of the Centennial Park bomb?

29 Which woman won a record fifth individual swimming gold in 1996?

30 Who held the record from 1980 for most individual golds in one Games?

48
RUGBY 4

1 Who has been an Irish international and the head of HJ Heinz?

2 In which decade of which century did the first league varsity match take place?

3 In which city were Barbarians RFC founded?

4 Which was the first league side to score 1,000 points in a season?

5 In 2006, who skippered Argentina when England lost their seventh game in a row?

6 Rob Andrew is qualified in what profession?

7 Where did Brian Moore begin his career?

8 How old was Will Carling when he played for Terra Nova Under 11s?

9 Against which side did Jeremy Guscott make his international debut?

10 Which league side was the first to win all its league games in a season?

11 In which month and year did Andy Robinson take over as England's head coach?

12 In 1986 St Helens beat Carlisle 112-0 in which competition?

13 Who was the first union player to kick eight penalties in an international?

14 What was Jason Leonard's first club?

15 Who were the beaten finalists in the first league Knockout Trophy?

16 Who captained Ireland in their centenary season?

17 Whom did the All Blacks beat 106-4 in 1987?

18 Where was the first floodlit rugby union match played?

19 What name was given to the breakaway clubs from the Rugby Union in 1895?

20 Which club won the first Middlesex Sevens at Twickenham?

21 What position did JJ Williams play for Llanelli?

22 Who returned to England from the Rugby World Cup in 2003 for the birth of daughter Eva?

23 Who recorded the then highest score draw 46-46 in 1994?

24 Who sponsored the rugby league before Courage?

25 In which country was the first rugby league World Cup held?

26 Who was the first UK rugby league club side to play in Australia?

27 Who played a record 17 appearances on five tours with the British Lions?

28 Which New Zealand fly half scored 26 points against England in November 2006?

29 Who made the lowest score (0-0) in the BBC's Floodlit Rugby League competition?

30 Who were the first Scottish rugby union club champions?

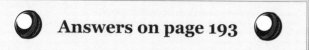
Answers on page 193

Answers on page 193

49 FOOTBALL: GOALKEEPERS

1 Who was in goal for Nottingham Forest in the 1992 League Cup Final?

2 Who was in goal for England in the 1997 World Cup qualifier v Italy at Wembley?

3 Who was in goal for Leeds Utd in the 1972 and 1973 FA Cup Finals?

4 John Burridge made his League debut for which club that's now no longer in the League?

5 Who, in the 1990s, saved five penalties in three days – three v Tranmere in a League Cup semi-final and two v Tottenham Hotspur?

6 At which League club did Chris Turner make his debut?

7 Which club did Coventry sign Steve Ogrizovic from?

8 Harry Dowd was in an FA Cup-winning 1960s team at which club?

9 Phil Parkes made his League debut at which club?

10 Which club did Jim Leighton join when he finally left Manchester Utd?

11 Who was in goal for Oldham Athletic in the 1990 League Cup Final?

12 Who went down from the top flight with Millwall in 1990 and Bolton in 96?

13 Which veteran keeper became player/manager of Exeter in 1995?

14 Which League Cup Final-winning side did Alan Judge play for?

15 Which keeper spent 20 years with Portsmouth?

16 Which keeper was injured in the 1957 FA Cup Final?

17 Northern Ireland's Harry Gregg was first capped while at which League club?

18 Who was in goal for Brighton in the 1980s FA Cup Final?

19 At which club did Bobby Mimms make his League debut?

20 Dave Gaskell was in an FA Cup-winning 1960s team at which club?

21 Who was England's goalkeeper when they lost 3–2 to Croatia in 2007?

22 Which goalkeeper kept the most clean sheets in the Premier League in 2005–06?

23 Which goalkeeper played 11 League matches for Chelsea in 2006–07?

24 Which goalkeeper played for six minutes as a striker for Manchester City in 2005?

25 Which Cornish goalkeeper played for England in the 2000s?

26 Who equalled David James's record of 166 consecutive Premiership games in 2008?

27 Who angered Joe Kinnear when he said Shay Given should join an Italian club?

28 Name the former goalkeeper who managed Norwich City in the Premiership.

29 Who began his career at York City before joining Leeds United aged 16 in 1995?

30 Who was Blackburn Rovers' No. 1 goalkeeper when they won the Premier League?

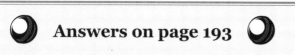
Answers on page 193

50 GOLF 2

1 Who was Tiger Woods's caddie for his first Masters win?

2 When did Great Britain first win the Walker Cup?

3 Where did Nick Faldo win his first British Open?

4 What was Jack Nicklaus's nickname in his first Walker Cup in the '50s?

5 What is the name of Hole 8 at Troon?

6 In the 1996 US Masters, by how many strokes did Norman lead Faldo before the final round?

7 Who won the British Open the year after Lee Trevino's first triumph?

8 Henry Cotton won the British Open at Sandwich, Muirfield and where?

9 Who was the first South African to win the British Open?

10 Which champion's father was a pro at Hawkstone Park golf course?

11 On which course did Tiger Woods win his first British Open?

12 Where in America did Great Britain and Ireland first win the Walker Cup?

13 Who got the nickname the Walrus?

14 What did Jack Nicklaus score on his last Major round at the British Open in 2005?

15 After World War Two, who got the first three-in-a-row hat-trick of British Opens?

16 Who set the course record of 64 at Troon in the Open of 1989?

17 Horton Smith was the first winner of which major event?

18 Which management group did Tiger Woods sign up to on turning pro?

19 What was the original prize for winning the British Open?

20 Michael Campbell won the 2005 US Open by how many shots from Tiger Woods?

21 Who was the first New Zealander to win the British Open?

22 In which decade was the Walker Cup staged at an English course?

23 Who got the nickname Dough Boy?

24 In what capacity did Devereux Emmet leave his mark on golf?

25 Who was the last golfer before Faldo to be BBC Sports Personality of the Year?

26 What first did Peter Butler manage in the 1973 Ryder Cup?

27 Which golfer's first tour victory was the 1982 Swiss Open?

28 Which course contains the Rabbit and the Seal?

29 Tom Lehman became the first American since whom to win an Open at Royal Lytham?

30 Where was the great Harry Vardon born?

Answers on page 193

51 HORSE RACING

1 In which county was the first steeplechase held?

2 Which horse won the first post-WWII Grand National?

3 Which jockey rode the 2,000 Guineas-winner four times between 1972 and 1989?

4 Which horse ran the fastest Epsom Derby of the 1990s?

5 Who sponsored the Derby at the turn of the century?

6 Who resigned as the Queen's trainer towards the end of the 1990s?

7 Who was the first jockey in the 1990s to ride 200 winners?

8 Who owned Sagamix when he won the Prix de l'Arc de Triomphe in 1998?

9 The steeplechaser One Man had to be put down after being injured in which race?

10 Which horse finished first in the last Grand National of the millennium to be abandoned?

11 Which was the first filly to win the Derby?

12 Which horse won the Derby the year WWI began?

13 What was Frankie Dettori's first 1000 Guineas win of the 1990s?

14 Which horse ran the fastest Grand National of the 1990s?

15 What was Mick Kinane's second 2000 Guineas win of the 1990s?

16 Which horse won the Grand National the year that Nijinsky won the Derby?

17 Which jockey won his third successive Prix de l'Arc de Triomphe in 1998?

18 Which horse won the St Leger the year that Mill Reef won the Derby?

19 Who rode the only Derby winner with Shirley in its name?

20 Which member of the Royal family got married the year Aldaniti won the National?

21 Which horse won the Derby the year after the legendary Shergar?

22 Which horse won the Grand National the year of the first 1990s General Election?

23 What was Lester Piggott's first 1000 Guineas winner in the second half of the 20th century?

24 Rodrigo de Triano was which jockey's thirtieth Classic winner?

25 What was the last year before 1993 that the Grand National was not run?

26 Before Royal Athlete which was the last Grand National winner to have Royal in its name?

27 In which park is Ireland's Clonmel Racecourse?

28 Which was the first 1000 Guineas winner of the 1990s to have two words in its name?

29 Which was the fastest of the first four British horses in the 1998 French 2000 Guineas?

30 Which horse ran the fastest Epsom Derby of the 1980s?

52 TENNIS

1 Jamie Murray teamed up with which Miss Jankovic to win at Wimbledon in 2007?

2 Which Becker beat Andre Agassi in his final Grand Slam, the 2006 US Open?

3 Where was former British No. 1 Elena Baltacha born?

4 Who lost both his singles for Britain in their 2008 World Group relegation play-off?

5 What feature is at Melbourne's Rod Laver Arena and was at Wimbledon in 2009?

6 Which woman tennis player's mother was a Wimbledon finalist in 1962?

7 With which doubles partner did John McEnroe have most success?

8 Which British man got to three Wimbledon semi-finals in the '60s and 70s?

9 How are Mrs Barrett and Mrs Janes better known?

10 What nationality did Hana Mandlikova take after leaving Czechoslovakia?

11 Who knocked Steffi Graf out of Wimbledon in the first round in 1994?

12 Whom did Becker beat to become the youngest Wimbledon champion?

13 What are Aranxia Sanchez-Vicario's tennis-playing brothers' names?

14 Who was the first player Martina Navratilova beat to win Wimbledon after her first three victories over Chris Evert?

15 Which French tennis player gave his name to a range of sportswear?

16 What "first" happened at Wimbledon in 1937?

17 Who was the first player to win the Grand Slam?

18 Who was tennis's first millionaire?

19 Which exiled Czech beat Ken Rosewall at Wimbledon in 1954?

20 Who played her first professional match against Tracy Austin in 1982?

21 In which year did Wimbledon go open?

22 Who were the only two women to win Grand Slams before Steffi Graf?

23 What is Yvon Petra famous for being the last man to do?

24 Who said on losing his title in the second round at Wimbledon, "I lost a tennis match, not a war. Nobody got killed"?

25 Which future king played a doubles match at Wimbledon?

26 Who was the first player to win all four US Girls Under 12 titles in 1979?

27 Who were the first siblings to win the Wimbledon Mixed Doubles?

28 Who did the LTA take over from in the management of tennis?

29 Who won the Men's Singles at Wimbledon in 1996 and lost in the first round the following year?

30 Who was the only American to win the Men's Singles at Wimbledon in the '60s?

 Answers on page 194

 Answers on page 194

53
TENNIS 2

1 Who was the first male to win the Junior Grand Slam?

2 Before Henman and Rusedski, who were the last two Brits to be in the men's last eight together at Wimbledon?

3 In which country did Henman and Murray first play each other?

4 Where was Martina Hingis born?

5 How many times did Navratilova win the Wimbledon singles as a Czech?

6 Which unseeded player reached the final of the 2006 Australian Open?

7 What was Chris Evert's second married name?

8 Who is Vera Puzejova's daughter?

9 Who won the women's singles at the 1992 Olympics?

10 Tim Henman reached his first US Open quarter final when who withdrew in 2004?

11 Where was the US Open played before Flushing Meadow?

12 What is Boris Becker's eldest son called?

13 What did Major Wingfield call lawn tennis when he first showed off his new game?

14 Who were known as the "Three Musketeers"?

15 Who was the first European to win the women's singles at Roland Garros in the 70s?

16 Whom did Billie Jean Moffitt win her first women's doubles with?

17 With whom did Ann Jones win the Wimbledon mixed doubles in 69?

18 Who was the first male Brit to win a Wimbledon title after Fred Perry?

19 Where did Fred Perry die?

20 Whom did Chris Evert beat to win her first Wimbledon title?

21 Who was known as the "Rockhampton Rocket"?

22 Who was the first Swede to win the Australian men's singles?

23 Who contested Wimbledon's longest-ever match?

24 Which tennis trophy did Hazel Hotchkiss donate?

25 Who was the first man to hold all four Grand Slam titles at once?

26 Which two countries has Hana Mandlikova played for?

27 Where were the very first US Championships held?

28 Who was the last men's singles champion at Wimbledon before it became open?

29 Who was the first person to lose in the opening round in the defence of his championship?

30 Where were the Australian Championships held in 1906 and 1912?

54
SPORTING MOMENTS

1 Which Grand National winner was the first to be trained by a woman?

2 David Broome was the first British showjumping champion on which horse?

3 Who had his spot kick saved in the first FA Cup Final decided on penalties?

4 How many deliveries were sent down in the final innings of the 2005 Ashes?

5 Jesse Owens was part of which university team when he set his three world records?

6 Who was the second player to hit a maximum 36 runs off one over?

7 In which road in Oxford did Roger Bannister run his four-minute mile?

8 How many people witnessed Brazil's defeat by Uruguay in the 1950 World Cup Final?

9 Who was the first athlete to break 13 minutes for the 5,000m?

10 Who made Chris Boardman's winning bicycle in Barcelona?

11 Which famous pacemaker founded the London Marathon?

12 Which Grand National horse was the first to cross the line the year the race was abandoned?

13 By what score did Steve Davis lose the World Professional Championship Final in 1985?

14 Who was the first man to break one minute for the 100m breaststroke in a 25m pool?

15 With whom did Steve Redgrave take the second of his four Olympic golds?

16 Which British man ran the fastest mile in the 1980s?

17 Why did Susan Brown make history in 1981?

18 Which was the last horse before Lammtarra in 1995 to win the classic triple?

19 How many times did Nadia Comaneci score a perfect 10 at Montreal in 1976?

20 To the nearest 10 minutes, how long did it take Brian Lara to score his record 501 against Durham in 1994?

21 Who caddied for Tiger Woods on his first US Masters victory?

22 How many races out of the 16 did Nigel Mansell win to become World Champion?

23 Who was the first player since WWII to score more than 30 goals in three consecutive seasons?

24 Where was Harvey Smith when he made his infamous V sign?

25 Whom did Virginia Wade beat to win her Wimbledon Singles title?

26 How many League games had Stanley Matthews played before his final match aged 50?

27 Seb Coe simultaneously held three world records, at which distances?

28 To the nearest 100, what were the odds against Frankie Dettori's seven Ascot wins?

29 Who broke the 1500, 3000 and 5000m records in 1994?

30 Whom did Mike Tyson beat to become the youngest WBC champion?

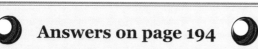 **Answers on page 194**

 Answers on page 194

55
FOOTBALL POT LUCK

1 At which club did Terry Paine finish his playing career?

2 Who was the first black player to be named in an England under-21 squad?

3 Frank O'Farrell became manager of which country?

4 At which club did Paul Parker make his League debut?

5 In which decade did Leeds Utd first win the championship?

6 Which club had a fanzine called *Deranged Ferret*?

7 Frank Worthington followed Bryan Hamilton as manager of which club?

8 Who moved from Oxford Utd to Derby County in 1988 to set a club record for a transfer fee received?

9 What was Grimsby Town once known as?

10 To one each way, how many international goals did Steve Coppell score?

11 Peter Nicholas and Clive Wilson were together at which club?

12 Which Steve became boss of Colchester Utd in January 1995?

13 Chris Waddle first played in an FA Cup Final for which team?

14 Who is Bolton Wanderers' all-time leading goalscorer?

15 Who scored 11 goals in QPR's first European season?

16 Who was boss of Millwall between 1982 and 1986?

17 Which club started out playing at Headington Quarry?

18 What is Reggie Blinker's middle name?

19 Who resigned as Tottenham Hotspur manager on June 23rd 1976?

20 Who retired as a player in 1975, following the Celtic v Airdrie Scottish Cup Final?

21 Which club did Tony Mowbray leave to manage West Bromwich Albion?

22 In which country would you watch Sheriff Tiraspol take on Zimbru Chisinau?

23 Who lost to Tottenham Hotspur in the 1984 UEFA Cup Final?

24 At which club, no longer in the League, did Peter Withe make his League debut?

25 In which decade did Blackburn Rovers first win the championship?

26 Which club had a fanzine called *Windy and Dusty*?

27 Alex Smith followed Ian Porterfield as manager of which club?

28 What is the name of Glenn Hoddle's brother, once with Barnet?

29 Which club was once known as "Pine Villa"?

30 To one each way, how many international goals did Francis Lee score?

56
CRICKET 5

1 In which city was Yorkshire's Michael Vaughan born?

2 Which was the first English county that Anil Kumble played for?

3 Who was the last England captain to play South Africa before the ban?

4 Who won the county championships in every season from 1951 to 1958?

5 Where in the West Indies did Brian Lara score his record-breaking 375?

6 Who was the first player to make over 1,000 catches in first-class cricket?

7 What did ICC stand for before 1965?

8 Who were the first winners of the Women's World Cup in 1973?

9 What is Bob Willis's middle name?

10 Which England batsmen each scored double centuries against India in 1985 in the same innings?

11 Who was the first batsman to score 10,000 runs in Test cricket?

12 In which country are the first-class sides United Bank and National Bank?

13 Who were the first three members of the ICC?

14 What was the Nat West Trophy previously called?

15 Which New Zealander hit a double century in 153 balls vs England in 2002?

16 Who kept wicket for Yorkshire in 412 consecutive county championship games?

17 Who was England's most capped cricketer at the end of the 2002/03 Ashes series?

18 Who scored 322 runs against Warwickshire in less than a day in 1985?

19 In which country do first-class teams compete for the Plunkett Shield?

20 Who was Man of the Match in the 2003 World Cup Final?

21 What is the trophy played for by first-class inter-state sides in India?

22 Who captained England during the "bodyline" series?

23 Who was the first bowler to take 300 Test wickets?

24 Which bowler is nicknamed "The King of Spain"?

25 What was the title of Andrew Flintoff's autobiography?

26 Who said, "The bowler's Holding, the batsman's Willey"?

27 To three each way, how many Tests did it take Muttiah Muralitharan to reach the 400 wicket mark?

28 Michael Vaughan made his international debut against which country?

29 Which ex-England cricketer made his county debut in 1981 and retired on 22 June 2004?

30 Which cup succeeded the Shell Shield in the West Indies?

 Answers on page 194

 Answers on page 194

57
FOOTBALL 5

1 Nanninga was the first sub to score in a World Cup Final for whom?

2 Which team are known as the Cherries?

3 What was strange about the tackle that ended the career of keeper Chic Brodie of Brentford back in 1970?

4 How many countries played in World Cup 2002 in Japan and South Korea?

5 Which club did Glenn Hoddle leave to become England manager?

6 Which country won the first World Cup held in 1930?

7 Which German club did Kevin Keegan play for?

8 Mike Walker and Martin O'Neill walked out on which chairman?

9 Who was the first uncapped player sold for over £1,000,000 in Britain?

10 What name is shared by Scunthorpe, Southend and Rotherham?

11 Fabien Barthez began his career with which French club?

12 Who was England's final substitute in the 2002 quarter-final defeat by Brazil?

13 Which country did Emlyn Hughes play for?

14 Emmanuel Petit joined Arsenal from which soccer club?

15 Which 4th Division team reached the first League Cup Final in 1962?

16 Who played in the first FA Cup Final ever to end 3–3?

17 Which team paid a record £1,000 for Alf Common in 1905?

18 Newcastle play at St James' Park but who plays at St James Park?

19 Who captained the Man Utd team that won the 1968 European Cup?

20 Who scored Scotland's only goal in the 1986 World Cup Finals in Mexico?

21 Where in England do you go to shout "Come on, you greens"?

22 An Italian boss replacing a Dutchman was a first at which English club?

23 Stokoe (Sunderland) and Revie (Leeds) were rival managers in the 1973 FA Cup Final. For which teams were they rivals as Cup Final players?

24 If you are at Turf Moor who is playing at home?

25 Which keeper played three games for Man Utd in the early 1990s and 23 games in 1999–2000?

26 Which club has been managed by Brian Clough and Jimmy Armfield?

27 Which player went from Juventus to Real Madrid for £46.5m in 2001? 28 Which team is known as "The Bairns"?

29 Which non-League team held Man Utd to a 0–0 draw in the third round of the 2005/6 FA Cup?

30 At which Lane did Wimbledon play when they entered the League?

  Answers on page 194

58
FOOTBALL: EXTRA TIME

1 Who came on in extra time for the Republic of Ireland in the Italia 90 World Cup game against Romania?

2 Preud'homme was in goal for which team knocked out of Italia 90 in extra time?

3 An extra-time goal by which country sent Nigeria out of the 1994 World Cup?

4 A 1940s extra-time FA Cup goal by Duffy won the cup for which club?

5 Who was sent off during extra time in the 2008 Champions League final?

6 In Italia 90 which country played extra time in both the quarter-finals and semi-finals?

7 English-based Guentchev came on in extra time in USA 1994 against which side?

8 What was the 90-minute score in the Arsenal v Liverpool 1971 FA Cup Final?

9 What was the score after extra time in the France v West Germany 1982 World Cup semi-final?

10 Which team won three Scottish FA Cup Finals in a row – all after extra time?

11 An extra-time goal by Ian St John beat which team in an FA Cup Final?

12 Andersson and Raducioiu hit 1994 World Cup extra time goals in which game?

13 How many quarter-finals went to extra time in the 1986 World Cup?

14 Which keeper was beaten by Jeff Astle's 1968 FA Cup winner?

15 What was the 90-minute score in England v Cameroon in Italia 90?

16 Which club beat Tottenham Hotspur after extra time in a League Cup Final?

17 After World War II, which team first won an FA Cup Final a.e.t.?

18 In Mexico 1986 who beat the USSR 4–3 after an extra-time gripper?

19 Which German had a "goal" disallowed v England in extra time of Euro 96?

20 How many minutes of extra time were needed in the Euro 96 Final?

21 In which competition did England last score an extra-time goal?

22 Which club did Porto defeat after extra time to win the 2002 UEFA Cup?

23 Who scored Tottenham's League Cup-winning goal in 2008?

24 When did Chelsea need extra time to win an FA Cup semi-final and final?

25 In which year was the last Scottish Cup Final decided in extra time?

26 Who was the first player sent off in extra time in the World Cup Final?

27 Which club beat Middlesbrough 1–0 after extra time in the 1997 League Cup final?

28 Name the team which won the 2005 League Cup final in extra time.

29 Name the two teams and score after extra time in the 1994 World Cup final.

30 Which World Cup first introduced a penalty shoot-out after extra time?

Answers on page 194

59 POP ALBUMS

1 Who recorded *Rubber Soul*?
2 What goes after *What's the Story* in the title of Oasis's album?
3 Which Phil recorded *No Jacket Required*?
4 Who recorded "The Dark Side of the Moon"?
5 Which Rod had six consecutive No. 1 albums in the 70s?
6 Who recorded "Purple Rain"?
7 Which group had a *Night at the Opera* and *A Day at the Races*?
8 Who recorded "Blue Hawaii"?
9 Paul McCartney was in which group for *Band on the Run*?
10 Who called their greatest hits album *End of Part One*?
11 Which legendary guitarist recorded "From the Cradle"?
12 Who recorded *Off the Wall*?
13 Mike Oldfield presented what type of "Bells"?
14 Who recorded "The Colour of My Love"?
15 *The Breakthrough* is the seventh album by which artist?
16 Who recorded "Breakfast in America"?
17 Which Abba album had a French title?
18 Neil Diamond's film soundtrack album was about what type of singer?
19 What was the Kaiser Chiefs' debut album called?
20 Who recorded *Brothers in Arms*?
21 Which group were of *A Different Class* in 1995?
22 In the 90s, who broke out with "The Great Escape"?
23 Which Bruce spent most weeks in the album charts in 1985?
24 Who recorded "Bridge Over Troubled Water"?
25 In the 70s who recorded "Goodbye Yellow Brick Road"?
26 Which Simply Red album featured "For Your Babies" and "Stars"?
27 *Rumours* provided over 400 weeks on the album chart for whom?
28 Who recorded *Bat out of Hell*?
29 Which Michael – not Jackson – spent most weeks in the 1991 charts?
30 What was "Definitely" the first No. 1 album from Oasis?

60 POP DIVAS

1 Which Spice Girl advertised Milky Bars as a child?
2 Was Billie Piper 10, 15 or 20 when she first went to No. 1?
3 Which Tina sang the title song from "Whistle Down the Wind"?
4 Who put her famous Union Jack dress up for auction?
5 Who had a No. 1 single with "Toxic"?
6 How many girls made up N-Tyce?
7 Janet and La Toyah are from which famous family?
8 What is the first name of the Welsh singer from Catatonia?
9 Whose album "Always and Forever" gives a clue to their name?
10 Which '60s singer's first hit was written by the Rolling Stones?
11 Heather Small found fame with which band?
12 What is the surname of sisters Kylie and Dannii?
13 Who made the big-selling album "J.LO"?
14 Whose third No. 1 was titled "Day & Night"?
15 Where do Scary Spice and Princess Anne's daughter have a stud?
16 Who share their name with an Egyptian queen?
17 Which Aussie soap did Natalie Imbruglia appear in?
18 How many singers make up B*witched?
19 How did the Bangles Walk?
20 Shaznay is in which all-girl band?
21 Which '60s singer hosted *Surprise Surprise*?
22 Which Capstan sang with the B52s and guested with REM?
23 Who was the lead singer for Blondie?
24 Which musical instrument is Vanessa Mae famous for?
25 Which musical star Alicia sang before the 2005 Super Bowl?
26 Alanis Morissette and Celine Dion are from which country?
27 Who sang about "Baboushka" and "Wuthering Heights"?
28 In which decade did Bananarama have their first hit?
29 Miss Nurding dropped her surname and became known as whom?
30 Which singing star married Kevin Federline?

 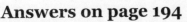 **Answers on page 194**

 Answers on page 194

61
OASIS

1 Which city do Oasis come from?

2 Which Gallagher brother was lead vocalist in the mid-90s?

3 With which band was there a media feud to decide on the top BritPop act?

4 What is Paul McGuigan's nickname?

5 How many people were in Oasis when they had their first No. 1 single?

6 What was the band's debut album?

7 What goes in brackets before "Morning Glory" on the album title?

8 Who is the elder of the two Gallagher brothers?

9 Which actress Patsy married Liam in the 90s?

10 Which drug was Liam charged with possessing in 1996?

11 Which football team do the Gallaghers support?

12 What is the nationality of Noel and Liam's parents?

13 What is their mother called?

14 Which musical instrument does Noel play?

15 In which country was a tour cancelled in 1996 when Liam returned home?

16 After which TV pop show did Oasis sack their drummer in 1995?

17 Which Wonder record was a 1995 hit for the band?

18 In 1996, how did Oasis say "Don't Look Back"?

19 At which Somerset Festival did Oasis perform in front of 30,000 fans in 1994?

20 What goes "With It" on the record title in 1995?

21 Which son of a Beatles drummer joined Oasis in 2004?

22 What did Oasis want you to "Dig Out" according to their 2008 album title?

23 Where did Oasis receive its Outstanding Contribution to Music award in 2007?

24 What "milestone" birthday did Noel celebrate in 2007?

25 "The Importance of Being..." what was the title of the eighth British No. 1 in 2005?

26 Liam and Noel both support the same football team. Name the club.

27 What is the name of the double compilation album released by the band in 2006?

28 "Definitely ..." was the name of the band's first album. Complete the title.

29 What type of "Chemistry" did Oasis release in 2002?

30 Can you name the fast-sounding title of Oasis's first single?

62
POP CHARTS

1 Whose first chart success was "Your Song"?

2 Which David has charted with both Bing Crosby and Mick Jagger?

3 Which Frank Sinatra hit has charted on more than ten occasions?

4 "The Show," "No Good Advice" and "Biology" are singles by which Popstars?

5 Which Rod has had over 50 chart hits?

6 "Swear It Again" was which record-breaking boy band's debut single?

7 "Red Red Wine" was the first No. 1 for which group?

8 Dido's song "Thank You" was sampled by which rapper on his song "Stan"?

9 In the 80s, which Paul first charted with "Wherever I Lay My Hat"?

10 Where in London did the Kinks watch the Sunset?

11 Which song was No. 1 for Jimmy Young and Robson and Jerome?

12 Who were Alone in the charts, 30 years after their first hit?

13 Which New Kids had seven singles in the charts in 1990?

14 "Work It" and "Get Ur Freak On" are singles by which artist?

15 "Independent Women Part 1" was the first No. 1 single for which group?

16 In which decade did Belinda Carlisle first hit the UK charts?

17 Debbie Harry fronted which chart busters in the late 70s early 80s?

18 Whose first chart entry was "Space Oddity"?

19 Which Olivia charted with John Travolta and ELO?

20 Which Ben E. King classic made No. 1 25 years after it was recorded?

21 Which song gave Robbie Williams and Nicole Kidman a No. 1 in 2001?

22 "Waterloo" was the first chart success for which group?

23 Which Judy Collins song amazingly charted eight times in the '70s?

24 "Song for Whoever" was the first hit for which Beautiful group?

25 Which John had three No. 1s following his murder?

26 "I Don't Want to Miss a Thing" was the first Top Ten hit for which group?

27 Which early hit did Cliff Richard rerecord with the Young Ones?

28 Boyzone charted with "Words" in the '90s, but who made the original?

29 In which decade did Stevie Wonder first hit the UK charts?

30 In which decade did charts start to be compiled in the UK?

  Answers on page 195

Answers on page 195

63
'80S POP

1 Who went straight to No. 1 in 1981 with "Stand and Deliver"?

2 What colour Door gave Shakin' Stevens an 80s hit?

3 Which ex-Beatle had a hit with Stevie Wonder in 1982?

4 Whose album *Thriller* provided several hit singles?

5 Who was KC's backing Band?

6 Which Scot had chart success after Esther Rantzen's *The Big Time*?

7 Which BBC Radio station banned "Relax"?

8 Ravel's "Bolero" charted because of which skaters' Olympic success?

9 Which actor Robert was named in a Bananarama song title?

10 Which Superstar Rat sang "Love Me Tender"?

11 Which Alison's nickname was Alf?

12 Which Elaine and Barbara topped the charts in 1985?

13 Which Mrs Andrew Lloyd Webber had a hit with "Pie Jesu"?

14 David Bowie and Mick Jagger had a hit after which Concert?

15 Elton John charted with "Nikita" at the same time as Sting had which coincidental hit?

16 Who had hits as part of Visage and Ultravox?

17 Who told you that you were "In the Army Now"?

18 Who fronted Culture Club?

19 Graham McPherson of Madness was known as what?

20 Which Kim reached No. 2 in 1981, 24 years after dad Marty?

21 Which Spanish singer had the UK's first chart topper in Spanish?

22 David Sylvian was part of which Asian-sounding band?

23 Who was the first ventriloquist in the charts with Orville?

24 Who teamed up with Annie Lennox in The Eurythmics?

25 Who was the then oldest man in the charts with "New York New York"?

26 Who joined Cliff Richard for his 80s "Living Doll"?

27 Which TV puppets sang "The Chicken Song"?

28 Which red-haired Royal liked "Lady in Red"?

29 Which future England coach joined Waddle on "Diamond Lights"?

30 Who had a Xmas No. 1 in 1988 after 30 years in the charts?

64
KID'S STUFF

1 Which Little Jimmy wanted to be A Long Haired Lover from Liverpool?

2 Which "Roses" did his 14-year-old sister Marie sing about in 1973?

3 Which 10-year-old Lena took "Ma, He's Making Eyes at Me" to No. 10?

4 Where was the choirboy Aled Jones Walking in 1985?

5 Which Brenda was known as "Little Miss Dynamite"?

6 Which Helen said "Don't Treat Me Like a Child" aged 14 in 1961?

7 Which 15-year-old girl from Glasgow was heard to "Shout" in 1964?

8 Which Stevie was called Little in his early showbiz years?

9 Which late-80s teen group were revamped as NKOTB in 1993?

10 Which Michael first sang with his four brothers at the age of six?

11 Which Mary hit the No. 1 spot with "Those Were the Days" after winning *Opportunity Knocks*?

12 Which Australian teenager had a No. 1 with "I Should be So Lucky"?

13 To two years either way, how old was Cliff Richard when he had his first hit "Move It" in 1958?

14 Which dancer/singer called Bonnie won *Opportunity Knocks* aged six?

15 Which Donny sang professionally with his brothers from the age of six and had chart success with "Puppy Love" and "Too Young"?

16 Which 17-year-old Sandie had a '60s hit with "Always Something There to Remind Me"?

17 Which Neil wrote "Oh Carol" for Carole Klein, later Carole King, whom he met at high school?

18 Which Genesis drummer called Phil was a former child actor?

19 The kids from which TV dance show had chart success in the 80s?

20 Which girl, later the name of a famous princess, gave 16-year-old Paul Anka chart success in 1957?

21 What was the title of Vanessa Hudgens debut album?

22 What is the famous surname of Dream Street member Jesse?

23 Sisters Alyson and Amanda Michalka are better known as which singing duo?

24 "Baby One More Time" was the debut single and global hit for which teenager?

25 Sam Concepcion sang the theme song for which 2008 DreamWorks movie?

26 Which group's debut single was titled "Five Colours in Her Hair"?

27 Which group sang "I'm a Believer" and "All Star" in the movie *Shrek*?

28 Who sang "What's New Pussycat" for the movie *Flushed Away*?

29 Which Ben sang several songs for the 2006 movie *Over the Hedge*?

30 Elton John sang the theme song for which 1994 Walt Disney movie?

 Answers on page 195

 Answers on page 195

65 POP SINGERS

1 Who sang "Like a Virgin"?

2 Which Osmond sang "Puppy Love" and "Young Love"?

3 Mutya Buena left which group in December 2005?

4 Which Irish singer won Eurovision with "All Kinds of Everything"?

5 Which Lisa sang on the "Five Live EP"?

6 Which Noddy sang lead with Slade?

7 Which female singer went solo from Clannad?

8 Who sang "Coward of the County"?

9 Who sang lead with T. Rex?

10 Under what name did high-voiced William Robinson Jnr sing?

11 Chrissie Hynde was lead singer with which group?

12 Which writer and guitarist sang "Annie's Song"?

13 "(Everything I Do) I Do It for You" was a monster hit for which singer?

14 Who had a No. 1 with "A Groovy Kind of Love"?

15 Who had a Christmas No. 1 with "Saviour's Day"?

16 Who won the Best British Female Solo Artist award at the Brits 2006?

17 Who sang "Every Loser Wins"?

18 Which song gave Jackie Wilson a No. 1 years after his death?

19 Who sang "The Lady in Red"?

20 Who was lead singer with the Police?

21 Who hit No. 1 with "Any Dream Will Do"?

22 "Crazy in Love" was the first solo No. 1 for which singer?

23 Which singer's second album was called *Stripped*?

24 Who released the album *Fever* in 2001?

25 The album *Call Off the Search* was released by which artist?

26 Heather Small sang lead with which People?

27 Who had a huge '60s hit with "Release Me"?

28 Who sang with the Wailers?

29 Ali Campbell sings lead with which group?

30 Who released the album *The Story Goes* in 2005?

66 KARAOKE

1 Which *Grease* classic begins "I got chills, they're multiplyin'"?

2 Which Madonna hit contains the words, "Ring, ring ring"?

3 What is the first line of "Nessun Dorma"?

4 What did Tina Turner sing after "Do I love you, my oh my"?

5 What follows the Beatles' "will you still need me, will you still feed me"?

6 Which song begins, "I feel it in my fingers, I feel it in my toes"?

7 In "Candle in the Wind '98" how are England's hills described?

8 How many times is "submarine" sung in the chorus of "Yellow Submarine"?

9 Which hit began "Oh my love, my darlin', I hunger for your touch"?

10 Which song's second line is "and so I face the final curtain"?

11 Which song begins "First I was afraid I was petrified"?

12 In which song did Tammy Wynette complain "Sometime it's hard to be a woman"?

13 Which Slade Xmas hit has the line "Everybody's having fun"?

14 In the "Titanic" song what follows, "Near, far, wherever you are, I believe..."?

15 What follows Bryan Adams' "Everything I do"?

16 Which Dire Straits hit begins "Here comes Johnny"?

17 What follows "Two little boys had two little....."?

18 Which charity hit has the line "Feed the world"?

19 What follows The Spice Girls' "swing it, shake it, move it, make it"?

20 Which Abba hit states "I was defeated you won the war"?

21 What do neighbours become in the original "Neighbours" theme song?

22 What follows "I believe for every drop of rain that falls"?

23 Which football anthem speaks of "Jules Rimet still gleaming"?

24 Which song's second chorus line is "I just called to say I care"?

25 Which *Evita* song begins, "It won't be easy, you'll think it strange"?

26 What did Boy George sing after singing karma five times?

27 Which *Lion King* song began "From the day we arrive on the planet"?

28 Which Simon & Garfunkel hit begins "When you're weary, feeling small"?

29 Which traditional song has the line, "The pipes, the pipes are calling"?

30 What are the last three words of Queen's "We are the Champions"?

 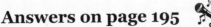 **Answers on page 195**

  Answers on page 195

67
SOUL & MOTOWN

1 Which musical instrument did Ray Charles play?
2 Which Motown star's real name is Steveland Judkins?
3 Which Dionne had a hit with "Walk on By" in 1964 and "Heartbreaker" 18 years later?
4 Who completed the Holland, Dozier trio and wrote many of the Motown hits of the '60s and 70s?
5 Which major all-male Tamla Motown group recorded "I'm Gonna Make You Love Me" with Diana Ross and the Supremes?
6 Which "Baby" gave the Supremes their first No. 1?
7 Who sang "Endless Love" with Diana Ross in 1981?
8 Which letters took the Jackson Five into the Top Ten in 1970?
9 What did Michael Jackson say to his "Summer Love" in 1984?
10 Which Marvin was "Too Busy Thinking 'Bout My Baby" in 1969?
11 Which Queen is Aretha Franklin known as?
12 Which Four were "Standing in the Shadows Of Love" in 1967?
13 Which Brothers charted with "This Old Heart Of Mine" in 1966 and 1968?
14 Which James was "Living in America" in 1986?
15 How were Martha Reeves and the Vandellas billed on their first Motown hits?
16 Who was Smokey Robinson's backing group?
17 How were Gladys Knight's brother Merald and cousins Edward and William known as collectively?
18 At the start of which decade did Berry Gordy set up the Tamla label?
19 Which Jackie recorded "Reet Petite" in 1957?
20 In which US city did Motown begin?
21 Which long-time Motown artist Diana left the label for the second time in 2002?
22 Which soul legend Isaac died in August 2008?
23 What was the title of Al Green's album released in 2008?
24 Whose debut album was titled "The Soul Sessions"?
25 What is the first name of the founder of the Motown label, Mr Gordy Jr?
26 Soul music is often said to have its roots in which type of Church music?
27 Can you name the famous record company founded by Berry Gordy?
28 Who had a major hit single with the soul classic "I Just Called to Say I Love You"?
29 What was Motown Records also known as?
30 Who "heard it through the grapevine" in 1968?

68
'60S POP

1 Who went "Surfin' USA"?
2 Micky Dolenz found fame in which simian-sounding group?
3 Who was "Crying in the Chapel"?
4 Which Beatles hit starts "Dear Sir or Madam, will you read my book"?
5 Brothers Barry, Maurice and Robin formed which group?
6 Who mocked the clothes conscious with "Dedicated Follower of Fashion"?
7 Diana Ross fronted which Tamla group?
8 Which group loved Jennifer Eccles?
9 Which part of her body did Sandie Shaw bare on stage?
10 Who sang "Don't Treat Me Like a Child" while still at school?
11 Were the Everley brothers actually brothers?
12 Which Dusty was "Goin' Back"?
13 Status Quo first charted with "Pictures of" what type of "Men"?
14 Which country-style singer was known as Gentleman Jim?
15 Who backed Brian Poole?
16 Which city did the Searchers come from?
17 Which Australian yodelled "I Remember You"?
18 Who completed the line-up with Dave Dee, Beaky, Mick and Tich?
19 Which trouser-splitting singer had the initials PJ?
20 Which city did the Flowerpot Men want to go to?
21 Whose Five were in "Bits and Pieces"?
22 Critics said Donovan was a British copy of which US performer?
23 Which Marianne was linked with Mick Jagger?
24 Which country did Roy Orbison come from?
25 Which George produced the Beatles' records?
26 Which group recorded "Flowers in the Rain"?
27 Who was backed by Hermits?
28 Who managed to get to No. 1 with a song about a dustman?
29 Which John wanted to "Give Peace a Chance" at the end of the '60s?
30 Which dance was Chubby Checker doing at the start of the '60s?

  Answers on page 195

 Answers on page 195

69 MUSIC CHARTS

1 Which Bob went to No. 1 with "Can We Fix It?"?
2 Which family had a hit with "Do the Bartman"?
3 Which "Rhapsody" was a chart topper for Queen?
4 What colour was the name of the boy band who had a No. 1 with Elton John?
5 Which female singer went straight to in the US with "Fantasy"?
6 Which actor Robson had a string of hits in 1995 with Jerome Flynn?
7 In which age group was Cher when she hit with "Believe"?
8 Where was the "Genie" in the 1999 hit of Christine Aguilera?
9 Which Jennifer sang "The Power of Love" in 1985?
10 Which band's singles include "No Matter What" and "Words"?
11 What type of single was Puff Daddy's "I'll be Missing You"?
12 Which Spice Girls' hit put a stop to a run of s?
13 Which controversial rapper's s include "The Real Slim Shady" and "Stan"?
14 Which British teenager's second was "Girlfriend"?
15 Which Irish group member had a solo with "Life is a Rollercoaster"?
16 Which US emergency phone number hit with "A Little Bit More"?
17 The Arctic Monkeys' first was "I Bet You Look Good on…" what?
18 Which band's singles include "Firestarter" and "Breathe"?
19 Which Spice Girl did Missy Misdemeanour Elliott record "I Want You Back" with?
20 In which decade did Wet Wet Wet have their huge hit "Love is All Around"?
21 Which Australian singer/actress is the most successful ex-soap star in the British pop charts?
22 Which "Prayer" was a millennium chart topper for Cliff Richard?
23 What went with "Beauty" in the title of Celine Dion's first UK chart success?
24 Which Kelly charted with "I Believe I Can Fly"?
25 Which "Lady" was a 1998 chart hit for All Saints?
26 Which ex-member of the Supremes has charted with Marvin Gaye and Lionel Richie?
27 Which future Mrs Evans charted with "Because We Want To"?
28 Whose follow-up to their first was "Say You'll be There"?
29 In which year did Elton John have the best-ever-selling single?
30 Who was "Not Such an Innocent Girl" in 2001?

70 LATE GREATS

1 Which group was Marc Bolan associated with?
2 Which Janis died in Hollywood in 1970?
3 Who won an award for his classic hit "Pretty Woman" after his death?
4 Whose death triggered "Bohemian Rhapsody"/"These are the Days of Our Lives" entering the charts at No. 1?
5 How did Buddy Holly meet his death?
6 Which Big star died at the same time as Buddy Holly?
7 Which live recording of a Frank Sinatra classic went into the Top Ten for Elvis Presley in January 1978?
8 Kurt Cobain was a member of which band?
9 Which famous Liverpudlian was murdered outside his New York flat?
10 Which musical instrument did Jimi Hendrix play?
11 Which Patsy became the first female solo performer to be inducted into the Country Music Hall of Fame?
12 Whose first Top Ten hit, "(Sittin' On) the Dock of the Bay" charted after his death?
13 Who was without his first name Harry when he sang "Without You"?
14 Which was the most famous group Mama Cass was a member of?
15 Which Rolling Stone died in 1969?
16 Whose pioneering rock 'n' roll career came to an end in 1981 after selling more than 60 million discs of "Rock Around the Clock"?
17 Which soul singer Marvin was shot by his own father?
18 Which highly successful female Motown group was the late Florence Ballard a member of?
19 Which band did Sid Vicious belong to?
20 Which Small group were fronted by the late Steve Marriott?
21 Syd Barrett was lead singer for which 1960s group?
22 Who was the second member of the Beatles to die?
23 Which R&B performer Mr Diddley died in 2008?
24 James Brown, who died in 2006, was known as the "Godfather of" what?
25 How close to Tulsa was Gene Pitney?
26 Which pioneer of rock 'n' roll died in a plane crash in 1959?
27 Which famous US female artist sang "Crazy" and died in 1963 aged just 30?
28 Who was the famous "Man in Black" who died in 2003?
29 What was Robert Palmer "Addicted to" in 1986?
30 Which ex-singer is better remembered for hosting TV's *The Record Breakers*?

  Answers on page 195

 Answers on page 195

71
WHO'S WHO?

1 Who married Patsy Kensit in April 1997?
2 Which singer's daughter is called Lourdes Maria?
3 Who has a backing group called the Waves?
4 Who took "Wannabe" to No. 1 in 1996?
5 Who was lead singer with Wet Wet Wet?
6 "Complicated" and "Sk8er Boi" are singles by which Canadian singer?
7 Who sang "Strangers in the Night"?
8 Who is the brother of the late Karen Carpenter?
9 Who wrote "Words", a 90s hit for Boyzone?
10 "PCD" was which group's debut album?
11 Who was Bernie Taupin's most famous songwriting partner?
12 Peter Kay resurrected the chart career of which vocalist Tony?
13 Who changed his name from Gordon Sumner to top the charts?
14 Which band's albums include *American Idiot* and *Nimrod*?
15 Who was the female vocalist with the Pretenders?
16 Who co-starred with Whitney Houston in *The Bodyguard*?
17 Who wrote the music for *Jesus Christ Superstar*?
18 Who were known on TV as Dave Tucker and Paddy Garvey?
19 Who sang that they were "Back for Good" in 1995?
20 Whose "new" single, "Free as a Bird", charted in 1995?
21 The title from which TV drama gave Jimmy Nail a hit in 1994?
22 Who was the subject of the biopic "What's Love Got to Do with It?"?
23 Whose first solo No. 1 was "Sacrifice/Healing Hands"?
24 Who was the British Monkee?
25 Which band released the single "I Believe in a Thing Called Love" in 2003?
26 Who had a hit with "Radio Ga Ga"?
27 Who was the father of the former Mrs Lisa Marie Jackson?
28 Which '80s duo included Andrew Ridgeley?
29 Who had his first UK solo No. 1 with "I Just Called to Say I Love You"?
30 Who was lead singer with Culture Club?

72
POP 2000

1 Which country does Ronan Keating come from?
2 The 2006 album *Love* featured which iconic 1960s band?
3 What was the occupation of chart topper Bob?
4 Which number follows S Club in the band's title?
5 How many boys are there in Destiny's Child?
6 How are the Street Preachers described?
7 What is the surname of the two brothers in Oasis?
8 Which "Pie" did Madonna sing about?
9 What did Geri Halliwell say to do "If You Want to Run Faster"?
10 What was Billie's surname when she first topped the charts?
11 Which sporting event did Kylie Minogue close in 2000?
12 Which Craig had a hit with "Fill Me In"?
13 Which Mariah had a hit with Westlife in 2000?
14 Which Robbie was a "Rock DJ"?
15 What was Mel B called during her brief first marriage?
16 What type of music is LeAnn Rimes famous for?
17 *Stop the Clocks* was a compilation of songs from which band?
18 Which teenage Charlotte wowed audiences on both side of the Atlantic?
19 What type of "Coffee" was a chart topper for All Saints?
20 "Never Had a Dream Come True" was the theme song to which children's TV charity?
21 Craig Phillips charted after winning on which Big TV show?
22 Who charted with The Bangles' "Eternal Flame"?
23 Who was "2 Faced" in 2000?
24 Whose third UK was "Oops I Did It Again"?
25 How many members of Westlife are there?
26 Which band named after a US state were "In Demand" in 2000?
27 Which Jones was a "Sex Bomb" with the Stereophonics in 2000?
28 Which band were formed from the *Popstars* TV show?
29 What is the surname of all the Corrs?
30 Who is controversial rapper Marshall Mathers better known as?

 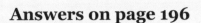 **Answers on page 196**

 **Answers on page 195**

73 MUSIC IN MOVIES

1 Who sang "The Shoop Shoop Song" in 1990?

2 Which Bob Dylan song was featured in Pat Garrett & Billy the Kid?

3 Which hero was the subject of the film for which Bryan Adams sang "(Everything I Do) I Do It For You"?

4 Who sang "Ben" from the film about a rat?

5 Which Meg Ryan/Billy Crystal film's songs were sung by Harry Connick Jr?

6 Who appeared in and had hits with songs from Grease and Xanadu?

7 Which Dire Straits guitarist played "Going Home" from Local Hero?

8 What was or were "Falling on My Head" in the theme music from Butch Cassidy and the Sundance Kid?

9 In which Lloyd Webber film did Madonna play the title role?

10 Which 1981 film starring Dudley Moore, Liza Minnelli and John Gielgud had a theme sung by Christopher Cross?

11 Who sang "Love is All Around" from Four Weddings and a Funeral?

12 Whose first film was A Hard Day's Night?

13 Which Welsh-born female vocalist had a hit with "Goldfinger"?

14 Which film about the 1924 Paris Olympics won an Oscar for the composer Vangelis?

15 Which classic film with Humphrey Bogart and Ingrid Bergman includes the song "As Time Goes By"?

16 Which duo sang "Mrs Robinson" from The Graduate in 1968?

17 Who "Does It Better" according to Carly Simon from The Spy Who Loved Me?

18 Which creatures were the subject of the film Born Free?

19 Which film featured "Stuck in the Middle With You" by Stealer's Wheel?

20 Who was Forever in the film to which Seal sang the theme song?

21 Which Derek and the Dominos hit was featured in Goodfellas?

22 Hans Zimmer's "Spider"-what from The Simpsons Movie was a UK chart hit?

23 Which song does Marty McFly play on guitar during Back to the Future?

24 "You Can Leave Your Hat On" was the theme for which stripping movie?

25 Shaun of the Dead has the theme tune of "Don't Stop Me Now" by which group?

26 Which Bee Gees album shares the same title as a 1977 disco movie?

27 Can you name Survivor's song which was the theme tune to Rocky III?

28 Which film featured "The End" by The Doors?

29 Which Bill Medley & Jennifer Warnes duet was the theme song to Dirty Dancing?

30 Which Kenny sang "Footloose" in the 1984 movie of the same name?

  Answers on page 196

74 POP NO. 1S

1 "Sound of the Underground" was the first No. 1 for which group?

2 Four Weddings and a Funeral made which song a No. 1?

3 In which decade did Elvis have his first UK No. 1?

4 "Where is the Love?" was the first No. 1 for which collective?

5 Which relative features in a Hollies song title?

6 Which other song was on Robson and Jerome's "Unchained Melody"?

7 Whose death gave "Bohemian Rhapsody" a second visit to No. 1?

8 Whom should you bring to the slaughter, according to Iron Maiden?

9 What was the imaginative title of Mr Blobby's first No. 1?

10 Who charted with a song about Heathcliff and Cathy?

11 Which soccer team were involved in "Come On You Reds"?

12 Who had No. 1s with "Call Me" and "Atomic"?

13 Who sang with Kiki Dee on "Don't Go Breaking My Heart"?

14 Which song was a No. 1 for both Nilsson and Mariah Carey?

15 Which English Sir has had No. 1s in the '50s, '60s, '70s, '80s and '90s?

16 Who had "Dreams" in 1993?

17 Which US state was the title of a Bee Gees No. 1?

18 Which band were "Back for Good" in 1995?

19 Which Beatle No. 1 featured the word "Yellow" in the title?

20 "The Winner Takes It All" was yet another No. 1 for which group?

21 Who wrote Simon and Garfunkel's "Bridge Over Troubled Water"?

22 What type of "House" did Blur take to the top of the charts?

23 George Michael first hit No. 1 as a member of which duo?

24 Who took "Lily the Pink" to No. 1?

25 Who thought it was fun to stay in the YMCA?

26 Whose first UK No. 1 was "Apache"?

27 In psychedelic '67, which old-time dance gave Engelbert Humperdinck a huge hit?

28 Who teamed up with Queen for "Under Pressure"?

29 Who had a No. 1 with "Cotton Eye Joe"?

30 Which singer first made No. 1 with "Livin' La Vida Loca"?

 Answers on page 196

75 MUSIC SUPERSTARS

1 Who was Simon's singing partner?

2 By which first name is Roderick David Stewart known?

3 Who has the surname Ciccone?

4 Freddie Mercury led which regal-sounding band?

5 Which superstar singer Barbra starred in the hit movie *Meet the Fockers*?

6 Which Elton John song was reworked and dedicated to Princess Diana?

7 What was the Spice Girls' first album called?

8 Which Elvis hit of 2005 has the line, "You ain't a never caught a rabbit"?

9 Which band's singles include "Country House" and "Beetlebum"?

10 Who made the album *Best of Bob Marley*?

11 Whose *Come On Over* album is a top-selling country album in the US?

12 Which ex-Take That member won a Brit Award for "She's the One" in 2000?

13 Whose hits include "Jesus to a Child" and "Outside"?

14 Which band has had the most gold albums of any band in the UK?

15 Which grandfather was a "Sex Bomb" in 2000?

16 In 2000 U2 received the keys to which city?

17 Which Beatle announced his engagement in 2001?

18 Which band's singles include "Common People" and "Disco 2000"?

19 Which band did Sting front?

20 Which late blue-eyed superstar had the first names Francis Albert?

21 Which "Jagged Little" album was a huge hit for Alanis Morissette?

22 Bjorn Again are a tribute band to which superstars?

23 Which Irish band made the album "By Request"?

24 Which Diana fronted The Supremes?

25 Eric Clapton had a transatlantic hit with "I Shot" who?

26 Who was in the news after the break-up of his marriage to Heather Mills?

27 Which George's early solo single was "Careless Whisper"?

28 Which band's singles include "Australia" and "A Design for Life"?

29 Who had hit albums "True Blue" and "Erotica"?

30 Who had huge hits with "Sacrifice" and "Rocket Man"?

76 CLIFF RICHARD

1 What is Cliff Richard's real name?

2 In which country was he born?

3 What was the name of his backing group, which included Bruce Welch?

4 In which film did Cliff head for the continent on a London Transport bus?

5 In 1996 where did Cliff give a concert with Martina Navratilova and Virginia Wade in his backing group?

6 Cliff came second with which song in the 1968 Eurovision Song Contest?

7 Which award did Cliff receive from the Queen in 1995?

8 In which musical based on a novel by Emily Bronte did Cliff play the title role?

9 With what type of "Doll" did Cliff chart accompanied by the Shadows and then the Young Ones?

10 Which '60s hit began with "When I was young my father said ..."?

11 What features in the title with Wine on Cliff's Christmas No. 1 in 1988?

12 Which blonde tennis star had her name linked with Cliff in the 80s?

13 What date of Never was a hit for Cliff in 1964?

14 What did Cliff say to Samantha when he said Goodbye to Sam?

15 Which wife of Andrew Lloyd-Webber did Cliff duet with in "All I Ask of You" from *Phantom of the Opera*?

16 Which Olivia sang with Cliff on "Suddenly" and "Had to be"?

17 Whose "Day" was the Christmas No. 1 in 1990?

18 What was Cliff's first hit single?

19 Which part of Cliff was "Lucky" in the title of his 1964 hit?

20 Which Everly did Cliff duet with in "She Means Nothing to Me"?

21 Which irreverent 1980s TV sitcom took its name from a Cliff Richard film?

22 How many decades in the music industry did Cliff Richard complete in 2008?

23 Which Iberian country gave Cliff the equivalent of a knighthood in 2006?

24 In which decade did Cliff Richard last have two British No. 1s?

25 Whose "List" reached No. 5 as Cliff's Christmas single in 2003?

26 Which was Cliff's first record label?

27 Which "Prayer" went to No. 1 in the Charts for Cliff at Christmas 1999?

28 Who is the only one solo artist with more weeks in the British singles charts than Cliff?

29 Which of his albums included "Devil Woman"?

30 In which decade did Cliff have a No. 1 hit with "We Don't Talk Anymore"?

 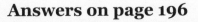 **Answers on page 196**

 Answers on page 196

77 MADONNA

1 What is the first name of Madonna's ex-husband Mr Ritchie?
2 Has Madonna ever written any of her own hits?
3 Which word completes her documentary movie title, *I Want to Tell You a ...*?
4 Is Madonna's husband a car salesman or a movie director?
5 In which movie did she play Eva Peron?
6 Is Maverick the name of her recording company or her son?
7 Which album came first, *Music* or *Like a Virgin*?
8 Which True album was No. 1 when the single "Papa Don't Preach" was No. 1?
9 In 1998 Madonna had album success with *Ray of...* what?
10 Was she in her 30s or 40s when she had success with the album *Music* in 2000?
11 Madonna was the most performed look and sound alike on which show?
12 Which "Pie" gave Madonna a 2000 No. 1 in the UK?
13 Which country follows "Don't Cry For Me" in her 1996 hit?
14 Which home of the US movie industry was the title of a 2003 hit?
15 Which "Life" was the name of a US No. 1?
16 Which 2002 Bond movie song gave Madonna a hit?
17 Which young singer joined her on "Me Against the Music"?
18 Did Madonna have her first hit albums in the 1980s or 1990s?
19 What type of stranger was the name of a 1999 hit?
20 What was the abbreviation of her *Greatest Hits Volume 2* album?
21 Which single was No. 1 when the album *Like a Prayer* was No. 1?
22 In which part of the UK did Madonna marry Guy Ritchie?
23 Which actor Sean was Madonna's first husband?
24 The single "Ray of Light" came from which album?
25 Who is older, her first son or daughter?
26 What had she fallen from when she suffered broken bones in 2005?
27 How many "Minutes" summed up Madonna's smash hit produced by Timbaland?
28 Was "Hung Up" the title of a single or album?
29 What was her debut album Madonna imaginatively retitled in 1985?
30 Which chart topper came first, "Hung Up" or "Frozen"?

78 '60S POP 2

1 Who was the drummer with the Dave Clark Five?
2 Which small Mod group were all under five foot six tall?
3 Who completed the line-up of Dave Dee, Dozy, Beaky and Mick?
4 In 1965 the Kinks sang about a "Dedicated Follower of..." what?
5 What did Marvin Gaye "Hear It Through" in 1969?
6 What did the Beatles "Want to Hold" on their first US No. 1?
7 Which Corner had Andy Fairweather-Low as lead singer?
8 Which Little girl sang "The Locomotion" in 1962?
9 Which head of the Diddymen shed "Tears" in 1965?
10 What is "Over" according to the Seekers in 1965?
11 Which Engelbert Humperdinck song's second line is "Let me go"?
12 Which '60s dance was popularized by Chubby Checker?
13 Which country were the Bachelors from?
14 What sort of "Vibrations" did the Beach Boys have in 1966?
15 Which Australian had the last No. 1 of the '60s with "Two Little Boys"?
16 What follows "Ob-La-Di" in the Marmalade No. 1?
17 Which lover of Romeo was a hit for the Four Pennies?
18 In 1960 what was the profession of Lonnie Donegan's dad?
19 Which "Pretty" pink bird was a No. 1 for Manfred Mann?
20 How old was the "Sweet" person Neil Sedaka wished Happy Birthday to in 1961?
21 Who came between Peter and Mary in the trio?
22 With what song did Sandie Shaw win the 1967 Eurovision Song Contest?
23 Where should you wear a flower if going to San Francisco?
24 Why did Jimi Hendrix play his Fender Stratocaster upside down?
25 Which Des sang about "Careless Hands" in 1967?
26 Who had a hit in 1960 with "Itsy Bitsy Teenie Weenie Yellow Polka Dot Bikini"?
27 Which 1967 chart hit became the signature song of Aretha Franklin?
28 Which fictional characters had a chart hit in 1969 with "Sugar Sugar"?
29 Which Beatles chart hit was created by Paul McCartney as a "song for Ringo"?
30 Who sang lead vocals on "Baby Love"?

  Answers on page 196

 Answers on page 196

79 KARAOKE

1 What line follows "Is this the real life"?

2 "Time goes by so slowly, And time can do so much," comes from which song?

3 What line comes before "Why, why, why, Delilah?"?

4 "And so I face the final curtain" comes from which song?

5 Which Robbie Williams song names Marlon Brando?

6 Finish the line: "If you want to know if he loves you so, It's..."

7 What do you hold up high when you walk through a storm?

8 Who sang "Never seen you looking so gorgeous as you did tonight"?

9 Jason Donovan closed his eyes and drew back what?

10 "The answer, my friend, is blowing..." where?

11 What line comes after "Her name was Lola"?

12 Where are you if you "wake up in a city that never sleeps"?

13 In which song by the Jam is there "a row going on, down in Slough"?

14 What did he paint apart from "Matchstalk Men"?

15 What line comes before "I feel it in my toes"?

16 How many times do you sing "Yeah" in the chorus of "She Loves You"?

17 To whom did Dolly Parton beg "Please don't take my man"?

18 If tonight is the night how is Whitney Houston feeling?

19 According to Pink Floyd, "We don't need no education, We don't need no..." what?

20 What word comes before "Not a sound from the pavement"?

21 Finish the line: "You never close your eyes anymore when I kiss..."

22 Which Elton John line follows "It's a little bit funny"?

23 Which two herbs go with "parsley, sage"?

24 In "Sultans of Swing" who "knows all the chords"?

25 In "Grease", what line comes before "Did she put up a fight?"?

26 Which David Gray song features the line, "Tell me something I don't already know"?

27 What four words go after "Do I love you, My oh my"?

28 Who was "wearing a face that she keeps in a jar by the door"?

29 "Do you really want to hurt me? Do you really want to" do what?

30 "Her face at first just ghostly turned" what kind of colour?

80 SOUND OF THE '70S

1 What was on the other side of Boney M's "Brown Girl in the Ring"?

2 Which Dawn single was in the charts for 39 weeks in the 1970s?

3 Which film did "You're the One that I Want" come from?

4 Which 1970s hit by Wings was the first UK single to sell two million copies?

5 Who made the album *Don't Shoot Me I'm Only the Piano Player*?

6 Which solo singer who died in 2001 recorded the album *And I Love You So*?

7 Whom did Elton John have a single with in 1976?

8 Julie Covington had a UK with a song from which Andrew Lloyd Webber/Tim Rice musical?

9 Who was the most successful solo star from the group which had a with "Message in a Bottle"?

10 "Matchstalk Men and Matchstalk Cats and Dogs" was about which artist?

11 With which song did Brotherhood of Man win the Eurovision Song Contest?

12 Who had the original hit with "Seasons in the Sun"?

13 Who had "Breakfast In America"?

14 How many times is Annie's name mentioned in John Denver's "Annie's Song"?

15 Who was the first Beatle to have a solo in the 1970s?

16 Which member of the cast of *Dad's Army* had a hit record?

17 Who hit with "Cum on Feel the Noize"?

18 Who declared that he was the Leader of the Gang?

19 Which star of the stage show *Evita* had a hit with "Hold Me Close"?

20 What was the title of the England World Cup squad's anthem of 1970?

21 On which new record label was Mike Oldfield's "Tubular Bells" released?

22 Which Tony featured on Dawn's "Tie a Yellow Ribbon"?

23 Which instrument did Suzi Quatro play on "Can the Can"?

24 Who had a hit with Nilsson's "Without You" 20 years later?

25 Which band made the super selling "Rumours"?

26 Which band did Roy Wood lead in "Angel Fingers"?

27 Whose "Sailing" was described by its performer as "one for the terraces"?

28 Which band's very first hit was "Debora"?

29 "I'd Like to Teach the World to Sing" was later used to advertised which drink?

30 Who recorded the album *Arrival*?

   Answers on page 196

 Answers on page 196

81
POP POT LUCK

1 In which decade did the Bee Gees have their first hit?

2 Whose backing group was the Blue Flames?

3 Who sang "Heart of Gold" in 1972?

4 Which colour "Monday" was a hit for New Order in 1983 and 1988?

5 How is Mary O'Brien better known?

6 In which "Park" were the Small Faces in 1967?

7 Who had a No. 1 with "Down Under"?

8 Which greeting linked Stevie Wonder and Altered Images in 1981?

9 Who was the first member to leave Take That in 1995?

10 Who was the female member of Blondie?

11 In which decade was Neil Sedaka born?

12 Who had a No. 1 with "I Can't Give You Anything (but My Love)"?

13 What was Sting's first solo single?

14 Who had a backing group called the Steelmen?

15 Whose man was So Macho in 1986?

16 Which Summer song did Abba sing in 1978?

17 What did Shanice say "I Love" in 1991 and 1992?

18 Whose first hit was "School's Out"?

19 Who had a '90s album called *Auberge*?

20 Whose "Clown" were the Everly Brothers in 1960?

21 Who had a big 2008 hit with "That's Not My Name"?

22 Which is the only song to be a big hit four times, all with different performers?

23 Which musical instrument does Ravi Shankar play?

24 Who was Johnny Kidd's backing group?

25 Which "drink" was the Four Seasons' first hit?

26 In which decade was Chris Rea's first Top Ten hit?

27 In which decade was Lionel Richie born?

28 Who starred as Bongo Herbert in a film?

29 Who had an album called *My People were Fair and Had Sky in Their Hair... But Now They're Content to Wear Stars on Their Brows*?

30 Which song title links Cars and R.E.M.?

82
SOUL & MOTOWN 2

1 The Four Tops had only one British . What was it?

2 Who was the boss of Tamla Motown?

3 Who sang with Sam on the hit "Soul Man"?

4 Which female soul star has recorded with Elton John, George Michael and George Benson?

5 Who made up the songwriting trio with Holland and Dozier?

6 Who was sitting on the dock of the bay?

7 Who according to Jimmy Ruffin "had love that has now departed"?

8 Which soul singer died in 1984 after lying in a coma for eight years?

9 Rudolph, Ronald and O'Kelley were which singing Brothers?

10 Who is known as "The Godfather of Soul"?

11 Which group featured Cindy Birdsong?

12 The Motown label was nearly called Tammy. After which Tammy?

13 Which Tamla song starts, "Set me free, why don't you babe"?

14 In the 1960s who was known as "The Wicked Pickett"?

15 Which group backed Martha Reeves?

16 Who recorded the soul classic "Sweet Soul Music"?

17 What was Diana Ross's first solo British ?

18 Which singer went solo after performing with the Commodores?

19 Who was backed by the Pips?

20 Which soul singer married Whitney Houston in 1992?

21 Who sang "I Was Made to Love Her"?

22 Eddie Kendricks and David Ruffin were lead singers with which group?

23 Whom did Martha Reeves want to "hurry back"?

24 What was Smokey Robinson's real first name?

25 Which hour did Cropper and Pickett write about?

26 Which was the first single in which the Supremes were billed as Diana Ross and the Supremes?

27 Who originally heard it through the grapevine?

28 On which label did Aretha Franklin record in the 1960s?

29 Who had a Tamla hit with "War"?

30 Who fronted the All Stars?

 Answers on page 197

 Answers on page 197

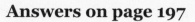

83
MUSIC CHARTS 2

1 What goes with "Inside In" in the title of The Kooks' first album?

2 Which veteran rockers had a 2005 hit with "The Party ain't Over Yet"?

3 Who sang "I'll be Missing You" with Puff Daddy?

4 Which Mariah Carey single was the first to debut at in the US, in 1995?

5 What was the title of Corinne Bailey Rae's debut album?

6 Who was the first male rapper to have two solo s?

7 S Club 7's "Never Had a Dream Come True" raised money for which charity?

8 Which was the first band to have seven successive s with their first seven releases?

9 Which British band had the first of the new millennium?

10 Which girl's name featured in a mega hit for Dexy's Midnight Runners?

11 Which was Wham!'s best-selling Christmas single?

12 Which 2000 Spiller song stopped Victoria Beckham from having her first solo ?

13 What was the English title of Sarah Brightman's "Con Te Partiro" which she sang with Andrea Bocelli?

14 Who first made the Top Twenty with "Linger"?

15 In 2000 Oxide & Neutrino charted with a reworking of the theme of which hospital series?

16 Who sang "How Do I Live" in 1998?

17 Whose "Killing Me Softly" was a top seller in 1996?

18 Which song from "Bridget Jones's Diary" did Geri Halliwell have a hit with in 2001?

19 What was Britney Spears' second UK ?

20 What was Elton John's first solo in the US?

21 "Three Lions" charted in which World Cup year?

22 Which family charted with "Mmmbop"?

23 Which Oasis member sang on The Chemical Brothers' "Setting Sun"?

24 What was Michael Jackson's last of the 20th century?

25 In which decade did Japan have their first Top Ten hit?

26 Who hit with "Deeper Underground" in 1999?

27 Chef's 1998 came from which cartoon series?

28 Who charted with "All Right Now" in the 1970s and with a 1990s remix?

29 "Vision of Love" was the first Top Ten hit for which singer?

30 In which decade did smooth soul group the Chi-Lites have most hits?

84
'50S POP

1 Who sang with the Checkmates?

2 Which film did "The Harry Lime Theme" come from?

3 Which girl was on the other side of "All I Have to Do Is Dream" for the Everly Brothers?

4 Which first No. 1 for Adam Faith was a question?

5 What was the '50s' best-selling single?

6 Who took "Mary's Boy Child" in to the charts in the '50s?

7 Which '50s classic begins "I'm so young and you're so old"?

8 Which singer was married to Debbie Reynolds and Elizabeth Taylor?

9 Who had a "Secret Love" in 1954?

10 Who sang "Yes Tonight Josephine"?

11 Which singer with which group had a hit with "Livin' Doll"?

12 Whose girl was "Only Sixteen" at No. 1 in 1959?

13 Which instrumentalist hit the top with "Let's Have Another Party"?

14 Which Buddy Holly hit was the first after his death and went to No. 1?

15 Who told the "Story of His Life" in 1958?

16 Who went from the "Green Door" to the "Garden of Eden"?

17 Who had a 1955 No. 1 with "Unchained Melody"?

18 Who had a "Dreamboat" in 1955?

19 Which '50s musical provided Vic Damone with a 1958 No. 1?

20 What does Anne Shelton finally sing after "Lay Down Your Arms" in her 1956 No. 1?

21 In which American state was Buddy Holly's fatal plane crash?

22 By what name was J. P. Richardson better known?

23 Which Carole was believed to be the subject of Neil Sedaka's "Oh Carol"?

24 What did Frankie Laine want you to do in his 1953 Christmas No. 1?

25 Which Shirley had her first British No. 1 in 1959?

26 What was wrong with the "Wings" which The Stargazers took to No. 1 in 1953?

27 This Perry Como No. 1 was used by Quality Street sweets in a TV advert.

28 What was "Cupid" in Connie Francis's No. 1 hit of 1958?

29 Which popular foreign-sounding radio station broadcast a sheet music Top 20?

30 What was the last UK No. 1 hit of the decade by Emile Ford & The Checkmates?

  Answers on page 197

 Answers on page 197

85
DANCE & DISCO

1 Which dance favourite became Kylie's first UK million-seller?

2 Which Village People chart hit was made up of initial letters?

3 Which boy's name took Sister Sledge to in 1985?

4 Cheryl Jones and Sandra Denton spiced up their names to what?

5 Who recorded the 2002 album "Come with Us"?

6 Which Doors song was given the disco treatment by Amii Stewart?

7 In which song does the line "Too Ra Loo Ra Loo Rye Aye" appear?

8 Which girl group backed Disco Tex?

9 Who was too sexy in 1991?

10 Whose name comes before the Mastermixers?

11 Which Richie Valens 1950s hit charted for Los Lobos in 1987?

12 Who was "Never Gonna Give You Up" in 1987?

13 Who did Madonna tell "don't preach" in the 1986 ?

14 Which country do Black Box come from?

15 Who recorded "Funky Stuff" and "Jungle Boogie"?

16 Which group found success in the 1970s with "Night Fever"?

17 Who teamed up with Take That in "Relight My Fire"?

18 Who recorded "Wham Rap"?

19 Who else was on "Keep On Pumpin' It" along with the Visionmasters and Tony Knight?

20 What was on the B side of Boney M's "Rivers of Babylon"?

21 Which disco hit singer thought that "Love's Unkind"?

22 What was a for The Simpsons?

23 Who had "A Night to Remember" in 1982?

24 While Tina Charles loved to love, what did her baby love to do?

25 In his baggy trousers, what name is rapper Stanley Burrell known as?

26 Who had "Heartache" in 1987?

27 Who had a 2001 dance hit with "Clint Eastwood"?

28 Who recorded the 1970s disco song "You're My First My Last My Everything"?

29 Who is credited on "Lady Marmalade" along with Christina Aguilera, Lil' Kim and Mya?

30 How is Robert Bell better known?

86
BANDS

1 Whose "Best of..." 1990s album was *Cross Road*?

2 Who embarked on their "Bigger Bang" tour in 2006?

3 Who had a hit with "Don't Let Go"?

4 *Happy Nation* was the debut album of which Scandinavian band?

5 What was the surname of the sisters in All Saints?

6 Which band had 18 consecutive UK Top Ten hits between July 1964 and March 1976?

7 What was Queen's best-selling single?

8 Which Beatles single was their first in the US?

9 Which band won the 2006 Eurovision Song Contest?

10 How many albums did the Spice Girls release in the 20th century?

11 Which was Blur's first UK ?

12 Which 1996 Boyzone hit was a previous hit by the Bee Gees?

13 Which 1999 Manic Street Preachers hit shares its name with a natural disaster?

14 Which was Take That's first UK of the 21st century?

15 Whose album *Fat of the Land* debuted at on both sides of the Atlantic?

16 Joe Elliot was vocalist with which heavy metal band?

17 Who had an "Appetite for Destruction" in 1987?

18 Whose album had some *Rattle and Hum* in 1988?

19 Who had the award-winning 1999 album *Surrender*?

20 Who were "Out of Time" in 1991?

21 Who had the original hit with Atomic Kitten's "Eternal Flame"?

22 Which city did the 1960s band The Animals come from?

23 What was Aqua's follow-up to "Barbie Girl"?

24 Which Catatonia hit shared its name with a TV duo?

25 Which part of the UK did Ash come from?

26 Which Blur album shared its name with a Steve McQueen film?

27 On which label did Oasis have their first Top Ten Hit?

28 Shane Lynch was a member of which band?

29 Arctic Monkeys hail from which city?

30 Which band had 16 consecutive UK Top Ten hits between December 1994 and December 1999?

  Answers on page 197

 Answers on page 197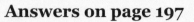

87
CHRISTMAS RECORDS

1 What did Dora Bryan want for Christmas in 1963?

2 In which decade did Bing Crosby's "White Christmas" first enter the UK charts?

3 What did John Lennon's "Happy Christmas" have in brackets in 1980?

4 According to Adam Faith, what was in a Christmas Shop in 1960?

5 Who said "Please Come Home for Christmas" in 1994?

6 Which "Christmas Rock" has been a hit for Max Bygraves and Chubby Checker with Bobby Rydell?

7 Who wished "It Could be Christmas Every Day" in 1973?

8 What was Johnny Mathis's 1976 Christmas hit?

9 What kind of Merry Christmas did a band of environmentalists wish us in 1974?

10 Who said "All I Want for Christmas is You" in 1994?

11 Which comedian was "Rockin' Around the Christmas Tree" in 1987?

12 Which Snowman did the Cocteau Twins sing about in 1993?

13 Who covered the Carpenters' "Santa Claus is Comin' to Town" in 1985?

14 Where was Santa Claus according to *Spitting Image* in 1986?

15 Who pleaded with Santa Baby in the 1990s?

16 Who sang with the Smurfs on "Christmas in Smurfland" in 1978?

17 Whose "Christmas Alphabet" went to No. 1 in 1955?

18 Who had a "Wonderful Christmas Time" in 1979?

19 What is the theme song from *The Snowman*?

20 Who had "White Christmas" on the other side of "Too Risky"?

21 The winner of which show 2005–07 also had the UK Christmas No. 1?

22 "Sound of the Underground" was the first Christmas No. 1 for which group?

23 Robbie Williams and Nicole Kidman covered whose No. 1 "Something Stupid"?

24 What did Bob the Builder ask if he could "Fix" in 2000?

25 What were Mud "This Christmas" in their 1974 Christmas No. 1 hit?

26 Can you name the School Choir who topped the charts at Christmas 1980?

27 Which Johnny Mathis classic was the 1976 Christmas No. 1 hit?

28 What were the Spice Girls saying with their 1998 Christmas No. 1?

29 Name the Westlife song which was the last Christmas No. 1 of the 20th century.

30 Which Christmas No. 1 from Dave Edmunds was his only ever No. 1 hit?

88
POP DUOS

1 How are Messrs Hodges and Peacock better known?

2 "It's four o'clock and we're in trouble deep" comes from which Everly Brothers song?

3 What relation was Sonny to Cher in their single-making days?

4 Pepsi and Shirlie provided backing vocals for which superstar group?

5 What was the first Eurythmics Top Ten single back in 1983?

6 What little animal did Nina and Frederick sing about?

7 Which duo were made up of Paul and Art?

8 Whom did Diano Ross duo with on "Endless Love"?

9 Which TV show gave Peters and Lee their first break?

10 Whom did Elton John sing with on his first British ?

11 What were the first names of the Ofarims?

12 Which artist did Brian and Michael sing about?

13 What was the Pipkins' only hit?

14 According to Peter and Gordon, to know you is to do what?

15 "It Takes Two" featured Tammi Terrell and who else?

16 Which duo has spent most weeks in the UK single charts?

17 Who were respectable in 1987?

18 How many of duo Miki and Griff were female?

19 Which duo had a with "Would I Lie to You"?

20 Which duo comprised Marc Almond and David Ball?

21 Who produced Ike and Tina Turner's "River Deep Mountain High"?

22 Which male/female singing duo had 16 weeks at in 1978?

23 According to "Tears for Fears", what did everyone want to rule?

24 Which duo charted with the "The Skye Boat Song"?

25 Which duo appeared in drag in an Abba tribute?

26 Tom Rowlands and Ed Simons make up which production dance duo?

27 Who charted with "(I Wanna Give You) Devotion"?

28 How many girls are in the duo Everything but the Girl?

29 Which Simon and Garfunkel song starts "I'm sitting in a railway station"?

30 How are Christopher Lowe and Neil Tennant better known?

  Answers on page 197

 Answers on page 197

89 COUNTRY & WESTERN

1 Who had a hit in 1972 with "A Thing Called Love"?

2 Which hit in letters followed "Stand by Your Man" for Tammy Wynette?

3 Which group had a No. 1 hit in 1976 with "Mississippi"?

4 Which best-selling country and pop star married Mutt Lange?

5 Whose song was a No. 1 for John Denver in 1974?

6 Which Patsy Cline hit was covered by Julio Iglesias in 1994?

7 In which year was "Achey Breaky Heart" a hit for Billy Ray Cyrus?

8 Who had a No. 11 UK hit with "Talking in Your Sleep" in 1978?

9 Hiram Williams is the real name of which singer?

10 Which opera singer joined John Denver to record "Perhaps Love"?

11 Who duetted with Ronan Keating on the chart hit "Last Thing on My Mind"?

12 Which Kris wrote "Help Me Make It Through the Night"?

13 Who had a hit in the summer of 1998 with "How Do I"?

14 Who wrote the autobiography *Coal Miner's Daughter*?

15 Who joined Kenny Rogers on the No. 7 hit "Islands in the Stream"?

16 What is Reba McEntire's real name?

17 Which specialist type of singing links Frank Ifield and Slim Whitman?

18 Who duetted with Mark Knopfler on the album "Neck and Neck"?

19 In the No. 1, which drums were heard by Jim Reeves?

20 Who sang "All I Have to do Is Dream" with Bobbie Gentry in 1969?

21 Who had a backing band called the Waylors?

22 What is the name of the theme park owned by Dolly Parton?

23 George Jones' 1975 hit "The Battle" told of the split from his wife. Who was she?

24 Which "Banks" were a hit in 1971 for Olivia Newton-John?

25 Which song was a No. 2 UK hit for Tammy Wynette and KLF in 1991?

26 Who wrote the classic song "Crazy"?

27 Who formed the Trio with Dolly Parton and Linda Ronstadt?

28 Who took "Cotton Eye Joe" to No. 1 in 1994?

29 Which No. 9 for Elvis was a No. 10 for Carl Perkins in 1956?

30 Which "modern girl" joined Kenny Rogers on "We've Got Tonight"?

90 '90S POP

1 Who sang about "Saturday Night" in 1994?

2 What was on the other side of Robson and Jerome's "I Believe"?

3 What goes after Meat Loaf's "I Would Do Anything for Love"?

4 Which soundtrack was a top-selling 1992 album in the UK and the US?

5 Which '91 chart toppers share a name with an instrument of torture?

6 Which band included Siobhan Fahey and Marcella Detroit?

7 Which '94 chart topper was written by the Troggs' Reg Presley?

8 Who were Baby, Posh, Scary, Ginger and Sporty?

9 Who had the album *Automatic for the People*?

10 Who was Take That's usual lead vocalist?

11 Which No. 1 artist was the creation of the TV producer Mike Leggo?

12 Whose first No. 1 was "End of the Road"?

13 What was Boyzone's first chart hit?

14 Which superstar did Bobby Brown marry in 1992?

15 Who had the bestselling album *Blue is the Colour*?

16 What was the Dunblane single called?

17 Which veteran band released "Voodoo Lounge" in 1994?

18 Whose 1994 Greatest Hits album was called *End of Part One*?

19 Which band included the bass player Paul McGuigan?

20 What was reported in the press as "Cliffstock"?

21 What did Kylie Minogue have on her "Pillow" in 1990?

22 In which year did Freddie Mercury die?

23 "It's in His Kiss" was the subtitle to which No. 1 enjoyed by Cher in 1991?

24 Whose only chart-topper was 1997's "The Drugs Don't Work"?

25 Who was the first Spice Girl to have a No. 1 as a solo artist?

26 What was Wamdue "King of" in their November 1999 No.1 hit?

27 Who had a worldwide hit in 1999 with "Livin' La Vida Loca"?

28 Can you recall what type of "Eye" Joe had in Rednex's only ever No. 1 single?

29 Which single gave Geri Halliwell her first solo UK No. 1?

30 What were Oasis "All Around" when they claimed their fourth UK No. 1 hit single?

  Answers on page 197

 Answers on page 197

91
JAZZ & BLUES

1 What was Louis Armstrong's nickname?
2 Which 1960s band featured Eric Clapton and Jimmy Page?
3 Which singer recorded the *When Harry Met Sally* soundtrack?
4 In which city were Kenny Ball and his jazzmen at midnight?
5 Which 1920s blues singer recorded "Down Hearted Blues"?
6 What was Chris Barber's only hit single?
7 Whose quartet famously decided to "Take Five"?
8 What was Jamie Cullum's breakthrough album?
9 What was John Mayall's group known as?
10 What instrument did Earl Hines play?
11 Which jazz-funk saxophonist had a hit in 1987 with "Songbird"?
12 Which jazz musician opened a London club in 1959?
13 Who played Billie Holiday in the film *Lady Sings the Blues*?
14 Which clarinettist lived from 1909 to 1986 and had his "Story" told in a 1955 film?
15 Which veteran blues performer recorded "The Healer"?
16 How is singer Clementina Dinah Campbell better known?
17 Which trumpeter talks of Mornington Crescent in a radio panel game?
18 Under what name did Marion Walter Jacobs record?
19 What instrument is associated with Courtney Pine?
20 Who sang "He's a Tramp" in Disney's "Lady and the Tramp"?
21 Who recorded "Hoochie Coochie Man" and "Got My Mojo Working"?
22 Which virtuoso jazz drummer started out in a vaudeville act as Baby Trapps the Drum Wonder?
23 In which country was Alexis Korner born?
24 Which bluesman had a with "Let the Heartaches Begin"?
25 What was the name of Mr Acker Bilk's Jazz Band?
26 Which instrument does Jamie Cullum play?
27 What instrument is associated with Monty Sunshine?
28 Which guitarist released the album "Ballads and Blues"?
29 Who turned "Three Blind Mice" into "Experiments with Mice"?
30 Which group were formed by Bruce, Baker and Clapton?

92
'70S POP

1 Which '70s hit by the Osmonds gave Boyzone a hit in '94?
2 Which Lieutenant's only UK No. 1 hit was "Mouldy Old Dough"?
3 Who sang that she was "born in the wagon of a travelling show"?
4 "(Hey There) Lonely Girl" was the only UK hit for which vocalist?
5 Tony Orlando sang in which group that had a girl's name?
6 The craze for streaking gave a No. 1 to which Ray?
7 Which part of the body was mentioned in the title of a Blondie hit?
8 Who were "Up The Junction" in 1979?
9 Which month links Pilot and part of a song title for Barbara Dickson?
10 Whose hits from 1970 include "Victoria" and "Apeman"?
11 What was the number of ELO's Overture in their first hit?
12 The No. 1 UK hit "Woodstock" was a one-hit wonder for which group?
13 Who had a No. 1 single in 2006, but first charted with "The Show Must Go On"?
14 Which Elton John '70s hit with a two-word title returned to the Top Ten in 2002?
15 What links Terry Wogan and the Brighouse and Rastrick Brass Band?
16 "Loving You" was a high-pitched No. 2 UK hit for which female singer?
17 Which group had a No. 1 UK hit with "Sad Sweet Dreamer"?
18 Who wanted to be taken to the Mardi Gras?
19 Which 1971 Supremes hit was later a hit for Bananarama?
20 Who had hits with "Bang Bang" and "Knocked It Off" in 1979?
21 The 1979 No. 6 hit "Since You've Been Gone" was a hit for whom?
22 Which US city was named twice in a Gerard Kenny hit from 1978?
23 Whom did Cliff Richard say "Hello" to when he said "Goodbye to Sam"?
24 In which song do the chorus beg, "Tell me more, tell me more!"?
25 Which group had hits in the 70s with "Easy", "Still" and "Sail On"?
26 What was on the other side of Boney M's "Brown Girl in the Ring"?
27 What time was Gladys Knight's train leaving for Georgia?
28 Which Mungo Jerry hit was used in an anti drink-drive campaign?
29 Which disco-style singer had the word "Love" in the title of four of her first five Top Ten hits?
30 Which No. 1 from 1972 was the theme for the Van Der Valk series?

  **Answers on page 198**

 Answers on page 198

93
STEVIE WONDER

1 Which three instruments could Stevie play by the age of seven?

2 How was Stevie known in his early days on stage?

3 What was the first record label he recorded on?

4 Which single had the subtitle "Everything's Alright"?

5 On whose *Duets II* album did he sing in 1994?

6 Which 1984 album was from a film soundtrack?

7 In which decade was Stevie Wonder born?

8 Who did he duet with on "My Love" in 1988?

9 To which monument did he sing "Happy Birthday" in Paris in 1989?

10 Who was his song "Sir Duke" dedicated to?

11 Which Miss Wright did Stevie Wonder marry in 1970?

12 Who sang with Stevie on his first No. 1?

13 To which black leader did he dedicate his Oscar?

14 Who were the other named Friends on Dionne Warwick's "That's What Friends are for"?

15 In which *Key* were the *Songs* on his 1976 album?

16 Who are Aisha Zakia and Kita Swan Di?

17 Who did he sing "Get It" with?

18 What was his first top five hit?

19 In 1984 Stevie was given the keys to which city, where he enjoyed much success?

20 For which song did he win an Oscar in 1985?

21 What is Stevie's real first name?

22 At which Olympics did Wonder play Lennon's "Imagine" to close the Games?

23 In which year did he begin his "A Wonder Summer's Night" Tour?

24 At which US Presidential candidate's acceptance did Wonder perform in 2008?

25 With which Italian classical singer did Wonder perform on the album *Amore*?

26 What "Happy" occasion was Stevie celebrating with this party song in 1981?

27 In 1974, what US boy band did he team-up with for "You Haven't Done Nothin'"?

28 Can you name the famous soul record label Stevie signed with when he was only 12?

29 What instrument was Stevie best known for playing in his early days?

30 Which Stevie Wonder hit from 1970 featured prominently in Barack Obama's presidential campaign?

94
SOLO STARS

1 Did John Lennon have a solo single in his lifetime?

2 Which Cliff Richard hit starts "Imagine a still summer's day"?

3 Colonel Tom Parker launched which star?

4 Which was Madonna's first UK top ten hit?

5 Which singer recorded "Every Picture Tells a Story"?

6 Who had a hit with the original version of "Sealed with a Kiss"?

7 Which former barber charted from 1953 to 1973?

8 Which lady was "Lost in France"?

9 What was a hit for both Frankie Vaughan and Shakin' Stevens?

10 Britney Spears had a hit with "My Prerogative", but who had the original hit?

11 Who had s with both "Dirrty" and "Beautiful"?

12 Which Jason Donovan single is made up of initials?

13 Tom Jones sang for which Bond film?

14 Which solo star had his first in a duo with Marc Almond in 1989?

15 Apart from Michael Jackson, which female singer charted with "Ben"?

16 Who had a in 2003 with "Friday's Child"?

17 Which Rod Stewart hit starts "Wake up, Maggie..."?

18 Can you remember who sang "I Remember You"?

19 What was George Michael's first solo?

20 Whose "Wonderful World" was a bigger hit as a reissue 26 years after the original?

21 Which Roy Orbison hit begins, "A candy-coloured clown they call the sandman"?

22 Mariah Carey was named after which song in "Paint Your Wagon"?

23 Which singer was "Crazy" with his first single success?

24 Which superstar has been chairman of Watford football club?

25 Which female singer recorded "Heaven is a Place on Earth"?

26 Which label did Michael Jackson first record on?

27 According to Tina Turner, what was the speed limit in "Nutbush"?

28 Who was born in the United States of Irish-Italian parents and with the middle names Frederick Joseph?

29 Who sang that she was "born in the wagon of a travelling show"?

30 Which country does Katie Melua come from?

 Answers on page 198

 Answers on page 198

95
KYLIE

1 Which was Kylie's first UK No. 1 of the new millennium?
2 Kylie voiced Florence in which 2006 movie?
3 Which tour was postponed when Kylie was diagnosed with cancer?
4 Which city does Kylie come from?
5 Which word completes her hits, "I Believe In ..." and "Giving ... Up"?
6 In 2001 which release returned her to No. 1 in the album charts?
7 Kylie moved to which UK label that launched The Beatles?
8 What was Kylie's first single to contain the word "Love"?
9 What is Kylie's star sign?
10 Who was the artist behind the original "The Loco-Motion"?
11 Which Abba classic did Kylie cover when closing the Sydney Olympics?
12 Which fungus-linked word names her early Australian recording label?
13 Which Kylie hit has the same title as a 2005 hit by Erasure?
14 Which charted first, "Chocolate" or "In Your Eyes"?
15 Which major British festival did Kylie pull out of in 2005?
16 Which No. 1 was promoted with a video showing Kylie in gold hot pants?
17 She played what colour of fairy in the movie *Moulin Rouge*?
18 What was Kylie's first Top Ten single with a colour in the title?
19 "On a Night Like This" was the first hit single on which she used which billing?
20 Which label handled Kylie's records in the UK for most of the 1990s?
21 What word completes her children's book, *The Showgirl...*?
22 What was Kylie's first million-seller single in the UK?
23 What kind of "Language" featured in the title of Kylie's 2003 hit album?
24 Love Kylie was the name of a range of what?
25 Kylie's first hit duet was with which artist?
26 Both "Chocolate" and "Slow" featured on which album?
27 In which decade of the twentieth century was Kylie born?
28 Kylie started off with how many consecutive Top Ten hits – 3, 9 or 13?
29 In which TV series did she play a cameo as Epponnee Rae?
30 What was the one-word title of Kylie's first album?

96
POP POT LUCK 2

1 Who had a 1989 hit with "Love Changes Everything"?
2 Which Baby girl did Rod Stewart sing about in 1983?
3 In which Park was Donna Summer in 1978?
4 Whose backing group was the Mindbenders?
5 Which musical instrument does Johnny Marr play?
6 Whose first hit was "Denis"?
7 Who has recorded under the name of Eivets Rednow?
8 Who was the female member of Wings?
9 Which Goffin and King song by the Chiffons shares its name with an aria from Puccini's *Madame Butterfly*?
10 Who was Cilla Black's first manager?
11 How did T. Rex's Marc Bolan meet his death?
12 Which duo with combined ages of over 80 topped the charts in September 1985 for four weeks?
13 Who were the first husband-and-wife team to top the charts?
14 Who had a 1990s album called *Waking Up The Neighbours*?
15 In which decade was Karen Carpenter born?
16 In which decade did the Beautiful South have their first hit?
17 Who had a No. 1 with "Caravan of Love"?
18 How is Michael Barratt better known?
19 Which "Summer" song did Lovin' Spoonful sing in 1966?
20 Who had a 1953 hit with "Don't Let the Stars Get in Your Eyes"?
21 Whose first album was "Alright, Still"?
22 Ana Matronic is a member of which glam rock group?
23 In which decade was Dusty Springfield born?
24 Which David released "David Live" in 1974?
25 Which state is "almost heaven" for John Denver?
26 Which group had a hit with "Son of My Father"?
27 Which member of the group Genesis left in 1975?
28 Whose second No. 1 album was *A Day at the Races*?
29 How many "vestal virgins" were leaving in "Whiter Shade of Pale"?
30 Who was "Doin' the Do" in 1990?

 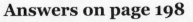 **Answers on page 198**

 Answers on page 198

97
FOLK & COUNTRY

1 Who was known as "Gentleman Jim"?

2 Which country anthem starts "Sometimes it's hard to be a woman"?

3 Which John Denver song did Peter, Paul and Mary take into the charts?

4 Which Dolly Parton song was a chart hit for Whitney Houston?

5 Which country music legend died in 2003 at the age of 71?

6 Which country star had a hit with "Kiss an Angel Good Morning"?

7 Which singer/songwriter penned "The Last Thing on My Mind"?

8 Which country star has had five husbands, including George Jones, and been kidnapped?

9 Which group was fronted by singer/songwriter Dave Cousins?

10 Which folk singer was called "Judas" for going electric?

11 Which city in eastern England has been the venue for a long-standing folk festival?

12 Who wrote "Your Cheatin' Heart"?

13 Which Rochdale Cowboy was a 1970s folk club favourite?

14 Who recorded the album *No Fences*?

15 Who is the long-time lead singer with Steeleye Span?

16 Who declared "Thank God I'm a Country Boy"?

17 In what language was Fairport Convention's only English hit sung?

18 Which guitarist teamed up with Mark Knopfler on "Neck and Neck"?

19 Who wrote US dust-bowl songs and "This Land is Your Land"?

20 How did Patsy Cline die?

21 Who took "There But for Fortune" into the UK single charts?

22 Under what name did Brenda Gail Webb become famous?

23 Who wrote the folk club classic "Streets Of London"?

24 Who wrote "Where Have All the Flowers Gone"?

25 How is Alexandra Denny better known?

26 Who recorded the album *Shotgun Willie*?

27 How are the trio of Yarrow, Stookey and Travers better known?

28 Who was on "Honky Tonk Angels" with Dolly Parton and Tammy Wynette?

29 Which Latin carol gave Steeleye Span a chart hit?

30 Which boy with a girl's name did Johnny Cash sing about?

98
'60S POP 3

1 Which No. 1 hit for the Archies was in the charts for 26 weeks?

2 Which "Park" was a hit for the Small Faces in 1967?

3 Who was singing about "Sheila" in 1962 and "Dizzy" in 1969?

4 Which '60s hit for Kitty Lester was an 80s hit for Alison Moyet?

5 When did the Shirelles want to know "Will You Still Love Me..."?

6 Which crime busting organisation gave the Shadows a 1961 hit?

7 What was Petula Clark's first No. 1 UK hit in 1961?

8 Which three numbers gave Len Barry his No. 3 hit in 1965?

9 Who had consecutive hits with "Daydream" and "Summer in the City"?

10 What was over for the Seekers in their 1965 UK No. 1 hit?

11 Charting again for Elvis in 2005, what was the name of "His Latest Flame"?

12 What were Emile Ford and the Checkmates "Counting" in 1960?

13 What was the Searchers' first No. 1?

14 What was on the other side of Shirley Bassey's "Reach for the Stars"?

15 Whose first Top Ten hit was "5-4-3-2-1" in 1964?

16 Which country was in the title of a '63 hit by Matt Monro?

17 Who recorded the original of the song used in *Four Weddings and a Funeral*?

18 What Girl was Neil Sedaka singing about in 1961?

19 The song "Starry Eyed" was a No. 1 on 1 January 1960 for which Michael?

20 Which words of exclamation were a 1960 No. 4 hit for Peter Sellers?

21 Which *Opportunity Knocks* star had a hit with "Those were the Days"?

22 What did The Move say they could hear grow in a 1967 hit title?

23 Which '60s hit for Kenny Lynch was a No. 1 for Robson and Jerome in 1995?

24 Who were "Glad All Over" in their No. 1 hit from 1963?

25 What was "skipped" in the lyrics of "Whiter Shade of Pale"?

26 What type of "Feelings" did Tom Jones have in his 1967 hit?

27 Which Group had consecutive No. 1s with "Keep On Running" and "Somebody Help Me"?

28 To which religious building were the Dixie Cups going in 1964?

29 Which weather sounding group had hits with "Robot" and "Globetrotter"?

30 Known by another name, Yusuf had his first Top Ten hit with which '60s song?

  Answers on page 198

 Answers on page 198

99
ONE-HIT WONDERS

1 Which school had a with "There's No One Quite Like Grandma"?

2 Which American answer to Band Aid sang "We are the World"?

3 Which musical did Lee Marvin's sole hit, "Wandrin' Star", come from?

4 According to 1950s star Kitty Kalen what do "Little Things Mean"?

5 Which pop duo recorded "In the Year 2525"?

6 Which member of the cast of *Dad's Army* sang "Grandad"?

7 Who recorded "Let It Be" in 1987 for a disaster fund?

8 Where had Charlene never been to in 1982?

9 Who said "Move Closer" in 1985?

10 What is Marie Osmond's only solo hit?

11 Which Beatles song did the Overlanders take to ?

12 With the theme song for which sporting event did Kiri Te Kanawa have her only chart hit in 1991?

13 Which music accompanied Des Lynam's top 50 hit?

14 Who had a hit in 1999 with "Everybody's Free (to Wear Sunscreen)"?

15 What colour were the spots on Mr Blobby?

16 Who were the first two one-hit wonders to reach the top with the same song?

17 Two members of which group sang on both of them?

18 Which Twins sang "When" in 1958?

19 Who did Ricky Valance say that he loved in 1960?

20 Which airways featured on Typically Tropical's only ?

21 What is John Denver's only solo UK single hit?

22 Who joined New Order on England New Order's "World in Motion"?

23 Which travel terminal provided a hit for Cats UK?

24 With which TV theme did Geoffrey Burgon have his only hit in 1981?

25 What was the Johnny Mann Singers' only hit?

26 Who got to No 3 in 1968 with "Judy in Disguise (With Glasses)"?

27 What did the Pipkins say "Gimme" in 1970?

28 Which qualification sang "I won't let you down" in 1982?

29 Which TV character gave Ken Barrie his only chart hit?

30 How many performers made up Las Ketchup who served up "The Ketchup Song"?

100
ALBUMS

1 Who released the biggest-selling album in Britain in the 1970s?

2 What was the final track on *Spice*?

3 Which 1988 album confirmed a comeback by Roy Orbison?

4 Dire Straits first albums came out on which label?

5 Which 6.5-minute hit was the title track of Queen's 7th No. 1 album?

6 Who charted with an album named after an English county?

7 Don McLean's "Vincent" came from which album?

8 Which superstar first charted with *Come Fly with Me*?

9 What was George Harrison's first solo album after the Beatles?

10 What was the first album to make its debut into the UK chart at No. 1?

11 Which album contains the line, "My kingdom for a horse"?

12 Who is not on the front cover of *Urban Hymns*, but features on an inside cover shot?

13 What was Phil Collins' first solo No. 1 album?

14 Who had a No. 1 album in 2005, nearly 30 years after his previous album success?

15 What was the main colour on the cover of Enya's *Shepherd Moons*?

16 Who along with Oasis gets production credits on *Definitely Maybe*?

17 Which group had five consecutive No. 1 albums from 1979 to 1986?

18 The soundtrack to which film was in the charts for a staggering 382 weeks?

19 Which album first featured "Candle in the Wind"?

20 Paul Weller has topped the charts in which three guises?

21 Who was the first artist to enter the Swiss album charts at No. 1?

22 What was the last Fleetwood Mac album released before the world smash "Rumours"?

23 Which double-album film soundtrack was a 30 million seller in 1978?

24 Why weren't the album charts published in 1971 for eight weeks?

25 What was the name of Mary Hopkin's debut album?

26 Which word appeared in the titles of Will Young's first and third albums?

27 Tubular Bells launched the Virgin label, but which label put out Tubular Bells II?

28 Which album originally featured "Perfect Day"?

29 Which Kate Bush album featured a song about Delius?

30 In 2005 which group took over as having most weeks on the UK album charts?

  Answers on page 198   **Answers on page 198**

101
MUSICAL GREATS

1 Which Pete Ham and Tom Evans song has been at No. 1 with two different artists?

2 The Isley Brothers and which other Motown act recorded "Grapevine" before Marvin Gaye?

3 To the nearest year, how long was there between Sinatra's first and second UK No. 1s?

4 Where is the singer's home in the lyrics of "On the Dock of the Bay"?

5 What was the first song to be Christmas No. 1 in two different versions?

6 Which group wrote the song that was Will Young's second No. 1?

7 Which 1970 seven-week No. 1 was best selling UK single of the year?

8 Whom did Billy Joel dedicate his 1983 version of "Uptown Girl" to?

9 What was Elvis Presley's closing number in his Las Vegas stage act?

10 What was Cliff Richard's first self-produced No. 1?

11 What was the chief of the Diddymen's only UK No. 1?

12 Which song has the line, "I see friends shaking hands saying how do you do"?

13 Which Beatles hit stayed in the UK Top 50 for 33 weeks in 1963?

14 Who had their first UK No. 1 with "Unchained Melody"?

15 Which film theme was the biggest-selling single of 1979?

16 Who took Led Zeppelin's "Stairway To Heaven" into the singles charts before Rolf Harris?

17 Who wrote "You'll Never Walk Alone"?

18 Which heavenly body is mentioned in the title of the song that gave George Michael his 4th solo and Elton John his 3rd No. 1?

19 Who played Buddy Holly in the 1978 movie *The Buddy Holly Story*?

20 Who wrote Aretha Franklin's first UK hit "Respect"?

21 What was Yusuf Islam's, once known as Cat Stevens, last Top Ten hit before "Father and Son"?

22 Which 1967 No. 1 recorded the longest-ever stay in the UK Top 50?

23 Which 1960s star, who died in 1988, charted with *Love Songs* album in 2001?

24 How many weeks in total did Whitney Houston top the US and UK charts with "I Will Always Love You"?

25 Which hit was the first No. 1 for writers Gerry Goffin and Carole King?

26 Which song includes the line, "nothing to kill or die for"?

27 What was the colour mentioned in the title of Tom Jones' final No. 1 in the 1960s?

28 What is the biggest international hit from the Eurovision Song Contest?

29 What was Sam Cooke's real name?

30 What was the Beatles' first No. 1 in America?

102
THE BEATLES

1 How many Beatles were still alive when the album *1* first became ?

2 What was John Lennon's middle name?

3 Which original Beatle did Ringo Starr replace?

4 What was on the other side of the single "We Can Work It Out"?

5 Which Beatles song was banned by the BBC because its initials were said to be drug-related?

6 What did Brian Epstein manage before the Beatles?

7 What are John Lennon's two sons called?

8 How was the double album, *The Beatles*, better known?

9 On which show did they make their first national TV appearance?

10 Which group did John Lennon form and name after his school in 1956?

11 Whom did the Beatles support on their first nationwide tour?

12 Which double-sided hit titles were Liverpool placenames?

13 On the *Royal Variety Show* John Lennon invited those in the cheaper seats to clap. What did he tell those in the more expensive seats to do?

14 Which Beatle died in Hamburg in 1962?

15 Which solo instrument did John Lennon play on "Love Me Do"?

16 How many Beatles appeared on *Juke Box Jury* in 1963?

17 What was George Harrison's first solo hit?

18 On which show were the Beatles watched by 73 million in the US?

19 Who made a record called "That's My Life" in 1965?

20 What was the first label the Beatles recorded on with George Martin?

21 Who was the last Beatle to marry twice?

22 In which paper was John Lennon's remark that the Beatles were more popular than Jesus?

23 Which cartoon film did the Beatles make in 1969?

24 What was John Lennon's book published in 1964 called?

25 How many letters were in the title of Cynthia Lennon's biography of her first husband?

26 Where was the last live Beatles' performance?

27 What were the group known as immediately before being known as the Beatles?

28 Which Beatles song is the most recorded song of all time?

29 Who was the first Beatle to have a solo single this century?

30 What were the Beatles awarded by the Queen in 1965?

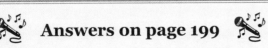

Answers on page 199

Answers on page 199

103
PEACE & LOVE

1 In which year was the so-called Summer of Love?

2 Whose only hit was "Let's Go to San Francisco"?

3 Which song described the history of the Mamas and Papas?

4 Whose melody was "A Whiter Shade of Pale" based on?

5 On which show did the Beatles sing "All You Need is Love" live to five continents?

6 Who did the Mamas and the Papas back on their first recordings?

7 Where did The Beatles plus Mick Jagger and Marianne Faithfull first attend one of the Maharishi's courses?

8 What did Ringo Starr compare to a Butlin's holiday camp in February 1968?

9 What colour jacket is John Lennon wearing on the Sgt Pepper cover?

10 Who recorded "Like an Old-Time Movie" in November 1967?

11 Who was paid the most to play at Woodstock?

12 Who took their name from the punchline to the joke, "What's purple and lives at the bottom of the sea?"?

13 Where in San Francisco was the first "Human Be-In"?

14 Who enjoyed "San Franciscan Nights" in 1967?

15 Who wrote "San Francisco (be Sure to Wear Some Flowers in Your Hair)"?

16 Which band had Grace Slick on lead vocals?

17 How was Ellen Cohen better known?

18 Who wrote "A Whiter Shade of Pale"?

19 What was Scott McKenzie's real name?

20 Which politician sued the Move over a promotional postcard for "Flowers in the Rain" which had a caricature of him in the nude?

21 On what date in 2005 did the ten Live 8 Concerts take place?

22 Who featured Jay-Z with the No. 1 "Umbrella"?

23 Leona Lewis won the 2008 Mobo award for which album?

24 Who, touring in Chicago on his 68th birthday, asked fans to say "Peace & Love"?

25 As advised by Beyonce in "Single Ladies", if you liked it what should you have done?

26 Which Elvis song was No. 1 in the UK charts in 1960 and February 2005?

27 What was in Mack's "Heart" when he reached No. 1 in 2006?

28 Whose first UK No. 1 single was entitled "Sexyback"?

29 What girl were Oasis singing about in their 2005 UK No. 1 hit?

30 Who got their first UK No. 1 with "Welcome to Black Parade"?

104
CLASSIC NO. 1S

1 Who were the first Scottish group to have three No. 1s?

2 Which 1955 American movie had "Unchained Melody" as its theme tune?

3 Which No. 1 was the first solo single by George Harrison?

4 Which Elvis hit made him the first artist with three consecutive British No. 1s?

5 Which Rod Stewart hit was originally the B-side of "Reason to Believe"?

6 Who was on top of the charts the week Everest was first climbed?

7 Who featured on the first No. 1 for Michael Andrews?

8 What was the first No. 1 from the Beatles' second film *Help!*?

9 Who wrote Chicago's No. 1 classic "If You Leave Me Now"?

10 Which lyricist of Aznavour's "She" was a writer on "Les Mis"?

11 What was on the other side of the double A No. 1 "Mull of Kintyre"?

12 Who co-wrote a No. 1 duet song under the pseudonym Ann Orson?

13 What finally knocked "(Everything I Do) I Do It for You" off the No. 1 spot?

14 Which film did Frank Ifield's "I Remember You" originally come from?

15 What was the third UK No. 1 single for the Sugababes?

16 What became the all-time best-UK selling single by a female duo?

17 Which Doris Day Oscar-winning song was from *The Man Who Knew Too Much* in 1956?

18 What was the first Westlife No. 1 single with a one-word title?

19 Which No. 1 hit by the Beatles equalled seven weeks at the top with "From Me to You"?

20 What is the only George Michael song for which Andrew Ridgeley takes equal writing credit?

21 Which album title track gave Simon and Garfunkel their biggest hit?

22 Which 1920s song gave Concetta Franconero a six-week No. 1 hit?

23 Which Commodores classic became Motown's best UK seller?

24 Who is the male half of the duo that have spent most weeks at No. 1?

25 Which single marked Madonna's 20-year span of having UK No. 1s?

26 Apart from "Cathy's Clown", which other No. 1 for the Everly Brothers had a girl's name in the title?

27 In 2000, who became the youngest male to write and perform a UK No. 1 single?

28 Which single was the first by a UK performer to top the US charts in the 1960s?

29 Which 1975 megahit remained at No. 1 for 9 weeks?

30 Which No. 1 hit was Cliff Richard's first million-seller?

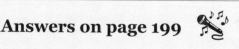 **Answers on page 199**

 Answers on page 199

105
ELVIS PRESLEY

1 What was Elvis Presley's middle name?

2 Which song did he sing to win a talent contest at the age of ten?

3 Which country guitarist produced Elvis's early RCA records?

4 What was his wife Priscilla's maiden name?

5 Which white gospel group provided vocal backings on Elvis's recordings in the 1950s and 1960s?

6 Which label signed Presley before selling his contract to RCA a year later?

7 What were Elvis's parents called?

8 What was Elvis's first film?

9 Where was he posted when he joined the army in 1958?

10 Which was his first ever recording, made at Sam Phillips' studio?

11 What was his first US ?

12 Who were vs Elvis in the 2002 remix that topped the singles charts?

13 Who took charge of Presley's career when he moved to RCA?

14 What was the fourth of four consecutive s between November 1960 and May 1961?

15 What was Elvis Presley's music publishing company called?

16 Which Elvis hit owes a debt to the Italian song "O Sole Mio"?

17 In what year was Elvis's last single of the 20th century?

18 What was his first UK ?

19 Which city was the focus of Presley's work in the 1970s?

20 Which record went to after his death in 1977?

21 Which dancer co-starred with Presley in *GI Blues*?

22 Which is the only part of Britain Presley set foot on?

23 Which Elvis film was a western?

24 Because his movements were so controversial, only which part of Elvis was it suggested should be shown on TV?

25 Which operation did James Peterson carry out on Presley in March 1958?

26 In 2005 which Elvis single replaced an Elvis single as a UK single?

27 What was the name of Elvis's famous mansion and where was it?

28 Which double-sided single was the top seller of the 1950s in the US?

29 Which Elvis hit was a for Dusty Springfield?

30 What was Elvis's last record in the UK in his lifetime?

106
KEYBOARDS

1 Who was the organist on "A Whiter Shade of Pale"?

2 Who left The Strawbs to join Yes?

3 Which band was Gary Brooker in before founding Procul Harum?

4 Who played keyboards with Erasure?

5 How is Rod Argent credited on San Jose's 1978 "Argentine Melody (Cancion de Argentina)"?

6 Which 1978 Elton John hit was an instrumental?

7 Which suitably-titled album did Billy Joel make in the US in 1974 although it was 10 years later that it was a minor UK hit?

8 Which band did Rod Argent found while still at school?

9 Who was keyboards player with the Doors?

10 Which pianist was one of the first Western musicians to visit China in 1991 with his Oriental Melody tour?

11 Who won a piano scholarship to the Juilliard School of Music in 1957?

12 Which jazz pianist had hits with "Take Five" and "Unsquare Dance"?

13 Who was keyboard player with the Moody Blues on "Go Now"?

14 Which Hammond organ specialist became Van Morrison's musical director in the early 1990s?

15 Who was the original keyboard player with Pink Floyd?

16 Whose debut solo album was *Between Today and Yesterday*?

17 How is Silsoe better known?

18 Which theme music did Silsoe record for ITV's coverage of the 1986 World Cup finals?

19 Which 1970s David Bowie album did Rick Wakeman work on as a backing session musician?

20 How is Ferdinand la Menthe Morton better known?

21 Which Chuck was the Rolling Stones' keyboardist on their A Bigger Bang Tour?

22 A Time to Love was the first album for a decade by whom?

23 Who played a 2005 concert in Gdansk in front of 170,000 people?

24 Robert Fripp and which Brian collaborated on "The Equatorial Stars"?

25 Which Rick has become *A Grumpy Old Man*?

26 Name the keyboard player who was with the group Genesis throughout their history.

27 Who in Emerson, Lake and Palmer was the keyboard player?

28 Who appeared alongside his dad in a television advert for R. White Lemonade?

29 Who played keyboards for Squeeze, Mike & the Mechanics and Roxy Music?

30 Which keyboard player was a founder member of both New Order and Joy Division?

 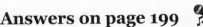
Answers on page 199

Answers on page 199

107
OLDIES & GOODIES

1 What was the first UK No. 1 in which the title posed a question?

2 Which traditional song provided instrumental and vocal versions that charted for 94 weeks?

3 What was Roy Orbison's final chart topper from 1964?

4 Which "Women" was the longest ever at No. 1 for the Rolling Stones?

5 Graham Gouldman and Eric Stewart wrote which 70s classic No. 1?

6 Which 1950s vocalist began singing with the Tony Pastor band?

7 What are the first three words of "San Francisco"?

8 How were the birds singing in the original title of the No. 1 "Why Do Fools Fall in Love"?

9 Which 1986 No. 1 was a cover of a 1970 No. 1?

10 Which artist took over the title of the youngest No. 1 hitmaker in 1972?

11 What is Ray Charles' only UK No. 1?

12 Which Canadian was next to No. 1 after Paul Anka?

13 Which hit gave producer Norrie Paramour his 27th and final No. 1?

14 Emile Ford shared his first week at No. 1 with which artist?

15 Which Chuck Berry hit was No. 1 at the same time in the UK and US?

16 Steve Miller's "The Joker" hit No. 1 in 1990 but when was it recorded?

17 Which hit gave The Searchers their second No. 1?

18 Who had a No. 1 with the original version of "Young Love"?

19 Who wrote and produced Nancy Sinatra's "These Boots are Made for Walking"?

20 Which John Leyton hit was covered in 1985 by Bronski Beat and Marc Almond?

21 Whose only UK hit was "Here Comes Summer"?

22 Who wrote "See My Baby Jive"?

23 What film theme gave Danny Williams his only No. 1 in 1961?

24 What was the first instrumental No. 1 after the Shadows' "Foot Tapper"?

25 What was the Kinks' third and final No. 1 hit in the summer of 1966?

26 What was the only Cliff Richard & the Shadows No. 1 double-A-side?

27 Which 1968 No. 1 was revived in the film *Good Morning Vietnam*?

28 What was "Wonderful" in the Shadows hit which stayed longest at No. 1?

29 Which act was the first beginning with a letter Z to have a No. 1 single?

30 What was Cilla Black's only US Top 40 hit?

Answers on page 199

108
MOR POP

1 Who wrote Katie Melua's hit "The Closest Thing to Crazy"?

2 Which partnership wrote "Walk On By" for Dionne Warwick?

3 Who has recorded with Neil Diamond, Barry Gibb and Don Johnson?

4 How many singles has Neil Diamond had?

5 Who recorded film themes "Moon River" and "Love Story"?

6 Who was the first artist to score three posthumous albums in the UK?

7 Who had a Top Twenty hit in 1969 with "Dick-A-Dum-Dum"?

8 Which Carpenters hit was the name of a food dish?

9 Whose hits mention Durham, Skye and the New World?

10 Which trumpeter was a co-founder of A & M Records?

11 Who in 1993 became second only to Elvis Presley with his number of album chart entries?

12 Which hugely successful orchestra leader was born Annunzio Paolo?

13 Who has recorded with northern brass bands and sung the songs of Fred Astaire and Hoagy Carmichael?

14 Who won *Opportunity Knocks* and was signed by the Apple label?

15 Which MOR singer's father was famous for his "Donkey Serenade"?

16 Which French singer's autobiography was called *Yesterday When I was Young*?

17 What was Perry Como's job before becoming a singer?

18 Who enquired about the whereabouts of Amarillo again in 2005?

19 Who has recorded with Deniece Williams and Gladys Knight?

20 Who was known as "The Tigress of Tiger Bay"?

21 Who had a transatlantic hit with "When I Need Love"?

22 Which German bandleader was the first to record the Beatles?

23 Who wrote the film themes "Days of Wine and Roses" and the "Pink Panther"?

24 Which British orchestra emulated the sound of Glenn Miller?

25 What was Tony Bennett's first chart entry and only UK No. 1?

26 Who was chosen for the role of Johnny Fontane (reputedly based on Frank Sinatra) in *The Godfather*?

27 Whose many hits included "When I Fall in Love" and "Too Young"?

28 Whose first US was the self-penned "I am a Woman"?

29 Who topped the bill in the first *Royal Variety Show* to be held in Wales?

30 Who was Carole King's songwriting partner in the 1960s?

Answers on page 199

109
POP DJS

1 Who was sacked from Radio 1 because he said the Transport Minister's wife had probably passed her driving test by slipping the examiner a fiver?

2 Which Belgian station did Steve Wright work for?

3 What was Chris Evans's 1992 Sunday show on Radio 1 called?

4 Who had a wife Sheila, four children and lived near Stowmarket?

5 Who was the first Radio 1 DJ to be knighted in 1990?

6 Which '60s singer presents a radio R&B show?

7 Which Radio DJ presented Confessions on TV?

8 Who presented the UK top 40 show on Radio 1 at the start of 1997?

9 Who is the only BBC national daily radio DJ to have had a No. 1 hit?

10 Who sang with Liz Kershaw and Bruno Brookes on "It Takes Two Baby"?

11 Who sang with Bruno and Liz on "Let's Dance"?

12 How was the former DJ J. P. Richardson better known?

13 What was John Peel's real surname?

14 Who presented the Radio 1 *Breakfast Show* between 1973 and 1978?

15 Who has been called the instigator of so called "zoo-radio"?

16 Who introduced Radio Luxembourg's "Under the Bedclothes Club"?

17 Whose catchphrase was "Your royal ruler, I wouldn't fool ya"?

18 Who was born on April Fool's Day in Oldham and has been a Capital Radio and Radio 1 DJ?

19 How was Michael Pasternak better known?

20 Whose autobiography was called *The Custard Stops at Hatfield*?

21 How old was Sir Jimmy Savile when he co-hosted the final *Top of the Pops*?

22 In which year did Chris Moyles take over BBC Radio's breakfast-time show?

23 Who became Radio 1's longest-serving DJ following the death of John Peel?

24 Who did Lisa Snowdon replace as Johnny Vaughan's co-presenter at Capital 95.8?

25 Which Jo hosted *Top of the Pops* 1995–98 and was a Radio 1 regular from 1993?

26 Which 2008 BBC Radio 2 DJ is the sister of the TV personality Keith Chegwin?

27 Which Radio 1 DJ was sacked in 2003 and joined Virgin Radio in January 2004?

28 Who began his career on BBC GLR in 1989 before joining Radio 1 in 1993?

29 Whose 1980s *Barbed Wireless* programme for local BBC won two Sony Awards?

30 Name the female Radio 1 DJ from 1995–99 who started out at Kiss FM in 1985.

110
ROCKERS

1 What was Eddie Cochrane's next UK single after "Three Steps to Heaven"?

2 Who played Jerry Lee Lewis in the 1989 biopic of his life?

3 How does Roger Peterson figure in rock history?

4 What was Billy Fury's first UK Top Ten hit from 1960?

5 In which city were R.E.M. formed?

6 As a teenager Morrissey ran a fan club for which group?

7 Who wrote the Buddy Holly classic "It Doesn't Matter Anymore"?

8 Which Elvis No. 1 is the only one written solely by Leiber and Stoller?

9 Which hard-rock band did the Scottish Young brothers form in Australia?

10 "Rock Around the Clock" came out on which label?

11 Who did Keith Richard work for before coming a full-time Stone?

12 Which Slade hit was No. 1 when US soldiers left Vietnam in 1973?

13 What did Rick Allen of Def Leppard lose in 1984?

14 What did an electrician fitting a burglar alarm find in Seattle in 1984?

15 Who first charted with "Rip It Up"?

16 James Jewel Osterberg took the stage under which name?

17 At which studio did the "Million Dollar Quartet" get together in the '50s?

18 In which month did Jim Morrison die in 1971?

19 Where in London was the Sex Pistols' first concert?

20 Which Dickie Valentine hit replaced "Rock Around the Clock" at No. 1?

21 Which place used to form part of The Stranglers name?

22 Who was Francis Rossi's school mate and long-time bass player in Status Quo?

23 How were the Rolling Stones billed for their first live concert?

24 Which Jerry Lee Lewis hit is the only version of the Ray Charles classic to reach the British charts?

25 Who ran the Clovis, New Mexico studio where Buddy Holly recorded?

26 Who was Phil Lynott's father-in-law?

27 Who recorded the album *Ma Kelly's Greasy Spoon*?

28 Which Led Zeppelin drummer died in 1980?

29 Who ran the Chelsea clothes shop called Let It Rock?

30 Which 1955 Glenn Ford movie featured "Rock Around the Clock"?

 Answers on page 199

 Answers on page 199

111
NOVELTY POP SONGS

1 What did Dora Bryan want for Christmas in 1963?

2 Who took his "Ding-a-ling" to ?

3 Which two versions of "Itsy Bitsy Teeny Weeny Yellow Polka Dot Bikini" have hit the charts 30 years apart?

4 On which of Rolf Harris's chart hits did we first hear a didgeridoo?

5 Which vocalist called himself the Joan Collins Fan Club?

6 Which TV series did the vocalists on "Whispering Grass" come from?

7 Which DJs were Laurie Lingo and the Dipsticks?

8 Which *EastEnders* star had a hit with "The Ugly Duckling"?

9 Who sang "Red Machine in Full Effect"?

10 Who was Mr Bean's backing group?

11 What are the only words on Lieutenant Pigeon's first ?

12 Who sang "They're Coming to Take Me Away Ha-Haaa" in 1966?

13 How was the Belgian Soeur Sourire known in Britain?

14 Which Jasper Carrott single was once banned by the BBC?

15 What was the title of Paul Gascoigne's Gazza rap?

16 Who was "Walking Backwards for Christmas" in the 1950s?

17 Who got to in 1958 with "Hoots Mon"?

18 Who argued about "Bangers and Mash" in 1961?

19 What was the first thing Scaffold said "Thank U Very Much" for?

20 Who recorded with the Red Nosed Burglars and the D Cups?

21 Which Superstar recorded "Love Me Tender" nearly 30 years after Elvis Presley?

22 How long did it take Mr Blobby to reach in December 1993?

23 Who helped the Stonkers get a hit with "The Stonk"?

24 Which duo had a minor hit with "Reet Petite" in 1993?

25 What was the full title of Harry Enfield's 1988 hit?

26 "Two Pints of Lager and a Packet of Crisps Please" was a hit for which band?

27 Which *Dad's Army* character had a hit?

28 Who accompanied Chas and Dave on "Snooker Loopy"?

29 What was on the other side of *Spitting Image*'s "Santa Claus is on the Dole"?

30 Which song did the Wurzels base their "Combine Harvester" on?

112
SOUL

1 What did "Three Times A Lady" replace as Motown's UK bestseller?

2 Which instrument did Lionel Richie play with the Commodores?

3 Who was Linda Womack's father?

4 Which group was Ronnie White in?

5 Who appeared in the films *Muscle Beach Party* and *Bikini Beach*?

6 Who was the eldest Jackson brother?

7 Who did Berry Gordy sell Motown to in 1988?

8 Where was Gamble and Huff's record label based in the '70s?

9 Which record label did Lionel Richie go to after leaving Motown?

10 Which Jackson's real name was Toriano Adaryll?

11 Who was the first major star to leave Motown in 1964?

12 Which song did Lou Rawls make after the Budweiser beer he advertised?

13 Who left Motown in 1967 to set up their own labels?

14 Where in the US were Gladys Knight and the Pips all from?

15 Who made an album called *The Wildest Organ in Town*?

16 Where did Motown relocate to in 1971?

17 Who did Randy Taraborelli write a biography of in 1991?

18 Who wrote "Reet Petite" with Jackie Wilson's cousin?

19 Who was Miss Wright – and Miss Right – for Stevie Wonder in 1970?

20 Which song did Lionel Richie write for Kenny Rogers?

21 Whose debut album was called *Rockferry*?

22 What genre of soul music does R. Kelly perform?

23 Which US gospel singer is featured with Eternal on "I Wanna be the One"?

24 *A Soulful Tale of Two Cities* was an album by stars from Philadelphia and where?

25 In which year was Isaac Hayes inducted into the Rock and Roll Hall of Fame?

26 With which Californian-based NBA team was Paula Abdul a cheerleader?

27 Whose 2008 album was entitled *Lay It Down*?

28 Who has many nicknames including "Mr Please Please Please Her"?

29 Which member of the Jackson family released the 1991 album "No Relations"?

30 Which soul sisters had hits with "Dancing in the Street" and "Jimmy Mack"?

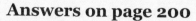Answers on page 200

Answers on page 200

113
MUSIC SUPERSTARS 2

1 Which veteran singer's first No. 1 album was *Foreign Affair*?

2 Who included Bono, Paul McCartney and Sting on his 2006 album *Duets*?

3 Who wrote "I'm a Believer" for The Monkees?

4 From which film was Elvis Presley's 2005 hit "Return to Sender"?

5 What was Elton John's first solo hit on his own Rocket label?

6 Which Leo Sayer hit gave the Chrysalis label their first No. 1?

7 In which decade did Barbra Streisand first make the UK charts?

8 Which hit was the first to be No. 1 over two separate Christmases?

9 Which singer/songwriter penned the lines, "The carpet, too, is moving under you"?

10 How many consecutive UK No. 1 hits did the Beatles have?

11 Who duetted with Peter Gabriel on "Games without Frontiers"?

12 What was Abba's only No. 1 in the USA?

13 Which opera does Pavarotti's anthem "Nessun Dorma" come from?

14 Which of the Gibb brothers wrote their first UK No. 1 "Massachusetts"?

15 Which David Bowie hit was his fourth UK and second US No. 1 in 1983?

16 Who replaced Diana Ross when she left The Supremes?

17 Who was the first person to duet on a single with Shania Twain?

18 Stephen Bray and Patrick Leonard have both co-written No. 1s with which singer?

19 Michael Jackson's "Thriller" and "Bad" came out on which label?

20 When did Tony Bennett first record "I Left My Heart in San Francisco"?

21 Which group singer put out a solo album called *Primitive Cool*?

22 A John Lennon song gave which group their only UK No. 1?

23 Which singing superstar once had a trial for Brentford FC?

24 Pete Townshend's first No. 1 as a producer was for which group?

25 Who sang the theme song to the film *Beauty and the Beast*?

26 What was the final No. 1 by any of the Osmond family?

27 Who conducted the Three Tenors for their Italia 90 concert?

28 Who is the only group to appear in the charts in every year of the 1970s?

29 Which Springsteen song was a hit for Manfred Mann's Earth Band?

30 Which David Essex hit was the soundtrack for "That'll be the Day"?

114
FOLK & BLUES

1 Who was the original female vocalist in Fairport Convention?

2 Who wrote "There but for Fortune"?

3 In which city was Alexis Korner born?

4 What was Bob Dylan's 1976 tour called?

5 Which cover version sneaked in the charts for Ian Campbell in 1965?

6 Whom did Ralph May take his stage name from?

7 What name did Billy Connolly and Gerry Rafferty sing under?

8 What was the name of Eric Clapton's son whose death inspired "Tears in Heaven"?

9 Who made up the trio with Yarrow and Stookey?

10 In the 1920s, who recorded "Match Box Blues" and "That Black Snake Moan"?

11 What was John Denver's first album called?

12 What is B. B. King's actual first name?

13 What was the name of London's leading folk club in the '60s?

14 Tom Paxton's *Ramblin' Boy* album came out on which label?

15 Simon and Garfunkel took the song "Scarborough Fair" from who?

16 Who used the pseudonyms Birmingham Sam and Delta John?

17 Who wrote "Who Knows Where the Time Goes"?

18 Which blues man had a speaking part on Hot Chocolate's hit "Brother Louis"?

19 Who recorded the album "Bedsitter Images"?

20 Pentangle's "Night Flight" came from which album?

21 What was Woody Guthrie's middle name?

22 Smitty's Corner and Pepper's Lounge were blues clubs in which city?

23 Who published in 1907 "English Folk Songs: Some Conclusions"?

24 John Mayall comes from which untraditional birthplace of bluesmen?

25 Who played organ on Dylan's "Like a Rolling Stone"?

26 Who made the album *Stormy Monday Blues*?

27 According to John Denver which state is "almost heaven"?

28 How did Sandy Denny die?

29 Which folk hero played piano in Bobby Vee's band the Shadows?

30 What was Lightnin' Hopkins's real name?

  Answers on page 200

 Answers on page 200

115
WHOSE MUSIC?

1 Who was knocked off No. 1 position by "Wannabe"?

2 Whose record has the longest playing time of any to make No. 1?

3 Howie Dorough was in which best-selling boy band?

4 Whose one-hit wonder replaced "Honky Tonk Women" at No. 1 in US and Britain?

5 Which singer left school in 1961 to appear in the film *It's Trad, Dad*?

6 Which No. 1 singer was born Arnold George Dorsey in Madras?

7 Which top musician produced Shakin' Stevens' "Merry Christmas Everyone"?

8 Who sang lead vocal on the chart topper "Babe"?

9 Who wrote the lines, "All alone, without a telephone"?

10 Who has recorded singles with Paul McCartney, Julio Iglesias and Diana Ross?

11 Who was the first drummer with The Stone Roses?

12 Joyce Vincent and Thelma Hopkins were the girls in which 1970s group?

13 Who joined Wendy Richard in the No. 1 from 1962 "Come Outside"?

14 Craig David's "Woman Trouble" featured Robbie Craig and who else?

15 Which chart topper started life in Leigh, Lancashire, as Clive Powell?

16 Who set up the DEP record label?

17 Which '60s artist was the first British-born artist with three No. 1 hits?

18 To two years, when did Tony Christie's "Amarillo" first hit the charts?

19 Who wrote "Chain Reaction" for Diana Ross?

20 Who joined the Beatles on their first hit to enter the charts at No. 1?

21 Who recorded the 1993 No. 1 written and produced by Shaw and Rogers?

22 Which actor was talking to the trees on the B side of "Wand'rin' Star"?

23 Who was No. 1 in the UK and US singles and album charts at the same time in 1971?

24 How many versions of "Spirit in the Sky" had made No. 1 before Gareth Gates did?

25 Which Creation Records boss signed Oasis?

26 Which duo made up the Righteous Brothers?

27 Who joined the Beautiful South after being roadie for The Housemartins?

28 Whose death moved Don McLean to write "American Pie"?

29 The Beatles apart, who first took a Lennon & McCartney song to No. 1, with the Dakotas?

30 In the 1950s who was the first instrumentalist to achieve two No. 1s?

116
THE ROLLING STONES

1 What was the name of the 2003 world tour?

2 Who wrote their first Top Twenty hit?

3 Which was their first to be written by Jagger and Richard?

4 In which blues band did both Mick Jagger and Charlie Watts perform?

5 From which album was the US chart entry "Mother's Little Helper"?

6 Which instrument did Brian Jones play, other than guitar, on "Their Satanic Majesties Request"?

7 How did Brian Jones die?

8 Which French director made The Stones film *One Plus One*?

9 Which Australian outlaw did Mick Jagger play on film?

10 What is the name of Mick Jagger's daughter by his first wife, Bianca?

11 Who designed the sleeve and logo on "Sticky Fingers"?

12 Where did they record the album *Goat's Head Soup*?

13 Which 1983 video for the title track was banned?

14 Which record was a hit for Bill Wyman in 1983?

15 Whom did Mick Jagger sing "Dancing in the Street" with at Live Aid?

16 What was the name of Bill Wyman's group that performed charity gigs?

17 In which sci-fi thriller did Mick Jagger appear in 1992?

18 Who was the subject of the film *Hail Hail Rock 'n' Roll*, for which Keith Richards directed the music?

19 Who were Keith Richards' band on "At the Hollywood Palladium"?

20 For which record label did the Stones sign a deal in 1991?

21 Who was dropped from the group in its early days because "he looked too normal"?

22 Whose song were the Rolling Stones named after?

23 Which Stone described his career as "five years of playing and 20 of hanging about"?

24 Which Jagger-Richard song was Marianne Faithfull's first hit?

25 Which famous guitarist played on Jagger's album *She's the Boss*?

26 Which 1960s Stones' hit had the longest title?

27 What was on the other side of "Ruby Tuesday"?

28 What was their first hit on their own Rolling Stones record label?

29 What was the Rolling Stones' second album called?

30 To a year either way, when did Mick Jagger become Sir Mick?

 Answers on page 200

 Answers on page 200

117
'40S & '50S FILMS

1 Which Disney film released in 1942 was about a little fawn?

2 How many days did it take David Niven to go *Around the World*?

3 In the 1957 film about Japanese prisoners of war, where was the bridge?

4 Which yuletide classic was first sung by Bing Crosby in "Holiday Inn"?

5 If Lady is a pedigree spaniel what is the name of the mongrel?

6 Which Ben won 11 Oscars in 1959?

7 In which 1940 film did Mickey Mouse conduct the orchestra?

8 In which film did Vivien Leigh play Scarlett O'Hara?

9 Who starred in the Road films with Dorothy Lamour and Bing Crosby?

10 Which film set in Rick's Café starred Humphrey Bogart and Ingrid Bergman?

11 Which distinguished actor, later a Lord, played the lead in *Henry V*?

12 Which film starred Celia Johnson, Trevor Howard and a train station?

13 Which Alfred directed the thrillers *Rebecca* and *Notorious*?

14 Which actor Orson starred in *Citizen Kane* and *The Third Man*?

15 Who played eight different characters in *Kind Hearts and Coronets*?

16 What was the series of comedies made in West London studios called?

17 Where was Gene Kelly "Singin'" in 1952?

18 How did *Some Like It* in the film with Jack Lemmon, Tony Curtis and Marilyn Monroe?

19 What was the name of the car that involved Kenneth More and Dinah Sheridan in the London to Brighton road run?

20 Which young star of *East of Eden* died in a car crash aged 24?

21 Which actress married Prince Rainier of Monaco?

22 Which French "sex kitten" starred with Dirk Bogarde in *Doctor at Sea*?

23 In the Charlton Heston film how many commandments were there?

24 Where was there *Room* in the film starring Laurence Harvey?

25 Who was the young star of *National Velvet* in 1945?

26 Which dancer/actress Ginger won an Oscar in 1940?

27 Which actor Marlon starred in *On the Waterfront*?

28 What goes with *Old Lace* in the title of the Cary Grant film?

29 What is *A Many Splendored Thing* in the film about the Korean War?

30 From *Here to* where is the Oscar-winning movie with Deborah Kerr, Burt Lancaster and Frank Sinatra?

118
BLOCKBUSTERS

1 Which early Spielberg blockbuster was about a shark?

2 What was Daniel Craig's first movie as James Bond?

3 In which 1990s musical film did Madonna change costume 85 times?

4 What was the name of the movie based on TV's *The X Files*?

5 Which Julianne played opposite Anthony Hopkins in *Hannibal*?

6 Martin Scorsese made a film about the *Gangs Of* which city?

7 *The Fellowship of the Ring* was based on which book?

8 Which creatures dominated "Jurassic Park"?

9 What was "Crocodile Dundee's" homeland?

10 "Hook" was based on which children's book?

11 Which lizard-like monster's name is a mix of the Japanese words for gorilla and whale?

12 Who left Kramer in the 1970s movie with Hoffman and Streep?

13 *From Here to Eternity* is set before the Japanese attack on where?

14 *Raging Bull* was about which sport?

15 Which film was an abbreviation of Extra Terrestrial?

16 *The Empire Strikes Back* was a sequel to what?

17 *Raiders of the Lost Ark* was about which Mr Jones?

18 Robin Hood was *Prince of* what in the 1991 blockbuster?

19 Was *Snow White and the Seven Dwarfs* released before or after World War II?

20 Where was Gary Oldman Lost in the 1998 hit movie?

21 Which Caped Crusader was the subject of one of the top 1980s films?

22 Which watery film succeeded *Waterworld* as the most costly to make?

23 Gene Kelly was An American ... where in the Vincente Minnelli movie?

24 Which star of *Grease* and *Saturday Night Fever* is a qualified pilot?

25 Was *The Sting* a hit in the 1950s, '70s or '90s?

26 Which Disney animal movie was a 1994 blockbuster set in Africa?

27 *Amadeus* told the story of which composer?

28 *Home Alone* shot which child star to fame?

29 Was *Schindler's List* in colour or black and white?

30 Which Kevin played Mariner in *Waterworld*?

  Answers on page 200

 Answers on page 200

119
'30S FILMS

1 *Anna Christie* was the first talkie for which Swedish star?

2 *The Blue Angel* with Marlene Dietrich was shot in English and which other language?

3 Which "modern" film was Chaplin's last silent movie?

4 In *Stagecoach* which actor John played the Ringo Kid?

5 Which 1939 movie featured a Yellow Brick Road?

6 Which dancers appeared in *The Story of Vernon* and *Irene Castle*?

7 *Mr Smith Goes* to where in the title of the 1939 movie?

8 Which Laurence played Heathcliff to Merle Oberon's Cathy in *Wuthering Heights*?

9 What were Katharine Hepburn and Cary Grant *Bringing Up* in the 1938 comedy?

10 Which King was a successful ape?

11 Which Clark Gable film, the name of a city, was about a Californian earthquake at the beginning of the 20th century?

12 The Adventures of which English hero was the title of a 1938 movie with Errol Flynn?

13 What type of character did James Cagney play in Angels with Dirty Faces?

14 *Thoroughbreds Don't Cry* teamed Judy Garland with which Mickey?

15 Which Busby did the choreography for *Footlight Parade*?

16 Which *Hotel* was the title of a Garbo movie?

17 Which zany brothers made *Animal Crackers* in 1930?

18 In which city is *The Hunchback of Notre Dame* set?

19 Bela Lugosi starred as the first sound version of which character?

20 Where was it *All Quiet* in the movies in 1930?

21 The movie *Scarface* was based on the life of which gangster?

22 Which 1939 movie was about a schoolmaster called Mr Chipperfield?

23 What was the heroine of *Gone with the Wind* called?

24 Boris Karloff starred in one of the first horror movies about which Mary Shelley character?

25 What completes the title of the Mae West movie, *She Done Him...*?

26 Who released *Snow White and the Seven Dwarfs* in 1938?

27 Which future US President began his acting career in the 1930s?

28 The soldiers of which country's army are depicted in *All Quiet on the Western Front*?

29 In which film is Rufus T. Firefly the lead character?

30 Who hoofs it with Fred Astaire in *Follow the Fleet*?

120
'60S FILMS

1 On which Side of New York was the musical *Story* about rival gangs?

2 Who starred as Cleopatra and married co-star Richard Burton?

3 With which country is Lawrence associated in the film with Peter O'Toole?

4 Which role did Warren Beatty play to Faye Dunaway's Bonnie?

5 What type of *Cowboy* was Jon Voight in the 1969 film?

6 Who was *The Graduate* in the film of the same name?

7 Who won an Oscar as Professor Higgins in *My Fair Lady*?

8 Which musical by Lionel Bart was based on a Dickens novel?

9 Which western actor won his only Oscar for *True Grit*?

10 Which actress Mia starred in the controversial *Rosemary's Baby*?

11 What were the hills alive with in the musical set in Austria?

12 What was the nationality of Zorba in the film with Anthony Quinn?

13 *Guess Who's Coming to* which meal in the Katharine Hepburn film?

14 Which nanny did Julie Andrews win an Oscar for playing?

15 Who played Alfie?

16 Which blonde Julie was a *Darling*?

17 Who played Fanny Brice in *Funny Girl*?

18 Which *Doctor* did Omar Sharif play in the film set in the USSR?

19 Which Gregory won an Oscar for *To Kill a Mockingbird*?

20 Which Miss was Maggie Smith whose Prime won an Oscar in '69?

21 Which actor Paul played Thomas More in *A Man for All Seasons*?

22 How many dalmatians starred in the 1961 Disney film?

23 Who was Butch Cassidy's partner?

24 In the 1968 film when was *The Space Odyssey*?

25 Which 1960 Hitchcock film has the most famous shower scene ever?

26 Which meal was taken at Tiffany's in the film with Audrey Hepburn?

27 Who played James Bond in *Dr No*?

28 What accompanied *the Bad and the Ugly* in the Clint Eastwood film?

29 Which *Sweet* girl was played by Shirley Maclaine in the 1968 musical?

30 Which film with Vanessa Redgrave was about King Arthur's court?

  **Answers on page 200**

 Answers on page 200

121
COMEDIES

1 Which Mr Atkinson created the spoof spy character Johnny English?

2 Sarah Michelle Gellar starred in the movie about which ghost-hunting dog?

3 What was the name of Sacha Baron Cohen's Kazakhstan character?

4 *Addams Family Values* was the follow-up to what?

5 Which west London borough is associated with classic comedies?

6 What age group are the performers in the gangster film *Bugsy Malone*?

7 Which cartoon set in Bedrock starred John Goodman in the human version?

8 What type of adventure did Bill and Ted have?

9 What sort of farm animal was Babe?

10 Which Tom starred in *Jerry Maguire*?

11 Which Hill in London was the location for a Hugh Grant / Julia Roberts movie?

12 Whose *World* did Mike Myers and Dana Garvey live in?

13 *A Fish Called...* what was a John Cleese & Jamie Lee Curtis classic?

14 What was Whoopi Goldberg disguised as in *Sister Act*?

15 Which group sang the theme song for *Four Weddings and a Funeral*?

16 Which Jim was the shy bank clerk in *The Mask*?

17 Forrest Gump said life was like a box of what?

18 Which Julia was the *Pretty Woman* in the film's title?

19 Which British comedy duo were the stars of *The Magnificent Two*?

20 What did Robin Williams in *Mrs Doubtfire* and Dustin Hoffman in *Tootsie* have in common?

21 What unusual handicap did Bernie have as a host in *A Weekend at Bernie's*?

22 Which film of a book featured "The Bare Necessities"?

23 Which Sid's first *Carry On* was *Carry On Constable*?

24 To whom did someone say *I Shrunk the Kids* in the film title?

25 Which spinach-loving cartoon character was played by Robin Williams?

26 Which Colin played Mark Darcy in the movie about Bridget Jones?

27 Was Patrick Swayze or Demi Moore the *Ghost* in the 1990 film?

28 *Look Who's Talking Too* was the sequel to what?

29 Who was the Queen of the Desert in the transvestite comedy?

30 Which inspector played by Peter Sellers was in *The Pink Panther*?

122
ANIMATION

1 Which Mel was the voice of Captain Smith in Pocahontas?

2 Who did Nick Park create as Wallace's faithful hound?

3 Who worked with Pixar to make *Toy Story*?

4 Which movie has the cub Simba and his evil uncle Scar?

5 Which Robin was the voice of the genie in *Aladdin*?

6 Who appeared with Beauty in the 1991 Disney movie?

7 Which alter ego of Mr Bean was the voice of Zazu in *The Lion King*?

8 Which Tarzan mate did Minnie Driver provide the voice for in Tarzan?

9 Who featured in *Knighty Knight Bugs* in 1958?

10 In which decade was *Fantasia* released?

11 Who provided the music for the Disney *Tarzan* film?

12 Pongo and Perdita were which types of black-and-white dog in the 1961 Disney movie?

13 The film of which book featured a jazz-loving bear, Baloo?

14 In which decade was *Jungle Book* released?

15 What type of creature was Felix, an early animation character?

16 Anne Bancroft provided a voice in which 1998 movie about insects?

17 Which felines were the stars of a 1970 Disney classic?

18 In which canine caper was there a "Twilight Bark"?

19 Which cartoon duck was usually dressed in blue and white?

20 In which decade was *Snow White and the Seven Dwarfs* released?

21 Which Bunny did Mel Blanc provide the voice for?

22 In which decade was *The Lion King* released?

23 Which film featured the song "The Bare Necessities"?

24 Which English actor Jeremy was the voice of Scar in *The Lion King*?

25 Which movie featured Buzz Lightyear and Mr Potato Head?

26 Which cartoon movie series has Mike Myers and Eddie Murphy as lead voices?

27 Which rare Chinese mammal is a kung fu expert in the 2008 movie?

28 Who wrote the music for the 1994 version of *Thumbelina*?

29 Who voices the part of Barry in *Bee Movie*?

30 Which 2007 animated film had a French culinary term as its title?

  Answers on page 201

 Answers on page 201

123
HOLLYWOOD

1 Which tough guy star of *Casablanca* married Lauren Bacall?

2 Who co-starred with Bob Hope in the *Road* films and died playing golf?

3 Which actress was shunned by Hollywood when she left her husband and children for director Roberto Rossellini?

4 What is the first name of actor Curtis, father of Jamie Lee?

5 Which *Officer and a Gentleman* married supermodel Cindy Crawford?

6 How was Ruth Elizabeth Davis better known?

7 Which director Cecil B. was famous for epic movies?

8 Which Kops were the creation of director Mack Sennett?

9 Which daughter of Judy Garland won an Oscar for *Cabaret*?

10 Who is Kirk Douglas's famous son?

11 Which actress Ava was Frank Sinatra's second wife?

12 What relation is Shirley Maclaine to fellow star Warren Beatty?

13 Which Katharine had a long relationship with Spencer Tracy?

14 Which actress Grace became Princess of Monaco?

15 Which British suspense film director worked in Hollywood from 1939?

16 Which actress daughter of Henry was known as Hanoi Jane because of her anti-Vietnam War activities in the 1970s?

17 Who co-starred with Vivien Leigh in *Gone with the Wind*?

18 How is Jack Lemmon's co-star in *The Odd Couple*, Walter Matasschanskavasky better known?

19 Who was Fred Astaire's most frequent dancing partner?

20 Which child star Shirley went on to be a US Ambassador?

21 Which silent movie star Rudolph died at an early age?

22 Hollywood legends Lionel, Ethel and John share what surname?

23 Which actor Paul is the husband of actress Joanne Woodward?

24 Who was married to Sean Penn and was chosen for the role of Evita?

25 Who was born Doris Kappelhoff and co-starred with Rock Hudson?

26 Which star of *Top Gun* married Nicole Kidman?

27 Which actor James, famous for gangster roles, is credited with the catchphrase "You dirty rat!"?

28 Why was Jimmy Durante nicknamed Schnozzle?

29 Who married Richard Burton twice?

30 Which actress Demi married Bruce Willis?

124
WHO'S WHO?

1 Which ex-James Bond has "Scotland Forever" tattooed on his arm?

2 Which Jools starred in *Spiceworld: The Movie*?

3 Which Irish-born 007 starred in *Tomorrow Never Dies*?

4 Which *Grease* actor danced with Princess Diana at the White House?

5 Which sleuth did Albert Finney play in Agatha Christie's *Murder on the Orient Express*?

6 Which top-selling rapper made his movie debut in *8 Mile*?

7 Who was the star of *Moonwalker* after being in The Jackson Five?

8 Which bespectacled US actor/director directed the musical *Everyone Says I Love You*?

9 What type of hat was Charlie Chaplin most famous for?

10 Who is Emma Forbes' actor/director dad?

11 Who was named after her home town of Winona?

12 Which knighted pop singer wrote the music for *The Lion King*?

13 Hayley Mills is the daughter of which knighted actor?

14 Who separated from husband Bruce Willis in 1998?

15 Which newspaper magnate bought 20th Century-Fox in 1985?

16 Who was Sid played by Gary Oldman in *Sid and Nancy*?

17 What name usually associated with a schoolbag did Woody Allen give his son?

18 Which Welsh actor Sir Anthony bought part of Mount Snowdon in 1998?

19 Which pop star Tina starred in *Mad Max Beyond the Thunderdome*?

20 Which Ms Foster swapped her real first name from Alicia?

21 In rhyming slang what financial term is Gregory Peck?

22 Which child star was Shirley MacLaine named after?

23 Who appeared first at Madame Tussaud's, Harrison Ford or Hugh Grant?

24 Who starred as Steed in the film version of *The Avengers*?

25 Which boxer played himself in *The Greatest*?

26 Film buff Barry Norman is a member of which club with the same name as a Marx brother?

27 Who sang "It's Not Unusual" *in Mars Attacks!*?

28 Which actress appeared on the cover of *The Sound of Music* movie DVD?

29 Judi Dench played which character known by a letter in the Bond movies?

30 *There's Something About Mary* and *Gangs of New York* starred which actress?

  Answers on page 201

 Answers on page 201

125
ARNOLD SCHWARZENEGGER

1 In which European country was he born?

2 What was he *Pumping* in the 1977 documentary film about himself?

3 What was the name of "the Barbarian" he played in 1982?

4 Which smash hit movie gave him the line "I'll be back"?

5 What colour went before "Sonja" in his 1985 movie?

6 Which Danny was his co-star in *Twins*?

7 What type of *Recall* was his 1990 movie?

8 In 1990 which Republican President made him chairman of the Council on Physical Fitness?

9 In which Californian city was *The Terminator* set?

10 Which muscleman relative of Jayne Mansfield did he play in the TV biopic?

11 What was *Conan the Destroyer* the sequel to?

12 Which Kelly co-starred in *Twins*?

13 Which journalist did he marry?

14 Which James, later famous for Titanic, directed *The Terminator*?

15 What very unmasculine condition was he in *Junior*?

16 In weightlifting circles he was billed as what type of Austrian tree?

17 Which *Terminator* film was subtitled *Judgment Day*?

18 What sort of *Lies* did he make for James Cameron in 1994?

19 What sort of *Action Hero* was he in 1993?

20 In which decade was he born?

21 What sort of *Cop* was he in 1990?

22 In *True Lies* Schwarzenegger is a salesman of what?

23 He married the niece of which late US President?

24 Which "Planet" restaurant chain did he back?

25 Who was Schwarzenegger's male co-star in *Stay Hungry*?

26 To which public office did Arnie win election in 2003?

27 Which country has a football stadium named in Arnold Schwarzenegger's honour?

28 Can you name the "fighting" occupation Arnie took up in 1965?

29 What competition did Arnie win for a record seventh time in 1980?

30 In which 2005 film did he play a cameo role as himself?

126
'70S FILMS

1 Which *Wars* were there in 1977?

2 Which 1972 film, with Marlon Brando, was about the Mafia?

3 What was *Herbie*?

4 Which creature took a starring role in "Jaws"?

5 What *Night* was there *Fever* in the movie with John Travolta?

6 Who was versus Kramer in the Dustin Hoffman film?

7 Who is Clark Kent better known as?

8 Which bird's nest did one fly over in 1975?

9 In which film did John Travolta and Olivia Newton-John sing "You're the One That I Want"?

10 What kind of *Close Encounters* were there in 1977?

11 On which Egyptian river was there death in the Agatha Christie film?

12 Which boxer did Sylvester Stallone play?

13 Name the frog in *The Muppet Movie*.

14 Which bird of prey landed in the war movie based on Jack Higgins' novel?

15 Which 1970s film about a giant ape was a remake of a 1933 movie?

16 Which disaster movie was about a fire in the world's tallest building?

17 Which film told of a mobile hospital in the Korean War?

18 Which fruit was *Clockwork* in the Stanley Kubrick film?

19 Which animal's day was it in the film about an assassin based on the Frederick Forsyth novel?

20 What was the first name of gangster Malone?

21 Who starred in the western *Every Which Way but Loose*?

22 What were forever in the James Bond movie?

23 What sort of *Hunter* was Robert de Niro in the film with Meryl Streep?

24 Where was Eddie Murphy a Cop in the film series?

25 Digby was the biggest what in the world?

26 Who starred with Paul Newman in *The Sting*?

27 How were *All Creatures* described in the 1974 film about a vet?

28 When was *Apocalypse* in the 1979 film?

29 Which planet features in the title of a 1979 Bond movie?

30 Which adventure was about a disaster on a luxury liner?

  Answers on page 201

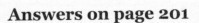 **Answers on page 201**

127
THE GREATS

1 Which great screen dancer is on the cover of "Sgt Pepper"?
2 Which wartime classic starred Ingrid Bergman and Humphrey Bogart?
3 Who is Jamie Lee Curtis's actor father?
4 Cary Grant was born in which west country port?
5 Was Rita Hayworth a blonde or a redhead?
6 Was it Bob Hope or Bing Crosby who was born in south London?
7 Which monster was arguably Boris Karloff's most famous role?
8 How was dancer Eugene Curran Kelly better known?
9 Who was the original "Candle in the Wind" dedicated to?
10 Which Anthony starred as the lead character in *Psycho*?
11 Which Sir Alec starred in, and had a share of the profits of, *Star Wars*?
12 Who was taller, Rock Hudson or Mickey Rooney?
13 Which James starred in *Harvey* and *The Philadelphia Story*?
14 Which Italian-born actor is best known for silent movies such as *The Sheikh*?
15 Which citizen was the subject of Orson Welles' first film?
16 Lauren Bacall was the wife of which Humphrey?
17 Tough guy Frank J. Cooper adopted which first name?
18 Which Joan starred in *Whatever Happened to Baby Jane*?
19 How was Ruth Elizabeth Davis better known?
20 Which Charlie was a founder of the film studio United Artists?
21 Bing Crosby had just finished a round of which game when he died?
22 William Claude Dunkenfield used his first two initials to become who?
23 Jane and Peter are the children of which screen great Henry?
24 Which Katharine enjoyed a long on and off screen relationship with Spencer Tracy?
25 Which Doris enjoyed popularity in films with Rock Hudson?
26 He was born John Uhler Lemmon III but how is he known in films?
27 Who is Michael Douglas's famous actor father?
28 In which German capital was Marlene Dietrich born?
29 Did Clark Gable die during his last film in the '40s, '50s or '60s?
30 Greta Garbo was born in which Scandinavian capital?

128
LATE GREATS

1 In what type of crash did James Dean meet his death?
2 Which Lillian was dubbed the "First Lady of the Silent Screen"?
3 Which Lee turned down George C. Scott's role in *Patton*?
4 Who won the Best Actor Oscar for *My Fair Lady*?
5 Which Clark's last movie was *The Misfits*?
6 Which David's autobiography was called *The Moon's a Balloon*?
7 Where was Jessica Tandy born?
8 In what type of building did Oliver Reed die?
9 Which British film star died as a result of head injuries sustained in a skiing accident in 2009?
10 Who won the Best Actress Oscar for *Gone with the Wind*?
11 Which Welsh actor directed and starred in *Dr Faustus* in 1968?
12 Which husband and wife starred in *The Great Dictator* in 1940?
13 Who was Bogart talking to when he said, "You look very soft for a rock"?
14 Which British actor won an Oscar for *Hamlet* in 1948?
15 Which Ava was Oscar-nominated for *Mogambo*?
16 Which Bette tested for the role of Scarlett O'Hara?
17 Which Sammy starred in *Sweet Charity*?
18 How was William Claude Fields known to cinema goers?
19 Jennifer Grant is the only daughter of which great from the heyday of Hollywood?
20 Which part of him did Jimmy Durante insure for $100,000?
21 How was John Gleason known in movies?
22 Which James died in 1997 aged 89?
23 What was Orson Welles's first film, in 1941?
24 Which doomed James starred in *Rebel Without a Cause*?
25 How was Elizabeth Ruth Grable better known?
26 Which Ledger died in 2008?
27 Which Jane, the first wife of Ronald Reagan, died in 2007?
28 Whose last screen role was in the 2002 film *Road to Perdition*?
29 Which star of Hollywood Biblical epics died in 2008?
30 Which acclaimed Swedish film director died in 2007?

 Answers on page 201

 Answers on page 201

129
'80S FILMS

1 What relation was Danny de Vito to Arnold Schwarzenegger in their 1988 film?

2 Which Bruce starred in *Die Hard*?

3 Which singer won an Oscar for *Moonstruck*?

4 *Out of* which continent were Meryl Streep and Robert Redford in 1985?

5 In which film did Dustin Hoffman dress up as a woman to get a job as a soap star?

6 What was Richard Gere in the film with Debra Winger?

7 What does an inventor tell Honey he has shrunk in the 1989 movie?

8 What does ET stand for in the 1982 film?

9 What sort of *Attraction* was there between Michael Douglas and Glenn Close?

10 Which bored housewife Shirley had an unforgettable Greek holiday?

11 Which disfigured man did John Hurt portray in the 1980 film?

12 Which film told the story of two athletes in the 1924 Olympics?

13 What is Australian adventurer Mick Dundee's nickname?

14 Which adventurer Indiana was played by Harrison Ford?

15 Which Indian leader was played by Ben Kingsley?

16 What sort of *Busters* were Dan Aykroyd and Sigourney Weaver?

17 Which composer did Tom Hulse play in *Amadeus*?

18 Which film with Bob Hoskins is also the name of a painting?

19 Which former actor became president of the USA in 1980?

20 What was the Fish called in the 1988 movie?

21 Which *Naked* film was the first in the series with Leslie Nielsen?

22 Who played James Bond in *For Your Eyes Only*?

23 What *Strikes Back* in the 1980 film?

24 Where was Eddie Murphy a cop in the film series?

25 Where was Michael J. Fox *Back to* in 1985?

26 *The Return of* what in 1983 was the sixth film in the *Star Wars* series?

27 Which US pop superstar starred in *Moonwalker*?

28 Which cartoon rabbit was framed in 1988?

29 Which famous ship did they try to raise in the 1980 film?

30 How many men looked after baby in 1987?

130
THE BRITS

1 What was the Spice Girls' first film?

2 Who with The Shadows starred in *The Young Ones*?

3 Which movie told of redundant steel workers becoming strippers?

4 *The Bridge on the River Kwai* prisoners are imprisoned by whom?

5 Nick Hornby's *Fever Pitch* is about which game?

6 Which Kenneth directed and starred in *Hamlet*?

7 *The Blue Lamp* preceded which TV series about PC George Dixon?

8 A BAFTA is a British Award for film and what?

9 What nationality was *The ... Patient* in the 1996 Oscar winner?

10 Which US food expert Loyd is the son-in-law of David Puttnam?

11 Mrs Blake Edwards won an Oscar for *Mary Poppins*; who was she?

12 What is the nationality of Sir Anthony Hopkins?

13 In which part of the UK was *Trainspotting* set?

14 Which one-time British Transport Minister twice won an Oscar?

15 Which Sir Richard directed *Chaplin*?

16 Which 1994 British hit shot Hugh Grant to superstardom?

17 Which Emma wrote the screenplay for *Sense & Sensibility*?

18 Jenny Agutter found fame in which movie about an Edwardian family?

19 Is Helena Bonham Carter a British Prime Minister's or a US President's granddaughter?

20 Elizabeth Taylor was twice married to this Welsh actor; who was he?

21 Who was born Maurice Micklewhite?

22 Which Julie was Oscar nominated in 1998?

23 Which Ewan plays the young Obi Wan Kenobi in Episode I of *Star Wars*?

24 In which film did Tom Conti play Pauline Collins' Greek lover?

25 Which blonde bombshell was born Diana Fluck?

26 Linus Roache's father has played which *Coronation Street* character since the soap began?

27 Who or what was the film *Wilde* with Stephen Fry about?

28 Which former James Bond became a goodwill ambassador for UNICEF?

29 In which part of the UK was Robert Carlyle born?

30 Hot Chocolate's "You Sexy Thing" was the theme for which 1997 film?

  Answers on page 201

 Answers on page 201

131
STARS OF THE '80S

1 Which pop superstar did Sean Penn marry in 1985?

2 Which ex-Mrs Sonny Bono played Loretta Castorini in *Moonstruck*?

3 When Billy Crystal was Harry, who was Meg Ryan?

4 Which 24-year-old Michael played teenager Marty in *Back to the Future*?

5 Which husband of Demi Moore played John McLane in *Die Hard*?

6 Which Kirstie appeared in *Star Trek II*?

7 Which tough guy actor has the nickname Sly?

8 Which Melanie was a "Working Girl" for Harrison Ford?

9 Who played Tom Cruise's autistic brother in *Rain Man*?

10 Which Patrick practised *Dirty Dancing* with Jennifer Grey?

11 Which Glenn's attraction looked fatal to Michael Douglas in 1987?

12 Which successful US talk show hostess appeared in *The Color Purple*?

13 Who changed her name from Susan Weaver before appearing in movies such as *Ghostbusters*?

14 In *Born on the Fourth of July*, Tom Cruise played a veteran from which war?

15 Which Canadian Leslie found big-screen fame as Lieutenant Frank Drebin?

16 Which Richard was the American Gigolo?

17 Which Mel played the title role in *Mad Max II*?

18 Which Kevin played opposite Meryl Streep in *Sophie's Choice*?

19 Which animal was a star with Clint Eastwood in *Any Which Way You Can*?

20 What did Elliott call his pet alien in the 80s Spielberg movie?

21 What sort of busters were Dan Aykroyd and Bill Murray?

22 Which Michael was in *Romancing the Stone* in 1984?

23 What was the name of the cartoon rabbit in the title of the movie with Bob Hoskins?

24 Michael Keaton starred as which caped crusader in 1989?

25 Which 007 joined Harrison Ford in *Indiana Jones and the Last Crusade*?

26 Which Tom played a cop who adopted the slobbering dog Hooch?

27 Whose demonic grin was on the movie posters for *The Shining*?

28 Who played opposite Billy Crystal in *When Harry Met Sally*?

29 Who plays Dale McKussic in *Tequila Sunrise*?

30 Which actress voiced the femme fatale in *Who Framed Roger Rabbit*?

132
'90S FILMS

1 Which male star shot to fame in *Four Weddings and a Funeral*?

2 In which film shot in Ireland did Australian Mel Gibson play a Scot?

3 Who had to *Carry On* 500 years after the discovery of America?

4 In which film did Robin Williams dress up as a Scottish nanny?

5 What was the name of the Dustin Hoffman film about Peter Pan?

6 In which film did Whoopi Golberg first get into the habit?

7 Who joined Walter Matthau in the film *Grumpy Old Men*?

8 What did Schindler draw up in the Spielberg film?

9 What is Beethoven in the 1992 film?

10 What is Casper?

11 Who won an Oscar for *Forrest Gump* and *Philadelphia*?

12 Who starred with Demi Moore in *Ghost*?

13 Who was Whitney Houston's bodyguard?

14 In which film did Anthony Hopkins play the role of Hannibal Lecter?

15 How was Macaulay Culkin left at home in 1990?

16 What did the cub Simba become in the 1994 Disney film?

17 What kind of proposal did Robert Redford make concerning Demi Moore?

18 What was Wrong in the Wallace and Gromit Oscar-winning film?

19 Who was the *Pretty Woman* in the 1990 film?

20 Whom did Harry meet in the film with Billy Crystal?

21 Which *Park* was the Spielberg film about dinosaurs?

22 Where was someone sleepless in the film with Meg Ryan?

23 Which Disney release told the story of an American Indian heroine?

24 In which series of films would you find Robin and the Joker?

25 Daniel Day-Lewis starred in the *Last of the...* what in 1992?

26 In which film was Robin Williams the voice of the genie?

27 Who was Nicole Kidman's co star in *Far and Away* whom she later married?

28 Which Judge does Sylvester Stallone play in the comic cult movie?

29 On which street was there a Miracle in the Xmas movie with Richard Attenborough?

30 What colour is the eye in the 007 film?

 Answers on page 202

 Answers on page 202

133
THE OSCARS

1 Which Oscar winner became a Labour MP?

2 Which actress received an Oscar for *Erin Brokovich*?

3 Which actress Ms Berry won an Oscar for *Monster's Ball*?

4 Which Kevin won Best Director and starred in *Dances with Wolves*?

5 *Braveheart* was set in which country?

6 Who won Best Actor for *The Silence of the Lambs*?

7 Who directed *Schindler's List*?

8 Which British actor Jeremy was a winner with *Reversal of Fortune*?

9 Was it Tom Hanks or Tom Cruise who won in 1993 and again in '94?

10 Sonny's ex-wife won Best Actress in *Moonstruck*; who was she?

11 Which Susan won for *Dead Man Walking*?

12 Which foot is named in the title of the movie with Daniel Day-Lewis?

13 Was Clint Eastwood Best Actor or Best Director for *Unforgiven*?

14 How often are the Oscars presented?

15 Which keyboard instrument gave its name to a film with Holly Hunter?

16 Kathy Bates won with *Misery* based on which Stephen's novel?

17 Which Kate was Oscar-nominated for *Titanic*?

18 Did Madonna receive one, two or no nominations for *Evita*?

19 What was Best Picture when Tom Hanks won Best Actor for *Forrest Gump*?

20 Which Al was Best Actor for *Scent of a Woman*?

21 Which Shirley won an Oscar at the age of five?

22 For which film did James Cameron win a 1997 Oscar?

23 Which British movie about the 1924 Olympics was a 1980s winner?

24 Which Oscar winner based in India holds the record for most extras?

25 Which son of Kirk Douglas won for *Wall Street*?

26 *Platoon* was about which Asian war?

27 Which Ralph was an *English Patient* winner?

28 *Talk to the Animals* came from which movie about a Doctor?

29 For her role in *The Hours* actress Nicole Kidman wore a false what?

30 *Dances with Wolves* was the first film of what type to win Best Picture for 60 years?

134
HORROR

1 Who directed Kenneth Branagh in Mary Shelley's Frankenstein?

2 Who, according to the movie, fathered Rosemary's Baby?

3 In which Dracula movie did Anthony Hopkins play Professor van Helsing?

4 What was the sequel to *Scream* called?

5 Who wrote the screenplay of William Peter Blatty's *The Exorcist*?

6 What was the first name of Dracula actor Lugosi?

7 What sort of "Man" was Claude Rains in 1933?

8 Which Stephen's first novel *Carrie* was a successful 70s movie?

9 Who was Transylvania's most famous vampire?

10 Which Tom played a vampire with Brad Pitt in *Interview with the Vampire: The Vampire Chronicles*?

11 Which creepy-crawlies are the subject of *Arachnophobia*?

12 Which Stanley made *The Shining* with Jack Nicholson?

13 What part did Boris Karloff play in the pre-World War II *Frankenstein*?

14 Which 1978 movie shares its name with the spooky 31st October?

15 Which Sissy played the title role in *Carrie*?

16 On which street was the nightmare in the 80s movie series?

17 In which decade was *The Exorcist* first released?

18 Who was the female star of *Rosemary's Baby*?

19 What was Frankenstein's first name in the Kenneth Branagh version?

20 Where was the *American Werewolf* in the 1981 movie with David Naughton?

21 Which Hitchcock movie featured feathered attackers?

22 Who directed and starred in *Psycho 3* in 1986?

23 Which British actor won an Oscar for *The Silence of the Lambs*?

24 Which Michelle co-starred with Jack Nicholson in *Wolf*?

25 Which British studios were famous for their horror movies?

26 Who did aliens meet in 2004?

27 Who played the lead in 2007's *I am Legend*?

28 Who directed the 2005 British horror film *The Descent*?

29 Which 2004 British zombie comedy starred Simon Pegg and Nick Frost?

30 Which 2006 American horror film had the tagline "They're Hungry ... You're Dinner"?

  Answers on page 202

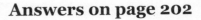 **Answers on page 202**

135
HOLLYWOOD 2

1 Which singer starred in *The Bodyguard*?
2 Which actress Keaton starred in *Father of the Bride II*?
3 *Walk the Line* was a biopic of which country music legend?
4 Which Holly won an Oscar for a silent role in *The Piano*?
5 Which silent movie star was played by Robert Downey Jr in 1992?
6 Which Welsh actor starred with Jodie Foster in *The Silence of the Lambs*?
7 Which Bob starred in *Mona Lisa* before finding it "good to talk"?
8 Which Steven directed *Schindler's List*?
9 Which actor Sylvester has the nickname Sly?
10 Who is Donald Sutherland's actor son?
11 What is the first name of *Pulp Fiction* director Tarantino?
12 Which actress Melanie married Don Johnson – twice?
13 Which Nick co-starred with Barbra Streisand in *The Prince of Tides*?
14 What is the first name of actress Sarandon ?
15 Which Johnny starred as Edward Scissorhands?
16 Which Scottish actor Sean has an actor son Jason?
17 Which Emilio starred in *Young Guns I* and *II*?
18 Which Macaulay became one of the highest-paid child stars ever?
19 Which actress Glenn had a *Fatal Attraction*?
20 Which Al starred in *The Godfather* and *Scent of a Woman*?
21 Which actor Mel was born in the US but brought up in Australia?
22 What is the surname of father and daughter Peter and Bridget?
23 Which Robin became Mrs Doubtfire?
24 Which blond Daryl had adventures with the *Invisible Man*?
25 Who was Alec Baldwin's real and screen wife in *The Getaway*?
26 What is the first name of Joanne Whalley-Kilmer's husband?
27 Liza Minnelli and Lorna Luft are daughters of which Hollywood great?
28 Which actor succeeded Timothy Dalton as James Bond?
29 Which film director's real name is Allen Stewart Konigsberg?
30 Which actor won an Oscar as director of *Dances with Wolves*?

136
MOVIES POT LUCK

1 Which film centre is also known as Tinseltown?
2 Which writer was *in Love* in the 1998 movie?
3 In which movie based on a Jane Austen novel did Gwyneth Paltrow play Emma Woodhouse?
4 What follows the names of Harry Connick and Robert Downey?
5 Who played the lead role in *The African Queen* after David Niven turned it down?
6 Who sang the title song of *Who's That Girl*?
7 In which decade was *Star Wars* first released?
8 Who played the villain in the 90s movie *Silence of the Lambs*?
9 Who won the Best Actor Oscar for *One Flew over the Cuckoo's Nest*?
10 In which decade was *Goldfinger* released?
11 How is Demetria Guynes better known?
12 Who won the Best Director Oscar for *Annie Hall*?
13 From which country did Mikhail Barishnikov defect to the USA?
14 In which country was Britt Ekland born?
15 In which eastern bloc country was the movie Reds set?
16 In which decade was *Mission: Impossible* released?
17 Who was Paul Newman's wife whom he directed in Rachel, Rachel?
18 What did T stand for in *E.T.*?
19 How is former Bond girl, Mrs Ringo Starr, Barbara Goldbach better known?
20 Which *Apollo* mission was the subject of a movie starring Tom Hanks?
21 Which comedian Bob has hosted the Oscars ceremony over 20 times?
22 Rupert Everett starred in *The Madness of...* which king?
23 Burt Bacharach was a former accompanist for which actress Marlene?
24 Which movie did the song *Fame* come from?
25 Which Phoebe of TV mini-series *Lace* married actor Kevin Kline?
26 *The Rise of the Machines* was the subtitle of which Schwarzenegger movie series?
27 What creature's curse did Wallace and Gromit encounter in 2005?
28 Which Claire starred in the 90s *Romeo and Juliet*?
29 Who sang "Call Me" in *America Gigolo*?
30 Which word goes before *Proposal* in a Demi Moore movie title?

  **Answers on page 202**

 Answers on page 202

137
ACTION

1 Which Bond film shares its name with Ian Fleming's Jamaican home?

2 What was the third of Oliver Stone's films about Vietnam?

3 Which English Oscar winner was the villain in *Die Hard III*?

4 Which Brit directed *Black Hawk Down* and *Hannibal*?

5 Who played Bernardo in *The Magnificent Seven* and Danny Velinski in *The Great Escape*?

6 Who was The Riddler in *Batman Forever*?

7 Which Oscar did Kevin Costner win for *Dances with Wolves*?

8 Who played the defrosted super-villain in *Demolition Man*?

9 What was Roger Moore's first Bond film in 1973?

10 Who had her first major starring role in *Bonnie & Clyde*?

11 Who plays the President in *Escape from New York*?

12 Which was the third *Die Hard* film?

13 Who played Indiana Jones?

14 Where was *French Connection II* set?

15 Astronaut Jim Lovell was portrayed by Tom Hanks in which film?

16 Who heads the crew which saves the world in *Armageddon*?

17 Whom did Gene Hackman play in *The French Connection*?

18 Who played Sonny Corleone in *The Godfather* and its sequel?

19 What nationality cop did Sean Connery play in *The Untouchables*?

20 Who co-starred with Morgan Freeman in *Seven*?

21 Which 1998 film of a '60s cult TV series starred Gary Oldman and William Hurt?

22 Who played the train robber of the title role in *Buster*?

23 What was Mel Gibson's job in the 1997 thriller *Conspiracy Theory*?

24 Which husband and wife were Oscar nominated for the song from *Live and Let Die*?

25 Which Oliver Stone movie with Kevin Costner was about events prior to Kennedy's assassination?

26 Which Yorkshireman played the IRA terrorist in *Patriot Games*?

27 Which British 90s Oscar winner featured in *The Man in the Iron Mask*?

28 Who played the construction worker who had flashbacks in *Total Recall*?

29 Where does the action of *Godzilla* take place?

30 Who played two roles in the 90s version of *The Man in the Iron Mask*?

138
ACTION 2

1 Which Bond villain has been played by Telly Savalas and Donald Pleasence?

2 Who directed *Hustle* and *The Dirty Dozen*?

3 What was the second Bond film?

4 Which role did Jim Carrey play in *Batman Forever*?

5 In which 1997 film does Pierce Brosnan play a vulcanologist?

6 Whose film biography was called *Dragon*?

7 What does "Ice Cold" refer to in the John Mills film *Ice Cold in Alex*?

8 Which sport features in *Million Dollar Baby*?

9 What was the occupation of the Fugitive?

10 Which means of transport dominates in *Speed*?

11 Which 1997 Mafia film starred Al Pacino and Johnny Depp?

12 In which US city is *Metro* set?

13 What was Pierce Brosnan's second film as James Bond?

14 What was the third *Die Hard* film called?

15 Who played Bond girl Solitaire in *Live and Let Die*?

16 In which decade does the action of *Raiders of the Lost Ark* take place?

17 What was Oliver Stone's final Vietnam trilogy film?

18 Which means of transport features in *The Hunt for Red October*?

19 Which country is the setting for Oliver Stone's *Platoon*?

20 Who plays the US captain escaping an Italian POW camp in *Von Ryan's Express*?

21 Who co-wrote and starred in *Cliffhanger* in 1993?

22 Which action movie is subtitled *Judgment Day*?

23 Who is the actress caught between an undercover cop and a drug dealer in *Tequila Sunrise*?

24 Which film critic's father produced *The Cruel Sea*?

25 Who directed the first three *Godfather* films?

26 Which 1995 film allegedly cost £1.3 million per minute screen time?

27 Which singer joined Mel Gibson for *Mad Max Beyond Thunderdome*?

28 Which city is the setting for *French Connection II*?

29 Which film's action begins with "Houston, we have a problem"?

30 Who played 007 in 1984 in *Never Say Never Again*?

  Answers on page 202

 Answers on page 202

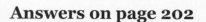

139
CARTOONS

1 Who was the voice of the dragon in Mulan?
2 Which 1997 movie featured the voices of Meg Ryan and John Cusack?
3 What was the first full-length animated movie to be Oscar-nominated for Best Film?
4 Whose songs feature in *Toy Story*?
5 Where do the characters live in *Who Framed Roger Rabbit?*?
6 Which 1945 Gene Kelly movie featured an animation sequence by Hanna and Barbera?
7 Which movie features Jiminy Cricket and Figaro?
8 *The Land Before Time* features an orphaned what?
9 Which 1995 movie saw Robin Williams being rescued from a board game?
10 Hakuna Matata is in which movie?
11 What are the Siamese cats called in *Lady and the Tramp*?
12 What was the name of the wicked uncle in *The Lion King*?
13 What is the name of the dinosaur in *Toy Story*?
14 *The Return of Jafar* was the sequel to which movie?
15 Which classic film has a rabbit called Thumper?
16 Which director provided a voice in *Antz*?
17 Which star of *Friends* provides a voice in *The Iron Giant*?
18 Who was the voice of John Smith in *Pocahontas*?
19 Who was the voice of Jessica in *Who Framed Roger Rabbit?*?
20 Which studio, famous for musicals, did Hanna and Barbera work for in the 40s?
21 Which 1999 movie featured the voices of Minnie Driver and Tony Goldwyn?
22 Which duo's first movie was in *Puss Gets the Boot*?
23 Lea Salonga sang on the soundtrack of *Aladdin* after making her name in which musical?
24 In *The Lion King* what sort of animal was Shenzi?
25 What is the name of "the king of the swingers" in Disney's *Jungle Book*?
26 What animal is voiced by Angelina Jolie in *Kung Fu Panda*?
27 *The Land of Far, Far Away* should be the domain of which swamp-dweller?
28 In what 1986 movie can you find Optimus Prime?
29 What Disney movies tells the story of a young prince's quest to rule the Pride Lands?
30 Can you recall the movie in which Bob Hoskins played Detective Eddie Valiant?

140
ANIMATION

1 Which Ponchielli piece features in *Fantasia*?
2 Which US-born Australian was the voice of John Smith in *Pocahontas*?
3 In which year was the Best Animated Feature Oscar first awarded?
4 What was the sequel to *Aladdin* called?
5 What colour are Mickey Mouse's gloves?
6 Perdita and Pongo are what type of animals?
7 How many Oscars, in total, was Disney given for *Snow White and the Seven Dwarfs*?
8 Which 1991 animated film was later a musical in London and the US?
9 Who is the best-known rabbit in *Bambi*?
10 Featuring Elton John songs, what was the highest-grossing animation movie of the 1990s?
11 Which of the Gabor sisters was a voice in *The Aristocats*?
12 Who created Tom and Jerry at MGM in the 40s?
13 What did Dumbo do immediately before his ears grew so big?
14 Which film of a fairy tale features the song "Bibbidy Bobbidy Boo"?
15 Which part did Kathleen Turner voice in *Who Framed Roger Rabbit?*?
16 Which Disney film was the first with a synchronised soundtrack?
17 "Colours of the Wind" was a hit song from which movie?
18 Which film with an animated sequence featured Angela Lansbury using her magic powers against the Nazis?
19 Who sings "He's a tramp" in *Lady and the Tramp*?
20 Where did Kim Basinger star as a sexy animated doodle, Holly, brought over to the real world?
21 Who sang in *Aladdin* after making her name in "Miss Saigon"?
22 Which 1990 film was about pizza-loving, sewer dwelling reptiles?
23 Which was the first film to feature, appropriately enough, computeranimated sequences?
24 What type of orphaned creature featured in *The Land Before Time*?
25 Which was the first animated film in the 90s which Tim Rice won an Oscar for?
26 Which dancer commissioned Hanna and Barbera to do an animation sequence in *Anchors Aweigh* in 1945?
27 Which Tchaikovsky ballet piece features in *Fantasia*?
28 In which film does Shere Khan appear?
29 Which characters made their debut in *Puss Gets the Boot* in 1940?
30 Who was the voice of Stuart in *Stuart Little 2*?

  Answers on page 202

 Answers on page 202

141
THRILLERS

1 In which film does Robert De Niro ask "are you talkin' to me?"?

2 Who wrote the book on which *The Russia House* was based?

3 Whom was the Jackal trying to assassinate in *The Day of the Jackal*?

4 Which president is being referred to in *All the President's Men*?

5 Who won an Oscar for *The Accused*?

6 Which movie was the first collaboration between Steven Spielberg and Tom Cruise?

7 What is Hitchcock said to have used for the blood in *Psycho*?

8 Which three actors have each played Richard Hannay in *The 39 Steps*?

9 Who played the role of South African Donald Woods in *Cry Freedom*?

10 What sort of establishment is the setting for *The China Syndrome*?

11 For which film did the reviewer write "Enough to make you kick the next pigeon you come across"?

12 What relation is Carter to Cain in *Raising Cain*?

13 On whose novel is the Sissy Spacek film *Carrie* based?

14 Who play the getaways in the remake of *The Getaway*?

15 What is the relationship between Tippi Hedren of Hitchcock's *Marnie* and Melanie Griffith of *A Stranger Among Us*?

16 What was the nationality of Alfonso Cuaron, who directed the third *Harry Potter* movie?

17 In which classic film do Mrs Danvers and Maxim de Winter appear?

18 Whose *Fatal Attraction* to Glenn Close cost him dear?

19 For which film did Steven Spielberg win his first Oscar as Director?

20 Who were the first performers to win the Best Actor and Actress Oscars in the same film after Henry Fonda and Katharine Hepburn in 1981?

21 Who starred in Hitchcock's *Dial M For Murder* and *Rear Window*?

22 Where was Jack Lemmon's son *Missing*?

23 In which classic film is "Rosebud..."a piece in the jigsaw puzzle?

24 In Hitchcock's *Frenzy* what are the victims strangled with?

25 Who costarred with Oscar-winner Jane Fonda in *Klute*?

26 In *The Crying Game* to which organization does the gunman belong?

27 Which filmed Anthony Shaffer play starred Michael Caine and Laurence Olivier?

28 Which *Apollo* mission was the subject of a film with Tom Hanks?

29 What was described as "Five criminals. One line up. No coincidence"?

30 Who causes terror in *The Hand That Rocks the Cradle*?

  Answers on page 203

142
ROBIN WILLIAMS

1 In which TV series did Robin Williams find fame in the 70s/80s?

2 Who played his ex-wife in *Mrs Doubtfire*?

3 Who was his male co-star in *Awakenings*?

4 In which decade did he make his first major movie?

5 In *Good Morning, Vietnam*, which President does Cronauer alias Williams impersonate?

6 Which 007 starred in *Mrs Doubtfire*?

7 Which 80s movie saw co-star Glenn Close win an Oscar nomination?

8 Which cartoon character did he play in a 1980 Robert Altman movie?

9 Which then-husband of Emma Thompson directed Dead Again?

10 In which movie does he play Daniel Hilliard?

11 What is the occupation of the grown-up Peter Pan in *Hook*?

12 Which member of the Bridges family was a co-star in *The Fisher King*?

13 Whose voice did he provide in *Aladdin*?

14 Who did he play in *Hook*?

15 Who played Olive to his Popeye?

16 Where in Scotland is the "nanny" from in *Mrs Doubtfire*?

17 In which film was he "released" from a board game after 26 years?

18 What was his job in *Good Morning, Vietnam*?

19 In which early film did he play a Russian saxophonist?

20 Which former Python Terry directed him in *The Fisher King*?

21 Which movie gave him his first Oscar nomination?

22 In which movie did he play an unorthodox prep school teacher?

23 Which Barry directed him in *Good Morning, Vietnam*?

24 In which film is he a car salesman held hostage by a jealous husband?

25 The 80s *Good Morning, Vietnam* featured songs from which decade on its soundtrack?

26 Which US President did Williams play in *Night at the Museum*?

27 How many times has Williams been nominated for the Best Actor Oscar?

28 What *Dead Society* did Williams star in in 1989?

29 What "helpful" role gave him an Oscar in the 1998 movie "Good Will Hunting"?

30 In which film did Williams play Reverend Frank?

Answers on page 203

143
BLOCKBUSTERS

1. How many crew members were there in the "Nostromo" in *Alien*?
2. What type of sauce was used in the shower scene in *Psycho*?
3. Which 1953 film was the first made in Cinemascope?
4. Who directed *The Godfather* and all its sequels?
5. *Saving Private Ryan* dealt with events in which part of France?
6. Which anti-war comedy did Robert Altman direct?
7. Which newspaper magnate was said to be the model for Orson Welles' Citizen Kane?
8. Which 80s film was the most profitable in Australian history?
9. Who played Christ in Mel Gibson's *The Passion of the Christ*?
10. What was John Schlesinger's first US film, made in 1969 with Dustin Hoffman and Jon Voight?
11. Who starred in, and co-wrote *Ghostbusters*?
12. Which film starred Juliette Binoche and Kristin Scott Thomas?
13. What was the name of Marlon Brando's character in *The Godfather*?
14. Which James Bond actor starred in *Dante's Peak*?
15. What was the name of Tom Cruise's character in *Born on the Fourth of July*?
16. In which classic did Olivia de Havilland play Melanie Wilkes?
17. In which film did Michael Douglas say "Greed is good"?
18. What was Mel Gibson's first film as actor, director and producer?
19. Which David Lynch space epic was based on the work of Frank Herbert?
20. Who was directing *The African Queen* when his daughter Anjelica was born?
21. Which sequel had the subtitle *Judgement Day*?
22. What is Schindler's nationality in *Schindler's List*?
23. What was the last film before *Titanic* to win 14 Oscar nominations?
24. In which decade was *Gone with the Wind* made?
25. Which Jeff was the mathematician in *Jurassic Park*?
26. Who became a human cartoon in *The Mask*?
27. Who played Princess Leia in the *Star Wars* Trilogy?
28. Who sang the theme song for *Titanic*?
29. In which movie did Tom Hanks play Captain Nathan Algren?
30. What was Michael Douglas' profession in *Basic Instinct*?

144
ACTION 3

1. Off which island is *Jaws* set?
2. Who played Harrison Ford's father in *Indiana Jones and the Last Crusade*?
3. Who is the cop battling with terrorists in *Die Hard*?
4. Which films are about the Corleone family?
5. What is Christopher Reeve's most famous role?
6. What is the name of the gem Harry Potter is looking for in the first Harry Potter movie?
7. In *Towering Inferno* Steve McQueen was the fireman: what was Paul Newman?
8. Which was the first Bond movie?
9. What was the final *Lord of the Rings* movie called?
10. Who was Bad in Spaghetti Westerns?
11. Which was the first of the *Indiana Jones* films to be released?
12. Which hero did Mel Gibson play in *Braveheart*?
13. In which city is *The Untouchables* set?
14. Who was involved in the writing of the *Rocky* and *Rambo* films?
15. Which was the first Bond film with Roger Moore?
16. Who played the starring role in *Last of the Mohicans*?
17. Who directed *Lawrence of Arabia*?
18. Which film starred Harrison Ford as an ex-CIA man?
19. For what did Kevin Costner win an Oscar in *Dances with Wolves*?
20. Which was George Lazenby's only Bond film?
21. Who starred as Jake La Motta in *Raging Bull*?
22. Which Clint Eastwood film won an Oscar for Gene Hackman as the sheriff of Big Whiskey?
23. Who played Bonnie to Warren Beatty's Clyde?
24. Who co-starred with Michael Douglas in *Romancing the Stone*?
25. What was the memorable, and at that time innovative, scene in *Bullitt*?
26. Which Bond film had the song "Nobody Does It Better"?
27. In which film did John Wayne win his only Oscar?
28. Which movie preceded *Magnum Force* and *The Enforcer*?
29. Who plays the title role in *Rob Roy*?
30. Who plays Miss Moneypenny in the early Bond films?

  Answers on page 203

 Answers on page 203

145
CLASSICS

1 In which classic did Paul Heinreid play Victor Laszlo?

2 Which animal sings "We're off to see the wizard, the wonderful Wizard of Oz" with Dorothy and co.?

3 In which movie did Trevor Howard play Alec Harvey?

4 What was deemed the cinema's first epic?

5 Which '50s movie told of Moses leading the children of Israel to the Promised Land?

6 "All right, Mr de Mille, I'm ready for my close-ups now" is the last line of which movie?

7 In which movie did Debra Winger begin with, "Anyone here named Loowis?"?

8 Was Debbie Reynolds 18, 20 or 22 when she made *Singin' in the Rain*?

9 Which inventor did Michael Redgrave play in *The Dam Busters*?

10 Which of the stars of *The Philadelphia Story* donated his salary for the movie to war relief?

11 Who was Spade in *The Maltese Falcon*?

12 In *The Third Man* who had Joseph Cotten come to Vienna to meet?

13 Which movie had the ad line, "Meet Benjamin. He's a little worried about his future"?

14 *A Man for All Seasons* is about whom?

15 Which 1946 Frank Capra movie with James Stewart became a Christmas classic?

16 Who did Marlene Dietrich play in *The Blue Angel*?

17 Who does James Cagney play in *White Heat*?

18 Which movie opens with the line, "What can you say about a 25-year-old girl who died"?

19 Which member of the Corleone family did Al Pacino play in the *Godfather* trilogy?

20 In which movie did Rita Hayworth remove a glove to "Put the Blame on Mame"?

21 What was Lauren Bacall's first film, in 1943?

22 In *Genevieve* who or what was Genevieve?

23 Which movie did Elvis Presley make next after *King Creole*?

24 Who played opposite Lana Turner in the original *The Postman Always Rings Twice*?

25 In which 1954 movie did Marlon Brando play a boxer?

26 In which year was the main action of *Titanic* set?

27 In *Philadelphia*, what is central character Andrew Beckett's profession?

28 This *Queen* earned Humphrey Bogart an Oscar in 1952.

29 How many *Flew Over the Cuckoo's Nest* in 1975?

30 Name the 1988 classic which starred Dustin Hoffman and Tom Cruise.

146
THE OSCARS

1 Who played Eddie to claim a Best Supporting Actor Oscar in a boxing movie?

2 Which World War II film would have been called Dar el-Beida had it been titled in the local language?

3 Which Michael Cimino film about Vietnam won five Oscars in the 70s?

4 Whom did Daniel-Day Lewis portray in *My Left Foot*?

5 Which veteran won an Oscar in 1981 two years after his daughter?

6 For which movie did Helen Hunt win in 1997?

7 For which film did Tom Hanks win playing a lawyer dying from AIDS?

8 Who overcame deafness to win for *Children of a Lesser God*?

9 Who won the Best Director award for *Titanic*?

10 For which films did Tom Hanks win in successive years?

11 Who won the Best Actor Oscar for *High Noon*?

12 What type of worker did John Gielgud play when he won his Oscar for *Arthur*?

13 In which decade did Katharine Hepburn win her first Oscar?

14 Who won three Oscars for *Annie Hall*?

15 For which film did Brando win his second Oscar?

16 Who won his first best actor Oscar for *Kramer vs. Kramer*?

17 Which singer won an Oscar for *From Here to Eternity*?

18 For which film did Steven Spielberg win his first award?

19 What was unusual about Holly Hunter's performance in *The Piano*?

20 Which father and son actor and director won for *The Treasure of the Sierra Madre*?

21 In the year *Gandhi* won almost everything who was Best Actress for *Sophie's Choice*?

22 Who won Oscars for *Dangerous*, *Jezebel* and *All About Eve*?

23 Who won as Dan Aykroyd's mother in *Driving Miss Daisy*?

24 How many times between 1990 and 1997 did Best Picture and Best Director Oscars go to the same film?

25 Who played the psychotic nurse in *Misery* and won Best Actress?

26 What did Anthony Hopkins win first, a knighthood or an Oscar?

27 Who won for her role as Blanch in *A Streetcar Named Desire*?

28 Who won Best Director for *The English Patient*?

29 Who won for her first film *Paper Moon*?

30 Which actress was nominated for *The Wings of the Dove*?

  Answers on page 203

 Answers on page 203

147
COMEDIES

1 In which 2002 movie did Nia Vardalos play a frumpy waitress in her Greek family's restaurant?

2 Who is Bridget Jones' boss in *Bridget Jones' Diary*?

3 In the 2001 movie directed by Gurinder Chadha, which footballer's surname is in the title?

4 Who was the baby's voice in *Look Who's Talking*?

5 Which tough guy was the star of *Kindergarten Cop*?

6 What was the subtitle of *Police Academy 6*?

7 Which film was about the activities of unemployed parapsychologists in New York?

8 Who won an Oscar for *Tootsie*?

9 Who was Richard Gere's co-star in *Pretty Woman*?

10 Which actors played the two revenging con men in *The Sting*?

11 In which area of New York is *Crocodile Dundee* set?

12 Which country singer starred in *Nine to Five*?

13 Which studios produced *Honey I Shrunk the Kids*?

14 Who plays the chauvinistic advertising executive in *What Women Want*?

15 Which English actor starred in *The Muppet Christmas Carol*?

16 Who played the title roles in *When Harry Met Sally*?

17 What was the profession of the Patrick Swayze character in *Ghost*?

18 Which was the first *Carry On* film?

19 Who is the police inspector in *The Pink Panther* films?

20 Which late superstar's wife stars in *The Naked Gun* films?

21 What was the sequel to *Three Men and a Baby*?

22 Which film included the song "Raindrops Keep Fallin' on My Head"?

23 What was the nationality of Mrs Doubtfire in the film of the same name?

24 Who played the role of Wendy in *Hook*?

25 In the film *Babe* who or what is Babe?

26 Who is Whoopi Goldberg hiding from in *Sister Act*?

27 In which film is Tom Hanks a small boy in a grown man's body?

28 Which historic event triggers the plot in *Some Like It Hot*?

29 Who directed *Annie Hall* and *Match Point*?

30 Who were Chico, Gummo and Zeppo's two brothers?

148
OSCARS: BEST ACTORS

1 Who was 80 when he won for *The Sunshine Boys*?

2 What was Michael Douglas's first nomination as performer?

3 For which movie did Ralph Fiennes receive his second nomination?

4 How is 1982 winner, Krishna Bahji, better known?

5 Which 1999 Oscar nominee played Lord Alfred Douglas in *Wilde*?

6 What was Bing Crosby's profession in *Going My Way*?

7 Who won the first Oscar for Best Actor?

8 What was John Gielgud's profession in the movie *Arthur* for which he won an award?

9 When Brenda Fricker first won as Best Actress which winner played her son?

10 For which movie did Woody Harrelson receive his first nomination?

11 What is the total number of Oscars won by Errol Flynn, Peter Cushing and Richard Burton?

12 Who was nominated for *Cleopatra* but won a year later as Professor Higgins?

13 Jon Voight's first nomination was for which X-rated movie?

14 How many Oscars did Sean Connery win for James Bond?

15 What was Michael Douglas's first win as Actor?

16 Which *King* gave Nigel Hawthorne a nomination?

17 For which Spielberg movie was Anthony Hopkins nominated in 1997?

18 What was the second of Jack Nicholson's three nominations between 1973 and 1975?

19 Who was the first actor to be awarded two posthumous Oscars?

20 Which 80s winner and 90s nominee is the son of Jill Balcon and a poet laureate?

21 Whose first award was for playing Terry Malloy in a '50s classic?

22 For which movie did John Hurt receive a nomination after *Midnight Express*?

23 Who did Robert De Niro play in *The Godfather Part II*?

24 Which Spielberg movie gave Liam Neeson his first nomination?

25 Which Brit won Best Actor in a musical the same year that Julie Andrews won for *Mary Poppins*?

26 Which former star of *ER* was nominated for the first time in 2007?

27 Disney's *Pirates of the Caribbean* won which Johnny a nomination in 2003?

28 Who holds the record for most nominations (8) without ever winning the award?

29 Name either one of the two male actors who declined to accept the award.

30 Which Western earned Gary Cooper his Oscar in 1952?

 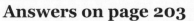 **Answers on page 203**

 Answers on page 203

149
WESTERNS

1 What was the first film in which Clint Eastwood starred as "The man with no name"?

2 Who played the sadistic sheriff in Eastwood's *Unforgiven*?

3 Which actor's films include *Big Jim McLain*, *McLintock* and *McQ*?

4 Which star of *Maverick* played Brett Maverick in the TV series?

5 Which Oscar did Kevin Costner win for *Dances with Wolves*?

6 What is the name of the original tale that the *Magificent Seven* is based on?

7 What weather feature was in the title of the song from *Butch Cassidy* won an Oscar?

8 Who was the star of *Jeremiah Johnson*?

9 Which comedy actor starred in the comedy western *The Paleface*?

10 Who starred with brother Charlie Sheen in *Young Guns*?

11 Which Oscar winner for *Fargo*, married director Joel Coen?

12 Who played the woman poker player in *Maverick*?

13 Which actor was *The Bad*?

14 Which *Back to the Future* film returns to the Wild West?

15 In which musical western does the song "Wandrin' Star" appear?

16 Which Hollywood legend was the narrator in *How the West was Won*?

17 Which film was originally called *Per un Pugno di Dollari*?

18 Which country singer was in *True Grit*?

19 Which son of a *M*A*S*H* star appeared in *Young Guns II*?

20 Whom did John Wayne play in *The Alamo*?

21 Clint Eastwood became mayor of which town?

22 Which 1985 film was a revised remake of the classic *Shane*?

23 Where is the village where the action of *The Magnificent Seven* centres?

24 Where was *The Good, the Bad and the Ugly* made?

25 What was the name of Mel Brooks' spoof western?

26 Which English comic appeared in *Desperado*?

27 Which '80s teenage western starred actors known as the Brat Pack?

28 What was Tonto's horse called?

29 Who was Gene Autry's most famous horse?

30 Traditionally, what colour is the western hero's hat?

150
WAR

1 About which conflict is the Sam Mendes film *Jarhead* about?

2 During which war was *Platoon* set?

3 Which Hollywood legend played Kurtz in *Apocalypse Now*?

4 Who played Hawkeye and Trapper John in *M*A*S*H*?

5 How was the film *Patton* known in the UK?

6 For which Robert de Niro film was *Cavatina* the theme music?

7 Who won an Oscar as the Colonel in *The Bridge on the River Kwai*?

8 In *The Colditz Story* what type of building was Colditz?

9 In which English county were the GIs billeted in *Yanks*?

10 What type of soldiers were the four Britons in *The Wild Geese*?

11 Which 1963 film about Allied POWs starred James Garner and Steve McQueen?

12 Hits from which decade were on the soundtrack of *Good Morning, Vietnam*?

13 Which George was the star of *Three Kings*?

14 How were the 12 convicts recruited for a suicide mission known in the 1967 movie?

15 Which novel was *Schindler's List* based on?

16 Which US singer played Von Ryan in *Von Ryan's Express*?

17 Whose café was a meeting place for war refugees in *Casablanca*?

18 Who wrote the novel on which *Where Eagles Dare* was based?

19 Which musical satire on war was directed by Richard Attenborough?

20 Where was it *All Quiet* in the classic film made in 1930?

21 At the time of which World War II event is *From Here to Eternity* set?

22 In *A Town Like Alice* what does "Alice" refer to?

23 Which anti-Vietnam War activist starred in *Coming Home*?

24 Who was the subject of the film *The Desert Fox*?

25 Which 1940 film starred Charlie Chaplin as despot Adenoid Hynkel?

26 Who directed *Born on the Fourth of July*?

27 Whose heroes were Clint Eastwood and Telly Savalas in 1970?

28 *The Eagle Has Landed* centres on a plot to kidnap whom?

29 Who won the Oscar for best actress in 1982 for *Sophie's Choice*?

30 In which country is *The Killing Fields* set?

   **Answers on page 203**

  Answers on page 203

151
JOHN WAYNE

1. What was his nickname?
2. In which classic western did he play the Ringo Kid?
3. Which sport did he play competitively when he was at college?
4. Which wife of Charlie Chaplin was his co-star in *Reap the Wild Wind*?
5. What was the first movie in which he starred with Maureen O'Hara?
6. Which singer was his drunken assistant in *Rio Bravo*?
7. What type of sportsman did he pay in *The Quiet Man*?
8. Which Hollywood great was his female co-star in *The Shootist*?
9. In which movie did he famously say, "Truly this man was the son of God"?
10. Which role did he play in *The Alamo*?
11. In which 1975 movie did he reprise his role from *True Grit*?
12. What was his real name?
13. He starred in and directed *The Green Berets* during which war?
14. What was the first movie for which he received an Oscar?
15. Which movie earned him his first Oscar nomination?
16. Which TV western series did he introduce the first episode of on camera?
17. Which legendary ruler did he play in *The Conqueror*?
18. What was the name of his first major movie?
19. Which director gave him the role in *She Wore a Yellow Ribbon*?
20. In which city was *Brannigan* set?
21. On what occasion was his last public appearance?
22. What was his directorial debut?
23. In which movie did he play Civil War veteran Ethan Edwards?
24. *El Dorado* was a virtual remake of which 1959 hit movie?
25. What was the name of his final movie?
26. Boxing grandnephew Tommy Morrison claimed to have beaten which condition?
27. Which eye was covered with a patch in *Rooster Cogburn*?
28. Which Vietnam War movie did he star in and direct in 1968?
29. What type of shop did the teenage Wayne work in?
30. Which one of the US armed services was Wayne rejected by prior to University?

152
DIRECTORS & PRODUCERS

1. Who is Ethan Coen's director brother?
2. Who directed *Moulin Rouge*, starring Nicole Kidman and Ewan McGregor?
3. Who directed the film *Flags of Our Fathers*?
4. What was George Lucas's role in the original *Star Wars*?
5. Who directed the movie about the most disastrous disaster at sea in peace time?
6. Who had the middle name Blount but only used his initial?
7. Which musical duo was the subject of a Mike Leigh movie with Jim Broadbent?
8. Which musical did Alan Parker direct before the drama *Angela's Ashes*?
9. How is Melvin Kaminski of *Young Frankenstein* better known?
10. Which Neil was Oscar-nominated as director and also writer for *The Crying Game*?
11. Who was the director of *When Harry Met Sally*?
12. In which city was Akira Kurosawa born?
13. Which lady was the director of the hit movies *Sleepless in Seattle* and *You Got M@il*?
14. Which father of a musical star directed *An American in Paris*?
15. How is the director of *Wolf* and *The Birdcage* born Michael Igor Peschkowsky better known?
16. Which actor directed *Rocky IV*?
17. Who was Oscar-nominated for *Dead Man Walking*?
18. Ken Russell's *The Music Lovers* was about which Russian composer?
19. For which movie with Robert De Niro did Martin Scorsese receive his first Oscar nomination?
20. Which brothers bought Shepperton Studios in 1994?
21. Which then husband and wife were the stars of Kubrick's *Eyes Wide Shut*?
22. What is the name of Garry Marshall's fellow director sibling, formerly married to the director of *When Harry Met Sally*?
23. Which president was the subject of the 1995 movie written and directed by Oliver Stone?
24. Who was the director of *Gandhi*?
25. Who was the subject of the biography *King Pulp*?
26. Which movie about an Apollo moon mission had Ron Howard as director?
27. Where in New York was Woody Allen born?
28. Terry Gilliam was a member of which comedy team?
29. In which decade did Stanley Kubrick direct *A Clockwork Orange*?
30. Which actor directed *Dances with Wolves* and *The Bodyguard*?

 Answers on page 204

 Answers on page 204

153
SCI-FI

1 Which character was described as "part man, part machine, all cop"?

2 Who played the part of the rebel princess in *Star Wars*?

3 *2001: A Space Odyssey* was based on a short story by whom?

4 What was the first in the five-film series of man and monkey conflict?

5 What planet did long-eared Mr Spock come from?

6 *Judge Dredd* was based on the character from which comic?

7 Which director said, "I'm embarrassed and ashamed that I get paid for doing this"?

8 In which film did Jane Fonda "do her own thing" in the 40th century?

9 What was the *Fahrenheit* reading in Truffaut's 1960s film?

10 Which hero has been portrayed by Christopher Reeve and Kirk Alyn?

11 Who was the star of *The Terminator* films?

12 Which rock band did the score for the 1970s romp *Flash*?

13 What was Darth Vader's spacecraft in *Star Wars*?

14 Who directed the 2005 version of *King Kong*?

15 Which creatures mutated in *Them*?

16 In which film did Claude Rains star as someone who was not seen?

17 Which rock star played Newton in *The Man Who Fell to Earth*?

18 In which film does Charlton Heston think he is Earth's last survivor?

19 Which vehicles set out to devour Paris?

20 In which film are people terminated at the age of 30?

21 In titles, which words go before *Stood Still* and *Caught Fire*?

22 Robbie the Robot and Dr Morbius appear in which film?

23 *Alien* posters said that "in space no one can hear you" do what?

24 In the 1953 film how many fathoms did the Beast come from?

25 *How I Learned to Stop Worrying and Love the Bomb* is known by what shorter title?

26 Which veteran actor played Ben (Obi-Wan) Kenobi?

27 In which 1960s film does rocket radiation activate flesh-eating zombies?

28 Who was the main star of *The Matrix* series of movies?

29 Who is the female companion of Flash Gordon?

30 In *The Incredible Shrinking Man* which creature does the man fight off with a needle?

154
ANIMALS ON SCREEN

1 Who or what was Andre in the film of the same name?

2 What sort of whale was Willy?

3 Which movie saw a creature threatening Amity off the Long Island coast?

4 What was the sequel to *Beethoven* called?

5 On whose novel was *101 Dalmatians* based?

6 Which creatures predominate in *Deep Blue Sea*?

7 Which actress founded the Born Free Foundation after appearing in the movie?

8 What sort of animal was the star of *Gus*?

9 In which film does Tom Hanks use the help of a dog to solve a murder?

10 Which veteran, and former child star, was one of the voices in the 80s *The Fox and the Hound*?

11 What sort of star was Rhubarb?

12 Which *X-Files* star played a villain in *Beethoven*?

13 Which animals were the stars of *Ring of Bright Water*?

14 What was Tom Mix's horse called?

15 The first dog to play which big-screen star was really called Pal?

16 What was the name of the basketball-playing golden retriever in *Air Bud* in 1997?

17 How many horses did Gene Autry have called Champion?

18 In which musical does Bill have a dog called Bullseye?

19 What type of animal was Digby in the Peter Sellers movie?

20 What breed of dog was K9 in the John Belushi movie?

21 How many dogs and cats make *The Incredible Journey*?

22 Which little girl had a dog as a nanny, called Nana?

23 What sort of animal featured in *My Friend Flicka*?

24 What was the cat called in *Breakfast at Tiffany's*?

25 What was the sequel to *The Incredible Journey* called?

26 What animal was Will Smith's only companion in I am Legend?

27 What creature's bite turned Peter Parker into a superhero?

28 What was the name of the pig in the *Toy Story* movies?

29 What type of animal was Skippy?

30 What was the name of King of the Jungle's chimpanzee in the *Tarzan* movies?

  Answers on page 204

 Answers on page 204

155
MOVIES 2000

1 Who was Nicole Kidman's co-star in *Moulin Rouge*?
2 Who directed *AI: Artificial Intelligence*?
3 Who played opposite Nicolas Cage in *Captain Corelli's Mandolin*?
4 Who plays Darcy Maguire in *What Women Want*, with Mel Gibson?
5 Who was the star of the computer-animated *Tomb Raider*?
6 What sort of farm features in *Chicken Run*?
7 Who directed *Gladiator*?
8 Who co-starred with Harry Enfield in *Kevin and Perry Go Large*?
9 Who became romantically linked with Russell Crowe during the making of *Proof of Life*?
10 For which movie did Julia Roberts win her first Oscar?
11 Who played the title role in Richard Attenborough's *Grey Owl*?
12 Who plays Johnny Depp's wife in *Blow*?
13 Which *Absolutely Fabulous* star was the voice of Ginger in *Chicken Run*?
14 Which movie starred Hugh Jackman as a computer hacker and John Travolta as a counter-terrorist?
15 In which country was *The Beach* filmed?
16 In *The Mexican*, what is the Mexican?
17 Who is the female corner of the love triangle in *Pearl Harbor*?
18 In *Meet the Parents* which animals is Robert De Niro particularly fond of?
19 Who was the voice of Shrek?
20 Which classes should Billy Elliot be going to when he is doing ballet?
21 Who played Lara Croft's father in the *Tomb Raider* film and in real life too?
22 Who plays the single mum in *Chocolat*?
23 Which new millennium movie on the drugs trade starred Michael Douglas?
24 Which English actor played the lawyer in *Erin Brokovich*?
25 Who plays the Marquis de Sade in *Quills*?
26 What was the sequel to *The Lost World* in the *Jurassic Park* films?
27 Who is the star of *The Family Man*, a remake of *It's a Wonderful Life*?
28 Who played Bridget's mum in *Bridget Jones's Diary*?
29 Which actress is the object of Jude Law's and Joseph Fiennes' affections in *Enemy at the Gates*?
30 What is John Hurt's profession in *Captain Corelli's Mandolin*?

156
PARTNERSHIPS

1 In which 1999 movie were Harvey Keitel and Jennifer Jason Leigh replaced by Tom Cruise and Nicole Kidman?
2 Who did Danny Boyle direct in both *Trainspotting* and *Shallow Grave*?
3 Which director was Geena Davis's third husband?
4 Harvey Keitel is particularly known for his work with which director?
5 How did Joanne Whalley style herself during her 1988–1996 marriage?
6 Marilyn Monroe divorced Arthur Miller a week after the premiere of which movie?
7 Who was Uma Thurman's on- and off-screen partner in *Gattaca*?
8 Fred Quimby was partly responsible for bringing which duo to the big screen?
9 Mimi Rogers was the first wife of which superstar of the 80s and 90s?
10 Which star of *Twins* married John Travolta?
11 Which wife of director James Keach was a Bond girl in *Live and Let Die*?
12 Which star of *The Horse Whisperer* married a French doctor?
13 Who married Danny DeVito during a break on *Cheers*?
14 Which tough guy played opposite Jill Ireland 12 times?
15 What was Abbot and Costello's first feature film?
16 Who played the mother of her daughter Rumer in *Striptease* in 1996?
17 Which brothers appeared in *The Fabulous Baker Boys*?
18 Which wife of Frank Sinatra was Oscar-nominated at the same time as him?
19 Which singer/actress was Mrs Bobby Brown?
20 *Dark Passage* featured which couple?
21 Who married Debbie Reynolds's daughter in 1983?
22 Which director did Rita Hayworth marry?
23 Who was Brad Pitt's on- and off-screen partner while they were making *Se7en*?
24 Vanessa Redgrave's affair with Franco Nero began on the set of which musical movie?
25 What was the name of Mrs Michael Douglas who divorced him in 1995?
26 Lyricist Alan Jay Lerner worked with composer Frederick who?
27 Which family, Lloyd, Jeff and Beau, have stars on Hollywood's Walk of Fame?
28 What is the name of Sherlock Holmes's assistant?
29 Abbott and Costello were a famous double-act but what were their Christian names?
30 Which husband and wife starred in *Who's Afraid of Virginia Woolf*?

  **Answers on page 204**

 Answers on page 204

157
SILENT CINEMA

1 Which comedian performed stunts in *Just Nuts* and *The Freshman*?

2 Who produced the *Keystone Kops* films?

3 Which actress starred in *Modern Times*?

4 About which actress did Kenneth Tynan say, "What one sees in other women drunk, one sees in her sober"?

5 Who was directed by D. W. Griffith in *Birth of a Nation* in 1916?

6 In which film does Rudolph Valentino play a father and his son?

7 Who directed the 1923 version of *The Ten Commandments*?

8 Which 1920 film with Douglas Fairbanks was based on the novel *The Curse of Capistrano*?

9 Who was the star of *The Paleface* in 1922?

10 In which year was the first version of *Ben Hur* made?

11 Which memorabilia were sold at Christie's in 1987 for £82,500?

12 Who was the "It" girl?

13 Who was the only woman in the quartet who founded United Artists?

14 What is Rudolph Valentino's job in *Blood and Sand*?

15 Which 1925 film starred John Gilbert as an American in the war in 1917?

16 Which 1926 film was remade in 1952 with James Cagney and Dan Dailey?

17 Although a silent movie, what did *Way Down East* contain?

18 Who played opposite Chaplin in *The Tramp*?

19 Which actress stars opposite Mack Sennett in *Mack and Mabel*?

20 Who asked D. W. Griffith to make the film *Hearts of the World*?

21 Who was Gaston de Tolignac, screenwriter of *Hearts of the World*?

22 Which English actor/playwright starred in *Hearts of the World*?

23 Who wrote and starred in the 1922 version of *Robin Hood*?

24 Which film about early aviation starred Clara Bow and Gary Cooper?

25 What nationality was the hero Valentino played in *The Four Horsemen of the Apocalypse*?

26 Which two roles did Mary Pickford play in *Little Lord Fauntleroy*?

27 What was Fatty Arbuckle's real first name?

28 Who played the title role in the 1928 version of *Sadie Thompson*?

29 Who won the first-ever Oscar for best actress for *Seventh Heaven*?

30 Where does the action of Buster Keaton's *The Navigator* take place?

 Answers on page 204

158
'50S FILMS

1 James Dean died during the filming of which film in 1955?

2 In which hospital would you find Sir Lancelot Spratt?

3 Who played George III in *Beau Brummell*?

4 Who played the blonde that James Stewart was hired to follow in *Vertigo*?

5 In which '50s film did Sean Connery sing?

6 Which actor wins Christ's robe in a dice game in *The Robe*?

7 Who played the younger Scrooge in the classic with Alistair Sim?

8 Who replaced Astaire for the *Holiday Inn* remake *White Christmas*?

9 Where does the climax of *North by Northwest* take place?

10 What was the second *Carry On* film?

11 What was the only film where Tony Curtis and Cary Grant starred together?

12 Whose voice was dubbed by Marilyn Horne in *Carmen Jones*?

13 Who won Best Supporting Actor for *All About Eve*?

14 Which film was based on *The Tin Star* by John W. Cunningham?

15 Which one-time husband of Elizabeth Taylor produced *Around the World in 80 Days*?

16 What was the second of Brando's four consecutive Oscar nominations for between 1951 and 1954?

17 Who contributed a song for his 1957 film *Fire Down Below*?

18 Ingrid Bergman won a second Oscar for which film, marking her return from Hollywood exile?

19 What was Shirley Maclaine's debut film in 1955?

20 What was the last film Grace Kelly made before becoming a princess?

21 Who played the Pharaoh in *The Ten Commandments*?

22 What was Sidney Poitier's first film, in 1950?

23 *The African Queen*, made in 1951, is about events in which year?

24 What was the first film in which Paul Newman and Joanne Woodward appeared together?

25 Which song did Rita Hayworth famously sing in *Pal Joey*?

26 What was Richard Burton's last UK film before turning to Hollywood?

27 Who won his third Best Director for his third Best Picture in 1959?

28 Which French superstar was the husband of the 1959 Oscar-winning Best Supporting Actress?

29 Who composed and played the music for *Genevieve*?

30 Who was replaced by Betty Hutton in *Annie Get Your Gun*?

 Answers on page 204

159
DISASTER MOVIES

1 What is the body count of *Die Hard 2* said to be?
2 Who played Ellis in *Die Hard*?
3 Who wrote the score for *Airport*?
4 Who directed *The Poseidon Adventure*?
5 Which character is the technical expert responsible for the *Towering Inferno*?
6 Who directed the '50s movie *Invasion USA*?
7 Who produced *Armageddon*?
8 Where does the character Jenny die in *Deep Impact*?
9 What is the occupation of the character played by Bill Paxton in *Titanic*?
10 Which company provided the computer-generated images for *Twister*?
11 Who directed *Apollo 13*?
12 Who plays the grandmother of the Mayor's children in *Dante's Peak*?
13 Within ten minutes, how long does *Towering Inferno* run?
14 Who wrote *Die Hard with a Vengeance*?
15 Who was Oscar-nominated for *Earthquake*?
16 *The Swarm* is based on a novel written by whom?
17 Who directed *Avalanche*?
18 Where is *Daylight* set?
19 Who wrote the score for *Meteor*?
20 Which David featured in *A Night to Remember*?
21 Which actor received an Oscar nomination for *San Francisco*?
22 Who wrote the novel that *The Devil at Four O'Clock* is based on?
23 For what did *Krakatoa, East of Java* receive an Oscar nomination?
24 Upon whose novel is *The Hindenburg* based?
25 Which two studios made the movie based on *The Tower* and *The Glass Inferno*?
26 In which year was the spoof *Disaster Movie* released?
27 What type of disaster occurs in *Dante's Peak*?
28 Which 1996 movie offers a fictional account of the invention of bubble fusion?
29 In what movie does a group of teenagers cheat death by avoiding a plane crash?
30 Who played Jim Scott in the 1997 movie *Danger Zone*?

160
BEST OF BRITISH

1 Which actor from 2005's *The Magic Roundabout* was born in Burnley?
2 For which film did Katharine Hepburn win the first best actress BAFTA?
3 In *Love Actually* what is the name of Rowan Atkinson's jewellery salesman?
4 Who played opposite Dirk Bogarde in *Doctor at Sea*?
5 Who directed *Four Weddings and a Funeral*?
6 Which Ealing comedy was based on Roy Horniman's *Noblesse Oblige*?
7 Which 1984 film was based on *The Death and Life of Dith Pran*?
8 Who was the most prolific writer of *Carry On* scripts?
9 In which film did Maggie Smith call her girls "The crème de la crème"?
10 Which *Carry On* film was (very) loosely based on the Scarlet Pimpernel?
11 In which Alec Guinness film does a bank clerk carry out a bullion robbery?
12 Which 1986 film had "O Mio Babbino Caro" as its theme?
13 In which Boulting Brothers film did Ian Carmichael star as a graduate who starts work in a factory and causes a national strike?
14 Which musical was "the most non-U subject ever to be given a U certificate"?
15 Who directed *Educating Rita* and *Shirley Valentine*?
16 Which British film was the first non-French film to win the prestigious Palme d'Or at the Cannes Film Festival in 1949?
17 In which city does *The Italian Job* take place?
18 On what instrument is the music for the film *Genevieve* played?
19 Who was played by Daniel Day-Lewis in *My Left Foot*?
20 Who played Miss Haversham in David Lean's *Great Expectations*?
21 In which film was Anne Bancroft writing to a London bookseller?
22 What is John Gordon Sinclair called in the credits to *Gregory's Girl*?
23 *The Last Emperor* was a collaboration on film between Britain and which two other countries?
24 In which Will Hay movie does he play a haunted stationmaster?
25 Who plays Peter's father in Kenneth Branagh's *Peter's Friends*?
26 Who starred opposite Cliff Richard in *Summer Holiday*?
27 Which three actors made up the love triangle in *Sunday Bloody Sunday*?
28 What was the alternative title of *Dr Strangelove*?
29 Who turned down the role of T. E. Lawrence in *Lawrence of Arabia*?
30 Which film opens with the dedication "No man's life can be encompassed in one telling"?

 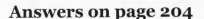 **Answers on page 204**

 Answers on page 204

161
'60S FILMS 2

1 In which '60s film did Richard Attenborough sing?
2 Who became head of production at EMI in 1969?
3 Between which two cities is *The Great Race* set?
4 Who directed the Civil War sequences of *How the West was Won*?
5 Who was Camembert in *Carry On – Don't Lose Your Head*?
6 Who inspired the David Hemmings role in Antonioni's *Blow Up*?
7 What is unusual about Christopher Lee's terrifying role in *Dracula – Prince of Darkness*?
8 What was the sequel to *A Million Years BC*?
9 Who devised the dance routines in *Half a Sixpence*?
10 Who is the only American in *King Rat*?
11 Who was the Doctor in the big screen *Doctor Who and the Daleks*?
12 Which film classic inspired Billy Wilder to make *The Apartment*?
13 Who played Princess Dala in "The Pink Panther"?
14 Who took over directing *Cleopatra* mid way through production?
15 Who was the singing voice of Tony in *West Side Story*?
16 Who wrote the music for *Lawrence of Arabia*?
17 In which film of her father's did Anjelica Huston make her screen debut?
18 Which golf course featured in *Goldfinger*?
19 What was Tracy and Hepburn's final movie together?
20 Which pop star starred in *Rag Doll* in 1960?
21 Which '62 Best Actor studied medicine at the University of California?
22 Who was Oscar-nominated for Pasha in *Doctor Zhivago*?
23 Which '60s Oscar winner was narrated by Michael MacLiammoir?
24 Who killed Ronald Reagan in his last film *The Killers*?
25 Whom did John Wayne play in *North to Alaska*?
26 For which film did Elizabeth Taylor win her second Oscar?
27 For which role was Dustin Hoffman nominated in 1969?
28 Which of the Redgrave clan appeared in *A Man for All Seasons*?
29 Who played opposite his then wife Claire Bloom in *The Illustrated Man*?
30 Who was the older winner of the shared Best Actress Oscar in 1968?

162
TOM CRUISE

1 Star of *Born on the Fourth of July*, when is his birthday?
2 What does he have in common with Robert De Niro and Charlie Chaplin?
3 What is his full real name?
4 What is the name of his character in *Days of Thunder*?
5 Who sang the title song of his first movie?
6 How old was he when he had his first movie role?
7 On which novel was *Taps* based?
8 Which 1999 movie was the last for its director?
9 Who directed him in the 1983 "brat pack" movie with Matt Dillon, Rob Lowe and others?
10 For which movie immediately after *Mission: Impossible* was he Oscar-nominated?
11 Who or what won an Oscar for *Top Gun*?
12 He received his first Oscar nomination for playing which role?
13 With which star of *Risky Business* did he have an off-screen romance?
14 Which 1986 movie won an Oscar for his co-star?
15 What is his job in the film which won his co-star Dustin Hoffman an Oscar?
16 Who was his wife prior to Nicole Kidman?
17 In which part of which state was he born?
18 Where did he spend a year before deciding to become an actor?
19 Which writer whose book a film was based on said, "He's no more my Vampire Lestat than Edward G. Robinson is Rhett Butler"?
20 What "award" did he win at high school?
21 What was his second film?
22 For which TV show did he make his directorial debut?
23 What was his next film after Rain Man?
24 What was the first movie he produced and starred in?
25 What was the first film he starred in with Nicole Kidman after their marriage?
26 Up to 2008, how many Oscar nominations had Tom received?
27 What is the name of his daughter, born in April 2006?
28 Which actress and competitive poker player did Tom marry in 1987?
29 What film studio did Tom and Paula Wagner take control of in 2005?
30 What did Tom train for and aspire to become before taking up a career in movies?

  Answers on page 205

 Answers on page 205

163
HOLLYWOOD HEYDAY

1 Which studio had a lion as its symbol?

2 Why didn't some of the cast of *Gone with the Wind* see its première?

3 Whose roles included characters called McLain, McLintock and McQ?

4 Which future politician was beaten by Elizabeth Taylor for the role of Velvet Brown in *National Velvet*?

5 Who starred with Bergman and Grant in *Notorious*?

6 In which film did Bette Davis play Margo Channingt?

7 How was Ronald Reagan overlooked for a cinematic "White House"?

8 For which film were live leeches imported to Africa?

9 Which artist devised the dream sequence in *Spellbound*?

10 Who was voted king of Hollywood in 1937?

11 Which Astaire-Rogers film had the Oscar-winner *Cheek to Cheek*?

12 What was the first film co-starring Humphrey Bogart and Lauren Bacall?

13 In 1933 who choreographed *42nd Street* in which Ginger Rogers had a lesser role as Anytime Annie?

14 In which film did James Cagney play vaudevillian George M. Cohan?

15 Who was *The Hunchback of Notre Dame* in 1923?

16 Which classic was based on *The Tin Star* by John W. Cunningham?

17 In which movie did Gary Cooper play a farmer who became a war hero?

18 Who played *Mildred Pierce*?

19 Which 1948 classic was described as "Greed, gold and gunplay on a Mexican mountain of malice"?

20 What was Citizen Kane's real first name?

21 What was shown at the beginning of Paramount pictures?

22 Which John Wayne western was described as "'Grand Hotel' on wheels"?

23 What was Cary Grant's real name?

24 Which musical was the first to pair Mickey Rooney and Judy Garland?

25 What were the names of the four Warner Brothers?

26 What is the name of the drunk played by James Stewart in *Harvey*?

27 What did Cary Grant donate his salary from *The Philadelphia Story* to?

28 Which film star's real name was Reginald Truscott-Jones?

29 Which western hero is the subject of *My Darling Clementine*?

30 Which film opens with an office memo including the words "I killed Dietrichson. Me. Walter Neff, insurance salesman, 35 years old…"?

164
MUSICAL MOVIES

1 Who sang the title song of a movie for which Marvin Hamlisch won two 1974 Oscars?

2 Who did Betty Hutton replace in *Annie Get Your Gun*?

3 *Fiddler on the Roof* and which other big musical did Norman Jewison direct in the 1970s?

4 Who was Gene Kelly's co-star in his Hollywood debut?

5 Which character did Debbie Allen play in the movie and TV show about Manhattan's High School for the Performing Arts?

6 For which song from *Lady be Good* did Oscar Hammerstein II win an Oscar?

7 Which novelist, when a Pinkerton detective in real life, investigated the gambling affairs of the man Barbra Streisand married in *Funny Girl*?

8 What was the Hollywood debut of the man born Harold Leek?

9 Who directed Nicole Kidman's first movie after divorcing Tom Cruise?

10 Whom did Miss Olsen fall in love with in the 1970s movie?

11 Where does Tony Manero do his day job in a big 1970s musical?

12 In which city is the song "Do Re Mi" sung in a musical?

13 Who wrote the music for the last Best Oscar-winning song of the 1990s?

14 Who played the male lead in the musical which included "Let's Hear It for the Boy"?

15 Who said, "I am simple, complex, generous, selfish, unattractive, beautiful, lazy, driven"?

16 In which musical do teenagers tune in to Wolfman Jack's rock 'n' roll show?

17 What is the name of the flower shop owner in *Little Shop of Horrors*?

18 Where is the 1983 musical with Jennifer Beals and Michael Nouri set?

19 Who plays the angry young intellectual in *Fiddler on the Roof*?

20 Who played Janet in the musical movie with the song "Dammit Janet"?

21 Who directed and choreographed the original production of *West Side Story* on stage before being involved in the movie?

22 In which state is the movie based on the life of Loretta Lynn set?

23 Which was the first Disney musical of the 1990s to win Best Song Oscar?

24 Who sang "Honeysuckle Rose" in *New York New York*?

25 What won the Best Song Oscar in Julie Andrews' first Oscar-winning film?

26 For which movie did Howard Ashman win his last Oscar in his own lifetime?

27 Which musical film included a psychopathic agricultural worker called Fry?

28 Who directed *Spiceworld: The Movie*?

29 What was Olivia Newton John's surname in *Grease*?

30 What was Jennifer Beals studying while she was making *Flashdance*?

  Answers on page 205

 Answers on page 205

165
MUSIC ON FILM

1. Who composed the score for the 1995 movie *August*?
2. Who wrote the title song for *When the Wind Blows*?
3. Who sang the theme song for *North to Alaska*?
4. Who was Oscar-nominated for music for *The Cider House Rules*?
5. The Oscar-nominated *Save Me* came from which movie?
6. Which three people successively sang the title song in *Someone to Watch Over Me*?
7. In which movie did jazz saxophonist Charlie Barnet play his hit recording of "Cherokee"?
8. For which movie did Bernard Herrmann receive his first Oscar?
9. Who wrote the music for *Lawrence of Arabia*?
10. Which Shostakovich piece was used in *Eyes Wide Shut*?
11. Whose recording of "Why Do Fools Fall in Love" featured on the soundtrack of *American Graffiti*?
12. Who wrote the score for *The Asphalt Jungle*?
13. Who provided the score for *Never on Sunday*?
14. Which music plays in the background in *10*?
15. Whose songs were on the soundtrack of *Philadelphia*?
16. Who wrote the songs for *Lady and the Tramp*?
17. Who was Oscar-nominated for the original score for *The Talented Mr Ripley*?
18. Who contributed a song for his 1957 film *Fire Down Below*?
19. "It Might be You" comes from which movie?
20. Who wrote the songs for Shanghai Surprise?
21. Which famous son appeared as Michael Jackson's friend in *Moonwalker*?
22. *Don't Look Back* is an account of whose tour of Britain?
23. Whose zither music is haunting part of *The Third Man*?
24. Who wrote the score for *Double Indemnity*?
25. Which piece of music accompanies the prehistoric section of *Fantasia*?
26. Which member of Abba had a small role in *Mamma Mia!*?
27. Which city's Philharmonic Orchestra performed the *Lord of the Rings* soundtrack?
28. Name the Argentine who won the Best Music Score Oscar in 2005 and 2006.
29. Can you name the Alfred who has won nine Academy Awards for his music?
30. Who composed the soundtrack for *Casablanca* and *Gone with the Wind*?

166
CHARLIE CHAPLIN

1. In which part of London did Chaplin spend his early life?
2. What was his elder brother and fellow performer called?
3. What did the troupe, the Eight Lancashire Lads, do?
4. With which company did Chaplin travel to the United States in 1910?
5. For which company did Chaplin make his first films?
6. Who played the title role in *The Kid* in 1921?
7. Which film appeared in 1925 and had sound added in 1942?
8. Which wife of Chaplin co-starred in *Modern Times*?
9. How many times did Chaplin marry altogether?
10. Which was Chaplin's first sound film?
11. Whom did he choose to play the young ballerina in *Limelight*?
12. Which type of sound was heard in *City Lights* in 1931?
13. From which film, for which Chaplin wrote the music, did Petula Clark have a with "This is My Song"?
14. Which former silent movie star joined Chaplin in *Limelight*?
15. What is odd about Chaplin's comments on his ex-wife, Lita Grey, in his autobiography?
16. Who was Chaplin's last father-in-law?
17. What was his last wife called?
18. Which film distributing company did Chaplin found with D.W. Griffith, Douglas Fairbanks and Mary Pickford?
19. Who bought the company out in 1940?
20. Which of Chaplin's sons starred with him in *A King in New York*?
21. Which was the last film Chaplin made in the United States?
22. In which split-reel film did the Tramp first appear?
23. Which daughter of Chaplin starred in *Doctor Zhivago*?
24. How did Emil Jannings score over Chaplin in 1929?
25. Where did Chaplin live after being banned from the US in 1953?
26. Which award did Chaplin receive in 1975?
27. What did Chaplin win his Oscar for in *Limelight*?
28. On which day of the year did Chaplin die?
29. What happened on March 2nd the following year?
30. Who played the roles of Chaplin's parents in a 1989 TV series *The Young Chaplin*?

 Answers on page 205

 Answers on page 205

167
'70S FILMS 2

1 What was Sting's debut movie?
2 What was Justin Henry's surname in a 70s Oscar winner?
3 In which film does railwayman Cleavon Little become sheriff?
4 *That's Entertainment* was a compilation of clips from which studio?
5 Who played Siegfried to Simon Ward's James in *All Creatures Great and Small*?
6 Which music plays in the background in *10*?
7 What was Alan Parker's first feature film?
8 Who starred in and produced *The China Syndrome*?
9 What was Tom Selleck's first film, in 1970?
10 Who played Winston's father in *Young Winston*?
11 Whose was the disembodied voice narrating Agatha Christie's *And Then There were None*?
12 Who wrote the music for *Shaft*?
13 Who was the landlord of *10 Rillington Place*?
14 Who sang the title song in *The Aristocats*?
15 For the trailer of which Hitchcock film was the director seen floating in the Thames?
16 Stacy Keach starred in *Fat City* after who turned it down?
17 Who directed *Death Wish*?
18 Who was the first director to cast Goldie Hawn in a non-comedy film?
19 Whom did Jane Fonda play in *Julia*?
20 Why did Peter Finch not collect his Oscar for *Network*?
21 Whose music did Malcolm McDowell like in *A Clockwork Orange*?
22 Who was the only female Oscar winner for *One Flew Over the Cuckoo's Nest*?
23 Who played the editor of the *Washington Post* in *All the President's Men*?
24 Which club features in *Cabaret*?
25 Who played the brother in *The Railway Children*?
26 Who was Maid Marian opposite Sean Connery in *Robin and Marian*?
27 What was the first film in which Julie Christie and Warren Beatty starred together?
28 What was Peter Ustinov's first film as Hercule Poirot?
29 What was the sequel to *Love Story*?
30 Which film of a Frederick Forsyth novel starred Jon Voight?

168
HORROR

1 Which actor was known professionally for a time as Ariztid Olt?
2 What is the name of the island that *The Wicker Man* is set upon?
3 Who played Sam in *The Lost Boys*?
4 What is Peter Vincent's occupation in *Fright Night*?
5 Where does Mitch live in *The Birds*?
6 What was the name of the 1959 sequel to *The Fly*?
7 Where is the action set in '50s classic *The Thing*?
8 Which actor was originally chosen to play Bela Lugosi's role in the 1931 film *Dracula*?
9 Where does Mia Farrow live in *Rosemary's Baby*?
10 Who directed *Night of the Living Dead*?
11 What is the father's occupation in *Poltergeist*?
12 Who directed *A Nightmare on Elm Street 5: The Dream Child*?
13 How is Jason brought back to life in *Friday the Thirteenth Part VI – Jason Lives*?
14 Who receives Gizmo as a gift in *Gremlins*?
15 Which low-budget horror movie did Oliver Stone direct in 1974?
16 Which star of *The Exorcist* is also known by the name Edna Rae?
17 Who starred in *The Final Terror* with then flat-mate Rachel Ward?
18 Who wrote the score for *Jaws*?
19 Within fifteen minutes, how long does *Scream* last?
20 On which day in America did Bram Stoker's *Dracula* open?
21 Who or what plays Thing in *The Addams Family*?
22 What is unusual about Christopher Lee's role in *Dracula – Prince of Darkness*?
23 What creatures were the stars of *Them!*?
24 Who made *The Damned* for Hammer?
25 Who directed *Interview with the Vampire: The Vampire Chronicles*?
26 Who played the vengeful Dr Anton Phibes in two movies?
27 How many Freddy Kruger *Nightmare* movies were there before *Freddy vs. Jason*?
28 Which 1896 Georges Melies movie is credited as being the first horror movie?
29 Who in the 1920s became the first American horror movie star?
30 Name the film studio which produced *Dracula* (1931) and *The Mummy* (1932).

 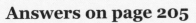 **Answers on page 205**

 Answers on page 205

169
SUPERSTARS

1 In which two films did Paul Newman play "Fast Eddie" Felson?

2 Whom did Tom Cruise play in *Born on the Fourth of July*?

3 Whose first film, for Disney, was called *Napoleon and Samantha*?

4 Who played Sherman McCoy in *Bonfire of the Vanities*?

5 Which two superstars collaborated on the massive flop *Ishtar*?

6 Which film gave Michelle Pfeiffer her first Oscar nomination?

7 Who has been married to Judy Carne and Loni Anderson?

8 For which film did Meryl Streep win her second Oscar?

9 Which role did Kim Basinger play in *Batman* in 1989?

10 Who co-wrote the screenplay for *Yentl* with Barbra Streisand?

11 Which role did Elizabeth Taylor play in *The Flintstones*?

12 What was Disney's first PG movie, which starred Michael J. Fox?

13 Who was the star and executive director of the remake of *The Return of Martin Guerre*?

14 Who won the Best Supporting Actress award for *Cactus Flower*?

15 Who starred with Natalie Wood in *Splendor in the Grass* in 1961?

16 In which film did Jack Lemmon first direct Walter Matthau?

17 In which film did Russell Crowe play the 1994 Nobel Prize for Economics winner?

18 Aged 21, who wrote his autobiography *Absolutely Mahvelous*?

19 Who has played the Boston Strangler and Houdini on screen?

20 Who won an Oscar for playing an Irish cop in *The Untouchables*?

21 Who won an Oscar nomination for her first feature-film role as Robin Williams's mother?

22 Who played Sean Connery's son and Matthew Broderick's father in the same film?

23 Who posed nude covered in paint which looked like a man's suit?

24 Who was the attorney played by Kevin Costner in *JFK*?

25 Whom did Jack Nicholson play in *One Flew Over the Cuckoo's Nest*?

26 Which actor's directorial debut was *Confessions of a Dangerous Mind*?

27 Which actor won Australia's equivalent of an Oscar for *Tim*?

28 Who played Horace Vandergelder in *Hello Dolly!*?

29 Who was the Penguin in *Batman Returns*?

30 Whom did Cher play in Robert Altman's *The Player*?

170
'80S FILMS 2

1 In whose stately home was the Tarzan film *Greystoke* filmed?

2 What was Sharon Stone's first film, in 1980?

3 *Uncle Buck* was the debut of which movie star?

4 May Day was the Bond girl in which film?

5 What was the occupation of Madame Sousatzka in the Shirley Maclaine film?

6 Who had a lead role in the movie version of *Rising Damp* who wasn't in the TV sitcom?

7 Whom did Alan Rickman play in *Die Hard*?

8 Who are the two letter writers in *84 Charing Cross Road*?

9 Which son of a pop star appears as Jackson's friend in *Moonwalker*?

10 In which film did Jack Nicholson say the catchphrase "Here's Johnny"?

11 Who played Mrs La Motta in *Raging Bull*?

12 Which film all but bankrupted United Artists in 1980?

13 Which ailing actor's voice was dubbed by Rich Little in *Curse of the Pink Panther*?

14 Who played Meryl Streep's eccentric friend in *Plenty*?

15 Who won an Oscar for his first major role in 1982?

16 Who was Glenn Close's character in *Dangerous Liaisons*?

17 Which film included the song "It Might be You"?

18 Who was the only Cambodian Oscar winner of the 80s?

19 Who was the only winner of an Oscar and a BAFTA for *Platoon*?

20 Who was nominated as Best Supporting Actress for *The Color Purple*?

21 In the film *A Royal Love Story*, who played Princess Diana?

22 *The Color of Money* re-created the character from which film?

23 Which father and son appeared in *Wall Street*?

24 Which role did Kevin Kline play in *A Fish Called Wanda*?

25 Which presidential candidate's cousin won an Oscar for *Moonstruck*?

26 Apart from Music and Visual Effects, which other Oscar did *E.T.* win?

27 Who directed *Psycho III*?

28 Whose music features on the soundtrack of *When Harry Met Sally*?

29 Whose novel was Warren Beatty's *Reds* based on?

30 Who was the aerobics instructor in *Perfect*?

  Answers on page 205

  Answers on page 205

171
HUMPHREY BOGART

1 What was his middle name?

2 What was the occupation of his father?

3 On which ship was he serving in World War I when he injured his lip, giving him his characteristic tough look?

4 In which short did he make his screen debut?

5 Which reviewer described his acting as "what is usually and mercifully described as inadequate"?

6 How many feature films did he make between 1936 and 1940?

7 Who did he marry after Helen Menken?

8 For which character was he Oscar-nominated in *The Caine Mutiny*?

9 Which studio was he working for at the outbreak of World War II?

10 What was the name of the killer he played in *The Petrified Forest*?

11 Who collaborated with W. R. Burnett to write the hit *High Sierra*?

12 In which Errol Flynn western did he play a Mexican bandit?

13 Who turned down the Sam Spade role in *The Maltese Falcon*?

14 Who insisted he get the screen role in *The Petrified Forest* which he had played on Broadway?

15 In which movie did he play Fred C. Dobbs?

16 In which movie did he say, "I stick my neck out for nobody"?

17 Whose daughter is Philip Marlowe hired to protect in *The Big Sleep*?

18 *The Breaking Point* was a remake of which Bogart movie?

19 Which film starred Bogart in John Huston's directorial debut?

20 Which company did he form in 1947?

21 In which movie did he play Mad Dog Earle?

22 Which of his co-stars said, "There was no bunkum with Bogart"?

23 What was the name of the film released shortly before his death?

24 What role did Mrs Bogart play in *The Big Sleep*?

25 In which movie did he say, "I don't mind if you don't like my manners. I don't like them myself"?

26 How old was Bogart when he died?

27 Who was Bogart's leading lady in *The Barefoot Contessa*?

28 In which movie does Bogart play a gang leader named Rocks Valentine?

29 In which 1947 film noir does Bogart star with Barbara Stanwyck and Alexis Smith?

30 In which film did he win his only Academy Award for Best Actor?

172
TOUGH GUYS

1 Who joined Robert De Niro and Joe Pesci on the poster for *Goodfellas*?

2 Who was lead villain to Clint Eastwood in *For a Few Dollars More*?

3 Which Mel Gibson movie tells of the first major battle of the Vietnam conflict?

4 Who played Goldfinger in 1964?

5 What did Humphrey Bogart study before entering the navy in the World War One?

6 Who was the star of the first four *Police Academy* films?

7 Which tough guy was Judas in Martin Scorsese's *The Last Temptation of Christ*?

8 Who was the violent hustler in *Looking for Mr Goodbar*?

9 Which film gave the real-life tough guy Steve McQueen his first lead role?

10 What was Robert De Niro's role in Scorsese's *Cape Fear* in 1991?

11 Who played Buck Barrow in *Bonnie and Clyde*?

12 Which film gave John Wayne his first Oscar nomination?

13 Who once said, "I look like a quarry that someone has dynamited"?

14 Which movie tough guy started out as a female impersonator?

15 Whose production company was called Malpaso?

16 What were Harrison Ford's first two films as the ex-CIA agent Jack Ryan?

17 Who played the crime boss to Lee Marvin's contract killer in "The Killers"?

18 What was Schwarzenegger's nickname after he won a record seven Mr Olympia titles?

19 Whom did Bogart play in one of his first movies, *The Petrified Forest*?

20 What was the first Martin Scorsese film Robert De Niro appeared in?

21 Who directed Schwarzenegger in the *Terminator* films?

22 For which movie did Rod Steiger win his first Oscar?

23 In which film was Sylvester Stallone a thug threatening Woody Allen?

24 In which 1954 film was Charles Bronson first credited as Charles Bronson?

25 Who was the tough knife-thrower James Coburn played in *The Magnificent Seven*?

26 In which 30s movie did James Cagney push half a grapefruit into Mae West's face?

27 What unusual character did Schwarzenegger play in *Junior*?

28 What was the name of Brando's character in *On the Waterfront*?

29 Whose autobiography was called *The Ragman's Son*?

30 In which film did Stallone first play Rambo?

 Answers on page 206

 Answers on page 206

173
WHO'S WHO?

1 Who said, "You can't get spoiled if you do your own ironing"?

2 How is Edna Gilhooley better known?

3 What was the name of the band Johnny Depp played in before turning to acting?

4 At which university did Richard E. Grant study?

5 In which city was Edward G. Robinson born?

6 Who said he would prefer "animal" on his passport to "actor"?

7 Who said, 'I look like a quarry someone has dynamited'?

8 How is Francoise Sorya Dreyfus better known?

9 Who was dubbed the "80s Errol Flynn" by *Vanity Fair* magazine?

10 Which star actor was born on exactly the same day as the late Laurence Harvey?

11 Who said, 'I stopped making pictures because I don't like taking my clothes off'?

12 Who played Woody Guthrie in *Bound for Glory*?

13 Which director did Theresa Russell marry?

14 Whose marriage to Michelle Phillips lasted just eight days?

15 Which film star wrote the novel *Adieu Volidia*?

16 About which of his co-stars did Anthony Hopkins say, "She's serious about her work but doesn't take herself seriously"?

17 What is Michael J. Fox's middle name?

18 Who starred in *Prom Night* and *Terror Train*?

19 Whom did Harrison Ford replace as Indiana Jones in *Raiders of the Lost Ark*?

20 Which actress's father was one of the Dalai Lama's first American Buddhist monks?

21 Which actor played drums in a band called *Scarlet Pride*?

22 Which actor is Sissy Spacek's cousin?

23 What does Tim Roth have tattooed on his arm?

24 What is Shirley MacLaine's real name?

25 Who played Francis Bacon in *Love Is the Devil*?

26 Maurice Micklewhite was Alfred in *Batman Begins*, but what is his stage name?

27 Paul Newman, who died in 2008, co-owned a motor racing team with whom?

28 Who played *Max Payne* in the 2008 movie of the same name?

29 Name the American actress whose career spanned 75 years, 1912–87.

30 Who was paid $50,000,000 for starring in *What Happens In Vegas*?

174
'90S FILMS 2

1 Which Barry Levinson film was used to satirise the US presidency during the Lewinsky crisis?

2 Who is the subject of *Love is the Devil*?

3 Which tough guy directed *Christmas in Connecticut*?

4 Who died during the filming of *Dark Blood* in 1993?

5 Which war is depicted in *Land and Freedom*?

6 Who was Lyon Gaultier in *AWOL*?

7 In which film did Tom Hanks make his directorial debut?

8 Which film's initial title was "$3,000"?

9 Who or what is Andre in the film of the same name?

10 Who was Leonardo DiCaprio's mother in *This Boy's Life*?

11 Who is Leslie Nielsen in the *Naked Gun* films?

12 What is Jim Carrey's job before he finds the mask in the hit movie?

13 Who was Tinkerbell when Spielberg met JM Barrie?

14 Who was the butler in *Princess Caraboo*?

15 What was director Tony Richardson's final film?

16 Which US presidents does Gump meet in *Forrest Gump*?

17 Who was the voice of Mufasa in *The Lion King*?

18 Muriel is a fan of which band in *Muriel's Wedding*?

19 Whom did Woody Allen cast as his ex-wife in *Deconstructing Harry*?

20 What was Hugh Grant's first Hollywood movie?

21 Who was Oscar winning best screen writer for *Sense and Sensibility*?

22 Who was John Goodman's mother-in-law in *The Flintstones*?

23 What is Macaulay Culkin's full name in the *Home Alone* movies?

24 Who designed The Riddler's costume in *Batman Forever*?

25 Who directed *White Men Can't Jump*?

26 In which film did Kate Winslet have her first nude scene?

27 Who played rat catcher Caesar in *Mousehunt*?

28 Who was the author in *The Muppet Christmas Carol*?

29 Which film was Gary Oldman's directorial debut?

30 In which comic did Sylvester Stallone's '95 futuristic police character appear?

  Answers on page 206

 Answers on page 206

175 AROUND ENGLAND

1 The Severn, the Trent and the Ouse are all what?
2 In which county are all ten of England's highest peaks?
3 Which is the second largest city in England?
4 Which London station was named after a long-reigning Queen?
5 In which county are the seaside resorts of Clacton and Southend?
6 Leeds Castle is in Kent. Where is Leeds?
7 Which seaside resort is famous for its Tower and its Golden Mile?
8 What might you see at Regent's Park, Chester and Whipsnade?
9 What is the name of the famous cathedral in York?
10 Which is the largest island in England?
11 What did Sunderland become in 1992 which Manchester, Liverpool and Birmingham became in the 19th century?
12 Which river runs through London?
13 Which is further north, Southport or Northampton?
14 Which stretch of water divides England and France?
15 What do the letters NEC stand for?
16 What is the area around Stoke-on-Trent known as?
17 Which northern city is served by Ringway airport?
18 Which motorway starts south of Birmingham and goes northwest towards Scotland?
19 Which part of the country would a Geordie come from?
20 Near which large city would you find the Wirral?
21 Which two cities are the home of England's two oldest universities?
22 Which range of northern hills is called the backbone of England?
23 Which moorland area of southwest Devon is the site of a high-security prison?
24 What were Dagenham, Luton and Cowley famous for producing?
25 Where would a Manx person come from?
26 Which famous stones can be seen on Salisbury Plain?
27 Whose birthplace might you be visiting in Stratford-on-Avon?
28 In which county is the English terminal of the Channel Tunnel?
29 How many square miles is the City of London?
30 Which was England's smallest county before the 1974 changes?

176 AROUND THE UK

1 Is Holy Island off the east or west coast of England?
2 What is a native of Aberdeen called?
3 Is London's Docklands, north, south, east or west of the city?
4 The Angel of the North was erected next to which major road?
5 Which English gorge takes its name from a nearby village famous for its cheese?
6 Which county has the abbreviation Beds?
7 St Anne's lies to the south of which British seaside resort?
8 Which Royal residence stands by the river Dee?
9 In which country is the UK's highest mountain?
10 What sort of an institution in London is Bart's?
11 On a London Tube map the Central Line is what colour?
12 In which Scottish city did you find the Gorbals?
13 Which motorway links London to Winchester?
14 Which Isle off the south coast of England is a county in its own right?
15 What is Britain's most southerly country?
16 Norwich is the administrative centre of which county?
17 In which city did the National Trust buy the childhood home of Paul McCartney?
18 Which motorway runs almost parallel to the A4?
19 With which profession is London's Harley Street associated?
20 What is Britain's largest international airport?
21 In which county is Land's End?
22 What colour are most London buses?
23 Which motorway goes from Lancashire to Yorkshire east to west?
24 What is the background colour of road signs to tourist sites?
25 In which part of the UK is "Land of My Fathers" a traditional song?
26 Winchester is the adminstrative seat of which county?
27 Aston University is near which Midlands city?
28 Most of the Lake District is in which county?
29 What red flower does Lancs have?
30 In which city is the Barbican Centre?

  Answers on page 206

 Answers on page 206

177
AROUND THE WORLD

1 The Bay of Biscay lies to the north of which country?
2 Which Gulf lies between Iran and Saudi Arabia?
3 Brittany is part of which country?
4 Which US city is known by its initials LA?
5 Which South American country shares its name with a nut?
6 Near which large city is the Wirral?
7 Which is Britain's most southerly point on the mainland?
8 In which country is Shanghai?
9 In which county is Lake Windermere?
10 To which country does the island of Bermuda belong?
11 What is the northernmost town in England?
12 Is San Francisco on the east or west coast of the USA?
13 Which Union was Ukraine once part of?
14 In which country is Zurich?
15 In which country is the holiday destination of Bali?
16 Which island lies to the south of India?
17 In which country would you hear the language Afrikaans?
18 Which group of islands does Gran Canaria belong to?
19 Where would you be if you had climbed Mount Olympus?
20 In which US state is Orlando?
21 Which Ocean is to the west of Portugal?
22 In which country is The Hague?
23 Monte Carlo is in which principality?
24 Which US state has the Arctic Circle running through it?
25 Which Land in Denmark is made up of bricks?
26 Which Falls are on the Canadian/US border?
27 Which country's women might wear a kimono?
28 Which Ocean's name means peaceful?
29 Which country originally produced Peugeot cars?
30 What is the English for what the French call an autoroute?

178
AROUND THE WORLD 2

1 Is Australia in the northern or the southern hemisphere?
2 What does each star on the flag of the United States stand for?
3 Which country does the holiday island of Ibiza belong to?
4 Which island would you visit to kiss the Blarney Stone?
5 In which country would you be if you were visiting the Taj Mahal?
6 The south of which continent is closest to the Falkland Islands?
7 In which mountain range would you find Mount Everest?
8 Which country is Luxembourg the capital of?
9 What colour is the spot in the middle of the Japanese flag?
10 The island of Sicily is at the toe of which country?
11 Which country is also known as the Netherlands?
12 In which country are Maoris the indigenous population?
13 In which Scandinavian country would you find fjords?
14 Which country's languages include English, Zulu and Afrikaans?
15 Which country's name could be part of a Christmas dinner?
16 In which city is the Vatican City?
17 What is K2?
18 In which country is the Yellow River, also known as Huang He?
19 Which country has four letters, the last one q?
20 Which country, capital Bangkok, used to be called Siam?
21 Which ocean lies between Europe and America?
22 Which European country has an area called Flanders?
23 Which stretch of water separates Anglesey and Wales?
24 Which Rock is on the south coast of Spain?
25 Which isle lies between England and Northern Ireland?
26 Which island to the south of India used to be called Ceylon?
27 Which sea separates Europe and Africa?
28 In which ocean is Fiji?
29 Which island, in the Arctic Ocean, is the largest in the world?
30 In which continent is the world's longest river, the Nile?

 Answers on page 206

 Answers on page 206

179 AROUND EUROPE

1 In which country would you find Jerez?
2 How would you travel if you left for France from a hoverport?
3 In which Sea is the island of Majorca?
4 In which country is Cologne?
5 Does London or Rome have the higher population?
6 The province of Flanders is in which country?
7 Which landlocked country is divided into cantons?
8 In which city would you find the Parthenon?
9 Bohemia is part of which Republic, formerly part of Czechoslovakia?
10 Is Schiphol an airport or a river in the Netherlands?
11 Which island is in the Bay of Naples?
12 Where is the Black Forest?
13 What type of country is Monaco?
14 Andorra lies between France and which other country?
15 In which Sea does Cyprus lie?
16 Belarus and Ukraine were formerly part of which huge republic?
17 What is the English name for the city known to Italians as Venezia?
18 Is Sweden a kingdom or a republic?
19 Vienna lies on which river?
20 Is Ibiza part of the Canaries or the Balearics?
21 In which Circle does about a third of Finland lie?
22 The Hague is the seat of government of which country?
23 Crete and Corfu belong to which country?
24 Which Scandinavian country is opposite Norway and Sweden?
25 Is Europe the second largest or the second smallest continent?
26 Which country marks the most westerly point of mainland Europe?
27 The Iberian Peninsula consists of Portugal and which other country?
28 Which French city is mainland Europe's largest?
29 What are the Balkans, the Apennines and the Pyrenees?
30 Which island is known to the French as Corse?

180 HOLIDAY DESTINATIONS

1 The holiday island of Ibiza belongs to which country?
2 Which European country popular with Brits has the rivers Guadiana and Tagos?
3 In which ocean is Fiji?
4 Is Tasmania to the north or south of Australia?
5 Majorca is part of which island group?
6 In which country is Vigo airport?
7 What is the principal seaside resort of the North Norfolk coast?
8 What name is given to America's most westerly time zone?
9 On which European island is the beach of Mazzaro?
10 The resort of Kuta is on which island – Bali or Malta?
11 What colour flag is awarded to quality beaches in Europe?
12 On which island is North Front airport?
13 The Californian coast fronts which ocean?
14 Which island are you on if you visit Mellieha?
15 In Australia, which state is commonly called the "Sunshine State"?
16 Tenerife is part of which island group?
17 In which country is the much-visited Saumur Castle?
18 The Isle of Tiree is part of which country?
19 In which country is Luxor airport?
20 Did *Captain Corelli's Mandolin* feature a Greek island or an Italian one?
21 What is another name for Tonga?
22 Which famous surfing beach is on the outskirts of Sydney?
23 Ludwig II built a fairytale style castle situated in which European country?
24 What is the largest city of Hawaii?
25 Which Italian island has a famous Blue Grotto?
26 The beautiful city of Florence stands on which river?
27 What is the oldest and largest city in Australia?
28 Salina Bay is on which island?
29 In which country would you find the capital city of Ankara?
30 Which US state are you visiting if you are in Miami?

 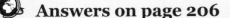 **Answers on page 206**

 Answers on page 206

181
AROUND SCOTLAND

1 Is Dundee on the east or west coast of Scotland?

2 Which is the most northerly point on the British mainland?

3 Which city is Scotland's capital?

4 Are Scottish banknotes legal tender in England?

5 Who built a wall to divide Scotland from England?

6 Where is the Royal and Ancient Golf Club?

7 The name of which Scottish product means "water of life"?

8 Where is the Queen's Scottish residence?

9 What is the name of the Games held at Braemar?

10 Which sport is Aviemore particularly famous for?

11 What are the Cairngorms?

12 Which east coast port is known as the Granite City?

13 Which islands give their name to ponies and wool?

14 In which Loch is there said to be a monster?

15 Which Isle was linked to the mainland by a bridge in 1995?

16 Which Mull was the title of a song by Paul McCartney?

17 Which river flows through Glasgow?

18 Which city holds an annual Arts Festival?

19 Which speciality's ingredients include sheep's stomach and oatmeal?

20 Which village was a popular destination for runaway couples?

21 What does the word "loch" mean?

22 What is Scotland's highest mountain?

23 Which city gives its name to a rich fruit cake?

24 Which city shares its name with a city in Australia?

25 Which river in the Borders gives its name to a woollen fabric?

26 Which sea is to the east of the Scottish mainland?

27 What is a glen?

28 In which city is Hampden Park Stadium?

29 Which is further north, Edinburgh or Dundee?

30 Who is Scotland's patron saint?

182
ON THE MAP

1 Which language other than English is an official language of the Channel Islands?

2 In which country did Saddam Hussein's 2005–06 trial take place?

3 You would find Delphi on a map of which country?

4 Which is further North, Clacton or Brighton?

5 Which continent has an Ivory Coast?

6 On which island would you find the Giant's Causeway?

7 If you were on a French autoroute what type of road would you be on?

8 Which Gulf lies between Saudi Arabia and Iran?

9 Lake Superior is on the border of the USA and which other country?

10 Which tiny European landlocked state is a Grand Duchy?

11 Macedonia was formerly a part of which communist republic?

12 Which Himalayan kingdom has been called the world's highest rubbish dump because of waste left behind by climbers?

13 Which Australasian capital shares its name with a Duke and a boot?

14 Which river which flows through Germany is Europe's dirtiest?

15 Where would you be if you saw Nippon on the map?

16 Whose address is often referred to as Number Ten?

17 Which motorway goes past Stoke on Trent?

18 On which continent is the Basque country?

19 The Home Counties surround which city?

20 Malta is to the south of which island to the south of Italy?

21 The Ural Mountains mark the eastern frontier to which continent?

22 How is the London Orbital Motorway better known?

23 Is Moldova in Europe or Africa?

24 Which island republic lies to the north west of the UK?

25 Miami is a port in which US state?

26 Kew Gardens are next to which London river?

27 Which country has Lakes Garda, Maggiore and Como?

28 Is Madagascar an island or is it an African peninsula?

29 In which city is Red Square?

30 Which country's official languages are Hebrew and Arabic?

  Answers on page 207

  Answers on page 207

183
AROUND IRELAND

1 Which is the main river of Dublin?
2 Which village with a shrine is found in Co. Mayo?
3 What sort of building was the focal point of the Easter Rising?
4 Which river is famous for Tara, home of the Kings of Ireland?
5 Which ocean does Cork border?
6 Which river flows through Belfast?
7 Blarney Castle is in which county?
8 Which shellfish does Dublin give its name to?
9 How many Irish counties are bigger than Co. Cork?
10 What is Ireland's biggest Lough?
11 Which famous 9th-century book is in Trinity College?
12 Which M is the county where Trim Castle is situated?
13 Which C is the river on which Galway stands?
14 Which city of Co. Londonderry is on the river Foyle?
15 Which leader has a home in Phoenix Park?
16 Which freshwater food fish is Lough Conn famous for?
17 Grafton Street is most famous for what?
18 What are the most famous mountains of County Down?
19 Donegal is famous for which fabric?
20 Is Larne to the north or south of Belfast?
21 Which Merseyside city is Dublin linked to by ferry?
22 Are the Aran Islands in the Atlantic or the Irish Sea?
23 Which K is Ireland's only inland city?
24 In which city is Crumlin Road gaol?
25 Which E is the county town of Fermanagh?
26 Armagh, the Orchard County, is known for which fruit?
27 Which is Dublin's main thoroughfare?
28 Which river S has a tidal estuary in Limerick?
29 In which Dublin street is St Patrick's Cathedral?
30 Is Dromore Castle in the north or south of Ireland?

184
AROUND THE WORLD 3

1 In which Swiss mountain range is the Jungfrau?
2 Which is the next largest island in the world after Australia?
3 Which seaside resort is Super-Mare?
4 On which continent is the Kariba Dam?
5 What are Lakes Michigan, Superior, Huron, Erie and Ontario known as collectively?
6 If the southern limit of the tropics is Capricorn what is the northern limit called?
7 Which island is to the south of Australia?
8 In the south of which country was Saigon?
9 If you were in Benidorm in which country would you be?
10 Which London palace has a maze?
11 Which isle off the west coast of England has three legs as its symbol?
12 Which country is connected to Wales by the Severn Bridge?
13 Which US state is a collection of islands in the Pacific?
14 Which language do natives of Hamburg speak?
15 Which county has a red rose as its symbol?
16 Which Queen gave her name to the capital of Hong Kong?
17 Which Bank is made of sand in the North Sea?
18 In which county is Penzance?
19 Which islands are Sark and Alderney part of?
20 Greece is in which continent?
21 What are the counties of Essex, Suffolk, Norfolk and Cambridgeshire collectively known as?
22 Is Japan in the northern or the southern hemisphere?
23 What is the name of the biggest Canyon in Arizona?
24 The London Eye was built by which river?
25 Is the Arctic Circle near the north or the south pole?
26 On the south of which continent are the Andes?
27 If you were looking at the Ganges which country would you be in?
28 Which country do the Scilly Isles belong to?
29 Which country originally produced Fiat cars?
30 What is the most westerly point of England?

  Answers on page 207

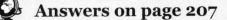 **Answers on page 207**

185
AROUND THE WORLD 4

1 Which long river has White and Blue tributaries?
2 Which religious leader is head of state of the Vatican?
3 Is Perth on the west or east coast of Australia?
4 Which country was the centre of operations for the Taliban?
5 Does Bombay or Tokyo have the higher population?
6 What sort of Snowman is another name for the Himalayan yeti?
7 What is the world's smallest, flattest and driest continent?
8 Is Argentina in the northern or southern half of South America?
9 Pakistan and Bangladesh both border which country?
10 Which country's name is an anagram of PURE?
11 The West Indies lie in which Sea?
12 Zambia is a neighbour of which country which also begins with Z?
13 Which Egyptian canal links the Red Sea and the Mediterranean?
14 Is Ghana on the African coast or wholly inland?
15 Which ocean is the world's deepest?
16 In which country is the homeland of KwaZulu?
17 Who is commemorated at Washington's Lincoln Memorial?
18 Which US state has the zipcode (postcode) AZ?
19 New South Wales is in which country?
20 Which African desert is the world's largest?
21 Is Swaziland a monarchy or a republic?
22 Mount Kilimanjaro is the highest point of which continent?
23 Which river runs through Belgrade, Budapest and Vienna?
24 Which ocean lies to the east of South America?
25 Which Islamic Republic used to be called Persia?
26 Two-thirds of Greenland lies in which Circle?
27 Is Namibia in northern or southern Africa?
28 In which country in Europe could you spend a forint?
29 Which People's Republic has the world's largest population?
30 Alberta is a province of which country?

186
ON THE MAP 2

1 If you were in France and crossed La Manche, where would you be?
2 In Scotland what does Ben mean in a place name?
3 Which Somerset city has a Spa railway station?
4 Which Canal links the Mediterranean and the Red Sea?
5 In which London street is the Chancellor of the Exchequer's official residence?
6 In which continent is the Hoover Dam?
7 In which city is England's oldest cathedral?
8 What do the Isle of Ely and the Isle of Dogs have in common?
9 In which city is the University of East Anglia?
10 By which letter and number is Mount Godwin-Austen known?
11 Which war memorial is in Whitehall?
12 Which country has the international vehicle registration letter B?
13 Which capital city stands on the Potomac river?
14 Which Australian rock is sacred to the aborigines?
15 The capital of Nova Scotia shares its name with which Yorkshire town?
16 Which German city hosted the 1972 Olympics?
17 What was man-made and stretches from Tyne and Wear to Cumbria?
18 On the London Underground what colour is the Central Line?
19 Glamis Castle was the childhood home of which late royal?
20 Which continent is the iciest?
21 Which Australian state is made up of three words?
22 In which country is Mount Fuji?
23 On which island is the volcanic Mount Etna?
24 In which area of the UK is the Black Country?
25 On which river are the Niagara Falls?
26 In which city would you find the Champs Elysées?
27 What does A stand for in the Middle Eastern UAE?
28 In which country is the port of Rotterdam?
29 Which of the Cinque Ports shares its name with a snack food?
30 Which European Sea's name means "Middle of the earth"?

  Answers on page 207

 Answers on page 207

187
AROUND WALES

1 What is Wales' highest mountain?

2 Which Welshman wrote *Portrait of the Artist as a Young Dog*?

3 Which Sea is to the north of Wales?

4 What are the Brecon Beacons?

5 Which island lies off the north west coast of Wales?

6 Which spring flower is a Welsh emblem?

7 What is the capital of Wales?

8 Which Channel is to the south of Wales?

9 Is Caernarvon Castle in the north or south of Wales?

10 Caerphilly is a town and also what type of food?

11 Which creature of legend is seen on the Welsh flag?

12 Which city in the south of the country is its second largest?

13 Which sport is played at Cardiff Arms Park?

14 Which wild cat gives its name to a Bay on Cardiff's quayside?

15 The production of which fuel affected the Welsh landscape until its decline in recent years?

16 Who was invested as Prince of Wales in 1969 at Caernarvon Castle?

17 Which vegetable is a Welsh emblem?

18 Which country lies to the east of Wales?

19 Who is the patron saint of Wales?

20 What is the mountainous area around Snowdon called?

21 Which Welsh Bay shares its name with a woollen jacket?

22 Which is the only Welsh county to have a first-class cricket team?

23 What is the currency of Wales?

24 Wales has the highest density in the world of which farm animal?

25 Which Welsh Secretary challenged John Major for the Tory Party leadership in the summer of 1995?

26 Which county is further north, Clwyd or Gwent?

27 Which Strait separates Anglesey from the mainland?

28 Which North Wales university town shares its name with a resort of Northern Ireland?

29 The UK's longest river rises in Wales. What is it called?

30 Which town is further south, Aberystwyth or Swansea?

188
AROUND THE UK 2

1 Is Aberdeen to the north or south of Glasgow?

2 Prestwick and Gatwick are both what?

3 The Dales are mainly in which county?

4 On which Devon moor is there a famous prison?

5 Denbighshire is in the north of which country?

6 Who is London's Downing Street's most famous resident?

7 What is the capital of Scotland's Dumfries and Galloway region?

8 Which of Eastbourne, Esher and Eccles is on the coast?

9 In London, Richmond is on which river?

10 In which county is Rutland Water?

11 Where in the UK is Armagh?

12 Dorchester is the county town of which county?

13 Salford is part of which city?

14 Who has their HQ at Scotland Yard?

15 Sherwood Forest is associated with which historical hero?

16 Which food item is associated with London's Smithfield market?

17 Durham is in which part of England?

18 What is Eton's most famous institution?

19 Who has a home at Sandringham?

20 What is the highest mountain in Snowdonia National Park?

21 Which S in central London is an area associated with clubs and nightlife?

22 In which county is Stansted airport?

23 The resort of Aberystwyth is on which coast of Britain?

24 Dudley in the West Midlands is near which major city?

25 Ealing is an area of which city?

26 What is the Savoy in London as well as a theatre?

27 Prince William chose to go to St Andrews university in which part of the UK?

28 What is Salisbury's most famous building?

29 Who are trained at Sandhurst?

30 Who would you be watching if you went to the JJB Stadium?

  **Answers on page 207**

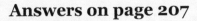 **Answers on page 207**

189
AROUND EUROPE 2

1 Reykjavik is the capital of which country?
2 Which is farther south – Corsica or Sardinia?
3 Which river runs through Belgrade, Budapest and Vienna?
4 Which Peter spent a Year in Provence?
5 The Acropolis overlooks which capital city?
6 Which is the highest mountain in the Alps?
7 Do the stripes go horizontally or vertically on the Austrian flag?
8 Belgium's coast touches which sea?
9 What is the currency of Greece?
10 Which capital takes its name from a prince of Troy?
11 Which ocean is Europe's northern boundary?
12 Which mountains divide Spain from France?
13 Ankara is the capital of which country?
14 What is the currency of Denmark?
15 Which tiny European country has the European Court of Justice?
16 Which two colours make up the Greek flag?
17 Nero fiddled while which city burned?
18 Which of the three Baltic states of the former USSR does not begin with L?
19 What is the tourist area of southern Portugal called?
20 What is the capital of Malta?
21 Which mountains are Europe's eastern boundary?
22 What is the currency of Austria?
23 The Black Forest is a mountain range in which country?
24 Which country has the regions Lazio and Calabria?
25 What is the colour of the middle of the French flag?
26 Which Sea is Europe's southern boundary?
27 Which two major European rivers begin with R?
28 What would an English-speaking person call Bretagne?
29 Sofia is the capital of which country?
30 Which country has the markka or finnmark as its currency?

190
AROUND THE WORLD 5

1 Which country can you easily walk to from Gibraltar?
2 Urdu is an important language in which two Asian countries?
3 Which is England's most northerly county?
4 What did Bejing used to be called?
5 Which is the Queen's London home?
6 In which European country is Salzburg?
7 Which county divides Cornwall from Somerset?
8 What "colour" is the Sea between Egypt and Saudi Arabia?
9 In which county is the Peak District?
10 In which country is the resort of Rimini?
11 Madagascar is to the east of which continent?
12 Is California on the east or west coast of the USA?
13 Which is the nearest country to the Falkland Islands?
14 Near which French city is the Disney Theme Park?
15 In which country is the Algarve?
16 Which is further west, Algeria or Ethiopia?
17 What is the highest point in England?
18 In which country is the county of Tayside?
19 Which Scandinavian capital begins and ends with the same letter?
20 Chad is in which continent?
21 What is Holland also known as?
22 In which US holiday state is Miami?
23 Which country is divided from Spain by the Pyrenees?
24 What is the largest city in the West Midlands?
25 Which town of Tyne and Wear shares its name with the US capital?
26 The Philippines are in which Ocean?
27 What is the largest country of South America?
28 In which continent is Slovenia?
29 Which country originally produced Volvo cars?
30 In which country do most Flemish speakers live?

  Answers on page 207

 Answers on page 207

191 AROUND EUROPE 3

1 In which Irish city is the Abbey Theatre?
2 What is the official language of Denmark?
3 What do the British call what the French call Dunkerque?
4 Dun Laoghaire is the port for which Irish city?
5 Rhodes is an island belonging to which country?
6 The Riviera is on the French/Italian coast on which sea?
7 St Moritz is famous for what type of sports?
8 St Peter's Basilica is in which Italian city?
9 Faro, or the Algarve, is in which country?
10 Rimini is a resort of the Adriatic in which country?
11 The Seine reaches the sea from which country?
12 Slovakia was formerly part of which country?
13 In which French city is the university called the Sorbonne?
14 Which European country is made up of cantons?
15 What are the Alps?
16 County Sligo is on which coast of Ireland?
17 Catalonia, Andalusia and Valencia are parts of which country?
18 The French town of Le Mans hosts what type of race?
19 Which Irish county has given its name to a comic rhyme?
20 Which German city is known locally as München?
21 In which country was the Academie Française founded?
22 Which city do the Portuguese call Lisboa?
23 Which city is also known locally as Bruxelles?
24 Which city replaced Bonn as Germany's capital?
25 Where would you have spent pesetas?
26 In which country are baguettes and brioches traditional breads?
27 Which country beginning with H is to the east of Austria?
28 The Shannon is which country's chief river?
29 Lapland is nearest to which ocean?
30 In which part of Europe is the Baltic Sea?

192 AROUND THE WORLD 6

1 Which islands share their name with Richard Branson's airline?
2 Which country beginning with S borders the east of France?
3 Dallas is in which US oil state?
4 What does the Dead Sea taste of?
5 Ecuador is on which continent?
6 In which US city is the Empire State Building?
7 What is another name for Inuit?
8 What is the nickname for the Rocky Mountains?
9 Algeria is to the north of which continent?
10 Which city comprises Old Delhi and New Delhi?
11 What is the official language of Russia?
12 In Spanish it's Rio de las Amazonas, what is it in English?
13 What name did Zimbabwe have in the 1960s?
14 Saudi Arabia is famous for producing which fuel?
15 The Sioux are a native tribe of which continent?
16 Scandinavia is in which continent?
17 Which continent is the next largest after Asia?
18 Soweto is a suburb of Johannesburg in which country?
19 In which harbour is the Statue of Liberty?
20 What type of waterway is at Suez?
21 Gran Canaria is in which islands?
22 What describes the famous Beach resort in California where the *Queen Mary* was brought?
23 Los Angeles suffers from a severe smog problem due to a high percentage of which vehicles?
24 Which is the only US state to begin with L?
25 Aborigines are from which Commonwealth country?
26 In which part of the USA is Alaska?
27 Quebec is a French-speaking part of which country?
28 Which of the following used to be called the Ivory Coast – Cote d'Ivoire, Gold Coast or Rhodesia?
29 What is Australia's largest city?
30 On which continent is Swahili spoken?

  **Answers on page 208**

 Answers on page 208

193
AROUND IRELAND 2

1 Which river runs through Dublin?

2 In which Irish county are the Mountains of Morne?

3 Which Sea is to the east of the Island of Ireland?

4 What is the capital city of Northern Ireland?

5 What sort of jewelled Isle is Ireland often called?

6 Which plant is the Irish emblem?

7 What is the capital of the Republic of Ireland?

8 In which Irish city is Queens University?

9 Which Irish town gives its name to a saucy rhyme?

10 Spell the Irish version of the drink the Scots call whisky.

11 Which Ocean is to the west of Ireland?

12 What are Ireland's two official languages?

13 Which type of glass is Waterford famous for?

14 Which Irish flute player James shares his name with a Bay ?

15 Which stone is kissed to receive the gift of smooth talking?

16 Which county shares its name with a fictional TV doctor?

17 Which sport is the Curragh famous for?

18 Which fabric made from flax is Ireland famous for?

19 Who is the patron saint of Ireland?

20 What do you put into Gaelic coffee apart from coffee?

21 Which fabric is Donegal famous for?

22 Is Belfast on the east or the west of the province?

23 What do the towns of Dun Laoghaire and Rosslare have in common?

24 O'Connell Street is which Irish city's main street?

25 How would you be travelling if you arrived at Shannon from abroad?

26 Which is further north, Belfast or Londonderry?

27 Which Irish town sounds like something in a wine bottle neck?

28 Which Causeway is said to have been built as a bridge from Ireland to Scotland?

29 Which stout is Dublin world-famous for?

30 What are the international registration letters for Ireland?

194
AROUND THE WORLD 7

1 The capital of Western Australia shares its name with which Scottish city?

2 How is Peking now more commonly known?

3 In which country would you see an emu fly?

4 Is French Provence nearer the Channel or the Mediterranean?

5 In which country do people speak Afrikaans?

6 Which bay to the west of France is notorious for its rough seas?

7 What is the principal language of Bulgaria?

8 If you were visiting the home of Parmesan cheese, in which country would you be?

9 Which country used to be called the DDR?

10 In which city is the Wailing Wall?

11 Is the Orinoco in North or South America?

12 How many consonants are there in Mississippi?

13 Which country has the international vehicle registration letter I?

14 Which major town of Morocco shares its name with a famous film?

15 In which country is Bavaria?

16 Which drug is Colombia's chief export?

17 On which long African river is the Aswan Dam?

18 Which Spanish city hosted the 1992 Olympics?

19 In which city is the University of Essex?

20 An Indian city gave its name to which style of riding breeches?

21 Andorra lies between which two countries?

22 Which country's national sport is Sumo wrestling?

23 The Cape of Good Hope is at the tip of which continent?

24 Which city has the cathedrals of Notre Dame and Sacre Coeur?

25 Which falls lie on the Zambesi river?

26 Which US state, capital Phoenix, is called the Grand Canyon state?

27 Which Baltic state has Tallinn as its capital?

28 Which is the only country in the world to begin with Q?

29 In which continent is Mount McKinley?

30 Which currency would you spend in Pakistan?

  Answers on page 208

  Answers on page 208

195
AROUND THE WORLD 8

1 Which country has the internet suffix .at?
2 Which wind blows from the Sahara to southern Italy?
3 Which Canadian island has Victoria as its capital?
4 Which country has the time zones Eastern, Central, Mountain and Pacific?
5 In which ocean are the Maldives?
6 Which US state is known as the Lone Star State?
7 In which country is Cotopaxi, the world's highest volcano?
8 How do the Argentinians refer to the Falkland Islands?
9 What is the USA's oldest educational institution called?
10 What did the Mason Dixon Line divide in the USA?
11 Which country has most neighbouring countries?
12 The Keys are islands off which US state?
13 Darwin is the capital of which Australian state?
14 Which river flows over the Victoria Falls?
15 Which two territories joined together to form Tanzania?
16 On which river are Quebec and Montreal?
17 Where are the US gold reserves?
18 In which country is the Mekong Delta?
19 Which capital is on the Moskva river?
20 Which river divides the USA and Mexico?
21 Where is Madison Square Garden?
22 How was Botswana known immediately prior to independence?
23 In which country is the world's highest waterfall?
24 Which US island was a registration point for immigrants until 1954?
25 Which of the world's highest mountains between India and China is not in the Himalayas?
26 How is Byzantium and Constantinople now known?
27 What is the second largest state of the US?
28 Tierra del Fuego is off which country?
29 Fuerteventura is in which island group?
30 Which is the highest mountain in North America?

196
AROUND THE WORLD 9

1 Baffin Island is between Baffin Bay and which island?
2 Bali is a mountainous island of which country?
3 The Falkland Islands are off which country?
4 Which US state is dubbed the Golden State?
5 Helsinki is on which Gulf?
6 Which city, also the name of a film, has the world's largest mosque?
7 How many islands make up Fiji?
8 Baku is the capital of which country on the Caspian Sea?
9 Where is the Forbidden City?
10 The Barbary Coast is the Mediterranean coast of where?
11 Which Egyptian city is Africa's largest city?
12 Greenwich Village is in which borough of New York City?
13 On which river is Ho Chi Minh City?
14 Where is Waikiki Beach?
15 Baghdad is on which river?
16 In which borough of New York City is Coney island?
17 In which mountains is the volcanic Cotopaxi?
18 Where are the Roaring Forties?
19 Which strait separates Australia from Tasmania?
20 What special sound is made in the language of the Hottentots of southwest Africa?
21 Which country was formerly the Dutch East Indies?
22 Which city gave its name to a type of riding breeches?
23 What is South Africa's largest city?
24 In which ocean are the Bahamas?
25 Which part of New York was named after Jonas Bronck?
26 The holy city of Qom is in which country?
27 Which country is between Nicaragua and Panama?
28 K2 is on the border of Pakistan and which country?
29 In which ocean are the Comoros?
30 Which is the most easterly of the Windward Islands in the Caribbean?

  Answers on page 208

 Answers on page 208

197 ON THE MAP 4

1 On which island is the holiday resort of Kuta?

2 What is the fault in San Francisco called?

3 What is the world's longest mountain range?

4 What is the third largest US state after Alaska and Texas?

5 Which country has IS as its international registration letters?

6 Where is Transylvania?

7 What is a sea containing many islands called?

8 What colour is the Bakerloo line on the London Underground map?

9 Which West Indian island has an active volcano named Soufrière?

10 What is the capital of Tasmania?

11 In Austria what is the Grossglockner?

12 Where are Waverley and Haymarket stations?

13 Where is the administrative HQ of Hampshire?

14 How was British Honduras subsequently known?

15 On which river is the Kariba Dam?

16 Herm is one of which group of islands?

17 Which South American country was named after Venice?

18 What is the capital of the US state of Ohio?

19 In which East Anglian town is the Greene King brewery based?

20 Which of the Cinque Ports has six letters in its name?

21 Which country has the longest coastline?

22 How is London Cathedral now known?

23 Which 77-acre site was founded at Kensal Green in London in 1832?

24 What is the largest country in Africa?

25 Which of the divisions of Yorkshire has the largest perimeter?

26 Which Square is in front of the Palace of Westminster?

27 After the Lake District which is England's largest National Park?

28 Which country of the British Isles has the largest county in terms of area?

29 What are the smallest units of local government in rural areas?

30 On which river does Sheffield stand?

198 AROUND THE UNITED STATES

1 Little Rock is the capital of which US state?

2 On which granite cliff are the faces of four presidents carved?

3 Which language is the first language of 6% of the population?

4 Which natural disaster is the San Andreas Fault prone to?

5 What does DC stand for in Washington DC?

6 In which city is the University of Virginia located?

7 In which state is the Grand Canyon?

8 What are a group of six states on the northeast coast known as collectively?

9 Which Kander and Ebb musical was set in a city in Illinois?

10 Which was the first of the original 13 states of the United States?

11 Where is the main space exploration centre in Florida?

12 In which city is almost half of the population of Illinois to be found?

13 How long is the motor race which Indianapolis is famous for?

14 Which town is famous for its jazz music?

15 Which mountainous forest state has a settlement of Crow Indians?

16 What is traditionally easily available in Reno?

17 In which city is La Guardia airport?

18 Which US state has the highest population?

19 Which two New York boroughs begin with B?

20 Key West and Key Largo are off the coast of which state?

21 Which US state used to be called the Sandwich Islands?

22 Which New York street is famous for its fashion stores?

23 The name of which state has four letters, the first and last the same?

24 The discovery of what in 1848 led to the expansion of California?

25 Kansas is the United States' chief producer of which grain?

26 Which Michigan town is famous for the production of motor vehicles?

27 Which New York borough is noted for its skyscraper skyline?

28 Other than White Americans what is the largest racial group on Hawaii?

29 Which US state is the title of a musical by Rodgers and Hammerstein?

30 Which city, the capital of Tennessee, is famous for its music?

  Answers on page 208

  Answers on page 208

199
AROUND EUROPE 4

1 In which city is the largest Christian church in the world?
2 What is the official home of the French President?
3 On which island is Ajaccio?
4 What is the French town of Limoges famous for?
5 Which part of Paris is famous as the artists' quarter?
6 Where is the European Court of Justice?
7 Ibiza and Majorca are part of which island group?
8 The Oise and the Marne are tributaries of which river?
9 Where is the Abbey Theatre?
10 What is Germany's highest mountain?
11 On which river does Florence stand?
12 Which Mediterranean island was the HQ of the Knights of St John?
13 Which country has most European neighbours?
14 The RER is part of which city's underground system?
15 The Azores belong to which European country?
16 How many Benelux countries are there?
17 Andorra is among which mountains?
18 Piraeus is the port of which city?
19 In which country is Lake Garda?
20 Where does the river Loire flow into the Atlantic?
21 In which central European country is Lake Balaton?
22 Which country do the Faeroe Islands belong to?
23 The Skagerrak links the Kattegat with which Sea?
24 Which country's official name is Konungariket Sverige?
25 The parliament of which country is called the Cortes?
26 Ljubljana is the capital of which country of the former Yugoslavia?
27 Which Republic lies between Poland and Hungary?
28 Utrecht is in which European country?
29 Where is Monegasque spoken?
30 Which is the southernmost and largest of Greece's many islands?

200
POP-MUSIC PLACES

1 Where is Sixties rock venue Eel Pie Island located?
2 Which Asian country provided Kim Wilde with a 1980s hit?
3 Which US state links with "Dreamin'" and "Girls" in song titles?
4 Which city did Scott McKenzie sing about in the 1967 summer of love?
5 Which city was the title of a Simple Minds EP in 1989?
6 Which geographical group had China, Tokyo and Cantonese in chart titles?
7 Who had a 1960s hit with "Do You Know the Way to San Jose?"?
8 Which city has given hit songs to Frank Sinatra, Gerard Kenny and Sting?
9 Who was in "Africa" in 1983?
10 Which female pop superstar sang about "Nutbush"?
11 Which Roger was "Leavin' Durham Town" in the 1960s?
12 "Wichita Lineman" and "Galveston" provided hits for which Glen?
13 Green Day made the top-selling 2004 album about what kind of "Idiot"?
14 In which Russian city was Michael Jackson a "Stranger" in 1996?
15 Which Queen was a hit for Billy Ocean?
16 Which popular New Jersey band made the popular album "New Jersey"?
17 Which US city links Elton John and Bruce Springsteen in song?
18 Which tropical paradise was the subject of a David Essex hit?
19 Which US state and river was a 1970s hit for Pussycat?
20 Who were "All the Way from Memphis" in 1973?
21 "London Calling" was a hit for which group?
22 How many hours was Gene Pitney away from Tulsa?
23 Which singer did Peter Kay aid on his way to "Amarillo"?
24 Which US state was the title of a Stereophonics 2005 ?
25 One-hit wonders Typically Tropical were going to which island?
26 In which city is "Penny Lane"?
27 Who had the 1990s hit version of "Don't Cry for Me Argentina"?
28 Which superstar declared he was "Made in England"?
29 Which G was the state on the mind of the late, great Ray Charles?
30 Who made the mega-selling "Born in the USA"?

  **Answers on page 208**

 Answers on page 208

201
AROUND THE UK 3

1 How many faces has the clock on Big Ben's tower?

2 In which port were Dickens and Brunel both born?

3 In which London building is the Lord Mayor's banquet held?

4 Which Womble was named after the town on the Isle of Mull?

5 Which Channel Island is famous for having no cars?

6 Where is Beaumaris Castle?

7 Girton and Newnham are colleges of which university?

8 Where in London is the Lutine Bell?

9 Bryher is part of which islands?

10 Which Hills divide England and Scotland?

11 Cumbernauld is near which British city?

12 Which Sea joins the St George's Channel and the North Channel?

13 In which county is Chequers, the Prime Minister's country residence?

14 What is England's second largest cathedral?

15 Which Firth lies between south-west Scotland and north-west England?

16 Where is The Cathedral Church of St Michael, consecrated in 1962?

17 Which Leicestershire town is famous for its pork pies?

18 What are the canals in Cambridge called?

19 In which county is the southern end of the Pennine Way?

20 Which Roman road shares its name with a type of fur?

21 What is ERNIE's original home town?

22 What is the high-security prison on the Isle of Wight called?

23 In which London Square is the US Embassy?

24 Which disaster does London's Monument commemorate?

25 Which waterway divides the Isle of Wight from the mainland?

26 Which castle has St George's Chapel?

27 What is the nearest seaside resort to London?

28 Where in London are there gates named after Margaret Thatcher?

29 Which theatre was founded in 1959 at Blackfriars in London?

30 Dogger Bank is off which English county?

202
AROUND THE UK 4

1 In London, which famous cathedral is near to the Barbican?

2 Where is the National Exhibition Centre?

3 Which Cross is at the west end of The Strand?

4 Cheddar is in which hills?

5 In which Essex town was Anglia University established?

6 Which area of London is famous for its Dogs' Home?

7 The Bristol Channel is an extension of which river?

8 Where is the University of Kent's main campus?

9 In which season would you see Blackpool's famous illuminations?

10 What is the name of Chesterfield's church with the famous twisted spire?

11 The Cheviot Hills run into which countries?

12 Barrow-in-Furness is on which county's coast?

13 In which county is the Prime Minister's country home?

14 What was Cleveland's county town?

15 On which island is Fingal's Cave?

16 The National Motor Museum is near which stately home?

17 Clydebank was famous for which industry?

18 In which county is the Forest of Dean?

19 What is Antony Gormley's famous sculpture near Gateshead?

20 What is London's second airport?

21 Which racecourse exclusively for flat racing is near Chichester?

22 Which city of south-west England was known to the Romans as Aqua Sulis?

23 In which part of London is the Natural History Museum?

24 Where did the Yvonne Arnaud theatre open in 1965?

25 Where in England is the Scott Polar Research Institute?

26 What is Hull's full name?

27 Which town of north-east Scotland is a terminus of the Caledonian Canal?

28 In which London borough is the National Maritime Museum?

29 What is the UK's electronic surveillance service at Cheltenham called?

30 In which London street are the offices of the Bank of England?

 Answers on page 209

 Answers on page 209

203
AROUND AUSTRALIA

1 Which city with 3 million inhabitants is Australia's largest?

2 What is the name of the world's longest reef?

3 Which sacred rock is the world's largest monolith?

4 What is the capital of Australia?

5 Which two oceans are to the east and west of Australia?

6 What is the name of the surfing beach on the outskirts of Sydney?

7 Darwin is the capital of which state?

8 At which famous east coast bay did James Cook arrive in April 1770?

9 Which meandering river is Brisbane built around?

10 Which state is commonly called the Sunshine State?

11 Perth is the capital of which Australian state?

12 Which mountain range to the west of Sydney was partly destroyed by bush fires in December 1993?

13 Which is the nearest major town to the southwest of Ayers Rock?

14 What is the capital of the state of Victoria?

15 Which granite formation, formed by the wind, is to the east of Perth?

16 What is the coastline to the south of Brisbane called?

17 Which national park, known for its Aboriginal rock paintings and wildlife, lies to the east of Darwin?

18 Which "village in the rainforest" at the highest end of the Barron Gorge is the home to the only permanent Aboriginal theatre in Australia?

19 What is the world's largest sand island northeast of Brisbane?

20 What is Queensland's most northerly city?

21 Which mountain range runs parallel to the east coast for 4000 kilometres?

22 Which famous surfing beach is to the south of Brisbane?

23 Where does the rainforest meet the sea in northern Queensland?

24 Which state capital lies on the Swan River?

25 Which range of domed mountains lies in Purnululu National Park?

26 Along the Great Ocean Road in Victoria what 12 off-coast formations would you discover?

27 Which mountain, at 1611 metres, is the highest in Queensland?

28 Which Australian city hosted its final Formula 1 race in 1995?

29 Which fossilized remains of an ancient forest are found in the Nambung?

30 Which cape is at the northernmost tip of Australia in Queensland?

204
AROUND EUROPE 5

1 In which county is Bantry Bay in the south of Ireland?

2 What is Italy's Capodimonte famous for?

3 In which city is the Pompidou Centre?

4 Which island is called Kefallinia in Greek?

5 From which resort at the foot of Mont Blanc does the highest cable car in the world rise?

6 What do the British call what the French call Les Iles Normands?

7 Which province of the Irish Republic includes Galway and Sligo?

8 The Amalienborg Palace is the home of which Royal Family?

9 Which Scandinavian country is called Suomi in its own language?

10 The Baltic states are made up of Latvia, Lithuania and where?

11 What is Germany's Schwarzwald?

12 Which monument is at the opposite end of Paris's Champs Elysées from the Place de la Concorde?

13 Where was a refugee camp built for asylum-seekers near the Channel Tunnel?

14 Where is the park called the Bois de Boulogne?

15 What is the capital of the state of the Tyrol?

16 Ithaca is off the west coast of which country?

17 Which Scandinavian strait has a name which means cat's throat?

18 In which Sea are the Balearic Islands?

19 Which breed of dog comes from Kerry in south-west Ireland?

20 In which city is the Prado art gallery?

21 Which town of Lombardy gave its name to a bright reddish mauve dye?

22 What is the Bourse in Paris?

23 On which Sea is Odessa?

24 Which country has the rivers Douro, Tagus and Guadiana?

25 What is the chief city of Catalonia, and Spain's second largest?

26 Which is the farthest north, Belarus, Ukraine or Estonia?

27 What was St Petersburg called for much of the 20th century?

28 Which Sea is to the west of Denmark?

29 Which is the most easterly city, Stuttgart, Munich or Hanover?

30 The Basque country surrounds which mountains?

  **Answers on page 209**

 Answers on page 209

205
AROUND SCOTLAND 2

1 Edradour is the smallest what in Scotland?

2 Which famous Scottish writer lived at Abbotsford by the Tweed?

3 In which direction from Edinburgh do the Pentland Hills lie?

4 What is Berwick Law?

5 What is the Bass Rock famous as?

6 Which cathedral is also known as the High Kirk of Edinburgh?

7 Rothesay is the chief town of which island?

8 What is at the foot of the Royal Mile in Edinburgh?

9 Which city is at the mouth of the rivers Don and Dee?

10 What is produced at Torness?

11 How many bridges are there over the Firth of Forth?

12 What lies between Charlotte Square and St Andrew's Square?

13 Where was the childhood home of the Queen Mother?

14 What is the industrial area in and around Livingston nicknamed?

15 Which canal links the lochs of the Great Glen?

16 Which historic island is off the southwest tip of the Isle of Mull?

17 What is the name of Edinburgh's stadium where the Commonwealth Games have been held?

18 Which rail bridge is the longest in Europe?

19 Which famous whisky is made at Blair Athol?

20 Which baronial castle is the seat of the only British subject allowed to maintain his own private army?

21 What is the most famous cave on Staffa?

22 Which palace was once the site of a famous coronation stone?

23 Which loch contains the largest volume of fresh water in the British Isles?

24 Which city is often called the Fair City?

25 Leanach farmhouse can be seen on which moorland field of battle?

26 On which river does Balmoral stand?

27 Remains of what type of building are at Kelso and Jedburgh?

28 What type of village can be seen at Skara Brae?

29 Which loch is the largest stretch of inland water in Britain?

30 Where is Scotland's largest malt whisky distillery?

206
AROUND THE WORLD 10

1 The Sargasso Sea is part of which ocean?

2 Which US city's name means "The Fields"?

3 How is New York's "Great White Way" also known?

4 Which Canadians speak Inuktitut?

5 Which Cape was originally called the Cape of Storms?

6 In America what type of natural phenomenon is a Chinook?

7 What is the principal island of Japan?

8 Where is the town of Kurri Kurri?

9 The Guangzhou TV & Sightseeing Tower was constructed in which country?

10 By which abbreviation is the mountain Chogori known?

11 What is the only permanent river in the Kalahari desert?

12 Which Ocean's deepest point is the Java Trench?

13 Where would you be if someone put a lei round your neck?

14 Where is the world's longest canal?

15 Afrikaans is the official language of which country in addition to South Africa?

16 In which desert is the Bactrian camel found?

17 What is the name of the index on the New York Stock Exchange?

18 Which group of people have a name meaning "eater of raw meat"?

19 Which is the only Great Lake wholly in the USA?

20 The Kariba Dam is on the border of which two countries?

21 Calypso is the traditional song form of which Caribbean island?

22 Which European language is spoken in Chad?

23 Las Palmas is in which island group?

24 Approximately where was Carthage to be found?

25 Wall Street and Broadway lie on which island?

26 Where is the Magellan Strait?

27 What is the largest island between the North Atlantic and the Arctic?

28 What is Africa's highest volcano?

29 Where is there a Parliament called the Knesset?

30 Which two countries does the Khyber Pass separate?

  Answers on page 209

Answers on page 209

207
AROUND ASIA

1 Which country has been officially called Myanmar since 1989?
2 Which country is made up of over 800 islands including Viti Levu?
3 Which desert covers part of China and Mongolia?
4 What title does the head of state of Nepal have?
5 Which 7000-island country lies in the Pacific, northeast of the South China Sea?
6 How is the Republic of China better known?
7 To which country does East Timor belong?
8 Which neighbouring countries' currency is the won?
9 What was the name of Bangladesh between 1947 and 1972?
10 In which country are the Cameron Highlands?
11 What are the majority of the islands of Micronesia composed of?
12 Which country is bordered by Laos, Vietnam and Thailand?
13 Which sea lies to the north of Iran?
14 What is Japan's highest mountain?
15 How many vowels are there in Kyrgyzstan?
16 Which country's official name in Hindi is Bharat?
17 What are China's famous "warriors" made from?
18 Which country's capital is Ulan Bator?
19 In which two countries is the Thar desert?
20 Which social system is divided into brahmins, ksatriyas vaisyas and sundras?
21 Where were Gurkhas originally from?
22 Which area of Russia has had the lowest temperatures in the world recorded there?
23 When *The Sound of Music* was shown in Korea what was missing?
24 What are the Seychelles' three official languages?
25 What is the capital of Singapore?
26 Which country's flag is a red circle on a green background?
27 Which Pacific islands share their name with a wise man in the Bible?
28 What did Ho Chi Minh City used to be called?
29 Which country has designated Chachoengsao as its new capital?
30 How many rivers does Tonga have?

208
ON THE MAP 5

1 Which South American city has a famous Copacabana beach?
2 The Bass Strait divides which two islands?
3 Which Middle East capital is known locally as El Qahira?
4 Where is the official country home of US Presidents?
5 Whose Vineyard is an island off Cape Cod?
6 Where was Checkpoint Charlie?
7 Which US state has a "pan handle" separating the Atlantic from the Gulf of Mexico?
8 In which two countries is the Dead Sea?
9 The site of ancient Babylon is now in which country?
10 On which river is the Aswan Dam?
11 The Trump International Hotel & Tower was built where in the USA?
12 The Fens were formerly a bay of which Sea?
13 What is Japan's highest peak?
14 To which country do the Galapagos Islands belong?
15 Aconcagua is an extinct volcano in which mountain range?
16 Where in California is the lowest point of the western hemisphere?
17 In which London Square is the US Embassy?
18 Ellis Island is in which harbour?
19 Which city is known to Afrikaners as Kaapstad?
20 On which Sea is the Gaza Strip?
21 What are the three divisions of Glamorgan?
22 Which river cuts through the Grand Canyon?
23 Where in India are Anjuna beach and Morjim beach?
24 Which continents are separated by the Dardanelles?
25 Which US state capital means "sheltered bay" in Hawaiian?
26 Hampstead is part of which London borough?
27 Which country owns the southernmost part of South America?
28 Where is the seat of the UN International Court of Justice?
29 The Golan Heights are on the border of which two countries?
30 Which is the saltiest of the main oceans?

  **Answers on page 209**

  Answers on page 209

209
AROUND AFRICA

1 The names of which two African countries begin with the letter Z?

2 What covers 85% of Algeria?

3 Famine in which country triggered the Band Aid Charity?

4 What do the initials OAU stand for?

5 Of which country is Ouagadougou the capital?

6 What is the Harmattan?

7 Which is further west, Uganda or Kenya?

8 Which country used to be called South West Africa?

9 Which substance, used to make a drink, is Ghana's main export?

10 Which lake lies between Kenya, Tanzania and Uganda?

11 What is Africa's highest mountain?

12 Which European language is an official language of Angola?

13 In which African country is El Alamein, scene of a World War II battle?

14 Which country is the main economic power in West Africa?

15 Which country is further north, Rwanda or Burundi?

16 Which language is Afrikaans derived from?

17 Near which major landmark is the Boiling Pot?

18 What is the area of savanna in West Africa called?

19 South Africa is the world's leading exporter of what?

20 Which Moroccan city is the name of a famous film?

21 The Kalahari Desert lies chiefly in which country?

22 What is the largest country in Africa?

23 What is the Okavango Swamp famous for?

24 In which country are the political parties ANC and Inkatha?

25 Which African country is the tiger native to?

26 Which man-made structures would you see at Aswan and Kariba?

27 Does most of Africa lie to the north or to the south of the Equator?

28 Which country occupies the Horn of Africa?

29 Which sound is unique to many African languages including Xhosa?

30 What is the administrative capital of South Africa?

210
AROUND ENGLAND 2

1 Which county did Huntingdonshire become part of in 1974?

2 What is High Wycombe famous for manufacturing?

3 Which atomic energy establishment used to be called Windscale?

4 Which two London boroughs begin with E?

5 Which seaside resort is on the Fylde?

6 What is the low-lying area of East Anglia called?

7 Which city was a Roman fortress called Deva and retains its medieval walls?

8 How many tunnels under the Mersey link Liverpool to the Wirral?

9 In which northern city is the National Railway Museum?

10 The Ribble is the chief river of which county?

11 In which city is the University of East Anglia?

12 Which county is Thomas Hardy associated with?

13 Which part of Oxford was famous for motor car manufacture?

14 Which Devon port has a famous Hoe?

15 Which county is also known as Salop?

16 Which Isle has Needles off its west coast?

17 Where would you find the 18th-century Assembly Rooms and Royal Crescent?

18 Which county does not exist: North, South, East or West Yorkshire?

19 In which town is the shopping complex, the Metro Centre?

20 Where would you find the Backs and the Bridge of Sighs?

21 Alphabetically what is the last county?

22 In which Metropolitan county are Trafford and Tameside?

23 In which National Park is Scafell Pike?

24 On which bank of the Thames is the City of London?

25 In which town is the modernist De La Warr Pavilion to be found?

26 Which city is served by John Lennon Airport?

27 Which county lies between the North Sea and Greater London?

28 What is Lindisfarne also known as?

29 In which county is Hadrian's Wall?

30 From which London station are there trains direct to the continent through the Channel Tunnel?

  Answers on page 209

 Answers on page 209

211
AROUND IRELAND 2

1 How many wheels does a jaunting car have?
2 On what would you see Ogham writing?
3 Which of two kinds of wood can a shillelagh be made from?
4 In which city was the Maze Prison?
5 Which is Ireland's chief river?
6 Which lake is the British Isles' largest?
7 What is the mine at Navan famous for?
8 What are the columns of the Giant's Causeway made from?
9 What is the county town of Fermanagh?
10 Which mountains stretch from Carlingford Lough to Dundrum Bay?
11 Which county's Irish name is Corcaigh?
12 What is Dublin's most famous theatre called?
13 What are the highest uplands in Ireland?
14 What is the name of the fertile vale in Limerick?
15 Which two of the counties of Northern Ireland begin with A?
16 What is Belfast's university called?
17 What are Slieve Donard and Slieve Commedagh?
18 Whose Saint's day is celebrated on 2nd February?
19 If you bought the *RTE Guide* what information would you receive?
20 In the early years of this millennium what was banned from pubs in Ireland?
21 Which is further north, Waterford or Cork?
22 What are the quartzite mountains in Connemara called?
23 What are drumlins?
24 What did Laoighis used to be called?
25 Which province of southeast Ireland includes the counties of Wexford and Wicklow?
26 What is St Ann's Shaldon Church famous for?
27 Which three counties of the Republic of Ireland begin with K?
28 Which county do Westlife come from?
29 Which university is at Coleraine?
30 Which three places in Northern Ireland may officially use the title "city"?

212
AROUND EUROPE 6

1 What are the three Baltic states?
2 In which country does the Douro reach the Atlantic?
3 What is the capital of Catalonia?
4 What is Northern Ireland's chief non-edible agricultural product?
5 What do the Germans call Bavaria?
6 Which European capital stands on the river Liffey?
7 What is the Eiffel Tower made from?
8 How is the Danish region of Jylland known in English?
9 In which forest does the Danube rise?
10 Which was the first country to legalise voluntary euthanasia?
11 What covers most of Finland?
12 In which country is the world's highest dam?
13 What is the capital of the Ukraine?
14 What is a remarkable feature of the caves at Lascaux in SW France?
15 What is Europe's highest capital city?
16 Where is France's Tomb of the Unknown Soldier?
17 Which area of the Rhone delta is famous for its nature reserve?
18 In which country would you find Kerkyra?
19 What are the two official European languages of Luxembourg?
20 The Magyars are the largest ethnic group of which country?
21 Where is Castilian an official language?
22 Abruzzi is a mountainous region of which country?
23 Which is the largest of the Balearic Islands?
24 On which island was the Mafia founded?
25 What is the UK's chief Atlantic port?
26 Tallinn is the capital of which Baltic state?
27 What is the main religion of Albania?
28 In which country would you meet Walloons?
29 In which country was the Millau Viaduct built?
30 Which country has Larisa and Volos amongst its chief towns?

  Answers on page 210

 Answers on page 210

213
AROUND EUROPE 7

1 Which country's capital is Tirana?
2 Where is a passion play staged every ten years?
3 Which state was Macedonia part of from 1945 to 1991?
4 Which island holds the George Cross?
5 Which country's highest mountain is the Grossglockner?
6 Which countries are on the Iberian Peninsula?
7 Where is the Netherlands' seat of government and administration?
8 What are the Dardanelles and where are they?
9 Which southern German city is famous for its October beer festival?
10 Which country is called Elleniki Dimokratia or Hellenic Republic?
11 Which country's chief river is the Po?
12 Which country, whose capital is Vaduz, has no armed forces?
13 Which sea lies to the north of Poland?
14 In which four countries are the Alps?
15 Which country covers 10% of the globe's land surface?
16 By what English name is Köln known?
17 Which country's landscape is made up of volcanoes and geysers?
18 Between which countries does the Skagerrak lie?
19 What are Bessarabia, Moldavia and a former part of the USSR now known as?
20 Which country has had a prime minister called Wim Kok?
21 Albert II became king of which country in 1993?
22 A region of eastern France has a girl's name with another girl's name as its capital. What are they?
23 Which country do Greenland and the Faeroe Islands belong to?
24 What is France's highest point?
25 Whose upper house of Parliament is called the Bundesrat?
26 Which country's currency is the lev?
27 What are the two official languages of Finland?
28 Which aid organization's emblem is the Swiss flag with its colours reversed?
29 Which Portuguese province borders Spain and the Atlantic Ocean?
30 Which is Europe's largest country after Russia?

214
AROUND THE UK 5

1 Which seaside resort has Lanes and a nudist beach?
2 Which Page Three blonde is Swindon's most famous export?
3 In which part of London is the Natural History Museum?
4 Where is the National Spinal Injuries Unit?
5 In which county is Sizewell nuclear power station?
6 What is Britain's longest tunnel?
7 The Old Bailey is on the site of which former prison?
8 Where in London would a Canary sit on Dogs?
9 What is a native of Shropshire called?
10 What is Salisbury Plain primarily used for?
11 In which two counties is Constable Country?
12 Where is the Clifton Suspension Bridge?
13 Spaghetti Junction is on which road?
14 Which Somerset town is said to be the burial place of King Arthur?
15 Which bell was named after Benjamin Hall?
16 Which pleasure beach was the UK's top tourist attraction in 2005?
17 What was the former name of Sellafield?
18 Which animals are kept in the Royal Mews near Buckingham Palace?
19 Holy Loch is an inlet of which river?
20 Which city has an annual Goose Fair?
21 In which English county is Europe's largest stone circle?
22 Which castle is at the west end of the Royal Mile?
23 How is the Sunday market in London's Middlesex Street better known?
24 Which Cambridgeshire hospital is famous for its transplant surgery?
25 Speaker's Corner is on the corner of what?
26 Where is the administrative headquarters of the Grampian region?
27 Which city has a famous Royal Crescent?
28 The Goodwin Sands are at the entrance to which straits?
29 What type of historic structures can be found at Framlingham, Orford and Windsor?
30 Where is Temple Meads railway station?

 Answers on page 210

 Answers on page 210

215 WORLD TOUR

1 Allegheny and Blue Ridge are in which mountain range?
2 Where is the N'Gorongoro Crater?
3 The Commonwealth of Australia set up in 1901 comprised two territories and how many states?
4 Flores, Corvo and Pico belong to which group of islands?
5 Which city had a street called the Bowery?
6 Who links the Cenotaph in London and New Delhi?
7 What do the straits of Magellan separate?
8 On which river does Adelaide stand?
9 What is the capital of the Canadian province Manitoba?
10 Fagatogo is the capital of what?
11 What are the three volcanic islands of the British Virgin Islands?
12 Avarua is on which of the Cook Islands?
13 What are the Monte Titano peaks made from?
14 Who owns Bouvet Island?
15 How many official languages does South Africa have?
16 In which country is the largest expanse of sand in the world?
17 The Fouta Djallon mountains are to the south of which country?
18 On which river does Nashville stand?
19 Lake Kivu forms much of the western boundary of which country?
20 What is the former name of Nizhny Novgorod?
21 Where is the Kara-Kum Desert?
22 Doi Inthanon is the highest point of which country?
23 What is the capital of Anguilla?
24 Where is the largest phosphate deposit in the world?
25 Flying Fish Cove is on which island?
26 Which country lies between Guyana and French Guiana?
27 What does the Nile split into at Khartoum?
28 Aruba is off which country's coast?
29 Which islands were annexed to the Clunies-Ross family until 1978?
30 In the US which state is immediately west of Colorado?

216 WHAT IN THE WORLD?

1 What was the name of the first storm to be given a name?
2 Which volcanic rock is named after a mountain range in South America?
3 What is our Solar System's nearest stellar neighbour?
4 Which Asian country has the greatest area of inland water?
5 What is the highest waterfall in Norway?
6 What is the next largest body in the Solar System after Venus?
7 What is the largest lake in the UK after Neagh?
8 In which US state is the Mammoth cave system?
9 What is V4641 Sgr?
10 What was the first asteroid to be discovered?
11 Where was the meteorite Hoba West found?
12 What is the world's highest island after New Guinea?
13 What is the name of the nearest planetary nebula to the Earth?
14 What percentage of the sky does the smallest constellation take up?
15 Which of the following is the brightest – Rigel, Sirius or Vega?
16 What was the second planet to have been visited by a spacecraft?
17 On which island is the Aceh province that was devastated by the 2004 tsunami?
18 Which state along with Texas and Nebraska is known as Tornado Alley?
19 About how many million years did the longest ice age last?
20 Which planet has the longest day in the solar system?
21 Which element discovered in 1931 is the rarest on Earth?
22 What is the defined visibility of a sea fog?
23 Which nebula is brightest in the night sky?
24 In which constellation is Procyon?
25 In which constellation is the Hyades cluster?
26 At which university is the McDonald Observatory?
27 Where was the meteorite Rowton found?
28 Which Asian Sea is the deepest?
29 From which country was the Andromeda Galaxy first observed?
30 After Pluto which is the next furthest body from the Sun?

  Answers on page 210

 Answers on page 210

217
EURO TOUR

1 The Croatian currency kuna is divided into 100 what?
2 On which river does Berlin stand?
3 Which three major Spanish international airports begin with "V"?
4 Miskoic and Debrecen are major towns in which country?
5 Where was the World Council of Churches established in 1948?
6 Which country's official name is Republika e Shqipërisë?
7 What is Europe's lowest point below sea level?
8 On which river does the capital city of Croatia stand?
9 Who are the two heads of state of Andorra?
10 What is the capital of Saxony?
11 Which country has Letzeburgish as its most widely used language?
12 What is Europe's highest waterfall called?
13 Where is the European Investment Bank?
14 In which country has Alfred Moisiu been President?
15 What are the only armed forces in Monaco?
16 The Aland Islands belong to which country?
17 Which is the most northerly capital city in the world?
18 The Glomma is one of the principal rivers of which country?
19 Which three French regions begin with A?
20 Which country's highest point is Rysys?
21 Which has the greater area, Iceland or Ireland?
22 What is San Marino's second-largest town?
23 Where is Ulemiste Airport?
24 Which is farther north, Moscow or Copenhagen?
25 Where was the UN peacekeeping mission UNPROFOR in force?
26 What is Belgium's highest point?
27 On which river does Amsterdam stand?
28 Other than Denmark where is Danish currency used?
29 Where is Italy's principal stock exchange?
30 Gozo and Comino are to the north west of which island?

218
WHAT ON EARTH?

1 In which US state is the Jewel cave system?
2 The largest man-made excavation in the world mines which element?
3 Which animal weighs the most – grizzly bear, polar bear or a walrus?
4 What is Europe's largest island which is not a country in its own right?
5 Which desert is on the US–Mexico border?
6 What is the most common element in the earth's crust after oxygen?
7 Which planet orbits the Sun fastest?
8 Acid rain results due to a pollution of the atmosphere with oxides of nitrogen and what?
9 What is another name for a tsunami?
10 What colour is apatite?
11 Where was the meteorite High Possil found?
12 Where is the highest waterfall outside South America?
13 What is the world's highest island?
14 How many states does Lake Michigan cover?
15 Which planet has the hottest surface?
16 Orogenesis is concerned with the formation of what?
17 Which unit measures distances beyond the solar system?
18 Where was the meteorite Armanty found on Earth?
19 Actinobiology studies the effect of what on living organisms?
20 Cryogenics studies materials under what conditions?
21 Of the five largest glaciers in the world which is the only one not in Antarctica?
22 Which part of planet Earth would a pedologist observe?
23 The Appleton layer plays a role in what – heat control, sifting of toxic gases or radio communication?
24 It isn't a sea, but what is the Afsluidijk Sea?
25 How many countries does the Mekong river flow through?
26 What is the most common element in the universe after hydrogen?
27 Which planet is the lightest?
28 Which scale measures the hardness of substances?
29 How many light years is Alpha Centauri from the Earth?
30 What substance is around 90% of the Earth's core made from?

  Answers on page 210

 Answers on page 210

219
AROUND THE UK 6

1 What is the highest peak in Scotland after Ben Nevis?
2 Where is the Whitworth Art Gallery?
3 On which river does Dumfries stand?
4 Where is the James Clerk Maxwell Telescope?
5 Which town has the car index mark AA?
6 Where is Dyce Airport?
7 Which Lough is in the centre of the Sperrin, Antrim and Mourne ranges?
8 Where is the National Library of Wales?
9 Which town's football ground is farthest away from any other?
10 Which English city has the first Jain temple in the western world?
11 In which county was there a £59 million robbery in February 2006?
12 What is Cambridge's county-class cricket ground called?
13 Which Milton Keynes theatre is named after a politician who was also a famous politician's wife?
14 How many bridges span the Tyne at Newcastle?
15 What was Scotland's capital in the 11th–15th centuries?
16 Where is Pontefract racecourse?
17 What is the longest river in Wales?
18 On which river does Winchester stand?
19 On which tube line is London's longest tunnel?
20 Which is farther north, Leeds or Halifax?
21 Where is Jurby Ronaldsway airport?
22 Where is the University College of North Wales?
23 Which town has a Theatre Royal and a Gardner Centre?
24 What is Bolton's theatre called?
25 Where is Queen of the South Football Club?
26 What are Edinburgh's two oldest universities called?
27 Which is farther east, Middlesbrough or York?
28 What is Oxford's county-class cricket ground called?
29 Where is the Royal and Ancient Golf Club?
30 On which river does Colchester stand?

220
AROUND THE WORLD 11

1 Which is further north – St Lucia or St Vincent?
2 Where was the world's largest shopping centre opened in 1985?
3 In 1990, in which country was the world's largest McDonald's?
4 Which Tower in Hong Kong is 100 storeys high?
5 In which country did fashion designer Cabeen launch his men's range of clothes?
6 What is Ecuador's largest Pacific seaport?
7 Where is the Seacon Square shopping centre?
8 Which is further south – Atlanta or Dallas?
9 Which country has the internet code .lk?
10 Where was the first state-subsidised theatre in the English-speaking world opened?
11 Which Canal links the Ebrie Lagoon and the Gulf of Guinea?
12 Which of these islands is the largest –Great Britain, Java or Sumatra?
13 What does the Mississippi-Missouri eventually flow into?
14 Which of these deserts is the smallest – Great Basin, Great Sandy or Great Victoria?
15 Why is Amarillo, Texas, so called?
16 On which river is Jordan's capital?
17 The capital of Maryland is on which river?
18 Which of these Seas is the largest – Arabian, Coral or South China?
19 The Appalachian mountains end in the centre of which state?
20 On which island does the Otira Rail Tunnel run?
21 Which of the following Australian cities is the most southerly – Melbourne, Perth or Sydney?
22 What is the Great Slave?
23 What was Brazil's first planned city?
24 What is the principal language of Andhra Pradesh?
25 Palmerston, Mangaia and Rarotonga are among which islands?
26 In which sea do the so-called ABC islands lie?
27 Which town is closest to the Everest base camp – Kathmandu, Namche or Sagarmatha?
28 In 2000 which was the largest city in the world by population?
29 Where is the "Leap the Dips" roller coaster?
30 The Dogon are inhabitants of where?

  Answers on page 210

 Answers on page 210

221
CAPITALS

1 Which British dependent territory has a capital called the Valley?

2 The name of the capital of which country means "good air"?

3 Other than in Scotland, where is there a capital called Edinburgh?

4 What is the capital of Venezuela?

5 What is the capital of Belarus?

6 What is the capital of the largest country in Europe after Russia?

7 Which US state's capital is the name of a lively 1920s' dance?

8 "One Night" in where is the name of a song from the musical *Chess*?

9 Oranjestad is the capital of Aruba but to whom does it belong?

10 Which fabric was originally made in Syria's capital?

11 In which US state's capital is the headquarters of the Mormon Church?

12 Which island's capital is Flying Fish Cove?

13 Which US state capital has the longest name?

14 In which capital was Gordon besieged for 10 months and then murdered?

15 Which African capital was sold to Italy in 1905?

16 What is the name of Greenland's capital, formerly Godthab?

17 Which country's capital is the end of a motor rally from Paris?

18 What shape is the Kremlin in Russia's capital, Moscow?

19 Which capital is linked to Almada by a bridge over the River Tagus?

20 Which US state capital is the name of the man credited with "discovering" America?

21 Which capital city has a state within it?

22 Which Arab capital's name is the name of a sweet dessert wine?

23 What did Abuja replace as Nigeria's capital?

24 Why is the Government Building in Wellington so notable?

25 Which Mexican state's name and state capital are also the name of a breed of small dog?

26 Which capital was founded in 1566 by the Knights of St John?

27 What is the capital of Malawi?

28 Which African capital's name was the name of a hit song by Tommy Steele in 1958?

29 *They Came to* which Middle Eastern capital in the title of a mystery by Agatha Christie?

30 Who sang about the capital of Catalonia in 1992?

222
AROUND EUROPE 8

1 Which is the largest province of the country which has Madrid as its capital?

2 Which building houses the Bayeux Tapestry?

3 France, Italy, Sweden – which does not have an internet code made up of its first two letters?

4 In which department of Basse Normandie is the village where the famous soft cheese is made?

5 Where are the Bakony Mountains?

6 Where is Switzerland's oldest university?

7 What is Europe's most southerly point?

8 Which country is to the immediate north of the Ukraine?

9 In which Sea are Gotland and Oland?

10 Which language is Euskara?

11 Which city is the burial place of William the Conqueror and Beau Brummel?

12 Which Austrian city was known as Thermae Helveticae to the Romans?

13 Anjou is now part of which French departement?

14 In Austria what is the Fohn?

15 The Campine coalfield is to the east of which country?

16 Which country is to the immediate south of Croatia?

17 Where is the Jotunheimen range of mountains?

18 Which Italian port takes its name from the Greek for elbow?

19 Which language is spoken in Wallonia?

20 What is the capital of Brabant?

21 How many countries border the Federal Republic of Germany?

22 In which country is the city of Esztergom?

23 What is the currency of Slovenia?

24 What is the capital of the German province to the south of Brandenburg?

25 What is the capital of the province to the west of Abruzzio?

26 In which country are the Pripet Marshes?

27 Which river bisects Andorra?

28 Who designed the Finlandia Concert Hall in Helsinki?

29 In which mountain range is Europe's highest peak?

30 Of the ten largest cities in Europe which three were once part of the Soviet Union?

  Answers on page 211

 Answers on page 211

223
AROUND ENGLAND 3

1 Which English county has the longest coastline?
2 Who is responsible for the blue plaques in London?
3 In which London borough are there the most blue plaques?
4 What was Marble Arch originally designed to be?
5 What is the stately home owned by the Spencer family in Northamptonshire called?
6 What are Grimes Graves and where are they?
7 Where is England's largest castle?
8 Which two English cathedrals have three spires each?
9 Which county used to be divided into Parts?
10 Which dukes are associated with Woburn Abbey?
11 Where would you go to watch a Furry dance?
12 Where are St Agnes, St Martin's and Bryher?
13 Which English county bordering the sea has the shortest coastline?
14 What is the eastern strait between the Isle of Wight and the English mainland called?
15 What is the main type of rock forming the North Downs?
16 Dunkery Beacon is the highest point where?
17 On which lake does Keswick stand?
18 Which part of England is associated with the novels of Arnold Bennett?
19 Under which London landmark are buried a razor, cigars and a portrait of Queen Victoria?
20 Where is there a Nelson's column other than the one in London ?
21 What is England's smallest mainland county?
22 Which stately home in Britain is the home of the Marquess of Bath?
23 In which city is Whip-ma-Whop-ma Gate?
24 How many parishes does Greater London have?
25 In which county is there a village called Middle Wallop?
26 Which Derbyshire village lost most of its population to plague in 1665 but prevented the spread of the disease?
27 Where would you find the Bell Harry tower?
28 Which English county has the smallest perimeter?
29 What are the chalk cliff headlands between Eastbourne and Seaford?
30 Where are trees laid out in the form of troops at a famous battle?

224
AROUND THE UK 7

1 In which Square is the UK's highest building?
2 How many capsules or pods does the London Eye have?
3 What did the Theatre of Small Convenience in Malvern used to be?
4 Where is the National Library of Wales?
5 Where does the Avon flow into what the French call La Manche?
6 Which Bridge spans the Beauly Firth?
7 What was London's first new underground railway line to open in the second half of the 20th century?
8 Which Welsh city is near the old Roman fort of Segontium?
9 What was Lord Camden's name before he became a Lord and before the London borough was named after him?
10 How many miles is it from Land's End to John O'Groats?
11 Which county is to the west of Hereford & Worcester?
12 At which northern railway station did Paul Simon write "Homeward Bound"?
13 In which county is the Cerne Giant?
14 Which of the Cinque Ports is nearest the beginning of the alphabet?
15 One of the founders of Fortnum and Mason was a footman in the service of which monarch?
16 Who inaugurated the Glyndebourne Festival?
17 Which is the UK's tallest structure built before the 20th century?
18 Where is the Cranfield Institute of Technology?
19 Where in Wales is the Royal Mint?
20 How long is Britain's longest river?
21 Which county is the largest to the east of Perth & Kinross?
22 When were the Broads designated a National Park?
23 Constable country is along which river?
24 What is the local name of the river which runs through Cambridge?
25 In what year were marriages at the famous blacksmith's shop in southern Scotland made illegal?
26 The founder of Guy's Hospital followed which profession?
27 Which county is to the south of Oxfordshire?
28 Where is the second largest castle in England and Wales?
29 What was Arsenal tube station called before it was called Arsenal?
30 Where did Britain's first nudist beach open in 1979?

 Answers on page 211

 Answers on page 211

225
WHAT IN THE WORLD? 2

1 Which Iranian city was partially destroyed by a Dec 2003 earthquake?

2 What is the highest standard cloud formation called?

3 Where is the most thundery place on earth?

4 What occurred in the Kalahari Desert on September 1st, 1981?

5 Where did the longest-lasting rainbow glow for three hours?

6 What name is given to the bending of the winds caused by the Earth spinning on its axis?

7 Which volcanic eruption gave the loudest sound ever recorded?

8 Which Indonesian island was nearest the epicentre of the earthquake in December 2004?

9 What is the name given to the lightning which clings to ships' masts?

10 What are the seven colours of the rainbow in their correct order?

11 What is the name for a column of swiftly spinning air?

12 What name is given to the phenomenon of bright lights in the atmosphere caused by the solar wind entering the ionosphere?

13 What are caused by changes in the level of the ocean floor?

14 What occurs when the central zone of the Sun is covered?

15 What are the "Ring of Fire" and "Alpine Belt"?

16 Which patrol group keeps track of all icebergs?

17 Which is the largest active volcano on Earth?

18 What forms when a tornado runs over water?

19 What is the scientific name for the Northern Lights?

20 Which island emerged from the sea off the coast of Iceland in 1963?

21 Which Greek philosopher made 5th-century BC studies of vulcanology?

22 Where did the strongest earthquake ever recorded take place in 1960?

23 Which is the only active volcano in Antarctica?

24 What is a vent in the Earth's crust that spouts a fountain of boiling water?

25 Which volcanic rock is so strongly charged with gas that it appears frothy and floats on water?

26 What occurs when a lunar eclipse take place?

27 What is a rising air current caused by heating from below called?

28 What are Tugela and the Buyoma?

29 What name is given to a volcanic opening that gives out gas and steam?

30 What scale, other than the Richter, measures earthquakes?

226
EXPLORATION

1 What is chiefly grown in Alabama's Canebrake country?

2 The Julian and Dinaric Alps extend into which two countries?

3 The Amur river forms much of the boundary between which two countries?

4 What is the Maori name for New Zealand?

5 Which two main metals are found in the Atacama Desert in Chile?

6 What is the currency of Malaysia?

7 Which country has the highest density of sheep in the world?

8 Which African country takes its name from the Shona for "House of Stone"?

9 Which volcanic peak is west of Cook inlet in Alaska?

10 San Miguel is the main island of which group?

11 What is the capital of the Lazio region of Italy?

12 What is the former name of the capital of Dominica?

13 Which Brazilian state is the centre of Amazonian tin and gold mining?

14 Aqaba is which country's only port?

15 On which island of the Philippines is Manila?

16 What is the world's flattest continent?

17 Which former fort in New York State is the home of the US Military Academy?

18 Which US state capital lies on the river Jordan?

19 In which country is Africa's lowest point?

20 What is the largest primeval forest left in Europe?

21 The Red Sea is the submerged section of which valley?

22 Regina in Saskatchewan was originally called what?

23 How many countries do the Andes pass through?

24 In which country do the Makua live?

25 What is the highest peak of the Apennines?

26 Which city south east of St Malo was the old capital of Brittany?

27 Which Alps lie north east of the Sea of Showers?

28 Robben Island is a prison in which Bay?

29 What is Malawi's largest city?

30 Which south American port's name means River of January?

  Answers on page 211

 Answers on page 211

227
WEATHER

1 Which country has the driest inhabited area in the world?

2 Which Cornish village suffered a freak flood in the summer of 2004?

3 What name is given to an occasion when the equator is furthest from the Sun?

4 Which county is England's wettest?

5 Which usually travels faster, a cold front or a warm front?

6 Which sea area is immediately to the south of Ireland?

7 Over which mountains does the chinook blow?

8 Which 1990s Eurovision Song Contest winner shares her name with a devastating hurricane?

9 The name of which type of cloud is Latin for a lock of hair?

10 What is Fata Morgana and where would you see it?

11 What is the belt of light variable winds near the equator called?

12 What sort of wind is föhn wind?

13 Where would you experience a williwaw?

14 What colour are altostratus clouds?

15 What is the buran?

16 What is the name of a front where a cold front has overtaken a warm front?

17 What is a hurricane called in the Pacific?

18 Where is the tramontana?

19 Which sea area lies due east of Dogger and Humber?

20 Where does the berg wind blow?

21 What number does the Beaufort scale go up to in international use?

22 In which two countries does the Seistan sand wind blow?

23 What is the hot, dry North African wind which blows from the Sahara called?

24 Down which valley does the mistral blow?

25 Where would you experience a southerly buster?

26 What are lines joining places of equal atmospheric pressure called?

27 What is the centre of a hurricane called?

28 What does a haboob create?

29 What causes a blue moon?

30 Over which mountains does the pampero blow?

228
WORLD TOUR 2

1 What is the currency of Bolivia?

2 Between which two rivers does Manhattan lie?

3 Where in Russia was a school besieged by extremists in September 2004?

4 In which country is the city of Curitiba?

5 What is the capital of Brunei?

6 In which country is the deep-water port of Lobito?

7 The islands of Taipa and Coloane are part of which possession?

8 Pluna Airlines are based in which country?

9 Which capital is further North – Khartoum or Addis Ababa?

10 What is the official language of Bhutan?

11 In which country is Kakadu National Park?

12 Which country is due North of Uruguay?

13 Which two countries border Morocco?

14 Which desert lies between the Kalahari and the Atlantic Ocean?

15 Where is the news agency Colprensa based?

16 What is Madison Square Garden situated over?

17 On which island is Nassau, the capital of the Bahamas?

18 In which US state was the first National Park?

19 How is Denali in Alaska also known?

20 The Negev desert tapers to which port?

21 Who designed New Delhi?

22 What is the third longest river in Africa?

23 Which country has the largest oil resources in Africa?

24 Chandrika Kumaratunga was president of which country hit by the 2004 tsunami?

25 In which country is the city of Medan?

26 What is the capital of Burundi?

27 What is South Africa's judicial capital?

28 What is the most north-eastern US state?

29 SAHSA Airlines are based in which country?

30 Which island is situated between Sumatra and Bali?

  Answers on page 211

 Answers on page 211

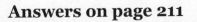

229
CAPITALS 2

1 What was the capital of Russia before Moscow?

2 What is the capital of Andorra?

3 What lies to the north of Algiers?

4 Which country has the last capital alphabetically?

5 What was Harare's former name?

6 Which Asian capital is at the head of the Mekong Delta?

7 Which capital is known as Leukosia or Lefkosa by its inhabitants?

8 Tashkent is the capital of which former Soviet republic?

9 Which capital is on the slopes of the volcano Pichincha?

10 Which is further north, Pakistan's new capital, Islamabad, or the former one, Karachi?

11 St John's is the capital of Antigua and Barbuda but on which island does it stand?

12 Which capital's former name was Christiania?

13 In Berlin which avenue runs east from the Brandenburg Gate?

14 Which capital is the largest city in Africa?

15 Where was Botswana's seat of government prior to 1965, after which it moved to Gaborone?

16 What was the capital of Italian East Africa between 1936 and 1941?

17 Which capital lies on the river Helmand?

18 In Paris what links the Arc de Triomphe and the Place de la Concorde?

19 Which new capital's main architect was Oscar Niemeyer?

20 Which capital's main industrial area is Piraeus?

21 In which capital is the Teatro Colón opera house?

22 What is the full name of the capital of Colombia?

23 Which capital's heating comes from natural hot springs?

24 What did New Delhi replace as the capital of British India in 1912?

25 On which sea is the Azerbaijani capital Baku?

26 Which capital is known as the Eternal City?

27 What is the capital of Bahrain?

28 Which capital began as the village of Edo?

29 Which capital in the West Indies is to be found on New Providence Island?

30 Which capital houses the Great Mosque and the Gate of God?

230
EURO TOUR 2

1 Which German hotel was home to the England WAGS during the 2006 World Cup?

2 Tarom Airlines are based in which country?

3 What is the capital of Georgia?

4 Which capital is further North – Budapest or Vienna?

5 Which Gulf is to the west of Estonia and Latvia?

6 Where is the news agency Centre d'Information Presse based?

7 In which country is Kranebitten International airport?

8 What is the chief port of Slovenia?

9 The Pelagian islands belong to which European country?

10 Bornholm is an island in which Sea?

11 Hoge Veluwe National Park is in which country?

12 Which European country has the internet code .ee?

13 St Petersburg is at the head of which gulf?

14 What is the largest island in Europe?

15 Which two Italian volcanoes erupted in 1994?

16 What is the world's highest dam?

17 Which country is called Suomen Tasavalta in its own language?

18 Which capital is further North – Berlin or London?

19 Aero Lloyd Airlines are based in which country?

20 Which European country has the highest life expectancy for men and women?

21 What is the highest waterfall in Europe?

22 Brest is a major town in which country other than France?

23 In which town did an earthquake claim nine lives in 1997?

24 In which country is the city of Bochum?

25 To which country do the islands of Stromboli and Vulcano belong?

26 What is the prominent religion of Lithuania?

27 Which is the northernmost and second largest of the Ionian islands?

28 What are Andorra's two main industries?

29 In which country is Sondica International airport?

30 Hardangervidda National Park is in which country?

  Answers on page 211

 Answers on page 211

231
GREAT BUILDINGS

1 Which is Britain's oldest cathedral?

2 Jørn Utzon designed the Sydney Opera House as a result of what?

3 What is the Taj Mahal made from?

4 In which Parisian square is the Arc de Triomphe?

5 What is the cathedral of the diocese of London?

6 What was the highest building in the world until 1930?

7 Who ordered the building of St Basil's Cathedral in Moscow?

8 Which library in Venice was described as "the richest and most ornate building since antiquity"?

9 Who had Hampton Court Palace built?

10 Which dukes does Chatsworth House in Derbyshire belong to?

11 Which stately home was used in the film *Brideshead Revisited*?

12 Why is the Washington Memorial smaller now than when it was built?

13 Which building did James Martin's cookery series *Castle in the Country* come from?

14 Other than in Egypt, where were pyramids built?

15 Which French château has a Hall of Mirrors?

16 In which US city is the Sears Tower?

17 Where was Europe's largest Gothic cathedral rebuilt after World War II?

18 Which chain store proprietor commissioned the then tallest inhabitable building in the world in 1913?

19 Which famous statue, brought back as war loot by Napoleon, is still housed in the Louvre?

20 When was Blackpool Tower built?

21 Which plan did Prince Charles describe as "a monstrous carbuncle"?

22 The memorial service for former *Countdown* presenter Richard Whiteley took place in which famous building?

23 In which area of Paris is the Basilica of Sacré Coeur?

24 Where is the largest church in the world?

25 Who designed it?

26 Where is the Shwa Dagon Pagoda?

27 In which city is Rastrelli's Winter Palace?

28 Which cathedral, opened in 1962, contains the ruins of the old cathedral?

29 Where in India is the Golden Temple, centre of the Sikh religion?

30 Why is the White House white?

232
AROUND THE UK 8

1 The Euroroute E24 is from Birmingham to which county town?

2 Which Scottish university was named after a jeweller and an inventor?

3 Which polo ground is in the park of a burnt-down former country house?

4 What is the smallest theatre at the Barbican in London called?

5 Where is Grimsetter Airport?

6 Which inlet of the Clyde was used as a US submarine base from the early '60s?

7 In which part of London is Kenwood?

8 Which shipping area is due north of Trafalgar?

9 In which county was the Open University founded?

10 John Peel lived in which county for the latter part of his life?

11 How many national parks does the Pennine Way pass through?

12 Which wall runs from the river Forth in the east to Clyde in the west?

13 What is the real name of "Petticoat Lane"?

14 Which county is due north of Buckinghamshire?

15 Where is the Post Office's main sorting office?

16 What name is given to someone born east of the Medway?

17 Which county is due South of Tyne and Wear?

18 Which colloquial name of the main church in Boston serves as a landmark for ships?

19 Who or what was London's Liverpool Street station named after?

20 Where is the official London residence of the Foreign Secretary?

21 What is the administration centre of Wiltshire?

22 How is London's Collegiate Church of St Peter better known?

23 Which House has an Egyptian Hall for banqueting?

24 Which important collection was given to the city of Glasgow in 1944?

25 Which World Heritage Site was built for the Duke of Marlborough?

26 Which house is headquarters and home to the BBC World Service?

27 What is MOMI on London's South Bank?

28 Which famous House is the only surviving part of Whitehall Palace?

29 Where is Scatsa Airport?

30 Which county is due south of Shropshire?

  Answers on page 212

 Answers on page 212

233
POT LUCK 1

1 What is the highest number used in a Sudoku puzzle?
2 What is the term for a positive electrode?
3 In *Last of the Summer Wine* what was Nora's husband called?
4 Which swimming stroke is named after an insect?
5 Which English queen has the same name as a type of plum?
6 Which Rovers does veteran cartoon character Roy play for?
7 How many dots are used in each letter in the Braille system?
8 Who won the Oscar for best actor in both 1993 and 1994?
9 What is a female deer called?
10 What does the letter B stand for in an ASBO?
11 What can be an island, a sweater or a potato?
12 What unit is used to measure horses?
13 Who is Reg Dwight better known as?
14 Who provided Aslan's voice in the 2005 movie of *The Lion, the Witch and the Wardrobe*?
15 Which Eamonn left the GMTV sofa in the summer of 2005?
16 How many tenpin bowling skittles need knocking down for a strike?
17 How is 77 represented in Roman numerals?
18 Who is the patron saint of music?
19 What are birds of a feather said to do?
20 *Kiss Me Kate* is a musical version of which play by Shakespeare?
21 The single "Papa Don't Preach" came from which Madonna album?
22 Betz cells are found in which part of the body?
23 What is the only bird that can hover in the air and also fly backwards?
24 Who earned the nickname "Slow-hand"?
25 In the Bible who goes after Mark and before John?
26 Which country does opera singer Pavarotti come from?
27 Which is the third largest of the Channel Islands?
28 Who was Liverpool's skipper in the 2005 European Champions League triumph?
29 In which Puccini opera does Mimi appear?
30 How many sides has an octagon?

234
POT LUCK 2

1 In international soccer, what is the main colour of Holland's shirts?
2 Who is older – Ruby Wax or Jennifer Saunders?
3 "Into the Groove" gave a first UK No. 1 for which singer?
4 Which two cities were linked by the M1 when it first opened?
5 Which song was a British No. 1 for Jimmy Young, the Righteous Brothers, Robson & Jerome and Gareth Gates?
6 What is Britain's smallest songbird?
7 How many sides are there in a pair of nonagons?
8 Which George was the main producer of The Beatles' hits?
9 EW Swanton wrote about which sport?
10 Was Joanna Lumley born in the 1940s, '50s or '60s?
11 How is Eithne Ni Bhraonain better known in the music world?
12 Mohawk, Seminole and Sioux are all names of what?
13 Which star group was Jason Orange a member of?
14 Is Riesling a red or white wine?
15 How many Teletubbies are there?
16 Russell Crowe starred in the movie *A Beautiful...* what?
17 Who links the films *Rebecca*, *Psycho* and *Vertigo*?
18 What's the most number of Sundays that could occur in December?
19 Which author created the reclusive character Miss Havisham?
20 On TV, did David Soul play Starsky or Hutch?
21 Which founder members of the Football League returned to the League in 2006?
22 What is England's most north easterly county?
23 Is Radio 5 Live broadcast on MW or FM?
24 What colour is verdigris which appears on copper or brass?
25 Who is killed if regicide is committed?
26 Ridings used to divide which county?
27 Is Robert Carrier linked with food, theatre or sport?
28 Pink gin is gin flavoured with what?
29 Who played the character Rachel in *Friends*?
30 Brisbane is the capital of which Australian state?

  Answers on page 212

 Answers on page 212

235
POP POT LUCK

1 Which song was a No. 1 for the Equals and Pato Banton?
2 Who formed a duo with Lyle?
3 How many c.c. were in the group which sang "I'm Not in Love"?
4 Which Yorkshire town's Fair was the subject of a Simon and Garfunkel song?
5 What Killed the Radio Star according to the Buggles?
6 What is the home country of Björk?
7 Which Elvis song has the line "I gave a letter to the postman, he put it in his sack"?
8 Where did the Police find a Message in 1979?
9 Which Orchestra joined Olivia Newton-John on "Xanadu"?
10 Which Bob wrote "Knockin' on Heaven's Door"?
11 Which instrument does Acker Bilk play?
12 Who took "Sloop John B" into the '60s charts?
13 Who was "Alone Again (Naturally)" in 1972?
14 How many members of the Thompson Twins were there?
15 Which surname is shared by Cat and Shakin'?
16 Which country star pleaded for Jolene not to take her man in 1976?
17 Whose first hit was "Love and Affection"?
18 How is Robert Zimmerman better known?
19 Who was lead singer with the Mechanics?
20 Which thoroughfare did Elton John say Goodbye to in 1973?
21 Mark Owen took lead vocals on which boy band's 2007 hit "Shine"?
22 What nationality are the Proclaimers?
23 Who makes up the trio with Crosby and Stills?
24 Which Canadian sang "Miss Chatelaine" in 1993?
25 Which Level had "Lessons in Love" in 1986?
26 What was Harold Melvin's backing group?
27 Where did Phyliss Nelson invite us to Move in the 80s and 90s?
28 Which Spanish insect was a hit for Herb Alpert?
29 Which Des had "Careless Hands" in 1967?
30 Which Daniel pondered "Whatever Happened to Old Fashioned Love" in 1993?

236
POT LUCK 3

1 The 2005–6 football season was the last that Arsenal played at which stadium?
2 The character Robert Langton is the hero of whose novels?
3 The discovery of what caused a rush to California in 1848?
4 What is the opposite of alkali?
5 In rhyme, who asked his way to Norwich when he came down too soon?
6 Which nutty chocolate is sold in triangular bars?
7 In which lane is the Great Fire of London said to have started?
8 Which lord was removed from the *Beano* in 1992?
9 In which game could an Australian's Chinaman beat an Englishman?
10 Which of the Wonders of the World was at Babylon?
11 Who presented a TV *Takeaway* on Saturday night?
12 A bob was the popular name of which old English coin?
13 What was the Teenage Mutant Turtles' favourite food?
14 What comes after red, orange and yellow in the rainbow's colours?
15 Which books and films featured Professor Dumbledore?
16 How many legs does a male insect have?
17 Which Grand Slam tournament did Andre Agassi win in 2000, 2001 and 2003?
18 Which workhouse boy asked for more?
19 Which language does the word kitsch come from?
20 What is the state capital of Massachusetts?
21 How many strings does a Spanish guitar have?
22 What did Old Mother Hubbard keep in her cupboard?
23 What kind of creature is an anchovy?
24 Dad, kayak and rotavator are examples of what type of words?
25 Which juicy green fruit is named after a New Zealand bird?
26 What is the name for a blanket-like cloak with a slit for the head?
27 Most snow crystals have how many sides?
28 What does an entomologist study?
29 In Britain a general election must be held after how many years?
30 What sort of creature is a treecreeper?

  Answers on page 212

 Answers on page 212

237
POT LUCK 4

1 What was the first soccer club to be managed by Roy Keane?

2 What are the metal loops that you place your feet in when horse riding?

3 Which bank is a dangerous sand bar in the North Sea?

4 How many players are there in a rounders team?

5 Whose official plane is *Air Force One*?

6 What does the letter P stand for in ESP?

7 Which group of countries did the Vikings come from?

8 How many Popes have been English – one, two or three?

9 What colour was Kojak's hair?

10 What kind of programmes are Hanna and Barbara famous for?

11 What is a man-made lake in which water is stored called?

12 What type of creature is a Black Widow?

13 Which overture has a date in its title and includes cannons and bells?

14 On what date did the St. Valentine's Day Massacre take place?

15 Which Tony won the first *I'm a Celebrity Get Me Out of Here*?

16 Melbourne is the capital of which Australian State?

17 How many walls surround a squash court?

18 In the Bible, who parted the sea?

19 Fiji is in which ocean?

20 Which part of your body has a coating of enamel?

21 In *Austin Powers International Man of Mystery* who was the leading actress?

22 Who milked the cow with the crumpled horn, in the rhyme?

23 Which parts of the Venus de Milo's body are missing?

24 In which city beginning with H was the 2005 World Athletics Championship held?

25 Would a vermicide be used to kill worms or mice?

26 How many presidents' faces are carved into Mount Rushmore?

27 Which green stone was buried by the Chinese with their dead?

28 How many New Testament Gospels are there?

29 What word describes a picture made from sticking scraps on to a background?

30 Which English coin was nicknamed the tanner?

238
MOVIES POT LUCK

1 Which Asian country is home to 'Bollywood'?

2 Which Emma starred in *Sense and Sensibility*?

3 To the nearest hour, how long does *Titanic* last?

4 Who directed *Four Weddings and a Funeral*?

5 In which 1997 movie did Daniel Day Lewis play a boxer?

6 Who won the Best Actor Oscar for *On the Waterfront*?

7 In which decade of the 20th century was Joan Collins born?

8 Which Nicolas starred in *Face/Off*?

9 Is *Raging Bull* about American football, boxing or bull-fighting?

10 *My Best Friend's Wedding* and *Sleeping with the Enemy* featured which actress?

11 The character Sonny Corleone was in which sequence of movies?

12 *Air Force One* starred which Gary?

13 What is the first name of the *Pulp Fiction* director?

14 Which actor links *Se7en*, *Sleepers* and *Thelma and Louise*?

15 What relation is Shirley MacLaine to Warren Beatty?

16 Which Tony starred in *Some Like It Hot*?

17 *The Secret Life of* which Walter formed a movie title?

18 Which early Spielberg blockbuster featured a shark?

19 Which Ms Ryder had her big break in *Beetlejuice*?

20 Which 70s actor Burt was *Cosmopolitan*'s first male nude centrefold?

21 Which Oliver won the Best Director Oscar for *Born on the Fourth of July*?

22 In which decade was *Batman* with Michael Keaton released?

23 Which famous Jean tested for the role of Scarlett O'Hara?

24 Which colour completes the film title, *How... Was My Valley*?

25 Which pop singer wrote the music for Disney's *The Lion King*?

26 In which year was *The Simpsons Movie* released?

27 Which villain did Arnold Schwarzenegger play in *Batman & Robin*?

28 What name is given to a situation in film where a suspense scene is temporarily left unresolved?

29 Which actor links *The Birdcage* and *Patch Adams*?

30 What number completes the title, *Naked Gun...: The Final Insult*?

  Answers on page 212   **Answers on page 212**

239
POT LUCK 5

1 Kelvedon Wonder and Little Marvel are types of what?
2 Which programme presented prizes on a conveyor belt?
3 In the 90s, who had a No. 1 with "I Believe"?
4 Which veteran comic Eric featured in the *Harry Potter* films?
5 On a Monopoly board, what colour is Pentonville Road?
6 The movie *Munich* is about which tragic event in this city?
7 Who wrote the novel *The Inimitable Jeeves*?
8 Which of Queen Elizabeth II's children was first to marry?
9 What is the administrative centre for the county of Suffolk?
10 In which decade of the 20th century was Joanna Lumley born?
11 Who went to sea with silver buckles on his knee?
12 How many fluid ounces in a pint?
13 Which band were formed from the *Popstars* TV show?
14 What is 1/6 as a percentage to two decimal places?
15 Would you expect Monty Don to cook, dance or garden on TV?
16 Who was England's manager for Gary Lineker's last international?
17 Which UK car manufacturer produced the Stag?
18 In music, what note is written on the bottom line of the treble clef?
19 On a dartboard what number is opposite 5?
20 RIBA is the Royal Institute of British what?
21 Which Prayer was a millennium chart topper for Sir Cliff Richard?
22 In which month is Independence Day in the USA?
23 Jason Wilcox played soccer for which country?
24 In which country is the city of Turin?
25 How are angles measured other than degrees?
26 The Battle of Waterloo was fought in which country?
27 The letter O is on which row of a typewriter or computer keyboard?
28 What colour is the centre of an archery target?
29 Pop and Ma Larkin appeared in which TV series?
30 Which kind of pear is usually served as a starter?

240
POT LUCK 6

1 If you die intestate you have not made what?
2 What's the least number of Mondays that can occur in July?
3 In which resort did the tragic deaths of the Shepherd children take place in Oct. 2006?
4 Which two animals are featured on the front of a British passport?
5 What is the German word for the number twenty?
6 Who had a No. 1 UK hit with "Everything I Do, I Do It for You"?
7 What is a prickly pear?
8 In which county, beginning with C, is "Goldplated" set?
9 Media person Janet Bull changed her last name to what in her search for "yoof"?
10 Bob Hawke was prime minister of which country?
11 The movie *Enigma* was set during which world conflict?
12 What colour is sable in heraldry?
13 For what was Capability Brown famous?
14 What is foolscap?
15 On TV who played the Equaliser?
16 What kind of plant is marjoram?
17 On which River are the Niagara Falls?
18 Which Disney movie includes the song "Heigh-Ho"?
19 For which sport is Willie Carson famous?
20 Sirloin, Rump and Topside are all joints of which meat?
21 What colour is Tinky Winky in the *Teletubbies*?
22 How many leaves are on a shamrock?
23 Which American state is the largest in area?
24 When Birmingham were relegated in 2006 Emile Heskey moved to which club?
25 According to the nursery rhyme, who met a pieman going to the fair?
26 Which two brothers made up the group Bros?
27 What is a bullace?
28 On which show did Chantelle Houghton first find fame?
29 A Model T Ford was nicknamed Tin what?
30 According to the proverb, imitation is the sincerest form of what?

 Answers on page 212

 Answers on page 212

241
MOVIES POT LUCK 2

1 Which Robert starred in *The Horse Whisperer*?
2 Who won the Best Actor Oscar for *Rain Man*?
3 Which pop group starred in *Spiceworld*?
4 Whose *World* was a 1992 film with Mike Myers and Dana Carvey?
5 *Shine* is about a musician playing which instrument?
6 Which actor links *Forrest Gump*, *You've Got Mail* and *A League of Their Own*?
7 Which colour goes before *Narcissus* and *mail* to form film titles?
8 Johnny Weissmuller portrayed which jungle hero?
9 Who are the two main characters in *The X-Files*?
10 Which Bo Derek film had a number as the title?
11 Who starred opposite Jennifer Gray in *Dirty Dancing*?
12 Which Donald played Hawkeye in the film *M*A*S*H*?
13 Who starred in and directed *Monsieur Hulot's Holiday*?
14 Which movie used the song "Everything I Do (I Do It for You)"?
15 In which decade of the 20th century was Jack Nicholson born?
16 Which colour links *Shoes* and *Dust* in film titles?
17 Which sergeant created by Phil Silvers featured in a 90s movie?
18 Which actress links *Fatal Attraction* and *101 Dalmatians*?
19 What is the name of Tatum O'Neal's actor father?
20 Which creatures dominated *Jurassic Park*?
21 *The First Wives' Club*, *Ruthless People* and *Hocus Pocus* all feature which actress?
22 A werewolf in London and a man in Paris were both of what nationality?
23 In which decade was *The Godfather* released?
24 What was the Bond theme for *The Living Daylights* called?
25 Who played opposite Patrick Swayze in *Ghost*?
26 *No... what for Old Men* won the Academy Award for Best Picture in 2007?
27 Whose adventure was *The Order of the Phoenix*?
28 Which former partner of Mick Jagger appeared in *Batman*?
29 Which John starred in *Face/Off*?
30 Which word completes the film title, Monty Python's *The... of Life*?

242
POT LUCK 7

1 Which Bette won an Oscar for Best Actress in "Dangerous"?
2 What is 10 cubed?
3 What is the administrative centre for the county of Shropshire?
4 What word can go after "music" and before "mark"?
5 How is Marvin Lee Addy better known?
6 In which best-selling book are Opus Dei entwined in the plot?
7 Who wrote the novel *The Shining*?
8 Tom Thumb and Little Gem are types of what?
9 In France, what is the abbreviation for Mademoiselle?
10 Which clown is Bart Simpson's idol?
11 Brian Jacks is associated with which sport?
12 What does the Y stand for in NIMBY?
13 C. J. Parker and Lt Mitch Bucannon appeared in which TV series?
14 Alan Pardew moved as boss of Reading to take over briefly at which London club?
15 What did Castleford's name become for the 1997 rugby league season?
16 The airline El Al is from which country?
17 Who was the outgoing American President when Jimmy Carter took office?
18 What is Ceylon now called?
19 What was the name of the tiny iPod launched in September 2005?
20 What word can follow "clay", "racing" and "wood"?
21 In which country is the city of Poana?
22 What happened to Victor Meldrew in the final episode of *One Foot in the Grave*?
23 Which Pink rock band reassembled at Live 8 in Hyde Park in 2005?
24 Shannon Lawson and Yasmin Salter are what type of TV wives?
25 Diamond denotes which wedding anniversary?
26 Which army rank is the higher – colonel or brigadier?
27 The character Kim Tate appeared in which TV soap?
28 What is the only English anagram of ACHES?
29 What was Lot's wife turned into?
30 A merino is what kind of creature?

  Answers on page 213

 Answers on page 213

243
POT LUCK 8

1 What was made "On a Dance Floor" according to Madonna's album title?
2 What is sugar added to, to make meringues?
3 Which poet laureate Sir John died in 1984?
4 What can pass through something if it is porous?
5 In which Scottish city are the *Rebus* novels set?
6 How many Oscars did *Titanic* win – 6, 11 or 14?
7 In the Bible, which angel foretold the birth of Jesus?
8 What youth group took to wearing parkas?
9 What is the German word for the number three?
10 Which children's favourite bear said he had "very little brain"?
11 Which English king reputedly commanded the sea to retreat?
12 What is the letter "V" if A is Alpha and B is Bravo?
13 Who is famous for saying, "Nice to see you, to see you nice"?
14 What is a popular name for the flower the antirrhinum?
15 Which Yorkshire city were Pulp from?
16 In music what does presto mean?
17 What object was invented by Lewis Waterman in 1884?
18 Tuscany is in which European country?
19 In the world of flying, what do the initials ETA stand for?
20 What is retsina?
21 Which soccer striker Robbie returned to Liverpool in 2006?
22 Which monster first hit the headlines in 1933?
23 How many edges are there around a 20-pence coin?
24 What are the New Zealand rugby union team called?
25 According to the rhyme, who killed Cock Robin?
26 The Samba originated in which South American country?
27 Who wrote *It Shouldn't Happen to a Vet*?
28 The port of Gdansk is in which country?
29 Would you eat, play or sit on a sitar?
30 Which Des presented the 1990s version of *Take Your Pick*?

244
MOVIES POT LUCK 3

1 Which film centre is also known as Tinseltown?
2 Which writer was "in Love" in the 1998 movie?
3 In which movie based on a Jane Austen novel did Gwyneth Paltrow play Emma Woodhouse?
4 What follows the names of Harry Connick and Robert Downey?
5 Who played the lead role in *The African Queen* after David Niven turned it down?
6 Who sang the title song of *Who's That Girl*?
7 In which decade was *Star Wars* first released?
8 Who played the villain in the 90s movie *Silence of the Lambs*?
9 Who won the Best Actor Oscar for *One Flew over the Cuckoo's Nest*?
10 In which decade was *Goldfinger* released?
11 How is Demetria Guynes better known?
12 Who won the Best Director Oscar for *Annie Hall*?
13 From which country did Mikhail Barishnikov defect to the USA?
14 In which country was Britt Ekland born?
15 In which eastern bloc country was the movie *Reds* set?
16 In which decade was *Mission: Impossible* released?
17 Who was Paul Newman's wife whom he directed in Rachel, Rachel?
18 What did T stand for in *E.T.*?
19 How is former Bond girl, Mrs Ringo Starr, Barbara Goldbach better known?
20 Which *Apollo* mission was the subject of a movie starring Tom Hanks?
21 Which comedian Bob has hosted the Oscars ceremony over 20 times?
22 Rupert Everett starred in *The Madness of...* which king?
23 Burt Bacharach was a former accompanist for which actress Marlene?
24 Which movie did the song "Fame" come from?
25 Which Phoebe of TV mini-series Lace married actor Kevin Kline?
26 *The Rise of the Machines* was the subtitle of which Schwarzenegger movie series?
27 What creature's curse did Wallace and Gromit encounter in 2005?
28 Which Claire starred in the 90s *Romeo and Juliet*?
29 Who sang "Call Me" in *America Gigolo*?
30 Which word goes before *Proposal* in a Demi Moore movie title?

  Answers on page 213

  Answers on page 213

245
POT LUCK 9

1 The characters Alf, Else and Rita appeared in which TV series?
2 Who was the first leader of Iraq in the 21st century?
3 Which UK car manufacturer produced the Hornet?
4 What word can go after "king" and before "man"?
5 How is the TV writer Lynda Titchmarsh better known?
6 Which Frenchman left Liverpool for Benitez to take over?
7 Who wrote the novel *Gridlock*?
8 What is the Roman numeral for one thousand?
9 How many gills in a pint?
10 In which decade of the 20th century was Mick Jagger born?
11 What are the two main parties in the US?
12 What name is given to a two-coloured oblong cake covered with almond paste?
13 In which country is the city of Dresden?
14 Which Brothers sang about the "Price of Love"?
15 Who wanted to ask the *Wizard of Oz* for courage?
16 In past times, what would a gentleman keep in his fob pocket?
17 What kind of creature is a cabbage white?
18 Who sang with the Miami Sound Machine?
19 Which US emergency phone number is also the name of a band to make No. 1?
20 What word can go before "holiday", "relations" and "school"?
21 Moving clockwise on a dartboard what number is next to 4?
22 How many Grand Slams did Roger Federer win in 2005 – one, two or three?
23 What type of triangle has equal sides and angles?
24 What is locked up in a tantalus?
25 Which planet is also referred to as the morning star?
26 Where is the HQ of the Scottish parliament?
27 What name is given to a starter dish of sliced raw vegetables?
28 Yelena Isinbayeva became the first woman to clear 5m in which athletic discipline?
29 Which country did Eidur Gudjohnsen play for?
30 Claustrophobia is the fear of what?

246
POT LUCK 10

1 Which snooker star Paul tragically died of cancer in October 2006?
2 Which alcoholic drink contains juniper as a flavour?
3 By what name is the mausoleum at Agra, India normally known?
4 Which dogs are a serious pest in Australia?
5 What would your profession be if you were a member of Equity?
6 Which instruments did Antonio Stradivari produce?
7 Which country is famous for moussaka?
8 In which month is Father's Day in the UK?
9 Pontoon and suspension are both types of which construction?
10 What did the "M" stand for in Louisa M. Alcott's name?
11 Who had the 2005 No. 1 single "Sometimes You Can't Make It on Your Own"?
12 What is a salary paid to a clergyman called?
13 What colour is cochineal?
14 The British Standards Institute uses what mark as a sign of approval?
15 Which American city is served by Kennedy Airport?
16 Which bird has the largest wing span?
17 Which soap is set in the city which hosted the 2002 Commonwealth Games?
18 What kind of drink is Amontillado?
19 What does an early bird catch, according to the proverb?
20 Which Beatle's daughter is a dress designer?
21 Bloomers and baps are both types of what?
22 How many years are there in four and a half decades?
23 Where are your incisors?
24 Who, together with Tim Rice, wrote *Evita*?
25 Where is Lord Nelson buried?
26 On a staircase are the risers flat or vertical?
27 Paddy Kenny was an ever present as which club reached the Premiership?
28 What are the two ingredients of marzipan?
29 Billy Graham is famous for which branch of Christianity?
30 Which black and white bird is usually accused of stealing?

  Answers on page 213

 Answers on page 213

247
FOOTBALL POT LUCK

1 Whose home, until May 1997, was the Baseball Ground?
2 Which city has a Wednesday and a United?
3 Rioch, Graham and Mee have all managed which club?
4 What second name is shared by Newcastle and Hartlepool?
5 Which country does diminutive striker John Spencer play for?
6 Which team are known as the Potters?
7 Which country do Ferencvaros come from?
8 With which football club did Ian Wright make his League debut?
9 Which club did Gordon Strachan join on leaving Manchester Utd?
10 What are the main colours on QPR's home shirts?
11 Which Tony was Port Vale's top League scorer in 1995–96?
12 What is Aston Villa's nickname?
13 Which overseas player was voted Footballer of the Year in 1996?
14 Bobby Robson became boss of which Spanish giants in 1996?
15 Which team does Danny Baker support?
16 Which Scotsman managed Galatasaray in 1995?
17 Which George of AC Milan was European Footballer of the Year in 1996?
18 Which country does Mikkel Beck play for?
19 What forename is shared by defenders Dodd and McAteer?
20 Which Robbie was PFA Young Player of the Year in 1995?
21 Which club ended a 50-year wait for the title by winning the 2005 Premiership?
22 Which Scottish city has had two UEFA Cup runners-up in the 21st century?
23 Which Kenny of Liverpool won the Footballer of the Year award in 1983?
24 Which Mark was Sheffield Wednesday's top League scorer in 1994–95?
25 Which team does Jasper Carrott support?
26 Fullback Gary Stevens played three FA Cup Finals for which club?
27 Which country staged the World Cup finals when "Nessun Dorma" became an anthem?
28 What is Scotland's national football stadium called?
29 What make of crisps has Gary Lineker advertised?
30 Which Tony of Arsenal was PFA Young Player of the Year in 1987?

248
POT LUCK 11

1 Which Ken starred as Rebus in the 2006 series based on Ian Rankin's novels?
2 Which major landmark is seen at the start of *News at Ten*?
3 In the 90s, who had a No. 1 with "Vogue"?
4 Who was the first British PM in this new millennium?
5 Prince Michael of Moldavia appeared in which TV soap?
6 In which country is the city of Berne?
7 Who wrote the novel *Cider With Rosie*?
8 The zodiac sign Gemini covers which two calendar months?
9 What does the Q stand for in IQ?
10 In which decade of the 20th century was Bob Dylan born?
11 Which famous chef has a wife known as Jules?
12 Which Helen starred in *Prime Suspect*?
13 Indira Gandhi International airport is in which country?
14 What word can go after "top" and before "trick"?
15 Which Mike directed Imelda Staunton in the movie *Vera Drake*?
16 What colour are Holland's international soccer shirts?
17 Whose No. 1 follow up to their first No. 1 was "Say You'll be There"?
18 What did Wigan's name become for the 1997 rugby league season?
19 What is the administrative centre for the county of Buckinghamshire?
20 The character Captain Kirk appeared in which TV series?
21 Is Turkey ahead of or behind Greenwich Mean Time?
22 What were the two colours of Andy Pandy's costume?
23 Who backed Buddy Holly?
24 What does ½ x ½ equal?
25 On a Monopoly board, what colour is Euston Road?
26 Which is closer to the sea – London or New York?
27 Who predicted that everyone would be famous for 15 minutes?
28 Who won an Oscar for Best Actor in *Ben Hur*?
29 What is the square root of 100?
30 Which unseeded player won the 2001 Wimbledon Men's Final?

 Answers on page 213

 Answers on page 213

249
POT LUCK 12

1 What is usually sold at reduced prices during a happy hour?
2 What are the two main ingredients of a ploughman's lunch?
3 Whose 2005 collection of hits was called "Curtain Call"?
4 Which UK daily newspaper has the shortest name?
5 Dame Barbara Cartland is famous for what type of fiction?
6 In which city is the Louvre Museum?
7 What does the E stand for in the acronym TESSA?
8 Steve McClaren left which soccer club to become England boss?
9 Which surviving tombs were built for the Pharaohs of Egypt?
10 What type of animal was the first successful adult cloning?
11 Which Bill is the world's richest businessman?
12 Twelfth Night marks the end of which festive season?
13 On which river does Cairo stand?
14 What type of animal is a Chihuahua?
15 2006 marked the 40th anniversary of which Welsh mining village disaster?
16 Which county does TV detective Hetty Wainthropp come from?
17 In motoring terms, what does the second A in AA stand for?
18 What is the national emblem of Scotland?
19 What type of animal does BSE affect?
20 In which decade of the 20th century was Prince William born?
21 What sort of tickets would a bucket shop sell?
22 On which Isle is Parkhurst prison?
23 What is hopscotch?
24 Which actress Cate starred in the movie *Charlotte Gray*?
25 Which British colony returned to China in July 1997?
26 In which city did rhyming slang originate?
27 Which alpine peak's name means White Mountain?
28 Which food is traditionally eaten on Shrove Tuesday?
29 If August 31st was a Wednesday what date would August Bank Holiday Monday be in England?
30 In which city is Tiananmen Square?

  Answers on page 213

250
POP POT LUCK 2

1 Which Liverpool lady had a No. 1 with "Anyone Who Had a Heart" in 1963?
2 Who was lead singer with Blondie?
3 Which Vanessa's album was called "The Violin Player"?
4 Which Music group was Bryan Ferry lead singer with?
5 Which Helen was "Walking Back to Happiness" in 1961?
6 Whose first hit was "Diana" in 1957?
7 Who were Steve Harley's backing group?
8 How is Noah Kaminsky better known?
9 What is the home country of Kylie Minogue?
10 Which musical instrument does Queen's Brian May play?
11 Which character with a Technicolor Dreamcoat did Jason Donovan play on the London stage?
12 What are the initials of the Canadian Ms lang?
13 Which country is Nana Mouskouri from?
14 Which Tina's life story was in the film *What's Love Got to Do with It?*?
15 Which Paula was Mrs Bob Geldof?
16 Which US city is mentioned with "Freedom" in a hit from 1975?
17 How were the Fugees "Killing Me" in 1996?
18 Which surname is shared by Edwin and Ringo?
19 Who did Little Richard say "Good Golly" to back in 1958?
20 Which Road famous for its recording studios is the title of a Beatles album?
21 Which show did Leon Jackson win in 2007?
22 Which No. 1 singer/actress/dancer married Guy Ritchie in 2000?
23 Which Ruby gave Melanie a 70s hit?
24 Which singer/songwriters were nicknamed Mr and Mrs Music?
25 Which Johnny joined Deneice Williams on "Too Much Too Little Too Late"?
26 Which male vocalist shared his name with late actress Miss Monroe?
27 Who had an album called "Everything Comes Up Dusty"?
28 Which US state were the Mamas and Papas Dreamin' of in 1966?
29 Which punk band was Malcolm McLaren manager of in the 70s?
30 How many members of the Hollies were there?

 Answers on page 213

251
POT LUCK 13

1 In which country is the city of Albuquerque?
2 What word can go before "baked", "measures" and "time"?
3 In which decade of the 20th century was Doris Day born?
4 What colour is Noddy's hat?
5 Who won the Women's Marathon gold medal at the 2005 World Championships?
6 Which Chancellor presented the first Budget of this new millennium?
7 Who wrote the novel *Tess of the D'Urbervilles*?
8 In the 70s, who had a No. 1 with "Long-Haired Lover from Liverpool"?
9 Who won an Oscar for Best Actor in *The Godfather*?
10 Which rugby league side added Giants to their name in the 90s?
11 Which 20th-century novelist used a Suffolk river as a pen name?
12 Which Bruce starred in *Moonlighting*?
13 Which Simon was vocalist with Duran Duran?
14 What word can go after "paper" and before "lifter"?
15 Henry Cecil is associated with which sport?
16 In the royal address HIH what does I stand for?
17 Whose autobiography about herself and her late husband was called *The Two of Us*?
18 In music, what note is written on the top line of the treble clef?
19 Timbuktu is on the edge of which desert?
20 What is the square root of 64?
21 Who was singer with Roxy Music?
22 The characters Fletcher and Godber appeared in which TV series?
23 Which general made a last stand at Little Big Horn?
24 The airline Iberia is from which country?
25 On a Monopoly board, what colour is Strand?
26 Which hurricane devastated New Orleans in September 2005?
27 What is the only English anagram of COULD?
28 What type of a rectangle has four equal sides and angles?
29 Who introduced "the eight who are going to generate"?
30 Who was the youngest leadership contender in the 2005 race for the Tory leadership?

252
POP POT LUCK 3

1 How is Reg Dwight better known?
2 Which Bryan's first hit was "Run to You"?
3 What is the home country of Celine Dion?
4 What was Blondie's Heart made of in 1979?
5 In 1985 Talking Heads were taking the "Road to..." where?
6 Who was lead singer with the Police?
7 Who joined Bennie on a 1976 hit by Elton John?
8 Which surname is shared by Carly and Paul?
9 How many members of the Carpenters were there?
10 What did Bill Haley sing after "See you later, alligator"?
11 Which musical instrument does Eric Clapton play?
12 Which David appeared on TV with the Partridge Family?
13 Which legendary dancer called Fred described Michael Jackson as "a wonderful mover"?
14 In which Queen No. 1 will you hear Beelzebub and Galileo?
15 Who led the Dreamers?
16 Who hit the top with "What Becomes of the Broken Hearted?" in 1996?
17 What was the Spice Girls' No. 1 album in late 1996?
18 What type of dance goes with Spandau in the charts?
19 Which Damon takes lead vocals with Blur?
20 Which London duo sang "You've got more rabbit than Sainsbury's"?
21 In 2005, Elvis Presley was at No. 1, celebrating which anniversary of his birth?
22 Who had a No. 1 with "Sometimes You Can't Make It on Your Own"?
23 Which '60s TV group included Mickey Dolenz and Mike Nesmith?
24 Which singer gave birth to baby Lourdes in 1996?
25 Suggs was the lead singer with which crazy-sounding group?
26 Which Scots pop star married the hairdresser John Freida?
27 How is George O'Dowd better known?
28 How many Lions feature on the Lightning Seeds' Euro 96 football anthem?
29 Which country are Japan from?
30 Which Eddy was lead singer with the Equals?

  Answers on page 214

 Answers on page 214

253
POT LUCK 14

1 Which Michael won an Oscar for Best Actor in *Wall Street*?

2 Which team did Michael Owen leave to go and play soccer in Spain?

3 In which decade of the 20th century was Jose Carreras born?

4 What word can go after "monk" and before "cake"?

5 In the 90s, who had a No. 1 with "Think Twice"?

6 How would 14 be written in Roman numerals?

7 Who wrote the novel *War and Peace*?

8 Who plays rugby union at the Recreation Ground, London Road?

9 In which UK No. 1 did Elvis Presley sing in German?

10 Whom did Margaret Thatcher follow as Conservative Party leader?

11 Quicksilver is another name for which element?

12 When Billie first topped the charts what was her surname?

13 Are the North Downs north of London?

14 In which country is the city of Kualalumpur?

15 How is Edward Stewart Mainwaring better known?

16 What colour are the shorts of Germany's international soccer side?

17 Dave Bedford is associated with which sport?

18 In the Bible, which book immediately follows St John's Gospel?

19 What word can follow "fruit", "rabbit" and "Suffolk"?

20 Where on the body could a cataract form?

21 Private Pike appeared in which TV series?

22 The airline Aeroflot is from which country?

23 Who wrote the *Messiah*?

24 What is the square root of 25?

25 Which planet is named after the Roman god of war?

26 Which scandal made US President Richard Nixon resign?

27 On a Monopoly board, what colour is Bond Street?

28 Which director is the subject of the movie *Gods and Monsters*?

29 Kurt Cobain was in which grunge group?

30 The character Cliff Barnes appeared in which TV soap?

254
POT LUCK 15

1 2005 marked which anniversary of the Gunpowder Plot?

2 What is the zodiac sign of the Bull?

3 On a dart board, which number is bottom centre?

4 Who had a hit with the song "Dancing Queen"?

5 Born Arthur Jefferson in 1890, what was this comic better known as?

6 What profession did Hillary Clinton previously practise?

7 Who partnered Robbie Williams on the hit single "Kids"?

8 In which sport are there madisons and pursuits?

9 Who is the only singer to have hits in the '50s, '60s, 70s, 80s and 90s?

10 According to proverb, what does the hand that rocks the cradle do?

11 What was founded in 859 at Fez, Morocco, that is reckoned to be the oldest of its type in the world?

12 Which writer established the Three Laws of Robotics?

13 Called hood in America, what's this part of the car called in the UK?

14 Titan is a moon of which planet?

15 What is hydrophobia the fear of?

16 How many furlongs in a mile?

17 Which Terry created the 2005 movie *The Brothers Grimm*?

18 Which annual race was first held in 1829?

19 What type of animal is a Lhasa Apso?

20 Garibaldi, Nice and Ginger Nut are all types of what?

21 In the USA, which are the two main political parties?

22 Which Noel said, "Television is something you appear on: you don't watch it"?

23 What was the trade of Thomas Wolsey's father?

24 What did Siam change its name to?

25 Which Colin played the title role in Oliver Stone's movie *Alexander*?

26 Which Bay housed the island prison Alcatraz?

27 What colours are on the flag of Argentina?

28 In which town did Jesus grow up?

29 Who set up Biba?

30 If a triangle has an angle of 58 degrees and an angle of 77 degrees, what is the third angle?

  Answers on page 214 **Answers on page 214**

255
POT LUCK 16

1. How many feet in a nautical mile?
2. In which country is the city of Osaka?
3. Which Phil won the US PGA in 2005?
4. What word can go before "hole", "pie" and "post"?
5. Ray Parlour and Kanu were colleagues with which London club?
6. Who was the original drummer with the Who?
7. Which Bob added his occupation to his name to top the UK charts?
8. If the first of June is a Monday what day is the 1st of July?
9. What sport is played by the San Francisco 49ers?
10. In the Bible, what is the first bok of the new Testament?
11. How many minutes in a day?
12. Which game show links Jim Davidson, Bruce Forsyth and Larry Grayson?
13. On a Monopoly board, what colour is Oxford Street?
14. Peggotty appears in which Charles Dickens novel?
15. Which UK car manufacturer produced the Cresta?
16. Which song mentions a jolly swagman?
17. The letter U is on which row of a typewriter or computer keyboard?
18. In legend, which bird rises from its own ashes?
19. In computing, what does the A stand for in RAM?
20. Alphabetically, what is the first sign of the zodiac?
21. What name is given to the horizontal bar of a window?
22. Which England cricketer won *Strictly Come Dancing* in partnership with Lilia Kopylova?
23. What day of the week did the Boomtown Rats not like?
24. What does a misogynist hate?
25. In baseball which city can support the Mets or the Yankees?
26. Moving clockwise on a dartboard, what number is next to 19?
27. Chris Old is associated with which sport?
28. Xenophobia is the fear of what?
29. The character Dennis Watts appeared in which TV soap?
30. In the 80s, who had a No. 1 with "True Blue"?

256
POT LUCK 17

1. Which John married actress Sheila Hancock?
2. Which pre-decimal coin had the value of two shillings?
3. Which group revived a previous hit in the 90s with the help of Roy "Chubby" Brown?
4. Which TV presenter's shows have had *Toothbrush* and *Breakfast* in their titles?
5. Were the Olympic Games last held in Russia in 1960, 1980 or 1988?
6. Who is Popeye's rival?
7. Was Sir Walter Scott Scottish?
8. Which English soccer side was managed by the late Bob Paisley?
9. What is the main language in Brazil?
10. Which Macaulay starred in the cartoon and live action film *The Pagemaster*?
11. Which is greater in distance, a mile or a kilometre?
12. Which MP Harriet was axed in Tony Blair's first Cabinet reshuffle?
13. Who had a 2005 No. 1 single with "I'll be OK"?
14. How many red cards are there in a standard pack of cards?
15. Ray Davies was writer and singer with which band?
16. Adonis, Apollo and Poseidon were all what?
17. Tara and Willow featured in which occult-based series?
18. Which dog is larger – a borzoi or a corgi?
19. The Micra was made by which car company?
20. *Crossroads* was set near which major city?
21. A vixen is the female of which animal?
22. Which alphabet is used by Muscovites?
23. What links the names Chamberlain, Heath and Wilson?
24. Which jockey Bob fought back from cancer to win the Grand National?
25. Who is Simply Red's lead singer?
26. Which was the first antibiotic to be discovered?
27. Which Welsh actress won an Oscar for her role in *Chicago*?
28. For which sport is Sunningdale famous?
29. A Muscovy is what type of bird?
30. Which musical Paul got involved with frogs and Rupert Bear?

  Answers on page 214

  Answers on page 214

257
POT LUCK 18

1 What do Manolo Blahnik and Jimmy Choo make?

2 If you perform a rim shot, what instrument are you playing?

3 In the Chinese calendar which year follows the year of the rat?

4 What are you in if you are caught in a Haboob?

5 What was wrestler Big Daddy's real name?

6 What trade did a webster follow?

7 Who wrote the book *The Prodigal Daughter*?

8 Where does the River Seine empty?

9 What is the fourth letter of the Greek alphabet?

10 What day of the week did Solomon Grundy get married?

11 Which bone is the hardest in the human body?

12 Who was the last Chancellor of West Germany prior to reunification?

13 What was the pen name of Eric Blair?

14 In which decade was *Jim'll Fix It* screened for the first time?

15 Who solved the crime in *Death on the Nile*?

16 Who was the first presenter of *Wheel of Fortune* in the UK?

17 Who was John Major's last Party Chairman?

18 Which breed of dog does not have a pink tongue?

19 Who portrayed Jesus in the TV adaptation *Jesus of Nazareth*?

20 Which novel by Louisa May Alcott sold millions of copies?

21 Which city in India has an airport called Dum Dum?

22 What links a group of whales to a group of peas?

23 If a Vietnamese was depositing a dong, where would he be?

24 Which hat originates from Ecuador?

25 What medical procedure was Iceland the first country to legalize?

26 What was crossed on a tightrope by Charles Blondin in 1855?

27 Which country hosted the 2006 Winter Olympics?

28 What colour smoke announces the election of a new Pope?

29 Which birthstone is linked to December?

30 Which Canadian province has Halifax as its capital?

258
POT LUCK 19

1 In which watery city is the Bridge of Sighs?

2 How would you get a note out of a bassoon?

3 Which letter is a Roman numerals and used in grading movies for viewing suitability?

4 The island of Majorca belongs to which country?

5 Which model Kate became the face of L'Oreal in 1998?

6 In a hospital what does E stand for in ER?

7 In the movies what colour is Superman's cape?

8 Which part of Monaco is famous for its car rally?

9 How many weeks are there in ten years?

10 The Murray is the main river of which country?

11 What sort of creature was the villain in the blockbuster movie *Jaws*?

12 Helen Sharman was the first female from the UK to go where?

13 In which country is there a Parliament called the Knesset?

14 Franz Klammer found fame in which sport?

15 What shape is a bagel?

16 In which branch of the creative arts did Stravinsky find fame?

17 What is mincemeat made from?

18 A mustang is a wild what?

19 Which famous Australian lit the Olympic torch in Sydney?

20 Which Peter directed the *Lord of the Rings* series of movies?

21 Which of these countries is the furthest south – India, Japan or New Zealand?

22 What is always the second line of a "Knock knock" joke?

23 People suffer when the pollen count is high if they have which fever?

24 In *Alice in Wonderland* which word is used to describe The Hatter?

25 What is needed for a game of canasta?

26 How did Maurice Greene win gold at Sydney 2000?

27 Thomas Chippendale was famous for making what?

28 Paul Azinger is linked to which sport?

29 In 1967 Christiaan Barnard performed the first transplant of what?

30 Which American city was named after the country's first President?

  Answers on page 214

 Answers on page 214

259
FOOTBALL POT LUCK 2

1 In which decade did Blackpool first win the FA Cup?
2 What colour are the stripes on Chester's home shirts?
3 What was Peter Shilton's first League club?
4 Which Tony of WBA was First Divison leading scorer in 1970–71?
5 Who was the regular keeper for Notts County in their 1991–92 relegation season?
6 Who plays at home at the Millmoor Ground?
7 Which England attacking midfielder was born in Bootle in February 1972?
8 Which club did Andy Thorn leave to join Newcastle United?
9 What is Torquay's nickname?
10 Ian Marshall and Graeme Sharpe were in the same team at which club?
11 Steve McManaman and which other player were League ever-presents for Liverpool in 1995–96?
12 In which decade was Sir John Hall born?
13 Which team were beaten 2–0 by Everton in the 1984 FA Cup Final?
14 John Trollope set a League appearance record at which club?
15 Which Ian became Southampton manager in 1991?
16 Which John of Villa won his only England cap in 1977?
17 David Harvey played over 300 games for which club?
18 What is Nigel Clough's middle name?
19 Which country did Harry Daft play for?
20 Which ex-Liverpool star was boss at Oxford Utd for a short time in 1988?
21 What position did Ricardo, the winning penalty-taker against England at Euro 2004, play?
22 Who is the only man to play in two Champions League Finals for Manchester United?
23 Which Scot played for Torino in 1961–62?
24 With which club did Trevor Sinclair make his League debut?
25 Which Ian become boss of Northampton Town in January 1995?
26 Which club moved ground from Gay Meadow to New Meadow in 2007?
27 Which team was beaten 3–1 by Tottenham Hotspur in the 1962 FA Cup final?
28 Ken Brown followed John Bond as boss of which club?
29 What colour are Exeter City's striped shirts?
30 Gordon Cowans was at which club when he made his international debut?

260
POT LUCK 20

1 Which river is nearest to Balmoral Castle?
2 Which country and western singer appeared in *Gunfight*?
3 Which US probe was sent to land on Mars in 1997?
4 Which London park would you be in to ride along Rotten Row?
5 Which Swiss resort awards the Golden Rose TV awards?
6 How did Jane Austen's character Mr Woodhouse like his boiled egg?
7 Who was the first non-Englishman to play James Bond?
8 Which British airport was the first with its own railway station?
9 In 2005, which Russian vessel was trapped off the Kamchatka peninsula?
10 How many wives are allowed at one time under Islamic Law?
11 In which century was religious reformer John Calvin born?
12 Who had a '50s No. 1 with "Who's Sorry Now"?
13 If it's 12 noon GMT what time is it in Oslo?
14 A red variety of which fruit went on sale in Marks & Spencer, Feb. 2006?
15 Who wrote the novel *Anna Karenina*?
16 Which bridge joins a palace and a prison in Venice?
17 What word can follow "band", "mass" and "pass"?
18 Which battle came first – Agincourt or Bosworth Field?
19 What is the next highest prime number above 53?
20 In which American state are the Everglades?
21 Who took over Leeds soccer club in Jan. 2005?
22 Hollyoaks featured a map of which city in its opening credits?
23 Which banned insecticide was the first to be man-made?
24 What was Britney Spears's second No. 1 single?
25 What is the capital of Georgia of the former USSR?
26 Whose motto is Ich Dien?
27 Who was the first presenter of *Tomorrow's World*?
28 Where was the Bayview Retirement Home in *Waiting for God*?
29 In which decade was *Blue Peter* screened for the first time?
30 Which river was Jesus Christ baptized in?

  Answers on page 214

  Answers on page 214

261
POT LUCK 21

1 Prince William graduated from which Scottish university in 2005?

2 Which album by The Beatles was released in 2006?

3 Who is the most well-known employee of cartoon character Mr Burns?

4 In which Australian city is the WACA cricket ground?

5 Which John wrote the book "Mission Song"?

6 Which singer Bob became a Tory Party's adviser on global warming in Nov. 2005?

7 Sam Walton founded which US-based chain of stores?

8 A bruschetta is fried or toasted what?

9 What is the first name of supermodel Ms MacPherson, dubbed "The Body"?

10 Queens is the largest borough in which famous American city?

11 Which David had a album with "Life in Slow Motion"?

12 Which Colin featured with Al Pacino in the movie *The Recruit*?

13 In *Cats* which showstopper does Grizabella remember to sing?

14 A millennium best seller, what is added to champagne to make Bucks Fizz?

15 In which city is the Dome of the Rock?

16 Which Keanu played the lead in *The Matrix* series of movies?

17 If IC stands for Inter-Continental what does M stand for in ICBM?

18 Pippa and Patrick lived next door to which elderly sitcom couple?

19 Which movie actress links *Gangs of New York* and *In Her Shoes*?

20 A sufferer from alopecia is likely to lose what?

21 Who or what are James M Cox and Norman Manley International?

22 In which programme did Desmond Lynam replace Richard Whiteley?

23 The term alter ego originated from which language?

24 Which Katie is better known as Jordan?

25 In a Sudoku what is usually fitted back into the frame?

26 Max and Dr Russell worked as what in *Inspector Morse*?

27 How is a footpath indicated on a modern map?

28 Who was the Labour Party's youngest ever leader of the 20th century?

29 In Roman Polanski's movie *Oliver Twist* which Ben was Fagin?

30 Who sold No. 32 Smith Square in February 2007?

262
POP POT LUCK 4

1 In which decade did the Smurfs have their first hit record?

2 How was Walden Robert Cassotto better known?

3 Which song title links Scott Walker and Kool and the Gang?

4 Whose first hit was "Shake, Rattle and Roll" in 1954?

5 Who was lead vocalist with the Zombies?

6 Whose album "Shepherd Moons" topped the charts in 1992?

7 How many hit singles did Frank Zappa have in the 70s?

8 Whose debut album was "No Parlez"?

9 How was Alvin Stardust previously known in the charts?

10 Which group's members included Neil Innes and Vivian Stanshall?

11 In which country were Boney M based?

12 In which decade was Dolly Parton born?

13 Whose first hit was "Get Down and Get With It"?

14 Who had an 80s hit with "Got My Mind Set on You"?

15 What is Clarence Henry's nickname?

16 What is the home country of Bjorn Again?

17 Who took part in the Eurovision Song Contest as a member of separate groups, Co-Co and Bucks Fizz?

18 Who did Sarah Brightman sing with on her first chart hit?

19 Which record label did Herb Alpert co-found?

20 What name was given to the new country stars of the 1990s?

21 Who had a UK chart hit in 2008 with "The Promise"?

22 Who put together and managed Westlife, having done the same with Boyzone?

23 What was the name of Harold Melvin's backing group?

24 Whose nickname was "Lady Leather"?

25 In the 1980s, which group's first hit was "Letter from America"?

26 What type of "Summer" was a 1980s hit for Style Council?

27 Who joined East 17 on the 1996 hit "If You Ever"?

28 Whose first album was called "Soul Provider"?

29 Who was told, "Don't be a hero" by Paper Lace in 1974?

30 Which country singer was born with the initials J.R.?

  Answers on page 215

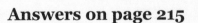 **Answers on page 215**

263
POT LUCK 22

1 What is a compote?

2 Which of Boeing's jets were launched in 1958, seating 189?

3 Who sang the theme song to the Bond film *Octopussy*?

4 Which mining town is named Berneslai in the *Domesday Book*?

5 What is the main edible export of Argentina?

6 Who was assassinated by Satwant and Beant Singh?

7 In *The Simpsons* who is reverend of Springfield?

8 Which family of fruit does the kumquat belong to?

9 Which Soviet football team was the first to make a European final?

10 Michael Henchard was the mayor of which fictional town?

11 Which character did Nicole Kidman play in *Moulin Rouge*?

12 What is the only English anagram of FIENDISH?

13 Which desert spreads into South West Africa from Botswana?

14 *The King of Barataria* is the subtitle of which light opera?

15 In which suburb was *The Good Life* set?

16 Hakan Sukor played soccer for which country?

17 Which play by George Bernard Shaw inspired *My Fair Lady*?

18 Which letter and number follow Albert Square, Walford?

19 Which England soccer keeper had the first names Raymond Neal?

20 Who wrote the novel *The French Lieutenant's Woman*?

21 Who sits on the Woolsack?

22 Athene is the Greek goddess of wisdom. Who is the Roman?

23 Who wrote "Hark, the Herald Angels Sing"?

24 Which state became the 50th American state?

25 Who created Perry Mason?

26 Which former film star was US Ambassador to Ghana in the 70s?

27 Who got the sack from the Beatles before they hit the big time?

28 What do H and G stand for in H. G. Wells's name?

29 What was called the Pluto Platter when it was originally sold?

30 In which century was Captain James Cook born?

264
POT LUCK 23

1 Robert Barclay founded what type of business?

2 For which sport is Jim Furyk famous?

3 Which Emma went from the Spice Girls to *Strictly Come Dancing*?

4 How many people were there in the original line-up of Hear'Say?

5 Which word means vocations and also means moves wildly?

6 Which Briton is the oldest 100m Olympic winner of the 20th century?

7 In which decade of the 20th century was Britney Spears born?

8 What did Michael Douglas and Catherine Zeta Jones call their baby son?

9 Which leader of the Palestine independence movement was buried in November 2004?

10 How many kidneys do humans normally have?

11 What was the name of the boat in which Ellen MacArthur sailed around the world?

12 The now extinct dodo was what type of creature?

13 Where does a hippopotamus spend most of its life?

14 What type of pattern is on a raccoon's tail?

15 What does a hyacinth grow from?

16 In *Dad's Army* which character often declared, "We're doomed"?

17 When texting, the word WHY is usually shown by which letter?

18 What type of food is associated with Harry Ramsden's?

19 What do you fear if you have bibliophobia?

20 A smolt or smelt is a young of which creature?

21 Manuel the waiter appeared in which classic comedy series?

22 Which soccer club has a stand dedicated to the late Bobby Moore?

23 What were the 19th-century Forty Niners searching for?

24 Which is not the name of a sea – Black Sea, North Sea or West Sea?

25 In the 1980s, young upwardly mobile persons became known as what?

26 In which country would you watch Nantes play a home soccer match?

27 What was manufactured by the business set up by Harvey Firestone?

28 How many English kings known as Henry came after Henry VIII?

29 What was Ken Barlow's main career throughout his many years as a *Coronation Street* character?

30 Which month was named after Mars, the god of war?

  Answers on page 215

 Answers on page 215

265
POP POT LUCK 5

1 In which decade did Stevie Wonder have his first hit record?
2 How is Concetta Rosemarie Franconero better known?
3 How did Charles Aznavour Dance in the 70s?
4 Who were Acker Bilk's backing band?
5 Whose first hit was "Year of Decision"?
6 Which musical instrument does Larry Adler play?
7 Whose album "Nobody Else" topped the charts in 1995?
8 What was the Who's first chart hit?
9 Who was like a "Rubber Ball" in 1961?
10 Who thought Elenore was swell in 1968?
11 Who sang "Nice One Cyril" in 1973?
12 Who was "Out of Time" in 1966?
13 What is the home country of Boris Gardiner?
14 Which song title links Len Barry and Gloria Estefan?
15 Whose first hit was "Love is Like a Violin"?
16 Who was on the "Marrakesh Express" in 1969?
17 How many times in the 80s did "Do They Know It's Christmas?" enter the charts?
18 In which decade was Sade born?
19 Which animals are on the cover of the Beach Boys album "Pet Sounds"?
20 Which creature links song titles by Elton John and Jimmy Nail?
21 "Bootie Call" was a hit for which girl group?
22 Who released a 2008 album "Let It be Me"?
23 What is the logo of the British record label Parlophone?
24 Who had the first instrumental No. 1 hit in 1953?
25 Who resigned as a Radio 1 DJ when he couldn't have Fridays off?
26 In which decade was Roberta Flack born?
27 Who was "Dancing on the Ceiling" according to his 1986 hit?
28 Who was a "junkie" according to David Bowie's "Ashes to Ashes"?
29 About which London Underground station did the New Vaudeville Band sing in 1967?
30 Which Mary Poppins song won an Oscar in 1964?

266
POT LUCK 24

1 Which bridge on the Thames is closest to the Tower of London?
2 Who seized power in Uganda in 1971?
3 What does "PB" against a runner's name indicate?
4 What was made by Sauron in a J. R. R. Tolkien book?
5 On TV, in which city is Ramsay Street?
6 Who is Charlie's sister in the CBeebies series based on Lauren Child's books?
7 Which character loves the little red-haired girl in "Peanuts"?
8 Which US space shuttle was the first to gain orbit into space?
9 Which annual holiday did the 1992 government want to move?
10 Which city provides the setting for *Nineteen Eighty-Four*?
11 What do the D and H stand for in D. H. Lawrence's name?
12 Which holiday date saw Michael Owen's first return to Anfield after his spell in Europe?
13 Who was the Greek god of time?
14 What musical instrument was played by Sherlock Holmes?
15 In which century was Sir Isaac Newton born?
16 If you were a resurrectionist, what would you steal?
17 In Morse code what letter is represented by one dot?
18 Which birthstone is linked to August?
19 Albert Tomba has been a world champion in which sport?
20 In which war was the Battle of Bunker Hill?
21 In which country did the fandango originate?
22 Which Man was discovered in East Sussex in 1912?
23 Which comic team included a Welshman, an Indian-born Anglo-Irishman and an Anglo-Peruvian?
24 Handel's *Messiah* was first put on for the public in which city?
25 What does karaoke mean?
26 In which decade was *The Antiques Roadshow* first screened?
27 What is the surname of the *Eurovision Song Contest* winner Katrina?
28 In which city was *Fame* set?
29 Who wrote the novel *Jamaica Inn*?
30 Which Scottish city has Saint Mungo as its patron saint?

  Answers on page 215

 Answers on page 215

267
FOOTBALL POT LUCK 3

1 Craig Johnston scored an FA Cup Final goal for which club?

2 Who in July 1986 moved to Rangers for £600,000, a new record fee for a keeper?

3 What was Steve Hodge's first League club?

4 What colour are Benfica's home shirts?

5 To ten years either way, when did Bury first win the FA Cup?

6 Who moved from Bristol Rovers in November 1989 to set a club record for transfer fee received?

7 Who plays at home at Boothferry Park?

8 Which club did Joey Jones leave to join Liverpool?

9 In which city was David Batty born?

10 Andy Goram was at which club when he made his international debut?

11 Who was Terry Venables's assistant at Barcelona?

12 Which team were beaten 1–0 by Ipswich in the 1978 FA Cup Final?

13 In which decade was Geoff Hurst born?

14 Alan Wright and Scott Sellars were in the same team at which club?

15 Which club did Wimbledon buy John Fashanu from?

16 Who holds the League appearance record at Celtic?

17 Which John became manager of Chelsea in March 1985?

18 Which country did Mick Robinson play for?

19 Ron Atkinson followed Dave Sexton as boss of which club?

20 Which club did Gary McAllister leave to join Leeds Utd?

21 Which club beat Arsenal 2–1 to win the last Football League Cup Final in Cardiff?

22 Which club won seven consecutive French League titles in the 21st century?

23 Which was Marcus Bent's first League club?

24 When did the USA first take part in the World Cup?

25 What is the first name of Joachim, formerly of Leicester City and Aston Villa?

26 In which decade did Hearts first win the Scottish FA Cup?

27 Whose 1992 £3,300,000 transfer to Blackburn from Southampton was a club record for a transfer fee received?

28 Cec Podd set an appearance record at which club?

29 Jim Baxter was at which club when he made his international debut?

30 Which England manager was born in London on 6 January 1943?

268
POP POT LUCK 6

1 What was Joan Baez's first top ten hit?

2 Which song was a hit for Shirley Bassey and Harry Belafonte in 1957?

3 Whose album "But Seriously" topped the charts in 1990?

4 Who duetted with Frank Sinatra on the 1993 single "I've Got You Under My Skin"?

5 Who sang "The Sun ain't Gonna Shine Any More" in 1966?

6 Which conservationists' "Minuetto Allegretto" charted in 1974?

7 Who was lead singer with the Troggs?

8 Which two 80s Wimbledon tennis champions had a top 100 hit in 1991?

9 Who took "Hallelujah" to No. 1 at Christmas in 2008?

10 According to Edison Lighthouse, what happens Where My Rosemary Goes?

11 In which decade was Donny Osmond born?

12 Which fellow-Western actor was on the flip side of Lee Marvin's "Wandrin' Star"?

13 Who had "Magic Moments" in 1958?

14 Whose first hit was "One of These Nights"?

15 Who was a "Yesterday Man" back in 1965?

16 Which day of the week was "Beautiful" to Daniel Boone in 1972?

17 How is Arnold Dorsey better known?

18 Which song title links Don Partridge and Elton John?

19 In which decade did Jackie Wilson have his first hit record?

20 What is the home country of Jimmy Cliff?

21 Which band's last album, released in 2005, was called "Home"?

22 How old was LeAnn Rimes when "Sittin' on Top of the World" was released in the US?

23 Which name links Freedom with Vanessa?

24 What was the Christians' first UK top ten hit?

25 Who had a '60s hit with "Come and Stay with Me"?

26 Andy Fairweather-Low was "Wide-Eyed" and what in his 1975 hit?

27 Which surname is shared by Rickie Lee and Quincy?

28 Which "Queen" was a 1970 hit for the Kinks?

29 What is the main colour on the album cover of Blur's "The Great Escape"?

30 Which word follows "Love and" in the song title by Cher?

  Answers on page 215

  Answers on page 215

269
POT LUCK 25

1 What would you measure on the cephalic index?

2 Which name links Gwent, Rhode Island, USA, and the Isle of Wight?

3 When was VAT introduced in Britain?

4 In the Tour de France, who wears the polka dot jersey?

5 Which breakfast dish was originally a hangover cure?

6 Who played Max in the 2005 movie remake of *The Producers*?

7 Where would you find the Doge's Palace?

8 What is the minimum number of points to win on a tennis tie-break?

9 What colour hair did Churchill have before he went bald?

10 What is the main range of hills in Gloucestershire?

11 Who wrote the novel *The Children of Men*?

12 What is the only English anagram of PIMENTOS?

13 What is studied by a heliologist?

14 In which century was Thomas à Becket born?

15 In Morse code what letter is represented by one dash?

16 Which golfer first won the US amateur title three years in a row?

17 Which London street is famous for men's tailoring?

18 Which was the frequency of Radio Luxembourg?

19 Which famous chair was kidnapped by students from the Cranfield Institute of Technology in 1978?

20 Which character did Bonnie Langford play in *Just William*?

21 What was Spain's General Franco's first name?

22 In the Chinese calendar which year follows the year of the dragon?

23 What is the RAF equivalent to the army rank of Major?

24 What was Jacques Cousteau's research ship called?

25 Which city does the Hallé Orchestra come from?

26 How many different venues were selected for the 2006 World Cup in Germany?

27 What is the Archbishop of Canterbury's official residence?

28 Where in London did the statue Alison Lapper Pregnant appear in 2005?

29 In which decade of the 20th century was Jack Nicholson born?

30 What is the main flavour of aioli?

270
POT LUCK 26

1 Tony Blair visited the Faisal mosque in which country in November 2006?

2 Which Niall took over as Sunderland chairman and manager?

3 Who is in the title with the Owl in Edward Lear's poem?

4 What went with *Hide* in the title of a 2005 Robert de Niro movie?

5 How many people are involved in a fencing match?

6 Which British PM during the 1970s "winter of discontent" died in 2005?

7 What are the sides of a stage called?

8 In music, the lines on which notes are written go in which direction?

9 Which people used C, D, L and M in their counting system?

10 John Glenn became the first person over 70 to do what?

11 What is the first name of Ms Hill who sang with the Fugees?

12 Which Texan gave his name to a tall hat – was it Homburg, Stetson or Tengallon?

13 A Bruxellois is a person coming from which city?

14 Marmite yeast extract is rich in which vitamin?

15 Which of these three spoons is the largest – a coffeespoon, a dessertspoon or a tablespoon?

16 What is the piece of the mushroom above the stalk called?

17 What were the pyramids made out of?

18 In the past, Kampuchea was known by which of these names: Cambodia, Sri Lanka or Thailand?

19 Which common kitchen item can also be a type of drum?

20 Which girl band made a movie called *Honest*?

21 Jonathan Edwards won an Olympic gold medal in which event?

22 What job did Peter and Andrew do before becoming disciples of Jesus?

23 Geometry is a branch of which subject?

24 Coal, diamonds, leather – which of these three items is not mined from underground?

25 What is the first of the three letters that invites you to turn over a piece of paper?

26 How many spaces are contained in a frame for noughts and crosses?

27 On a camera, what opens and closes to allow light in?

28 Is a kayak a type of currency, a hairy animal or a sailing craft?

29 Whose first hit was "Because We Want to"?

30 In the nursery rhyme "Hey Diddle Diddle", who did a runner with the dish?

  Answers on page 215

 Answers on page 215

271
MOVIES POT LUCK 4

1 In which film did King Jaffe Joffer appear?
2 Which Alan featured in *Die Hard*?
3 In which decade was *Rebecca* released?
4 In which movie did Winona Ryder play Cher's daughter?
5 Who won the Best Director Oscar for *One Flew over the Cuckoo's Nest*?
6 Which actor married US journalist Maria Shriver, one of the Kennedy clan?
7 Which character did Anthony Hopkins play in *Legends of the Fall*?
8 To the nearest hour, how long does *Dances with Wolves* last?
9 "King of the Cowboys" Leonard Slye was better known as whom?
10 Who directed *Goodfellas*?
11 A character named Rooster Cogburn first appeared in which film?
12 Who played Dolly in the '60s *Hello Dolly*?
13 In which decade was *A Streetcar Named Desire* released?
14 Which James was Professor Lindenbrook in *Journey to the Centre of the Earth*?
15 Who won the Best Actress Oscar for *Children of a Lesser God*?
16 *Anna and the King of Siam* and *Cleopatra* featured which Rex?
17 Who played Blofeld in *On Her Majesty's Secret Service*?
18 In which decade of the 20th century was Danny Glover born?
19 Which pop veteran featured in *The Man Who Fell to Earth*?
20 Who was Roger Moore's first Bond girl?
21 At what sport did Warren Beatty excel?
22 Who won the Best Actor Oscar for *Captains Courageous*?
23 Which conductor was Woody Allen's father-in-law?
24 Who directed *The Full Monty*?
25 Who played Lieutenant Schaffer in *Where Eagles Dare*?
26 Which 2008 action movie stars Nicolas Cage as an assassin in the Far East?
27 Which *Happy Days* actor has become a multi-Oscar-winning director?
28 What were the names of the Blues Brothers
29 Which Jeff featured in *The Big Chill*?
30 Which musician presided over the 1987 wedding of Bruce Willis and Demi Moore?

272
POT LUCK 27

1 Which range of hills has Cleeve Hill as its highest point?
2 Who painted a "Self Portrait with Bandaged Ear"?
3 Who co-wrote "We are the World" with Michael Jackson?
4 Where, on the River Stort, was the birthplace of Cecil Rhodes?
5 Which year was the Hiroshima bombing?
6 Which lager is the name of Britain's second-most important men's tennis tournament?
7 Which toll bridge crosses the River Severn?
8 In *The Sopranos* Dr Jennifer Melfi is played by which actress?
9 What is the first thing you should do if you have a motor accident?
10 What is Cape Kennedy now called?
11 What do P and G stand for in P. G. Wodehouse's name?
12 Which country has the internet code .se?
13 Morgan Freeman won 2005's best supporting actor Oscar for which film?
14 In which area of Greater Manchester did Dr Harold Shipman work?
15 What word can go after "gall" and before "hem"?
16 What is the capital of Vietnam?
17 Which actor portrayed Rowdy Yates in *Rawhide*?
18 In which century was Chopin born?
19 Whose was the voice of Dangermouse in the cartoon series?
20 Which Sheffield theatre opened in 1972?
21 Where are British monarchs crowned?
22 Whose Organ Symphony was used for the theme of *Babe*?
23 Who made the first non-stop double flight across the English Channel?
24 In which Dickens novel does Alfred Jingle appear?
25 What colour caps do the Australians cricket team wear?
26 Which girl's name means grace and favour in Hebrew?
27 Who wrote *The Rainbow*?
28 In which decade of the 20th century was Ray Charles born?
29 Alfresco, Golden Boy and Shirley are types of what?
30 What is the capital of Sri Lanka?

  Answers on page 216

 Answers on page 216

273
POT LUCK 28

1 Which Irish group were "Breathless" at making in the year 2000?

2 England keepers David Seaman and Richard Wright were together at which club in September 2001?

3 Which ocean is to the east of South Africa?

4 What part of the body goes after Winged to name golf's 2006 US Open venue?

5 Under which nationality did Navratilova play her final Wimbledon?

6 If an animal has not been sighted for 50 years it is described as what?

7 What kind of game is bridge?

8 Which country beginning with an E joined the European Union in 2004?

9 Which dance was connected with Marlon Brando and Paris?

10 A natural sponge is what colour?

11 What is the sport of Riddick Bowe and Buster Douglas?

12 Which insect carries the disease malaria?

13 In which decade did Wet Wet Wet have their first hit?

14 Which SIr George masterminded the Beatles album "Love"?

15 What is the first word sung in the popular carol "Away in a Manger"?

16 Which is the fastest speed – a gale, a hurricane or a storm?

17 Which country is directly west of southern Spain?

18 In which decade of last century was Thierry Henry born?

19 Suffragettes campaigned so that women had the right to do what?

20 Ornithophobia is a fear of what?

21 Which former US President died in June 2004?

22 Which bird shares its name with a famous nurse?

23 The disease tuberculosis is often abbreviated to which initials?

24 Which letter is the symbol of the euro currency?

25 What colour is a female blackbird?

26 The Marquis of Queensberry established rules relating to what?

27 How many noughts appear when one million is written in figures?

28 How does a venomous snake kill things?

29 A wishbone resembles letter of the alphabet?

30 What is the name of the system that enables humans to breathe?

274
MOVIES POT LUCK 5

1 To the nearest hour, how long does *Braveheart* last?

2 In which decade was *Trading Places* released?

3 How is Julia Wells better known?

4 Which Ashley featured in *Heat*?

5 In the 1930s who sang "Old Man River" in *Showboat*?

6 Who won the Best Director Oscar for *Reds*?

7 What was the name of Mel Gibson's character in *Ransom*?

8 Who married Lyle Lovett instead of Kiefer Sutherland?

9 Who played the Bond girl in *Goldfinger*?

10 *Wish You Were Here* and *The Real Thing* featured which actress?

11 Was *The Untouchables* with Kevin Costner set in the 1920s, 40s or '60s?

12 In which film did a character named Randie P. McMurphy appear?

13 Which Cliff featured in *Three Days of the Condor*?

14 Which screen gangster was born Emmanuel Goldenberg in Rumania in 1893?

15 Which Julianne starred in *The Lost World: Jurassic Park*?

16 A character named John Mason appeared in which film?

17 Who played Kristin Scott Thomas's husband in *The English Patient*?

18 Who was the blonde female star in *Marnie* and *The Birds*?

19 Who won the Best Actor Oscar for *Coming Home*?

20 In which decade was *The Greatest Show on Earth* released?

21 Who played the villain in *Robin Hood: Prince of Thieves*?

22 Who directed *Love Story*?

23 Which Matthew starred in *Married to the Mob*?

24 Who won the Best Actress Oscar for *Roman Holiday*?

25 *Who Framed Roger Rabbit?* and *Back to the Future III* featured which actor?

26 Which British actress won an Oscar for her role as Queen Elizabeth II?

27 Which Korean War medical drama/black comedy did Robert Altman direct?

28 What was the name of Robin Williams's character in *Mrs Doubtfire*?

29 In which decade was the biker classic *Easy Rider* released?

30 Who sang the Bond theme from *A Licence to Kill*?

  Answers on page 216

 Answers on page 216

275
POT LUCK 29

1 Which film featured the single "Vogue" by Madonna?
2 In medical terms, what does an ECG stand for?
3 Is Rolf Harris's birthday portrait of the Queen done in oils or watercolours?
4 With which two surnames did Aussie Evonne win Wimbledon?
5 Who played the con man in Spielberg's *Catch Me If You Can*?
6 Which canal linked Liverpool to London?
7 Which piece of attire took its name from a Pacific nuclear test site?
8 Who wrote the novel *Nostromo*?
9 Who was lost for six days in 1982's Paris–Dakar desert rally?
10 Which dessert is named after a ballerina?
11 Who invented the magnetic telegraph?
12 What word can go after "tea" and before "fast"?
13 Which word links a TV quiz show with space launches?
14 In which century was Botticelli born?
15 Who was Miss California in 1978?
16 What is the capital of Albania?
17 Which heroine was awarded Freedom of the City of London in 1908?
18 In Scrabble, how many points is the letter J worth?
19 In which country would you find the Great Sandy Desert?
20 In Morse code what letter is represented by four dots?
21 Alphabetically what is the last of the chemical elements?
22 What name is given to the larva of a fly?
23 Who became a Saint in 1909, nearly 500 years after she was killed?
24 In which Dickens novel does Jerry Cruncher appear?
25 What fruit can be made from the letters in TRANSCIENCE?
26 Which Asian capital city did George W. Bush visit in November 2005?
27 In which decade of the 20th century was Warren Beatty born?
28 Which pop star ran for Mayor of Detroit in 1989?
29 What name describes the loose rocks on the side of a mountain?
30 Which hat took its name from a novel by George Du Maurier?

276
POT LUCK 30

1 Stamp duty is normally paid on the sale of what?
2 In which country is Aceh province, scene of the 2004 tsunami?
3 What does a BACS system transfer?
4 Who wears a chasuble?
5 Who or what is your doppelganger?
6 Emphysema affects which part of the body?
7 Which term for school or university is from the Latin meaning "bounteous mother"?
8 Which salts are hydrated magnesium sulphate?
9 What was the last No. 1 single made by Steps?
10 What did Plaid Cymru add to its name in 1998?
11 Which punctuation mark would an American call a period?
12 For which film did George Clooney win Best Supporting Actor in 2006?
13 Where were the Elgin marbles from originally?
14 Which song starts, "Friday night and the lights are low"?
15 According to legend, what will happen to Gibraltar's ape population if the British leave?
16 Is BST before or behind GMT?
17 Which country does Man Utd's Nemanja Vidic represent?
18 How many valves does a bugle have?
19 What name is given to the compulsive eating disorder?
20 What is a Blenheim Orange?
21 Which childhood disease is also called varicella?
22 What do citronella candles smell of?
23 Which part of the anatomy shares its name with a punctuation mark?
24 Which tax did council tax immediately replace?
25 Which English archbishop signs his name Ebor?
26 Which saint was born in Lourdes?
27 Which proposal for a single currency shares its name with a bird?
28 Where is the auditory canal?
29 Where is a fresco painted?
30 How long must a person have had to be dead to qualify for a blue plaque?

  Answers on page 216

 Answers on page 216

277
POT LUCK 31

1 Who played the title character in the first *Doctor Who* movie?

2 In 2007 the isle of Inis Mor held a festival celebrating which TV show?

3 Which Grand National course fence, other than Becher's, contains the name Brook?

4 Stephen Cameron's 1996 death was a tragic first in which circumstances?

5 Which American was the first to achieve tennis's Men's Singles Grand Slam?

6 In song lyrics, where did Billie Jo Spears want to lay her blanket?

7 Which Roger was drummer with Queen?

8 Along with Doric and Corinthian, what is the third Greek order of architecture?

9 Who was the first British woman to win a world swimming title?

10 Which northern city has the dialling code 0113?

11 What nationality is Salman Rushdie?

12 What was the first hit album by The Killers?

13 Which population was devastated by myxomatosis?

14 Which is the brightest planet as seen from the Earth?

15 What do three horizontal lines represent in mathematics?

16 Which English King was the last to die in battle?

17 In rock opera, Tommy was deaf, dumb and what else?

18 How many times does the letter A appear in the first name of singer/ actress Streisand?

19 Sale Sharks won the Guinness Premiership title in 2006, beating which team in the final?

20 What is the next prime number above 100?

21 What is a quadrilateral with one pair of opposite sides parallel called?

22 Which telephone link service was established in July 1937?

23 What is lowered by a beta-blocker?

24 Which country has the greatest number of telephone subscribers?

25 In the song "Country Roads", which place is described as "almost heaven"?

26 Who was the most famous inhabitant of the fictitious village St Mary Mead?

27 Which composer's 6th Symphony is known as the *Pathétique*?

28 Who was 60 first – Gloria Hunniford, Cliff Richard or John Major?

29 Boxer Jack Dempsey was nicknamed which Mauler?

30 Which country suffered most loss of life in the Indian Ocean tsunami of December 2004?

278
POT LUCK 32

1 Who won the Best British Group award at the 2007 Brits?

2 Where did golfer Padraig Harrington win his first major, the Open Championship?

3 To which mammal family does the dingo belong?

4 Who preceded David Cameron as leader of the Conservative Party

5 Which tobacco company sponsored the *Football Yearbook* from 1970 to 2001?

6 What is the study of rocks and rock formations?

7 Who was short-listed for the Turner Prize for "Shark in Formaldehyde"?

8 Is the penguin native to the North Pole or the South Pole?

9 Which building, built on an island in San Francisco Bay, is now a tourist attraction?

10 On which two countries' borders is Mount Everest?

11 What is the world's largest mammal by weight?

12 Which former South African President was too ill to attend the 2007 Rugby World Cup final?

13 Which former comedy partner of Stephen Fry stars in the American hospital drama *House*?

14 Which Hungarian Communist politician proclaimed his country to be Soviet Republic in 1919?

15 In which city is the synthetic-turfed Luzhniki Stadium?

16 What is name of the world's largest ocean liner, which entered service in 2004?

17 Which East London station will be the arrival point for international railusers during the 2012 Olympics?

18 Which British decathlete won gold medals in both 1980 and 1984?

19 What was the name of the family that ran the Fiat motor company until the 1990s?

20 Where was Gianni Versace murdered in 1997?

21 Who did Forest Whitaker play in his Oscar-winning role in *The Last King of Scotland*?

22 Which of Tony Blair's children was born while he was Prime Minister?

23 What is the main currency of Malaysia?

24 What is the capital of Macedonia?

25 Which British musician and poet wrote the opera *Peter Grimes*?

26 What tourist attraction commemorates the Great Fire of London in 1666?

27 What was the name of the Duke of York's (Prince Andrew) father-in-law?

28 Which country toured England to play rugby league in both 1907 and 2007?

29 Which homonyms could be a primary colour or slang for wasted as in a chance?

30 Who was England cricket captain when they toured Australia in 2006–07?

 Answers on page 216

 Answers on page 216

279
POT LUCK 33

1 In which decade did Lester Piggott first win the Derby?
2 Who had hits with "My Perfect Cousin" and "Jimmy Jimmy"?
3 Which folklore fantasy tale is subtitled "There and Back Again"?
4 Who was Nelson Eddy's singing partner in many musical films?
5 Which famous sword is sometimes called Caliburn?
6 Which famous film director has a son called Satchel?
7 Which is further North, Chelmsford or Colchester?
8 Children's broadcaster Derek McCulloch was known on the radio as whom?
9 What is your mode of transport if you go by Walker's Bus?
10 Which Israeli leader suffered a severe stroke in January 2006?
11 Which Wizzard star formed ELO in 1971?
12 In which TV soap was Trevor Jordache buried under the patio?
13 Who played Old Mother Riley in films and on stage?
14 Which member of the Monty Python team was born on the same day as John Major?
15 What does the word piliferous mean?
16 What was the first Westlife No. 1 to feature the word "Love" in the title?
17 Which King George bought Buckingham Palace?
18 What kind of animal is a Schnauzer?
19 Which soccer boss was the first to win the English double twice?
20 In which famous Square is St Basil's cathedral?
21 In the series *Dad's Army* which soldier's daytime job was an undertaker?
22 Chris Woodhead and Mike Tomlinson have both been Chief Inspectors of what?
23 Which animals are attacked by a disease called Scrapie?
24 Which childhood disease affects the parotid salivary gland?
25 Which female MP was one of the founder members of the SDP?
26 What can be fired by a crossbow?
27 In which city was Anne Frank when she wrote her diary?
28 Which actress played lead in the films *Dimples* and *Curly Top*?
29 Lard is mainly produced from which animal?
30 Which king was the last Emperor of India?

280
POT LUCK 34

1 In which US National Park is the Old Faithful geyser?
2 What do the initials IMF stand for?
3 What is emitted from a fumarole?
4 What is the main ingredient in dhal, the Indian dish?
5 In which city is Bramall Lane?
6 Westlife had a No. 1 with "Mandy", but who had the original hit?
7 Who was in goal for the "great escape" run-in for Portsmouth 2006?
8 How is Josephina Jacques known in *Carry On* films?
9 To what would a codicil be added?
10 Which American annual celebration was first marked during 1789?
11 The first Girl Guides had to wear what colour stockings?
12 Which band claimed fifty per cent of Bob Marley's estate?
13 Cullen Skink is what kind of soup?
14 What does NEC stand for around Birmingham?
15 Who left Bow Wow Wow to form Culture Club?
16 What is the maximum score in blackjack?
17 Which building in France has a famous Hall of Mirrors?
18 Does one revolution of the London Eye take around 15, 30 or 70 minutes?
19 Which country did Arsenal keeper Bob Wilson play for?
20 In the Bible, which character saw the first writing on the wall?
21 A Daiquiri is made from fruit juice and which alcoholic drink?
22 Astraphobia is the fear of which meteorological event?
23 Which male pop superstar once played with the Frantic Elevators?
24 Machu Picchu is in which mountain range?
25 What is the English equivalent of the Melbourne Cup?
26 What is surrounded by amniotic fluid?
27 Who links *Fawlty Towers* and *After Henry*?
28 Which bird is India's national symbol?
29 Which sea is the least salty in the world?
30 Where was the Duke of Windsor buried in 1972?

  Answers on page 216

  Answers on page 216

281
POT LUCK 35

1 What do the initials NASA stand for?
2 What is a palmiped?
3 In which city would you find the house of the painter Rubens?
4 What had Chloe and Jack become in Great Britain by the dawn of the new millennium?
5 Who was duped by a "Fake Sheikh" in January 2006?
6 Dodonpa, Goliath and Phantom's Revenge are all names of what?
7 What do Romney Marsh, Suffolk, Clun and Forest have in common?
8 Who was the singer on the radio classic *Take It from Here*?
9 Who succeeded Pope John Paul II?
10 In *Dad's Army* what was the occupation of Private Frazer?
11 What was Casanova's occupation at the time of his death?
12 Which Dutchman won the World Darts Championship in 2006?
13 Who wrote the forensic thriller *Predator*?
14 Which organization was founded in Ontario, Canada, by Mrs Hoodless in 1897?
15 What is the British equivalent to the US trademark Plexiglas?
16 Monte Marmolada is the highest peak of which mountain range?
17 Where in Britain would you find Roedean Girls' School?
18 Which Guy Ritchie film has the tagline "a disgrace to criminals everywhere"?
19 What was referred to as Black Forty-Seven?
20 2005 was which anniversary of the game of Monopoly?
21 What are Prince Andrew's three other first names?
22 Concord is the capital of which US state?
23 What is the opposite of oriental?
24 Which of Charles Dickens' novels was left unfinished in 1870?
25 Which Scottish mathematician invented logarithms?
26 What is the longest bone in the human body?
27 Who wrote "Anything Goes" and "Can Can"?
28 In Greek legend, which prophetess was the foreteller of doom?
29 Who was nicknamed "The Beard" by the US intelligence service?
30 The carnation is the national flower of which country?

282
POT LUCK 36

1 A limited edition bank note issued in November 2006 featured which person?
2 Katie Holmes and Tom Cruise married in which castle in Italy?
3 When was the BT monopoly of directory enquiry service calls deregulated?
4 Around how many customers did Farepak have at the time of its 2006 collapse?
5 At which ground did Sven Goran Eriksson's England first lose a game?
6 Brian Littrell was in which best-selling boy band?
7 Which commission investigated KGB infiltration in the Italian government?
8 In which state does the action of *The Blair Witch Project* take place?
9 What was on the other side of Elvis' original release of "Little Sister"?
10 Mirza Tahir Hussain spent how many years on death row before his November 2006 pardon?
11 Which country were chosen to host cricket's 2015 World Cup?
12 Gemma Adams and Tania Nicol were victims murdered near which town?
13 How many players did Australia use in the 2006–07 Ashes series?
14 Which Mervyn was Governor of the Bank of England in 2007?
15 Caitlin McClatchey won Commonwealth Gold in which sport?
16 What is the name of the magazine company featured in TV's *Ugly Betty*?
17 Which former *A-Team* actor featured in *Celebrity Big Brother* in 2007?
18 Henrik Larsson missed a penalty against which team in Germany 2006?
19 Which contained the line, "They're going to crucify me"?
20 What name links a Joseph Conrad novel and the craft in the movie *Alien*?
21 Which year will be the centenary of when Joan of Arc became a Saint?
22 At which West End theatre did *The Woman In White* open?
23 Which middle name is shared by David Beckham and Kevin Keegan?
24 Whose artistic works include "Away from the Flock"?
25 Who shared the 1998 Nobel Peace Prize with David Trimble?
26 In which Jack Nicholson movie did Danny have an imaginary friend called Tony?
27 Who was 50 first – John Kettley, Tony Blair or Richard Madeley?
28 Which country did Asafa Powell run for?
29 Who was the first UK female to have four solo hit singles?
30 The Rt Rev. David Urquhart became Bishop of where in November 2006?

  Answers on page 217

 Answers on page 217

283
POP POT LUCK 7

1 Who was nicknamed the "Tycoon of Teen"?

2 Who had most weeks in the UK charts in 1970 and 1971?

3 In which film did Elvis play the role of Walter Gulick?

4 How is Patricia Louise Holt-Edwards better known?

5 What was the sixth of Rod Stewart's six No.1 albums between 1971 and 1976?

6 Which song begins "Almost heaven West Virginia"?

7 What was the best-selling single of 1980?

8 Whose first UK single was "Halfway Down the Stairs"?

9 In which musical will you find Grizabella and Rumpleteazer?

10 Who won the 1965 Grammy for Record of the Year for "A Taste of Honey"?

11 Who sang Norway's 1995 Eurovision winner "Nocturne"?

12 What was the first of Tom Jones's three No. 2 hits between 1967 and 1968?

13 Which David Bowie Top 30 hit has only two letters?

14 Which Desmond Dekker hit has a number in its title?

15 Which football team had a hit called "We Can Do It"?

16 What was the first of Slade's trio of No. 1 albums between 1973 and 1974?

17 How did the Beach Boy Dennis Wilson meet his death?

18 Who starred as Pink in Alan Parker's 1982 film *The Wall*?

19 Why did the Police dye their hair blond?

20 Which lady provided Kenny Rogers and Little Richard with hit records?

21 How is Norma Eggstrom better known?

22 What is the first of Sweet's three No. 2 hits between 1973 and 1974?

23 Which Who hit has a number in the title?

24 Which song was subtitled "Spurs are on Their Way to Wembley"?

25 Which song begins "Music is a world within itself with a language we all understand"?

26 Who had a breakthrough single in 2008 with "I Kissed a Girl"?

27 Which band is comprised of three brothers and a cousin all named Followill?

28 Which *American Idol* contestant had a US No. 1 in 2009 with "My Life Would Suck without You"?

29 What's the stage name of Stefani Joanne Angelina Germanotta?

30 Who has an alter-ego named Sasha Fierce?

284
POT LUCK 37

1 In 2005, who released the album "Affirmation"?

2 What colour was Rupert Bear's face in early books and annuals?

3 Where did the world's first controlled nuclear reaction take place in 1942?

4 What is the collective name for a group of bears?

5 In our solar system which planet is farthest from the Sun?

6 What colour was the Queen's outfit for the blessing of Charles and Camilla after their wedding?

7 Which big cat has the proper name Acinonyx jubatus?

8 Who ordered the building of the Pavilion at Brighton ?

9 What is the side away from the wind called on a ship?

10 What was Robin's real name in the *Batman* TV series?

11 Which fish walks on land?

12 What does the musical term Vivace mean?

13 What was the real title of the painting called *The Laughing Cavalier*?

14 Which king was known as "Silly Billy"?

15 Who designed the first mechanical adding machine in 1641?

16 In which country did a cultural revolution take place during 1966–69?

17 Who drew the Katzenjammer Kids for the *New York Journal* in 1910?

18 Who was the first Irish athlete to win gold in the European Championships?

19 Which scale measures the effects of an earthquake at a particular place?

20 What is the vitamin riboflavin?

21 Which is the second largest island in the world after Australia?

22 Which actress starred in *Bend It Like Beckham* and *ER*?

23 What was the surname of soul musician Booker T.?

24 What would the Chuckle Brothers be called if they used their real surnames?

25 In which Alpine range is the Swiss mountain, Jungfrau?

26 What nationality was the first non-US, non-Soviet spaceman?

27 To two years, in what year was the final episode of *Dad's Army* originally screened?

28 Where in Italy was Mussolini executed?

29 Which means of transport features on Darkness's album cover "One Way Ticket to Hell... and Back"?

30 What was the surname of the Windsors before they changed it?

 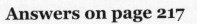 **Answers on page 217**

 Answers on page 217

285
POT LUCK 38

1 To ten years when was the Rotary Club founded?

2 Which horse with a John Wayne link won the first Grand National?

3 What does the second R stand for in the acronym RADAR?

4 Which monarch attended the very first Royal Ascot?

5 Which country was the first to introduce vehicle registration plates?

6 Jo-Raquel Tejad become known as which movie actress?

7 What is the largest castle in England?

8 Who scored the quickest ever FA Cup Final goal?

9 What was George II supposedly sitting on at the time of his death?

10 EOKA was an active terrorist organisation on which island?

11 Who wrote the novel *The Ordeal of Gilbert Pinfold*?

12 A cross between a Scottish draught horse and a Flemish horse produced which breed?

13 Under what name did Paul and Phil Hartnoll have hit records?

14 What is the name of the Royal Hong Kong Jockey Club's racecourse?

15 How is Denali in Alaska also known?

16 Which place used to form part of The Stranglers' name?

17 In which year did Bernhard Langer first play in a Ryder Cup?

18 What is the usual general temperature requirements for serving sake?

19 Who combined with Leiber to write the rock classic "Jailhouse Rock"?

20 Which food additive prevents fat and water separating out?

21 Who was Republic of Ireland boss when Sven was appointed?

22 What was the only Top Ten hit for US female group First Choice?

23 At which track did Michael Schumacher achieve his record-breaking 52nd career win?

24 Dyce Airport serves which city?

25 Who was born first, Albert Einstein or Charles Darwin?

26 In "Penny Lane", what is the occupation of the person selling poppies from a tray?

27 Alan Shearer scored his only England hat trick against which team?

28 In which country is the city of Tabris?

29 Which former member of Steps featured in *Celebrity Big Brother* in 2007?

30 What was the directorial debut of the screenwriter of *Gosford Park*?

286
MOVIES POT LUCK 6

1 Who directed *Groundhog Day*?

2 In which film does a character named Bud Fox appear?

3 In the '50s epic, what colour horses pull Ben Hur's chariot during the race?

4 Which Josh featured in *Teenage Mutant Ninja Turtles*?

5 Within five minutes, how long does *Mrs Doubtfire* last?

6 Who did Ray Milland play in *National Velvet*?

7 How many crew members were there in the Nostromo in *Alien*?

8 What movie is being watched in *Home Alone 2: Lost in New York*?

9 Which British actor won an Oscar for *Separate Tables*?

10 Within fifteen minutes, how long does *Lost in Space* last?

11 Which Nicholas featured in *Chariots of Fire*?

12 Who was the first non-professional actor to win an acting Oscar?

13 Which actress links *Drop Dead Fred* and *Soapdish*?

14 Which actor was originally set to play Tom Cruise's role in *Born on the Fourth of July*?

15 Which writer directed *Night Breed* in 1990?

16 Which 1988 film had the highest fee ever for a commissioned script?

17 Who played Brandi in the film *Boyz N the Hood*?

18 Which 1990 film had the highest ratio ever of stunt men to actors?

19 Who appears as a gravedigger in the film *LA Story*?

20 The song "Buttons and Bows" came from which movie?

21 Which Ron featured in *Swingers*?

22 Who won the Best Actress Oscar for *The Rose Tattoo*?

23 A character named Joe Turner appeared in which film?

24 Who directed *Gremlins*?

25 Who played Lucy Westenra in the film Bram Stoker's *Dracula*?

26 Which birthday did Will Smith celebrate in 2008?

27 Which star of *Semi Pro* decided not to appear in any sports movies after 2008?

28 Who directed *Deep Impact*?

29 Edith Head won eight Oscars and received 35 nominations in which department?

30 In which year did David Niven die?

 Answers on page 217

 Answers on page 217

287
POT LUCK 39

1 Which queen of England had 11 fingers?

2 In *The Lone Ranger* what was the name of Tonto's horse?

3 Which world-famous scientist said that any man who likes marching had been given a brain for nothing: just the spinal column would have done?

4 To £5 either way, how much did a colour TV licence cost in 1974?

5 Former Tory Party leader Michael Howard was born in which country?

6 What type of fish is a torpedo fish?

7 In which year was Nelson Mandela sentenced to life imprisonment?

8 Who followed Hussein as King of Jordan?

9 To ten years either way, when was the Victoria Cross instituted?

10 Who said, "There but for the Grace of God, goes God"?

11 Into how many international time zones is the world divided?

12 What was Walt Disney's middle name?

13 What is the link between the words act, flow, loin and shore?

14 In the Rocky Mountains what is the dry wind that is warm in winter and cool in summer?

15 Published in 2001, which male novelist writes as a first-person female narrator in *How to be Good*?

16 Which group were made up of Douglas, Ginger, Henry and William?

17 When did Rhodesia declare UDI?

18 What is the physics of friction properly called?

19 What is the collective noun for several moles?

20 What does hydrogen fuse into in the Sun's core?

21 Who was Mary Queen of Scots' first husband?

22 What is the longest snake in the world?

23 Which character gave the name to the series *It ain't Half Hot Mum*?

24 Which duke owns Badminton, setting for the well-known horse trials?

25 To ten years, when did Hong Kong become a British crown colony?

26 Who invented the caricature John Bull?

27 How else is the star Sirius known?

28 Who played the White Witch in the 2005 movie version of *The Lion, The Witch and the Wardrobe*?

29 Who became editor of *The Oldie* magazine in 1992?

30 Who won the first British Open Golf Championship?

288
POT LUCK 40

1 In motor racing, who was the first driver to be sacked twice by Benetton?

2 Who was the first *Coronation Street* actress to be awarded an OBE?

3 A brochette is another name for what type of food?

4 Who adapted *The Cider House Rules* into a movie?

5 In which country is the city of Makeyevka?

6 What does a lapidary deal in?

7 On 19th February 2007, Notting Hill, Kensington, Westminster became subjected to what?

8 Which group had 1970 top ten hits with "Sunny", "Belfast" and "Painter Man"?

9 What did D stand for in Franklin D Roosevelt's name?

10 In which 1980s movie did Mr & Mrs Harvey Keitel star?

11 Victor Emmanuel was the first King of which European country?

12 Leander is the oldest club in the world in which sport?

13 In 2007 who won the Orange Rising Star Award at the BAFTAS?

14 What is Sebastian Coe's middle name?

15 Which 1990s English soccer champions have a ground with the Darwen End?

16 Where in the US was the first artificial turf soccer pitch?

17 What was the first Top Ten single for Iron Maiden?

18 Which city hosts the oldest modern-day marathon race?

19 Whose wives included Helen Menken and Mary Philips?

20 On TV for many years Michael Miles invited contestants to do what?

21 Paris and which other capital city were the first to be linked by telephone?

22 What was Gary Cooper's job before he became an actor?

23 The Strathcona Cup is competed for in which sport?

24 What was the first Top Ten single for James?

25 Which folk singer and writer who inspired Dylan, passed away in February 2007?

26 Who dropped out of *The Godfather, Part III*, allowing Sofia Coppola to play the role?

27 Michael Fagan made the headlines when he broke into where?

28 In which film did a pilot named Klaatu appear?

29 How does Roger Peterson fit into the history of pop music?

30 Geraldine Rees was the first woman jockey to finish which race?

 Answers on page 217

 Answers on page 217

289
POP POT LUCK 8

1 What is on David Bowie's face on the album cover of Aladdin Sane?
2 Which instrumental group had a hit with "Perfidia" in the 1960s?
3 Who played bass on Manfred Mann's "Pretty Flamingo"?
4 Who first played Dorothy and the Scarecrow in *The Wiz* on Broadway?
5 Which Isley Brothers song was recorded by the Beatles?
6 Which British trio released the gold album "Brain Salad Surgery"?
7 What was the first-ever UK reggae No. 1, in 1969?
8 Who wrote "Baby Come Back" for the Equals?
9 Who was the first French solo singer to get to No. 1 in the UK?
10 Which Stones album cover had peel-off sticky labels on the front?
11 Who recorded the title track for "Twins" with Philip Bailey?
12 What is Evelyn King's middle nickname?
13 Who had a minor hit with "Gin and Juice" in 1994?
14 Whose first album was called "Postcard"?
15 Which British pop festival was founded in 1968?
16 What was the Oscar-winning song from the 1985 film *White Nights*?
17 How is Apollo C. Vermouth, producer of "I'm the Urban Spaceman" by The Bonzo Dog Doo-Dah Band, better known?
18 About whom did John Lennon say, "We might have had him in the group"?
19 Which severe illness did Joni Mitchell suffer from when she was nine?
20 Which song title links the Supremes and Dannii Minogue?
21 At which 1998 awards ceremony did Chumbawamba throw water at John Prescott?
22 Who released the 2004 album "Mind, Body & Soul"?
23 What is the predominant colour of the "Making Movies" album cover?
24 Who made a comedy album called "Hedgehog Sandwich"?
25 Which Jackson brother suggested, "Let's get serious"?
26 Which brothers starred in a weekly television series in Australia in the 1960s?
27 How old is Marie in the Chuck Berry hit "Memphis Tennessee"?
28 Which artist spent the most weeks in the UK charts in 1990?
29 On which Eurythmics album cover is Annie Lennox wearing a black mask?
30 What single and album gave the Steve Miller Band chart success in 1982?

290
POT LUCK 41

1 In which decade was flogging abolished in Britain?
2 What sort of word is made up from initial letters of other words?
3 What is a necropolis?
4 Where did the Vikings originally come from?
5 What is the coldest substance?
6 Who wrote the book *Chitty Chitty Bang Bang*?
7 In which sport is there a york round?
8 Who wrote the song "If"?
9 In cricket how many runs is a Nelson?
10 Which British prime minister once said, "Is a man an ape or an angel? Now I am on the side of the angels"?
11 By what name is Jim Moir better known?
12 When was the first free vertical flight of a twin-rotor helicopter?
13 What does an aphyllous plant not have?
14 For how long did Alexander the Great rule?
15 What is the central administrative body of the Catholic Church?
16 Which decade saw the introduction of instant coffee?
17 In which city was Ray Davies of the Kinks shot in the leg in 2004?
18 Who launched the *Daily Mail*?
19 Which co founder of *The Guinness Book Of Records* passed away in 2004?
20 Which film did newspaper magnate William Randolph Hearst inspire?
21 Which city is built on the site of the Aztec capital Tenochtitlan?
22 To which king in the Bible was Jezebel married?
23 Which famous American singer was described in *Life* magazine in 1974 as having a "half-melted vanilla face"?
24 What do you do in music when you play a piece "con brio"?
25 What punishment did the Vestal Virgins of Rome suffer if they betrayed their vows of chastity?
26 Which movie actress has twins Phinnaeus and Hazel?
27 Which is the largest seed in the world?
28 To 20 years each way, when was Hyde Park opened to the public?
29 Which country built the *Mars* probe known as Beagle 2?
30 Gilberto Silva joined Arsenal from which club side?

 Answers on page 217

 Answers on page 217

291
POT LUCK 42

1 *Titanic* overtook which movie as the most costly ever made?
2 Which animal is linked with the US state of Minnesota?
3 In which American city sharing its name with a European city were R.E.M. formed?
4 In which month did the Japanese launch the 1941 attack on Pearl Harbor?
5 Who or what is a merlon?
6 The unlikely-sounding writing duo Ham and Evans penned which song that made for two different artists?
7 Who wrote the book on which *101 Dalmatians* was based?
8 England led Australia by what score at half time in the 2003 rugby World Cup Final?
9 How long was the run of Arthur Miller's first Broadway play?
10 What was the creature-named publishing company set up by Paul Hamlyn?
11 What was the occupation of Louis Washkansky, the first heart transplant recipient?
12 Who played Ava Gardner in the movie *The Aviator*?
13 What was Eternal's first single not to make the Top Ten?
14 Who drew the caricature sequences at the start of TV's *Yes Minister*?
15 Which character did Jim Davidson play in *Up the Elephant and Round the Castle*?
16 In 1824 William Buckland named the first what?
17 What was the middle name of sub-four-minute-miler Roger Bannister?
18 Which creatures were wild in the title of a Jung Chang novel?
19 In which royal residence did Queen Victoria die?
20 To which Olympic thrower was runner Mary Decker married?
21 What was the first – and only – Top Ten hit for Silver Convention?
22 What celestial body is portrayed in the seventh movement of Gustav Holst's *Planet Suite*?
23 From which play was the movie *Casablanca* adapted?
24 "June is Bustin' Out All Over" features in which musical?
25 Which horse was the first ever winner of the Derby?
26 In which country is the city of Kumasi?
27 Which player scored the first penalty in the 2006 FIFA World Cup Final shoot-out?
28 How many Motown acts recorded "I Heard It Through the Grapevine" before Marvin Gaye?
29 Laennec is credited with inventing which medical aid?
30 What percentage of zebras have exactly the same pattern of stripes?

292
MOVIES POT LUCK 7

1 Jackie Brown is based on whose bestseller, *Rum Punch*?
2 Which Diane featured in *The Wicker Man*?
3 Who directed *Lost in Space*?
4 Who starred with Terence Stamp in '60s movie *The Collector*?
5 Which actress links *Raising Arizona* and *Once Around*?
6 Within five minutes, how long does *Pale Rider* last?
7 Who was Daniel Day-Lewis's actress mother?
8 Who played Charlie's handsome colleague in *Roxanne*?
9 What was the name of Edward Woodward's character in *The Wicker Man*?
10 Who played Addy in the film *City Heat*?
11 Who won the Best Director Oscar for *The Divine Lady*?
12 In which land is *The Neverending Story* set?
13 Within ten minutes, how long does *Invasion of the Body Snatchers* last?
14 Which Paul featured in *Romeo and Juliet*?
15 What was the name of Anthony Hopkins's character in *The Elephant Man*?
16 Who directed *Butterfield 8*?
17 Who won the Best Director Oscar for *The Last Emperor*?
18 Who played Peter Falk's grandson in *The Princess Bride*?
19 Who played Bonnie Rayburn in the film *City Slickers*?
20 In which film did a character named Griffin Mill appear?
21 The song "Swinging on a Star" came from which movie?
22 Who played opposite Elliott Gould in the 70s remake of *The Lady Vanishes*?
23 Which Carrie featured in *Pale Rider*?
24 Who won the Best Actress Oscar for *Two Women*?
25 Who directed *The Cable Guy*?
26 Who plays Elliot Moore in *The Happening*?
27 How many Oscar nominations and awards did Meryl Streep receive 1979–2007?
28 What was the name of Gary Cooper's character in *High Noon*?
29 Which actress worked at a pineapple cannery in Hawaii before finding fame?
30 Whose first writing credit, with Alice Arlen, received an Oscar nomination for *Silkwood*?

 Answers on page 218

 Answers on page 218

293
POT LUCK 43

1 Australia's Barossa Valley is noted for which industry?
2 Who succeeded Ted Hughes as Poet Laureate?
3 Which French building did architects Nervi, Breuer and Zehrfuss create?
4 Which programme did the late John Peel present on Saturday mornings on Radio 4?
5 Who was the voice of Stuart Little in the 1999 movie?
6 After which mythological Greek character was the drug morphine named?
7 In which year did Britain go decimal?
8 What is the world's fastest-moving insect?
9 What was the capital of the Roman province of Britain before Londinium (London)?
10 How many minutes approximately does it take for one revolution of the London Eye?
11 At what height does a pony become a horse?
12 Which bird was selected in 1961 as the British national bird?
13 Who invented neon lights in 1911?
14 Which country was the first to insist upon car registration plates?
15 What was the original name of the flagship the *Golden Hind*?
16 Who was the first sovereign to be addressed as "Your Majesty"?
17 Which painting was stolen and kept for two years by V. Peruggio?
18 When did the first televised debate of the House of Lords take place?
19 What is the capital of Samoa?
20 In which country did the first Christmas stamp appear in 1898?
21 Which volcano erupted to give the greatest explosion in recorded history?
22 For what did the Swede Jenny Lind achieve fame?
23 How many legs has a lobster?
24 Who won the last FA Cup Final of the 20th century?
25 Which is the largest of the anthropoid apes?
26 Who is the magical spirit of the air in Shakespeare's *The Tempest*?
27 Who wrote the lyrics to "A Whiter Shade of Pale"?
28 How many Oscars for best director did Alfred Hitchcock win?
29 Which paper was first published as the *Daily Universal Register*?
30 Which grain is used to make malt whisky?

294
POT LUCK 44

1 At which meeting was the establishing of an International Monetary Fund proposed?
2 How is Iran's Dasht e Kavir also known?
3 Which is farthest north – Kerry, Limerick or Munster?
4 Which famous car did Issigonis design as well as the Mini?
5 WG Grace died on which future England captain's 15th birthday?
6 Where was the first permanent English settlement in the New World?
7 The lady born Sheila Gilhooly wrote the second part of whose autobiography?
8 Who described Herbert Von Karajan as "a kind of musical Malcolm Sargent"?
9 What does M stand for in HTML?
10 In 1994 Johannesburg was made capital of which region?
11 Which painter, and sister of a famous painter was the model and mistress of Rodin?
12 What is the southernmost city of New Zealand?
13 Who is the heroine of *Fear of Flying*?
14 Who made his debut in *The Wise Little Hen* in 1934?
15 Which classic did Kylie Minogue sing when she starred in the show which opened the Fox Studios in Sydney in 1999?
16 On which Channel is Alaska's capital?
17 Who broke the solo flight record to Cape Town in 1932?
18 What was the speed limit raised to when it no longer required a person with a red flag to walk in front of a motor vehicle?
19 Where did *The Mousetrap* have its first night in the West End?
20 Which newspaper published the first crossword?
21 Where is Yupik or Yuk spoken?
22 How are the Sandwich Islands now known?
23 Which UN Secretary General negotiated peace in the Iran–Iraq War?
24 Who did Helmut Kohl overtake as Germany's longest serving Chancellor in 1995?
25 What was Prince Philip's military rank when he married Princess Elizabeth?
26 Which Great Britain forward was sacked by Leeds Rhinos in January 2006?
27 What is the English title of the play *La Cantatrice Chauve*?
28 "Whom the Gods Would Destroy" was an episode in a series about which TV detective?
29 In which city did Tchaikovsky die?
30 In which month did Margaret Thatcher announce her resignation as Prime Minister?

  Answers on page 218

  Answers on page 218

295 FOOTBALL POT LUCK 4

1 Alphabetically, which is the last Scottish League club?
2 Which two English clubs have a badge with a horse on it?
3 Who was manager of Wales for 47 days?
4 In the 1920s, 1930s and 1940s which club used to play at the Recreation Ground, Hanley?
5 What are the two middle names of Noel Blake?
6 Wark and Walsh scored in the same European game for which club?
7 Who scored for Manchester Utd in the Cantona Kung-Fu game?
8 Jurgen Kohler moved for £4 million plus from Bayern Munich to which club?
9 Who commentated, "Stuart Pearce has got the taste of Wembley in his nostrils"?
10 Jimmy Hampson established a record for most League goals in a season at which club?
11 Talbot and Ford were in the same team at which club?
12 Which Alan became boss of Wycombe Wanderers in June 1995?
13 Clive Woods first played in an FA Cup Final for which team?
14 At which club did Mark Bright make his League debut?
15 In what decade did Kilmarnock first win the championship?
16 Which club has a fanzine called *Ferry Cross the Wensum*?
17 Neil Warnock followed John Barnwell as manager of which club?
18 Joe Allon moved to Chelsea in 1991 to set a record for a transfer fee received at which club?
19 Which club was once known as Ardwick FC?
20 To one each way, how many international goals did Chris Nichol score?
21 Which club was 2007–08 League champions in Poland?
22 Which father and son were managing Football League/ Premiership clubs in 2008?
23 What is Matt Le Tissier's middle name?
24 Lovett, Collard and Hope played for which 1960s FA Cup finalists?
25 Which England player hit 22 goals in just 23 games?
26 Which League do FC Sion play in?
27 Grant and Rideout scored Euro goals in the same 1990s game for which club?
28 What FA Cup Final tradition was altered in 1992?
29 Which former Bournemouth player became their manager in 2008?
30 Who lost 1–0 to AC Milan in the final of the 1990 European Cup?

296 POT LUCK 45

1 Who shot the Archduke Franz Ferdinand?
2 In fiction, what were Milly Molly Mandy's proper names?
3 Which monarchs sat on the Peacock Throne?
4 Of what is a lux a unit?
5 In the early 19th century what did George Shillibeer bring to London?
6 Who first claimed that the world was not flat but a sphere?
7 Who was the first woman to fly the Atlantic single-handed?
8 Which animals communicate by touch, smell and dance?
9 Around which French town is the champagne industry centred?
10 A track by which female artist was used as the theme to ITV's *Celebrity Love Island*?
11 At what speed in mph does a wind become a hurricane?
12 Who officially opened the 1936 Olympiad?
13 What was the name of the first talking cartoon?
14 Which competition was organized by Mecca Ltd to coincide with the 1951 Festival of Britain?
15 Who invented the coordinate system to compare relationships on a graph?
16 What colour is the ribbon of the Victoria Cross?
17 Who or what lived in Honalee?
18 Which profession would use the terms occlusion, isohyet and adiabatic?
19 What name is used to describe a baby salmon?
20 In which building did Charles and Camilla hold their civil wedding ceremony?
21 Who is the husband of Meera Syal?
22 Who anonymously entered a contest in Monaco to find his lookalike and came third?
23 Where in Spain was Pablo Picasso born?
24 Who was Edward VI's mother?
25 Which sea has no coast?
26 Who was the first Briton to organize a continental holiday tour?
27 What was the first US for Destiny's Child?
28 Who discovered oxygen in 1774?
29 Which bird can fly the fastest?
30 Which is the largest human organ?

  Answers on page 218   **Answers on page 218**

297
POT LUCK 46

1 YouTube was founded in which year?

2 Which constituency did MP Alan B'Stard's represent in TV's *The New Statesman*?

3 "Atom Heart Mother" was the first album to top the UK charts by which long-lasting group?

4 Which film studio released the first talking film?

5 Roger Bannister's first sub-four-minute mile was recorded at 3 minutes and how many seconds?

6 Which club did Mark Hughes join when he left Chelsea?

7 In which sport has Bob Nudd been world champion?

8 Which Commonwealth country was the first to issue a special Christmas stamp?

9 What was the nationality of the first manager to win the European Cup with an English club?

10 Which initials are linked to the discovery by Paul Muller?

11 What was the first top ten hit for Seal?

12 When was the last manned moon landing of the last century?

13 Which musical is based on the writing of Christopher Isherwood?

14 TV presenter Alison Holloway became the third wife of which comic?

15 *Stare Back and Smile* was the autobiography of which actress?

16 Who was the first winner on Wimbledon's new court in the 1990s?

17 In which country is the city of Nara?

18 Concord and Louise Bonne are both types of what?

19 Whose one and only UK top ten hit was "Jeans On"?

20 Who was Queen Elizabeth II's first Prime Minister?

21 How many wickets did Shane Warne take in his final Test series?

22 Which two countries share the world's longest frontier?

23 Which planet's day is actually longer than its year?

24 For which film did Geena Davis first win an Oscar?

25 Which renowned Danish furniture designer engaged in a lifelong quest to design the perfect chair?

26 Which former golfer shares a birthday with opera star Placido Domingo?

27 Who or what was the fabulous Cullinan Diamond named after?

28 The first solo transatlantic flight started in New York but where did it finish?

29 Usually known by its initials, what was set up at the Bretton Wood Agreement of 1944?

30 Which office item was registered by Wolfgang Dabisch in 1962?

298
FOOTBALL POT LUCK 5

1 In which decade did Chester add City to their name?

2 Which Nigel went on from non-League St Blazey to play for England?

3 How many points did Newcastle Utd take from their first 10 games of the 1995–96 League season?

4 What is Peter Beagrie's middle name?

5 Which club used to play at the Antelope Ground?

6 Which Brian of Burnley made his only England appearance in 1961?

7 What was the first club that Arthur Cox managed?

8 Peter Allen set a League appearance record at which London club?

9 Gerry Ryan took temporary charge of which club in November 1991?

10 Manchester City in 1995 and Blackburn in 1996 both played how many League games before a win?

11 David Seaman and Peter Reid were in the same team at which club?

12 Which John first became boss of Millwall in 1986?

13 Clive Goodyear played in an FA Cup Final for which team?

14 At which club did England's Mark Wright make his League debut?

15 In what decade did Dundee first win the championship?

16 Which club had a fanzine called *Marching Altogether*?

17 Dave Bassett followed Billy McEwan as manager of which club?

18 Rufus Brevett moved for £250,000 to QPR in 1991 to set a record for a transfer fee received at which club?

19 Which club was once known as Singers FC?

20 To two each way, how many international goals did John Toshack score?

21 Which club was 2007–08 League champions in the Czech Republic?

22 Who left the board of Manchester United to join the board of Chelsea in 2004?

23 Marvin Hinton and Peter Houseman played for which 1970s FA Cup finalists?

24 What is Darren Huckerby's middle name?

25 Which ex-Manchester City keeper recommended Eike Immel to his old club?

26 Who lost on penalties to Steaua Bucharest in the final of the 1986 European Cup?

27 Who holds the record for the fastest-ever England goal?

28 Which Arsenal player was booked for the first time in his career in the 1993 FA Cup Final replay?

29 Viv Anderson was player/manager of which club in 1993–94?

30 Ray Graydon scored a League Cup Final winner for which club?

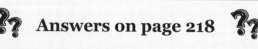 **Answers on page 218**

 Answers on page 218

299
POP POT LUCK 9

1 Who sang "Raindrops Keep Falling on My Head" in the film?

2 What colour was the Island 45 record label in the '60s?

3 Who was the first artist to have two Oscar-winning songs in the same decade?

4 Whose first UK hit was "I'm a Man"?

5 What was Engelbert Humperdinck's last No. 1 in the '60s?

6 From which film did "Rock Around the Clock" come from?

7 Which film had the song "The Morning After"?

8 What was the Bachelors' only No. 1?

9 Which London group failed an EMI audition and had 15 top ten hits?

10 What is the main colour on the "Beggar's Banquet" album?

11 Who was known as the "Godfather of Rhythm and Blues"?

12 Who wrote Jackie Wilson's "The Sweetest Feeling"?

13 On which label was Lionel Richie's 1992 album "Back to Front"?

14 Who was the first solo artist to have a No. 1 album?

15 Whose real surname was Ivanhoe?

16 Who had a '60s album called "Please Get My Name Right"?

17 In which film did Elvis play the role of Pacer Burton?

18 How is Charles Westover better known?

19 In which country was Danny Williams born?

20 Which hit was based on a stay by Justin Hayward in Jamaica?

21 Which famous American chart celebrated its 50th anniversary in August 2008?

22 Which Elton John hit does he refuse ever to play in public?

23 What follows in brackets in the title of Phil Collins's hit "Against All Odds"?

24 What group were asking "Don't Bring Me Down" in 1964?

25 Who sang the theme song from *The Man with the Golden Gun*?

26 What time is the Rocket Man's zero hour?

27 Who had a great success with "Poetry in Motion" in 1960?

28 Who played bass synthesizer on Whitney Houston's "I Wanna Dance with Somebody (Who Loves Me)"?

29 Which 1980s No. 1 translates from Spanish as "the goat"?

30 Which Beach Boy died in 1984?

300
POT LUCK 47

1 Who were tennis's "Four Musketeers"?

2 Which tennis player appeared in *Octopussy*?

3 Who had the car number plate X CZECH?

4 Who won the first US Men's Open?

5 Who, in 1986, became the youngest woman semi-finalist at Wimbledon for 99 years?

6 Who won the inaugural Grand Slam Cup in Munich in 1990?

7 What was Monica Seles's first Grand Slam title?

8 Who was the first Australian woman to win the Wimbledon Singles?

9 How does a Golden Grand Slam differ from a Grand Slam?

10 With whom did Billie Jean Moffitt win her first Wimbledon Doubles title?

11 What year was the world's first Open tournament?

12 Who was the first German to win the Wimbledon Men's Singles after reunification?

13 At Wimbledon who won an unseeded men's final in the 90s?

14 Whom did Roger Federer beat to win his third US Open?

15 In 2005, who won the women's German Open for the third time?

16 Who were the winners of the 2006 Davis Cup?

17 Who gave Virginia Wade her trophy when she won Wimbledon?

18 Which new competition was included in the Wimbledon championships in 1884 along with the Women's Singles?

19 Which Grand Slam title has Boris Becker never won?

20 Which Grand Slam title did Roger Federer not win in 2006?

21 In 1992 John McEnroe won the Wimbledon Doubles title with whom?

22 Who replaced Martina Hingis as World No. 1 in October 1998?

23 Whom did Boris Becker beat to become Wimbledon's youngest Men's Singles winner?

24 Whom did Greg Rusedski sack as his coach during Wimbledon 1998?

25 Who won his first Open title in 1985 two years after winning the Junior Grand Slam?

26 Which mentor of Pete Sampras died in May 1996?

27 Who was the last British man before Tim Henman to reach a Wimbledon quarter-final?

28 Where was Martina Hingis born?

29 How is Wimbledon semi-finalist Mrs Lampard better known?

30 Which Helena won two titles in one day at Wimbledon 1996?

 Answers on page 218

 **Answers on page 218**

301
PLANTS

1 Which green plant is widely seen on St Patrick's Day?
2 Which term describes a plant crossed from different species?
3 Where in London are the Royal Botanical Gardens?
4 If a leaf is variegated it has two or more what?
5 What is the flower truss of a willow tree called?
6 Which flower became the emblem of the Labour Party in the 80s?
7 Which part of a tree is cork made from?
8 Which former Tory minister shares his name with a type of tree?
9 Which Busy plant is also called *Impatiens walleriana*?
10 Which part of a plant may be called tap?
11 Which word describes a plant which can withstand the cold and frost?
12 Which "trap" shares its name with a planet?
13 What name is given to a plant which completes its life cycle in less than a year?
14 Are conifers evergreen or deciduous?
15 Which London borough hosts an annual flower show?
16 The thistle may be a weed to some but it's the symbol of which country?
17 What does a fungicide do to fungi?
18 Which garden vegetable – often used as a fruit – has edible stems and poisonous leaves?
19 What is the study of plants called?
20 A type of crocus produces which yellow spice or flavouring?
21 What are the fruits of the wild rose called?
22 Which holly trees are the only ones to bear berries?
23 Which plant associated with the seaside is used to make laver bread?
24 The cone or flower cluster of which plant is used to make beer?
25 Which tree can be white or weeping?
26 Archers made their bows from which wood commonly found in churchyards?
27 Does a crocus grow from a bulb or a corm?
28 On which continent did potatoes originate?
29 The maple is the national emblem of which country?
30 Is the cocoa tree native to North or South America?

302
SEA LIFE

1 The whale shark is the largest what?
2 Which fish shares its name with a sports boot?
3 What is the name of the heaviest mammal which lives in the sea?
4 A mollusc's body is covered in what?
5 What is a baby whale called?
6 Great white and hammerhead are types of what?
7 Which one of these creature has pincers – dolphin, lobster or seal?
8 Which nationality Man o' War is a sea creature?
9 The word "octo" means an octopus has how many tentacles?
10 Where would you find plankton?
11 How many legs does a seahorse have?
12 Which of these is not a fish – cod, osprey or perch?
13 A fish breathes through what?
14 A sardine is a young what?
15 How many tentacles does a squid have?
16 Where does a marine creature live?
17 Blue, fin and humpback are all types of what?
18 What do marine mammals feed their babies on?
19 Approximately how much of the Earth's water is in the oceans – 67%, 87% or 97%?
20 Which term best describes the eyesight of a whale – excellent, outstanding or poor?
21 What is the name for a whale's layer of fat?
22 What do fish absorb through their gills?
23 Which fish was at the centre of the so-called fishing Wars involving Great Britain and Iceland?
24 What colour fur does a baby grey seal have?
25 How much of an iceberg is visible on or above the surface of the sea – 12%, 50% or 90%?
26 Caviar is the name given to which fish's eggs, seen by many as a great delicacy?
27 Nurse and tiger are both types of what?
28 Which of the following is not a type of whale – Blue, Gold or White?
29 Which hole helps a dolphin to breathe?
30 Which of the following is the crayfish related to – lobster, sardine or whale?

   Answers on page 219

 Answers on page 219

303
SCIENCE & NATURE

1 What force makes the Earth orbit the Sun?
2 What colour is the Great Spot on Jupiter?
3 Is Jupiter larger or smaller than Earth?
4 Which gas is present in the Earth's atmosphere which is not present on any other planet?
5 A solar eclipse occurs when the Moon gets between Earth and what?
6 Which is the seventh planet from the Sun?
7 What is the layer around the Earth called?
8 What is the name given to matter so dense that even light cannot escape its pull?
9 Which planet's name comes nearest the end of the alphabet?
10 Herschel planned to name Uranus after the King; which one?
11 What would you find on a celestial map?
12 Is the science of celestial bodies, astrology or astronomy?
13 Which colour in the rainbow has the shortest name?
14 Which TV programme called space "The Final Frontier"?
15 Were the first US Shuttle flights in the 1950s, '60s, or 80s?
16 Which show with Reeves & Mortimer shared its name with another term for meteors?
17 What is a group of stars which make a recognisable pattern called?
18 What does "S" stand for in NASA?
19 In which decade was the US's first satellite launched?
20 What is the English name for the lunar sea Mare Tranquillitas?
21 Castor and Pollux are two stars in which constellation?
22 John Young ate which item of fast food in space in 1968?
23 Was Apollo a US or USSR space programme?
24 Prior to being an astronaut was John Glenn in the Air Force or the Marines?
25 How long does it take the Earth to orbit the Sun?
26 Mishka, the 1980 Olympic mascot, was the first of which toy in space?
27 How is Ursa Major better known?
28 How many times did Gagarin orbit the Earth on his first space flight?
29 What travels at 186,272 miles per second?
30 Edward White was the first American to walk where?

304
ANIMALS

1 In mammals, the Asian elephant is second but man has the longest – what?
2 A papillon is a breed of what?
3 What is the term for a group of beavers?
4 Alphabetically, which animal always comes first?
5 Dromedary and Bactrian are types of what?
6 What is a male fox called?
7 How many teats does a cow usually have?
8 In Britain, which is the only venomous snake?
9 What type of leaves does a koala feed on?
10 The cairn terrier was originally bred in which country?
11 What type of animal is a natterjack?
12 What type of "ology" is the study of animals?
13 What colour are the markings on a skunk?
14 A jenny is a female what?
15 What is the term for a group of elephants?
16 Which monkey has a blue and red face?
17 What type of animal is an ibex?
18 Which animal lives in an earth or sett?
19 What type of animal eats meat?
20 What name is given to a baby kangaroo?
21 Which creature provides a mole's main source of food?
22 What type of animal was Baloo in *The Jungle Book*?
23 The common and the grey are types of which creature that breed around the coast of Britain?
24 What kind of *Naked* creature did Desmond Morris write about?
25 A leveret is a young what?
26 Which animal's home is called a drey?
27 Which creature is the fastest land mammal?
28 Which is the largest land animal?
29 What is the term for a group of foxhounds?
30 The wild dog the dingo comes from which country?

  **Answers on page 219**

 Answers on page 219

305
PLANTS & ANIMALS

1 What sort of creature is an aardvark?

2 What colour are a daisy's petals?

3 Which of the following dogs is the biggest: Pekinese, Labrador or St Bernard?

4 The dove is a member of which bird family?

5 What is the largest and most powerful land mammal?

6 What sort of feet do antelopes have?

7 A caribou is a type of what?

8 What is a rhododendron?

9 What is a Scots pine?

10 The lynx belongs to which family?

11 What do herbivores eat?

12 Where is a horse's muzzle?

13 How many nostrils does a dog have?

14 In the animal world what is an adder?

15 What colour are rhubarb stalks?

16 In the very early part of which season do snowdrops appear?

17 Which big cat has a mane?

18 What is an antirrhinum?

19 Mushrooms and puffballs are what types of living things?

20 Which of cacti, root vegetables or water lilies can survive in the desert?

21 In plants, pollination is the transfer of what?

22 Where do wetland plants grow?

23 What do carnivorous plants eat?

24 What colour are natural sponges?

25 How many tentacles does a starfish have?

26 Which animal can be field or harvest?

27 Where would an insect have its antenna?

28 In animals what is another name for the backbone?

29 Which is the heaviest of chimpanzee, gorilla or man?

30 Where are a deer's antlers?

306
GARDENING

1 What is the most common colour for a daffodil?

2 What is decking usually made from?

3 Which Monty took over on BBC's *Gardener's World*?

4 What is a plant's foliage?

5 Which vegetables can be globe or Jerusalem?

6 Where does a cloche go?

7 What are tulips grown from?

8 What do secateurs do?

9 What are culinary herbs used for?

10 Which piece of garden equipment can be hover or rotary?

11 Which heap provides fertiliser for the garden?

12 Which vegetables can be French or broad?

13 If you grew a box in your garden what would it be?

14 Which prickly green shrub with red berries is a Christmas decoration?

15 Which purple aromatic plant takes its name from the Latin *Lavo*, meaning I wash?

16 What colour is peat?

17 How many wheels does a wheelbarrow usually have?

18 What is significant about bonsai plants?

19 Hybrid tea and floribunda are types of what?

20 Which part of the garden has decorative stones?

21 What is the most common colour of a cornflower?

22 Which peas are decorative flowers?

23 What do conifers produce?

24 Which house is used for rearing delicate plants?

25 What sort of fruit do you grow if you grow Cox's Orange Pippin and Bramley?

26 Which princely name follows "sweet" in a cottage garden plant?

27 Which word describes cutting a lawn?

28 What do lilies grow from?

29 What is the most common colour for a delphinium?

30 Which fruits follow elderflowers?

  Answers on page 219

 Answers on page 219

307
ANIMALS 2

1 Which tree can be Dutch, English or wych?
2 What type of creature is a stingray?
3 How does a boa kill?
4 Which bird can be bald, golden or harpy?
5 How many humps does a Bactrian camel have?
6 What sort of animal is a Dandie Dinmont?
7 What is a mamba?
8 Would a tuber grow above or below the ground?
9 What is a chameleon famous for being capable of changing?
10 What is a monkey puzzle?
11 To which hemisphere do penguins belong?
12 Which creature constructs dams and lodges?
13 What is a female fox called?
14 What does a rattlesnake rattle when it is disturbed?
15 What is the larva of a butterfly or moth called?
16 Which country were Newfoundland dogs originally from?
17 The moose or elk are species of which creature?
18 What sort of plant is a common puffball?
19 On which continent is the opossum found in its natural habitat?
20 Which American creature is renowned for its foul-smelling defence mechanism?
21 What can be great white, tiger or whale?
22 What colour is a West Highland terrier?
23 Bile is a secretion of which organ of the body?
24 What colour are the bracts of a poinsettia?
25 What is snake poison called?
26 A shoal is a group of what type of creatures?
27 How many sets of teeth do most mammals have?
28 Which is larger, the wallaby or the kangaroo?
29 Does a skipjack jump, skip or swim?
30 Where are emus found in their natural habitat?

308
PLANTS 2

1 Where is water stored in a cactus plant?
2 Are most conifers evergreen or deciduous?
3 Ceps and chanterelles are types of what?
4 Flax is grown to produce which fabric?
5 Which drug is obtained from the coca plant?
6 Bamboo is the tallest type of what?
7 Which Mexican drink comes from the agave plant?
8 Is it true or false that laurel has poisonous leaves?
9 The petiole is on which part of a plant?
10 What colour is cuckoo spit?
11 What colour are the flowers on a gorse bush?
12 Which perennial herb can be grown to create lawns?
13 What goes before lavender and holly to make another plant's name?
14 What can be obtained from the cassava plant which would have gone in a typical school dinner pudding?
15 Harebells are usually what colour?
16 Does a polyanthus have a single or several blooms?
17 Which ingredient in tonic water comes from the bark of the cinchona?
18 Which plants would a viticulturist grow?
19 Wild cornflowers are usually what colour?
20 Which paintbrush cleaner is found in the resin of a conifer?
21 Which pear has the most protein?
22 In the garden what would you use secateurs for?
23 Do peanuts grow on trees or low plants?
24 What colour is chlorophyll?
25 In which Gardens is the Princess of Wales Conservatory?
26 Cacti are native to which continent?
27 What would you find in an arboretum?
28 Which fast grower is nicknamed the mile-a-minute vine?
29 Which yellow flower is nicknamed the Lent lily?
30 Which trees carry their seeds in cones?

 Answers on page 219

 Answers on page 219

309
FOOD & DRINK

1 Tikka is a dish in which country's cookery?
2 A strudel is usually filled with which fruit?
3 What relation is Albert to fellow chef and restaurateur Michel Roux?
4 Which pasta sauce originated in Bologna in Italy?
5 What is a frankfurter?
6 How are eggs usually cooked in the breakfast dish bacon and eggs?
7 What is fromage frais a soft type of?
8 Does an Italian risotto contain rice or pasta?
9 Over what would you normally pour a vinaigrette dressing?
10 Rick Stein's restaurant and cooking specialises in what?
11 What colour wine is a Valpolicella?
12 In which country did Chianti originate?
13 What is the main filling ingredient of a quiche?
14 Is a poppadum crisp or soft?
15 What sort of drink is espresso?
16 Is brioche a type of bread or a fruit?
17 What shape is the pasta used to make lasagne?
18 What is mozzarella?
19 What colour is fudge?
20 Which north of England county is famous for its hotpot?
21 Do you eat or drink a loyal toast?
22 What type of meat is found in a cock-a-leekie soup?
23 In restaurant chains, what type of food would you buy from a Hut?
24 What is the alcoholic ingredient of Gaelic coffee?
25 Which fruit is usually used in marmalade?
26 At what age can you legally drink alcohol in an pub?
27 What does G stand for in G and T?
28 Which country produces more wine – Bulgaria or France?
29 Would you eat or drink schnapps?
30 A Conference is what type of fruit?

310
BIRD BRAINS

1 Which bird has a red breast?
2 Which birds can be barn, tawny or snowy?
3 What two colours is a magpie?
4 Which birds are associated with the Tower of London?
5 What colour is a female blackbird?
6 The teal belongs to which family group?
7 What word can go in front of sparrow or martin to name a bird?
8 Which bird lays its eggs in the nests of others?
9 Which bird has the same name as a chess piece?
10 Which bird featured in the film *Kes*?
11 Which part of the golden eagle is gold?
12 Which part of a bird was used as a pen?
13 An early riser is said to be up before which bird?
14 What colour is the plumage on the head of a male mallard?
15 What is special about a swallow's tail?
16 Which bird starts its name with the word "Bull"?
17 The jay is a member of which family?
18 Which seashore bird has a colourful triangular bill?
19 Which reddish-brown songbird sings just before dawn or after dusk?
20 What colour is a tufted duck?
21 Which game bird is a word meaning grumble?
22 Which bird is the symbol of peace?
23 Which bird was said to deliver babies?
24 Which bird is so called because of its fast flight?
25 What is the largest bird in the world?
26 Which flying toy shares its name with a bird?
27 What is a baby swan called?
28 Which letter of the alphabet sounds like a bird's name?
29 What is Britain's smallest bird?
30 Is a fledgling a young or old bird?

  Answers on page 219

 Answers on page 219

311
LIVING WORLD

1 Glaucoma affects which part of the body?

2 Which flightless bird lays the world's largest egg?

3 What is a puffball?

4 What happens to a female butterfly after it has laid its eggs?

5 In what type of environment do most crustaceans live?

6 Which natural disaster is measured on the Richter scale?

7 What is the main ingredient of glass?

8 Does a millipede have more, fewer, or exactly 1000 feet?

9 An ore is a mineral which contains a what?

10 Is the whale shark a mammal like the whale, or a fish like the shark?

11 Which bird is the symbol of the USA?

12 Are butterflies more colourful in warmer or cooler countries?

13 What sort of rock is lava?

14 Which is larger, the dolphin or the porpoise?

15 Which organ of the body has the aorta?

16 How many bones does a slug have?

17 Are worker ants male or female?

18 Altocumulus is a type of what?

19 What is the main source of energy in our ecosystem?

20 Which name for remains of plants and animals which lived on Earth means "dug up"?

21 On which continent is the world's largest glacier?

22 Kelp is a type of what?

23 What order of mammals does the gibbon belong to?

24 What is the staple food of over half of the world's population?

25 Which creatures are larvae and pupae before being adults?

26 Are most bats visible at night or by day?

27 Which part of a jellyfish has stinging cells?

28 Natural rubber is obtained from what?

29 What is the mother of all the bees in a colony called?

30 The giant sequoia is the largest living what?

312
FOOD & DRINK 2

1 What is an anchovy?

2 What would you find in the middle of a damson?

3 Darjeeling is a type of what?

4 Guinness was first made in which Irish city?

5 What is endive?

6 What would you do with a claret?

7 Saffron tinges food what colour?

8 Which vegetable shares its name with a fruit drink?

9 Which village in Leicestershire gives its name to a classic British blue cheese?

10 All citrus fruits are rich in which vitamin?

11 The island of Madeira shares its name with a cake and also what?

12 What colour is root ginger?

13 What are the tops of asparagus called?

14 Which of the following are not types of tomatoes – plum, orange, cherry?

15 What is rocket?

16 What is the most common fuel for a barbecue?

17 Sirloin is which meat?

18 What ingredient is balsamic?

19 What is the most common colour of an aubergine's skin?

20 Which food item is sold at London's Billingsgate market?

21 How is white wine usually served?

22 Mangetout and sugar snaps are types of what?

23 What is feta?

24 If coffee is drunk without milk or cream how is it described?

25 Which Earl gave his name to a type of mild tea?

26 Ciabatta bread originated in which country?

27 What sort of wine is chardonnay?

28 A shallot is a type of what?

29 What shape is the pasta used to make lasagne?

30 Seville is famous for which fruit used to make marmalade?

 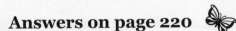 **Answers on page 220**

 Answers on page 220

313
ANIMALS 3

1 Where does a kangaroo keep its young?
2 Which black and white mammal lives in China's bamboo forests?
3 Where do koalas live?
4 How many legs does an adult insect have?
5 What type of creature is a black widow?
6 Which animal's nickname is "ship of the desert"?
7 Which breed of spaniel shares its name with a king?
8 Which sea creature is known as a Portuguese man-of-war?
9 What is a female sheep called?
10 What do carnivorous animals live on?
11 Which animals are described as canine?
12 What is a fox's tail called?
13 Which saint is the heaviest breed of dog named after?
14 What is special about a guinea pig's tail?
15 What are pigs' feet called?
16 Which elephants have the smaller ears, African or Indian?
17 What are edible sturgeon eggs called?
18 What name is given to the period of winter sleep by some animals?
19 What is Britain's hardiest and shaggiest bovine breed?
20 What would a billy and a nanny produce?
21 Which black and white mammal sprays a foul smelling liquid when attacked?
22 How does a boa constrictor kill its prey?
23 Why does a fish need gills?
24 What does a scorpion have at the end of its tail?
25 What does a chameleon change to camouflage itself?
26 What does an Isle of Man Manx cat not have?
27 What type of insect is a Red Admiral?
28 What is another name for an Alsatian dog?
29 What kind of animal is a Suffolk Punch?
30 A lynx is a member of which family group?

314
ANIMALS 4

1 Which land mammal has the largest ears?
2 Which wild animal is the domesticated dog descended from?
3 Are mammals warm blooded or cold blooded?
4 Which part of the body has a crown and a root?
5 What is another name for the larynx?
6 Do tigers hunt in packs or alone?
7 Which group of animals shares its name with an archbishop?
8 What type of creature is an Aylesbury?
9 What was the first animal to be domesticated?
10 Cheviot and Suffolk are both types of what?
11 Shrews have acute sense of smell and hearing to compensate for which weak sense?
12 The opossum and the skunk are famous for what?
13 What colour is a grizzly bear?
14 The llama is native to which continent?
15 Which part of a human's body has a cornea?
16 A leveret is a young what?
17 What part of a Basset Hound is particularly long?
18 Which northerly US state is famous for the brown bear?
19 Does the moose live in a warm or cold climate?
20 Are crocodiles carnivorous or herbivores?
21 Which farm animals chew the cud?
22 Which primate species is the closest genetic cousin to humanity?
23 Where is a human's jugular vein?
24 Are most animals vertebrates or invertebrates?
25 How many young does a kangaroo usually produce at any one time?
26 What part of the body of a Manx cat is missing which is present on most other cats?
27 Which bear is the largest meat-eating land animal?
28 What do all mammals feed their babies on?
29 Which part of a human includes loops and whorls?
30 In which hemisphere do penguins live in the wild?

   Answers on page 220

 Answers on page 220

315
FOOD & DRINK 3

1 Which batter mix is an accompaniment to roast beef?
2 Which chef replaced Fern Britton on *Ready Steady Cook*?
3 What colour wine is Beaujolais Nouveau?
4 What colour is the flesh of an avocado?
5 What is the traditional colour for the outside of a stick of rock?
6 Would you eat or drink a Sally Lunn?
7 What type of egg is covered in sausage meat?
8 Scrumpy is a rough form of what?
9 Which mashed vegetable tops a shepherd's pie?
10 Which food has given its name to a road network near Birmingham?
11 Is a Spotted Dick a first course or a pudding?
12 Which fruit is associated with tennis at Wimbledon?
13 Champagne originated in which country?
14 Is a Melton Mowbray pie sweet or savoury?
15 What is a pistachio?
16 What sort of fruit is in a teacake?
17 Which chef Antony appeared in *I'm a Celebrity Get Me Out of Here*?
18 Which is more substantial, afternoon tea or high tea?
19 If you ate al fresco would you be indoors or out of doors?
20 What is the usual shape of a Camembert cheese?
21 Which soft pulpy peas are eaten with fish and chips?
22 What type of food may be served clotted?
23 What would you make in a cafetière?
24 What type of drink is Bristol Cream?
25 Is chowder a soup or a pudding?
26 A "pinta" is usually a pint of what?
27 Should red wine normally be drunk chilled or at room temperature?
28 Is there milk in a cappuccino coffee?
29 Are you more likely to eat a croissant at breakfast or supper?
30 Does celebrity chef Nick Nairn come from England, Scotland or Wales?

316
TIME & SPACE

1 Which planet is closest to the sun?
2 Which Big theory explains the formation of the universe?
3 What is another name for the star constellation the Plough?
4 Which Helen became the first Briton in space?
5 What is the term for a giant group of stars held together by gravity?
6 In 1981, *Columbia I* was the first flight of which distinctive craft?
7 What can be a red dwarf or a white dwarf?
8 Which planet is the largest in our solar system?
9 Who or what was Hale-Bopp?
10 In 1986, what happened to *Challenger 52* after take-off?
11 Cape Canaveral took on board the name of which US President?
12 Where is the Sea of Tranquillity?
13 What is the name of the force that keeps planets moving round the sun?
14 Tiros, Echo and Sputnik were types of what?
15 What is the name for the study of the structure of the universe?
16 Which John was the first American to orbit Earth?
17 What was the name of the project that first put man on the moon?
18 Alphabetically, which is last in the list of planets in our solar system?
19 What is Yuri Gagarin's famous first?
20 Approximately how long does it take the Earth to travel round the sun?
21 Which bright comet visits Earth every 76 years?
22 Which country launched the Pioneer space probes?
23 What is the popular name for the star Sirius?
24 Quasi-stellar sources are in short usually known as what?
25 Who is the long-time presenter of *The Sky at Night*?
26 The moons of Uranus are named after which playwright's characters?
27 Jodrell Bank is in which English county?
28 What units are used for measuring distance in space?
29 What was the first animal in space?
30 Our solar system lies in which galaxy?

  Answers on page 220

 Answers on page 220

317
SCIENCE & THE NATURAL WORLD

1 Which part of the body is associated with Achilles?

2 Dairy farming is usually associated with the rearing of which animals?

3 A drone is a type of which insect?

4 What does the Kelvin scale measure?

5 In what sort of climate do rainforests appear?

6 What colour is amber?

7 What characteristic of reptiles is also a phrase used to describe a callous act?

8 What is the framework of ribs called?

9 What colour is a robin's breast?

10 Anorexia nervosa is what type of disorder?

11 Which continent grows the most rice?

12 Saliva is produced in which part of the body?

13 What sort of trail does a slug leave behind?

14 If you have laryngitis what may you lose?

15 Lumbago causes pain in which part of the body?

16 What is inserted in the body in acupuncture?

17 The Florida cougar is a member of which family?

18 Which eight-legged creature do many people have a phobia about?

19 On which continent are most elephants found?

20 What do arteries in the body carry?

21 Chimpanzee, gorilla and man – present company excepted – which is the most intelligent?

22 What is a black mamba?

23 Cats, dogs and sheep – which of these animals are sheared?

24 Which contains more lines a plus or a minus sign?

25 Mars is called what colour planet?

26 What colour are a flamingo's feathers?

27 Koalas are natives to which country?

28 If water freezes what does it become?

29 Which plant increases in popularity at Christmas when you kiss under it?

30 Which metal is used in thermometers?

318
FOOD: HEALTHY EATING

1 Which celeb chef was credited with removing "Turkey Twizzlers" from school menus?

2 Which has most fat, cream cheese or cottage cheese?

3 How many portions of fruit and vegetables a day are recommended?

4 What colour are the bottle tops on semi-skimmed milk?

5 Which has the lower fat content, chicken with skin or chicken without?

6 Which helps to maintain strong bones and teeth, calcium or carbohydrate?

7 Which porridge ingredient helps keep cholesterol levels down?

8 Which B is a piece of equipment used to make a smoothie?

9 Which is the healthier way to cook green vegetables, boiling or steaming?

10 Which salad ingredient can be Iceberg or Little Gem?

11 Which "pea" is an ingredient of houmous or falafels?

12 Mozzarella is a low-fat cheese originally from which country?

13 By eating too much salt do you run the risk of high or low blood pressure?

14 Beta-carotene is responsible for which colour in carrots and sweet potatoes?

15 Glucose and sucrose are types of what?

16 Which is less healthy, saturated or non-saturated fat?

17 Which anagram of brief is an important food element?

18 How much fat is there in watermelon and cucumber, 0% or 50%?

19 Which has a lower fat content, poached eggs or fried eggs?

20 Is it healthier to eat a high-protein meal in the middle of the day or right at the end?

21 Which processed food product did Jamie Oliver campaign to get removed from school menus?

22 Is milk high in Vitamin A or Vitamin C?

23 What colour is the rind on Edam cheese?

24 Which nutrient, the name of a metal, ensures healthy blood and prevents anaemia?

25 Which Vitamin in fruit and vegetables is destroyed by over-cooking?

26 Sunflower, linseed, sesame and pumpkin are all types of what?

27 Which is usually larger, a satsuma or an orange?

28 Carb is an abbreviation of which food term?

29 Which has less fat, skimmed milk or Channel Islands milk?

30 What colour is the salad ingredient radicchio?

  Answers on page 220

 Answers on page 220

319
FOOD & DRINK 4

1 What is the main ingredient in an omelette?
2 Which animal does venison come from?
3 Which garden herb is made into a sauce often eaten with lamb?
4 In which country did the word biscuit originate?
5 What is traditionally eaten on Shrove Tuesday?
6 What is another name for French fries?
7 What is a slice of bacon called?
8 Which edible sugary substance do bees make?
9 What is done to a herring to make it into a kipper?
10 Which vegetable can be King Edward or Desirée?
11 Which country does Edam cheese originate from?
12 What do you add to milk to make porridge?
13 What is minestrone?
14 What is bottled tomato sauce called?
15 What colour is vodka?
16 Where did the dish paella originate?
17 Which fruit is covered with toffee at a fairground?
18 Which nuts are used to make marzipan?
19 Is a Spotted Dick usually eaten hot or cold?
20 What meat dish is Cumberland famous for?
21 Which pudding is eaten with roast beef?
22 Which vegetables can be French, runner or baked?
23 What colour is piccalilli?
24 What sort of food is a rollmop?
25 Is wholemeal bread brown or white?
26 If something is cooked "au gratin" what must it contain?
27 Petits pois are small what?
28 In which country is Peroni beer bottled?
29 What are the two main ingredients of a shandy?
30 Which Scottish island has seven working whisky distilleries on it?

320
THE UNIVERSE

1 What is the largest planet in our Solar System?
2 In space, what is Mir?
3 What's the name of the explosion that began Universe?
4 A constellation is a group of what?
5 To make a rainbow what weather conditions are needed?
6 In a storm what can be forked or sheet?
7 If the Moon looks like an illuminated circle what is it called?
8 What is a moving sheet of ice called?
9 In which country is the tropical rain forest of Amazonia?
10 Which layer above Antarctica has a hole in it?
11 Which of these is a danger to the environment – heavy rain, acid rain, drizzly rain?
12 The term fauna refers to what?
13 Which ocean is the deepest?
14 Which M is the largest lake in the USA?
15 What type of natural phenomenon is K2?
16 Which is the most valuable metal – gold, platinum or silver?
17 A monsoon is a wind which brings what along with it?
18 Which river is the longest – Amazon, Mississippi or Nile?
19 What is a meteorite made from?
20 In which southern hemisphere country is Ayers Rock?
21 Which Sea is the lowest point on Earth?
22 Reservoirs are man made to hold what?
23 Europe's longest river the Volga flows in which country?
24 Which of these regions has the most glaciers – Antarctica, Asia or Europe?
25 The water in rivers is provided by either melting snow or what?
26 Cumulus and Nimbostratus are types of what?
27 Which is the world's largest desert?
28 Which "effect" is associated with global warming?
29 What colour is linked to caring for nature and the environment?
30 The Yangtze, Congo and Mekong are all types of what?

  Answers on page 220

 Answers on page 220

321
ANIMAL STARS

1 What was the first *Lassie* film called?
2 What was the most successful "creature" film of the 1970s?
3 What was Clint Eastwood's co-star in *Every Which Way But Loose*?
4 What breed of dog was Beethoven?
5 Which country is the setting for *Born Free*?
6 Which animal adopts the piglet in *Babe*?
7 How many movie versions of *Black Beauty* had been made up to 1997?
8 In which decade was the first *Lassie* film made?
9 White Fang is a cross between which two animals?
10 What is Dorothy's dog called in *The Wizard of Oz*?
11 What was the sequel to *The Incredible Journey* called?
12 Which animals starred with Sigourney Weaver in a biopic of Dian Fossey?
13 Which film about rats had a theme song with lyrics by Don Black?
14 Which horse eventually had co-star billing with Gene Autry?
15 Which film was described as "Eight legs. Two fangs. And an attitude"?
16 What was the Lone Ranger's horse called?
17 What sort of creature is Flicka in *My Friend Flicka*?
18 Which two types of animal feature in *Oliver and Company*?
19 Which nation's army dog was Rin Tin Tin?
20 What is the principal lioness called in *Born Free*?
21 In which decade was one of the first successful animal films *Rescued by Rover* released?
22 Which studio made the seven official *Lassie* films?
23 Which fictional whale did Keiko play in a 1993 movie?
24 Who wrote the book on which *Babe* was based?
25 Which film was directed by Hitchcock from a Daphne Du Maurier novel, other than *Rebecca*?
26 What was the sequel to *Beethoven* called?
27 What breed of dog features in *K-9*?
28 Which 1971 film was the predecessor of *Ben* a year later?
29 Which creatures contributed to the most successful film of 1993?
30 What animal is the star of Disney's 1964 classic *The Three Lives of Thomasina*?

322
FLOWERS

1 What is the common name for the antirrhinum?
2 Which hanging basket favourite is also called pelargonium?
3 What qualities do the flowers helichrysum and acroclinium have?
4 By what name is solidago known?
5 What type of bell is a campanula?
6 Which yellow, pink-flushed rose was bred by Meilland in 1945?
7 Which wild flower is also known as the knapweed?
8 Which flower has rung-like leaflets?
9 What would you find in an anther on a stamen?
10 What is the common name for the plant *Impatiens*?
11 Which flowers are said to symbolize the Crucifixion?
12 Which flower, also called chalk plant or baby's breath, is a favourite with flower arrangers?
13 Bachelor's buttons are a variety of which yellow wild flower?
14 Which flower's seeds are pickled to make capers?
15 Which animals love nepeta, giving the latter its common name?
16 What sort of hyacinth is a muscari?
17 Which flower – *Lychnis* – shares its name with a fictional detective?
18 Which two flowers would you find in an orchestra?
19 Which flower gets its name from a Persian or Turkish word for turban?
20 Which plant is grown not for its flowers but for its silvery seed pods?
21 Which family do azaleas belong to?
22 Jonquils are members of which family?
23 Which plant is also called the torch lily?
24 Which climbing plant has the variety 'Nelly Moser'?
25 Which flower's foundation varieties are alba, gallica and damascena?
26 Which plant was named after the Greek goddess of the rainbow?
27 What sort of purplish-blue daisies are types of aster?
28 Which bloom's name means golden flower, although it can be many different colours?
29 What colour is the rose 'Silver Jubilee'?
30 Which country sent the first dahlia seeds to Europe?

 Answers on page 221

 Answers on page 221

323
TREES

1 What do conifers have in their cones?
2 Which tree's leaves are the symbol of the National Trust?
3 Which three coniferous trees are native to Britain?
4 Which garden tree with yellow flowers has poisonous seeds?
5 What colour are the flowers of the horse chestnut tree?
6 In which country did the bonsai technique develop?
7 Which tree do we get turpentine from?
8 In which continent did the monkey-puzzle tree originate?
9 Which tree produces cobs and filberts?
10 Aspen is from which family of trees?
11 Is the wood of a coniferous tree hard or soft?
12 What is the more common name for the great maple?
13 What sort of environment do alder trees grow in?
14 Which tree is cork obtained from?
15 In which county is England's largest forest?
16 Which tree is sago obtained from?
17 Which beech tree has purplish leaves?
18 What is the Spanish chestnut also called?
19 Which tree can be English, American or Eurasian?
20 To which family does the umbrella tree belong?
21 The teak is native to which continent?
22 Which wood is used for piano keys?
23 Which maple's sap is used to make maple syrup?
24 To which family does the osier belong?
25 Which is thought to be the tallest tree in the world and one of the longest-lived?
26 Which tree produces "keys"?
27 What colour flowers does a jacaranda tree have?
28 Which tree produces the seeds from which cocoa is made?
29 To which group of trees do blue gum and red gum belong?
30 What is the linden tree also called?

324
PLANTS 3

1 What can follow "milk" and "rag" in the plant world?
2 What sort of fruit is a mirabelle?
3 Which Princess had a rose named after her at the 1997 Chelsea Flower Show?
4 Which grain is used to make semolina?
5 Which term is used for plants which store moisture in their thick fleshy leaves or stems?
6 Which part of a plant protects it as a bud?
7 What shape is a campanulate flower?
8 What is a morel?
9 What does lamina mean when referring to a leaf?
10 Which part of the tree is cinnamon obtained from?
11 Which parts of the potato are poisonous?
12 If a leaf is dentate what does it mean?
13 What colour are the flowers of a St John's wort?
14 What is a prickly pear?
15 What is the main vegetation of the South African veld?
16 Why is the grapefruit so called?
17 What colour are borage flowers?
18 What is kelp?
19 Which plant's name means lion's tooth?
20 What is another name for the lime tree?
21 What is to be found in a plant's anther?
22 How long is the life cycle of a biennial plant?
23 The sycamore is native to which continent?
24 How many leaves does the twayblade orchid have?
25 What colour are the fruits on the deadly nightshade?
26 What type of plants are traditionally seen in a herbarium?
27 Which tree did archers need to cultivate to make bows?
28 Which King reputedly sought refuge in an oak tree?
29 The loganberry is a cross between which fruits?
30 What colour is the blossom of the blackthorn?

  **Answers on page 221**

 Answers on page 221

325
LIVING WORLD 2

1 Tsunami is another name for what type of wave?
2 Where would a melanoma appear?
3 Which disease in humans has been linked to the cattle disease BSE?
4 What sort of creature is a fluke?
5 Which branch of medicine is concerned with disorders of the blood?
6 What name is given to an organism which is both male and female?
7 What sort of bird is a Merlin?
8 Which part of the body might suffer from labyrinthitis?
9 What sort of creature is an abalone?
10 Where is a bird's patella?
11 Which racing creatures live in lofts?
12 What condition is caused by a shortage of haemoglobin?
13 What colour are the spots on a plaice?
14 What is a puffball?
15 Which part of the body does scabies affect?
16 Which digestive organ lies below the thorax in invertebrates?
17 Where is a human's scapula?
18 What do most sharks live on?
19 If a person has myopia what problem does he or she have?
20 How many pairs of ribs does a human have?
21 Which putative monarch was portrayed in the film *The Last King of Scotland*?
22 Which skin disorder is caused by inflammation of the sebaceous glands?
23 What is the popular name for mouth-to-mouth resuscitation?
24 A BCG is a vaccination against which disease?
25 Where is the pituitary gland?
26 Which tendon pins the calf muscle to the heel bone?
27 Hepatic refers to which organ of the body?
28 What colour head does a male mallard usually have?
29 The adrenal gland is above which organ?
30 The pilchard is a member of which fish family?

326
FISH

1 Where is a fish's caudal fin?
2 What colour are the spots on a plaice?
3 What sort of fish is a skipjack?
4 Which family does the anchovy belong to?
5 Caviare is which part of the sturgeon?
6 *Tinca tinca* is the Latin name of which fish?
7 Alevin and parr are stages in the development of which fish?
8 What is the world's largest fish?
9 What is a young pilchard called?
10 What colour is a live lobster?
11 From which part of the cod is a beneficial oil produced?
12 The minnow is the smallest member of which family?
13 What is pisciculture?
14 Which fish has been nicknamed "tin plate"?
15 What is a buckie another name for?
16 What sort of fish is a dogfish?
17 What is a dogfish called when it is bought for food?
18 Which type of crab lives in hollow objects such as snail shells?
19 Where is a fish's dorsal fin?
20 Which fish has the varieties brown, sea or rainbow?
21 How many arms does a squid have?
22 Who wrote *The Compleat Angler*?
23 Flounder is a common name for which type of fish?
24 What are brisling also called?
25 Where would you find barbels on a fish?
26 What starts an oyster developing a pearl in its shell?
27 Which fish has the same name as an early infantry weapon?
28 Which fish is also called goatfish or surmullet?
29 What is another name for the common European sole?
30 What is a geoduck?

  **Answers on page 221**

 Answers on page 221

327
FOOD & DRINK 5

1 What is ciabatta?
2 What is the predominant flavour of fennel?
3 What type of pulses are used in hummus?
4 What flavour is the drink Kahlua?
5 What is added to butter in a *beurre manié*?
6 What type of wine is traditionally used in zabaglione?
7 What is radicchio?
8 What do the Spanish call a medium dry sherry?
9 What is panettone?
10 What are the three main ingredients of an Hollandaise sauce?
11 In the kitchen, what would a mandolin be used for?
12 What is harissa?
13 Which liqueur is used in a White Lady?
14 What sweet substance is added to whisky to make Drambuie?
15 From which continent does couscous originate?
16 What is the dish of stuffed vine leaves called?
17 In wine bottle sizes what is another name for a double magnum?
18 In the food world what is rocket?
19 From which country does balsamic vinegar originate?
20 Which spirit is used in a Daiquiri?
21 In which century was chocolate introduced into the UK?
22 Everards beers were originally based near which town?
23 What type of meat is used in moussaka?
24 What is the main ingredient of rosti?
25 Which traditional pudding ingredient comes from the cassava plant?
26 What is ghee?
27 Slivovitz is made from which fruit?
28 From what is angostura obtained?
29 What type of milk is a basic ingredient of Thai cookery?
30 What is a bruschetta?

328
PLANTS 4

1 Which cereal can survive in the widest range of climatic conditions?
2 The hellebore is known as what type of rose?
3 What colour are edelweiss flowers?
4 Which plant is St Patrick said to have used to illustrate the Holy Trinity?
5 Succulents live in areas lacking in what?
6 How many points does a sycamore leaf have?
7 What is the ornamental shaping of trees and shrubs called?
8 What is an alternative name for the narcotic and analgesic aconite?
9 What colour are laburnum flowers?
10 What is another name for a yam?
11 What shape are flowers which include the name campanula?
12 What is a frond on a plant?
13 Which climbing plant is also called hedera helix?
14 Agronomy is the study of what?
15 What is a Sturmer?
16 Which fruit is called "earth berry" in German from where the plant grows?
17 What is another name for belladonna?
18 What is the effect on the nervous system of taking hemlock?
19 Are the male, female or either hop plants used to make beer?
20 What is the most common plant grown in Assam in India?
21 Aspen is what type of tree?
22 Which flowering plant is named after the sixteenth-century German botanist Leonhart Fuchs?
23 The ground powder form turmeric dyes food which colour?
24 The pineapple plant is native to which continent?
25 What is the purpose of a plant's petals?
26 Which type of pesticide is used to kill weeds?
27 What colour are the leaves of a poinsettia?
28 What name is given to the wild yellow iris?
29 Which plant is famous for having a "clock"?
30 What colour are borage flowers?

 Answers on page 221

 Answers on page 221

329
WINE

1 Claret wine is produced in the region surrounding which French city?
2 What would be the term to describe a dry champagne?
3 In which country is the wine-growing Barossa Valley?
4 Which white wine grape variety is most widely planted in California?
5 In which country is the Marlborough wine region?
6 Retsina is native to which country?
7 Which wine has the varieties Malmsey and Sercial?
8 What is the normal capacity for a bottle of wine?
9 In which country is Rioja produced?
10 Along which river is most of France's Sauvignon Blanc cultivated?
11 What colour are most English wines?
12 Which scientist discovered that yeast causes fermentation?
13 What is a crate of twelve bottles of wine called?
14 Which country does Sukhindol wine come from?
15 In which part of the United States is the Zinfandel grape chiefly cultivated?
16 What is the first name of wine writer Ms Robinson?
17 In which country is the wine-making area of Stellenbosch?
18 How many normal-size wine bottles would you have in a Methuselah?
19 How are fizzy wines, other than champagnes, described?
20 In which area of Italy is Chianti Classico produced?
21 Would a French wine described as "*doux*" be medium sweet or medium dry?
22 What are the three styles of port?
23 What colour are most of the wines from France's Anjou region?
24 In which South American country is Casablanca Valley?
25 Which red wine is drunk when young and is called "nouveau"?
26 In which country was a vine variety called "vegetable dragon pearls"?
27 Which wine can be "fino" or "oloroso"?
28 What is Moët et Chandon?
29 Who was the female wine expert on the BBC's *Food and Drink* programme?
30 Along which river and its tributaries do the German vineyards lie?

330
ANIMALS 5

1 What does the aardvark feed on?
2 What colour is an ocelot?
3 What is the only member of the giraffe family other than the giraffe itself?
4 What sort of animal feeds on plants and other animals?
5 Which ape's natural habitat is restricted to Sumatra and Borneo?
6 What are ossicles?
7 Which group has more teeth – mammals or reptiles?
8 What is the North American equivalent of the reindeer?
9 What colour is a coyote's coat?
10 What name is given to a creature equally at home on land and in water?
11 What term describes an animal which cannot control its body temperature and has to rely on its environment?
12 What was the first animal to be domesticated?
13 Which special mouth parts inject poison into prey?
14 The llama is a relative of which African animal?
15 Which is the only vertebrate capable of sustained flight?
16 The wapiti is a member of which family of animals?
17 What protects a vertebrate's nerve cord?
18 Which extinct animal's name is the Portuguese for "stupid"?
19 What is another name for the Russian wolfhound?
20 What colour tongue does a chow chow have?
21 Other than the Australian mainland the platypus is native to where?
22 Where does a gopher make its home?
23 What is the most intelligent of land animals after man?
24 What type of apes were imported into Gibraltar in the 18th century?
25 What do mammary glands produce?
26 The brown bear is also known by what name?
27 What is the only true amphibious member of the weasel family?
28 Which American native has a black masked face and a distinctive ringed tail?
29 The anteater is native to which continent?
30 What is a marmoset?

   Answers on page 221

 **Answers on page 221**

331
PLANTS 5

1 What is the main characteristic of the wood of the balsa tree?
2 Plantain is a type of which fruit?
3 What is another name for the blackthorn?
4 Which industry's demands meant that rubber production increased in the last century?
5 What does a berry typically contain?
6 In a biennial plant, when do flower and seed production usually occur?
7 What name is given to small hardy plants ideal for rockeries, such as saxifraga?
8 The name tulip is derived from a Turkish word meaning what type of headgear?
9 What type of soil is vital for growing rhododendrons?
10 What is the most common colour of *Primula vulgaris* or common primrose?
11 Clematis is a member of which family of wild flowers?
12 How many petals does an iris usually have?
13 What nationality was the botanist who gave his name to the dahlia?
14 How is the wild *Rosa canina* better known?
15 What colour is the Rose of York?
16 Antirrhinums are also called what?
17 What is gypsophilia mainly grown for?
18 Which busy plant has the name *Impatiens*?
19 Forget Me Nots are usually which colour?
20 Which TV cook Ms Lawson shares her name with the Love in a Mist flower?
21 How are the papery daisy-like flowers of helichrysum better known?
22 In which season do Michaelmas daisies flower?
23 Which best describes leaves of a hosta – scalloped, spiky or very large?
24 Which of the following flowers are not grown from bulbs – pansies, snowdrops and tulips?
25 What sort of bell is a campanula?
26 Muscari are what type of hyacinth?
27 What is used to make a mulch – chemicals, organic material or seeds?
28 What makes the seeds of the laburnum potentially dangerous?
29 What colour are the ripe fruits of the mulberry tree?
30 What is the most common colour for alyssum, often used in borders and hanging baskets?

332
BIRD BRAINS 2

1 Was bird flu first detected in America, Asia or Europe?
2 What species of kite breeds in Britain?
3 What is the study of birds' eggs called?
4 An exaltation is a group of which birds?
5 What would you see if there was a Turdus on your window sill?
6 What colour are wild budgerigars?
7 A scapular on a bird is a type of what?
8 Which bird song sounds like chiff-chaff chiff-chaff?
9 Which bird is sacred in Peru?
10 What is the smallest British bird?
11 What type of birds are ratites?
12 Which birds group to mate and are shot in braces?
13 What name is given to a flock or gathering of crows?
14 What is special about the bones of most birds?
15 Which family of birds does the robin belong to?
16 Golden and argus are varieties of which bird?
17 Which of the senses is poorly developed in most birds?
18 What is special about a palmiped?
19 Which bird lays the largest egg?
20 What is the oldest known fossil bird?
21 What is the main food of the oyster catcher?
22 What is the shaft of a feather called?
23 Which extinct bird was last sighted in Mauritius?
24 What does a syrinx help a bird to do?
25 Which three features distinguish birds from other creatures?
26 What name is given to a castrated cockerel?
27 What is the common name for all small birds of prey?
28 Which bird is the symbol of the RSPB?
29 What name is given to a flock or gathering of starlings?
30 What is the main group in the family Phasianidae?

 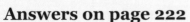 **Answers on page 222**

 Answers on page 222

333
TIME & SPACE 2

1 Which planet appears brightest to the naked eye?

2 What creatures were Laska and Beny, who went into space in 1958?

3 Which space first was Vladimir Komarov in 1967?

4 Who first predicted correctly the intermittent return of a famous comet?

5 In which US state is the Keck Telescope?

6 Which planet's moons have names of Shakespearean characters?

7 How are Corona Australis and Corona Borealis also known?

8 How many *Apollo* missions resulted in successful moon landings?

9 When the Earth or the moon enters the other's shadow what is it called?

10 Which is the only sign of the zodiac named after two living things?

11 Jodrell Bank is the observatory of which university?

12 Which planet did Johann Galle discover in 1846?

13 What is the system of numbering asteroids?

14 Which *Star Trek* character is asteroid No. 2309 named after?

15 Whose spacecraft was called *Vostok VI*?

16 In moon exploration what was EVA?

17 Which planet lies between Venus and Mars?

18 How many orbits of the Earth did Gagarin make in *Vostok I*?

19 What are the Northern Lights also known as?

20 Ganymede and Io are moons of which planet?

21 How long does it take the moon to complete a revolution of Earth?

22 Which planet did Clyde Tombaugh discover in 1930?

23 Which planet's rings and moons were photographed by *Voyager 1* in 1980?

24 Which theory states that the universe came into being as a result of an explosion?

25 What does the abbreviation "ly" stand for?

26 Which planet has two moons called Phobos and Demos?

27 In relation to the sun in which direction does a comet's tail point?

28 Which planet in our solar system is only slightly smaller than Earth?

29 What is the nearest star to our sun?

30 The sidereal period is the time it takes a planet to orbit what?

334
NATURAL PHENOMENA

1 What is another name for calcium oxide?

2 What is the next largest body in our solar system after the Sun?

3 What is the only planet to have been discovered by an American – Mars, Pluto or Venus?

4 What is the next deepest ocean after the Pacific?

5 What is the longest river on the American continent?

6 Which is the largest lake on the UK mainland?

7 Which country has the largest area of inland water?

8 In which waters is the EEC's largest island?

9 Which home of the Queen is one of the coldest places in the UK?

10 In December 2006 which natural disaster befell Kensal Rise in North London?

11 The Congo river is in the Democratic Republic of Congo and where else?

12 Which county of mainland England is the warmest?

13 What is the most common element in the universe?

14 Which is the heaviest – plutonium, gold or uranium?

15 What is England's second largest lake?

16 What is the chemical name for chalk?

17 Kaolin is what type of clay?

18 Denmark comprises how many islands – 26, 300 or 500?

19 Which mountain is the highest in the Alaska Range?

20 The Caucasus Mountains divide Georgia and Azerbaijan from where?

21 In which US state is the volcanic mountain of Mount St Helens which erupted in 1980?

22 Which metallic element has its natural occurrence in wolfram?

23 In which country are most of Europe's volcanoes?

24 Where in Japan did a massive earthquake kill over 5,000 people in 1995?

25 What is the most popular form of green beryl called?

26 What was the first name of Richter whose scale measures the intensity of an earthquake?

27 How much of the Earth's area is covered in ice – 5%, 10% or 20%?

28 What colour is the quartz known as citrine?

29 Where is the volcanic island of Sumatra?

30 Which river burst its banks to flood York in 2002?

  Answers on page 222

 Answers on page 222

335
FOOD & DRINK 6

1 What country is Pecorino cheese from?
2 What type of pastry are profiteroles made from?
3 Which fruits are usually served *belle hélène*?
4 What is the main flavour of aïoli?
5 Which vegetable can be oyster, chestnut or shitaki?
6 What is wiener schnitzel?
7 How is steak tartare cooked?
8 Which drink is Worcester sauce traditionally added to?
9 Which fish is the main ingredient of Scotch Woodcock?
10 Which area of England are Singing Hinnies from?
11 What is beef fillet cooked in puff pastry called?
12 What gives Windsor Red cheese its colour and flavour?
13 What is a Worcester Pearmain?
14 Which meat is used in Glamorgan sausages?
15 Which vegetables can be Pentland Crown or Maris Bard?
16 What type of food is basmati?
17 What is Roquefort cheese made from?
18 What are the two main ingredients of angels on horseback?
19 Which fruit is a cross between a blackberry and a raspberry?
20 Which type of pasta's name means "little worms"?
21 What ingredient is included in food in a florentine style?
22 What is pancetta?
23 What is the main ingredient of a black pudding?
24 Which herb is in pesto sauce?
25 In Indian cookery what is naan?
26 What type of food is Cullen Skink?
27 What type of fish is in an Omelette Arnold Bennett?
28 What shape is the pasta called rigatoni?
29 What is couscous made from?
30 What does a Pomfret or Pontefract cake taste of?

336
FOOD & DRINK 7

1 Which type of wheat is used in gnocchi?
2 What type of meat is used in osso bucco?
3 What is the flavour of kummel?
4 Which cream has more fat, clotted cream or double cream?
5 What are suntinas?
6 What is special about porcini mushrooms?
7 How is Parmigiano Reggiano usually known in the UK?
8 Burtonwood Ales were originally based near which town?
9 What sort of meat is silverside?
10 What is the Italian equivalent of a French vin de table?
11 Which spirit is used in a Manhattan?
12 Which fruit flavour is used in crêpes suzette?
13 What are the two main ingredients of a coulibiac?
14 What is sake wine made from?
15 Which flavoured liqueur is used to make Kir?
16 What are the two main ingredients of kedgeree?
17 Which breeds of cow produce so-called gold-top milk?
18 Which liqueur is used in a sidecar?
19 Which type of pastry is usually bought frozen in wafer-thin slices?
20 Which two cheeses are layered in a Huntsman cheese?
21 How many standard bottles of wine are equivalent to a methuselah?
22 What is pancetta?
23 What type of flour is traditionally used in blinis?
24 What are flageolet and cannellini?
25 Which country does chorizo sausage come from?
26 From which part of France does Calvados originate?
27 What is focaccia?
28 Which two main ingredients would you add to spaghetti to make spaghetti alla carbonara?
29 What type of milk has a bottle with a blue-and-silver-checked cap?
30 What is arborio?

  **Answers on page 222**

 Answers on page 222

337
ANIMALS 6

1 What type of creature is a mandrill?
2 The bandicoot is a marsupial from which country?
3 What is a young penguin called?
4 What sort of creature is a Tasmanian devil?
5 Which cord connects the placenta to the embryo in mammals?
6 Which country has the most Asian elephants in their natural habitat?
7 Which extinct flightless bird has the Latin name *Didus ineptus*?
8 Which weighs the most – African elephant, hippopotamus or white rhinoceros?
9 What can be Persian long hair, British short hair or Oriental short hair?
10 Which word would describe a wombat's diet?
11 The chipmunk is related to which creature?
12 Where do sloths live?
13 What percentage of all living mammals are rodents?
14 Which of the primates' senses is the weakest?
15 Which is the most intelligent – baboon, chimpanzee or gorilla?
16 How does a tiger hunt?
17 The orang utan in the wild is restricted to Sumatra and where?
18 Who has the most teeth, reptiles, fish or mammals?
19 What is the neck region of the cobra called?
20 What sort of feet do tortoises have?
21 Which is the most intelligent breed of dog?
22 Which of the following animals has the greatest length or height – African elephant, giraffe or tapeworm?
23 What can be minke, grey or bowhead?
24 Which snake is traditionally used by snake charmers?
25 What are the fertilised eggs of amphibians called?
26 Which is the fastest – hare, horse or greyhound?
27 Which fish are members of the class Asteroidea?
28 Which is the only "finger" of a bat that is free from the membrane that forms its wing?
29 Which deadly snakes can be Egyptian, Indian or Forest?
30 Which is the heaviest – black bear, grizzly bear or polar bear?

338
ANIMALS 7

1 What is a common name for the asteroidea which have five arms?
2 At what stage of development is the imago stage of an insect?
3 What is the aquatic larva of an amphibian more commonly called?
4 What is a chameleon capable of changing?
5 What does a reptile shed in the process of sloughing?
6 What is another name for snake poison?
7 The aardvark is a native of which continent?
8 Which is the only mammal able to fly?
9 Which type of dark-coloured bear is the largest?
10 What do Americans call reindeer?
11 Man has seven vertebrae in his neck. How many does a giraffe have?
12 What is the main diet of hedgehogs?
13 Which two colours are wolves?
14 What is the fastest land animal?
15 From which border do Border collies originate?
16 What colour is a chow chow's tongue?
17 What is the mammal *homo sapiens* better known as?
18 Where does an arboreal animal live?
19 What is the smallest breed of dog?
20 Do dolphins have teeth?
21 Which part of the rhino is regarded as an aphrodisiac?
22 Which is the largest of the cats?
23 The ibex is a member of which animal family?
24 Which is generally larger, a wallaby or a kangaroo?
25 How many sets of teeth do most mammals have?
26 What is the black leopard more commonly known as?
27 What do moles mainly feed on?
28 Which country does the breed of dog, shih tzu, come from?
29 What would the Europeans call what the Americans call a moose?
30 What do beavers build?

  Answers on page 222

  Answers on page 222

339
LIVING WORLD 3

1 What is the male honey bee known as?
2 Hermit and spider are types of what?
3 What is another name for an insect's feelers?
4 What name is given to the body a parasite feeds on?
5 How many eyes does a bee have?
6 Which beetle was sacred to the Egyptians?
7 What is the process of casting skin, hair or feathers called?
8 What is a gurnard?
9 Which bird is associated with Lundy Island?
10 What is a conch?
11 What sort of animal is a papillon?
12 What is the olfactory sense?
13 What does the term "metamorphosis" mean?
14 What is a hummingbird's hum caused by?
15 Which is the largest member of the crow family?
16 What and where is Minsmere?
17 What is another name for thunderflies or thunderbugs?
18 How many parts are there to an insect's body?
19 What do lugworms live in?
20 What is a dunnock?
21 Which system controls touch, sight and hearing?
22 From which language does the word budgerigar come?
23 What do the Americans call what the British call a ladybird?
24 How many wings does a flea have?
25 For whom is the Glorious Twelfth not glorious?
26 What is another name for cartilage?
27 How does a stoat's appearance change in the winter?
28 What is a mavis?
29 What is the smallest living unit called?
30 What do polled cattle not have?

340
FOOD & DRINK 8

1 If bread is left to "prove" what does it do?
2 Which initials indicate the highest-quality brandy – AC, RSVP or VSOP?
3 What is a chanterelle?
4 What is aioli flavoured with?
5 What type of sauce was named after the Marquis de Bechamel?
6 What would you be eating if you were served calamari?
7 Enchiladas were originally part of which country's cooking?
8 What shape is the pasta called fusilli?
9 Mozzarella was originally made from which type of milk?
10 Which herb is usually used in gremolata?
11 Which pulses are used to make hummus?
12 Other than tomatoes and onions which is the main vegetable used in moussaka?
13 In which country is the famous wine-growing area of the Barossa valley?
14 Chianti comes from which area of Italy?
15 If a dish is cooked *en papillote* what is it cooked in?
16 Passata is pureed what?
17 A brochette is another word for what?
18 What is prosciutto?
19 What flavour do ratafia biscuits have?
20 What makes a *salsa verde* green – celery leaves, herbs or spinach?
21 Schnapps is distilled from what?
22 What type of white wine is Barsac famous for?
23 What type of oven is traditionally used for a tandoori?
24 Which Japanese dish is made from rice, seaweed and raw fish?
25 Which herb is usually used in a pesto sauce?
26 What type of dough is calzone made from?
27 What is a bisque?
28 When would antipasto be served?
29 What does baking powder produce when water is added, which makes dough rise?
30 How is something cooked if it is sauté?

 Answers on page 222

 Answers on page 222

341
ANIMALS 8

1 What does a browser forage for?

2 What is the largest living rodent?

3 What type of owl featured on the British Nature Conservation stamps of the 80s?

4 Where would a mammal have a malleus?

5 Echidna feed chiefly on what?

6 How many chambers does a camel have in its stomach?

7 What sort of creatures were the now extinct aurochs?

8 Which camelid is the ancestor of the llama and the alpaca?

9 What does a therian mammal produce?

10 In the animal world what is a bongo?

11 How many bones are there in the human arm?

12 What is an erythrocyte?

13 What is another name for the bearded collie?

14 Where is the world's largest zoological library?

15 Which marsupial has the highest reproductive rate?

16 What is another name for the flying lemur?

17 What is the world's largest pedigree cat registry?

18 Which unusual sexual characteristic does the Patagonian hare have?

19 The lemur is native to where?

20 Which species of marten can penetrate a porcupine's defences?

21 What shape are a bushbuck's horns?

22 In mongooses what is the tripod position?

23 What is the principal food of the sperm whale?

24 Which order of reptiles do snakes and lizards belong to?

25 What is a poikilotherm?

26 What is a taipan?

27 What were Dandie Dinmonts originally bred for?

28 Which two main features do reptiles have which amphibians don't?

29 What is a krait?

30 How is the German mastiff also known?

342
FOOD & DRINK 9

1 What culinary item is produced by Filippo Berio?

2 What type of milk was first processed in 1899?

3 In which year did Bird's Eye Fish Fingers first go on sale in the UK?

4 Which drink had the first registered British trademark?

5 Which French city is famous for Cointreau?

6 Which author of *La Bonne Chère* ran the French Pavilion at Disneyworld, Orlando?

7 Which type of pasta lends it name to a type of chocolate decoration?

8 Who created vichysoisse?

9 Who founded the restaurant with Rose Gray where Jamie Oliver was "discovered"?

10 Which area is the only one not to grow a Muscat which is sweet?

11 The Chardonnay grape is a native of where?

12 Which food or drink was named after American John McAdam?

13 Where did Balti cooking originate?

14 In wine making what is another name for tartrate?

15 What are the most common herbs in a bearnaise sauce?

16 Which herb is used in gremolata?

17 When were pressure cookers invented – 1891, 1905 or1933?

18 Where was Anton Mosimann's first post as chef in the UK?

19 Which size of wine bottle is the equivalent of 12 standard bottles?

20 Which monk was responsible for putting the liqueur Chartreuse on sale?

21 Which nuts are usually used in a pesto sauce?

22 Which food item comes form the Hindi meaning pounded meat?

23 Pyrex was made originally to be used where?

24 What is arborio?

25 Auslese is usually made from which grape?

26 Which food comes from the Tamil word meaning pepper water?

27 Dom Bernardo Vincelli devised which drink?

28 Who opened the Miller Howe restaurant in 1971?

29 Fitou is made from which grape?

30 What is unusual about the harvesting of Spätlese grapes?

 Answers on page 223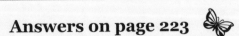

 Answers on page 223

343
FOOD & DRINK 10

1 What is hanepoot?
2 Who or what was Buck's Fizz named after?
3 Which snack's name comes from the Turkish for rotating?
4 Where is the yeastless beer faro made?
5 Where was Anton Mosimann's first position as chef in the UK?
6 Kummel is a Russian liqueur extracted from what?
7 The macadamia is native to where?
8 What is the main ingredient of a brandade?
9 Who opened the Miller Howe restaurant in 1971?
10 In his diary what did Pepys call "jucalette"?
11 Where in a dish would you put gremolata?
12 Which country has a wine-growing area called O'Higgins?
13 Which term indicates the amount of wine by which a container falls short of being full?
14 Who is credited with creating camembert cheese in about 1790?
15 What is the base of a florentine biscuit made from?
16 Where did malmsey wine originate?
17 Balti is the Indian word for what?
18 Which abbreviation indicates wine between the qualities of vin de pays and appellation contrôlée?
19 What are the ingredients of a Mr Callaghan?
20 What is cocose?
21 What did TV cook Sophie Grigson study at university?
22 In Swiss cooking what is a leckerli?
23 What is added to an omelette to make an omelette Argenteuil?
24 Which herbs are put in a béarnaise sauce?
25 Which fruit is used to make slivovitz?
26 Foie gras is the liver of which creatures?
27 In ceviche raw fish is marinated in what?
28 What is a mesclun?
29 A brochette is another name for what?
30 In Mexican cookery what is a quesadilla?

344
PLANTS 6

1 Who bred the first 'Peace' rose?
2 What sort of tree is a gean?
3 How are Boston or pinto beans also known?
4 Where did liquorice originate?
5 Which part of asafoetida is used as a spice?
6 What is a clouded agaric?
7 What is the practice of growing plants in liquid nutrients instead of soil called?
8 What colour is the pigment leghaemoglobin found in legumes?
9 The breakdown of what produces malic acid?
10 What is the milky juice of the dandelion called?
11 What colour is a cloudberry?
12 What term applies to a plant which is lime-hating?
13 What does the bladderwort live on?
14 Which shrubs are also known as bush honeysuckles?
15 What does a batologist study?
16 What is litmus obtained from?
17 A halophyte tolerates soil or water containing what?
18 What is the ring of fine down on a dandelion called?
19 What would you grow if you grew Peruvian apples?
20 What fruit is produced on a banyan tree?
21 Which common vegetable family does chervil belong to?
22 What is a toadstool's pileus?
23 Cauliflowers are vegetables but technically what are caulis?
24 Where would you normally find a bracket fungus?
25 What is phytopathology?
26 What is *Camellia sinensis* more commonly called?
27 From what is the oil copra obtained?
28 What does edaphic mean?
29 What is a saguaro?
30 Which part of the plants are the cloves you buy as a spice?

 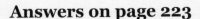 **Answers on page 223**

 Answers on page 223

345
PLANET EARTH

1 In which US state is the Jewel cave system?
2 The largest man-made excavation in the world mines which element?
3 Which animal weighs the most – grizzly bear, polar bear or a walrus?
4 What is Europe's largest island which is not a country in its own right?
5 Which desert is on the US–Mexico border?
6 What is the most common element in the earth's crust after oxygen?
7 Which planet orbits the Sun fastest?
8 Acid rain results due to a pollution of the atmosphere with oxides of nitrogen and what?
9 What is another name for a tsunami?
10 What colour is apatite?
11 Where was the meteorite High Possil found?
12 Where is the highest waterfall outside South America?
13 What is the world's highest island?
14 How many states does Lake Michigan cover?
15 Which planet has the hottest surface?
16 Orogenesis is concerned with the formation of what?
17 Which unit measures distances beyond the solar system?
18 Where was the meteorite Armanty found on Earth?
19 Actinobiology studies the effect of what on living organisms?
20 Cryogenics studies materials under what conditions?
21 Of the five largest glaciers in the world which is the only one not in Antarctica?
22 Which part of planet Earth would a pedologist observe?
23 The Appleton layer plays a role in what – heat control, sifting of toxic gases or radio communication?
24 It isn't a sea, but what is the Afsluidijk Sea?
25 How many countries does the Mekong river flow through?
26 What is the most common element in the universe after hydrogen?
27 Which planet is the lightest?
28 Which scale measures the hardness of substances?
29 How many light years is Alpha Centauri from the Earth?
30 What substance is around 90% of the Earth's core made from?

346
FOOD & DRINK 11

1 Which wine comes from Worms?
2 How is sake usually drunk?
3 In which Berkshire village is Heston Blumenthal's Fat Duck restaurant to be found?
4 What were angostura bitters originally used for?
5 In the US if a dessert is served *à la mode* what is served with it?
6 Which vegetable is a passata made from?
7 What shape is a rugelach?
8 What is chenin blanc wine known as in South Africa?
9 Which term describes the fermented grape juice added to wine that has lost its strength to perk it up?
10 If a wine is madeirised what has happened to it?
11 Where is Marsala, famed for its fortified wine?
12 In wine terms what is the difference between frizzante and spumante?
13 Which folded pizza dough dish takes its name from the Italian for trouser leg?
14 Which cereal is polenta made from?
15 How does Malaga wine achieve its dark colour?
16 In which London borough did Jamie Oliver's healthy school dinner campaign begin?
17 Where does Dao wine come from?
18 In addition to Sauternes itself which four communes can call their wine Sauternes?
19 Where did balti cooking originate?
20 Who was the winner of *Masterchef Goes Large* in the early part of 2006?
21 Other than Spain and Portugal where does sack come from?
22 What is a red biddy?
23 Which food is also called the vegetable oyster?
24 In wine making which term describes turning the bottles so the sediment collects at the cork end?
25 In which district of Bordeaux is Chateau Petrus produced?
26 What is pradikat?
27 Which classic French sauce was named after a courtier of Louis XIV?
28 What is the study of wine called?
29 Which chef created the Bombe Nero and the peche melba?
30 Which sweet rice wine is used in Japanese cookery?

  Answers on page 223

 Answers on page 223

347
FOOD & DRINK 12

1 A batavia is a variety of what?

2 From where is rennet normally obtained?

3 Which part of France does Cantal cheese come from?

4 What was mozzarella cheese originally made from?

5 What is the chemical name of vitamin B1?

6 A rhyton was a drinking vessel in the shape of what?

7 Which chicken dish was named after a Napoleonic battle of June 1800?

8 What sort of nuts are used to make a pesto sauce?

9 What does authentic Parmesan cheese have stamped on its rind?

10 The leaves of which plant are the main ingredient of absinthe?

11 What do you add to a white sauce to make an aurore sauce?

12 How do you cook food en papillote?

13 Where is the home of the Anheuser-Busch Inc. brewery?

14 What is Ameleon?

15 What does the name of the pasta capelli d'angelo mean?

16 What sort of drink is Volvic?

17 Where is the Kirin Brewery based?

18 Who had signed the wine bottle sold for £105,000 at Christie's in 1985?

19 What are the ingredients with E numbers 200–29 used for in foods?

20 In which restaurant did Escoffier begin his career?

21 What is the main ingredient of a piperade?

22 Which drink is Les Bouillens famous for?

23 Which fast-food chain opened its first UK outlet in London in 1954?

24 What do the Chinese call "lively fellows"?

25 What is ricotta cheese made from?

26 What was Reuben Mattus's most famous creation of 1961?

27 What does a baron of lamb consist of?

28 Which type of avocado has a knobbly skin?

29 What shape is farfalle pasta?

30 What is a kugelhopf?

348
SCIENCE

1 What did the word astronaut originally mean?

2 Who discovered the mystery object Chiron?

3 What was the third planet to have been visited by a spacecraft?

4 In which US state is the Fisher Ridge cave system?

5 Which company introduced Photo CD?

6 What was the third country to have a man in space?

7 Which is the longest bone in the arm?

8 What is another name for slaked lime?

9 Where was the meteorite Mbosi found?

10 In which constellation is Rigel?

11 Which bone is named after the Italian for flute?

12 What is emetophobia a fear of?

13 What is Saturn's biggest moon?

14 Willem Johan Kolff devised which item of equipment, a pioneer in medicine and health?

15 How much faster does the strongest wind blow on Neptune than on Earth?

16 How many miles below the Earth' surface do diamonds form?

17 What is the next largest body in the Solar System after Uranus?

18 Which company created Dolly the Sheep?

19 What is the next largest human organ after the brain?

20 Asteroids usually appear between the orbits of Mars and which other planet?

21 In which decade were contact lenses first devised?

22 Who discovered the asteroid Flora?

23 Which device did Apple CEO Steve Jobs say would "reinvent" telecommunications in 2007?

24 What is the most common element in the human body after oxygen?

25 Which satellite has the thickest atmosphere?

26 What name is given to the animal and plant life which lives at the bottom of the sea?

27 What does a limnologist study?

28 How many people were in space on 14th March 1995, a then record?

29 What is Neptune's largest moon?

30 What is D2O?

  Answers on page 223

 Answers on page 223

349
ANIMALS 9

1 What is the only mammal to live as a parasite?
2 How is a Sibbald's rorqual also known?
3 For how many hours in a period of 24 does a giraffe sleep?
4 What is the world's largest rodent?
5 What gives the sloth its greenish appearance?
6 Which mammal lives at the highest altitude?
7 Which animals are famously sold at Bampton Fair?
8 The mammal which can live at the greatest depth is a species of what?
9 From which part of a sperm whale is ambergris obtained?
10 Where does a cane toad squirt poison from?
11 What is the longest type of worm?
12 Where would you find a shark's denticles?
13 What does the male mouse deer have that no other deer has?
14 Where does a browser find food?
15 What is the Latin name for the Blue Whale?
16 A Clydesdale was originally a cross between a Scottish draught horse and a what?
17 What colour is a mandrill's beard?
18 The wisent is native to where?
19 Lemurs are only found in their natural habitat where?
20 What is the oldest indigenous breed of cat in the US?
21 What is a koikoi?
22 What is the average life expectancy of the mayfly?
23 Which protein is cartilage made up of?
24 The term monkey refers to all primates except apes, humans and what?
25 Why were Samoyeds originally bred?
26 Falabellas are native to where?
27 What is another name for the aye-aye?
28 Which animal has the longest tail?
29 What name is given to the smaller of a rhino's horns?
30 What does it mean if an animal is homoiothermic?

350
LIVING WORLD 4

1 RSPB founders campaigned specifically against the slaughter of birds for what purpose?
2 Which faunal region covers South/Central America and the Caribbean?
3 What is the largest class of sponges called?
4 Sea fans and sea whips are types of what?
5 What colour is the underside of the pipesnake's tail?
6 What is the world's largest eagle?
7 Which sense does the New World vulture have which the Old World vulture doesn't?
8 How many eyes does a tuatara have?
9 A sunstar is a type of what?
10 How is the early bird from Australasia, the butcherbird, also known?
11 How does the flamingo get its colour?
12 Where does a blenny live?
13 What is a ratite?
14 Which bird can walk up to 20 miles a day?
15 What do oystercatchers eat?
16 To which family does the grampus belong?
17 Which continent is the home of the electric eel?
18 What has the largest wingspan of any living bird?
19 The Puerto Rican boa is endangered due to which predator?
20 What does a white bait grow into?
21 Where does the axolotl come from?
22 Which part of a turtle is its carapace?
23 How is the goat fish also known?
24 Which flightless bird in addition to the emu is native to Australia?
25 What is a skink?
26 Which bone of birds is also called the furcula?
27 Which Australian male bird incubates the eggs and raises the young?
28 Where is the mesite native to?
29 Which fish is known as rock salmon when sold for food?
30 How does the monitor lizard consume its prey?

  Answers on page 223

Answers on page 223

351
NATURAL PHENOMENA 2

1 What was the name of the first storm to be given a name?
2 Which volcanic rock is named after a mountain range in South America?
3 What is our Solar System's nearest stellar neighbour?
4 Which Asian country has the greatest area of inland water?
5 What is the highest waterfall in Norway?
6 What is the next largest body in the Solar System after Venus?
7 What is the largest lake in the UK after Neagh?
8 In which US state is the Mammoth cave system?
9 What is V4641 Sgr?
10 What was the first asteroid to be discovered?
11 Where was the meteorite Hoba West found?
12 What is the world's highest island after New Guinea?
13 What is the name of the nearest planetary nebula to the Earth?
14 What percentage of the sky does the smallest constellation take up?
15 Which of the following is the brightest – Rigel, Sirius or Vega?
16 What was the second planet to have been visited by a spacecraft?
17 On which island is the Aceh province that was devastated by the 2004 tsunami?
18 Which state along with Texas and Nebraska is known as Tornado Alley?
19 About how many million years did the longest ice age last?
20 Which planet has the longest day in the solar system?
21 Which element discovered in 1931 is the rarest on Earth?
22 What is the defined visibility of a sea fog?
23 Which nebula is brightest in the night sky?
24 In which constellation is Procyon?
25 In which constellation is the Hyades cluster?
26 At which university is the McDonald Observatory?
27 Where was the meteorite Rowton found?
28 Which Asian Sea is the deepest?
29 From which country was the Andromeda Galaxy first observed?
30 After Pluto which is the next furthest body from the Sun?

352
PLANTS 7

1 How is the maidenhair tree also known?
2 Which acid makes rhubarb leaves poisonous?
3 What is a tissue which forms on a damaged plant surface called?
4 The *Sequoia* takes its name from what?
5 What makes the death cap mushroom so toxic?
6 Which European country produces more than half of Europe's rice?
7 Where would you find the home of the bristlecone pine?
8 The Venus flytrap is found naturally in which US states?
9 A meadow clary has flowers of what colour?
10 What sort of plants are cryptogams?
11 The world's tallest tree is native only to where?
12 If a leaf is sessile what is missing?
13 What is another name for the *Saintpaulia*?
14 How does a bladderwort receive its nourishment?
15 If a plant suffers from chlorosis what happens to it?
16 How is the entada known in Australia?
17 What is the only plant which can change its shape?
18 What is the fruit of the blackthorn bush?
19 What type of plant is a saguaro?
20 To which family does the greater celandine belong?
21 The largest known giant redwood is named after whom?
22 How is the plant *Lactuca sativa* better known?
23 If something is coprophilous where does it grow?
24 The tree sometimes known as Wellingtonia is native to which mountains?
25 Atropine is derived from which plant?
26 Which part of the flax plant is used to make linen?
27 If a plant is halophytic where does it grow?
28 Which tree is the tallest native to Europe?
29 On which two islands would you find the sea coconut?
30 Which plant has the largest leaves?

 Answers on page 224

 Answers on page 224

353
ANIMALS 10

1 What creature is unique to Skomer Island, off the Pembrokeshire coast of Wales?

2 Which is the only snake to be found regularly north of the Arctic Circle?

3 What is the smallest tiger subspecies?

4 What is a dik-dik?

5 Which animal is the symbol of the US Republican Party?

6 What are goannas and anoles?

7 Which breed of dog is a cross between an Irish wolfhound and a greyhound?

8 What general name is given to manatees and dugongs?

9 Of which family is the linsang a member?

10 What is unusual about a chameleon's eyes?

11 What region is the arrow-poison frog a native of?

12 What group of insects include German, American and common?

13 Which animal might be Siberian or Caspian?

14 What do entomophagous animals eat?

15 What are the five groups of vertebrates?

16 What are oviparous animals?

17 What do horse, snake and scorpion have in common?

18 Which largest rodent became a serious pest in East Anglia?

19 What is the world's largest burrowing herbivorous mammal?

20 Which is the largest of all the animal phyla?

21 What are stag, rhinoceros and tiger other than animals in their own right?

22 What sort of animal is a fennec?

23 Where are the ayaye the remaining endangered animals?

24 What does an impala do when frightened?

25 What country are Père David's deer native to?

26 What name is given to a mammal which bears live young?

27 What is a group of hedgehogs called?

28 What is another name for an Old English terrier?

29 What is a sand mason?

30 What is a Clydesdale?

354
ANIMALS 11

1 What is the second largest species of fish?

2 What type of animals were space travellers Sam and Miss Sam?

3 Which animals spends the largest amount of time asleep?

4 Who first named the gorilla?

5 Which usually weighs the most – a bison, a moose or a polar bear?

6 What are Pacific leatherbacks and Atlantic leatherbacks?

7 Which of these swims the fastest – marlin, sailfish or swordfish?

8 Kittis's hognosed bat is native to which country?

9 What is Rhincodon typus?

10 The devil's hole pupfish restricts its habitat to an isolated part of which US state?

11 What is a Ruppell's griffon?

12 What has the highest reproductive rate of all marsupials?

13 What is another name for the colugo?

14 Approximately how many domestic breeds of dog are there?

15 What is the most socially organised member of the cat family?

16 Which is the largest – giant African snail, giant clam or giant squid?

17 Which creature is unique in its ability to penetrate the quills of a porcupine?

18 What is the only truly amphibious member of the weasel family?

19 The skunk is a major carrier of which disease?

20 The greatest number of feathers counted on a bird was on a what?

21 Which is the largest of the toothed whales?

22 What is the smallest of the Ratitae order?

23 Which flies the fastest – mallard, pintail or teal?

24 Which sense does the Old World vulture lack?

25 What is the most beautiful part of the bulbul?

26 What does the tuatara have on top of its head?

27 What is the only marsupial which specialises in burrowing?

28 Where is the Bolson tortoise native to?

29 What is the San Joaquin leopard lizard also known as?

30 What is the largest living rodent?

  Answers on page 224

 Answers on page 224

355
LIVING WORLD 5

1 What is another name for the North American nightjar?
2 Who was the first woman to have a partial face transplant?
3 How is the disease trypanosomiasis also known?
4 What is meant by a haemorrhage which is "occult"?
5 Which protein is present in a hair?
6 What does it mean if a cell is haploid?
7 In addition to tea and coffee where is caffeine found?
8 Where is the *flexor carpi radialis*?
9 What is an erythrocyte?
10 How is the sand hopper also known?
11 Guano is used as fertiliser but what is it made from?
12 Cranes are found on all continents except which two?
13 What is an alternative name for leptospirosis?
14 Carragheen is a type of what?
15 Where is a caterpillar's spinneret?
16 Which bird flies highest?
17 What is an insect's Malpighian tubes?
18 How does a mamba differ from a cobra?
19 Which part of the brain controls muscular movements, balance and co-ordination?
20 Which bird can swim as fast as a seal?
21 An urodele is another name for which reptile?
22 Which bird builds the largest nest?
23 The world's largest spider is named after which Biblical character?
24 What is a bird's furcula?
25 Disulfiram is used in the treatment of what?
26 What is a hairstreak?
27 On which island would you find the bee hummingbird?
28 Which bird produces the largest egg in relation to its body size?
29 Why should you avoid a chigger?
30 How many hearts does an earthworm have?

356
FOOD & DRINK 13

1 What do you add to béchamel to make an aurore sauce?
2 What three main ingredients are added to mayonnaise to make a Waldorf salad?
3 What is a Kugelhupf?
4 In which country do red onions originate?
5 What is added to cheddar cheese to make Ilchester cheese?
6 What is laver?
7 What type of fish are Arbroath smokies?
8 What size eggs are between 60 and 65 grams?
9 What type of milk was mozzarella cheese originally made from?
10 What sort of meat is used in a guard of honour?
11 What is something cooked in if cooked *en papillote*?
12 What do you add to vegetables to make a salmagundi?
13 What are Pershore eggs and Marjorie's seedlings?
14 What are the two main ingredients of a Hollandaise sauce?
15 What colour top do bottles of unpasteurized milk have?
16 What is the chief ingredient of boxty bread?
17 In which English county is Brie made?
18 What is the main meat ingredient of faggots?
19 Which has most fat: double cream, crème fraîche or whipping cream?
20 What is Cornish yarg cheese coated with?
21 Which country does skordalia come from?
22 What shape is the pasta called farfalle?
23 What is the main ingredient of dal?
24 In Indian cuisine what is ghee?
25 Where does coulibiac originate and what is it?
26 Which term in Italian cooking means "soft but firm"?
27 What is a carbonade cooked in?
28 How is steak cooked if cooked blue?
29 How does paella get its name?
30 What is the main vegetable ingredient of moussaka?

 Answers on page 224

 Answers on page 224

357
PLANTS 8

1 In which US state is the Tongass National Forest?

2 Which of the following do algae have – chlorophyll, roots and stems?

3 What does a saphrophyte feed on?

4 Urtica ferox is a deadly tree nettle native to where?

5 How much chlorophyll does spinach have – 0.9%, 0.12% or 0.17%?

6 Which of the following originated in the Middle East – barley, maize or millet?

7 What is another name for the blade of a plant?

8 What name is given to a plant whose seed is not enclosed in an ovary?

9 Which of the following are in the Aquilfoliacae group – conifers, hollies or ivies?

10 What name is given to a plant which grows on another without damaging it?

11 The whistler tree is what type of tree?

12 Myosotis is another name for which flower?

13 What is a funicle?

14 According to legend which plant did Adam take from the Garden of Eden?

15 How is Lunaria biennis better known?

16 What type of plant is a silver slipper?

17 What colour are the blooms of the rose "Zéphirine Drouhin"?

18 What is another name for the meadow saffron?

19 What is the rose of Lancaster also called?

20 What are Alice Forbes and Bailey's Delight?

21 What is Crocus sativus?

22 How is chionodoxa also known?

23 The agapanthus is native to where?

24 Which part of asafoetida is used?

25 The borlotti bean also takes its name from which city?

26 Which part of a mooli is edible?

27 How is rock cress better known?

28 Which herb reputedly travels seven times to the devil before it will emerge?

29 The amaryllis is related to which popular spring flower?

30 What is the nationality of the man who gave his name to the plant Lobelia?

  Answers on page 224

358
FOOD & DRINK: GOURMET

1 Who set up the Society of British Gastronomes?

2 Which couple had a TV show called Gourmet Ireland?

3 Whose restaurant was named Best Restaurant in The World by Restaurant magazine in 2005?

4 At which London hotels did Auguste Escoffier gain his reputation?

5 Which chef is associated with the world-class "Waterside Inn" at Bray?

6 Whose cookery book is called Food of the Sun?

7 What type of food does Valentina Harris specialize in?

8 Who is the chef/proprietor of "Le Manoir aux Quat' Saisons"?

9 Vatcharin Bhumichitr has written about the taste of which country?

10 Which writer, raconteur and food expert was a former Liberal MP for Ely?

11 In which city is Murphy's Irish stout brewed?

12 Which chef is the restaurant "Bibendum" associated with?

13 Which cook and writer produced a Cook's Tour of France?

14 Which expert on Indian cooking is also an accomplished actress?

15 Who founded a School of Food and Wine and was instrumental in improving British Rail sandwiches?

16 Where was Gary Rhodes chef when he shot to fame on TV?

17 Who founded the Ballymaloe Cook School in Ireland?

18 Which cook was a founder of Classic FM?

19 Who wrote the foreword to the collection of recipes in book form Delia Smith compiled as a response to Live Aid?

20 Who is chef/patron of the Miller Howe, Windermere?

21 Where did Delia Smith have a cookery column before achieving fame on TV?

22 What type of cuisine does Sarah Brown specialize in?

23 Which cook has been married to the founder of "Habitat"?

24 In which county is Hugh Fearnley-Whittingstall's River Cottage?

25 What was the name of the chef played by Lenny Henry?

26 What was the first name of Sophie Grigson's mother?

27 Who founded the magazine where Mrs Beeton's articles were printed?

28 Which TV programme consists of chefs producing a dish from a limited list of ingredients against the clock?

29 Which team wrote the Daily Telegraph's "Bon Viveur" column?

30 Who wrote "Man in the Kitchen" and was a TV cookery pioneer?

 Answers on page 224

1 ❋ PENALTY KICKS

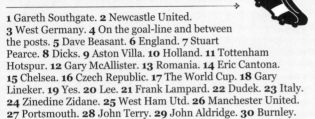

1 Gareth Southgate. **2** Newcastle United.
3 West Germany. **4** On the goal-line and between the posts. **5** Dave Beasant. **6** England. **7** Stuart Pearce. **8** Dicks. **9** Aston Villa. **10** Holland. **11** Tottenham Hotspur. **12** Gary McAllister. **13** Romania. **14** Eric Cantona. **15** Chelsea. **16** Czech Republic. **17** The World Cup. **18** Gary Lineker. **19** Yes. **20** Lee. **21** Frank Lampard. **22** Dudek. **23** Italy. **24** Zinedine Zidane. **25** West Ham Utd. **26** Manchester United. **27** Portsmouth. **28** John Terry. **29** John Aldridge. **30** Burnley.

2 ❋ SUMMER SPORTS

1 Cricket. **2** Lewis. **3** Shane Warne. **4** Pole vault. **5** Tim Henman. **6** Cricket. **7** Tour de France. **8** Bicycle. **9** USA. **10** Europe. **11** Four. **12** Bounce. **13** Triple jump. **14** Australia. **15** Greg Norman. **16** Navratilova. **17** Tour de France. **18** Steffi Graf. **19** Ireland. **20** Four. **21** Novotna. **22** High jump. **23** Hambledon CC. **24** Six. **25** John McEnroe. **26** Viv Richards. **27** Mark McGwire. **28** Connors. **29** Argentinean. **30** Europe.

3 ❋ QUOTE UNQUOTE

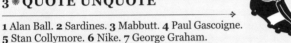

1 Alan Ball. **2** Sardines. **3** Mabbutt. **4** Paul Gascoigne. **5** Stan Collymore. **6** Nike. **7** George Graham. **8** Graham Taylor. **9** Pele. **10** Neal. **11** Beardsley. **12** George Best. **13** Paul Gascoigne. **14** Jurgen Klinsmann. **15** Tomatoes. **16** Before the Euro 96 semi-final. **17** Argentina. **18** Glenn Hoddle. **19** Gareth Southgate. **20** Paul Gascoigne. **21** Steve McClaren. **22** Luiz Felipe Scolari. **23** Arsene Wenger. **24** Strachan. **25** The bus. **26** David Bentley. **27** Gianfranco Zola. **28** Mike Ashley. **29** Harry Redknapp. **30** Paul Ince.

4 ❋ THE '80S

1 Lineker. **2** Bob Champion. **3** Geoff Boycott. **4** Ovett. **5** Liverpool. **6** Davis. **7** Australia. **8** Hailwood. **9** Watson. **10** Everton. **11** Navratilova. **12** Bolero. **13** Italy. **14** Zola Budd. **15** Los Angeles. **16** Lyle. **17** Brazil. **18** Dennis Taylor. **19** Belgium. **20** Javelin. **21** Boxing. **22** Boris Becker. **23** Maradona. **24** Flo Jo. **25** Bryan Robson. **26** Somerset. **27** France. **28** Czechoslovakia. **29** Rangers. **30** Jack Charlton.

5 ❋ HORSE RACING

1 Lester Piggott. **2** Red Rum. **3** Doncaster. **4** *The Sporting Life*. **5** Ireland. **6** November. **7** Peter Scudamore. **8** The Dip. **9** St Leger. **10** Mon Mome. **11** National. **12** Chantilly. **13** Corbiere. **14** Richards. **15** United States. **16** Goodwood. **17** Derby. **18** Kildare. **19** Ascot. **20** Australia. **21** Czech Republic. **22** Mick Fitzgerald. **23** Tipperary. **24** Dubai. **25** Aintree. **26** Kauto Star. **27** Seabiscuit. **28** Mick Channon. **29** £500. **30** Longchamp.

6 ❋ FOOTBALL

1 Newcastle. **2** Vieira. **3** Blue and white. **4** Houllier. **5** USA. **6** Bristol. **7** Goal. **8** Newcastle. **9** Cole. **10** Blackpool. **11** Schmeichel. **12** Spain. **13** Rangers. **14** Manchester United. **15** Northern Ireland. **16** Red. **17** France. **18** Tottenham. **19** Bolton. **20** As hosts they automatically qualified. **21** Pleat. **22** Own goal. **23** 2005. **24** Keegan. **25** Bramall. **26** Liverpool. **27** 3.00pm. **28** Man Utd. **29** Everton. **30** Chelsea.

7 ❋ FOOTBALL LEGENDS

1 Outside right. **2** George Best. **3** Johan Cruyff. **4** Chelsea. **5** Bobby Moore. **6** Poland. **7** Wolves. **8** Jackie Milburn. **9** Hungary. **10** Manchester City. **11** Franz Beckenbauer. **12** One. **13** Lev Yashin. **14** Gordon Banks. **15** Pele. **16** Jennings. **17** Michel Platini. **18** Manchester. **19** Diego Maradona. **20** Stoke City. **21** Alan Ball. **22** Le Tissier. **23** Jinky. **24** Tottenham. **25** Gianfranco Zola. **26** George Weah. **27** Stanley Matthews. **28** George Best. **29** Eric Cantona. **30** Ruud Gullit.

8 ❋ WHO'S WHO?

1 Martina Navratilova. **2** Pele. **3** Ginola. **4** South Africa. **5** Tim Henman. **6** New Zealand. **7** Army. **8** Paula Radcliffe. **9** Reardon. **10** Monocle. **11** Boxing. **12** Seles. **13** USA. **14** Michael Schumacher. **15** India. **16** Red Rum. **17** Rusedski. **18** Wisden. **19** Women's cricket. **20** Canada. **21** Anne. **22** David James. **23** John McEnroe. **24** Pitman. **25** Ricky Ponting. **26** Frank Bruno. **27** Shergar. **28** Jackie Stewart. **29** Dickie Bird. **30** Ruud Gullit.

9 ❋ THE '70S

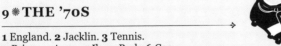

1 England. **2** Jacklin. **3** Tennis. **4** Princess Anne. **5** Ibrox Park. **6** Coe. **7** Boxing. **8** Arsenal. **9** Swimming. **10** Richards. **11** Goolagong. **12** Reardon. **13** Celtic. **14** Red Rum. **15** Brian Clough. **16** Foster. **17** Sweden. **18** Sheene. **19** Thompson. **20** Virginia Wade. **21** Liverpool. **22** Cricket. **23** France. **24** Ipswich. **25** Argentina. **26** Rugby League. **27** Lauda. **28** Kerry Packer. **29** Stewart. **30** Scotland.

10 ❋ MANCHESTER UNITED

1 Alex Ferguson. **2** 17. **3** George Best. **4** Keith Gillespie. **5** Scotland. **6** West Ham. **7** Barcelona and Chelsea. **8** Crystal Palace. **9** Wolves. **10** Gary. **11** 10. **12** First sending off in a final. **13** Greenhoff. **14** Ron Atkinson. **15** Eric Cantona. **16** The Republic of Ireland. **17** George Best. **18** David. **19** Bobby Charlton and Nobby Stiles. **20** Andy Cole. **21** Tottenham Hotspur. **22** Wayne Rooney. **23** 2–0. **24** Ryan Giggs. **25** Portugal. **26** The Red Devils. **27** Ten. **28** 1968, 1999 & 2008. **29** Eric Cantona. **30** Ron Atkinson.

11 ✳ CRICKET

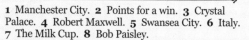

1 Australia and England. 2 Manchester.
3 Before. 4 Cork. 5 Andrew Flintoff. 6 Jack Russell.
7 Lord's. 8 Randall. 9 Jerusalem. 10 England.
11 Two. 12 Yorkshire. 13 Wicket keeper. 14 Nottingham.
15 None. 16 India. 17 W. G. 18 Yorkshire. 19 Stewart.
20 Caught and bowled. 21 Left. 22 Lancashire. 23 Sunday.
24 Six. 25 Brian Johnson. 26 Terence. 27 Australia.
28 Six. 29 Middlesex. 30 None.

12 ˙ RECORD BREAKERS

1 Swimming. 2 Brazil. 3 10 years. 4 Long jump.
5 Australia. 6 Gunnell. 7 Glenn Hoddle. 8 Oxford.
9 15. 10 Jason Leonard. 11 Mansell. 12 Coe.
13 Jacklin. 14 Ben Johnson. 15 Davis. 16 East Germany.
17 American football. 18 Ten. 19 Sampras. 20 Edwards.
21 France. 22 Long jump. 23 Linford Christie. 24 Gower.
25 Africa. 26 14. 27 Jack Nicklaus. 28 Hurdles.
29 Alan Shearer. 30 Swimming.

13 ✳ THE '80S

1 Manchester City. 2 Points for a win. 3 Crystal
Palace. 4 Robert Maxwell. 5 Swansea City. 6 Italy.
7 The Milk Cup. 8 Bob Paisley.
9 Tottenham Hotspur. 10 Kevin Keegan. 11 Gary Lineker.
12 Liverpool. 13 Jock Stein. 14 France. 15 England.
16 France. 17 Terry Venables. 18 Arsenal. 19 Chelsea.
20 Play-offs. 21 Watford. 22 Wimbledon. 23 Liverpool.
24 Ruud Gullit. 25 Arsenal. 26 Bobby Robson. 27 Aston Villa.
28 West Ham United. 29 Ipswich Town. 30 Manchester United.

14 ✳ MOURINHO'S CHELSEA

1 2004. 2 Newcastle United. 3 "The Special One".
4 John Terry. 5 Manchester City. 6 France. 7 Frank
Lampard. 8 Czech Republic. 9 William Gallas. 10 Porto.
11 Terry. 12 Argentina. 13 West Ham. 14 Portugal. 15 Roman
Abramovich. 16 Carlo Cudicini. 17 Ukraine. 18 1960s. 19 Claudio
Ranieri. 20 Liverpool. 21 Tottenham Hotspur. 22 Newcastle
United. 23 Ghana. 24 1950s (1955). 25 Wayne Bridge.
26 Rafael Benitez. 27 Drug taking. 28 League Cup. 29 Holland.
30 Rosenborg.

15 ✳ CRICKET

1 1987. 2 Surrey. 3 Duck. 4 Devon Malcolm.
5 Lancashire. 6 Bradman. 7 40. 8 Ian Botham.
9 Wide. 10 Wicket keeper. 11 Three. 12 Shane
Warne. 13 Slips. 14 Leicestershire. 15 A finger. 16 New Zealand.
17 Chappell. 18 Yorkshire. 19 Lara. 20 Extras. 21 Stumped.
22 Pakistan. 23 A six. 24 A pair. 25 Jonathan Agnew.
26 Edgbaston. 27 Australia. 28 Yes. 29 Glenn McGrath.
30 Simon Jones.

16 ✳ MIDFIELD MEN

1 Blackburn Rovers. 2 Arsenal. 3 Michel Platini.
4 Osvaldo Ardiles. 5 Bremner. 6 Manchester City. 7
Graeme Souness. 8 Lothar Matthaus. 9 Parker.
10 Arsenal. 11 Scott. 12 Belgium. 13 Fulham. 14 Paul
McStay. 15 Liverpool. 16 Wolfgang. 17 Bryan Robson.
18 Everton. 19 Manchester Utd. 20 Yes. 21 2007.
22 Lampard. 23 Aston Villa. 24 France. 25 David Beckham.
26 Steven Gerrard. 27 West Ham Utd. 28 Roy Keane.
29 Tim Cahill. 30 Michael Carrick.

17 ✳ FOOTBALL UK

1 Manchester Utd. 2 Karren Brady. 3 Alan
Curbishley. 4 Matthews. 5 Blackburn. 6 Sweden.
7 Kenny Dalglish. 8 Japan. 9 Black & white.
10 Sunderland. 11 £15 million. 12 Northern Ireland. 13 Dutch.
14 Petr Cech. 15 Paul Jewell. 16 Leeds Utd. 17 Ince. 18 Terry
Venables. 19 Ian Wright. 20 FA Cup. 21 Rush. 22 Charlton
Athletic. 23 Red. 24 Clough. 25 Middlesbrough. 26 Bobby.
27 Cantona. 28 Duncan Ferguson. 29 Rangers. 30 Aston Villa.

18 ✳ FOOTBALL 2

1 Blackburn Rovers. 2 Arsenal. 3 Red. 4 Sweden.
5 Everton. 6 Sheffield. 7 FC Porto. 8 Celtic. 9 45. 10
City. 11 Red. 12 Berlin. 13 Wales. 14 Souness.
15 Norwich City. 16 22. 17 Brazil. 18 Aston Villa. 19 Liverpool.
20 Edinburgh. 21 1. 22 Robinson. 23 Sweden. 24 Everton. 25
Celtic. 26 Forest. 27 Blue. 28 Sven Goran Eriksson. 29 Yes.
30 White Hart.

19 ✳ THE '90S

1 Leeds Rhinos. 2 The Tri Nations. 3 A. P. 4 Baker
Finch. 5 Auckland. 6 Hastings. 7 Rangers. 8 Taylor.
9 South Africa. 10 Atlanta. 11 Grand National. 12
Wigan. 13 Gunnell. 14 George Graham.
15 It was cancelled. 16 Kriss. 17 Swimming. 18 Ireland.
19 Platt. 20 Skis. 21 France. 22 Scotland. 23 Dalglish.
24 John. 25 Conchita. 26 Michael Schumacher.
27 Manchester United. 28 Triple Jump. 29 Javelin. 30 Denmark.

20 ✳ DAVID BECKHAM

1 No 7. 2 Leytonstone. 3 Alex Ferguson.
4 Argentina. 5 Posh Spice. 6 Joseph. 7 New York
(Brooklyn). 8 My Side. 9 Romeo. 10 Spain. 11 None.
12 Adams. 13 Hansen. 14 White. 15 Parents. 16 Colombia.
17 Ireland. 18 Sven Goran Eriksson. 19 Fledglings.
20 Beckingham Palace. 21 Austria. 22 No 23.
23 Wimbledon. 24 Commonwealth Games. 25 £25m.
26 Brazil. 27 He was sent off. 28 Michael Owen.
29 Glenn Hoddle. 30 Victoria.

21 ✸ FOOTBALL: LONDON CLUBS

1 Dave Beasant. 2 Alan McDonald. 3 Croatian.
4 QPR. 5 No. 6 Fulham. 7 Ron Harris. 8 Watford,
Arsenal and Tottenham Hotspur. 9 Leyton Orient.
10 Brentford. 11 Wimbledon. 12 Billy Bonds. 13 Michael
Thomas. 14 Frank McAvennie. 15 Watford. 16 Barry Hearn.
17 Dean Holdsworth. 18 Tottenham Hotspur. 19 Liverpool.
20 Leyton Orient. 21 Emirates Stadium. 22 Chelsea. 23 Barnet.
24 Crystal Palace. 25 Millwall. 26 13. 27 Woolwich Arsenal.
28 Spurs (1901). 29 Queens Park Rangers. 30 Brentford.

22 ✸ RUGBY

1 Australia. 2 Gavin Hastings. 3 22. 4 Shane
Williams. 5 Two (England and France). 6 Davies.
7 Paul Sculthorpe (injured). 8 Bath. 9 Wales. 10 Wembley.
11 New Zealand. 12 England. 13 1970s. 14 Castleford.
15 Lynagh. 16 Salford Reds. 17 Toulouse. 18 Harlequins.
19 Australia, New Zealand. 20 Ivory Coast. 21 Centre.
22 1940s. 23 New Zealand. 24 Michael Owen. 25 Widnes.
26 Phillippe Sella. 27 Mike Gibson. 28 Fan-Jones.
29 Twenty. 30 Knowsley Road.

23 ✸ WHO'S WHO? 2

1 Sonny Liston. 2 Natalie Tauziat. 3 Rocky Marciano.
4 Al Joyner. 5 Joe DiMaggio. 6 Jake La Motta.
7 Silver. 8 Ray Reardon. 9 Raymond van Barnevald.
10 Mary Decker Slaney. 11 Italy. 12 Ernie Els. 13 Nick Faldo.
14 Steve Davis. 15 Cook book. 16 Paul Azinger. 17 Chris Evert.
18 Davis. 19 Squash. 20 Denise Lewis. 21 Graeme Smith.
22 Rocket. 23 John Conteh. 24 Judo. 25 Mike Tyson.
26 Conchita Martinez. 27 Bernard Gallacher.
28 Snooker. 29 Peter Fleming. 30 Nigel Benn.

24 ✸ SPORTING RECORDS

1 Bobby Robson. 2 Squash. 3 Bob Taylor.
4 Salford. 5 New England Patriots. 6 Ruud Gullit.
7 Sandwich. 8 First £1,000 soccer transfer. 9 David Campese.
10 Kapil Dev. 11 Pole vaulting. 12 Leyton Orient. 13 Smallwood.
14 Table tennis. 15 Notts County. 16 Tiger Woods.
17 60s. 18 Alan Shearer. 19 Angling. 20 Jim Clark.
21 Gipsy Moth IV. 22 Bonds. 23 Asaafa Powell. 24 Imran Khan.
25 Emerson Fittipaldi. 26 Liz McColgan. 27 Gliding.
28 Allan Border. 29 Most aces in a match (51). 30 Newbold.

25 ✸ SPORTING LEGENDS

1 Severiano Ballesteros. 2 Doctor.
3 Manchester United. 4 1970s. 5 Four. 6 Sydney.
7 1950s. 8 Aberdeen. 9 Chelsea. 10 1970s. 11 400m
hurdles. 12 14. 13 Stephen Hendry. 14 Tony Jacklin.
15 Barry John. 16 Michael Johnson. 17 Kapil Dev.
18 Chess. 19 Hamburg. 20 Squash. 21 20. 22 Bjorn Borg.
23 452. 24 Australian. 25 Ravel's Bolero. 26 Ipswich Town.
27 Baseball. 28 Refused to do military service. 29 French.
30 Willie Carson.

26 ✸ HORSE RACING

1 Grand National. 2 12th. 3 1977.
4 Jim Culloty. 5 2,000 Guineas, Derby, St Leger.
6 Committed suicide. 7 Pat Eddery. 8 1954. 9 The Oaks.
10 Dick Francis. 11 Bay. 12 1 mile 4 furlongs. 13 Four.
14 Ten. 15 Peter Scudamore. 16 Corky. 17 Lester Piggott.
18 1920s. 19 Frankie Dettori. 20 Desert Orchid. 21 L'Escargot.
22 Once. 23 Kentucky Derby. 24 Buckle. 25 Sam Arnull.
26 Lanfranco. 27 Laffit Pincay Jr. 28 Oath. 29 Bay. 30 54.

27 ✸ WORLD FOOTBALL

1 Japan. 2 Lazio. 3 Ruud Gullit. 4 Gary Lineker.
5 Australia. 6 Croatia. 7 Barcelona. 8 Prague.
9 Graham Poll. 10 Mario Zagallo. 11 Benfica.
12 Germany. 13 Davor Suker. 14 Argentina.
15 Roger Milla. 16 Uruguay. 17 Gerard Houllier.
18 Edson Arrentes do Nascimento. 19 Italy. 20 Switzerland.
21 Emmanuel Petit. 22 Ronaldo's. 23 Zinedine Zidane.
24 Dennis Bergkamp. 25 Matthias Sammer. 26 St Denis. 27 Dunga.
28 Stanley Matthews. 29 Marco Materazzi. 30 Alexi Lalas.

28 ✸ GOLDEN OLDIES

1 Stanley Matthews. 2 Preston North End. 3
Leicester City. 4 West Ham Utd. 5 Billy Wright. 6 Dixie
Dean. 7 Huddersfield Town. 8 Ted Drake. 9 Joe Mercer. 10 Nat
Lofthouse. 11 33 years. 12 Alex James. 13 Mackay. 14 Newcastle
Utd. 15 Middlesbrough. 16 Manchester Utd. 17 Scotland. 18
Hungary. 19 Pat Jennings. 20 Yes. (He played once for Scotland.)
21 Fatty. 22 David Jack. 23 Johnny Carey. 24 Len Shackleton.
25 Alf Ramsey. 26 Stanley Matthews. 27 Ivor Broadis. 28 Danny
Blanchflower. 29 Joe Mercer. 30 Bert Trautmann.

29 ✸ WORLD FOOTBALL 2

1 Black. 2 Hamburg. 3 Porto. 4 Argentina.
5 Roberto Baggio. 6 1990s. 7 AC Milan. 8 Sweden.
9 Argentina. 10 Frans Thijssen. 11 Colombia.
12 Ukraine. 13 Rotterdam. 14 Real Madrid. 15 Michael Owen.
16 Blue. 17 16. 18 Franco Baresi. 19 AC Milan. 20 Kaiserslautern.
21 Tony Yeboah. 22 Bruce Rioch. 23 Every two years.
24 Cameroon. 25 Sweden. 26 Bayern Munich.
27 Lisbon. 28 Green. 29 Argentina. 30 1980s.

30 ✸ FOOTBALL: ITALY

1 AC Milan. 2 Juventus. 3 Roberto Baggio. 4 29.
5 Sampdoria. 6 Internazionale. 7 Juventus. 8 Lazio.
9 Argentina. 10 Foreign players. 11 Northern Ireland.
12 Paolo Rossi. 13 Liverpool. 14 Diego Maradona. 15 1930s.
16 AC Milan. 17 Parma. 18 Roberto Baggio. 19 Rome.
20 Arrigo Saachi. 21 Turin. 22 Paolo Maldini. 23 South Korea.
24 Christian Vieri. 25 Grosso. 26 Dino Zoff. 27 Fabrizio
Ravanelli. 28 Francesco Totti. 29 Gianluca Zambrotta.
30 Luca Toni.

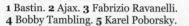

31 ✳ FOOTBALL: GOLDEN GOALS

1 Bastin. 2 Ajax. 3 Fabrizio Ravanelli.
4 Bobby Tambling. 5 Karel Poborsky.
6 Southampton. 7 Gerd Muller. 8 Derby County.
9 Jurgen Klinsmann. 10 349. 11 Crystal Palace and Arsenal.
12 Stockport County. 13 Arsenal. 14 Peter Schmeichel.
15 Mark Hughes. 16 Romario. 17 Arsenal. 18 Dundee Utd.
19 Ally McCoist. 20 Geoff Hurst. 21 Abel Xavier. 22 Paraguay.
23 David Trezeguet. 24 Silver goal. 25 2001. 26 1993. 27 Euro 1996.
28 Laurent Blanc. 29 FIFA Beach World Cup 30 Oliver Bierhoff.

32 ✳ WAYNE ROONEY

1 Liverpool. 2 Macedonia. 3 David Moyes.
4 1985. 5 7th. 6 Australia. 7 Birmingham. 8 BBC Young
Sportsperson of the Year. 9 Number 8. 10 Nicky Butt.
11 Arsenal. 12 Richard Wright. 13 Scorpio. 14 Portugal.
15 Newcastle. 16 Ferenbache. 17 Three. 18 Arsenal.
19 Switzerland. 20 Shrek. 21 Villarreal. 22 England won 4–2.
23 9. 24 6 goals. 25 Arsenal. 26 17 years 111 days old.
27 Tomasz Radzinkski. 28 Third. 29 Mark. 30 Wrexham.

33 ✳ FOOTBALL UK 2

1 Gerry Francis. 2 St Mirren. 3 David Platt.
4 Vinnie Jones. 5 Gareth Southgate. 6 Robbie
Fowler. 7 Christian Gross. 8 Harry Redknapp.
9 Blackpool. 10 Doddle. 11 Blackburn Rovers. 12 Karren Brady.
13 Chelsea v Man Utd. 14 Ron Atkinson. 15 Villarreal. 16 Graeme
Souness. 17 Roy Hodgson. 18 Coventry. 19 Craig Bellamy.
20 Sir Bobby Robson. 21 Andy Johnson. 22 Lawrie McMenemy.
23 David Beckham. 24 Estonia. 25 Chris Waddle. 26 Leeds Utd.
27 John Jensen. 28 Graham Taylor. 29 1990–91. 30 Sevilla.

34 ✳ AMERICAN SPORT

1 All 16. 2 Boston Celtics. 3 Nextel. 4 Alberta.
5 The White Sox. 6 Ice hockey. 7 Houston.
8 Washington. 9 Georgman Herman Ruth. 10 USSR and
Yugoslavia. 11 Roy Wegerle. 12 London Ravens. 13 American
football. 14 Los Angeles Rams. 15 1970. 16 Six. 17 Basketball.
18 Yogi. 19 New York. 20 Basketball. 21 The visiting team.
22 1994. 23 American football. 24 Canada. 25 Scott Hamilton
and Brian Boitano. 26 The Pro Bowl. 27 Nancy Kerrigan and
Tonya Harding. 28 Green Bay Packers. 29 Baseball. 30 Nine.

35 ✳ SPEED STARS

1. Argentina. 2 Ronnie O'Sullivan. 3 Devon
Malcolm. 4 Julio was a horse. 5 Coxless Pairs
(Rowing). 6 Alain Prost. 7 Glasgow. 8 500 cc.
9 Decker. 10 Glenn McGrath. 11 1976. 12 Cycling. 13 Dakar Car
Rally. 14 37. 15 First Derby winner. 16 Brazilian Grand Prix.
17 Kidney in a transplant. 18 Germany. 19 Jacques Villeneuve.
20 Roger Black. 21 Canada. 22 Finnish. 23 Monaco. 24 Johnny
Weismuller. 25 John Aston. 26 Francis Morgan. 27 Australia.
28 Brian Statham. 29 Never Say Die. 30 Alpine skiing.

36 ✳ CRICKET 3

1 Durham. 2 Shane Warne. 3 Andrew Strauss.
4 "Tich". 5 Glamorgan. 6 Warwickshire. 7 Dragon.
8 Phil Edmonds, John Emburey. 9 New Zealand. 10 Yellow.
11 Derbyshire. 12 Bangladesh. 13 Australia. 14 David Lloyd.
15 Mike Denness. 16 Jim Laker. 17 Worcestershire.
18 Left-handed. 19 Tree on the playing area
(blown over in a gale). 20 Bob Willis. 21 25. 22 Dominic Cork.
23 Victoria. 24 Essex. 25 1981. 26 Hampshire. 27 1870s.
28 Matthew Hoggard. 29 Australia. 30 Yes.

37 ✳ FOOTBALL: INTERNATIONALS

1 Billy Meredith. 2 1970s. 3 Bryan Hamilton.
4 John Toshack. 5 Lansdowne Road. 6 McParland.
7 Gillingham. 8 1990. 9 Wales. 10 Ivor Allchurch.
11 Jimmy. 12 Danny Blanchflower. 13 Liam Brady. 14 Northern
Ireland. 15 Johnny Giles. 16 1986. 17 Northern Ireland, England
and Scotland. 18 Terry Neill. 19 Iain Dowie. 20 1958. 21 Zagreb.
22 Spain. 23 Southampton. 24 Australia. 25 Peter Taylor.
26 Slaven Bilic. 27 Kenny Dalglish. 28 Gianfranco Zola.
29 Toto Scilacci. 30 Andrei Kanchelskis.

38 ✳ RUGBY 2

1 David Campese. 2 Jonny Wilkinson.
3 Rory Underwood. 4 Italy. 5 Blue, black and white.
6 Gareth Edwards. 7 Fulham. 8 Andy Farrell. 9 Warrington.
10 Northern. 11 Gavin Hastings. 12 Martin Offiah.
13 Leeds. 14 Wasps. 15 Fiji. 16 Oxford University and
Cambridge University. 17 Leicester. 18 Jonah Lomu.
19 White. 20 Ellery Hanley. 21 Bath Rugby Club.
22 Errol Tobias. 23 Wigan. 24 1920s. 25 22. 26 Rob Andrew.
27 Bill Beaumont. 28 Twickenham. 29 Eight. 30 Widnes.

39 ✳ CRICKET 4

1 Brisbane. 2 Chris Read. 3 Tony Lewis.
4 Trevor McDonald. 5 Terrence. 6 Kapil Dev.
7 Somerset. 8 Denis Compton. 9 Shakoor Rana.
10 Dennis Lillee. 11 Michael Atherton. 12 The Oval.
13 Graham Alan Gooch. 14 Langer & Hayden. 15 Headingley.
16 Muthiah Muralitharan. 17 William Gilbert. 18 David Gower.
19 Northants. 20 Lancashire. 21 Sunglasses. 22 Sunil Gavaskar.
23 Hansie Cronje. 24 Don Bradman. 25 Graeme Hick.
26 Imran Khan. 27 Antigua. 28 *The Times*. 29 Sri Lanka. 30 Left.

40 ✳ FOOTBALL: HAT TRICKS

1 Alan Shearer. 2 Matt Le Tissier.
3 Gary McAllister. 4 Mortensen. 5 West Germany.
6 Everton. 7 John Wark. 8 Ian Wright. 9 Coventry City.
10 Rangers. 11 Alan Shearer. 12 Turkey. 13 Mike Newell.
14 Andy Cole. 15 Gary Lineker. 16 Manchester City.
17 Gordon Durie. 18 Les Ferdinand. 19 Jimmy Greaves.
20 Eric Cantona. 21 David Villa. 22 Theo Walcott.
23 Ian Wright. 24 Ronaldo. 25 Munich. 26 Wayne Rooney.
27 Ronaldo. 28 Fernando Torres. 29 Peter Crouch. 30 Darren Bent.

41 ✸ FOOTBALL 3

1 Netherlands (in 1978). **2** Bournemouth. **3** It was against a dog that ran on to the field. **4** 32. **5** Chelsea. **6** Uruguay. **7** Hamburg. **8** Robert Chase. **9** Steve Daley (in 1979). **10** United. **11** Toulouse. **12** Teddy Sheringham. **13** England. **14** Monaco. **15** Rochdale. **16** Crystal Palace v Man Utd (1990). **17** Middlesbrough. **18** Exeter. **19** Bobby Charlton. **20** Gordon Strachan. **21** Plymouth. **22** Chelsea (Vialli replacing Gullit). **23** Stokoe, Birmingham and Revie, Manchester City in 1956. **24** Burnley. **25** Mark Bosnich. **26** Leeds United. **27** Zinedine Zidane. **28** Falkirk. **29** Burton Albion. **30** Plough.

42 ✸ FOOTBALL 4

1 Wilf McGuinness. **2** First woman ref of men's soccer. **3** Italy (1990). **4** Man City. **5** Richard Branson. **6** Liverpool. **7** Everton. **8** Wigan Athletic. **9** 67 games. **10** Morocco. **11** Torino. **12** Brazil. **13** Peter Schmeichel. **14** Thomas Ravelli. **15** Diego Maradona. **16** Bari. **17** Chesterfield. **18** Bulgaria. **19** Inter Milan. **20** Gillespie Road. **21** Arnold Muhren. **22** West Brom. **23** Spurs v. Wolves. **24** Ajax. **25** 90. **26** Ivar Ingimarsson. **27** Boston, USA. **28** Santos. **29** Ugo Ehiogu. **30** Rangers and Hearts.

43 ✸ FOOTBALL: WORLD CUP

1 Cameroon. **2** USA. **3** Patrick Battiston. **4** Italy. **5** Bonner and Coyne. **6** Norway. **7** Tomas Skuhravy. **8** Russia. **9** None. **10** Italy (1934). **11** Sweden 4 v Bulgaria 0. **12** Argentina. **13** Bulldog Bobby. **14** Brazil (1970). **15** McCall and Johnston (1 each). **16** Gerd Muller. **17** Mexico. **18** East Germany. **19** Mark Wright. **20** Greece. **21** Argentina. **22** Hakan Sukur. **23** 3-0. **24** Uruguay. **25** 12. **26** Italy (1934 and 1938). **27** Oleg Salenko (v Cameroon in 1994). **28** Mexico. **29** Three. **30** Ukraine.

44 ✸ RUGBY 3

1 New Zealand. **2** Five. **3** 1959. **4** David Ward. **5** Bay of Plenty. **6** Hugo Porta. **7** Neil Back. **8** Widnes. **9** Simon Culhane. **10** Durham. **11** Andrew Stoddart. **12** Jonah Lomu. **13** Paul Newlove. **14** France. **15** 27. **16** Ian Millward. **17** Middlesbrough. **18** Nwokocha. **19** 44. **20** Bradford Northern. **21** 1920s. **22** Cardiff. **23** Jonathan Davies. **24** Marc Ellis, Jonah Lomu. **25** Lesley Vainikolo. **26** Halifax. **27** Flanker. **28** Roger Uttley. **29** Malaysia. **30** 3 games.

45 ✸ OLYMPICS

1 Singapore. **2** Ice hockey. **3** Yachting. **4** St Moritz. **5** Bars and beam. **6** Michael Johnson. **7** Long jump. **8** Al Oerter. **9** Five. **10** Two. **11** Retained 10,000m and won 5,000m and marathon. **12** Evander Holyfield. **13** Lake Lanier. **14** Simone Jacobs. **15** Michelle Smith. **16** Izzy. **17** Seoul. **18** Allan Wells. **19** Spain. **20** Soling. **21** Poland's Renata Mauer. **22** Tim Henman & Chris Broad. **23** Jayne Torvill. **24** 4 x 400m relay. **25** 1900. **26** Quarantine laws. **27** Denise Lewis. **28** Montreal. **29** Robin Cousins. **30** Japan.

46 ✸ GOLF

1 Valhalla. **2** Justin Rose. **3** Bobby Locke. **4** Ted Ray. **5** Gary Player (South Africa). **6** Ben Hogan. **7** Ian Baker-Finch. **8** Tony Jacklin. **9** Supermex. **10** Cricket (Rod Marsh). **11** Byron Nelson. **12** Southport. **13** Wentworth. **14** Jack Nicklaus. **15** Portugal. **16** Newport, Rhode Island. **17** Muirfield. **18** Great Britain and Ireland. **19** Nick Faldo. **20** Curtis Cup. **21** British Open. **22** Ted Dexter. **23** Bobby Jones. **24** Amateurs. **25** Lee Trevino. **26** Richard Burton. **27** Christy O'Connor. **28** Bernard Gallacher. **29** Peter Oosterhuis. **30** Dwight D. Eisenhower.

47 ✸ OLYMPICS 2

1 200m. Individual Medley. **2** Marie-Jose Perec. **3** Cuba, Japan. **4** Lanier. **5** Belarus. **6** Marlo Kindelan. **7** Garmisch-Partenkirchen & Neil Broad. **8** Christa Luding, née Rothenburger. **9** Cortina (1956). **10** St Moritz. **11** Twice (1908, 1948). **12** Head garland of wild olive leaves. **13** Three. **14** Equestrian dressage. **15** Armenia, Azerbaijan. **16** Kenny Harrison. **17** Penny Heyns. **18** 1994. **19** Carl Lewis. **20** Ian Walker, John Merricks. **21** Seppo Raty. **22** Mark Phillips. **23** Paul Palmer. **24** Steve Redgrave. **25** Mountain biking. **26** Over transport problems. **27** One. **28** Krisztina Egerszegi. **29** Eric Heiden (speed skating).

48 ✸ RUGBY 4

1 Tony O'Reilly. **2** 1981. **3** Bradford. **4** St Helens. **5** Agustin Pichot. **6** Chartered surveyor. **7** Nottingham. **8** Six. **9** Romania. **10** Hull. **11** Oct, 2004. **12** Lancashire Cup. **13** Canada's Mark Wyatt. **14** Barking. **15** Wakefield Trinity. **16** Willie John McBride. **17** Japan. **18** Rodney Parade, Newport. **19** Northern Union. **20** Harlequins. **21** Right wing. **22** Martin Corry. **23** Sheffield Eagles & Leeds. **24** Slalom lager. **25** France. **26** St Helens. **27** Willie John McBride. **28** Dan Carter. **29** Salford & Warrington. **30** Hawick.

49 ✸ FOOTBALL: GOALKEEPERS

1 Andy Marriott. **2** Ian Walker. **3** David Harvey. **4** Workington. **5** Mark Bosnich. **6** Sheffield Wednesday. **7** Shrewsbury Town. **8** Manchester City. **9** Walsall. **10** Dundee. **11** Andy Rhodes. **12** Keith Branagan. **13** Peter Fox. **14** Oxford Utd. **15** Alan Knight. **16** Ray Wood. **17** Doncaster Rovers. **18** Graham Moseley. **19** Rotherham Utd. **20** Manchester Utd. **21** Scott Carson. **22** Jose Reina. **23** Hilario. **24** David James. **25** Nigel Martyn. **26** Brad Friedel. **27** Giovanni Trapattoni. **28** Mike Walker. **29** Paul Robinson. **30** Tim Flowers (1994-95).

50 ✸ GOLF 2

1 Mike "Fluff" Cowan. **2** 1938. **3** Muirfield. **4** Snow White. **5** The Postage Stamp. **6** Six. **7** Lee Trevino. **8** Carnoustie. **9** Bobby Locke. **10** Sandy Lyle. **11** St Andrews. **12** Peachtree, Georgia. **13** Craig Stadler. **14** 72. **15** Peter Thomson. **16** Greg Norman. **17** US Masters. **18** IMG. **19** A championship belt. **20** Two. **21** Bob Charles. **22** 1950s. **23** John Daly. **24** Designed courses. **25** Dai Rees (1957). **26** A hole in one. **27** Ian Woosnam. **28** Troon. **29** Bobby Jones. **30** Jersey.

51 ✻ HORSE RACING

1 Limerick, Ireland. 2 Lovely Cottage. 3 Willie Carson. 4 Lammtarra. 5 Vodaphone. 6 Lord Huntingdon. 7 Pat Eddery. 8 Jean Luc Lagardere. 9 Melling Chase. 10 Esha Ness. 11 Eleanor. 12 Durbar II. 13 Cape Verdi. 14 Mr Frisk. 15 Entrepreneur. 16 Gay Trip. 17 Olivier Peslier. 18 Athens Wood. 19 Greville Starkey. 20 Prince Charles. 21 Golden Fleece. 22 Party Politics. 23 Humble Duty. 24 Lester Piggott. 25 1945. 26 Royal Tan. 27 Powerstown Park. 28 Las Meninas. 29 Victory Note. 30 Kahyasi.

52 ✻ TENNIS

1 Jelena. 2 Benjamin. 3 Kiev. 4 Alex Bogdanovich. 5 A retractable roof. 6 Helena Sukova. 7 Peter Fleming. 8 Roger Taylor. 9 Angela Mortimer, Christine Truman. 10 Australian. 11 Lori McNeil. 12 Kevin Curren. 13 Emilio, Javier. 14 Andrea Jaeger. 15 Lacoste. 16 It was televised. 17 Donald Budge. 18 Rod Laver. 19 Jaroslav Drobny. 20 Steffi Graf. 21 1968. 22 Margaret Court, Maureen Connolly. 23 Wear white flannels instead of shorts. 24 Boris Becker. 25 George VI (1926). 26 Kathy Rinaldi. 27 John and Tracy Austin. 28 MCC. 29 Manuel Santana. 30 Chuck McKinley.

53 ✻ TENNIS 2

1 Stefan Edberg. 2 Bobby Wilson, Mike Sangster. 3 Switzerland. 4 Kosice, Slovakia. 5 Twice. 6 Marcos Baghdatis. 7 Mill. 8 Helena Sukova. 9 Jennifer Capriati. 10 Nicolas Kiefer. 11 Forest Hills. 12 Noah. 13 Sphairistike. 14 Borotra, Cochet, Lacoste. 15 Sue Barker. 16 Karen Hantze. 17 Fred Stolle. 18 John Lloyd (Mixed 1983-4). 19 Australian Championships in 1995. 20 Olga Morozova. 21 Rod Laver. 22 Mats Wilander. 23 Pancho Gonzales, Charlie Pasarell. 24 Wightman Cup (she became Mrs Wightman). 25 Donald Budge. 26 Czechoslovakia, Australia. 27 Staten Island. 28 John Newcombe. 29 Manuel Santana. 30 New Zealand.

54 ✻ SPORT MOMENTS

1 Corbiere. 2 Beethoven. 3 Paul Scholes (in 2005). 4 Four. 5 Ohio State University. 6 Ravi Shastri. 7 Iffley Road. 8 200,000. 9 Said Aouita. 10 Lotus. 11 Chris Brasher (pacemaker for Bannister). 12 Esha Ness. 13 18-17. 14 Adrian Moorhouse. 15 Andrew Holmes. 16 Steve Cram. 17 First woman to take part in the boat race. 18 Mill Reef (1971). 19 Seven. 20 7hr 54 mins. 21 Mike "Fluff" Cowan. 22 Nine. 23 Alan Shearer. 24 Hickstead. 25 Betty Stove. 26 700. 27 800m, 1000m, 1500m. 28 25,095-1. 29 Noureddine Morceli. 30 Trevor Berbick.

55 ✻ FOOTBALL POT LUCK

1 Hereford Utd. 2 Laurie Cunningham. 3 Iran. 4 Fulham. 5 1960s. 6 Lincoln City. 7 Tranmere Rovers. 8 Dean Saunders. 9 Grimsby Pelham. 10 7. 11 Chelsea. 12 Wignall. 13 Tottenham Hotspur. 14 Nat Lofthouse. 15 Stan Bowles. 16 George Graham. 17 Oxford Utd. 18 Waldie. 19 Terry Neill. 20 Billy McNeill. 21 Hibernian. 22 Moldova. 23 Anderlecht. 24 Southport. 25 1910s. 26 Rotherham. 27 Aberdeen. 28 Carl. 29 Oldham Athletic. 30 10.

56 ✻ CRICKET 5

1 Manchester. 2 Northants. 3 M. J. K. Smith. 4 Surrey. 5 Antigua. 6 Frank Woolley. 7 Imperial Cricket Conference. 8 England. 9 Dylan. 10 Mike Gatting, Graeme Fowler. 11 Sunil Gavaskar. 12 Pakistan. 13 England, Australia, South Africa. 14 Gillette Cup. 15 Nathan Astle. 16 Jimmy Binks. 17 Alec Stewart. 18 Ian Botham. 19 New Zealand. 20 Ricky Ponting (Australia). 21 Ranji Trophy. 22 Douglas Jardine. 23 Fred Trueman. 24 Ashley Giles. 25 *Being Freddie*. 26 Brian Johnston. 27 72 Tests. 28 South Africa. 29 Jack Russell. 30 Red Stripe Cup.

57 ✻ FOOTBALL 5

1 Netherlands (in 1978). 2 Bournemouth. 3 It was against a dog that ran on to the field. 4 32. 5 Chelsea. 6 Uruguay. 7 Hamburg. 8 Robert Chase. 9 Steve Daley (in 1979). 10 United. 11 Toulouse. 12 Teddy Sheringham. 13 England. 14 Monaco. 15 Rochdale. 16 Crystal Palace v Man Utd (1990). 17 Middlesbrough. 18 Exeter. 19 Bobby Charlton. 20 Gordon Strachan. 21 Plymouth. 22 Chelsea (Vialli replacing Gullit). 23 Stokoe, Birmingham and Revie, Manchester City in 1956. 24 Burnley. 25 Mark Bosnich. 26 Leeds United. 27 Zinedine Zidane. 28 Falkirk. 29 Burton Albion. 30 Plough.

58 ✻ FOOTBALL: EXTRA TIME

1 David O'Leary. 2 Belgium. 3 Italy. 4 Charlton Athletic. 5 Didier Drogba. 6 Argentina. 7 Mexico. 8 0-0. 9 3-3. 10 Aberdeen. 11 Leeds Utd. 12 Sweden v Romania. 13 Three. 14 Gordon West. 15 2-2. 16 Liverpool. 17 Derby (1946). 18 Belgium. 19 Stefan Kuntz. 20 Five. 21 Euro 2004. 22 Celtic. 23 Jonathan Woodgate. 24 2007. 25 1991. 26 Zinedine Zidane (2006). 27 Leicester City. 28 Chelsea. 29 Brazil v Italy, 0-0. 30 Spain 1982.

59 ✻ POP ALBUMS

1 The Beatles. 2 "Morning Glory". 3 Collins. 4 Pink Floyd. 5 Stewart. 6 Prince. 7 Queen. 8 Elvis Presley. 9 Wings. 10 Wet Wet Wet. 11 Eric Clapton. 12 Michael Jackson. 13 "Tubular". 14 Celine Dion. 15 Mary J. Blige. 16 Supertramp. 17 "Voulez-Vous". 18 A jazz singer. 19 "Employment". 20 Dire Straits. 21 Pulp. 22 Blur. 23 Springsteen. 24 Simon & Garfunkel. 25 Elton John. 26 "Stars". 27 Fleetwood Mac. 28 Meat Loaf. 29 Bolton. 30 "Definitely Maybe".

60 ✻ POP DIVAS

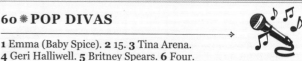

1 Emma (Baby Spice). 2 15. 3 Tina Arena. 4 Geri Halliwell. 5 Britney Spears. 6 Four. 7 Jackson. 8 Nerys. 9 Eternal. 10 Marianne Faithfull. 11 M People. 12 Minogue. 13 Jennifer Lopez. 14 Billie Piper. 15 Tongue. 16 Cleopatra. 17 Home & Away. 18 Four. 19 Like an Egyptian. 20 All Saints. 21 Cilla Black. 22 Kate. 23 Debbie Harry. 24 Violin. 25 Alicia Keys. 26 Canada. 27 Kate Bush. 28 1980s. 29 Louise. 30 Britney Spears.

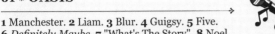

61 ❋ OASIS

1 Manchester. 2 Liam. 3 Blur. 4 Guigsy. 5 Five.
6 *Definitely Maybe*. 7 "What's The Story". 8 Noel.
9 Kensit. 10 Cocaine. 11 Manchester City. 12 Irish.
13 Margaret (Peggy). 14 Guitar. 15 USA. 16 *Top of the Pops*.
17 "Wonderwall". 18 In Anger. 19 Glastonbury. 20 "Roll".
21 Zak Starkey. 22 "Your Soul". 23 The Brit Awards.
24 40th. 25 "Idle". 26 Manchester City. 27 *Stop the Clocks*.
28 "Definitely Maybe". 29 *Heathen Chemistry*. 30 "Supersonic".

62 ❋ POP CHARTS

1 Elton John. 2 Bowie. 3 "My Way". 4 Girls Aloud.
5 Stewart. 6 Westlife. 7 UB40. 8 Eminem. 9 Young.
10 Waterloo. 11 "Unchained Melody". 12 Bee Gees.
13 On the Block. 14 Missy Elliott. 15 Destiny's Child.
16 80s. 17 Blondie. 18 David Bowie. 19 Newton-John.
20 "Stand by Me". 21 "Somethin' Stupid". 22 Abba.
23 "Amazing Grace". 24 Beautiful South. 25 Lennon.
26 Aerosmith. 27 "Living Doll". 28 The Bee Gees.
29 1960s. 30 1950s.

63 ❋ '80S POP

1 Adam and the Ants. 2 Green. 3 Paul McCartney.
4 Michael Jackson. 5 Sunshine Band.
6 Sheena Easton. 7 Radio One. 8 Torvill & Dean.
9 Robert de Niro. 10 Roland. 11 Moyet. 12 Paige, Dickson.
13 Sarah Brightman. 14 Live Aid. 15 "Russians". 16 Midge Ure.
17 Status Quo. 18 Boy George. 19 Suggs. 20 Kim Wilde.
21 Julio Iglesias. 22 Japan. 23 Keith Harris. 24 Dave Stewart.
25 Frank Sinatra. 26 The Young Ones. 27 Spitting Image.
28 Duchess of York. 29 Hoddle. 30 Cliff Richard.

64 ❋ KID'S STUFF

1 Osmond. 2 "Paper". 3 Zavaroni.
4 "In the Air". 5 Lee. 6 Shapiro. 7 Lulu. 8 Wonder.
9 New Kids on the Block. 10 Jackson. 11 Hopkin.
12 Kylie Minogue. 13 17. 14 Langford. 15 Osmond.
16 Shaw. 17 Sedaka. 18 Collins. 19 "Fame". 20 Diana.
21 "V". 22 McCartney. 23 Aly and AJ. 24 Britney Spears.
25 *Kung Fu Panda*. 26 McFly. 27 Smash Mouth.
28 Tom Jones. 29 Ben Folds. 30 *The Lion King*.

65 ❋ POP SINGERS

1 Madonna. 2 Donny. 3 Sugababes. 4 Dana.
5 Stansfield. 6 Holder. 7 Enya. 8 Kenny Rogers.
9 Marc Bolan. 10 Smokey Robinson. 11 Pretenders.
12 John Denver. 13 Bryan Adams. 14 Phil Collins.
15 Cliff Richard. 16 K. T. Tunstall. 17 Nick Berry.
18 "Reet Petite". 19 Chris de Burgh. 20 Sting. 21 Jason Donovan.
22 Beyoncé. 23 Christina Aguilera. 24 Kylie Minogue.
25 Katie Melua. 26 M. 27 Engelbert Humperdinck.
28 Bob Marley. 29 UB40. 30 Craig David.

66 ❋ KARAOKE

1 "You're the One that I Want". 2 "Wannabe". 3 Nessun
dorma, nessun dorma. 4 River deep mountain high.
5 When I'm sixty-four. 6 "Love is All Around". 7 Greenest.
8 Six. 9 "Unchained Melody". 10 "My Way". 11 "I Will Survive".
12 "Stand by Your Man". 13 "Merry Christmas Everybody". 14 That the
heart does go on. 15 I do it for you. 16 "Walk of Life". 17 Toys.
18 "Do They Know It's Christmas?". 19 Who do you think you are?
20 "Waterloo". 21 Good friends. 22 A flower grows. 23 "Three Lions".
24 "I Just Called to Say I Love You". 25 "Don't Cry for Me Argentina".
26 Chameleon. 27 "Circle of Life". 28 "Bridge Over Troubled Water".
29 "Danny Boy". 30 Of the world.

67 ❋ SOUL & MOTOWN

1 Piano. 2 Stevie Wonder. 3 Warwick. 4 Holland.
5 The Temptations. 6 "Baby Love". 7 Lionel Richie.
8 "ABC". 9 Farewell. 10 Gaye. 11 Queen of Soul.
12 Tops. 13 Isley Brothers. 14 Brown.
15 Martha and the Vandellas. 16 The Miracles.
17 The Pips. 18 '60s. 19 Wilson. 20 Detroit. 21 Ross.
22 Hayes. 23 *Lay It Down*. 24 Joss Stone. 25 Berry.
26 Gospel. 27 Motown Records. 28 Stevie Wonder.
29 Tamla Motown. 30 Marvin Gaye.

68 ❋ '60S POP

1 The Beach Boys. 2 Monkees. 3 Elvis Presley.
4 "Paperback Writer". 5 The Bee Gees. 6 The Kinks.
7 Supremes. 8 The Hollies. 9 Her feet. 10 Helen
Shapiro. 11 Yes. 12 Springfield. 13 "Matchstick". 14 Jim Reeves.
15 The Tremeloes. 16 Liverpool. 17 Frank Ifield. 18 Dozy.
19 Proby. 20 San Francisco. 21 Dave Clark. 22 Bob Dylan.
23 Faithfull. 24 US. 25 Martin. 26 Move. 27 Herman.
28 Lonnie Donegan. 29 John Lennon. 30 The Twist.

69 ❋ MUSIC CHARTS

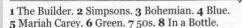

1 The Builder. 2 Simpsons. 3 Bohemian. 4 Blue.
5 Mariah Carey. 6 Green. 7 50s. 8 In a Bottle.
9 Rush. 10 Boyzone. 11 Rap. 12 Stop. 13 Eminem.
14 Billie. 15 Ronan Keating. 16 911. 17 "The Dance Floor".
18 Prodigy. 19 Mel B. 20 1990s. 21 Kylie Minogue.
22 Millennium Prayer. 23 And the Beast.
24 R. 25 Marmalade. 26 Diana Ross. 27 Billie.
28 Spice Girls. 29 1997. 30 Victoria Beckham.

70 ❋ LATE GREATS

1 T. Rex. 2 Joplin. 3 Roy Orbison.
4 Freddie Mercury. 5 Plane crash. 6 Big Bopper.
7 "My Way". 8 Nirvana. 9 John Lennon. 10 Guitar.
11 Cline. 12 Otis Redding. 13 Nilsson. 14 The Mamas and the Papas.
15 Brian Jones. 16 Bill Haley. 17 Gaye. 18 The Supremes.
19 Sex Pistols. 20 Small Faces. 21 Pink Floyd. 22 George
Harrison. 23 Bo. 24 Soul. 25 24 Hours. 26 Buddy Holly.
27 Patsy Cline. 28 Johnny Cash. 29 Love. 30 Roy Castle.

71 ✳ WHO'S WHO?

1 Liam Gallagher. 2 Madonna. 3 Katrina.
4 The Spice Girls. 5 Marti Pellow. 6 Avril Lavigne.
7 Frank Sinatra. 8 Richard. 9 The Bee Gees.
10 The Pussycat Dolls. 11 Elton John. 12 Tony Christie.
13 Sting. 14 Green Day. 15 Chrissie Hynde. 16 Kevin Costner.
17 Andrew Lloyd Webber. 18 Robson and Jerome. 19 Take That.
20 The Beatles. 21 *Crocodile Shoes*. 22 Tina Turner.
23 Elton John. 24 Davy Jones. 25 The Darkness. 26 Queen.
27 Elvis Presley. 28 Wham! 29 Stevie Wonder. 30 Boy George.

72 ✳ POP 2000

1 Ireland. 2 The Beatles. 3 Builder. 4 7.
5 None. 6 Manic. 7 Gallagher. 8 American.
9 Scream. 10 Piper. 11 Olympics. 12 David.
13 Carey. 14 Williams. 15 Mel G. 16 Country. 17 Oasis.
18 Church. 19 Black. 20 Children in Need. 21 *Big Brother*.
22 Atomic Kitten. 23 Louise. 24 Britney Spears. 25 Five.
26 Texas. 27 Tom. 28 Hear'say. 29 Corr. 30 Eminem.

73 ✳ FILM LINKS

1 Cher. 2 "Knockin' On Heaven's Door". 3 Robin Hood.
4 Michael Jackson. 5 *When Harry Met Sally*.
6 Olivia Newton-John. 7 Mark Knopfler. 8 Raindrops.
9 *Evita*. 10 *Arthur*. 11 Wet Wet Wet. 12 The Beatles. 13 Shirley
Bassey. 14 *Chariots of Fire*. 15 *Casablanca*. 16 Simon and Garfunkel.
17 Nobody. 18 Lions. 19 *Reservoir Dogs*. 20 *Batman*. 21 "Layla". 22
Pig. 23 "Johnny B. Goode". 24 *The Full Monty*. 25 Queen.
26 *Saturday Night Fever*. 27 "Eye of the Tiger". 28 *Apocalypse Now*. 29 "The Time of My Life". 30 Kenny Loggins.

74 ✳ POP NO. 1S

1 Girls Aloud. 2 "Love is All Around". 3 1950s.
4 Black Eyed Peas. 5 Brother. 6 "White Cliffs of
Dover". 7 Freddie Mercury. 8 Your Daughter.
9 "Mr Blobby". 10 Kate Bush. 11 Man. Utd. 12 Blondie.
13 Elton John. 14 "Without You". 15 Cliff Richard. 16 Gabrielle.
17 Massachusetts. 18 Take That. 19 "Yellow Submarine".
20 Abba. 21 Paul Simon. 22 Country. 23 Wham!. 24 Scaffold.
25 Village People. 26 The Shadows. 27 Waltz. 28 David Bowie.
29 Rednex. 30 Ricky Martin.

75 ✳ MUSIC SUPERSTARS

1 Garfunkel. 2 Rod. 3 Madonna. 4 Queen.
5 Streisand. 6 "Candle in the Wind". 7 *Spice*.
8 Hound Dog. 9 Blur. 10 Bob Marley. 11 Shania
Twain. 12 Robbie Williams. 13 George Michael.
14 Queen. 15 Tom Jones. 16 Dublin. 17 Paul McCartney.
18 Pulp. 19 Police. 20 Sinatra. 21 "Pill". 22 Abba. 23 Boyzone.
24 Ross. 25 "The Sheriff". 26 Sir Paul McCartney. 27 George
Michael. 28 Manic Street Preachers. 29 Madonna.
30 Elton John.

76 ✳ CLIFF RICHARD

1 Harry Webb. 2 India. 3 The Shadows.
4 *Summer Holiday*. 5 Wimbledon.
6 "Congratulations". 7 Knighthood. 8 *Heathcliff*.
9 "Livin'". 10 "Bachelor Boy". 11 Mistletoe. 12 Sue Barker.
13 Twelfth. 14 Hello. 15 Sarah Brightman. 16 Newton-John.
17 "Saviour's". 18 "Move It". 19 "Lips". 20 Phil. 21 *The Young Ones*. 22 Five. 23 Portugal. 24 1990s. 25 Santa's. 26 EMI.
27 "Millennium Prayer". 28 Elvis Presley.
29 *I'm Nearly Famous*. 30 1970s.

77 ✳ MADONNA

1 Guy. 2 Yes. 3 Secret. 4 Movie director. 5 *Evita*.
6 Recording company. 7 Music. 8 *True Blue*.
9 *Light*. 10 40s. 11 *Stars in Their Eyes*.
12 "American Pie". 13 Argentina. 14 Hollywood. 15 "American
Life". 16 "Die Another Day". 17 Britney Spears. 18 1980s.
19 Beautiful. 20 GHV2. 21 "Like a Prayer". 22 Scotland.
23 Penn. 24 *Ray of Light*. 25 Her daughter. 26 Horse. 27 "4
Minutes". 28 Single. 29 *The First Album*. 30 "Frozen".

78 ✳ '60S POP 2

1 Dave Clark. 2 Small Faces. 3 Tich. 4 "Fashion".
5 "The Grapevine". 6 "Your Hand". 7 Amen. 8 Eva.
9 Ken Dodd. 10 "The Carnival". 11 "Release Me".
12 The Twist. 13 Ireland. 14 "Good". 15 Rolf Harris.
16 Ob-La-Da. 17 "Juliet". 18 Dustman. 19 "Flamingo".
20 "16". 21 Paul. 22 "Puppet on a String". 23 Your hair.
24 He was left-handed. 25 O'Connor. 26 Brian Hyland.
27 "Respect". 28 The Archies. 29 "Yellow Submarine".
30 Diana Ross.

79 ✳ KARAOKE

1 Is this just fantasy? 2 Unchained Melody. 3 My, my,
my Delilah. 4 "My Way". 5 "Advertising Space". 6 In his
kiss. 7 Your head. 8 Chris de Burgh. 9 The curtain. 10 In
the wind. 11 She was a showgirl. 12 New York. 13 "Eton Rifles".
14 Matchstalk cats and dogs. 15 I feel it in my fingers. 16 10. 17 Jolene.
18 All right. 19 Thought control. 20 Midnight. 21 Your lips. 22 This
feeling inside. 23 Rosemary and thyme. 24 Guitar George. 25 Tell me
more. 26 "Hospital Food". 27 River deep mountain high. 28 Eleanor
Rigby. 29 Make me cry. 30 A whiter shade of pale.

80 ✳ SOUND OF THE '70S

1 "Rivers of Babylon". 2 "Tie a Yellow Ribbon".
3 *Grease*. 4 "Mull of Kintyre". 5 Elton John.
6 Perry Como. 7 Kiki Dee. 8 *Evita*. 9 Sting. 10 LS Lowry.
11 "Save Your Kisses for Me". 12 Terry Jacks. 13 Supertramp.
14 Never. 15 George Harrison. 16 Clive Dunn. 17 Slade.
18 Gary Glitter. 19 David Essex. 20 "Back Home". 21 Virgin.
22 Orlando. 23 Bass guitar. 24 Mariah Carey. 25 Fleetwood Mac.
26 Wizzard. 27 Rod Stewart. 28 T. Rex. 29 Coca-Cola. 30 Abba.

81 ❋ POP POT LUCK

1 1960s. 2 Georgie Fame. 3 Neil Young. 4 "Blue". 5 Dusty Springfield. 6 "Itchycoo". 7 Men at Work. 8 Happy Birthday. 9 Robbie Williams. 10 Debbie Harry. 11 1930s. 12 The Stylistics. 13 "Spread a Little Happiness". 14 Tommy Steele. 15 Sinitta. 16 "Summer Night City". 17 "Your Smile". 18 Alice Cooper. 19 Chris Rea. 20 "Cathy's". 21 Ting Tings. 22 "Unchained Melody". 23 Sitar. 24 The Pirates. 25 "Sherry". 26 1980s (1989). 27 1940s. 28 Sir Cliff Richard. 29 Tyrannosaurus Rex. 30 "Drive".

82 ❋ SOUL & MOTOWN 2

1 "Reach Out, I'll be There". 2 Berry Gordy. 3 Dave. 4 Aretha Franklin. 5 Holland. 6 Otis Redding. 7 The Broken Hearted. 8 Jackie Wilson. 9 The Isley Brothers. 10 James Brown. 11 The Supremes. 12 After the song "Tammy" by Debbie Reynolds. 13 "You Keep Me Hangin' On". 14 Wilson Pickett. 15 The Vandellas. 16 Arthur Conley. 17 "I'm Still Waiting". 18 Lionel Richie. 19 Gladys Knight. 20 Bobby Brown. 21 Stevie Wonder. 22 The Temptations. 23 Jimmy Mack. 24 William. 25 Midnight. 26 "Reflections". 27 Marvin Gaye. 28 Atlantic. 29 Edwin Starr. 30 Junior Walker.

83 ❋ MUSIC CHARTS 2

1 "Inside Out". 2 Status Quo. 3 Faith Evans. 4 "Fantasy". 5 *Corinne Bailey Rae*. 6 Eminem. 7 Children in Need. 8 Westlife. 9 Manic Street Preachers. 10 Eileen. 11 "Last Christmas". 12 "Groovejet". 13 "Time to Say Goodbye". 14 Cranberries. 15 *Casualty*. 16 LeAnn Rimes. 17 The Fugees. 18 "It's Raining Men". 19 "Born to Make You Happy". 20 "Crocodile Rock". 21 1998. 22 Hanson. 23 Noel Gallagher. 24 "Blood on the Dance Floor". 25 1980s. 26 Jamiroquai. 27 *South Park*. 28 Free. 29 Mariah Carey. 30 1970s.

84 ❋ '50S POP

1 Emile Ford. 2 *The Third Man*. 3 Claudette. 4 "What Do You Want?". 5 "Rock Around the Clock". 6 Harry Belafonte. 7 "Diana". 8 Eddie Fisher. 9 Doris Day. 10 Johnny Ray. 11 Cliff Richard and the Drifters. 12 Craig Douglas. 13 Winifred Atwell. 14 "It Doesn't Matter Anymore". 15 Michael Holliday. 16 Frankie Vaughan. 17 Jimmy Young. 18 Alma Cogan. 19 *My Fair Lady* ("On the Street Where You Live"). 20 "And surrender to mine". 21 Iowa. 22 The Big Bopper. 23 Carole King. 24 Answer Me. 25 Bassey. 26 They were Broken. 27 "Magic Moments". 28 "Stupid". 29 Radio Luxembourg. 30 "What Do You Want to Make Those Eyes at Me For".

85 ❋ DANCE & DISCO

1 "Can't Get You Out of My Head". 2 "YMCA". 3 "Frankie". 4 Salt 'N' Pepa. 5 Chemical Brothers. 6 "Light My Fire". 7 "Come On Eileen" by Dexy's Midnight Runners. 8 The Sex-O-Lettes. 9 "Right Said Fred". 10 Jive Bunny. 11 "La Bamba". 12 Rick Astley. 13 Papa. 14 Italy. 15 Kool and the Gang. 16 The Bee Gees. 17 Lulu. 18 Wham! 19 Kylie Minogue. 20 "Brown Girl in the Ring". 21 Donna Summer. 22 "Do the Bartman". 23 Shalamar. 24 Dance. 25 M. C. Hammer. 26 Pepsi and Shirlie. 27 Gorillaz. 28 Barry White. 29 Pink. 30 Kool, of Kool and the Gang.

86 ❋ BANDS

1 Bon Jovi. 2 The Rolling Stones. 3 En Vogue. 4 Ace of Base. 5 Appleton. 6 Beatles. 7 Bohemian Rhapsody. 8 I Want to Hold Your Hand. 9 Lordi. 10 Two. 11 Country House. 12 Words. 13 Tsunami. 14 Patience. 15 Prodigy. 16 Def Leppard. 17 Guns N' Roses. 18 U2. 19 Chemical Brothers. 20 REM. 21 The Bangles. 22 Newcastle. 23 Doctor Jones. 24 Mulder & Scully. 25 Northern Ireland. 26 The Great Escape. 27 Creation. 28 Boyzone. 29 Sheffield. 30 Boyzone.

87 ❋ CHRISTMAS RECORDS

1 A Beatle. 2 1970s. 3 "War is Over". 4 Lonely Pup. 5 Bon Jovi. 6 "Jingle Bell Rock". 7 Wizzard. 8 "When a Child is Born". 9 "Wombling Merry Christmas". 10 Mariah Carey. 11 Mel Smith. 12 Frosty. 13 Bruce Springsteen. 14 On the Dole. 15 Madonna. 16 Father Abraham. 17 Dickie Valentine. 18 Wings. 19 "Walking in the Air". 20 Jim Davidson. 21 "X-Factor". 22 Girls Aloud. 23 Frank and Nancy Sinatra. 24 It. 25 Lonely. 26 St. Winifred's. 27 "When a Child is Born". 28 Goodbye. 29 "I Have a Dream/Seasons in the Sun". 30 "I Hear You Knockin'".

88 ❋ POP DUOS

1 Chas and Dave. 2 Wake Up Little Suzie. 3 Husband. 4 Wham! 5 Sweet Dreams (are Made of This). 6 Donkey. 7 Simon and Garfunkel. 8 Lionel Richie. 9 Opportunity Knocks. 10 Kiki Dee. 11 Esther and Abi. 12 L. S. Lowry. 13 Gimme Dat Ding. 14 Love you. 15 Marvin Gaye. 16 Everly Brothers. 17 Mel and Kim. 18 One. 19 Charles and Eddie. 20 Soft Cell. 21 Phil Spector. 22 John Travolta and Olivia Newton-John. 23 The World. 24 Roger Whittaker, Des O'Connor. 25 Erasure. 26 Chemical Brothers. 27 Nomad. 28 One. 29 Homeward Bound. 30 Pet Shop Boys.

89 ❋ COUNTRY & WESTERN

1 Johnny Cash. 2 "D.I.V.O.R.C.E.". 3 Pussycat. 4 Shania Twain. 5 "Annie's Song". 6 "Crazy". 7 1992. 8 Crystal Gayle. 9 Hank Williams. 10 Placido Domingo. 11 LeAnn Rimes. 12 Kristofferson. 13 LeAnn Rimes. 14 Loretta Lynn. 15 Dolly Parton. 16 Reba McEntire. 17 Yodelling. 18 Chet Atkins. 19 "Distant Drums". 20 Glen Campbell. 21 Waylon Jennings. 22 Dollywood. 23 Tammy Wynette. 24 "The Ohio". 25 "Justified and Ancient". 26 Willie Nelson. 27 Emmylou Harris. 28 Rednex. 29 "Blue Suede Shoes". 30 Sheena Easton.

90 ❋ '90S POP

1 Whigfield. 2 "Up on the Roof". 3 "But I Won't Do That". 4 *The Bodyguard*. 5 Iron Maiden. 6 Shakespear's Sister. 7 "Love is All Around". 8 The Spice Girls. 9 R. E. M. 10 Gary Barlow. 11 Mr Blobby. 12 Boyz II Men. 13 "Love Me for a Reason". 14 Whitney Houston. 15 The Beautiful South. 16 "Knockin' on Heaven's Door". 17 The Rolling Stones. 18 Wet Wet Wet. 19 Oasis. 20 Cliff Richard's impromptu singing during rain at Wimbledon tennis. 21 Tears. 22 1991. 23 "The Shoop Shoop Song". 24 Verve. 25 Mel B (Scary). 26 "My Castle". 27 Ricky Martin. 28 Cotton. 29 Mi Chico Latino. 30 The world.

91 ✳ JAZZ & BLUES

1 Satchmo. 2 The Yardbirds. 3 Harry Connick Jnr. 4 Moscow. 5 Bessie Smith. 6 "Petite Fleur". 7 Dave Brubeck. 8 *Twentysomething*. 9 Bluesbreakers. 10 Piano. 11 Kenny G. 12 Ronnie Scott. 13 Diana Ross. 14 Benny Goodman. 15 John Lee Hooker. 16 Cleo Laine. 17 Humphrey Lytlelton. 18 Little Walter. 19 Saxophone. 20 Peggy Lee. 21 Muddy Waters. 22 Buddy Rich. 23 France. 24 Long John Baldry. 25 Paramount. 26 Piano. 27 Clarinet. 28 Gary Moore. 29 John Dankworth. 30 Cream.

92 ✳ '70S POP

1 "Love Me for a Reason". 2 Pigeon. 3 Cher. 4 Eddie Holman. 5 Dawn. 6 Ray Stevens. 7 Heart. 8 Squeeze. 9 January. 10 The Kinks. 11 10538. 12 Matthews Southern Comfort. 13 Leo Sayer. 14 "Your Song". 15 "The Floral Dance". 16 Minnie Riperton. 17 Sweet Sensation. 18 Paul Simon. 19 "Nathan Jones". 20 B A Robertson. 21 Rainbow. 22 New York. 23 "Samantha". 24 "Summer Nights". 25 The Commodores. 26 Rivers of Babylon. 27 Midnight. 28 "In the Summertime". 29 Donna Summer. 30 "Eye Level".

93 ✳ STEVIE WONDER

1 Piano, drums, harmonica. 2 Little Stevie Wonder. 3 Tamla Motown. 4 "Uptight". 5 Frank Sinatra's. 6 *Woman in Red*. 7 1950s. 8 Julio Iglesias. 9 Eiffel Tower. 10 Duke Ellington. 11 Syreeta. 12 Paul McCartney. 13 Nelson Mandela. 14 Elton John, Gladys Knight. 15 "Of Life". 16 His daughters. 17 Michael Jackson. 18 "I was Made to Love Her". 19 Detroit. 20 "I Just Called to Say I Love You". 21 Stevland. 22 Atlanta (1996). 23 2007. 24 Barack Obama. 25 Andrea Bocelli. 26 "Birthday". 27 The Jackson 5. 28 Motown (Tamla). 29 The harmonica. 30 "Signed, Sealed, Delivered I'm Yours."

94 ✳ SOLO STARS

1 No. 2 "The Day I Met Marie". 3 Elvis Presley. 4 "Holiday". 5 Rod Stewart. 6 Bryan Hyland. 7 Perry Como. 8 Bonnie Tyler. 9 "Green Door". 10 Bobby Brown. 11 Christina Aguilera. 12 "RSVP". 13 *Thunderball*. 14 Gene Pitney. 15 Marti Webb. 16 Will Young. 17 "Maggie May". 18 Frank Ifield. 19 "Careless Whisper". 20 Sam Cooke. 21 "In Dreams". 22 "They Call the Wind Mariah". 23 Seal. 24 Elton John. 25 Belinda Carlisle. 26 Tamla Motown. 27 25 mph. 28 Bruce Springsteen. 29 Cher - "Gypsies, Tramps and Thieves". 30 Georgia.

95 ✳ KYLIE

1 "Spinning Around". 2 *The Magic Roundabout*. 3 Showgirl. 4 Melbourne. 5 "You". 6 Fever. 7 Parlophone. 8 "Love at First Sight". 9 *Gemini*. 10 Little Eva. 11 "Dancing Queen". 12 Mushroom. 13 Breathe. 14 In Your Eyes. 15 Glastonbury. 16 Spinning Around. 17 Green Fairy. 18 Red Blooded Woman (2004). 19 Kylie. 20 Deconstruction. 21 Princess. 22 Can't Get You Out of My Head. 23 Body Language. 24 Lingerie. 25 Jason Donovan. 26 *Body Language*. 27 1960s. 28 13. 29 Kath & Kim. 30 *Kylie*.

96 ✳ POP POT LUCK 2

1 Michael Ball. 2 "Baby Jane". 3 MacArthur. 4 Wayne Fontana. 5 Guitar. 6 Blondie. 7 Stevie Wonder (his name backwards!). 8 Linda McCartney. 9 "One Fine Day". 10 Brian Epstein. 11 His car hit a tree. 12 Mick Jagger, David Bowie. 13 Hatch and Trent. 14 Bryan Adams. 15 1950s. 16 1980s. 17 The Housemartins. 18 Shakin' Stevens. 19 "Summer in the City". 20 Perry Como. 21 Lily Allen. 22 Scissor Sisters. 23 1930s. 24 David Bowie. 25 West Virginia. 26 Chicory Tip. 27 Peter Gabriel. 28 Queen. 29 "16". 30 Betty Boo.

97 ✳ FOLK & COUNTRY

1 Jim Reeves. 2 "Stand by Your Man". 3 "Leaving on a Jet Plane". 4 "I Will Always Love You". 5 Johnny Cash. 6 Charlie Pride. 7 Tom Paxton. 8 Tammy Wynette. 9 The Strawbs. 10 Bob Dylan. 11 Cambridge. 12 Hank Williams. 13 Mike Harding. 14 Garth Brooks. 15 Maddy Prior. 16 John Denver. 17 French. 18 Chet Atkins. 19 Woody Guthrie. 20 In an air crash. 21 Joan Baez. 22 Crystal Gayle. 23 Ralph McTell. 24 Pete Seeger. 25 Sandy Denny. 26 Willie Nelson. 27 Peter, Paul, Mary. 28 Loretta Lynn. 29 Gaudete. 30 Sue.

98 ✳ '60S POP 3

1 "Sugar Sugar". 2 "Itchycoo Park". 3 Tommy Roe. 4 "Love Letters". 5 "Tomorrow". 6 "FBI". 7 "Sailor". 8 "1-2-3". 9 Lovin' Spoonful. 10 "The Carnival is Over". 11 Marie. 12 "Teardrops". 13 "Sweets for My Sweet". 14 "Climb Ev'ry Mountain". 15 Manfred Mann. 16 Russia. 17 Troggs. 18 "Calendar Girl". 19 Holliday. 20 "Goodness Gracious Me". 21 Mary Hopkin. 22 "The Grass". 23 "Up on the Roof". 24 Dave Clark Five. 25 The Light Fandango. 26 "Funny Familiar Forgotten". 27 Spencer Davis. 28 "Chapel of Love". 29 Tornadoes. 30 "Matthew and Son" (Cat Stevens).

99 ✳ ONE-HIT WONDERS

1 St Winifred's. 2 USA for Africa. 3 Paint Your Wagon. 4 A lot. 5 Zager and Evans. 6 Clive Dunn. 7 Ferry Aid. 8 Me. 9 Phyllis Nelson. 10 Paper Roses. 11 Michelle. 12 Rugby World Cup. 13 Fauré's Pavane. 14 Baz Luhrmanne. 15 Yellow. 16 Band Aid, Band Aid II, Do They Know It's Christmas. 17 Bananarama. 18 Kalin Twins. 19 Laura. 20 Coconut Airways. 21 Annie's Song. 22 England World Cup Squad. 23 Luton Airport. 24 Brideshead Revisited. 25 Up, Up and Away. 26 John Fred and the Playboy Band. 27 Dat Ding. 28 PhD. 29 Postman Pat. 30 Three.

100 ✳ ALBUMS

1 Simon & Garfunkel. 2 If U Can't Dance. 3 *Mystery Girl*. 4 Vertigo. 5 Innuendo. 6 Alison Moyet (Essex). 7 *American Pie*. 8 Frank Sinatra. 9 *All Things Must Pass*. 10 *Help!* - The Beatles. 11 *Sheer Heart Attack*. 12 A black dog. 13 *Face Value*. 14 Tony Christie. 15 Blue. 16 Mark Coyle. 17 The Police. 18 *The Sound of Music*. 19 *Goodbye Yellow Brick Road*. 20 As a soloist, with Style Council and the Jam. 21 Chris De Burgh. 22 *Fleetwood Mac*. 23 *Saturday Night Fever*. 24 A postal strike. 25 Postcard. 26 On. 27 WEA. 28 *Transformer*. 29 *Never for Ever*. 30 Queen.

101 ✳ MUSICAL GREATS

1 "Without You". 2 The Miracles. 3 12 years. 4 Georgia. 5 "Mary's Boy Child". 6 The Doors. 7 "In the Summertime". 8 Christie Brinkley. 9 "Can't Help Falling in Love". 10 "Mistletoe and Wine". 11 "Tears". 12 "What a Wonderful World". 13 "She Loves You". 14 Jimmy Young. 15 "Bright Eyes". 16 Far Corporation. 17 Rodgers and Hammerstein. 18 Sun. 19 Gary Busey. 20 Otis Redding. 21 "Morning Has Broken". 22 "Release Me". 23 Roy Orbison. 24 24 weeks. 25 "I'm Into Something Good". 26 "Imagine". 27 Green. 28 "Waterloo" by Abba. 29 Cook without an "e". 30 "I Wanna Hold Your Hand".

102 ✳ THE BEATLES

1 Three. 2 Winston. 3 Pete Best. 4 "Day Tripper". 5 "Lucy in the Sky with Diamonds." 6 A record store. 7 Julian and Sean. 8 "The White Album". 9 *Thank Your Lucky Stars*. 10 The Quarrymen. 11 Helen Shapiro. 12 "Penny Lane"/"Strawberry Fields Forever". 13 Rattle their jewellery. 14 Stuart Sutcliffe. 15 Harmonica. 16 All four. 17 "My Sweet Lord". 18 *The Ed Sullivan Show*. 19 Fred Lennon (John's long-absent father). 20 Parlophone. 21 Paul McCartney. 22 *Evening Standard*. 23 *Yellow Submarine*. 24 *In His Own Write*. 25 Four (John). 26 San Francisco (1966). 27 Silver Beetles. 28 "Yesterday". 29 George Harrison. 30 MBE.

103 ✳ PEACE & LOVE

1 1967. 2 The Flowerpot Men. 3 "Creeque Alley". 4 Bach. 5 "Our World". 6 Barry McGuire. 7 Bangor, North Wales. 8 The Maharishi's retreat. 9 Yellow. 10 The Voice of Scott McKenzie. 11 Jimi Hendrix. 12 Moby Grape. 13 Golden Gate Park. 14 Eric Burdon and the Animals. 15 John Phillips. 16 Jefferson Airplane. 17 Mama Cass Elliot. 18 Keith Reid, Gary Brooker. 19 Philip Blondheim. 20 Harold Wilson. 21 2 July. 22 Rihanna. 23 *Bleeding Love*. 24 Ringo Starr. 25 "Put a Ring on It". 26 "It's Now or Never". 27 "Thunder". 28 Justin Timberlake. 29 Lyla. 30 My Chemical Romance.

104 ✳ CLASSIC NO. 1S

1 Wet Wet Wet. 2 *Unchained*. 3 "My Sweet Lord". 4 "Wooden Heart". 5 "Maggie May". 6 Frankie Laine. 7 Gary Jules (Mad World). 8 "Ticket to Ride". 9 Peter Cetera. 10 Herbert Kretzmer. 11 "Girls' School". 12 Elton John. 13 "The Fly" (U2). 14 *The Fleet's In*. 15 "Hole in the Head". 16 "I Know Him So Well". 17 "Whatever Will Be Will Be". 18 "Mandy" 19 "Hello Goodbye". 20 "Careless Whisper". 21 "Bridge Over Troubled Water". 22 "Who's Sorry Now?" 23 "Three Times a Lady". 24 John Travolta. 25 "Hung Up". 26 "Claudette". 27 Craig David. 28 "Stranger on the Shore" (Acker Bilk). 29 "Bohemian Rhapsody". 30 "Living Doll".

105 ✳ ELVIS PRESLEY

1 Aaron. 2 "Old Shep". 3 Chet Atkins. 4 Beaulieu. 5 The Jordanaires. 6 Sun Records. 7 Vernon and Gladys. 8 *Love Me Tender*. 9 West Germany. 10 "My Happiness". 11 "Heartbreak Hotel". 12 JXL. 13 Colonel Tom Parker. 14 "Surrender". 15 Elvis Presley Music. 16 It's Now or Never. 17 1977 (Way Down). 18 "All Shook Up". 19 Las Vegas. 20 "Way Down". 21 Juliet Prowse. 22 Scotland. 23 *Charro*. 24 Waist up. 25 Cut his hair for the army. 26 "One Night"/"I Got Stung". 27 Graceland, Memphis. 28 "Hound Dog"/"Don't be Cruel". 29 "You Don't Have to Say You Love Me". 30 "The Wonder of You".

106 ✳ KEYBOARDS

1 Matthew Fisher. 2 Rick Wakeman. 3 The Paramounts. 4 Vince Clarke. 5 Rodriguez Argentina. 6 "Song for Guy". 7 *Piano Man*. 8 The Zombies. 9 Ray Manzarek. 10 Richard Clayderman. 11 Neil Sedaka. 12 Dave Brubeck. 13 Mike Pinder. 14 Georgie Fame. 15 Rick Wright. 16 Alan Price. 17 Rod Argent. 18 "Aztec Gold". 19 *Hunky Dory*. 20 Jelly Roll Morton. 21 Leavell. 22 Stevie Wonder. 23 Jean-Michel Jarre. 24 Eno. 25 Wakeman. 26 Tony Banks. 27 Keith Emerson. 28 Elvis Costello. 29 Paul Carrack. 30 Bernard Sumner.

107 ✳ OLDIES & GOODIES

1 "(How Much is) That Doggie in the Window?" 2 "Amazing Grace". 3 "Oh Pretty Woman". 4 "Honky Tonk". 5 "I'm not in Love". 6 Rosemary Clooney. 7 If you're going. 8 "So Gay". 9 "Spirit in the Sky". 10 Little Jimmy Osmond. 11 "I Can't Stop Loving You". 12 Terry Jacks. 13 "Lily the Pink". 14 Adam Faith. 15 "My Ding-a-Ling". 16 1973. 17 "Needles and Pins". 18 Tab Hunter. 19 Lee Hazelwood. 20 "Johnny Remember Me". 21 Jerry Keller. 22 Roy Wood. 23 "Moon River". 24 "The Good, the Bad and the Ugly". 25 "Sunny Afternoon". 26 "The Next Time"/"Bachelor Boy". 27 "What a Wonderful World". 28 "Land". 29 Zager & Evans. 30 "You're My World".

108 ✳ MOR POP

1 Mike Batt. 2 Burt Bacharach and Hal David. 3 Barbra Streisand. 4 None. 5 Andy Williams. 6 Eva Casssidy. 7 Des O'Connor. 8 "Jambalaya". 9 Roger Whittaker. 10 Herb Alpert. 11 James Last. 12 Mantovani. 13 Peter Skellern. 14 Mary Hopkin. 15 Jack Jones. 16 Charles Aznavour. 17 Barber. 18 Tony Christie. 19 Johnny Mathis. 20 Shirley Bassey. 21 Leo Sayer. 22 Bert Kaempfert. 23 Henry Mancini. 24 Syd Lawrence. 25 "Stranger in Paradise". 26 Al Martino. 27 Nat King Cole. 28 Helen Reddy. 29 Shirley Bassey. 30 Gerry Goffin.

109 ✳ POP DJS

1 Kenny Everett. 2 Radio Atlantis. 3 *Too Much Gravy*. 4 John Peel. 5 Jimmy Savile. 6 Paul Jones. 7 Simon Mayo. 8 Mark Goodier. 9 Jimmy Young. 10 Jive Bunny and London Beat. 11 Radio 1 DJ Posse. 12 The Big Bopper. 13 Ravenscroft. 14 Noel Edmonds. 15 Chris Tarrant. 16 Jimmy Savile. 17 Tony Prince. 18 Phillip Schofield. 19 Emperor Rosko. 20 Kenny Everett. 21 79. 22 2004. 23 Annie Nightingale. 24 Denise Van Outen. 25 Whiley. 26 Janice Long. 27 Gary Davies. 28 Danny Baker. 29 Terry Christian 30 Lisa l'Anson.

110 ✳ ROCKERS

1 "Sweetie Pie". 2 Dennis Quaid. 3 Pilot in the crash that killed Holly. 4 Colette. 5 Athens, Georgia. 6 The New York Dolls. 7 Paul Anka. 8 "Jailhouse Rock." 9 AC/DC. 10 Decca. 11 The Post Office. 12 "Cum On Feel the Noize". 13 An arm (in a car crash). 14 Kurt Cobain's body. 15 Little Richard. 16 Iggy Pop. 17 Sun Studio, Memphis. 18 July. 19 St Martin's School of Art. 20 "Christmas Alphabet". 21 Guildford. 22 Alan Lancaster. 23 Rollin' Stones. 24 "What'd I Say". 25 Norman Petty. 26 Leslie Crowther. 27 Status Quo. 28 John Bonham. 29 Malcolm McLaren. 30 *Blackboard Jungle*.

111 ✸ NOVELTY POP SONGS

1 A Beatle. 2 Chuck Berry. 3 Bryan Hyland and Bombalurina. 4 "Tie Me Kangaroo Down". 5 Julian Clary. 6 *It Ain't Half Hot Mum.* 7 DLT, Paul Burnett. 8 Mike Reid. 9 Liverpool FC. 10 Smear Campaign. 11 Mouldy Old Dough. 12 Napoleon XIV. 13 The Singing Nun. 14 "Magic Roundabout". 15 "Geordie Boys". 16 The Goons. 17 Lord Rockingham's XI. 18 Peter Sellers, Sophia Loren. 19 Aintree Iron. 20 Ivor Biggun. 21 Roland Rat. 22 7 days. 23 Hale, Pace. 24 Pinky, Perky. 25 "Loadsamoney". 26 Splodgenessabounds. 27 Corporal Jones. 28 The Matchroom Mob. 29 1st Atheist Tabernacle Choir. 30 Brand New Key.

112 ✸ SOUL

1 "I'm Still Waiting". 2 Saxophone. 3 Sam Cooke. 4 The Miracles. 5 Stevie Wonder. 6 Jackie. 7 MCA. 8 Philadelphia. 9 Mercury. 10 Tito. 11 Mary Wells. 12 "When You've Heard Lou You've Heard It All". 13 Holland Dozier Holland. 14 Atlanta. 15 Billy Preston. 16 Los Angeles. 17 Michael Jackson. 18 Berry Gordy. 19 Syreeta. 20 "Lady". 21 Duffy. 22 Chicago Soul. 23 Bebe Winans. 24 Detroit. 25 2002. 26 Los Angeles Lakers. 27 Al Green. 28 James Brown. 29 La Toya Jackson. 30 Martha and the Vandellas.

113 ✸ MUSIC SUPERSTARS 2

1 Tina Turner. 2 Tony Bennett. 3 Neil Diamond. 4 *Girls! Girls! Girls!* 5 "Sorry Seems to be the Hardest Word". 6 "When I Need You". 7 1960s. 8 "Bohemian Rhapsody". 9 Bob Dylan. 10 Eleven. 11 Kate Bush. 12 "Dancing Queen". 13 *Turandot.* 14 Barry, Robin & Maurice Gibb. 15 "Let's Dance". 16 Jean Terrell. 17 Mark McGrath. 18 Madonna. 19 Epic. 20 1962. 21 Mick Jagger. 22 Roxy Music. 23 Rod Stewart. 24 Thunderclap Newman. 25 Celine Dion and Peabo Bryson. 26 "Love Me for a Reason". 27 Zubin Mehta. 28 Hot Chocolate. 29 "Blinded by the Light". 30 "Rock On".

114 ✸ FOLK & BLUES

1 Judy Dyble. 2 Phil Ochs. 3 Paris. 4 Rolling Thunder Review. 5 "The Times They are A-Changin'". 6 Blind Willie McTell (Ralph McTell). 7 The Humblebums. 8 Conor. 9 Travers (Peter, Paul and Mary). 10 Blind Lemon Jefferson. 11 *Rhymes and Reasons.* 12 Riley. 13 Troubador. 14 Elektra. 15 Martin Carthy. 16 John Lee Hooker. 17 Sandy Denny. 18 Alexis Korner. 19 Al Stewart. 20 "Basket of Light". 21 Wilson. 22 Chicago. 23 Cecil Sharp. 24 Macclesfield. 25 Al Kooper. 26 T-Bone Walker. 27 West Virginia. 28 Brain haemorrhage. 29 Bob Dylan. 30 Sam Hopkins.

115 ✸ WHOSE MUSIC?

1 Gary Barlow. 2 Meat Loaf. 3 Backstreet Boys. 4 Zager and Evans - "In the Year 2525". 5 Helen Shapiro. 6 Engelbert Humperdinck. 7 Dave Edmunds. 8 Mark Owen. 9 Marc Bolan (Metal Guru). 10 Stevie Wonder. 11 Alan "Remi" Wren. 12 Dawn. 13 Mike Sarne. 14 Artful Dodger. 15 Georgie Fame. 16 UB40. 17 Frank Ifield. 18 1971. 19 The Gibb Brothers. 20 Billy Preston on "Get Back". 21 Mr Blobby. 22 Clint Eastwood. 23 Rod Stewart. 24 Two versions. 25 Alan McGhee. 26 Bill Medley and Bobby Hatfield. 27 Dave Stead. 28 Buddy Holly. 29 Billy J. Kramer. 30 Eddie Calvert.

116 ✸ THE ROLLING STONES

1 40 Licks. 2 Lennon and McCartney. 3 The Last Time. 4 Alexis Korner's. 5 *Aftermath.* 6 Sitar. 7 Drowned in pool. 8 Jean-Luc Godard. 9 Ned Kelly. 10 Jade. 11 Andy Warhol. 12 Jamaica. 13 *Undercover.* 14 "Je suis un rock star". 15 David Bowie. 16 Willie and the Poor Boys. 17 Freejack. 18 Chuck Berry. 19 X-Pensive Winos. 20 Virgin. 21 Ian Stewart. 22 Muddy Waters. 23 Charlie Watts. 24 "As Tears Go By". 25 Jeff Beck. 26 "Have You Seen Your Mother Baby Standing in the Shadow?" 27 "Let's Spend the Night Together". 28 "Brown Sugar". 29 *Rolling Stones No 2.* 30 2002.

117 ✸ '40S & '50S FILMS

1 *Bambi.* 2 80 days. 3 Over the River Kwai. 4 "White Christmas". 5 Tramp. 6 Ben Hur. 7 *Fantasia.* 8 *Gone with the Wind.* 9 Bob Hope. 10 *Casablanca.* 11 Laurence Olivier. 12 *Brief Encounter.* 13 Hitchcock. 14 Welles. 15 Alec Guinness. 16 Ealing Comedies. 17 "In the Rain". 18 *Hot.* 19 *Genevieve.* 20 James Dean. 21 Grace Kelly. 22 Brigitte Bardot. 23 Ten. 24 *At the Top.* 25 Elizabeth Taylor. 26 Rogers. 27 Brando. 28 *Arsenic.* 29 *Love.* 30 *Eternity.*

118 ✸ BLOCKBUSTERS

1 *Jaws.* 2 *Casino Royale.* 3 *Evita.* 4 *The X Files.* 5 Julianne Moore. 6 *New York.* 7 The Lord of the Rings. 8 Dinosaurs. 9 Australia. 10 *Peter Pan.* 11 Godzilla. 12 Kramer. 13 Pearl Harbor. 14 Boxing. 15 *E.T.* 16 *Star Wars.* 17 Indiana Jones. 18 *Thieves.* 19 Before. 20 Space. 21 Batman. 22 Titanic. 23 Paris. 24 John Travolta. 25 70s. 26 *The Lion King.* 27 Mozart. 28 Macaulay Culkin. 29 Black & white. 30 Costner.

119 ✸ '30S FILMS

1 Greta Garbo. 2 German. 3 *Modern Times.* 4 Wayne. 5 *The Wizard of Oz.* 6 Fred Astaire & Ginger Rogers. 7 *Washington.* 8 Olivier. 9 *Baby.* 10 *King Kong.* 11 San Francisco. 12 *Robin Hood.* 13 Gangster. 14 Rooney. 15 Berkeley. 16 *Grand.* 17 Marx Brothers. 18 Paris. 19 Dracula. 20 *On the Western Front.* 21 Al Capone. 22 *Goodbye Mr Chips.* 23 Scarlett O'Hara. 24 Frankenstein. 25 *Wrong.* 26 Walt Disney. 27 Ronald Reagan. 28 Germany. 29 *Duck Soup.* 30 Ginger Rogers.

120 ✸ '60S FILMS

1 West. 2 Elizabeth Taylor. 3 Arabia. 4 Clyde. 5 *Midnight.* 6 Dustin Hoffman. 7 Rex Harrison. 8 *Oliver!* 9 John Wayne. 10 Farrow. 11 *The Sound of Music.* 12 Greek. 13 *Dinner.* 14 Mary Poppins. 15 Michael Caine. 16 Christie. 17 Barbra Streisand. 18 *Zhivago.* 19 Peck. 20 Jean Brodie. 21 Scofield. 22 101. 23 The Sundance Kid. 24 2001. 25 *Psycho.* 26 Breakfast. 27 Sean Connery. 28 *The Good.* 29 *Charity.* 30 *Camelot.*

121 ✳ COMEDIES

1 Rowan. **2** *Scooby Doo*. **3** Borat. **4** The Addams Family. **5** Ealing. **6** Children. **7** *The Flintstones*. **8** Excellent. **9** Pig. **10** Cruise. **11** *Notting Hill*. **12** *Wayne's*. **13** *Wanda*. **14** Nun. **15** Wet Wet Wet. **16** Carrey. **17** Chocolates. **18** Roberts. **19** Morecambe & Wise. **20** Dressed in drag. **21** Dead. **22** *The Jungle Book*. **23** James. **24** Honey. **25** Popeye. **26** Colin Firth. **27** Patrick Swayze. **28** *Look Who's Talking*. **29** Priscilla. **30** Clouseau.

122 ✳ ANIMATION

1 Gibson. **2** Gromit. **3** Disney. **4** *The Lion King*. **5** Williams. **6** The Beast. **7** Rowan Atkinson. **8** Jane. **9** Bugs Bunny. **10** 1940s. **11** Phil Collins. **12** Dalmatians. **13** *Jungle Book*. **14** 1960s. **15** Cat. **16** *Antz*. **17** *The Aristocats*. **18** *101 Dalmatians*. **19** Donald. **20** 1930s. **21** Bugs Bunny. **22** 1990s. **23** Jungle Book. **24** Irons. **25** *Toy Story*. **26** *Shrek*. **27** Panda. **28** Barry Manilow. **29** Jerry Seinfeld. **30** *Ratatouille*.

123 ✳ HOLLYWOOD

1 Humphrey Bogart. **2** Bing Crosby. **3** Ingrid Bergman. **4** Tony. **5** Richard Gere. **6** Bette. **7** De Mille. **8** Keystone. **9** Liza Minnelli. **10** Michael Douglas. **11** Gardner. **12** Sister. **13** Hepburn. **14** Kelly. **15** Alfred Hitchcock. **16** Jane Fonda. **17** Clark Gable. **18** Walter Matthau. **19** Ginger Rogers. **20** Temple. **21** Valentino. **22** Barrymore. **23** Newman. **24** Madonna. **25** Doris Day. **26** Tom Cruise. **27** Cagney. **28** Nose. **29** Elizabeth Taylor. **30** Moore.

124 ✳ WHO'S WHO?

1 Sean Connery. **2** Holland. **3** Pierce Brosnan. **4** John Travolta. **5** Poirot. **6** Eminem. **7** Michael Jackson. **8** Woody Allen. **9** Bowler. **10** Bryan Forbes. **11** Winona Ryder. **12** Sir Elton John. **13** Sir John Mills. **14** Demi Moore. **15** Rupert Murdoch. **16** Vicious. **17** Satchel. **18** Hopkins. **19** Turner. **20** Jodie Foster. **21** Cheque. **22** Shirley Temple. **23** Harrison Ford. **24** Ralph Fiennes. **25** Muhammad Ali. **26** Groucho. **27** Tom Jones. **28** Julie Andrews **29** M. **30** Cameron Diaz.

125 ✳ ARNOLD SCHWARZENEGGER

1 Austria. **2** *Iron*. **3** Conan. **4** *The Terminator*. **5** Red. **6** DeVito. **7** *Total*. **8** George Bush. **9** Los Angeles. **10** Her husband. **11** *Conan the Barbarian*. **12** Preston. **13** Maria. **14** Cameron. **15** Pregnant. **16** Austrian Oak. **17** Terminator 2. **18** *True Lies*. **19** *The Last*. **20** 1940s. **21** *Kindergarten*. **22** Computers. **23** J. F. Kennedy. **24** Planet Hollywood. **25** Jeff Bridges. **26** Governor of California. **27** Austria. **28** He joined the Austrian army. **29** Mr Olympia. **30** *The Kid & I*.

126 ✳ '70S FILMS

1 *Star Wars*. **2** *The Godfather*. **3** A car. **4** A shark. **5** *Saturday*. **6** Kramer. **7** Superman. **8** Cuckoo's. **9** Grease. **10** Third. **11** Nile. **12** Rocky. **13** Kermit. **14** Eagle. **15** *King Kong*. **16** *Towering Inferno*. **17** *M*A*S*H*. **18** *Orange*. **19** Jackal. **20** Bugsy. **21** Clint Eastwood. **22** Diamonds. **23** *Deer*. **24** Beverly Hills. **25** Dog. **26** Robert Redford. **27** *Great and Small*. **28** *Now*. **29** Moon. **30** Poseidon.

127 ✳ THE GREATS

1 Fred Astaire. **2** *Casablanca*. **3** Tony Curtis. **4** Bristol. **5** Redhead. **6** Bob Hope. **7** Frankenstein's monster. **8** Gene Kelly. **9** Marilyn Monroe. **10** Perkins. **11** Guinness. **12** Rock Hudson. **13** Stewart. **14** Rudolph Valentino. **15** Citizen Kane. **16** Bogart. **17** Gary. **18** Crawford. **19** Bette Davis. **20** Chaplin. **21** Golf. **22** W.C. Fields. **23** Fonda. **24** Hepburn. **25** Day. **26** Jack Lemmon. **27** Kirk Douglas. **28** Berlin. **29** 60s. **30** Stockholm.

128 ✳ LATE GREATS

1 Car. **2** Gish. **3** Marvin. **4** Rex Harrison. **5** Gable. **6** Niven. **7** England. **8** Pub. **9** Natasha Richardson. **10** Vivien Leigh. **11** Richard Burton. **12** Charlie Chaplin & Paulette Goddard. **13** Rock Hudson. **14** Laurence Olivier. **15** Gardner. **16** Davis. **17** Davis. **18** W. C. Fields. **19** Cary Grant. **20** Nose. **21** Jackie Gleason. **22** Stewart. **23** *Citizen Kane* **24** Dean. **25** Betty Grable. **26** Heath. **27** Wyman. **28** Paul Newman. **29** Charlton Heston. **30** Ingmar Bergman.

129 ✳ '80S FILMS

1 Twin. **2** Willis. **3** Cher. **4** *Africa*. **5** *Tootsie*. **6** *An Officer and a Gentleman*. **7** The Kids. **8** *Extra Terrestrial*. **9** *Fatal*. **10** Valentine. **11** *Elephant Man*. **12** *Chariots of Fire*. **13** Crocodile. **14** Jones. **15** Gandhi. **16** *Ghost*. **17** Mozart. **18** *Mona Lisa*. **19** Ronald Reagan. **20** Wanda. **21** *Naked Gun*. **22** Roger Moore. **23** *The Empire*. **24** Beverly Hills. **25** *The Future*. **26** *The Jedi*. **27** Michael Jackson. **28** Roger. **29** The Titanic. **30** Three.

130 ✳ THE BRITS

1 *Spiceworld The Movie*. **2** Cliff Richard. **3** *The Full Monty*. **4** Japanese. **5** Football. **6** Branagh. **7** Dixon of Dock Green. **8** Television. **9** *English*. **10** Grossman. **11** Julie Andrews. **12** Welsh. **13** Scotland. **14** Glenda Jackson. **15** Attenborough. **16** *Four Weddings and a Funeral*. **17** Thompson. **18** *The Railway Children*. **19** British Prime Minister's. **20** Richard Burton. **21** Michael Caine. **22** Christie. **23** McGregor. **24** Shirley Valentine. **25** Diana Dors. **26** Ken Barlow. **27** Oscar Wilde. **28** Roger Moore. **29** Scotland. **30** The *Full Monty*.

131 ❋ STARS OF THE '80S

1 Madonna. 2 Cher. 3 Sally. 4 J. Fox. 5 Bruce Willis. 6 Alley. 7 Sylvester Stallone. 8 Griffith. 9 Dustin Hoffman. 10 Swayze. 11 Close. 12 Oprah Winfrey. 13 Sigourney Weaver. 4 Vietnam. 15 Nielsen. 16 Gere. 17 Gibson. 18 Kline. 19 Orang Utan. 20 E.T. 21 *Ghostbusters*. 22 Douglas. 23 Roger. 24 Batman. 25 Sean Connery. 26 Hanks. 27 Jack Nicholson. 28 Meg Ryan. 29 Mel Gibson. 30 Kathleen Turner.

132 ❋ '90S FILMS

1 Hugh Grant. 2 *Braveheart*. 3 Columbus. 4 *Mrs Doubtfire*. 5 *Hook*. 6 *Sister Act*. 7 Jack Lemmon. 8 List. 9 A dog. 10 A ghost. 11 Tom Hanks. 12 Patrick Swayze. 13 Kevin Costner. 14 *The Silence of the Lambs*. 15 Alone. 16 *The Lion King*. 17 Indecent. 18 Trousers. 19 Julia Roberts. 20 Sally. 21 *Jurassic*. 22 Seattle. 23 *Pocahontas*. 24 *Batman*. 25 *Mohicans*. 26 *Aladdin*. 27 Tom Cruise. 28 *Dredd*. 29 34th. 30 Golden.

133 ❋ THE OSCARS

1 Glenda Jackson. 2 Julia Roberts. 3 Halle Berry. 4 Costner. 5 Scotland. 6 Anthony Hopkins. 7 Steven Spielberg. 8 Irons. 9 Hanks. 10 Cher. 11 Sarandon. 12 Left Foot. 13 Director. 14 Once a year. 15 *The Piano*. 16 King. 17 Winslet. 18 None. 19 Forrest Gump. 20 Pacino. 21 Temple. 22 *Titanic*. 23 *Chariots of Fire*. 24 *Gandhi*. 25 Michael. 26 Vietnam. 27 Fiennes. 28 Doolittle. 29 Nose. 30 Western.

134 ❋ HORROR

1 Kenneth Branagh. 2 The Devil. 3 Bram Stoker's *Dracula*. 4 *Scream 2*. 5 William Peter Blatty. 6 Bela. 7 Invisible. 8 King. 9 Dracula. 10 Cruise. 11 Spiders. 12 Kubrick. 13 The creature. 14 *Halloween*. 15 Spacek. 16 Elm Street. 17 1970s. 18 Mia Farrow. 19 Victor. 20 In London. 21 *The Birds*. 22 Anthony Perkins. 23 Anthony Hopkins. 24 Pfeiffer. 25 Hammer. 26 Predator. 27 Will Smith. 28 Neil Marshall. 29 *Shaun of the Dead*. 30 *Feast*.

135 ❋ HOLLYWOOD 2

1 Whitney Houston. 2 Diane. 3 Johnny Cash. 4 Hunter. 5 Charlie Chaplin. 6 Anthony Hopkins. 7 Hoskins. 8 Spielberg. 9 Stallone. 10 Kiefer. 11 Quentin. 12 Griffith. 13 Nolte. 14 Susan. 15 Depp. 16 Connery. 17 Estevez. 18 Culkin. 19 Close. 20 Pacino. 21 Gibson. 22 Fonda. 23 Williams. 24 Hannah. 25 Kim Basinger. 26 Val. 27 Judy Garland. 28 Pierce Brosnan. 29 Woody Allen. 30 Kevin Costner.

136 ❋ MOVIES POT LUCK

1 Hollywood. 2 *Shakespeare*. 3 *Emma*. 4 Junior. 5 Humphrey Bogart. 6 Madonna. 7 1970s. 8 Anthony Hopkins. 9 Jack Nicholson. 10 1960s. 11 Demi Moore. 12 Woody Allen. 13 USSR - Latvia. 14 Sweden. 15 USSR. 16 1990s. 17 Joanne Woodward. 18 Terrestrial. 19 Barbara Bach. 20 13. 21 Hope. 22 George. 23 Dietrich. 24 Fame. 25 Cates. 26 Terminator. 27 The Were-Rabbit. 28 Danes. 29 Blondie. 30 *Indecent*.

137 ❋ ACTION

1 *Goldeneye*. 2 *Platoon*. 3 Jeremy Irons. 4 Ridley Scott. 5 Charles Bronson. 6 Jim Carrey. 7 Best Director. 8 Wesley Snipes. 9 *Live and Let Die*. 10 Faye Dunaway. 11 Donald Pleasance. 12 *Die Hard With a Vengeance*. 13 Harrison Ford. 14 Marseilles. 15 *Apollo*. 16 Bruce Willis. 17 Popeye Doyle. 18 James Caan. 19 Irish. 20 Brad Pitt. 21 *Lost In Space*. 22 Phil Collins. 23 Cabbie. 24 Paul and Linda McCartney. 25 *JFK*. 26 Sean Bean. 27 Jeremy Irons. 28 Arnold Schwarzenegger. 29 New York. 30 Leonardo DiCaprio.

138 ❋ ACTION 2

1 Blofeld. 2 Robert Aldrich. 3 *From Russia with Love*. 4 The Riddler. 5 *Dante's Peak*. 6 Bruce Lee. 7 Beer. 8 Boxing. 9 Doctor. 10 Bus. 11 *Donnie Brasco*. 12 San Francisco. 13 *Tomorrow Never Dies*. 14 *Die Hard with a Vengeance*. 15 Jane Seymour. 16 1930s. 17 *Heaven and Earth*. 18 Submarine. 19 *Vietnam*. 20 Frank Sinatra. 21 Sylvester Stallone. 22 *Terminator 2*. 23 Michelle Pfeiffer. 24 Barry Norman. 25 Francis Ford Coppola. 26 *Waterworld*. 27 Tina Turner. 28 Marseilles. 29 *Apollo 13*. 30 Sean Connery.

139 ❋ CARTOONS

1 Eddie Murphy. 2 *Anastasia*. 3 *Beauty and the Beast*. 4 Randy Newman. 5 Toontown. 6 *Anchors Aweigh*. 7 Pinocchio. 8 Dinosaur. 9 *Jumanji*. 10 *The Lion King*. 11 Si & Am. 12 Scar. 13 Rex. 14 *Aladdin*. 15 *Bambi*. 16 Woody Allen. 17 Jennifer Aniston. 18 Mel Gibson. 19 Kathleen Turner. 20 MGM. 21 *Tarzan*. 22 Tom & Jerry. 23 Miss Saigon. 24 Hyena. 25 King Louie. 26 Tigress. 27 Shrek. 28 *Transformers: The Movie*. 29 *The Lion King*. 30 *Who Framed Roger Rabbit?*

140 ❋ ANIMATION

1 *Dance of the Hours*. 2 Mel Gibson. 3 2002. 4 *The Return of Jafar*. 5 White. 6 Dalmatians. 7 Eight. 8 *Beauty and the Beast*. 9 Thumper. 10 *The Lion King*. 11 Eva. 12 Hanna & Barbera. 13 He sneezed. 14 *Cinderella*. 15 Jessica Rabbit. 16 *Steamboat Willie*. 17 Pocahontas. 18 *Bedknobs & Broomsticks*. 19 Peggy Lee. 20 Cool World. 21 Lea Salonga. 22 *Teenage Mutant Ninja Turtles*. 23 *Tron*. 24 Dinosaur. 25 *Aladdin*. 26 Gene Kelly. 27 *Nutcracker Suite*. 28 *Jungle Book*. 29 Tom & Jerry. 30 Michael J. Fox. PAGE 203

141 ✳ THRILLERS

1 *Taxi Diver.* **2** John Le Carré. **3** Charles de Gaulle. **4** Richard Nixon. **5** Jodie Foster. **6** *Minority Report.* **7** Chocolate sauce. **8** Robert Donat, Kenneth More, Robert Powell. **9** Kevin Kline. **10** Nuclear power plant. **11** *The Birds.* **12** Twin brother. **13** Stephen King's. **14** Alec Baldwin and Kim Basinger. **15** Mother and daughter. **16** Mexican. **17** *Rebecca.* **18** Michael Douglas. **19** *Schindler's List.* **20** Anthony Hopkins and Jodie Foster. **21** Grace Kelly. **22** Chile. **23** *Citizen Kane.* **24** Necktie. **25** Donald Sutherland. **26** IRA. **27** *Sleuth.* **28** 13. **29** *The Usual Suspects.* **30** The nanny.

142 ✳ ROBIN WILLIAMS

1 *Mork & Mindy.* **2** Sally Field. **3** Robert De Niro. **4** 1980s. **5** Nixon. **6** Pierce Brosnan. **7** *The World According to Garp.* **8** Popeye. **9** Kenneth Branagh. **10** *Mrs Doubtfire.* **11** Lawyer. **12** Jeff. **13** The genie. **14** Peter Pan. **15** Shelley Duvall. **16** Aberdeen. **17** *Jumanji.* **18** Disc jockey. **19** *Moscow on the Hudson.* **20** Gilliam. **21** *Good Morning, Vietnam.* **22** *Dead Poets Society.* **23** Levinson. **24** *Cadillac Man.* **25** 1960s. **26** Teddy Roosevelt. **27** Three. **28** *Poets.* **29** Best Supporting Actor. **30** *License to Wed.*

143 ✳ BLOCKBUSTERS

1 Five. **2** Chocolate. **3** *The Robe.* **4** Francis Ford Coppola. **5** Normandy. **6** *M*A*S*H.* **7** Hearst. **8** *Crocodile Dundee.* **9** James Caviezel. **10** *Midnight Cowboy.* **11** Dan Aykroyd. **12** *The English Patient.* **13** Vito Corleone. **14** Pierce Brosnan. **15** Ron Kovic. **16** *Gone with the Wind.* **17** *Wall Street.* **18** *Braveheart.* **19** *Dune.* **20** John Huston. **21** *Terminator II.* **22** Austrian. **23** *All About Eve.* **24** 1930s. **25** Goldblum. **26** Jim Carrey. **27** Carrie Fisher. **28** Celine Dion. **29** *The Last Samurai.* **30** Cop.

144 ✳ ACTION 3

1 Long Island. **2** Sean Connery. **3** Bruce Willis. **4** *The Godfather.* **5** Superman. **6** The philosopher's stone. **7** The architect. **8** *Dr No.* **9** *The Return of the King.* **10** Lee Van Cleef. **11** *Raiders of the Lost Ark.* **12** William Wallace. **13** Chicago. **14** Stallone. **15** *Live and Let Die.* **16** Daniel Day-Lewis. **17** David Lean. **18** *Patriot Games.* **19** Directing. **20** *On Her Majesty's Secret Service.* **21** Robert De Niro. **22** *Unforgiven.* **23** Faye Dunaway. **24** Kathleen Turner. **25** Car chase. **26** *The Spy Who Loved Me.* **27** *True Grit.* **28** *Dirty Harry.* **29** Liam Neeson. **30** Lois Maxwell.

145 ✳ CLASSICS

1 *Casablanca.* **2** Lion. **3** *Brief Encounter.* **4** *Birth of a Nation.* **5** *The Ten Commandments.* **6** *Sunset Boulevard.* **7** *Shadowlands.* **8** 20. **9** Barnes Wallis. **10** Cary Grant. **11** Humphrey Bogart. **12** Harry Lime. **13** The Graduate. **14** Thomas More. **15** *It's a Wonderful Life.* **16** Lola Lola. **17** Cody Jarrett. **18** *Love Story.* **19** Michael. **20** *Gilda.* **21** *To Have and Have Not.* **22** Car. **23** *GI Blues.* **24** John Garfield. **25** *On the Waterfront.* **26** 1912. **27** Lawyer. **28** *African.* **29** *One.* **30** *Rain Man.*

146 ✳ THE OSCARS

1 Morgan Freeman. **2** *Casablanca.* **3** *The Deer Hunter.* **4** Christy Brown. **5** Henry Fonda. **6** *As Good as It Gets.* **7** *Philadelphia.* **8** Marlee Matlin. **9** James Cameron. **10** *Philadelphia, Forrest Gump.* **11** Gary Cooper. **12** Butler. **13** 1930s. **14** Woody Allen. **15** *The Godfather.* **16** Dustin Hoffman. **17** Frank Sinatra. **18** *Schindler's List.* **19** She never spoke. **20** Walter & John Huston. **21** Meryl Streep. **22** Bette Davis. **23** Jessica Tandy. **24** Eight (all of them). **25** Kathy Bates. **26** Oscar. **27** Vivien Leigh. **28** Anthony Minghella. **29** Tatum O'Neal. **30** Helena Bonham-Carter.

147 ✳ COMEDIES

1 *My Big Fat Greek Wedding.* **2** Daniel. **3** *(Bend It Like) Beckham.* **4** Bruce Willis. **5** Arnold Schwarzenegger. **6** City Under Siege. **7** *Ghostbusters.* **8** Jessica Lange. **9** Julia Roberts. **10** Paul Newman and Robert Redford. **11** Manhattan. **12** Dolly Parton. **13** Disney. **14** Mel Gibson. **15** Michael Caine. **16** Meg Ryan and Billy Crystal. **17** Stockbroker. **18** *Carry On Sergeant.* **19** Clouseau. **20** Priscilla Presley. **21** *Three Men and a Little Lady.* **22** *Butch Cassidy and the Sundance Kid.* **23** Scottish. **24** Maggie Smith. **25** A pig. **26** The Mafia. **27** *Big.* **28** St Valentine's Day Massacre. **29** Woody Allen. **30** Harpo and Groucho (Marx).

148 ✳ OSCARS: BEST ACTORS

1 George Burns. **2** *Wall Street.* **3** *The English Patient.* **4** Ben Kingsley. **5** Jude Law. **6** Priest. **7** Emil Jannings. **8** Manservant. **9** Daniel Day-Lewis. **10** *The People versus Larry Flint.* **11** None. **12** Rex Harrison. **13** *Midnight Cowboy.* **14** None. **15** Wall Street. **16** *George III.* **17** *Amistad.* **18** *Chinatown.* **19** James Dean. **20** Daniel Day-Lewis. **21** Marlon Brando. **22** *The Elephant Man.* **23** Don Corleone. **24** *Schindler's List.* **25** Rex Harrison. **26** George Clooney. **27** Depp. **28** Peter O'Toole. **29** George C. Scott and Marlon Brando. **30** *High Noon.*

149 ✳ WESTERNS

1 *A Fistful of Dollars.* **2** Gene Hackman. **3** John Wayne. **4** James Garner. **5** Best Director. **6** *The Seven Samurai.* **7** Raindrops. **8** Robert Redford. **9** Bob Hope. **10** Emilio Estevez. **11** Frances McDormand. **12** Jodie Foster. **13** Lee van Cleef. **14** No. III. **15** *Paint Your Wagon.* **16** Spencer Tracy. **17** *A Fistful of Dollars.* **18** Glen Campbell. **19** Kiefer Sutherland. **20** Davy Crockett. **21** Carmel. **22** Pale Rider. **23** Mexico. **24** Italy. **25** *Blazing Saddles.* **26** John Cleese. **27** *Young Guns.* **28** Scout. **29** Champion. **30** White.

150 ✳ WAR

1 1991 Gulf War. **2** Vietnam War. **3** Marlon Brando. **4** Donald Sutherland and Elliott Gould. **5** Patton - Lust for Glory. **6** The Deer Hunter. **7** Alec Guinness. **8** A castle. **9** Lancashire. **10** Mercenaries. **11** *The Great Escape.* **12** The 1960s. **13** Clooney. **14** The Dirty Dozen. **15** Schindler's Ark. **16** Frank Sinatra. **17** Rick's Café. **18** Alistair MacLean. **19** *Oh! What a Lovely War.* **20** *On the Western Front.* **21** Pearl Harbor. **22** Alice Springs. **23** Jane Fonda. **24** Rommel. **25** *The Great Dictator.* **26** Oliver Stone. **27** *Kelly's Heroes.* **28** Winston Churchill. **29** Meryl Streep. **30** Cambodia.

151 ✷ JOHN WAYNE

1 Duke. 2 *Stagecoach*. 3 (American) Football.
4 Paulette Goddard. 5 *Rio Grande*. 6 Dean Martin.
7 Boxer. 8 Lauren Bacall. 9 *The Greatest Story Ever Told*. 10 Davy Crockett. 11 Rooster Cogburn. 12 Marion Morrison. 13 Vietnam. 14 *True Grit*. 15 *Sands of Iwo Jima*.
16 *Gunsmoke*. 17 Genghis Khan. 18 *The Big Trail*. 19 John Ford.
20 London. 21 1979 Oscar ceremony. 22 *The Alamo*. 23 *The Searchers*. 24 *Rio Bravo*. 25 *The Shootist*. 26 HIV. 27 His left.
28 *The Green Berets*. 29 Ice Cream. 30 Navy.

152 ✷ DIRECTORS & PRODUCERS

1 Joel. 2 Baz Luhrmann. 3 Clint Eastwood. 4 Director.
5 James Cameron. 6 Cecil B de Mille. 7 Gilbert & Sullivan (Topsy Turvy). 8 Evita. 9 Mel Brooks. 10 Jordan. 11 Rob Reiner. 12 Tokyo. 13 Nora Ephron. 14 Vincente Minnelli. 15 Mike Nichols. 16 Sylvester Stallone. 17 Tim Robbins.
18 Tchaikovsky. 19 *Raging Bull*. 20 Tony and Ridley Scott.
21 Nicole Kidman and Tom Cruise. 22 Penny. 23 Nixon. 24 Richard Attenborough. 25 Quentin Tarantino. 26 *Apollo 13*. 27 Brooklyn.
28 Monty Python's Flying Circus. 29 1970s. 30 Kevin Costner.

153 ✷ SCI-FI

1 Robocop. 2 Carrie Fisher. 3 Arthur C. Clarke.
4 *Planet of the Apes*. 5 Vulcan. 6 2000 A.D.
7 Steven Spielberg. 8 Barbarella. 9 *451*.
10 Superman. 11 Arnold Schwarzenegger. 12 Queen. 13 The Death Star. 14 Peter Jackson. 15 Ants. 16 *The Invisible Man*.
17 David Bowie. 18 *The Omega Man*. 19 Cars. 20 *Logan's Run*.
21 *The Day the Earth*. 22 *Forbidden Planet*. 23 *Scream*.
24 20,000. 25 *Dr Strangelove*. 26 Alec Guinness. 27 *The Night of the Living Dead*. 28 Keanu Reeves. 29 Dale Arden. 30 Spider.

154 ✷ ANIMALS ON SCREEN

1 Seal. 2 Orca (Killer Whale). 3 *Jaws*. 4 *Beethoven's Second*. 5 Dodie Smith. 6 Sharks. 7 Virginia McKenna. 8 *Mule*. 9 Turner and Hooch. 10 Mickey Rooney. 11 Cat. 12 David Duchovny. 13 Otters. 14 Tony.
15 Lassie. 16 Buddy. 17 Three. 18 *Oliver!*. 19 Dog. 20 German Shepherd. 21 Two dogs, one cat. 22 Wendy (Peter Pan).
23 Horse. 24 Cat. 25 *Homeward Bound: The Incredible Journey*. 26 A German Shepherd dog. 27 A spider. 28 Hamm.
29 A bush kangaroo. 30 Cheeta.

155 ✷ MOVIES 2000

1 Ewan McGregor. 2 Spielberg. 3 Penelope Cruz.
4 Helen Hunt. 5 Lara Croft.
6 Egg farm. 7 Ridley Scott. 8 Kathy Burke. 9 Meg Ryan. 10 Erin Brokovich. 11 Pierce Brosnan. 12 Penelope Cruz.
13 Julia Sawalha. 14 *Swordfish*. 15 Thailand. 16 Pistol. 17 Kate Beckinsale. 18 Cats. 19 Mike Myers. 20 Boxing. 21 Jon Voight.
22 Juliette Binoche. 23 Traffic. 24 Albert Finney. 25 Geoffrey Rush. 26 Jurassic Park III. 27 Nicolas Cage. 28 Gemma Jones.
29 Rachel Weisz. 30 Doctor.

156 ✷ PARTNERSHIPS

Eyes Wide Shut. 2 Ewan McGregor. 3 Renny Harlin.
4 Martin Scorsese. 5 Joanne Whalley-Kilmer. 6 *The Misfits*. 7 Ethan Hawke. 8 Tom & Jerry. 9 Tom Cruise.
10 Kelly Preston. 11 Jane Seymour. 12 Kristin Scott Thomas. 13 Rhea Perlman. 14 Charles Bronson. 15 *One Night in the Tropics*. 16 Demi Moore. 17 Jeff & Beau Bridges. 18 Ava Gardner. 19 Whitney Houston.
20 Bogart & Bacall. 21 Paul Simon. 22 Orson Welles. 23 Gwyneth Paltrow. 24 *Camelot*. 25 Diandra. 26 Loewe. 27 The Bridges. 28 Dr Watson. 29 Bud and Lou. 30 Richard Burton and Elizabeth Taylor.

157 ✷ SILENT CINEMA

1 Harold Lloyd. 2 Mack Sennett. 3 Paulette Goddard.
4 Garbo. 5 Lillian Gish. 6 *Son of the Sheikh*. 7 Cecil B. de Mille. 8 *The Mark of Zorro*. 9 Buster Keaton. 10 1926.
11 Chaplin's hat and cane. 12 Clara Bow. 13 Mary Pickford. 14 Matador.
15 *The Big Parade*. 16 *What Price Glory?* 17 A colour sequence.
18 Edna Purviance. 19 Mabel Normand. 20 British government.
21 D. W. Griffith. 22 Noel Coward. 23 Douglas Fairbanks. 24 Wings.
25 Argentinian. 26 Young Cedric and his mother. 27 Roscoe. 28 Gloria Swanson. 29 Janet Gaynor. 30 Transatlantic liners.

158 ✷ '50S FILMS

1 *Giant*. 2 St Swithin's. 3 Robert Morley. 4 Kim Novak.
5 *Darby O'Gill and the Little People*. 6 Richard Burton.
7 George Cole. 8 Danny Kaye. 9 Mount Rushmore.
10 *Carry On Nurse*. 11 *Operation Petticoat*. 12 Dorothy Dandridge.
13 George Sanders. 14 *High Noon*. 15 Mike Todd. 16 *Viva Zapata!*.
17 Jack Lemmon. 18 *Anastasia*. 19 *The Trouble with Harry*. 20 *The Swan*. 21 Yul Brynner. 22 *No Way Out*. 23 1915. 24 *The Long Hot Summer*. 25 "Bewitched, Bothered and Bewildered". 26 *Green Grow the Rushes*. 27 William Wyler. 28 Yves Montand. 29 Larry Adler.
30 Judy Garland.

159 ✷ DISASTER MOVIES

1 264. 2 Hart Bochner. 3 Alfred Newman. 4 Ronald Neame.
5 Roger Simmons. 6 Alfred E. Green. 7 Jerry Bruckheimer.
8 On the beach. 9 Salvage hunter. 10 Industrial Light and Magic. 11 Ron Howard. 12 Elizabeth Hoffman. 13 158 mins. 14 Jonathon Hensleigh. 15 Philip Lathrop. 16 Arthur Herzog. 17 Corey Allen. 18 New York to New Jersey tunnel. 19 Laurence Rosenthal. 20 McCallum.
21 Spencer Tracy. 22 Max Catto. 23 Special effects. 24 Michael M. Mooney's. 25 Fox & MGM (Towering Inferno). 26 2008. 27 A volcano.
28 *Chain Reaction*. 29 *Final Destination*. 30 Robert Downey Jnr.

160 ✷ BEST OF BRITISH

1 Sir Ian McKellen. 2 *Lion in Winter*. 3 Rufus.
4 Brigitte Bardot. 5 Mike Newell. 6 Kind Hearts and Coronets. 7 Killing Fields. 8 Talbot Rothwell. 9 *Prime of Miss Jean Brodie*. 10 *Don't Lose Your Head*. 11 *Lavender Hill Mob*. 12 *Room with a View*. 13 I'm All Right Jack. 14 *Oliver!*
15 Lewis Gilbert. 16 *Third Man*. 17 Turin. 18 Harmonica. 19 Christy Brown. 20 Martita Hunt. 21 *84 Charing Cross Road*. 22 Gordon John Sinclair. 23 Italy, China. 24 *Oh, Mr Porter!* 25 Richard Briers.
26 Lauri Peters. 27 Peter Finch, Glenda Jackson, Murray Head.
28 How I Learned to Stop Worrying and Love the Bomb. 29 Albert Finney. 30 *Gandhi*.

161 ✳ '60S FILMS 2

1 *Doctor Dolittle*. 2 Bryan Forbes. 3 New York & Paris. 4 John Ford. 5 Kenneth Williams. 6 David Bailey. 7 He has no dialogue. 8 When Dinosaurs Ruled the Earth. 9 Gillian Lynne. 10 George Segal. 11 Peter Cushing. 12 *Brief Encounter*. 13 Claudia Cardinale. 14 Joseph Mankiewicz. 15 Jimmy Bryant. 16 Maurice Jarre. 17 *A Walk with Love and Death*. 18 Stoke Poges. 19 *Guess Who's Coming to Dinner*. 20 Jess Conrad. 21 Gregory Peck. 22 Tom Courtenay. 23 *Tom Jones*. 24 Lee Marvin. 25 Big Sam. 26 *Who's Afraid of Virginia Woolf?*. 27 Ratso Rizzo. 28 Corin. 29 Rod Steiger. 30 Katharine Hepburn.

162 ✳ TOM CRUISE

1 3rd July. 2 Left-handed. 3 Thomas Cruise Mapother IV. 4 Cole. 5 Lionel Richie ("Endless Love"). 6 18. 7 Father Sky. 8 *Eyes Wide Shut* (Stanley Kubrick). 9 Francis Ford Coppola. 10 Jerry Maguire. 11 Song ("Take My Breath Away"). 12 Ron Kovic (*Born on the Fourth of July*). 13 Rebecca De Mornay. 14 *The Color of Money*. 15 Salesman. 16 Mimi Rogers. 17 Syracuse, New York. 18 Franciscan monastery. 19 Anne Rice (Interview with the Vampire). 20 Least Likely to Succeed. 21 *Taps*. 22 *Fallen Angels*. 23 *Cocktail*. 24 Mission: Impossible. 25 *Far and Away*. 26 Three. 27 Suri. 28 Mimi Rogers. 29 United Artists. 30 A Catholic priest.

163 ✳ HOLLYWOOD HEYDAY

1 MGM. 2 All-white cinema. 3 John Wayne. 4 Shirley Williams. 5 Claude Rains. 6 *All About Eve*. 7 Rejected for Rick in *Casablanca* (White House). 8 *The African Queen*. 9 Salvador Dali. 10 Clark Gable. 11 *Top Hat*. 12 To Have and to Have Not. 13 42nd Street. 14 *Yankee Doodle Dandy*. 15 Lon Chaney. 16 *High Noon*. 17 *Sergeant York*. 18 Joan Crawford. 19 *Treasure of the Sierra Madre*. 20 Charles (Foster). 21 Mountain. 22 *Stagecoach*. 23 Archie Leach. 24 *Babes in Arms*. 25 Jack, Harry, Samuel, Albert. 26 Elwood. 27 War relief. 28 Ray Milland. 29 Wyatt Earp. 30 *Double Indemnity*.

164 ✳ MUSICAL MOVIES

1 Barbra Streisand. 2 Judy Garland. 3 *Jesus Christ Superstar*. 4 Judy Garland. 5 Lydia. 6 "The Last Time I Saw Paris". 7 Dashiel Hammett. 8 *Annie Get Your Gun*. 9 Baz Luhrmann. 10 Danny Zuko. 11 DIY store. 12 Salzburg. 13 Phil Collins. 14 Kevin Bacon. 15 Barbra Streisand. 16 *American Graffiti*. 17 Mr Mushnik. 18 Pittsburgh. 19 Paul Michael Glaser. 20 Susan Sarandon. 21 Jerome Robbins. 22 Kentucky. 23 *Beauty & the Beast*. 24 Diahnne Abbott. 25 "Chim Chim Cheree". 26 *Beauty & the Beast*. 27 *Oklahoma!* 28 Bob Spiers. 29 Olsen. 30 US Literature.

165 ✳ MUSIC ON FILM

1 Anthony Hopkins. 2 David Bowie. 3 Johnny Horton. 4 Rachel Portman. 5 Magnolia. 6 Sting, Gene Ammons & Roberta Flack. 7 Jam Session. 8 *All That Money Can Buy*. 9 Maurice Jarre. 10 *Jazz Suite No. 2*. 11 Frankie Lymon's. 12 Miklos Rozsa. 13 Monos Hadjidakis. 14 Ravel's *Bolero*. 15 Bruce Springsteen & Neil Young's. 16 Peggy Lee & Sonny Burke. 17 Gabriel Yared. 18 Jack Lemmon. 19 *Tootsie*. 20 George Harrison. 21 Sean Lennon. 22 Bob Dylan's. 23 Anton Karas's. 24 Miklos Rozsa. 25 Stravinsky's *Rite of Spring*. 26 Benny Andersson. 27 Prague. 28 Gustavo A. Santaolalla. 29 Alfred Newman. 30 Max Steiner.

166 ✳ CHARLIE CHAPLIN

1 Lambeth. 2 Sydney. 3 Clog dancing. 4 Fred Karno. 5 Keystone. 6 Jackie Coogan. 7 *The Gold Rush*. 8 Paulette Goddard. 9 Four. 10 *The Great Dictator*. 11 Claire Bloom. 12 Music. 13 *A Countess from Hong Kong*. 14 Buster Keaton. 15 He never mentions her. 16 Eugene O'Neill. 17 Oona. 18 United Artists. 19 Sam Goldwyn. 20 Michael. 21 *Limelight*. 22 *Kid Auto Races at Venice*. 23 Geraldine. 24 Beat him to the first-ever Oscar. 25 Switzerland. 26 Knighthood. 27 Music score. 28 Christmas Day. 29 Coffin stolen. 30 Ian McShane and Twiggy.

167 ✳ '70S FILMS

1 *Quadrophenia*. 2 Kramer. 3 *Blazing Saddles*. 4 MGM. 5 Anthony Hopkins. 6 Ravel's Bolero. 7 *Bugsy Malone*. 8 Michael Douglas. 9 *Myra Breckinridge*. 10 Robert Shaw. 11 Orson Welles. 12 Isaac Hayes. 13 John Reginald Christie. 14 Maurice Chevalier. 15 *Frenzy*. 16 Marlon Brando. 17 Michael Winner. 18 Spielberg (*The Sugarland Express*). 19 Lilian Hellman. 20 He died shortly after it was made. 21 Beethoven. 22 Louise Fletcher. 23 Jason Robards. 24 The Kit Kat Club. 25 Gary Warren. 26 Audrey Hepburn. 27 *McCabe and Mrs Miller*. 28 *Death on the Nile*. 29 *Oliver's Story*. 30 *The Odessa File*.

168 ✳ HORROR

1 Bela Lugosi. 2 Summer Isle. 3 Corey Haim. 4 TV horror film host. 5 Bodega Bay. 6 Return of the Fly. 7 The Arctic. 8 Lon Chaney. 9 Manhattan. 10 George A. Romero. 11 Property developer. 12 Stephen Hopkins. 13 His body is struck by lightning. 14 Billy. 15 *Seizure*. 16 Ellen Burstyn. 17 Daryl Hannah. 18 John Williams. 19 110 minutes. 20 Friday the 13th. 21 The right hand of Christopher Hart. 22 He did not speak. 23 Ants. 24 Joseph Losey. 25 Neil Jordan. 26 Vincent Price. 27 Seven. 28 *Le Manoir du Diable (The House of the Devil)*. 29 Lon Chaney. 30 Universal Pictures Co. Inc.

169 ✳ SUPERSTARS

1 *The Hustler, The Color of Money*. 2 Ron Kovic. 3 Jodie Foster. 4 Tom Hanks. 5 Warren Beatty, Dustin Hoffman. 6 *Dangerous Liaisons*. 7 Burt Reynolds. 8 *Sophie's Choice*. 9 Vicki Vale. 10 Jack Rosenthal. 11 Pearl Slaghoople. 12 *Midnight Madness*. 13 Richard Gere. 14 Goldie Hawn. 15 Warren Beatty. 16 *Kotch*. 17 *A Beautiful Mind*. 18 Billy Crystal. 19 Tony Curtis. 20 Sean Connery. 21 Glenn Close. 22 Dustin Hoffman. 23 Demi Moore. 24 Jim Garrison. 25 Randall Patrick McMurphy. 26 George Clooney. 27 Mel Gibson. 28 Walter Matthau. 29 Danny De Vito. 30 Herself.

170 ✳ '80S FILMS 2

1 Duke of Roxburghe's. 2 *Stardust Memories*. 3 Macaulay Culkin. 4 *A View to a Kill*. 5 Piano teacher. 6 Denholm Elliott. 7 Hans Gruber. 8 Helene Hanff & Frank Doel. 9 Sean Lennon. 10 *The Shining*. 11 Cathy Moriarty. 12 *Heaven's Gate*. 13 David Niven. 14 Tracey Ullman. 15 Ben Kingsley. 16 Marquise de Merteuil. 17 *Tootsie*. 18 Haing S. Ngor. 19 Oliver Stone. 20 Oprah Winfrey. 21 Catherine Oxenberg. 22 *The Hustler*. 23 Martin & Charlie Sheen. 24 Otto. 25 Olympia Dukakis. 26 Sound. 27 Anthony Perkins. 28 Harry Connick Jr. 29 John Reed's. 30 Jamie Lee Curtis.

171 ✷ HUMPHREY BOGART

1 DeForest. **2** Surgeon. **3** *Leviathan.* **4** *Broadway's Like That.* **5** Alexander Woollcott. **6** 28. **7** Mary Philips. **8** Captain Queeg. **9** Warner Brothers. **10** Duke Mantee. **11** John Huston. **12** *Virginia City.* **13** George Raft. **14** Leslie Howard. **15** *The Treasure of the Sierra Madre.* **16** *Casablanca.* **17** General Sternwood (Charles Waldron). **18** *To Have And Have Not.* **19** *The Maltese Falcon.* **20** Santana Pictures. **21** *High Sierra.* **22** Katharine Hepburn. **23** *The Harder They Fall.* **24** Vivian Sherwood Rutledge. **25** The Big Sleep. **26** 57. **27** Ava Gardner. **28** *The Amazing Dr Clitterhouse.* **29** *The Two Mrs Carrolls.* **30** *The African Queen.*

172 ✷ TOUGH GUYS

1 Ray Liotta.. **2** Lee Van Cleef. **3** We were Soldiers. **4** Gert Frobe. **5** Medicine. **6** Steve Guttenberg. **7** Harvey Keitel. **8** Richard Gere. **9** The Blob. **10** Max Cady. **11** Gene Hackman. **12** *Sands of Iwo Jima.* **13** Charles Bronson. **14** James Cagney. **15** Clint Eastwood. **16** *Patriot Games, Clear and Present Danger.* **17** Ronald Reagan. **18** The Austrian Oak. **19** Duke Mantee. **20** *Mean Streets.* **21** James Cameron. **22** *In the Heat of the Night.* **23** *Bananas.* **24** *Drum Beat.* **25** Britt. **26** *The Public Enemy.* **27** A pregnant man. **28** Terry Molloy. **29** Kirk Douglas. **30** *First Blood.*

173 ✷ WHO'S WHO?

1 Meryl Streep. **2** Ellen Burstyn. **3** The Kids. **4** Cape Town. **5** Bucharest. **6** Mickey Rourke. **7** Charles Bronson. **8** Anouk Aimee. **9** Kevin Kline. **10** George Peppard. **11** Debbie Reynolds. **12** David Carradine. **13** Nicholas Roeg. **14** Dennis Hopper. **15** Simone Signoret. **16** Emma Thompson. **17** Andrew. **18** Jamie Lee Curtis. **19** Tom Selleck. **20** Uma Thurman. **21** Ewan McGregor. **22** Rip Torn. **23** The birthdates of his children. **24** Shirley Maclean Beaty. **25** Derek Jacobi. **26** Michael Caine. **27** Carl Haas. **28** Mark Wahlberg. **29** Lillian Gish. **30** Cameron Diaz.

174 ✷ '90S FILMS 2

1 *Wag the Dog.* **2** Francis Bacon. **3** Arnold Schwarzenegger. **4** River Phoenix. **5** Spanish Civil War. **6** Jean-Claude Van Damme. **7** *That Thing You Do!.* **8** *Pretty Woman.* **9** Seal. **10** Ellen Barkin. **11** Frank Drebin. **12** Banker. **13** Julia Roberts. **14** Kevin Kline. **15** Blue Sky. **16** Kennedy & Nixon. **17** James Earl Jones. **18** Abba. **19** Kirsty Alley. **20** *Nine Months.* **21** Emma Thompson. **22** Elizabeth Taylor. **23** Kevin McCallister. **24** Jim Carrey , who played The Riddler. **25** Ron Shelton. **26** *Jude.* **27** Christopher Walken. **28** Gonzo. **29** *Nil by Mouth.* **30** *2000 AD.*

175 ✷ AROUND ENGLAND

1 Rivers. **2** Cumbria. **3** Birmingham. **4** Victoria. **5** Essex. **6** Yorkshire. **7** Blackpool. **8** Zoo. **9** The Minster. **10** Isle of Wight. **11** A city. **12** Thames. **13** Southport. **14** English Channel. **15** National Exhibition Centre. **16** The Potteries. **17** Manchester. **18** M6. **19** Northeast. **20** Liverpool. **21** Oxford. Cambridge. **22** Pennines. **23** Dartmoor. **24** Cars. **25** Isle of Man. **26** Stonehenge. **27** Shakespeare's. **28** Kent. **29** One. **30** Rutland.

176 ✷ AROUND THE UK

1 East. **2** Aberdonian. **3** East. **4** A1. **5** Cheddar. **6** Bedfordshire. **7** Blackpool. **8** Balmoral. **9** Scotland. **10** Hospital. **11** Red. **12** Glasgow. **13** M3. **14** Isle of Wight. **15** England. **16** Norfolk. **17** Liverpool. **18** M4. **19** Medical profession. **20** Heathrow. **21** Cornwall. **22** Red. **23** M62. **24** Brown. **25** Wales. **26** Hampshire. **27** Birmingham. **28** Cumbria. **29** Rose. **30** London.

177 ✷ AROUND THE WORLD

1 Spain. **2** Persian Gulf. **3** France. **4** Los Angeles. **5** Brazil. **6** Liverpool. **7** Lizard. **8** China. **9** Cumbria. **10** Britain. **11** Berwick-upon-Tweed. **12** West. **13** Soviet. **14** Switzerland. **15** Indonesia. **16** Sri Lanka. **17** South Africa. **18** Canary Islands. **19** Greece. **20** Florida. **21** Atlantic. **22** Holland. **23** Monaco. **24** Alaska. **25** Legoland. **26** Niagara. **27** Japan. **28** Pacific. **29** France. **30** Motorway.

178 ✷ AROUND THE WORLD 2

1 Southern. **2** A state. **3** Spain. **4** Ireland. **5** India. **6** South America. **7** Himalayas. **8** Luxembourg. **9** Red. **10** Italy. **11** Holland. **12** New Zealand. **13** Norway. **14** South Africa. **15** Turkey. **16** Rome. **17** Mountain. **18** China. **19** Iraq. **20** Thailand. **21** Atlantic. **22** Belgium. **23** Menai Strait. **24** Gibraltar. **25** Isle of Man. **26** Sri Lanka. **27** Mediterranean. **28** Pacific. **29** Greenland. **30** Africa.

179 ✷ AROUND EUROPE

1 Spain. **2** Hovercraft. **3** Mediterranean. **4** Germany. **5** London. **6** Belgium. **7** Switzerland. **8** Athens. **9** Czech Republic. **10** Airport. **11** Capri. **12** Germany. **13** Principality. **14** Spain. **15** Mediterranean. **16** USSR. **17** Venice. **18** Kingdom. **19** Danube. **20** Balearics. **21** Arctic Circle. **22** Netherlands. **23** Greece. **24** Denmark. **25** Second smallest. **26** Portugal. **27** Spain. **28** Paris. **29** Mountain ranges. **30** Corsica.

180 ✷ HOLIDAY DESTINATIONS

1 Spain. **2** Portugal. **3** Pacific. **4** South. **5** Balearics. **6** Spain. **7** Cromer. **8** Pacific. **9** Sicily. **10** Bali. **11** Blue. **12** Gibraltar. **13** Pacific. **14** Malta. **15** Queensland. **16** Canaries. **17** France. **18** Scotland. **19** Egypt. **20** Greek. **21** Friendly Islands. **22** Bondi beach. **23** Germany. **24** Honolulu. **25** Capri. **26** River Arno. **27** Sydney. **28** Malta. **29** Turkey. **30** Florida.

181 ✳ AROUND SCOTLAND

1 East. 2 John o' Groat's. 3 Edinburgh. 4 Yes. 5 Hadrian. 6 St Andrews. 7 Whisky. 8 Balmoral. 9 Highland Games. 10 Skiing. 11 Mountains. 12 Aberdeen. 13 Shetland. 14 Ness. 15 Skye. 16 Kintyre. 17 Clyde. 18 Edinburgh. 19 Haggis. 20 Gretna Green. 21 Lake. 22 Ben Nevis. 23 Dundee. 24 Perth. 25 Tweed. 26 North Sea. 27 Valley. 28 Glasgow. 29 Dundee. 30 St Andrew.

182 ✳ ON THE MAP

1 French. 2 Iraq. 3 Greece. 4 Clacton. 5 Africa. 6 Ireland. 7 Motorway. 8 Persian Gulf. 9 Canada. 10 Luxembourg. 11 Yugoslavia. 12 Nepal. 13 Wellington. 14 Rhine. 15 Japan. 16 Prime Minister. 17 M6. 18 Europe. 19 London. 20 Sicily. 21 Europe. 22 M25. 23 Europe. 24 Iceland. 25 Florida. 26 Thames. 27 Italy. 28 Island. 29 Moscow. 30 Israel.

183 ✳ AROUND IRELAND

1 Liffey. 2 Knock. 3 Post Office. 4 Boyne. 5 Atlantic. 6 Lagan. 7 Cork. 8 Dublin Bay Prawn. 9 None. 10 Lough Neagh. 11 Book of Kells. 12 Meath. 13 Corrib. 14 Derry. 15 President. 16 Trout. 17 Shopping. 18 Mountains of Mourne. 19 Tweed. 20 North. 21 Liverpool. 22 Atlantic. 23 Kilkenny. 24 Belfast. 25 Enniskillen. 26 Apple. 27 O'Connell Street. 28 Shannon. 29 Patrick Street. 30 North.

184 ✳ AROUND THE WORLD 3

1 Alps. 2 Greenland. 3 Weston. 4 Africa. 5 Great Lakes. 6 Tropic of Cancer. 7 Tasmania. 8 Vietnam. 9 Spain. 10 Hampton Court. 11 Isle of Man. 12 England. 13 Hawaii. 14 German. 15 Lancashire. 16 Victoria. 17 Dogger Bank. 18 Cornwall. 19 Channel Islands. 20 Europe. 21 East Anglia. 22 Northern. 23 Grand Canyon. 24 River Thames. 25 North. 26 America. 27 India. 28 United Kingdom. 29 Italy. 30 Land's End.

185 ✳ AROUND THE WORLD 4

1 Nile. 2 Pope. 3 West. 4 Afghanistan. 5 Bombay. 6 Abominable. 7 Australia. 8 Southern. 9 India. 10 Peru. 11 Caribbean. 12 Zimbabwe. 13 Suez. 14 Coast. 15 Pacific. 16 South Africa. 17 Abraham Lincoln. 18 Arizona. 19 Australia. 20 Sahara. 21 Monarchy. 22 Africa. 23 Danube. 24 Atlantic. 25 Iran. 26 Arctic Circle. 27 Southern. 28 Hungary. 29 China. 30 Canada.

186 ✳ ON THE MAP 2

1 England. 2 Mountain. 3 Bath. 4 Suez Canal. 5 Downing Street. 6 America. 7 Canterbury. 8 They're not surrounded by water. 9 Norwich. 10 K2. 11 The Cenotaph. 12 Belgium. 13 Washington DC. 14 Ayers Rock. 15 Halifax. 16 Munich. 17 Hadrian's Wall. 18 Red. 19 The Queen Mother. 20 Antarctica. 21 New South Wales. 22 Japan. 23 Sicily. 24 Midlands. 25 Niagara. 26 Paris. 27 Arab. 28 Holland. 29 Sandwich. 30 Mediterranean.

187 ✳ AROUND WALES

1 Snowdon. 2 Dylan Thomas. 3 Irish Sea. 4 Mountains. 5 Anglesey. 6 Daffodil. 7 Cardiff. 8 Bristol Channel. 9 North. 10 Cheese. 11 Dragon. 12 Swansea. 13 Rugby. 14 Tiger. 15 Coal. 16 Prince Charles. 17 Leek. 18 England. 19 St David. 20 Snowdonia. 21 Cardigan. 22 Glamorgan. 23 Pound sterling. 24 Sheep. 25 John Redwood. 26 Clwyd. 27 Menai Strait. 28 Bangor. 29 Severn. 30 Swansea.

188 ✳ AROUND THE UK 2

1 North. 2 Airports. 3 Yorkshire. 4 Dartmoor. 5 Wales. 6 The Prime Minister. 7 Dumfries. 8 Eastbourne. 9 Thames. 10 Rutland. 11 Northern Ireland. 12 Dorset. 13 Manchester. 14 Metropolitan Police. 15 Robin Hood. 16 Meat. 17 North east. 18 School/College. 19 The Queen. 20 Snowdon. 21 Soho. 22 Essex. 23 West. 24 Birmingham. 25 London. 26 Hotel. 27 Scotland. 28 Cathedral. 29 Soldiers. 30 Wigan Athletic.

189 ✳ AROUND EUROPE 2

1 Iceland. 2 Sardinia. 3 Danube. 4 Mayle. 5 Athens. 6 Mont Blanc. 7 Horizontally. 8 North Sea. 9 Drachma. 10 Paris. 11 Arctic. 12 Pyrenees. 13 Turkey. 14 Krone. 15 Luxembourg. 16 Blue and white. 17 Rome. 18 Estonia. 19 The Algarve. 20 Valetta. 21 Urals. 22 Schilling. 23 Germany. 24 Italy. 25 White. 26 Mediterranean. 27 Rhine, Rhone. 28 Brittany. 29 Bulgaria. 30 Finland.

190 ✳ AROUND THE WORLD 5

1 Spain. 2 India and Pakistan. 3 Northumberland. 4 Peking. 5 Buckingham Palace. 6 Austria. 7 Devon. 8 Red. 9 Derbyshire. 10 Italy. 11 Africa. 12 West. 13 Argentina. 14 Paris. 15 Portugal. 16 Algeria. 17 Scafell Pike. 18 Scotland. 19 Oslo. 20 Africa. 21 Netherlands. 22 Florida. 23 France. 24 Birmingham. 25 Washington. 26 Pacific. 27 Brazil. 28 Europe. 29 Sweden. 30 Belgium.

191 ✹ AROUND EUROPE 3

1 Dublin. 2 Danish. 3 Dunkirk. 4 Dublin. 5 Greece.
6 Mediterranean. 7 Winter sports. 8 Rome.
9 Portugal. 10 Italy. 11 France. 12 Czechoslovakia.
13 Paris. 14 Switzerland. 15 Mountains. 16 West. 17 Spain.
18 Car. 19 Limerick. 20 Munich. 21 France. 22 Lisbon.
23 Brussels. 24 Berlin. 25 Spain. 26 France. 27 Hungary.
28 Ireland. 29 Arctic. 30 North.

192 ✹ AROUND THE WORLD 6

1 Virgin. 2 Switzerland. 3 Texas. 4 Salt. 5 South
America. 6 New York. 7 Eskimo. 8 Rockies.
9 Africa. 10 Delhi. 11 Russian. 12 Amazon river.
13 Rhodesia. 14 Oil. 15 America. 16 Europe. 17 Africa. 18 South
Africa. 19 New York. 20 Canal. 21 Canaries. 22 Long. 23 Cars.
24 Louisiana. 25 Australia. 26 Northwest. 27 Canada. 28 Cote
d'Ivoire. 29 Sydney. 30 Africa.

193 ✹ AROUND IRELAND 2

1 Liffey. 2 County Down. 3 Irish Sea. 4 Belfast.
5 Emerald Isle. 6 Shamrock. 7 Dublin. 8 Belfast.
9 Limerick. 10 Whiskey. 11 Atlantic. 12 Irish and
English. 13 Crystal. 14 Galway. 15 Blarney Stone. 16 Kildare.
17 Horse racing. 18 Linen. 19 Patrick. 20 Whiskey and cream.
21 Tweed. 22 East. 23 Ferry ports. 24 Dublin. 25 Air.
26 Londonderry. 27 Cork. 28 Giant's Causeway. 29 Guinness.
30 IRL.

194 ✹ AROUND THE WORLD 7

1 Perth. 2 Beijing. 3 Emus don't fly.
4 Mediterranean. 5 South Africa. 6 Bay of Biscay.
7 Bulgarian. 8 Italy. 9 East Germany.
10 Jerusalem. 11 South. 12 Seven. 13 Italy. 14 Casablanca.
15 Germany. 16 Cocaine. 17 Nile. 18 Barcelona. 19 Colchester.
20 Jodhpurs. 21 France and Spain. 22 Japan. 23 Africa.
24 Paris. 25 Victoria. 26 Arizona. 27 Estonia. 28 Qatar.
29 America. 30 Rupee.

195 ✹ AROUND THE WORLD 8

1 Austria. 2 Sirocco. 3 Vancouver. 4 USA. 5 Indian.
6 Texas. 7 Ecuador. 8 Las Malvinas. 9 Harvard.
10 States with and without slavery. 11 China (16).
12 Florida. 13 Northern Territory. 14 The Zambesi.
15 Tanganyika, Zanzibar. 16 St Lawrence. 17 Fort Knox.
18 Vietnam. 19 Moscow. 20 Rio Grande. 21 New York.
22 Bechuanaland. 23 Venezuela. 24 Ellis Island. 25 K2.
26 Istanbul. 27 Texas. 28 Argentina. 29 Canaries. 30 McKinley.

196 ✹ AROUND THE WORLD 9

1 Greenland. 2 Indonesia. 3 Argentina.
4 California. 5 Gulf of Finland. 6 Casablanca.
7 Two. 8 Azerbaijan. 9 Bejing. 10 North Africa.
11 Cairo. 12 Manhattan. 13 Saigon. 14 Hawaii. 15 Tigris.
16 Brooklyn. 17 Andes. 18 Cape Horn. 19 Bass. 20 Click.
21 Indonesia. 22 Jodhpur. 23 Johannesburg. 24 Atlantic.
25 Bronx. 26 Iran. 27 Costa Rica. 28 China. 29 Indian.
30 Barbados.

197 ✹ ON THE MAP 4

1 Bali. 2 San Andreas Fault. 3 Andes. 4 California.
5 Iceland. 6 Romania. 7 Archipelago. 8 Brown.
9 St Vincent. 10 Hobart. 11 Mountain. 12
Edinburgh. 13 Winchester. 14 Belize. 15 Zambesi. 16 Channel
Islands. 17 Venezuela. 18 Columbus. 19 Bury St Edmunds.
20 Romney. 21 Canada. 22 St Paul's. 23 Cemetery. 24 Sudan.
25 North. 26 Parliament Square. 27 Yorkshire Dales.
28 Scotland (Highland Region). 29 Parishes. 30 Don.

198 ✹ AROUND THE UNITED STATES

1 Arkansas. 2 Mount Rushmore. 3 Spanish.
4 Earthquakes. 5 District of Columbia.
6 Charlottesville. 7 Arizona. 8 New England.
9 Chicago. 10 Delaware. 11 Cape Canaveral. 12 Chicago. 13 500
miles. 14 New Orleans. 15 Montana. 16 Divorce. 17 New York.
18 California. 19 Bronx, Brooklyn. 20 Florida. 21 Hawaii.
22 Fifth Avenue. 23 Ohio. 24 Gold. 25 Wheat. 26 Detroit.
27 Manhattan. 28 Japanese. 29 Oklahoma. 30 Nashville.

199 ✹ AROUND EUROPE 4

1 Rome. 2 Elysée Palace. 3 Corsica. 4 Porcelain.
5 Montmartre. 6 Luxembourg. 7 Balearics. 8 Seine.
9 Dublin. 10 Zugspitze. 11 Arno. 12 Malta.
13 Germany (six). 14 Paris. 15 Portugal. 16 Three. 17 Pyrenees.
18 Athens. 19 Italy. 20 Nantes. 21 Hungary. 22 Denmark.
23 North Sea. 24 Sweden. 25 Spain. 26 Slovenia. 27 Czech
Republic. 28 The Netherlands. 29 Monaco. 30 Crete.

200 ✹ POP MUSIC PLACES

1 The River Thames. 2 Cambodia. 3 California.
4 San Francisco. 5 Amsterdam. 6 Japan. 7 Dionne
Warwick. 8 New York. 9 Toto. 10 Tina Turner.
11 Roger Whittaker. 12 Glen Campbell. 13 American Idiot.
14 Moscow. 15 Caribbean. 16 Bon Jovi. 17 Philadelphia.
18 Tahiti. 19 Mississippi. 20 Mott the Hoople. 21 The Clash.
22 Twenty-four. 23 Tony Christie. 24 Dakota. 25 Barbados.
26 Liverpool. 27 Madonna. 28 Elton John. 29 Georgia. 30 Bruce
Springsteen.

201 ❋ AROUND THE UK 3

1 Four. **2** Portsmouth. **3** The Guild Hall.
4 Tobermory. **5** Sark. **6** Anglesey. **7** Cambridge.
Lloyd's of London. **9** Scillies. **10** Cheviots.
11 Glasgow. **12** Irish Sea. Buckinghamshire. **14** York Minster.
15 Solway Firth. **16** Coventry. **17** Melton Mowbray. **18** The Backs.
19 Derbyshire. **20** Ermine Street. **21** Lytham St Annes.
22 Parkhurst. **23** Grosvenor Square. **24** The Great Fire of
London. **25** The Solent. **26** Windsor. **27** Southend. **28** Downing
Street. **29** Mermaid. **30** Northumberland.

202 ❋ AROUND THE UK 4

1 St Paul's. **2** (near) Birmingham. **3** Charing Cross.
4 Mendips. **5** Chelmsford. **6** Battersea. **7** Severn.
8 Canterbury. **9** Autumn. **10** All Saints.
11 England/Scotland. **12** Cumbria. **13** Buckinghamshire.
14 Middlesbrough. **15** Staffa. **16** Beaulieu. **17** Shipping.
18 Gloucestershire. **19** Angel of the North. **20** Gatwick.
21 Goodwood. **22** Bath. **23** South Kensington. **24** Guildford.
25 Cambridge. **26** Kingston Upon Hull. **27** Inverness.
28 Greenwich. **29** GCHQ. **30** Threadneedle Street.

203 ❋ AROUND AUSTRALIA

1 Sydney. **2** Great Barrier Reef. **3** Ayers Rock or Uluru.
4 Canberra. **5** Pacific and Indian. **6** Bondi Beach. **7** The
Northern Territory. **8** Botany Bay. **9** Brisbane river.
10 Queensland. **11** Western Australia. **12** The Blue Mountains.
13 Alice Springs. **14** Melbourne. **15** Wave Rock. **16** The Gold Coast.
17 Kakadu National Park. **18** Kuranda, Queensland. **19** Fraser Island.
20 Cairns. **21** Great Dividing Range. **22** Surfers' Paradise. **23** Cape
Tribulation. **24** Perth. **25** The Bungle Bungle Range. **26** The Twelve
Apostles. **27** Mount Bartle Frere. **28** Adelaide. **29** The Pinnacles.
30 Cape York.

204 ❋ AROUND EUROPE 5

1 Cork. **2** Porcelain. **3** Paris. **4** Cephallonia.
5 Chamonix. **6** Channel Islands. **7** Connacht
(Connaught). **8** Danish. **9** Finland. **10** Estonia.
11 Black Forest. **12** Arc de Triomphe. **13** Sangatte. **14** Paris.
15 Innsbruck. **16** Greece. **17** Kattegat. **18** Mediterranean.
19 Kerry blue. **20** Madrid. **21** Magenta. **22** Stock Exchange.
23 Black. **24** Portugal. **25** Barcelona. **26** Estonia. **27** Leningrad.
28 North Sea. **29** Munich. **30** Pyrenees.

205 ❋ AROUND SCOTLAND 2

1 Distillery. **2** Sir Walter Scott. **3** Southwest.
4 Extinct volcano. **5** Bird sanctuary. **6** St Giles
Cathedral. **7** Bute. **8** Holyrood House. **9** Aberdeen.
10 Nuclear power. **11** Two. **12** Princes Street. **13** Glamis Castle.
14 Silicon Glen. **15** Caledonian Canal. **16** Iona. **17** Meadowbank.
18 Tay Bridge. **19** Bell's. **20** Blair Castle. **21** Fingal's Cave.
22 Scone Palace. **23** Loch Ness. **24** Perth. **25** Culloden. **26** Dee.
27 Abbeys. **28** Stone Age. **29** Loch Lomond. **30** Tomatin.

206 ❋ AROUND THE WORLD 10

1 Atlantic. **2** Las Vegas. **3** Broadway. **4** Inuit
(Eskimos). **5** Cape of Good Hope. **6** Wind.
7 Honshu. **8** Australia. **9** China. **10** K2.
11 Okovango. **12** Indian. **13** Hawaii. **14** China. **15** Namibia.
16 Gobi. **17** Dow Jones. **18** Eskimo. **19** Michigan. **20** Zambia and
Zimbabwe. **21** Trinidad. **22** French. **23** Canaries. **24** North coast
of Africa. **25** Manhattan. **26** Tip of South America. **27** Greenland.
28 Kilimanjaro. **29** Israel. **30** Pakistan & Afghanistan.

207 ❋ AROUND ASIA

1 Burma. **2** Fiji. **3** Gobi. **4** King. **5** Philippines.
6 Taiwan. **7** Indonesia. **8** North and South Korea.
9 East Pakistan. **10** Malaysia. **11** Coral.
12 Cambodia. **13** Caspian. **14** Mount Fujiyama. **15** One.
16 India. **17** Terracotta. **18** Mongolia's. **19** India and Pakistan.
20 Caste system. **21** Nepal. **22** Siberia. **23** Music. **24** English,
French and Creole. **25** Singapore. **26** Bangladesh. **27** Solomon
Islands. **28** Saigon. **29** Thailand. **30** None.

208 ❋ ON THE MAP 5

1 Rio de Janeiro. **2** Australia & Tasmania. **3** Cairo.
4 Camp David. **5** Martha's Vineyard. **6** Between
East and West Berlin. **7** Florida. **8** Israel & Jordan.
9 Iraq. **10** Nile. **11** Chicago. **12** North Sea. **13** Mount Fujiyama.
14 Ecuador. **15** Andes. **16** Death Valley. **17** Grosvenor. **18** New
York. **19** Cape Town. **20** Mediterranean. **21** Mid, South, West.
22 Colorado. **23** Goa. **24** Europe & Asia. **25** Honolulu.
26 Camden. **27** Chile. **28** The Hague. **29** Israel & Syria.
30 Atlantic.

209 ❋ AROUND AFRICA

1 Zamia, Zimbabwe. **2** Sahara Desert. **3** Ethiopia.
4 Organization of African Unity. **5** Burkina Faso.
6 A wind. **7** Uganda. **8** Namibia. **9** Cocoa.
10 Victoria. **11** Kilimanjaro. **12** Portuguese. **13** Libya. **14** Nigeria.
15 Rwanda. **16** Dutch. **17** Victoria Falls. **18** Sahel. **19** Gold.
20 Casablanca. **21** Botswana. **22** Sudan. **23** Wildlife. **24** South
Africa. **25** None, it is native to Asia not Africa. **26** Dams.
27 North. **28** Somalia. **29** A click, made in the throat.
30 Pretoria.

210 ❋ AROUND ENGLAND 2

1 Cambridgeshire. **2** Furniture. **3** Sellafield.
4 Ealing, Enfield. **5** Blackpool. **6** The Fens.
7 Chester. **8** Two. **9** York. **10** Lancashire.
11 Norwich. **12** Dorset. **13** Cowley. **14** Plymouth. **15** Shropshire.
16 Isle of Wight. **17** Bath. **18** East. **19** Gateshead. **20** Cambridge.
21 Worcestershire. **22** Greater Manchester. **23** Lake District.
24 North. **25** Bexhill-on-Sea. **26** Liverpool. **27** Essex. **28** Holy
Island. **29** Northumberland. **30** Waterloo. Quiz 211

211 ✳ AROUND IRELAND 2

1 Two. 2 Stone. 3 Oak or blackthorn. 4 Belfast.
5 Shannon. 6 Lough Neagh. 7 Lead-zinc. 8 Lava.
9 Enniskillen. 10 Mountains of Mourne. 11 Cork.
12 Abbey Theatre. 13 Macgillicuddy's Reeks. 14 Golden Vale.
15 Antrim, Armagh. 16 Queen's. 17 Mountain peaks. 18 St Brigit.
19 TV listings. 20 Smoking. 21 Waterford. 22 The Twelve Bens.
23 Hills. 24 Queen's County. 25 Leinster. 26 Bells. 27 Kerry,
Kildare, Kilkenny. 28 Sligo. 29 University of Ulster. 30 Armagh,
Belfast, Derry/Londonderry.

212 ✳ AROUND EUROPE 6

1 Estonia, Latvia and Lithuania. 2 Portugal.
3 Barcelona. 4 Flax. 5 Bayern. 6 Dublin. 7 Iron.
8 Jutland. 9 Black Forest. 10 Netherlands.
11 Trees. 12 Switzerland. 13 Kiev. 14 Cave paintings. 15 Madrid.
16 Under L'Arc de Triomphe. 17 Camargue. 18 Greece. 19 French
& German. 20 Hungary. 21 Spain. 22 Italy. 23 Majorca.
24 Sicily. 25 Liverpool. 26 Estonia. 27 Muslim. 28 Belgium.
29 France. 30 Greece.

213 ✳ AROUND EUROPE 7

1 Albania. 2 Oberammergau. 3 Yugoslavia.
4 Malta. 5 Austria's. 6 Spain and Portugal. 7 The
Hague. 8 Strait, Turkey. 9 Munich. 10 Greece.
11 Italy. 12 Liechtenstein. 13 Baltic. 14 France, Italy,
Switzerland and Austria. 15 Russia. 16 Cologne. 17 Iceland.
18 Denmark and Norway. 19 Moldova. 20 The Netherlands.
21 Belgium. 22 Lorraine and Nancy. 23 Denmark. 24 Mont
Blanc. 25 Germany's. 26 Bulgaria. 27 Finnish and Swedish.
28 Red Cross. 29 The Algarve. 30 Ukraine.

214 ✳ AROUND THE UK 5

1 Brighton. 2 Melinda Messenger. 3 South
Kensington. 4 Stoke Mandeville. 5 Suffolk.
6 Severn Tunnel. 7 Newgate. 8 Canary Wharf (Isle
of Dogs). 9 Salopian. 10 Army exercises. 11 Essex & Suffolk.
12 Bristol. 13 M6. 14 Glastonbury. 15 Big Ben. 16 Blackpool.
17 Windscale. 18 Horses. 19 Clyde. 20 Nottingham. 21 Wiltshire.
22 Edinburgh. 23 Petticoat Lane. 24 Papworth. 25 Hyde Park.
26 Aberdeen. 27 Bath. 28 Straits of Dover. 29 Castle. 30 Bristol.

215 ✳ WORLD TOUR

1 Appalachian Mountains. 2 Serengeti National Park,
Tanzania. 3 Six. 4 Azores. 5 New York. 6 Sir Edward
Lutyens (designed the first, planned the second). 7
Tierra de Fuego and South American mainland. 8 Torrens.
9 Winnipeg. 10 American Samoa. 11 Tortola, Virgin Gorda, Jost
van Dyke. 12 Rarotonga. 13 Limestone. 14 Norway. 15 11. 16 Saudi
Arabia. 17 Senegal. 18 Cumberland. 19 Rwanda. 20 Gorky.
21 Turkmenistan. 22 Thailand. 23 The Valley. 24 Bu Craa, Western
Sahara. 25 Christmas Island. 26 Suriname. 27 Blue Nile, White Nile.
28 Venezuela. 29 Cocos Islands. 30 Utah.

216 ✳ NATURAL PHENOMENA

1 Carol. 2 Andesite. 3 Proxima centauri. 4 India.
5 Utigard. 6 Mars. 7 Erne. 8 Kentucky. 9 Black
hole. 10 Ceres. 11 Namibia. 12 Akutan. 13 Helix. 14
0.16%. 15 Sirius. 16 Venus. 17 Sumatra. 18 Iowa. 19 70.
20 Venus. 21 Astatine. 22 1000 yds. 23 Orion. 24 Canis minor.
25 Taurus. 26 Texas. 27 Shropshire. 28 SouthChina.
29 Germany. 30 Neptune.

217 ✳ EURO TOUR

1 Para. 2 Spree. 3 Valencia, Vigo, Vitoria. 4 Hungary.
5 Amsterdam. 6 Albania. 7 Caspian Sea. 8 Sava (capital:
Zagreb). 9 President of France, Spanish Bishop of Urgel.
10 Dresden. 11 Luxembourg. 12 Ormeli. 13 Luxembourg City.
14 Albania. 15 Palace guard. 16 Finland. 17 Reykjavik, Iceland.
18 Norway. 19 Alsace, Aquitaine, Auvergne. 20 Poland. 21 Iceland.
22 Serraville. 23 Tallinn, Estonia. 24 Moscow. 25 Bosnia-Herzegovina
and Macedonia. 26 Mount Botrange. 27 Amstel. 28 Greenland and the
Faeroe Islands. 29 Milan. 30 Malta.

218 ✳ PLANET EARTH

1 South Dakota. 2 Copper. 3 Walrus. 4 West
Spitsbergen. 5 Sonoran. 6 Silicon. 7 Mercury.
8 Sulphur. 9 Seismic wave. 10 Green.
11 Strathclyde. 12 South Africa. 13 New Guinea. 14 Four.
15 Venus. 16 Mountain chains. 17 Parsec. 18 Western Mongolia.
19 Radiation. 20 Low temperatures. 21 Novaya Zemlya.
22 Soil. 23 Radio communication. 24 Dam. 25 Six. 26 Helium.
27 Saturn. 28 Moh. 29 4.35. 30 Iron.

219 ✳ AROUND THE UK 6

1 Ben Macdui. 2 Manchester. 3 Nith. 4 Edinburgh.
5 Bournemouth. 6 Aberdeen. 7 Neagh.
8 Aberystwyth. 9 Carlisle. 10 Leicester. 11 Kent.
12 Fenner's. 13 Jennie Lee. 14 Ten. 15 Perth. 16 Wakefield.
17 Towy. 18 Itchen. 19 Northern. 20 Leeds. 21 Douglas, Isle of
Man. 22 Bangor. 23 Brighton. 24 The Octagon. 25 Dumfries.
26 Edinburgh, Heriot-Watt. 27 York. 28 The Parks. 29 St
Andrews. 30 Colne.

220 ✳ AROUND THE WORLD 11

1 St Lucia. 2 Alberta, Canada. 3 Russia. 4 Nina.
5 China. 6 Guayaquil. 7 Bangkok. 8 Dallas. 9 Sri
Lanka. 10 Dublin. 11 Vridi. 12 Sumatra. 13 Gulf of
Mexico. 14 Great Sandy. 15 Yellow colour of a creek bank.
16 Zarqa. 17 Severn. 18 Coral. 19 Alabama. 20 South island,
New Zealand. 21 Perth. 22 Lake. 23 Aracaju. 24 Telugu. 25 Cook
Islands. 26 Caribbean. 27 Namche. 28 Tokyo. 29 Lakemont
Park, Pennsylvania. 30 Mali.

221 ✸ CAPITALS I

1 Anguilla. 2 Argentina. 3 Tristan da Cunha.
4 Caracas. 5 Minsk. 6 Kiev, Ukraine. 7 West
Virginia. 8 Bangkok. 9 Netherlands. 10 Damask.
11 Utah. 12 Christmas Island. 13 Jefferson City. 14 Khartoum.
15 Mogadishu. 16 Nuuk. 17 Senegal. 18 Triangular. 19 Lisbon.
20 Ohio. 21 Rome. 22 Muscat. 23 Lagos. 24 It's made of wood.
25 Chihuahua. 26 Valletta. 27 Lilongwe. 28 Nairobi.
29 *Baghdad*. 30 Montserrat Caballé, Freddie Mercury.

222 ✸ AROUND EUROPE 8

1 Badajoz. 2 William the Conqueror Cultural
Centre. 3 Sweden. 4 Orne. 5 Hungary. 6 Basle.
7 Tarifa Point. 8 Belarus. 9 Baltic. 10 Basque.
11 Caen. 12 Baden. 13 Maine et Loire. 14 Wind. 15 Belgium.
16 Bosnia Herzegovina. 17 Norway. 18 Ancona. 19 French.
20 Brussels. 21 Nine. 22 Poland. 23 Jolar. 24 Dresden.
25 Rome. 26 Belarus. 27 Valira. 28 Alvar Aalto. 29 Caucasus.
30 Moscow, St Petersburg and Kiev.

223 ✸ AROUND ENGLAND 3

1 Cornwall. 2 English Heritage. 3 Westminster.
4 Gateway to Buckingham Palace. 5 Althorp. 6 Flint
mines, Norfolk. 7 Windsor. 8 Lichfield and Truro.
9 Lincolnshire. 10 Bedford. 11 Helston, Cornwall. 12 Scilly Isles.
13 Durham. 14 Spithead. 15 Chalk. 16 Exmoor. 17 Derwent
Water. 18 The Potteries. 19 Cleopatra's Needle. 20 Great
Yarmouth. 21 Tyne and Wear. 22 Longleat. 23 York. 24 None.
25 Hampshire. 26 Eyam. 27 Canterbury cathedral. 28 Isle of
Wight. 29 Seven Sisters. 30 Blenheim.

224 ✸ AROUND THE UK 7

1 Canada. 2 32. 3 Gentlemen's toilet.
4 Aberystwyth. 5 Christchurch. 6 Kessock.
7 Victoria. 8 Caernarvon. 9 Pratt. 10 603.
11 Powys. 12 Widnes. 13 Dorset. 14 Dover. 15 Anne. 16 John
Christie. 17 Lincoln Cathedral. 18 Bedford. 19 Llantrisant.
20 220 miles. 21 Angus. 22 1988. 23 Stour. 24 Granta. 25 1940.
26 Book dealer. 27 Berkshire. 28 Caerphilly. 29 Gillespie Road.
30 Brighton.

225 ✸ WHAT IN THE WORLD? 2

1 Bam. 2 Cirrus. 3 Bogor, Java. 4 Snow. 5 Bracknell, north
Wales. 6 Coriolis effect. 7 Krakatoa, near Java.
8 Sumatra. 9 St Elmo's fire. 10 Red, orange, yellow, green,
blue, indigo, violet. 11 Tornado. 12 Aurora. 13 Tsunami (not tidal waves).
14 An annular eclipse. 15 Earthquake areas. 16 The International Ice
Patrol. 17 Mauna Loa, Hawaii. 18 A waterspout. 19 Aurora Borealis.
20 Surtsey. 21 Empedocles. 22 Lebu, Chile. 23 Mount Erebus.
24 Geyser. 25 Pumice. 26 The Earth passes between the Sun and Moon.
27 Thermal. 28 Stalactites. 29 Fumarole. 30 The Mercalli scale.

226 ✸ EXPLORATION

1 Cotton. 2 Albania & Yugoslavia. 3 China &
Russia. 4 Aotearoa. 5 Silver & copper. 6 Ringgit.
7 Wales. 8 Zimbabwe. 9 Mount Redoubt.
10 Azores. 11 Rome. 12 Charlotte Town. 13 Rondonia. 14 Jordan.
15 Luzon. 16 Australia. 17 West Point. 18 Salt Lake City.
19 Djibouti. 20 Hainburg in Austria. 21 Great Rift Valley. 22 Pile
of Bones. 23 Seven. 24 Mozambique. 25 Gran Sasso d'Italia.
26 Rennes. 27 Lunar Alps. 28 Table Bay. 29 Blantyre. 30 Rio de
Janeiro.

227 ✸ THE WEATHER

1 Egypt. 2 Boscastle. 3 Solstice. 4 Cumbria. 5 Cold
front. 6 Fastnet. 7 Rockies. 8 Katrina. 9 Cirrus.
10 Mirage, Strait of Messina, Italy. 11 Doldrums.
12 Dry, warm, blowing down a mountain. 13 Alaska (wind).
14 Grey. 15 Russian wind. 16 Occluded front. 17 Typhoon.
18 Spain. 19 German Bight. 20 South Africa. 21 12. 22 Iran and
Afghanistan. 23 Sirocco. 24 Rhône. 25 Australia. 26 Isobars.
27 Eye of the storm. 28 Sandstorm. 29 Excessive dust, e.g. after
a volcanic eruption. 30 Andes.

228 ✸ WORLD TOUR 2

1 Boliviano. 2 Hudson & East. 3 Beslan. 4 Brazil.
5 Bandar Seri Begawan. 6 Angola. 7 Macao.
8 Uruguay. 9 Khartoum. 10 Dzongkha.
11 Australia. 12 Brazil. 13 Algeria and Mauritania. 14 Namib
desert. 15 Bogota. 16 Pennsylvania Station. 17 New Providence
Island. 18 Wyoming. 19 Mount McKinley. 20 Eilat. 21 Edwin
Lutyens. 22 Niger. 23 Nigeria. 24 Sri Lanka. 25 Indonesia.
26 Bujumbura. 27 Bloemfontein. 28 Maine. 29 Honduras.
30 Java.

229 ✸ CAPITALS 2

1 St Petersburg. 2 Andorra la Vella.
3 Mediterranean. 4 Croatia (Zagreb). 5 Salisbury.
6 Phnom Penh. 7 Nicosia (Cyprus). 8 Uzbekistan.
9 Quito (Ecuador). 10 Islamabad. 11 Antigua. 12 Oslo. 13 Unter
den Linden. 14 Cairo. 15 Mafeking. 16 Addis Ababa. 17 Kabul.
18 Champs Elysées. 19 Brasilia. 20 Athens. 21 Buenos Aires.
22 Santa Fé de Bogotà. 23 Reykjavik (Iceland). 24 Calcutta. 25
Caspian. 26 Rome. 27 Manama. 28 Tokyo. 29 Nassau.
30 Damascus (Syria).

230 ✸ EURO TOUR 2

1 Brenner's Park Hotel. 2 Romania. 3 Tbilisi.
4 Vienna. 5 Gulf of Riga. 6 Brussels. 7 Austria.
8 Koper. 9 Italy. 10 Baltic. 11 Netherlands.
12 Estonia. 13 Gulf of Finland. 14 Great Britain. 15 Mount Etna
and Stromboli. 16 Grande Dizence in Switzerland. 17 Finland.
18 London. 19 Germany. 20 Liechtenstein. 21 Ormeli in Norway.
22 Belarus. 23 Assisi in Central Italy. 24 Germany. 25 Italy.
26 Roman Catholic. 27 Corfu. 28 Tourism and tobacco.
29 Spain. 30 Norway.

231 ✳ GREAT BUILDINGS

1 Canterbury. 2 Winning an international competition. 3 Marble. 4 Etoile. 5 St Paul's. 6 Eiffel Tower. 7 Ivan the Terrible. 8 San Marco. 9 Cardinal Wolsey. 10 Devonshire. 11 Castle Howard. 12 It has sunk. 13 Castle Howard. 14 Mexico. 15 Versailles. 16 Chicago. 17 Cologne. 18 F. W. Woolworth. 19 Venus de Milo. 20 1894. 21 Extension to the National Gallery. 22 York Minster. 23 Montmartre. 24 Vatican, Rome. 25 Michelangelo. 26 Rangoon, Myanmar (Burma). 27 St Petersburg. 28 Coventry. 29 Amritsar. 30 To cover smoke stains. (It was set on fire by the British in 1814.)

232 ✳ AROUND THE UK 8

1 Ipswich. 2 Heriot-Watt. 3 Cowdray Park. 4 The Pit. 5 Orkney. 6 Holy Loch. 7 Hampstead. 8 Finisterre. 9 Buckinghamshire. 10 Suffolk. 11 Three. 12 Antonine Wall. 13 Middlesex Street. 14 Northamptonshire. 15 Mount Pleasant. 16 Man of Kent. 17 Durham. 18 The Boston Stump. 19 PM Earl of Liverpool. 20 Carlton House Terrace. 21 Trowbridge. 22 Westminster Abbey. 23 Mansion House. 24 The Burrell Collection. 25 Blenheim Palace. 26 Bush House. 27 Museum of the Moving Image. 28 Banqueting House. 29 Shetlands. 30 Hereford and Worcester.

233 ✳ POT LUCK

1 9. 2 Anode. 3 Wally. 4 Butterfly. 5 Victoria. 6 Melchester. 7 Six. 8 Tom Hanks. 9 Doe. 10 Behaviour. 11 Jersey. 12 Hands. 13 Elton John. 14 Liam Neeson. 15 Eamonn Holmes. 16 Ten. 17 LXXVII. 18 St Cecilia. 19 Flock together. 20 The Taming of the Shrew. 21 True Blue. 22 The brain. 23 Hummingbird. 24 Eric Clapton. 25 Luke. 26 Italy. 27 Alderney. 28 Steven Gerrard. 29 La Bohème. 30 Eight.

234 ✳ POT LUCK 2

1 Orange. 2 Jennifer Saunders. 3 Madonna. 4 London & Birmingham. 5 Unchained Melody. 6 Goldcrest. 7 18. 8 Martin. 9 Cricket. 10 1940s. 11 Enya. 12 Red Indian tribes. 13 Take That. 14 White. 15 Four. 16 Mind. 17 Alfred Hitchcock. 18 Five. 19 Charles Dickens. 20 Hutch. 21 Accrington Stanley. 22 Northumberland. 23 MW. 24 Green. 25 A king. 26 Yorkshire. 27 Food. 28 Angostura Bitters. 29 Jennifer Aniston. 30 Queensland.

235 ✳ POP POT LUCK

1 "Baby Come Back". 2 Gallagher. 3 10. 4 Scarborough. 5 Video. 6 Iceland. 7 "Return to Sender". 8 In a Bottle. 9 Electric Light. 10 Dylan. 11 Clarinet. 12 Beach Boys. 13 Gilbert O'Sullivan. 14 Three. 15 Stevens. 16 Dolly Parton. 17 Joan Armatrading. 18 Bob Dylan. 19 Mike Rutherford. 20 Yellow Brick Road. 21 Take That. 22 Scottish. 23 Nash. 24 k. d. lang. 25 42. 26 The Bluenotes. 27 Closer. 28 Flea. 29 O'Connor. 30 O'Donnell.

236 ✳ POT LUCK 3

1 Highbury. 2 Dan Brown. 3 Gold. 4 Acid. 5 The man in the moon. 6 Toblerone. 7 Pudding Lane. 8 Snooty. 9 Cricket. 10 The Hanging Gardens. 11 Ant & Dec. 12 A shilling (now 5p). 13 Pizza. 14 Green. 15 *Harry Potter* series. 16 Six. 17 Australian Open. 18 Oliver Twist. 19 German. 20 Boston. 21 Six. 22 Nothing. 23 A fish. 24 Palindromes. 25 Kiwi fruit. 26 Poncho. 27 Six. 28 Insects. 29 Five. 30 Bird.

237 ✳ POT LUCK 4

1 Sunderland. 2 Stirrups. 3 Dogger Bank. 4 Nine. 5 US President. 6 Perception. 7 Scandinavia. 8 One. 9 He was bald. 10 Animated cartoons. 11 A reservoir. 12 A spider. 13 The 1812 Overture. 14 14th February. 15 Tony Blackburn. 16 Victoria. 17 Four. 18 Moses. 19 The Pacific Ocean. 20 Teeth. 21 Elizabeth Hurley. 22 The maiden all forlorn. 23 Arms. 24 Helsinki. 25 Worms. 26 Four. 27 Jade. 28 Four. 29 A collage. 30 Sixpence.

238 ✳ MOVIES POT LUCK

1 India. 2 Thompson. 3 3 hours. 4 Mike Newell. 5 *The Boxer*. 6 Marlon Brando. 7 1930s. 8 Cage. 9 Boxing. 10 Julia Roberts. 11 *The Godfather*. 12 Oldman. 13 Quentin. 14 Brad Pitt. 15 Sister. 16 Curtis. 17 Mitty. 18 *Jaws*. 19 Winona. 20 Reynolds. 21 Stone. 22 1980s. 23 Harlow. 24 Green. 25 Elton John. 26 2007. 27 Mr Freeze. 28 Cliffhanger. 29 Robin Williams. 30 331/ 2

239 ✳ POT LUCK 5

1 Pea. 2 *The Generation Game*. 3 Robson and Jerome. 4 Eric Sykes. 5 Light blue. 6 Massacre at 1972 Olympics. 7 P. G. Wodehouse. 8 Princess Anne. 9 Ipswich. 10 40s. 11 Bobby Shaftoe. 12 20. 13 Hear'say. 14 16.66. 15 Garden. 16 Graham Taylor. 17 Triumph. 18 E. 19 17. 20 Architects. 21 Millennium Prayer. 22 July. 23 England. 24 Italy. 25 Radians. 26 Belgium. 27 Top letters row. 28 Gold. 29 *The Darling Buds of May*. 30 Avocado.

240 ✳ POT LUCK 6

1 A will. 2 Four. 3 Corfu. 4 Lion & Unicorn. 5 Zwanzig. 6 Bryan Adams. 7 A cactus. 8 Cheshire. 9 Street-Porter. 10 Australia. 11 World War II. 12 Black. 13 Landscape gardening. 14 A size of paper. 15 Edward Woodward. 16 A herb. 17 River Niagara. 18 Snow White. 19 Horse racing. 20 Beef. 21 Purple. 22 Three. 23 Alaska. 24 Wigan. 25 Simple Simon. 26 Luke and Matt Goss. 27 A kind of plum. 28 *Celebrity Big Brother*. 29 Lizzie. 30 Flattery.

241 ✱ MOVIES POT LUCK 2

1 Redford. 2 Dustin Hoffman. 3 The Spice Girls.
4 *Wayne's*. 5 Piano. 6 Tom Hanks. 7 *Black*.
8 Tarzan. 9 Mulder & Scully. 10 *10*. 11 Patrick
Swayze. 12 Sutherland. 13 Jacques Tati. 14 *Robin Hood: Prince of Thieves*. 15 1930s. 16 *Red*. 17 Sergeant Bilko. 18 Glenn Close.
19 Ryan O'Neal. 20 Dinosaurs. 21 Bette Midler. 22 American.
23 1970s. 24 "The Living Daylights". 25 Demi Moore.
26 Country. 27 Harry Potter. 28 Jerry Hall. 29 Travolta.
30 Meaning.

242 ✱ POT LUCK 7

1 Davis. 2 1,000. 3 Shrewsbury. 4 "Hall". 5 Meat
Loaf. 6 *Da Vinci Code*. 7 Stephen King. 8 Lettuce.
9 Mlle. 10 Krusty the Clown. 11 Judo. 12 Yard.
13 *Baywatch*. 14 West Ham. 15 Castleford Tigers. 16 Israel. 17
Gerald Ford. 18 Sri Lanka. 19 Nano. 20 "Pigeon". 21 India. 22
Died. 23 Pink Floyd. 24 *Footballers' Wives*. 25 Sixtieth.
26 Brigadier. 27 *Emmerdale*. 28 Chase. 29 Pillar of salt.
30 Sheep.

243 ✱ POT LUCK 8

1 Confessions. 2 Egg whites. 3 Betjeman. 4 Liquid
or gas. 5 Edinburgh. 6 11. 7 Gabriel. 8 Mods. 9 Drei.
10 Winnie The Pooh. 11 Canute. 12 Victor. 13 Bruce
Forsyth. 14 Snap-dragon. 15 Sheffield. 16 Quickly. 17 Fountain
pen. 18 Italy. 19 Estimated Time of Arrival. 20 Wine. 21 Robbie
Fowler. 22 Loch Ness Monster. 23 Seven. 24 The All Blacks.
25 The sparrow. 26 Brazil. 27 James Herriot. 28 Poland.
29 Play. 30 Des O'Connor.

244 ✱ MOVIES POT LUCK 3

1 Hollywood. 2 Shakespeare. 3 *Emma*. 4 Junior.
5 Humphrey Bogart. 6 Madonna. 7 1970s.
8 Anthony Hopkins. 9 Jack Nicholson. 10 1960s.
11 Demi Moore. 12 Woody Allen. 13 USSR - Latvia. 14 Sweden.
15 USSR. 16 1990s. 17 Joanne Woodward. 18 Terrestrial.
19 Barbara Bach. 20 13. 21 Hope. 22 George. 23 Dietrich.
24 Fame. 25 Cates. 26 *Terminator*. 27 The Were-Rabbit.
28 Danes. 29 Blondie. 30 *Indecent*.

245 ✱ POT LUCK 9

1 *Till Death Us Do Part*. 2 Saddam Hussein.
3 Wolseley. 4 "Fisher". 5 Lynda La Plante.
6 Houllier. 7 Ben Elton. 8 M. 9 Four. 10 40s.
11 Democrat, Republican. 12 Battenberg. 13 Germany. 14 The
Everly Brothers. 15 Cowardly Lion. 16 Watch. 17 Butterfly.
18 Gloria Estefan. 19 911. 20 "Public". 21 13. 22 Two.
23 Equilateral. 24 Decanters. 25 Venus. 26 Edinburgh.
27 Crudités. 28 Pole Vault. 29 Iceland. 30 Enclosed spaces.

246 ✱ POT LUCK 10

1 Paul Hunter 2 Gin. 3 Taj Mahal. 4 Dingoes.
5 Actor/Actress. 6 Violins. 7 Greece. 8 June.
9 Bridges. 10 May. 11 U2. 12 A stipend. 13 Red.
14 Kite-mark. 15 New York. 16 Albatross. 17 *Coronation Street*.
18 Sherry. 19 The worm. 20 Paul McCartney. 21 Bread.
22 45. 23 In the mouth. 24 Andrew Lloyd Webber. 25 St Paul's
Cathedral. 26 Vertical. 27 Sheffield Utd. 28 Sugar, almonds.
29 Evangelism. 30 Magpie.

247 ✱ FOOTBALL POT LUCK

1 Derby County. 2 Sheffield. 3 Arsenal. 4 United.
5 Scotland. 6 Stoke City. 7 Hungary. 8 Crystal
Palace. 9 Leeds Utd. 10 Blue and white. 11 Naylor.
12 The Villains. 13 Eric Cantona. 14 Barcelona. 15 Millwall.
16 Graeme Souness. 17 Weah. 18 Denmark. 19 Jason.
20 Fowler. 21 Chelsea. 22 Glasgow. 23 Dalglish. 24 Bright.
25 Birmingham City. 26 Everton. 27 Italy. 28 Hampden Park.
29 Walkers. 30 Adams.

248 ✱ POT LUCK 11

1 Ken Stott. 2 Big Ben. 3 Madonna. 4 Tony Blair.
5 *Dynasty*. 6 Switzerland. 7 Laurie Lee. 8 May and
June. 9 Quotient. 10 40s. 11 Jamie Oliver.
12 Mirren. 13 India. 14 "Hat". 15 Mike Leigh. 16 Orange.
17 Spice Girls. 18 Wigan Warriors. 19 Aylesbury. 20 *Star Trek*.
21 Ahead. 22 Blue and white. 23 The Crickets. 24 1/4. 25 Light
blue. 26 New York. 27 Andy Warhol. 28 Charlton Heston. 29 10.
30 Goran Ivanisevic.

249 ✱ POT LUCK 12

1 Drinks. 2 Bread & cheese. 3 Eminen. 4 *The Sun*.
5 Romantic. 6 Paris. 7 Exempt. 8 Middlesbrough.
9 Pyramids. 10 Sheep. 11 Gates. 12 Christmas.
13 Nile. 14 Dog. 15 Aberfan. 16 Lancashire. 17 Association.
18 Thistle. 19 Cattle. 20 80s. 21 Travel. 22 Wight. 23 Game.
24 Blanchett. 25 Hong Kong. 26 London. 27 Mont Blanc.
28 Pancakes. 29 29th. 30 Beijing.

250 ✱ POP POT LUCK 2

1 Cilla Black. 2 Debbie Harry. 3 Mae. 4 Roxy Music.
5 Shapiro. 6 Paul Anka. 7 Cockney Rebel. 8 Neil
Diamond. 9 Australia. 10 Guitar. 11 Joseph. 12 k. d.
13 Greece. 14 Turner. 15 Yates. 16 "Philadelphia". 17 "Softly".
18 Starr. 19 Miss Molly. 20 Abbey Road. 21 *X-Factor*.
22 Madonna. 23 Tuesday. 24 Jackie Trent and Tony Hatch.
25 Mathis. 26 Marilyn Manson. 27 Dusty Springfield.
28 California. 29 The Sex Pistols. 30 Five.

251 ✳ POT LUCK 13

1 USA. 2 "Half". 3 20s. 4 Blue. 5 Paula Radcliffe.
6 Gordon Brown. 7 Thomas Hardy. 8 Little Jimmy
Osmond. 9 Marlon Brando. 10 Huddersfield.
11 Orwell. 12 Willis. 13 Le Bon. 14 "Weight". 15 Horse racing.
16 Imperial. 17 Sheila Hancock. 18 F. 19 Sahara. 20 8. 21 Bryan
Ferry. 22 *Porridge*. 23 Custer. 24 Spain. 25 Red. 26 Katrina.
27 Cloud. 28 Square. 29 Bruce Forsyth. 30 David Cameron.

252 ✳ POP POT LUCK 3

1 Elton John. 2 Adams. 3 Canada. 4 Glass.
5 "Nowhere". 6 Sting. 7 The Jets. 8 Simon. 9 Two.
10 "In a while, crocodile". 11 Guitar. 12 Cassidy.
13 Astaire. 14 "Bohemian Rhapsody". 15 Freddie. 16 Robson and
Jerome. 17 *Spice*. 18 Ballet. 19 Albarn. 20 Chas and Dave.
21 70th. 22 U2. 23 The Monkees. 24 Madonna. 25 Madness.
26 Lulu. 27 Boy George. 28 Three. 29 UK. 30 Grant.

253 ✳ POT LUCK 14

1 Douglas. 2 Liverpool. 3 40s. 4 "Fish". 5 Celine
Dion. 6 XIV. 7 Leo Tolstoy. 8 Bath. 9 Wooden
Heart. 10 Edward Heath. 11 Mercury. 12 Piper.
13 No. 14 Malaysia. 15 Ed Stewart. 16 Black. 17 Athletics. 18 The
Acts of the Apostles. 19 "Punch". 20 The eye. 21 *Dad's Army*.
22 Russia. 23 Handel. 24 5. 25 Mars. 26 Watergate. 27 Green.
28 James Whale. 29 Nirvana. 30 "Dallas".

254 ✳ POT LUCK 15

1 400th. 2 Taurus. 3 3. 4 Abba. 5 Stan Laurel.
6 Lawyer. 7 Kylie Minogue. 8 Cycling. 9 Cliff
Richard. 10 Rule the world. 11 University. 12 Isaac
Asimov. 13 Bonnet. 14 Saturn. 15 Water. 16 Eight. 17 Terry
Gilliam. 18 Oxford and Cambridge boat race. 19 Dog. 20 Biscuit.
21 Democrats and Republicans. 22 Coward. 23 Butcher.
24 Thailand. 25 Colin Farrell. 26 San Francisco. 27 Blue and
white. 28 Nazareth. 29 Barbara Hulanicki. 30 45 degrees.

255 ✳ POT LUCK 16

1 6,080. 2 Japan. 3 Phil Mickelson. 4 "Pigeon".
5 Arsenal. 6 Keith Moon. 7 Bob the Builder.
8 Wednesday. 9 American Football. 10 Matthew.
11 1,440. 12 *The Generation Game*. 13 Green. 14 *David
Copperfield*. 15 Vauxhall. 16 "Waltzing Matilda". 17 Top letters
row. 18 Phoenix. 19 Access. 20 Aries. 21 Transom. 22 Darren
Gough. 23 Monday. 24 Women. 25 New York. 26 7. 27 Cricket.
28 Foreigners. 29 *EastEnders*. 30 Madonna.

256 ✳ POT LUCK 17

1 Thaw. 2 Florin. 3 Smokie. 4 Chris Evans.
5 1980. 6 Bluto. 7 Yes. 8 Liverpool. 9 Portuguese.
10 Culkin. 11 Mile. 12 Harman. 13 McFly. 14 26.
15 The Kinks. 16 Greek gods. 17 *Buffy the Vampire Slayer*.
18 Borzoi. 19 Nissan. 20 Birmingham. 21 Fox. 22 Cyrillic.
23 British Prime Ministers. 24 Champion. 25 Mick Hucknall.
26 Penicillin. 27 Catherine Zeta Jones. 28 Golf. 29 Duck.
30 McCartney.

257 ✳ POT LUCK 18

1. Shoes. 2 Drums. 3 Ox. 4 A sandstorm. 5 Shirley
Crabtree. 6 Weaving. 7 Jeffrey Archer. 8 The
English Channel. 9 Delta. 10 Wednesday. 11 The
jawbone. 12 Helmut Kohl. 13 George Orwell. 14 1970s.
15 Hercule Poirot. 16 Nicky Campbell. 17 Brian Mawhinney.
18 Chow. 19 Robert Powell. 20 Little Women. 21 Calcutta.
22 They both collect in pods. 23 A Bank. 24 Panama.
25 Abortion. 26 Niagara Falls. 27 Italy. 28 White. 29 Turquoise.
30 Nova Scotia.

258 ✳ POT LUCK 19

1 Venice. 2 Blow it. 3 X. 4 Spain. 5 Moss.
6 Emergency. 7 Red. 8 Monte Carlo. 9 521.
10 Australia. 11 Shark. 12 Space. 13 Israel.
14 Skiing. 15 Round. 16 Music. 17 Dried fruit. 18 Horse.
19 Cathy Freeman. 20 Peter Jackson. 21 New Zealand. 22 Who's
there?. 23 Hay Fever. 24 Mad. 25 Playing cards. 26 Running.
27 Furniture. 28 Golf. 29 Heart. 30 Washington.

259 ✳ FOOTBALL POT LUCK 2

1 1950s. 2 Blue and white. 3 Leicester City. 4 Brown.
5 Steve Cherry. 6 Rotherham Utd. 7 Steve McManaman.
8 Wimbledon. 9 The Gulls. 10 Oldham Athletic. 11
David James. 12 1930s. 13 Watford. 14 Swindon Town. 15 Branfoot.
16 Gidman. 17 Leeds Utd. 18 Howard. 19 England. 20 Mark
Lawrenson. 21 Goalkeeper. 22 Ryan Giggs. 21 Goalkeeper. 22 Ryan
Giggs. 23 Denis Law. 24 Blackpool. 25 Atkins. 26 Shrewsbury Town.
27 Burnley. 28 Norwich City. 29 Red and white. 30 Aston Villa.

260 ✳ POT LUCK 20

1 The Dee. 2 Johnny Cash. 3 Pathfinder. 4 Hyde
Park. 5 Montreux. 6 Very soft. 7 Sean Connery.
8 Gatwick. 9 Priz. 10 Four. 11 16th. 12 Connie
Francis. 13 1 p.m. 14 Bananas. 15 Leo Tolstoy. 16 The Bridge of
Sighs. 17 "Age". 18 Agincourt. 19 59. 20 Florida. 21 Ken Bates.
22 Chester. 23 DDT. 24 "Born to Make You Happy". 25 Tbilisi.
26 The Prince of Wales. 27 Raymond Baxter. 28 Bournemouth.
29 1950s. 30 The Jordan.

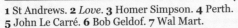

261 ✷ POT LUCK 21

1 St Andrews. 2 *Love*. 3 Homer Simpson. 4 Perth.
5 John Le Carré. 6 Bob Geldof. 7 Wal Mart.
8 Bread. 9 Elle. 10 New York. 11 David Gray.
12 Firth. 13 Memory. 14 Orange juice. 15 Jerusalem. 16 Reeves.
17 Missile. 18 The Meldrews. 19 Cameron Diaz. 20 Hair.
21 Airports. 22 *Countdown*. 23 Latin. 24 Katie Price.
25 Numbers. 26 Pathologists. 27 A dotted line. 28 Tony Blair.
29 Ben Kingsley. 30 The Conservative Party.

262 ✷ POP POT LUCK 4

1 1970s. 2 Bobby Darin. 3 "Joanna". 4 Bill Haley
and His Comets. 5 Colin Blunstone. 6 Enya. 7 None.
8 Paul Young. 9 Shane Fenton. 10 Bonzo Dog Doo-
Dah Band. 11 Germany. 12 1940s. 13 Slade. 14 George Harrison.
15 Frogman. 16 Australia. 17 Cheryl Baker. 18 Hot Gossip. 19 A
& M. 20 The Men in Hats. 21 Girls Aloud. 22 Louis Walsh.
23 The Blue Notes. 24 Suzi Quatro. 25 The Proclaimers.
26 Long Hot Summer. 27 Gabrielle. 28 Michael Bolton. 29 Billy.
30 Johnny Cash.

263 ✷ POT LUCK 23

1 Stewed fruit. 2 The 707. 3 Rita Coolidge.
4 Barnsley. 5 Beef. 6 Mrs Indira Gandhi.
7 Reverend Lovejoy. 8 Citrus. 9 Moscow Dynamo.
10 Casterbridge. 11 Satine. 12 Finished. 13 Kalahari. 14 The
Gondoliers. 15 Surbiton. 16 Turkey. 17 Pygmalion. 18 E20.
19 Clemence. 20 John Fowles. 21 Lord Chancellor. 22 Minerva.
23 Charles Wesley. 24 Hawaii. 25 Erle Stanley Gardner.
26 Shirley Temple Black. 27 Pete Best. 28 Herbert George.
29 The Frisbee. 30 18th.

264 ✷ POT LUCK 24

1 Bank. 2 Golf. 3 Emma Bunton. 4 Five. 5 Careers.
6 Linford Christie. 7 1980s. 8 Dylan. 9 Yasser
Arafat. 10 Two. 11 Kingfisher. 12 Bird. 13 In water.
14 Stripes. 15 Bulb. 16 Private Frazer. 17 Y. 18 Fish and chips.
19 Books. 20 Salmon. 21 Fawlty Towers. 22 West Ham United.
23 Gold. 24 West. 25 Yuppies. 26 France. 27 Tyres. 28 None.
29 Teaching. 30 March.

265 ✷ POP POT LUCK 5

1 1960s. 2 Connie Francis. 3 In the Old-Fashioned
Way. 4 His Paramount Jazz Band. 5 Three Degrees.
6 Harmonica. 7 Take That. 8 "I Can't Explain".
9 Bobby Vee. 10 The Turtles. 11 Cockerel Chorus. 12 Chris
Farlowe. 13 Jamaica. 14 "1-2-3". 15 Ken Dodd. 16 Crosby, Stills
and Nash. 17 Three. 18 1950s. 19 Goats. 20 Crocodile (Rock,
Shoes). 21 All Saints. 22 Jason Donovan. 23 A pound sterling.
24 Mantovani. 25 Chris Evans. 26 1930s. 27 Lionel Richie.
28 Major Tom. 29 Finchley Central. 30 "Chim Chim Cheree".

266 ✷ POT LUCK 25

1 Tower Bridge. 2 Idi Amin. 3 Personal best.
4 The ring. 5 Melbourne. 6 Lola. 7 Charlie Brown.
8 Columbia. 9 May Day. 10 London. 11 David
Herbert. 12 Boxing Day - 26th December. 13 Chronos. 14 Violin.
15 17th. 16 Bodies from graves. 17 E. 18 Sardonyx. 19 Skiing.
20 American Independence. 21 Spain. 22 Piltdown Man.
23 The Goons. 24 Dublin. 25 Without an orchestra. 26 1970s.
27 Leskanich. 28 New York. 29 Daphne du Maurier.
30 Glasgow.

267 ✷ FOOTBALL POT LUCK 3

1 Liverpool. 2 Chris Woods. 3 Nottm Forest. 4 Red.
5 1900. 6 Nigel Martyn. 7 Hull City. 8 Wrexham.
9 Leeds. 10 Oldham Athletic. 11 Alan Harris. 12
Arsenal. 13 1940s. 14 Blackburn Rovers. 15 Millwall. 16 Billy
McNeill. 17 Hollins. 18 The Republic of Ireland. 19 Manchester
Utd. 20 Leicester City. 21 Chelsea. 22 Olympique Lyonnais
(Lyon). 23 Brentford. 24 1930. 25 Julian. 26 1890s. 27 Alan
Shearer. 28 Bradford City. 29 Rangers. 30 Terry Venables.

268 ✷ POP POT LUCK 6

1 "There but for Fortune". 2 "Banana Boat Song".
3 Phil Collins. 4 Bono. 5 The Walker Brothers.
6 The Wombles. 7 Reg Presley. 8 John McEnroe,
Pat Cash. 9 Alexandra Burke. 10 Love Grows. 11 1950s. 12 Clint
Eastwood. 13 Perry Como. 14 The Eagles. 15 Chris Andrews.
16 "Sunday". 17 Engelbert Humperdinck. 18 "Blue Eyes".
19 1950s. 20 Jamaica. 21 The Corrs. 22 15. 23 Williams.
24 "Harvest for the World". 25 Marianne Faithfull. 26 Legless.
27 Jones. 28 "Victoria". 29 Blue. 30 "Understanding".

269 ✷ POT LUCK 26

1 Human head. 2 Newport. 3 1973. 4 The King of
the Mountains. 5 Eggs Benedict. 6 Nathan Lane.
7 Venice. 8 Seven. 9 Red. 10 The Cotswolds.
11 P. D. James. 12 Nepotism. 13 The sun. 14 12th. 15 T. 16 Tiger
Woods. 17 Savile Row. 18 208. 19 Mastermind chair. 20 Violet
Elizabeth Bott. 21 Francisco. 22 Snake. 23 Squadron Leader.
24 *The Calypso*. 25 Manchester. 26 Twelve. 27 Lambeth Palace.
28 Trafalgar Square. 29 30s. 30 Garlic.

270 ✷ POT LUCK 27

1 Pakistan. 2 Quinn. 3 The Pussy Cat. 4 *Seek*.
5 Two. 6 James Callaghan. 7 Wings. 8 Horizontally.
9 Romans. 10 Travel in space. 11 Lauryn.
12 Stetson. 13 Brussels. 14 B. 15 Tablespoon. 16 Cap. 17 Stone.
18 Cambodia. 19 Kettle. 20 All Saints. 21 Triple jump.
22 Fishermen. 23 Mathematics. 24 Leather. 25 P. 26 Nine.
27 Shutter. 28 Sailing craft. 29 Billie. 30 The spoon.

271 ✳ MOVIES POT LUCK 4

1 *Coming to America*. 2 Rickman. 3 1940s. 4 *Moonstruck*. 5 Milos Forman. 6 Arnold Schwarzenegger. 7 Colonel Ludlow. 8 3 hours. 9 Roy Rogers. 10 Martin Scorsese. 11 True Grit. 12 Barbra Streisand. 13 1950s. 14 Mason. 15 Marlee Matlin. 16 Harrison. 17 Telly Savalas. 18 1940s. 19 David Bowie. 20 Jane Seymour. 21 American Football. 22 Spencer Tracy. 23 Andre Previn. 24 Peter Cattaneo. 25 Clint Eastwood. 26 *Bangkok Dangerous*. 27 Ron Howard. 28 Jake and Elwood. 29 Goldblum. 30 Little Richard.

272 ✳ POT LUCK 28

1 The Cotswolds. 2 Van Gogh. 3 Lionel Richie. 4 Bishop's Stortford. 5 1945. 6 Stella Artois. 7 The Severn Bridge. 8 Lorraine Braco. 9 Stop. 10 Cape Canaveral. 11 Pelham Grenville. 12 Sweden. 13 *Million Dollar Baby*. 14 Hyde. 15 "Ant". 16 Hanoi. 17 Clint Eastwood. 18 19th. 19 David Jason. 20 The Crucible. 21 Westminster Abbey. 22 Saint-Saens. 23 Charles Rolls. 24 *Pickwick Papers*. 25 Green. 26 Hannah. 27 D. H. Lawrence. 28 30s. 29 Tomato. 30 Colombo.

273 ✳ POT LUCK 29

1 Corrs. 2 Arsenal. 3 Indian. 4 Foot. 5 American. 6 Extinct. 7 Card game. 8 Estonia. 9 Tango. 10 Yellow. 11 Boxing. 12 Mosquito. 13 1980s. 14 Martin. 15 Away. 16 Hurricane. 17 Portugal. 18 1970s. 19 Vote. 20 Birds. 21 Ronald Reagan. 22 Nightingale. 23 TB. 24 E. 25 Brown. 26 Boxing. 27 Six. 28 Poisoning. 29 Y. 30 Respiratory system.

274 ✳ MOVIES POT LUCK 5

1 3 hours. 2 1980s. 3 Julie Andrews. 4 Judd. 5 Paul Robeson. 6 Warren Beatty. 7 Tom Mullen. 8 Julia Roberts. 9 Honor Blackman. 10 Emily Lloyd. 11 1920s. 12 *One Flew Over the Cuckoo's Nest*. 13 Robertson. 14 Edward G. Robinson. 15 Moore. 16 *The Rock*. 17 Colin Firth. 18 Tippi Hedren. 19 Jon Voight. 20 1950s. 21 Alan Rickman. 22 Arthur Hiller. 23 Modine. 24 Audrey Hepburn. 25 Christopher Lloyd. 26 Helen Mirren. 27 *M*A*S*H*. 28 Daniel Hillard. 29 1960s. 30 Gladys Knight.

275 ✳ POT LUCK 30

1 Dick Tracy. 2 Electrocardiogram. 3 Oils. 4 Goolagong/Cawley. 5 Leonardo DiCaprio. 6 Grand Union Canal. 7 Bikini. 8 Joseph Conrad. 9 Mark Thatcher. 10 Pavlova. 11 Morse. 12 "Break". 13 Countdown. 14 15th. 15 Michelle Pfeiffer. 16 Tirana. 17 Florence Nightingale. 18 Eight. 19 Australia. 20 H. 21 Zirconium. 22 Maggot. 23 Joan of Arc. 24 A Tale of Two Cities. 25 Nectarines. 26 Beijing. 27 30s. 28 Stevie Wonder. 29 Scree. 30 Trilby.

276 ✳ POT LUCK 31

1 House. 2 Indonesia. 3 Money. 4 Priest. 5 Double. 6 Lungs. 7 Alma Mater. 8 Epsom salts. 9 Stomp. 10 the Party of Wales. 11 Full stop. 12 *Syriana*. 13 Greece. 14 "Dancing Queen". 15 It will die out. 16 Before. 17 Serbia & Montenegro. 18 None. 19 Bulimia. 20 Apple. 21 Chicken pox. 22 Lemons. 23 Colon. 24 Community Charge or Poll Tax. 25 York. 26 Bernadette. 27 EMU. 28 In the ear. 29 On a wall. 30 20 years.

277 ✳ POT LUCK 32

1 Peter Cushing. 2 Father Ted. 3 Valentine's. 4 Road rage attack. 5 Donald Budge. 6 On the ground. 7 Taylor. 8 Ionic. 9 Karen Pickering. 10 Leeds. 11 British. 12 *Hot Fuss*. 13 Rabbit. 14 Venus. 15 Identically equal to. 16 Richard III. 17 Blind. 18 Twice. 19 Leicester. 20 101. 21 Trapezium. 22 999 service. 23 Heart rate and/ or blood pressure. 24 USA. 25 West Virginia. 26 Miss Marple. 27 Tchaikovsky. 28 Gloria Hunniford (April 2000). 29 Manassa. 30 Indonesia.

278 ✳ POT LUCK 33

1 Arctic Monkeys 2 Carnoustie. 3 Dog. 4 Michael Howard 5 Rothmans. 6 Geology. 7 Damien Hirst. 8 South Pole. 9 Alcatraz Prison. 10 Tibet and Nepal. 11 The blue whale. 12 Nelson Mandela. 13 Hugh Laurie. 14 Béla Kun. 15 Moscow. 16 Queen Mary 2. 17 Stratford. 18 Daley Thompson. 19 Agnelli. 20 Miami Beach. 21 Idi Amin. 22 Leo. 23 Ringgit. 24 Skopje. 25 Benjamin Britten. 26 The Monument. 27 Ronald Ferguson. 28 New Zealand. 29 Blue/ Blew. 30 Andrew (Freddie) Flintoff.

279 ✳ POT LUCK 34

1 1950s. 2 The Undertones. 3 *The Hobbit*. 4 Jeanette MacDonald. 5 Excalibur. 6 Woody Allen. 7 Colchester. 8 Uncle Mac. 9 You walk. 10 Ariel Sharon. 11 Roy Wood. 12 *Brookside*. 13 Arthur Lucan. 14 Eric Idle. 15 Hairy. 16 My Love (2000). 17 George III. 18 A dog. 19 Alex Ferguson. 20 Red Square, Moscow. 21 Private Fraser. 22 Schools. 23 Sheep & goats. 24 Mumps. 25 Shirley Williams. 26 A bolt or quarrel. 27 Amsterdam. 28 Shirley Temple. 29 Pig. 30 George VI.

280 ✳ POT LUCK 35

1 Yellowstone National Park. 2 International Monetary Fund. 3 Volcanic gases. 4 Lentils. 5 Sheffield. 6 Barry Manilow. 7 Dean Kiely. 8 Hattie Jacques. 9 A will. 10 Thanksgiving. 11 Black. 12 The Wailers. 13 Fish soup. 14 National Exhibition Centre. 15 Boy George. 16 21. 17 Versailles. 18 30 minutes. 19 Scotland. 20 Belshazzar. 21 White rum. 22 Thunder & lightning. 23 Mick Hucknall. 24 The Andes. 25 The Derby. 26 An unborn baby. 27 Prunella Scales. 28 The peacock. 29 The Baltic. 30 Frogmore.

281 ❋ POT LUCK 36

1 National Aeronautics and Space Administration. **2** A web-footed bird. **3** Antwerp. **4** Most popular first names for babies. **5** Sven-Goran Eriksson. **6** Roller coasters. **7** Breeds of sheep. **8** Alma Cogan. **9** Pope Benedict XVI. **10** Undertaker. **11** Librarian. **12** Jelle Klaasen. **13** Patricia Cornell. **14** Women's Institute. **15** Perspex. **16** Dolomites. **17** Brighton. **18** *Lock, Stock and Two Smoking Barrels.* **19** The potato famine in Ireland. **20** 75th. **21** Albert Christian Edward. **22** New Hampshire. **23** Occidental. **24** *The Mystery of Edwin Drood.* **25** John Napier. **26** The femur (thigh bone). **27** Cole Porter. **28** Cassandra. **29** Fidel Castro. **30** Spain.

282 ❋ POT LUCK 37

1 George Best. **2** Bracciano. **3** December 2002. **4** 150,000. **5** White Hart Lane (vs. Holland). **6** Backstreet Boys. **7** Mitrokhin commission. **8** Maryland. **9** His Latest Flame. **10** 17 years. **11** Australia. **12** Ipswich. **13** 12 players. **14** Mervyn King. **15** Swimming (freestyle). **16** Mead Publications. **17** Dirk Benedict. **18** Germany. **19** The Ballad of John & Yoko. **20** Nostromo. **21** 2009. **22** The Palace. **23** Joseph. **24** Damien Hirst. **25** John Hume. **26** *The Shining.* **27** John Kettley (2002). **28** Jamaica. **29** Geri Halliwell. **30** Birmingham.

283 ❋ POP POT LUCK 7

1 Phil Spector. **2** Elvis Presley. **3** *Kid Gallahad.* **4** Patti Labelle. **5** *A Night on the Town.* **6** Take Me Home Country Roads. **7** "Don't Stand Too Close to Me". **8** Muppets. **9** *Cats.* **10** Herb Alpert and the Tijuana Brass. **11** Secret Garden. **12** "I'll Never Fall in Love Again". **13** "D.J.". **14** 007. **15** Liverpool. **16** *Slayed?* **17** Drowned. **18** Bob Geldof. **19** For a chewing gum ad. **20** Lucille. **21** Peggy Lee. **22** "Hell Raiser". **23** 5:15. **24** "Ossie's Dream". **25** Sir Duke. **26** Katy Perry. **27** Kings of Leon. **28** Kelly Clarkson. **29** Lady Gaga. **30** Beyonce Knowles.

284 ❋ POT LUCK 38

1 Beverley Knight. **2** Brown, although he was white-faced on inside colour pages. **3** Chicago. **4** A sleuth. **5** Pluto. **6** Cream. **7** Cheetah. **8** George IV, as Prince Regent. **9** The leeside. **10** Dick Grayson. **11** The climbing perch of India. **12** Lively. **13** Portrait of a Man. **14** William IV. **15** Blaise Pascal. **16** China. **17** Rudolph Dirks. **18** Sonia O'Sullivan. **19** Mercalli scale. **20** B2. **21** Greenland. **22** Parminder Nagra. **23** Jones. **24** The Elliot Brothers. **25** Bernese Alps. **26** Czech. **27** 1977. **28** Como. **29** Train. **30** House of Saxe-Coburg.

285 ❋ POT LUCK 39

1 1905. **2** The Duke. **3** Ranging. **4** Queen Anne. **5** France. **6** Raquel Welch. **7** Windsor. **8** Roberto di Matteo. **9** A toilet. **10** Cyprus. **11** Evelyn Waugh. **12** Clydesdale. **13** Orbital. **14** Happy Valley. **15** Mount McKinley. **16** Guildford. **17** 1981. **18** Warm. **19** Stoller. **20** Stabiliser. **21** Mick McCarthy. **22** Smarty Pants. **23** Spa Francorchamps. **24** Aberdeen. **25** Darwin. **26** Nurse. **27** Luxembourg. **28** Iran. **29** Ian "H" Watkins. **30** Separate Lives (Julian Fellowes).

286 ❋ MOVIES POT LUCK 6

1 Harold Ramis. **2** *Wall Street.* **3** White. **4** Pais. **5** 125 minutes. **6** Don Birman. **7** Five. **8** It's a Wonderful Life (in Spanish). **9** David Niven. **10** 109 minutes. **11** Farrell. **12** Harold Russell (*Best Years of Our Lives*). **13** Carrie Fisher. **14** Al Pacino. **15** Clive Barker. **16** *Rain Man.* **17** Nia Long. **18** *The Rookie.* **19** Rick Moranis. **20** *The Paleface.* **21** Livingston. **22** Anna Magnani. **23** *Three Days of the Condor.* **24** Joe Dante. **25** Sadie Frost. **26** 40th. **27** Will Ferrell. **28** Mimi Leder. **29** Costume design. **30** 1983.

287 ❋ POT LUCK 40

1 Anne Boleyn. **2** Scout. **3** Albert Einstein. **4** £12. **5** Wales. **6** A ray. **7** 1964. **8** Abdullah. **9** 1856. **10** Winston Churchill (about Stafford Cripps). **11** 24. **12** Elias. **13** All anagrams of animals. **14** The chinook. **15** Nick Hornby. **16** The Outlaws (in Richmal Crompton's books). **17** 1965. **18** Tribophysics. **19** A labour. **20** Helium. **21** Francis II of France. **22** A reticulated python. **23** Gunner Parkin. **24** The Duke of Beaufort. **25** In 1842, after the First Opium War. **26** John Arbuthnot. **27** The Dog Star. **28** Tilda Swinton. **29** Richard Ingrams. **30** Tom Morris.

288 ❋ POT LUCK 41

1 Johnny Herbert. **2** Violet Carson. **3** Kebab. **4** John Irving. **5** Ukraine. **6** Gemstones. **7** Congestion charge. **8** Boney M. **9** Delano. **10** *The Naples Connection.* **11** Italy. **12** Rowing. **13** Eva Green. **14** Newbold. **15** Blackburn Rovers. **16** Houston. **17** Run to the Hills. **18** Boston. **19** Humphrey Bogart. **20** *Take Your Pick.* **21** Brussels. **22** Cartoonist/illustrator. **23** Curling. **24** "Sit Down". **25** Eric von Schmidt. **26** Winona Ryder. **27** Buckingham Palace. **28** *The Day the Earth Stood Still.* **29** In charge of the flight that claimed the life of Buddy Holly. **30** Grand National.

289 ❋ POP POT LUCK 8

1 A red lightning flash. **2** The Ventures. **3** Jack Bruce. **4** Diana Ross and Michael Jackson. **5** "Twist and Shout". **6** Emerson, Lake and Palmer. **7** "The Israelites". **8** Eddy Grant. **9** Charles Aznavour. **10** *Undercover.* **11** Little Richard. **12** Champagne. **13** Snoop Doggy Dogg. **14** Mary Hopkin. **15** Isle of Wight. **16** "Say You, Say Me". **17** Paul McCartney. **18** Billy Preston. **19** Polio. **20** "Baby Love". **21** BRITS. **22** Joss Stone. **23** Red. **24** Not the Nine o'Clock News. **25** Jermaine. **26** The Gibbs. **27** Six. **28** New Kids on the Block. **29** *Touch.* **30** *Abracadabra.*

290 ❋ POT LUCK 42

1 1940s. **2** Acronym. **3** Cemetery. **4** Gotland. **5** Solid helium. **6** Ian Fleming. **7** Archery. **8** David Gates. **9** 111. **10** Benjamin Disraeli. **11** Vic Reeves. **12** 1907, by Paul Cornu. **13** Leaves. **14** 12 years. **15** The Curia. **16** 1938, Nescafé. **17** New Orleans. **18** Alfred Harmsworth, Viscount Northcliffe, in 1896. **19** Norris McWhirter. **20** *Citizen Kane.* **21** Mexico City. **22** Ahab. **23** Elvis Presley. **24** Play vigorously. **25** Live burial. **26** Julia Roberts. **27** Double coconut. **28** 1637. **29** Britain. **30** Athletico Madrid.

291 ❋ POT LUCK 43

1 *Waterworld.* **2** Gopher. **3** Athens. **4** December.
5 Part of a parapet. **6** "Without You". **7** Dodie Smith.
8 14-5. **9** One week. **10** Octopus. **11** Dentist.
12 Kate Beckinsale. **13** So Good. **14** Gerald Scarfe. **15** Jim
London. **16** Dinosaur. **17** Gilbert. **18** Swans. **19** Osborne House.
20 Bob Slaney. **21** Get Up and Boogie. **22** Neptune.
23 *Everybody Comes to Rick's.* **24** *Carousel.* **25** Diomed.
26 Ghana. **27** Pirlo. **28** Two. **29** Stethoscope. **30** None.

292 ❋ MOVIES POT LUCK 7

1 Elmore Leonard. **2** Cilento. **3** Stephen Hopkins.
4 Samantha Eggar. **5** Holly Hunter. **6** 115 minutes.
7 Jill Balcon. **8** Rick Rossovich. **9** Sergeant Neil
Howie. **10** Jane Alexander. **11** Frank Lloyd. **12** Fantasia. **13** 80
minutes. **14** Sorvino. **15** Dr Frederick Treves. **16** Daniel Mann.
17 Bernardo Bertolucci. **18** Fred Savage. **19** Helen Slater. **20** *The
Player.* **21** *Going My Way.* **22** Cybill Shepherd. **23** Snodgrass.
24 Sophia Loren. **25** Ben Stiller. **26** Mark Wahlberg. **27** 14.
28 Will Kane. **29** Bette Midler. **30** Nora Ephron.

293 ❋ POT LUCK 44

1 Wine production. **2** Andrew Motion. **3** The
Unesco headquarters. **4** *Home Truths.* **5** Michael
J. Fox. **6** Morpheus. **7** 1971. **8** Tropical cockroach.
9 Camulodunum (Colchester). **10** 30 minutes. **11** 14.2 hands
and over. **12** The robin. **13** Georges Claude. **14** France. **15** The
Pelican. **16** Henry VIII. **17** *The Mona Lisa.* **18** 1985. **19** Apia.
20 Canada. **21** Krakatoa. **22** Soprano singer. **23** Eight. **24** Man
Utd. **25** The gorilla. **26** Ariel. **27** Keith Reid. **28** None. **29** The
Times. **30** Barley.

294 ❋ POT LUCK 45

1 Bretton Woods Conference. **2** Great Salt Desert.
3 Limerick. **4** Morris Minor. **5** Douglas Jardine.
6 Jamestown. **7** John Peel's. **8** Thomas Beecham. **9** Mark
up. **10** Gauteng. **11** Gwen John. **12** Invercargill. **13** Isadora Wing.
14 Donald Duck. **15** *Diamonds are a Girl's Best Friend.* **16** Gastineau.
17 Amy Johnson. **18** 14 mph. **19** Ambassadors Theatre. **20** *New York
World.* **21** Southern Alaska/Siberia. **22** Hawaii. **23** Perez De Cuellar. **24**
Konrad Adenauer. **25** Lieutenant. **26** Danny Ward. **27** *The Bald Prima
Donna.* **28** Lewis. **29** St Petersburg. **30** November.

295 ❋ FOOTBALL POT LUCK 4

1 Stranraer. **2** Gillingham & Ipswich Town. **3** John
Toshack. **4** Port Vale. **5** Lloyd George. **6** Liverpool. **7**
David May. **8** Juventus. **9** John Motson.
10 Blackpool. **11** WBA. **12** Smith. **13** Ipswich Town. **14** Port Vale.
15 1960s. **16** Norwich City. **17** Notts County. **18** Hartlepool Utd.
19 Manchester City. **20** Three. **21** Wisla Krakow. **22** Sir Alex and
Darren Ferguson. **23** Paul. **24** WBA. **25** Tommy Lawton.
26 Swiss Super League. **27** Everton. **28** Losers received their
medals first. **29** Jimmy Quinn. **30** Benfica.

296 ❋ POT LUCK 46

1 Gavrilo Princip. **2** Millicent Margaret Amanda.
3 The shahs of Persia. **4** Illumination. **5** A bus service
(using horses). **6** Pythagoras. **7** Amelia Earhart.
8 Bees. **9** Epernay. **10** Jem. **11** 73 mph. **12** Adolf Hitler.
13 *Steamboat Willie.* **14** Miss World. **15** René Descartes. **16** Purple.
17 Puff the Magic Dragon. **18** Meteorology. **19** Parr. **20** Guildhall,
Windsor. **21** Sanjeev Bhaskar. **22** Charlie Chaplin. **23** Málaga.
24 Jane Seymour. **25** The Sargasso Sea. **26** Thomas Cook. **27** Bills,
Bills, Bills. **28** Joseph Priestley. **29** The homing pigeon. **30** The liver.

297 ❋ POT LUCK 47

1 2005. **2** Haltemprice. **3** Pink Floyd. **4** Warner
Brothers. **5** 59.4. **6** Everton. **7** Freshwater angling.
8 Canada. **9** Scottish. **10** DDT. **11** "Crazy".
12 972. **13** *Cabaret.* **14** Jim Davidson. **15** Joanna Lumley. **16** Tim
Henman. **17** Japan. **18** Grapes. **19** David Dundas. **20** Winston
Churchill. **21** 23 wickets. **22** Canada/ USA. **23** Venus. **24** *The
Accidental Tourist.* **25** Hans Wegner. **26** Jack Nicklaus. **27** Sir
Thomas Cullinan, superintendent at Premier Mine. **28** Paris.
29 IMF. **30** Tipp-Ex.

298 ❋ FOOTBALL POT LUCK 5

1 1980s. **2** Martyn. **3** 27. **4** Sydney. **5** Southampton.
6 Miller. **7** Chesterfield. **8** Leyton Orient.
9 Brighton. **10** 12. **11** QPR. **12** Docherty.
13 Wimbledon. **14** Oxford Utd. **15** 1960s. **16** Leeds Utd.
17 Sheffield Utd. **18** Doncaster Rovers. **19** Coventry City. **20** 13.
21 Slavia Prague. **22** Peter Kenyon. **23** Chelsea. **24** Carl. **25** Bert
Trautmann. **26** Barcelona. **27** Tommy Lawton. **28** Alan Smith.
29 Barnsley. **30** Aston Villa.

299 ❋ POP POT LUCK 9

1 B. J. Thomas. **2** Pink. **3** Frank Sinatra. **4** Chicago.
5 "The Last Waltz". **6** Blackboard Jungle. **7** The
Poseidon Adventure. **8** "Diane". **9** The Who.
10 White. **11** Johnny Otis. **12** Van McCoy. **13** Motown. **14** Freddy
Cannon. **15** Burl Ives. **16** Twiggy. **17** Flaming Star. **18** Del Shannon.
19 South Africa. **20** "Dreadlock Holiday". **21** Billboard Hot 100.
22 Candle in the Wind 1997/England's Rose. **23** "Take a Look at Me
Now". **24** The Pretty Things. **25** Lulu. **26** 9.00 am. **27** Johnny
Tillotson. **28** Randy Jackson. **29** "La Bamba". **30** Dennis Wilson.

300 ❋ POT LUCK 48

1 Borotra, Brugnon, Cochet & Lacoste. **2** Vijay Amritraj.
3 Martina Navratilova. **4** Arthur Ashe. **5** Gabriela Sabatini.
6 Pete Sampras. **7** French Open. **8** Margaret Smith. **9** Plus
an Olympic gold medal. **10** Karen Hantze. **11** 1968. **12** Michael Stich.
13 Richard Krajicek. **14** Andy Roddick. **15** Justine Henin Ardenne.
16 Russia. **17** The Queen. **18** Men's doubles. **19** French. **20** French Open.
21 Michael Stich. **22** Lindsay Davenport. **23** Kevin Curren. **24** Tony
Pickard. **25** Stefan Edberg. **26** Tim Gullikson. **27** Roger Taylor. **28** Kosice,
Slovakia. **29** Sue Barker. **30** Sukova.

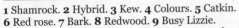

301 ✱ PLANTS

1 Shamrock. 2 Hybrid. 3 Kew. 4 Colours. 5 Catkin.
6 Red rose. 7 Bark. 8 Redwood. 9 Busy Lizzie.
10 Root. 11 Hardy. 12 Venus Flytrap. 13 Annual.
14 Evergreen. 15 Chelsea. 16 Scotland. 17 Kills them.
18 Rhubarb. 19 Botany. 20 Saffron. 21 Hips. 22 Females.
23 Seaweed. 24 Hop. 25 Willow. 26 Yew. 27 Corm. 28 America.
29 Canada. 30 South.

302 ✱ SEA LIFE

1 Fish. 2 Skate. 3 Blue whale. 4 Shell. 5 Calf.
6 Sharks. 7 Lobster. 8 Portuguese. 9 Eight. 10 In
the sea. 11 None. 12 Osprey. 13 Gills. 14 Herring. 15
10. 16 In the sea. 17 Whale. 18 Milk. 19 97%. 20 Poor.
21 Blubber. 22 Oxygen. 23 Cod. 24 White. 25 12%. 26 Sturgeon.
27 Shark. 28 Gold. 29 Blowhole. 30 Lobster.

303 ✱ SCIENCE & NATURE

1 Gravity. 2 Red. 3 Larger. 4 Oxygen. 5 The Sun.
6 Uranus. 7 Atmosphere. 8 Black Hole. 9 Venus.
10 George. 11 Stars. 12 Astronomy. 13 Red. 14 *Star
Trek*. 15 80s. 16 *Shooting Stars*. 17 Constellation. 18 Space.
19 1950s. 20 Sea of Tranquillity. 21 Gemini. 22 Burger. 23 USA.
24 Marines. 25 A year. 26 Teddy bear. 27 Great Bear. 28 Once.
29 Light. 30 Space.

304 ✱ ANIMALS

1 Life span. 2 Dog. 3 Colony. 4 Aardvark. 5 Camels.
6 Dog. 7 Four. 8 Adder. 9 Eucalyptus. 10 Scotland.
11 Toad. 12 Zoology. 13 Black and white.
14 Donkey. 15 Herd. 16 Mandrill. 17 Goat. 18 Badger.
19 Carnivore. 20 Joey. 21 Earthworm. 22 Bear. 23 Seal.
24 *Ape.* 25 Hare. 26 Squirrel. 27 Cheetah. 28 Elephant.
29 Pack. 30 Australia.

305 ✱ PLANTS & ANIMALS

1 Mammal. 2 White. 3 St Bernard. 4 Pigeon.
5 Elephant. 6 Hooves. 7 Reindeer. 8 Plant. 9 Tree.
10 Cat. 11 Plants. 12 Head. 13 Two. 14 Snake. 15
Pink. 16 Spring. 17 Lion. 18 Plant. 19 Fungus. 20 Cacti.
21 Pollen. 22 In water. 23 Insects. 24 Yellow. 25 Five.
26 Mouse. 27 Head. 28 Spine. 29 Gorilla. 30 Head.

306 ✱ GARDENING

1 Yellow. 2 Wood. 3 Monty Don. 4 Leaves.
5 Artichokes. 6 Over plants. 7 Bulbs. 8 Cut.
9 Cooking. 10 Lawnmower. 11 Compost. 12 Beans.
13 Hedge. 14 Holly. 15 Lavender. 16 Brownish/black. 17 One.
18 Small. 19 Roses. 20 Rockery. 21 Blue. 22 Sweet. 23 Cones.
24 Greenhouse. 25 Apples. 26 William. 27 Mowing.
28 Bulbs. 29 Blue. 30 Elderberries.

307 ✱ ANIMALS 2

1 Elm. 2 Fish. 3 Constriction. 4 Eagle. 5 Two.
6 Breed of terrier. 7 Snake. 8 Below. 9 Its colour.
10 Tree. 11 Southern. 12 Beaver. 13 Vixen. 14 Its
tail. 15 Caterpillar. 16 Canada. 17 Deer. 18 Fungus. 19 America.
20 Skunk. 21 Shark. 22 White. 23 Liver. 24 Red. 25 Venom.
26 Fish. 27 Two. 28 Kangaroo. 29 Swim (type of tuna fish).
30 Australia.

308 ✱ PLANTS 2

1 Stem. 2 Evergreen. 3 Fungi. 4 Linen. 5 Cocaine.
6 Grass. 7 Tequila. 8 True. 9 Leaf stalk. 10 White.
11 Yellow. 12 Camomile. 13 Sea. 14 Tapioca.
15 Blue. 16 Several. 17 Quinine. 18 Vines. 19 Blue.
20 Turpentine. 21 Avocado. 22 Cutting, pruning. 23 Low plants.
24 Green. 25 Kew. 26 America. 27 Trees. 28 Russian Vine.
29 Daffodil. 30 Conifers.

309 ✱ FOOD & DRINK

1 India. 2 Apple. 3 Brother. 4 Bolognese. 5 Sausage.
6 Fried. 7 Cheese. 8 Rice. 9 Salad. 10 Fish. 11 Red.
12 Italy. 13 Eggs. 14 Crisp. 15 Coffee. 16 Bread.
17 Rectangular. 18 Cheese. 19 Light brown. 20 Lancashire.
21 Drink (toast to the queen). 22 Chicken. 23 Pizza. 24 Whiskey.
25 Oranges. 26 18. 27 Gin. 28 France. 29 Drink. 30 Pear.

310 ✱ BIRD BRAINS

1 Robin. 2 Owls. 3 Black and white. 4 Ravens.
5 Brown. 6 Duck. 7 House. 8 Cuckoo. 9 Rook.
10 Kestrel. 11 Neck feathers. 12 Feather. 13 Lark.
14 Green. 15 Forked. 16 Bullfinch. 17 Crow. 18 Puffin.
19 Nightingale. 20 Black and white. 21 Grouse. 22 Dove.
23 Stork. 24 Swift. 25 Ostrich. 26 Kite. 27 Cygnet. 28 Jay.
29 Wren. 30 Young.

311 ✸ LIVING WORLD

1 Eyes. 2 Ostrich. 3 Fungus. 4 It dies. 5 Water.
6 Earthquake. 7 Sand. 8 Fewer. 9 Metal. 10 Fish.
11 Eagle. 12 Warmer. 13 Volcanic rock. 14 Dolphin.
15 Heart. 16 None. 17 Female. 18 Cloud. 19 Sun. 20 Fossil.
21 Antarctica. 22 Seaweed. 23 Primates (also accept apes).
24 Rice. 25 Insects. 26 At night. 27 Tentacles. 28 Rubber Tree.
29 Queen. 30 Tree.

312 ✸ FOOD & DRINK 2

1 Fish. 2 Stone. 3 Tea. 4 Dublin. 5 Salad plant.
6 Drink it. 7 Yellow. 8 Squash. 9 Stilton. 10 C. 11 A
wine. 12 Brown. 13 Spears. 14 Orange. 15 Salad leaf.
16 Charcoal. 17 Beef. 18 Vinegar. 19 Purple. 20 Fish. 21 Chilled.
22 Peas. 23 Cheese. 24 Black. 25 Grey. 26 Italy. 27 White.
28 Onion. 29 Rectangular. 30 Oranges.

313 ✸ ANIMALS 3

1 In a pouch. 2 Panda. 3 Australia. 4 Six. 5 Spider.
6 Camel. 7 King Charles. 8 Jellyfish. 9 Ewe.
10 Meat. 11 Dogs. 12 Brush. 13 St Bernard.
14 It doesn't have one. 15 Trotters. 16 Indian. 17 Caviar.
18 Hibernation. 19 Highland cattle. 20 Kids. 21 Skunk.
22 Squeezing. 23 To breathe. 24 Sting. 25 Colour. 26 A tail.
27 Butterfly. 28 German Shepherd. 29 Horse. 30 Cat.

314 ✸ ANIMALS 4

1 (African) elephant. 2 Wolf. 3 Warm blooded.
4 Tooth. 5 Voice box. 6 Alone. 7 Primate. 8 Duck.
9 Dog. 10 Sheep. 11 Sight. 12 Offensive smell.
13 Brown. 14 (South) America. 15 Eye. 16 Hare. 17 Its ears.
18 Alaska. 19 Warm. 20 Carnivorous. 21 Cows. 22 Chimpanzee.
23 Neck. 24 Invertebrates. 25 One. 26 Tail. 27 Polar bear.
28 Milk. 29 Fingerprints. 30 Southern.

315 ✸ FOOD & DRINK 3

1 Yorkshire pudding. 2 Ainsley Harriott. 3 Red.
4 Green. 5 Pink. 6 Eat. 7 Scotch egg. 8 Cider.
9 Potato. 10 Spaghetti (junction). 11 Pudding.
12 Strawberries. 13 France. 14 Savoury. 15 Nut. 16 Currants
and/or other dried fruit. 17 Antony Worrall Thompson. 18 High
tea. 19 Out of doors. 20 Round. 21 Mushy peas. 22 Cream.
23 Coffee. 24 Sherry. 25 Soup. 26 Milk. 27 Room temperature.
28 Yes. 29 Breakfast. 30 Scotland.

316 ✸ TIME & SPACE

1 Mercury. 2 Big Bang. 3 Ursa Major (the Great
Bear). 4 Sharman. 5 Galaxy. 6 Space Shuttle. 7 Star.
8 Jupiter. 9 Comet. 10 It exploded. 11 Kennedy.
12 The Moon. 13 Gravity. 14 Satellites. 15 Cosmology. 16 Glenn.
17 Apollo. 18 Uranus. 19 First man in space. 20 A year.
21 Halley's comet. 22 USA. 23 The Dog Star. 24 Quasars.
25 Patrick Moore. 26 Shakespeare. 27 Cheshire. 28 Light years.
29 A dog. 30 The Milky Way.

317 ✸ SCIENCE & THE NATURAL WORLD

1 Heel. 2 Cows/cattle. 3 Bee. 4 Temperature.
5 Tropical. 6 Orange/yellow. 7 Coldblooded. 8 Rib
cage. 9 Red. 10 Eating. 11 Asia. 12 Mouth. 13 Slime. 14 Your
voice. 15 Back. 16 Needles. 17 Cat. 18 Spider. 19 Africa.
20 Blood. 21 Man. 22 Snake. 23 Sheep. 24 Plus. 25 Red.
26 Pink. 27 Australia. 28 Ice. 29 Mistletoe. 30 Mercury.

318 ✸ HEALTHY EATING

1 Jamie Oliver. 2 Cottage cheese. 3 Five. 4 Green.
5 Without. 6 Calcium. 7 Oats. 8 Blender.
9 Steaming. 10 Lettuce. 11 Chickpea. 12 Italy.
13 High. 14 Orange. 15 Sugars. 16 Saturated. 17 Fibre. 18 0%.
19 Poached. 20 Middle. 21 Turkey Twizzlers. 22 Vitamin A.
23 Red. 24 Iron. 25 Vitamin C. 26 Seeds. 27 Orange.
28 Carbohydrate. 29 Skimmed. 30 Red.

319 ✸ FOOD & DRINK 4

1 Eggs. 2 Deer. 3 Mint. 4 France. 5 Pancakes.
6 Chips. 7 Rasher. 8 Honey. 9 Smoked. 10 Potato.
11 Holland. 12 Oats. 13 Soup. 14 Ketchup.
15 Colourless. 16 Spain. 17 Apples. 18 Almonds. 19 Hot.
20 Sausage. 21 Yorkshire. 22 Beans. 23 Yellow. 24 Fish.
25 Brown. 26 Cheese. 27 Peas. 28 Italy. 29 Beer and lemonade.
30 Isle of Islay.

320 ✸ THE UNIVERSE

1 Jupiter. 2 Space station. 3 Big Bang. 4 Stars.
5 Sun and rain. 6 Lightning. 7 Full moon. 8 Glacier.
9 Brazil. 10 Ozone layer. 11 Acid rain. 12 Animals.
13 Pacific. 14 Michigan. 15 Mountain. 16 Gold. 17 Rain.
18 Nile. 19 Rock. 20 Australia. 21 Dead Sea. 22 Water.
23 Russia. 24 Antarctica. 25 Rain. 26 Cloud. 27 Sahara.
28 Greenhouse. 29 Green. 30 River.

321 ❋ ANIMAL STARS

1 *Lassie Come Home.* 2 *Jaws.* 3 Orang-utan. 4 St Bernard. 5 Kenya. 6 Sheepdog. 7 Three.
8 1940s. 9 Dog and wolf. 10 Toto. 11 Homeward Bound. 12 Gorillas. 13 *Ben.* 14 Champion. 15 *Arachnophobia.*
16 Silver. 17 Horse. 18 Cats and dogs. 19 German. 20 Elsa.
21 1900s. 22 MGM. 23 Willy. 24 Dick King-Smith. 25 The Birds.
26 Beethoven's 2nd. 27 Alsatian. 28 *Willard.* 29 Dinosaurs (Jurassic Park). 30 A tabby cat.

322 ❋ FLOWERS

1 Snapdragon. 2 Geranium. 3 Everlasting. 4 Golden Rod. 5 Canterbury bell. 6 Peace. 7 Cornflower.
8 Jacob's ladder. 9 Pollen. 10 Busy Lizzie.
11 Passion flower. 12 Gypsophila. 13 Buttercups. 14 Nasturtium.
15 Cats (Catmint). 16 Grape hyacinth. 17 Campion. 18 Viola, Bugle. 19 Tulip (tuliban). 20 Honesty. 21 Rhododendron.
22 Narcissus. 23 Red hot poker. 24 Clematis. 25 Rose. 26 Iris.
27 Michaelmas daisy. 28 Chrysanthemum. 29 Pink. 30 Mexico.

323 ❋ TREES

1 Seeds. 2 Oak. 3 Yew, Scots Pine, Juniper.
4 Laburnum. 5 White/cream. 6 Japan. 7 Pine.
8 South America. 9 Hazel. 10 Poplar. 11 Soft.
12 Sycamore. 13 Wet. 14 Cork oak. 15 Northumberland. 16 Palm.
17 Copper beech. 18 Sweet chestnut. 19 Elm. 20 Magnolia.
21 Asia. 22 Ebony. 23 Sugar maple. 24 Willow. 25 Redwood.
26 Ash. 27 Blue/violet. 28 Cacao. 29 Eucalyptus. 30 Lime.

324 ❋ PLANTS 3

1 "Wort". 2 Plum. 3 Princess of Wales. 4 Wheat.
5 Succulent. 6 Sepal. 7 Bellshaped. 8 Mushroom.
9 Blade. 10 Bark. 11 Green parts including leaves.
12 Toothed or notched. 13 Yellow. 14 Cactus. 15 Grass. 16 Grows in grape-like clusters. 17 Blue. 18 Seaweed. 19 Dandelion (*dent de lion*). 20 Linden. 21 Pollen. 22 More than one year, but less than two. 23 Europe. 24 Two. 25 Black. 26 Dried plants. 27 Yew.
28 Charles II. 29 Raspberry and blackberry. 30 White.

325 ❋ LIVING WORLD 2

1 Tidal wave. 2 On the skin. 3 CJD. 4 Worm.
5 Haematology. 6 Hermaphrodite. 7 Falcon. 8 Ear.
9 Marine snail. 10 Knee. 11 Pigeons. 12 Anaemia.
13 Orange. 14 Fungus. 15 Skin. 16 Abdomen. 17 Shoulder blade.
18 Fish. 19 Short-sighted. 20 12. 21 Idi Amin. 22 Acne. 23 The kiss of life. 24 Tuberculosis. 25 Base of the brain. 26 Achilles tendon. 27 Liver. 28 Green. 29 Kidney. 30 Herring.

326 ❋ FISH

1 The tail. 2 Red/orange. 3 Tuna. 4 Herring.
5 Roe. 6 Tench. 7 Salmon. 8 Whale shark.
9 Sardine. 10 Blue/black. 11 Liver. 12 Carp. 13 Fish rearing. 14 Silver bream. 15 Whelk. 16 Small shark. 17 Rock salmon. 18 Hermit crab. 19 On its back. 20 Trout. 21 Ten.
22 Izaak Walton. 23 Flatfish. 24 Sprats. 25 Round its mouth.
26 A grain of sand. 27 Pike. 28 Red mullet. 29 Dover sole.
30 Clam.

327 ❋ FOOD & DRINK 5

1 An Italian bread. 2 Aniseed. 3 Chick peas.
4 Coffee. 5 Flour. 6 Marsala. 7 Redleaved lettuce.
8 Amontillado. 9 Fruit bread. 10 Butter, egg yolk, wine vinegar. 11 Slicing. 12 Hot spicy paste. 13 Cointreau.
14 Heather honey. 15 Africa. 16 Dolmas. 17 Jeroboam. 18 Salad leaf. 19 Italy. 20 Dark rum. 21 17th. 22 Leicester. 23 Lamb.
24 Potatoes. 25 Tapioca. 26 Clarified butter. 27 Plums. 28 Tree bark. 29 Coconut milk. 30 Fried or toasted bread.

328 ❋ PLANTS 4

1 Barley. 2 Christmas rose. 3 White. 4 Shamrock.
5 Water. 6 Five. 7 Topiary. 8 Monkshood. 9 Yellow.
10 Sweet potato. 11 Bell-shaped. 12 Leaf. 13 Ivy.
14 Crops and soils. 15 Apple. 16 Strawberry. 17 Deadly nightshade. 18 Paralysis. 19 Female. 20 Tea. 21 Poplar.
22 Fuchsia. 23 Yellow. 24 South America. 25 Attract pollinators.
26 Herbicide. 27 Red. 28 Flag. 29 Dandelion. 30 Blue.

329 ❋ WINE

1 Bordeaux. 2 Brut. 3 Australia. 4 Chardonnay.
5 New Zealand. 6 Greece. 7 Madeira. 8 75 centilitres. 9 Spain. 10 Loire. 11 White. 12 Louis Pasteur. 13 Case. 14 Bulgaria. 15 California. 16 Jancis. 17 South Africa. 18 Eight. 19 Sparkling. 20 Tuscany. 21 Medium sweet.
22 Ruby, tawny and vintage. 23 Rosé. 24 Chile. 25 Beaujolais.
26 China. 27 Sherry. 28 Champagne. 29 Jilly Goolden.
30 Rhine.

330 ❋ ANIMALS 5

1 Ants and termites. 2 Yellow with black markings.
3 Okapi. 4 Omnivore. 5 Orangutan. 6 Bones.
7 Mammals. 8 Caribou. 9 Grey. 10 Amphibian.
11 Cold-blooded. 12 Dog. 13 Fangs. 14 Camel. 15 Bat. 16 Deer.
17 Backbone. 18 Dodo. 19 Borzoi. 20 Blue. 21 Tasmania.
22 Underground. 23 Gorilla. 24 Barbary apes. 25 Milk.
26 Grizzly. 27 Otter. 28 Racoon. 29 America. 30 A monkey.

331 ✱ PLANTS 5

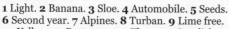

1 Light. 2 Banana. 3 Sloe. 4 Automobile. 5 Seeds.
6 Second year. 7 Alpines. 8 Turban. 9 Lime free.
10 Yellow. 11 Buttercup. 12 Three. 13 Swedish.
14 Dog rose. 15 White. 16 Snapdragons. 17 Flower arranging.
18 Lizzie. 19 Blue. 20 Nigella. 21 Everlasting flowers.
22 Autumn. 23 Very large. 24 Pansies. 25 Canterbury bell.
26 Grape. 27 Organic material. 28 Poisonous. 29 Dark red.
30 White.

332 ✱ BIRD BRAINS 2

1 Asia. 2 Red. 3 Oology. 4 Larks. 5 A thrush.
6 Green. 7 Feather. 8 Chiffchaff. 9 Condor.
10 Wren. 11 Flightless. 12 Pheasants. 13 Murder.
14 They are hollow. 15 Thrush. 16 The pheasant. 17 Smell. 18 It
has webbed feet. 19 Ostrich. 20 Archaeopteryx. 21 Mussels.
22 Quill. 23 The dodo. 24 Sing. 25 Beaks, feathers and wings.
26 Capon. 27 Hawks. 28 Avocet. 29 A chattering. 30 Pheasants.

333 ✱ TIME & SPACE 2

1 Venus. 2 Mice. 3 First human fatality. 4 Halley.
5 Hawaii. 6 Uranus. 7 Southern Crown and
Northern Crown. 8 Six. 9 Eclipse. 10 Gemini.
11 Manchester. 12 Neptune. 13 Order of discovery. 14 Mr Spock.
15 Valentina Tereshkova. 16 Extra Vehicular Activity. 17 Earth.
18 One. 19 Aurora Borealis. 20 Jupiter. 21 27.3 days. 22 Pluto.
23 Saturn. 24 Big Bang Theory. 25 Light year. 26 Mars. 27 Away
from it. 28 Venus. 29 Proxima Centauri. 30 The Sun.

334 ✱ NATURAL PHENOMENA

1 Quicklime. 2 Jupiter. 3 Pluto. 4 Indian. 5 Amazon.
6 Loch Lomond. 7 Canada. 8 North Atlantic (Great
Britain). 9 Balmoral. 10 Tornado. 11 Angola.
12 Cornwall. 13 Hydrogen. 14 Plutonium. 15 Ullswater.
16 Calcium carbonate. 17 China clay. 18 500. 19 Mouount
McKinley. 20 Russia. 21 Washington. 22 Tungsten. 23 Iceland.
24 Kobe. 25 Emerald. 26 Charles. 27 10%. 28 Yellow.
29 Indonesia. 30 River Ouse.

335 ✱ FOOD & DRINK 6

1 Italy. 2 Choux pastry. 3 Pears. 4 Garlic.
5 Mushroom. 6 Veal. 7 It's served raw. 8 Tomato
juice. 9 Anchovy. 10 North East. 11 Beef Wellington.
12 Red wine. 13 Apple. 14 None, they are made from cheese.
15 Potatoes and cabbage. 16 Rice. 17 Ewe's milk. 18 Oysters and
bacon. 19 Tayberry. 20 Vermicelli. 21 Spinach. 22 Bacon.
23 Blood. 24 Basil. 25 Bread. 26 Soup. 27 Smoked haddock.
28 Tube-shaped. 29 Semolina. 30 Liquorice.

336 ✱ FOOD & DRINK 7

1 Semolina. 2 Veal. 3 Caraway. 4 Clotted cream.
5 Citrus fruits. 6 Dried. 7 Parmesan cheese.
8 Warrington. 9 Beef. 10 Vino da tavola. 11 Whiskey
or Bourbon. 12 Orange. 13 Fish, pastry. 14 Rice. 15 Blackcurrant.
16 Smoked fish, rice. 17 Guernseys and Jerseys. 18 Cointreau.
19 Filo. 20 Double Gloucester and Stilton. 21 Eight. 22 Bacon.
23 Buckwheat. 24 Dried beans. 25 Spain. 26 Normandy. 27 An
Italian bread. 28 Bacon and eggs. 29 Skimmed. 30 Italian rice.

337 ✱ ANIMALS 6

1 Monkey. 2 Australia. 3 Chick. 4 Marsupial.
5 Umbilical. 6 India. 7 Dodo. 8 African elephant.
9 Cat. 10 Herbivorous. 11 Squirrel. 12 Trees.
13 40%. 14 Smell. 15 Chimpanzee. 16 Alone. 17 Borneo.
18 Reptiles. 19 Hood. 20 Clawed. 21 Border collie.
22 Tapeworm. 23 Whale. 24 Indian cobra. 25 Spawn.
26 Hare. 27 Starfish. 28 Thumb. 29 Cobra. 30 Grizzly bear.

338 ✱ ANIMALS 7

1 Starfish. 2 Adult. 3 Tadpole. 4 Colour. 5 Skin.
6 Venom. 7 Africa. 8 Bat. 9 Grizzly. 10 Caribou.
11 Seven. 12 Insects. 13 Grey, red. 14 Cheetah.
15 Scottish. 16 Blue. 17 Man. 18 Trees. 19 Chihuahua. 20 Yes.
21 Horn. 22 Tiger. 23 Goat. 24 Kangaroo. 25 Two. 26 Panther.
27 Earthworms. 28 China. 29 Elk. 30 Dams.

339 ✱ LIVING WORLD 3

1 Drone. 2 Crab. 3 Antennae. 4 Host. 5 Five.
6 Scarab. 7 Moulting. 8 Fish. 9 Puffin. 10 Shell or
shellfish. 11 Dog. 12 Smell. 13 Change of shape.
14 Beating its wings. 15 Raven. 16 Bird sanctuary in Suffolk.
17 Thrips. 18 Three. 19 Sand or mud. 20 Bird (hedge sparrow).
21 Nervous system. 22 Aboriginal Australian. 23 Ladybug.
24 None. 25 Grouse - it is the start of the grouse shooting season.
26 Gristle. 27 Its coat turns white. 28 Song thrush. 29 Cell.
30 Horns.

340 ✱ FOOD & DRINK 8

1 Rise. 2 VSOP. 3 Mushroom. 4 Garlic. 5 White
sauce. 6 Squid. 7 Mexico. 8 Spirals. 9 Buffalo's.
10 Parsley. 11 Chick peas. 12 Aubergine.
13 Australia. 14 Tuscany. 15 Paper. 16 Tomatoes. 17 Kebab.
18 Ham. 19 Almond. 20 Herbs. 21 Potatoes. 22 Sweet. 23 Clay.
24 Sushi. 25 Basil. 26 Pizza. 27 Soup. 28 Before a meal.
29 Carbon dioxide. 30 Fried.

341 ✳ ANIMALS 8

1 Vegetation above ground. 2 Capybara. 3 Barn Owl. 4 In its ear. 5 Insects. 6 Three. 7 Oxen. 8 Guanaco. 9 Live young. 10 Antelope. 11 30. 12 Red blood cell. 13 Highland collie. 14 London Zoo. 15 Bandicoot. 16 Colugo. 17 The Cat Fanciers Association of the US. 18 Strictly monogamous. 19 Madagascar. 20 Fisher. 21 Spiral. 22 When they stand up on hind legs and tail. 23 Squid. 24 Squamata. 25 Coldblooded animal. 26 Snake. 27 Fox, badger or otter hunting. 28 Scaled waterproof skins, shelled yolk-bearing eggs. 29 Venomous snake. 30 Great Dane.

342 ✳ FOOD & DRINK 9

1 Olive oil. 2 Evaporated milk. 3 1955. 4 Bass Pale Ale. 5 Angers. 6 Paul Bocuse. 7 Vermicelli. 8 Louis Diat. 9 Ruth Rogers. 10 Alsace. 11 Burgundy. 12 Macadamia nuts. 13 Britain. 14 Argol. 15 Tarragon & chervil. 16 Parsley. 17 1905. 18 Dorchester. 19 Salmanazar. 20 Jerome Maubee. 21 Pine nuts. 22 Kofta. 23 Railroad kitchens. 24 Rice. 25 Riesling. 26 Mulligatawny. 27 Benedictine. 28 John Tovey. 29 Carignan. 30 Harvested late.

343 ✳ FOOD & DRINK 10

1 Type of grape. 2 Buck's Club in London. 3 Doner kebab. 4 Belgium. 5 The Dorchester. 6 Caraway seeds. 7 Australia. 8 Salt cod. 9 John Tovey. 10 Chocolate. 11 Top (garnish). 12 Chile. 13 Ullage. 14 Madame Harel, a French farmer's wife. 15 Chocolate. 16 Greece. 17 Bucket. 18 VDQS. 19 Cinzano, apricot brandy & angostura bitters. 20 Butter made from coconut. 21 Maths. 22 Biscuit. 23 Asparagus. 24 Tarragon, chervil. 25 Plums. 26 Geese or ducks. 27 Lime juice. 28 Mixed green salad. 29 Kebab. 30 Filled tortilla or pancake.

344 ✳ PLANTS 6

1 Meilland. 2 Wild cherry. 3 Borlotti beans. 4 Egypt. 5 Sap. 6 Poisonous mushroom. 7 Hydroponics. 8 Red. 9 Starch. 10 Latex. 11 Gold/orange. 12 Calcifuge. 13 Insects. 14 Weigelas. 15 Brambles. 16 Lichens. 17 Salt. 18 Pappus. 19 Tomatoes. 20 Figs. 21 Carrot. 22 Its cap. 23 The stems of plants. 24 Old tree or log. 25 Study of plant diseases. 26 Tea. 27 Coconut palm. 28 Pertaining to the soil. 29 Giant cactus. 30 Unopened flower buds.

345 ✳ PLANET EARTH

1 South Dakota. 2 Copper. 3 Walrus. 4 West Spitsbergen. 5 Sonoran. 6 Silicon. 7 Mercury. 8 Sulphur. 9 Seismic wave. 10 Green. 11 Strathclyde. 12 South Africa. 13 New Guinea. 14 Four. 15 Venus. 16 Mountain chains. 17 Parsec. 18 Western Mongolia. 19 Radiation. 20 Low temperatures. 21 Novaya Zemlya. 22 Soil. 23 Radio communication. 24 Dam. 25 Six. 26 Helium. 27 Saturn. 28 Moh. 29 4.35. 30 Iron.

346 ✳ FOOD & DRINK 11

1 Liebfraumilch. 2 Warm. 3 Bray. 4 Stomach remedy. 5 Ice cream. 6 Tomatoes. 7 Crescent-shaped (roll). 8 Steen. 9 Stum. 10 Browned at the edges due to age. 11 Sicily. 12 Semi-sparkling, fully sparkling. 13 Calzone. 14 Maize. 15 Grapes are partly sun-dried before use. 16 Greenwich. 17 Portugal. 18 Barsac, Bommes, Fargues, Preignac. 19 Britain. 20 Peter Bayless. 21 Canary Islands. 22 Wine and methylated spirits. 23 Salsify. 24 Remuage. 25 Pomerol. 26 Wine award in Germany. 27 Bechamel. 28 Oenology. 29 Escoffier. 30 Mirin.

347 ✳ FOOD & DRINK 12

1 Lettuce. 2 Calves' stomachs. 3 Auvergne. 4 Buffalo milk. 5 Thiamin. 6 Ram's horn. 7 Chicken Marengo. 8 Pine nuts. 9 Parmigiano-Reggiano. 10 Wormwood. 11 Tomato purée. 12 In foil or paper. 13 USA. 14 A type of cider. 15 Angel hair. 16 Still water. 17 Japan. 18 President Thomas Jefferson. 19 Preservative. 20 Moulin Rouge. 21 Eggs. 22 Perrier water. 23 Wimpy. 24 Chopsticks. 25 Whey. 26 Haagen-Dazs ice cream. 27 Two legs and saddle. 28 Hass. 29 Bows - means butterflies. 30 Cake.

348 ✳ SCIENCE

1 Star sailor. 2 Charles Kowal. 3 Mars. 4 Kentucky. 5 Kodak. 6 Czechoslovakia. 7 Humerus. 8 Calcium hydroxide. 9 Tanzania. 10 Orion. 11 Tibia. 12 Vomiting. 13 Titan. 14 Dialysis machine. 15 Five. 16 90+. 17 Neptune. 18 Therapeutics plc. 19 Lungs. 20 Jupiter. 21 1880s. 22 John Russell Hind. 23 iPhone. 24 Carbon. 25 Titan. 26 Benthos. 27 Lakes. 28 13. 29 Triton. 30 Heavy water.

349 ✳ ANIMALS 9

1 Vampire bat. 2 Blue whale. 3 One. 4 Capybara. 5 Algae which grow on it. 6 Mount Everest pika. 7 Exmoor ponies. 8 Bat. 9 Intestine. 10 Behind its eyes. 11 Bootlace worm. 12 On its skin. 13 Canine teeth. 14 Anywhere above ground. 15 *Balaenoptera musculus*. 16 Flemish horse. 17 Yellow. 18 Europe (bison). 19 Madagascar. 20 Maine coon. 21 Poisonous frog. 22 Couple of hours. 23 Collagen. 24 Tarsiers. 25 Herd reindeer. 26 Argentina. 27 Lemur. 28 Asian elephant. 29 Forehead horn. 30 Warm-blooded.

350 ✳ LIVING WORLD 4

1 Use of feathers for the fashion trade. 2 Neotropical. 3 Demospongia. 4 Corals. 5 Red. 6 Harpy eagle. 7 Smell. 8 Three. 9 Starfish. 10 Bushman's clock. 11 Its diet. 12 On the sea bed. 13 Flightless bird. 14 Secretary bird. 15 Shellfish (not oysters!), worms, insects. 16 Cetacean or dolphin. 17 South America. 18 Andean condor. 19 Mongoose. 20 Sprat. 21 Mexico. 22 Dome of the shell. 23 Red mullet. 24 Cassowary. 25 Lizard. 26 Wishbone. 27 Plains wanderer. 28 Madagascar. 29 Dogfish. 30 Whole.

351 ✳ NATURAL PHENOMENA 2

1 Carol. **2** Andesite. **3** *Proxima centauri.* **4** India.
5 Utigard. **6** Mars. **7** Erne. **8** Kentucky. **9** Black hole.
10 Ceres. **11** Nwamibia. **12** Akutan. **13** Helix.
14 0.16%. **15** Sirius. **16** Venus. **17** Sumatra. **18** Iowa. **19** 70.
20 Venus. **21** Astatine. **22** 1000 yds. **23** Orion. **24** Canis Minor.
25 Taurus. **26** Texas. **27** Shropshire. **28** South China.
29 Germany. **30** Neptune.

352 ✳ PLANTS 7

1 Ginkgo. **2** Oxalic. **3** Callus. **4** Cherokee leader.
5 It dissolves blood corpuscles. **6** Italy. **7** Rockies.
8 North & South Carolina. **9** Blue. **10** Ferns &
mosses. **11** Pacific coast of North America. **12** Stalk. **13** African
violet. **14** From insects. **15** It loses its green colour. **16** Matchbox
bean. **17** Rose of Jericho. **18** Sloes. **19** Cactus. **20** Poppy.
21 General Sherman. **22** Lettuce. **23** On dung. **24** Sierra Nevada.
25 Belladonna. **26** Stalk. **27** By the sea. **28** Silver Fir. **29** Praslin
& Curiense. **30** Giant waterlily.

353 ✳ ANIMALS 10

1 Skomer vole. **2** Adder. **3** Sumatran tiger. **4** A small
African antelope. **5** Ass. **6** Lizards. **7** Kangaroo hound.
8 Sea-cows. **9** Mongoose. **10** They act independently of
each other. **11** South America. **12** Cockroaches. **13** Tiger. **14** Insects.
15 Fish, amphibians, reptiles, birds and mammals. **16** Animals which
lay eggs. **17** Can precede "fly" to give the name of another creature. **18**
Coypu. **19** Wombat. **20** Arthropods. **21** Types of beetle. **22** Desert fox.
23 Madagascar. **24** Leap. **25** China. **26** Viviparous. **27** Array.
28 Airedale terrier. **29** Worm. **30** Heavy horse.

354 ✳ ANIMALS 11

1 Basking shark. **2** Monkeys. **3** Koala bear.
4 Thomas Savage. **5** Bison. **6** Turtles. **7** Sailfish.
8 Thailand. **9** Whale shark. **10** Nevada. **11** Vulture.
12 Bandicoot. **13** Flying lemur. **14** 400. **15** Lion. **16** Giant squid.
17 Fisher marten. **18** Otter. **19** Rabies. **20** Swan. **21** Sperm whale.
22 Kiwi. **23** Teal. **24** Smell. **25** Voice. **26** Third eye. **27** Marsupial
mole. **28** Mexico. **29** Blunt nose lizard. **30** Capybara.

355 ✳ LIVING WORLD 5

1 Whippoorwill. **2** Isabelle Diniore. **3** Sleeping
sickness. **4** Internal. **5** Keratin. **6** Single set of
chromosomes. **7** Kola nuts. **8** Human's forearm.
9 Red blood cell. **10** Beachflea. **11** Bird droppings. **12** South
America & Antarctica. **13** Weil's disease. **14** Seaweed. **15** Head.
16 Ruppell's vulture. **17** Excretory organs. **18** Not hooded.
19 Cerebellum. **20** Penguin. **21** Salamander. **22** Male malle fowl.
23 Goliath. **24** Wishbone. **25** Alcoholism. **26** Butterfly. **27** Cuba.
28 Kiwi. **29** Harvest mite (which bites). **30** Ten.

356 ✳ FOOD & DRINK 13

1 Tomato purée. **2** Apple, celery and walnuts.
3 Cake. **4** Italy. **5** Beer and garlic. **6** Seaweed.
7 Haddock. **8** Three. **9** Buffalo. **10** Neck of lamb.
11 Paper. **12** Duck and chicken. **13** Plums. **14** Egg yolks and
butter. **15** Green. **16** Potatoes. **17** Somerset. **18** Liver. **19** Double
cream. **20** Nettle leaves. **21** Greece. **22** Bows or butterflies.
23 Lentils. **24** Clarified butter. **25** Russia, fish pie. **26** Al dente.
27 Beer. **28** Very rare. **29** From the pan it's cooked in.
30 Aubergines.

357 ✳ PLANTS 8

1 Alaska. **2** Chlorophyll. **3** Dead matter.
4 New Zealand. **5** 0.9%. **6** Barley. **7** Lamina.
8 Gymnosperm. **9** Hollies. **10** Epiphyte. **11** Cork.
12 Forget Me Not. **13** Small stalk. **14** Myrtle sprig. **15** Honesty.
16 Azalea. **17** Pink. **18** Autumn crocus. **19** Rosa gallica.
20 Carnations. **21** Saffron. **22** Glory of the snow. **23** South
Africa. **24** Sap. **25** Boston. **26** Root. **27** Aubretia. **28** Parsley.
29 Daffodil. **30** Flemish.

358 ✳ FOOD & DRINK: GOURMET

1 Egon Ronay. **2** Paul and Jeanne Rankin. **3** Heston
Blumenthal. **4** Savoy, Carlton. **5** Michel Roux. **6** Alastair
Little. **7** Italian. **8** Raymond Blanc. **9** Thailand. **10**
Clement Freud. **11** Cork. **12** Simon Hopkinson. **13** Mireille Johnston.
14 Madhur Jaffrey. **15** Prue Leith. **16** The Greenhouse restaurant.
17 Darina Allen. **18** Michael Barry. **19** Terry Wogan. **20** John Tovey.
21 *Evening Standard.* **22** Vegetarian. **23** Caroline Conran. **24** Dorset.
25 Gareth Blackstock. **26** Jane. **27** Mr Beeton. **28** *Ready Steady
Cook.* **29** Fanny and Johnny Cradock. **30** Philip Harben.